THE UPANISHADS

Translated by F. MAX MÜLLER

The Upanishads
Translated by F. Max Müller

Print ISBN 13: 978-1-4209-7470-6
eBook ISBN 13: 978-1-4209-7637-3

Cover Image: a detail of a painting of gods paying homage to Shiva and Krishna, Kathmandu Valley, 19th century / Pictures from History / Bridgeman Images.

Please visit *www.digireads.com*

CONTENTS

VOLUME I

VOLUME II

TO

THE RIGHT HONOURABLE
THE MARQUIS OF SALISBURY, K*G*.

CHANCELLOR OF THE UNIVERSITY OF OXFORD,
LATELY SECRETARY OF STATE FOR INDIA,

SIR HENRY J. S. MAINE, K.*OS*.I.
MEMBER OF THE COUNCIL OF INDIA,

AND

THE VERY REV. H. G. LIDDELL, DD.
DEAN OF CHRIST CHURCH,

TO WHOSE KIND INTEREST AND EXERTIONS

THIS ATTEMPT TO MAKE KNOWN TO THE ENGLISH PEOPLE

THE SACRED BOOKS OF THE EAST

IS SO LARGELY INDEBTED,

I NOW DEDICATE THESE VOLUMES

WITH SINCERE RESPECT AND GRATITUDE,

F. MAX MÜLLER.

'The general inclinations which are naturally implanted in my soul to some religion, it is impossible for me to shift off: but there being such a multiplicity of religions in the world, I desire now seriously to consider with my self which of them all to restrain these my general inclinations to. And the reason of this my enquiry is not, that I am in the least dissatisfied with that religion I have already embraced; but because 'tis natural for all men to have an overbearing opinion and esteem for that particular religion they are born and bred-up in. That, therefore, I may not seem biassed by the prejudice of education, I am resolved to prove and examine them all; that I may see and hold fast to that which is best ....

'Indeed there was never any religion so barbarous and diabolical, but it was preferred before all other religions whatsoever, by them that did profess it; otherwise they would not have professed it ....

'And why, say they, may not you be mistaken as well as we? Especially when there is, at least, six to one against your Christian religion; all of which think they serve God aright; and expect happiness thereby as well as you And hence it is that in my looking out for the truest religion, being conscious to my self how great an ascendant Christianity holds over me beyond the rest, as being that religion whereinto I was born and baptized, that which the supreme authority has enjoined and my parents educated me in; that which every one I meet withal highly approves of, and which I my self have, by a long continued profession, made almost natural to me: I am resolved to be more jealous and suspicious of this religion, than of the rest, and be sure not to entertain it any longer without being convinced by solid and substantial arguments, of the truth and certainty of it. That, therefore, I may make diligent and impartial enquiry into all religions and so be sure to find out the best, I shall for a time, look upon my self as one not at all interested in any particular religion whatsoever, much less in the Christian religion; but only as one who desires, in general, to serve and obey Him that made me, in a right manner, and thereby to be made partaker of that happiness my nature is capable of.'

BISHOP BEVERIDGE (1636-1707).
Private Thoughts on Religion, Part 1, Article 2.

Preface to the Sacred Books of the East

I must begin this series of translations of the Sacred Books of the East with three cautions:—the first, referring to the character of the original texts here translated; the second, with regard to the difficulties in making a proper use of translations; the third, showing what is possible and what is impossible in rendering ancient thought into modern speech.

Readers who have been led to believe that the Vedas of the ancient Brahmans, the Avesta of the Zoroastrians, the Tripi*t*aka of the Buddhists, the Kings of Confucius, or the Koran of Mohammed are books full of primeval wisdom and religious enthusiasm, or at least of sound and simple moral teaching, will be disappointed on consulting these volumes. Looking at many of the books that have lately been published on the religions of the ancient world, I do not wonder that such a belief should have been raised; but I have long felt that it was high time to dispel such illusions, and to place the study of the ancient religions of the world on a more real and sound, on a more truly historical basis. It is but natural that those who write on ancient religions, and who have studied them from translations only, not from original documents, should have had eyes for their bright rather than for their dark sides. The former absorb all the attention of the student, the latter, as they teach nothing, seem hardly to deserve any notice. Scholars also who have devoted their life either to the editing of the original texts or to the careful interpretation of some of the sacred books, are more inclined, after they have disinterred from a heap of rubbish some solitary fragments of pure gold, to exhibit these treasures only than to display all the refuse from which they had to extract them. I do not blame them for this, perhaps I should feel that I was open to the same blame myself, for it is but natural that scholars in their joy at finding one or two fragrant fruits or flowers should gladly forget the brambles and thorns that had to be thrown aside in the course of their search.

But whether I am myself one of the guilty or not, I cannot help calling attention to the real mischief that has been done and is still being done by the enthusiasm of those pioneers who have opened the first avenues through the bewildering forest of the sacred literature of the East. They have raised expectations that cannot be fulfilled, fears also that, as will be easily seen, are unfounded. Anyhow they have removed the study of religion from that wholesome and matter-of-fact atmosphere in which alone it can produce valuable and permanent results.

The time has come when the study of the ancient religions of mankind must be approached in a different, in a less enthusiastic, and more discriminating, in fact, in a more scholarlike spirit. Not that I object to dilettanti, if they only are what by their name they profess to be, devoted lovers, and not mere amateurs. The religions of antiquity must always be approached in a loving spirit, and the dry and cold-blooded scholar is likely to do here as much mischief as the enthusiastic sciolist. But true love does not ignore all faults and failings: on the contrary, it scans them keenly, though only in order to be able to understand, to explain, and thus to excuse them. To watch in the Sacred Books of the East the dawn of the religious consciousness of man, must always remain one of the most inspiring and hallowing sights in the whole history of the world; and he whose heart cannot quiver with the first quivering rays of human thought and human faith, as revealed in those ancient documents, is, in his own way, as unfit for these studies as, from another side, the man who shrinks from copying and collating ancient MSS., or toiling through volumes of tedious commentary. What we want here, as everywhere else, is the truth, and the whole truth; and if the whole truth must be told, it is that, however radiant the dawn of religious thought, it is not without its dark clouds, its chilling colds, its noxious vapours. Whoever does not know these, or would hide them from his own sight and from the sight of others, does not know and can never understand the real toil and travail of the human heart in its first religious aspirations; and not knowing its toil and travail, can never know the intensity of its triumphs and its joys.

In order to have a solid foundation for a comparative study of the religions of the East, we must have before all things complete and thoroughly faithful translations of their sacred books. Extracts will no longer suffice. We do not know Germany, if we know the Rhine; nor Rome, when we have admired St. Peter's. No one who collects and publishes such extracts can resist, no one at all events, so far as I know, has ever resisted, the temptation of giving what is beautiful, or it may be what is strange and startling, and leaving out what is commonplace, tedious, or it may be repulsive, or, lastly, what is difficult to construe and to understand. We must face the problem in its completeness, and I confess it has been for many years a problem to me, aye, and to a great extent is so still, how the Sacred Books of the East should, by the side of so much that is fresh, natural, simple, beautiful, and true, contain so much that is not only unmeaning, artificial, and silly, but even hideous and repellent. This is a fact, and must be accounted for in some way or other.

To some minds this problem may seem to be no problem at all. To those (and I do not speak of Christians only) who look upon the sacred books of all religions except their own as necessarily the outcome of human or superhuman ignorance and depravity, the mixed nature of their contents may seem to be exactly what it ought to be, what they expected it would be. But there are other and more reverent minds who can feel a divine afflatus in the sacred books, not only of their own, but of other religions also, and to them the mixed character of some of the ancient sacred canons must always be extremely perplexing.

I can account for it to a certain extent, though not entirely to my own satisfaction. Most of the ancient sacred books have been handed down by oral tradition for many generations before they were consigned to writing. In an age when there was nothing corresponding to what we call literature, every saying, every proverb, every story handed down from father to son, received very soon a kind of hallowed character. They became sacred heirlooms, sacred, because they came from an unknown source, from a distant age. There was a stage in the development of human thought, when the distance that separated the living generation from their grandfathers or great-grandfathers was as yet the nearest approach to a conception of eternity, and when the name of grandfather and great-grandfather seemed the nearest expression of God[1]. Hence, what had been said by these half-human, half-divine ancestors, if it was preserved at all, was soon looked upon as a more than human utterance. It was received with reverence, it was never questioned and criticised.

Some of these ancient sayings were preserved because they were so true and so striking that they could not be forgotten. They contained eternal truths, expressed for the first time in human language. Of such oracles of truth it was said in India that they had been heard, *s*ruta, and from it arose the word sruti, the recognised term for divine revelation in Sanskrit.

But besides those utterances which had a vitality of their own, strong enough to defy the power of time, there were others which might have struck the minds of the listeners with great force under the peculiar circumstances that evoked them, but which, when these circumstances were forgotten, became trivial and almost unintelligible. A few verses sung by warriors on the eve of a great battle would, if that battle ended in victory, assume a charm quite independent of their poetic merit. They would be repeated in memory of the heroes who conquered, and of the gods who granted victory. But when the heroes, and the gods, and the victory were all forgotten, the song of victory and thanksgiving would often survive as a relic of the past, though almost unintelligible to later generations.

Even a single ceremonial act, performed at the time of a famine or an inundation, and apparently attended with a sudden and almost miraculous success, might often be preserved in the liturgical code of a family or a tribe with a superstitious awe entirely beyond our understanding. It might be repeated for some time on similar

[1] Bishop Callaway, Unkulunkulu, or the Tradition of Creation, as existing among the Amazulu and other tribes of South Africa, p. 7.

emergencies, till when it had failed again and again it survived only as a superstitious custom in the memory of priests and poets.

Further, it should be remembered that in ancient as in modern times, the utterances of men who had once gained a certain prestige, would often receive attention far beyond their merits, so that in many a family or tribe the sayings and teachings of one man, who had once in his youth or manhood uttered words of inspired wisdom, would all be handed down together, without any attempt to separate the grain from the chaff.

Nor must we forget that though oral tradition, when once brought under proper discipline, is a most faithful guardian, it is not without its dangers in its incipient stages. Many a word may have been misunderstood, many a sentence confused, as it was told by father to son, before it became fixed in the tradition of a village community, and then resisted by its very sacredness all attempts at emendation.

Lastly, we must remember that those who handed down the ancestral treasures of ancient wisdom, would often feel inclined to add what seemed useful to themselves, and what they knew could be preserved in one way only, namely, if it was allowed to form part of the tradition that had to be handed down, as a sacred trust, from generation to generation. The priestly influence was at work, even before there were priests by profession, and when the priesthood had once become professional, its influence may account for much that would otherwise seem inexplicable in the sacred codes of the ancient world.

These are some of the considerations which may help to explain how, mixed up with real treasures of thought, we meet in the sacred books with so many passages and whole chapters which either never had any life or meaning at all, or if they had, have, in the form in which they have come down to us, completely lost it. We must try to imagine what the Old Testament would have been, if it had not been kept distinct from the Talmud; or the New Testament, if it had been mixed up not only with the spurious gospels, but with the records of the wranglings of the early Councils, if we wish to understand, to some extent at least, the wild confusion of sublime truth with vulgar stupidity that meets us in the pages of the Veda, the Avesta, and the Tripi*t*aka. The idea of keeping the original and genuine tradition separate from apocryphal accretions was an idea of later growth, that could spring up only after the earlier tendency of preserving whatever could be preserved of sacred or half-sacred lore, had done its work, and wrought its own destruction.

In using, what may seem to some of my fellow-workers, this very strong and almost irreverent language with regard to the ancient Sacred Books of the East, I have not neglected to make full allowance for that very important intellectual parallax which, no doubt, renders it most difficult for a Western observer to see things and thoughts under exactly the same angle and in the same light as they would appear to an Eastern eye. There are Western expressions which offend Eastern taste as much as Eastern expressions are apt to offend Western taste. A symphony of Beethoven's would be mere noise to an Indian ear, an Indian Saṅgîta seems to us without melody, harmony, or rhythm. All this I fully admit, yet after making every allowance for national taste and traditions, I still confidently appeal to the best Oriental scholars, who have not entirely forgotten that there is a world outside the four walls of their study, whether they think that my condemnation is too severe, or that Eastern nations themselves would tolerate, in any of their classical literary compositions, such violations of the simplest rules of taste as they have accustomed themselves to tolerate, if not to admire, in their sacred books.

But then it might no doubt be objected that books of such a character hardly deserve the honour of being translated into English, and that the sooner they are forgotten, the better. Such opinions have of late been freely expressed by some eminent writers, and supported by arguments worthy of the Khalif Omar himself. In these days of anthropological research, when no custom is too disgusting to be recorded, no rules of intermarriage too complicated to be disentangled, it may seem strange that the few genuine relics of ancient religion which, as by a miracle, have been preserved to us, should thus have been judged from a purely aesthetic, and not from an historical point of view. There was some excuse for this in the days of Sir William Jones and Colebrooke. The latter, as is well known, considered 'the Vedas as too voluminous for a complete translation of the whole,' adding that (what they contain would hardly reward the labour of the reader; much less that of the translator[2].' The former went still further in the condemnation which he pronounced on Anquetil Duperron's translation of the Zend-avesta. Sir W. Jones, we must remember, was not only a scholar, but also a man of taste, and the man of taste sometimes gained a victory over the scholar. His controversy with Anquetil Duperron, the discoverer of the Zend-avesta, is well known. It was carried on by Sir W. Jones apparently with great success, and yet in the end the victor has proved to be the vanquished. It was easy, no doubt, to pick out from Anquetil Duperron's translation of the sacred writings of Zoroaster hundreds of passages which were or seemed to be utterly unmeaning or absurd. This arose partly, but partly only, from the imperfections of the translation. Much, however, of what Sir W. Jones represented as ridiculous, and therefore unworthy of Zoroaster, and therefore unworthy of being translated, forms an integral part of the sacred code of the Zoroastrians. Sir W. Jones smiles at those who 'think obscurity sublime and venerable, like that of ancient cloisters and temples,

[2] Colebrooke's Miscellaneous Essays, 1873, vol. ii, p. 102.

shedding,' as Milton expresses it, 'a dim religious light[3].' 'On possédait déjà,' he writes in his letter addressed to Anquetil Duperron, and composed in very good and sparkling French, 'plusieurs traités attribués à Zardusht ou Zeratusht, traduits en Persan moderne; de prétendues conférences de ce législateur avec Ormuzd, des prières, des dogmes, des lois religieuses. Quelques savans, qui ont lu ces traductions, nous ont assure que les originaux étaient de la plus haute antiquité, parce qu'ils renfermaient beaucoup de platitudes, de bévues, et de contradictions: mais nous avons conclu par les mêmes raisons, qu'ils étaient très-modernes, ou bien qu'ils n'étaient pas d'un homme d'esprit, et d'un philosophe, tel que Zoroastre est peint par nos historiens. Votre nouvelle traduction, Monsieur, nous confirme dans ce jugement: tout le collège des Guèbres aurait beau nous l'assurer; nous ne croirons jamais que le charlatan le moins habile ait pu écrire les fadaises dont vos deux derniers volumes sont remplis[4].' He at last sums up his argument in the following words: 'Ou Zoroastre n'avait pas le sens commun, ou il n'écrivit pas le livre que vous lui attribuez: s'il n'avait pas le sens commun, il fallait le laisser dans la foule, et dans l'obscurité; s'il n'écrivit pas ce livre, il était impudent de le publier sous son nom. Ainsi, ou vous avez insulté le goût du public en lui présentant des sottises, ou vous l'avez trompé en lui donnant des faussetés: et de chaque côté vous méritez son mépris[5].'

This alternative holds good no longer. The sacred code of Zoroaster or of any other of the founders of religions may appear to us to be full of absurdities, or may in fact really be so, and it may yet be the duty of the scholar to publish, to translate, and carefully to examine those codes as memorials of the past, as the only trustworthy documents in which to study the growth and decay of religion. It does not answer to say that if Zoroaster was what we believe him to have been, a wise man, in our sense of the word, he could not have written the rubbish which we find in the Avesta. If we are once satisfied that the text of the Avesta, or the Veda, or the Tripi*t*aka is old and genuine, and that this text formed the foundation on which, during many centuries, the religious belief of millions of human beings was based, it becomes our duty, both as historians and philosophers, to study these books, to try to understand how they could have arisen, and how they could have exercised for ages an influence over human beings who in all other respects were not inferior to ourselves, nay, whom we are accustomed to look up to on many points as patterns of wisdom, of virtue, and of taste.

The facts, such as they are, must be faced, if the study of the

---

[3] Sir W. Jones's Works, vol. iv, p. 113.

[4] Ib., vol. x, p. 408.

[5] Works, vol. x, p.437.

ancient religions of the world is ever to assume a really historical character; and having myself grudged no praise to what to my mind is really beautiful or sublime in the early revelations of religious truth, I feel the less hesitation in fulfilling the duty of the true scholar, and placing before historians and philosophers accurate, complete, and unembellished versions of some of the sacred books of the East. Such versions alone will enable them to form a true and just estimate of the real development of early religious thought, so far as we can still gain a sight of it in literary records to which the highest human or even divine authority has been ascribed by the followers of the great religions of antiquity. It often requires an effort to spoil a beautiful sentence by a few words which might so easily be suppressed, but which are there in the original, and must be taken into account quite as much as the pointed ears in the beautiful Faun of the Capitol. We want to know the ancient religions such as they really were, not such as we wish they should have been. We want to know, not their wisdom only, but their folly also; and while we must learn to look up to their highest points where they seem to rise nearer to heaven than anything we were acquainted with before, we must not shrink from looking down into their stony tracts, their dark abysses, their muddy moraines, in order to comprehend both the height and the depth of the human mind in its searchings after the Infinite.

I can answer for myself and for those who have worked with me, that our translations are truthful, that we have suppressed nothing, that we have varnished nothing, however hard it seemed sometimes even to write it down.

There is only one exception. There are in ancient books, and particularly in religious books, frequent allusions to the sexual aspects of nature, which, though perfectly harmless and innocent in themselves, cannot be rendered in modern language without the appearance of coarseness. We may regret that it should be so, but tradition is too strong on this point, and I have therefore felt obliged to leave certain passages untranslated, and to give the original, when necessary, in a note. But this has been done in extreme cases only, and many things which we should feel inclined to suppress have been left in all their outspoken simplicity, because those who want to study ancient man, must learn to study him as he really was, an animal, with all the strength and weaknesses of an animal, though an animal that was to rise above himself, and in the end discover his true self, after many struggles and many defeats.

After this first caution, which I thought was due to those who might expect to find in these volumes nothing but gems, I feel I owe another to those who may approach these translations under the impression that they have only to read them in order to gain an insight into the nature and character of the religions of mankind. There are philosophers who have accustomed themselves to look upon religions as things that can be studied as they study the manners and customs of savage tribes, by glancing at the entertaining accounts of travellers or missionaries, and. then classing each religion under such wide categories as fetishism, polytheism, monotheism, and the rest. That is not the case. Translations can do much, but they can never take the place of the originals, and if the originals require not only to be read, but to be read again and again, translations of sacred books require to be studied with much greater care, before we can hope to gain a real understanding of the intentions of their authors or venture on general assertions.

Such general assertions, if once made, are difficult to extirpate. It has been stated, for instance, that the religious notion of sin is wanting altogether in the hymns of the Rig-veda, and some important conclusions have been based on this supposed fact. Yet the gradual growth of the concept of guilt is one of the most interesting lessons which certain passages of these ancient hymns can teach us[6]. It has been asserted that in the Rig-veda Agni, fire, was adored essentially as earthly sacrificial fire, and not as an elemental force. How greatly such an assertion has to be qualified, may be seen from a more careful examination of the translations of the Vedic hymns now accessible[7]. In many parts of the Avesta fire is no doubt spoken of with great reverence, but those who speak of the Zoroastrians as fire-worshippers, should know that the true followers of Zoroaster abhor that very name. Again, there are certainly many passages in the Vedic writings which prohibit the promiscuous communication of the Veda, but those who maintain that the Brahmans, like Roman Catholic priests, keep their sacred books from the people, must have for gotten the many passages in the Brâhma*n*as, the Sûtras, and even in the Laws of Manu, where the duty of learning the Veda by heart is inculcated for every Brâhma*n*a, Kshatriya, Vaisya, that is, for every man except a *S*ûdra.

These are a few specimens only to show how dangerous it is to generalise even where there exist complete translations of certain sacred books. It is far easier to misapprehend, or even totally to misunderstand, a translation than the original; and it should not be supposed, because a sentence or a whole chapter seems at first sight unintelligible in a translation, that therefore they are indeed devoid of all meaning.

What can be more perplexing than the beginning of the *Kh*ândogya-upanishad? 'Let a man meditate,' we read, or, as others translate it, 'Let a man worship the syllable Om.' It may seem

---

[6] M. M., History of Ancient Sanskrit Literature, second edition, 1859, p.540 seq.

[7] Ludwig, Rig-veda, übersetzt, vol. iii, p. 331 seq. Muir, Sanskrit Texts, vol. v, p. 199 seq. On the later growth of Agni, see a very useful essay by Holtzmann, 'Agni, nach den Vorstellungen des Mahâbhârata,' 1878.

impossible at first sight to elicit any definite meaning from these words and from much that follows after. But it would be a mistake, nevertheless, to conclude that we have here vox et præterea nihil. Meditation on the syllable Om consisted in a long continued repetition of that syllable with a view of drawing the thoughts away from all other subjects, and thus concentrating them on some higher object of thought of which that syllable was made to be the symbol. This concentration of thought, ekâgratâ or one-pointedness, as the Hindus called it, is something to us almost unknown. Our minds are like kaleidoscopes of thoughts in constant motion; and to shut our mental eyes to everything else, while dwelling on one thought only, has become to most of us almost as impossible as to apprehend one musical note without harmonics. With the life we are leading now, with telegrams, letters, newspapers, reviews, pamphlets, and books ever breaking in upon us, it has become impossible, or almost impossible, ever to arrive at that intensity of thought which the Hindus meant by ekâgratâ, and the attainment of which was to them the indispensable condition of all philosophical and religious speculation. The loss may not be altogether on our side, yet a loss it is, and if we see the Hindus, even in their comparatively monotonous life, adopting all kinds of contrivances in order to assist them in drawing away their thoughts from all disturbing impressions and to fix them on one subject only, we must not be satisfied with smiling at their simplicity, but try to appreciate the object they had in view.

When by means of repeating the syllable Om, which originally seems to have meant 'that,' or 'yes,' they had arrived at a certain degree of mental tranquillity, the question arose what was meant by this Om, and to this question the most various answers were given, according as the mind was to be led up to higher and higher objects. Thus in one passage we are told at first that Om is the beginning of the Veda, or, as we have to deal with an Upanishad of the Sâma-veda, the beginning of the Sâma-veda, so that he who meditates on Om, may be supposed to be meditating on the whole of the Sâma-veda. But that is not enough. Om is said to be the essence of the Sâma-veda, which, being almost entirely taken from the Rig-veda, may itself be called the essence of the Rig-veda. And more than that. The Rig-veda stands for all speech, the Sâma-veda for all breath or life, so that Om may be conceived again as the symbol of all speech and all life. Om thus becomes the name, not only of all our physical and mental powers, but especially of the living principle, the Prâ*n*a or spirit. This is explained by the parable in the second chapter, while in the third chapter, that spirit within us is identified with the spirit in the sun. He therefore who meditates on Om, meditates on the spirit in man as identical with the spirit in nature, or in the sun; and thus the lesson that is meant to be taught in the beginning of the *Kh*ândogya-upanishad is really this, that none of the Vedas with their sacrifices and ceremonies could ever secure the salvation of the worshipper, i.e. that sacred works, performed according to the rules of the Vedas, are of no avail in the end , but that meditation on Om alone, or that knowledge of what is meant by Om alone, can procure true salvation, or true immortality. Thus the pupil is led on step by step to what is the highest object of the Upanishads, viz. the recognition of the self in man as identical with the Highest Self or Brahman. The lessons which are to lead up to that highest conception of the universe, both subjective and objective, are no doubt mixed up with much that is superstitious and absurd; still the main object is never lost sight of. Thus, when we come to the eighth chapter, the discussion, though it begins with Om or the Udgîtha, ends with the question of the origin of the world; and though the final answer, namely, that Om means ether (âkâ*s*a), and that ether is the origin of all things, may still sound to us more physical than metaphysical, still the description given of ether or âkâsa, shows that more is meant by it than the physical ether, and that ether is in fact one of the earlier and less perfect names of the Infinite, of Brahman, the universal Self. This, at least, is the lesson which the Brahmans themselves read in this chapter[8]; and if we look at the ancient language of the Upanishads as representing mere attempts at finding expression for what their language could hardly express as yet, we shall, I think, be less inclined to disagree with the interpretation put on those ancient oracles by the later Vedânta philosophers[9], or, at all events, we shall hesitate before we reject what is difficult to interpret, as altogether devoid of meaning.

This is but one instance to show that even behind the fantastic and whimsical phraseology of the sacred writings of the Hindus and other Eastern nations, there may be sometimes aspirations after truth which deserve careful consideration from the student of the psychological development and the historical growth of early religious thought, and that after careful sifting, treasures may be found in what at first we may feel inclined to throw away as utterly worthless.

And now I come to the third caution. Let it not be supposed that a text, three thousand years old, or, even if of more modern date, still widely distant from our own sphere of thought, can be translated in the same manner as a book written a few years ago in French or German. Those who know French and German well enough, know how difficult, nay, how impossible it is, to render justice to certain touches of genius

---

[8] The Upanishad itself says: 'The Brahman is the same as the ether which is around us; and the ether which is around us, is the same as the ether which is within us. And the ether which is within, that is the ether within the heart. That ether in the heart is omnipresent and unchanging. He who knows this obtains omnipresent and unchangeable happiness.' *Kh*. Up. III, 12, 7-9.

[9] Cf. Vedânta-sûtras I, 1, 22.

which the true artist knows how to give to a sentence. Many poets have translated Heine into English or Tennyson into German, many painters have copied the Madonna di San Sisto or the so-called portrait of Beatrice Cenci. But the greater the excellence of these translators, the more frank has been their avowal, that the original is beyond their reach. And what is a translation of modern German into modern English compared with a translation of ancient Sanskrit or Zend or Chinese into any modern language? It is an undertaking which, from its very nature, admits of the most partial success only, and a more intimate knowledge of the ancient language, so far from facilitating the task, of the translator, renders it only more hopeless. Modern words are round, ancient words are square, and we may as well hope to solve the quadrature of the circle, as to express adequately the ancient thoughts of the Veda in modern English.

We must not expect therefore that a translation of the sacred books of the ancients can ever be more than an approximation of our language to theirs, of our thoughts to theirs. The translator, however, if he has once gained the conviction that it is impossible to translate old thought into modern speech, without doing some violence either to the one or to the other, will hardly hesitate in his choice between two evils. He will prefer to do some violence to language rather than to misrepresent old thoughts by clothing them in words which do not fit them. If therefore the reader finds some of these translations rather rugged, if he meets with expressions which sound foreign, with combinations of nouns and adjectives such as he has never seen before, with sentences that seem too long or too abrupt, let him feel sure that the translator has had to deal with a choice of evils, and that when the choice lay between sacrificing idiom or truth, he has chosen the smaller evil of the two. I do not claim, of course, either for myself or for my fellow-workers, that we have always sacrificed as little as was possible of truth or idiom, and that here and there a happier rendering of certain passages may not be suggested by those who come after us. I only wish to warn the reader once more not to expect too much from a translation, and to bear in mind that, easy as it might be to render word by word, it is difficult, aye, sometimes impossible, to render thought by thought.

I shall give one instance only from my own translation of the Upanishads. One of the most important words in the ancient philosophy of the Brahmans is Âtman, nom. sing. Âtmâ. It is rendered in our dictionaries by 'breath, soul, the principle of life and sensation, the individual soul, the self, the abstract individual, self, one's self, the reflexive pronoun, the natural temperament -or disposition, essence, nature, character, peculiarity, the person or the whole body, the body, the understanding, intellect, the mind, the faculty of thought and reason, the thinking faculty, the highest principle of life, Brahma, the supreme deity or soul of the universe, care, effort, pains, firmness, the

Sun, fire, wind, air, a son.'

This will give classical scholars an idea of the chaotic state from which, thanks to the excellent work done by Boehtlingk, Roth, and others, Sanskrit lexicology is only just emerging. Some of the meanings here mentioned ought certainly not to be ascribed to Âtman. It never means, for instance, the understanding, nor could it ever by itself be translated by sun, fire, wind, air, pains or firmness. But after deducting such surplusage, there still remains a large variety of meanings which may, under certain circumstances, be ascribed to Âtman.

When Âtman occurs in philosophical treatises, such as the Upanishads and the Vedânta system which is based on them, it has generally been translated by soul, mind, or spirit. I tried myself to use one or other of these words, but the oftener I employed them, the more I felt their inadequacy, and was driven at last to adopt self and Self as the least liable to misunderstanding.

No doubt in many passages it sounds strange in English to use self, and in the plural selfs instead of selves; but that very strangeness is useful, for while such words as soul and mind and spirit pass over us unrealised, self and selfs will always ruffle the surface of the mind, and stir up some reflection in the reader. In English to speak even of the I and the Non-I, was till lately considered harsh; it may still be called a foreign philosophical idiom. In German the Ich and Nicht-ich have, since the time of Fichte, become recognised and almost familiar, not only as philosophical terms, but as legitimate expressions in the literary language of the day. But while the Ich with Fichte expressed the highest abstraction of personal existence, the corresponding word in Sanskrit, the Aham or Ahaṅkâra, was always looked upon as a secondary development only and as by no means free from all purely phenomenal ingredients. Beyond the Aham or Ego, with all its accidents and limitations, such as sex, sense, language, country, and religion, the ancient sages of India perceived, from a very early time, the Âtman or the self, independent of all such accidents.

The individual âtman or self, however, was with the Brahmans a phase or phenomenal modification only of the Highest Self, and that Highest Self was to them the last point which could be reached by philosophical speculation. It was to them what in other systems of philosophy has been called by various names, τὸ ὄν, the Divine, the Absolute. The highest aim of all thought and study with the Brahman of the Upanishads was to recognise his own self as a mere limited reflection of the Highest Self, to know his self in the Highest Self, and through that knowledge to return to it, and regain his identity with it. Here to know was to be, to know the Âtman was to be the Âtman, and the reward of that highest knowledge after death was freedom from new births, or immortality.

That Highest Self which had become to the ancient Brahmans the goal of all their mental efforts, was looked upon at the same time as the starting-point of all phenomenal existence, the root of the world, the only thing that could truly be said to be, to be real and true. As the root of all that exists, the Âtman was identified with the Brahman, which in Sanskrit is both masculine and neuter, and with the Sat, which is neuter only, that which is, or Satya, the true, the real. It alone exists in the beginning and for ever; it has no second. Whatever else is said to exist, derives its real being from the Sat. How the one Sat became many, how what we call the creation, what they call emanation (πρόοδος), constantly proceeds and returns to it, has been explained in various more or less fanciful ways by ancient prophets and poets. But what they all agree in is this, that the whole creation, the visible and invisible world, all plants, all animals, all men are due to the one Sat, are upheld by it, and will return to it.

If we translate Âtman by soul, mind, or spirit, we commit, first of all, that fundamental mistake of using words which may be predicated, in place of a word which is a subject only, and can never become a predicate. We may say in English that man possesses a soul, that a man is out of his mind, that man has or even that man is a spirit, but we could never predicate Âtman, or self, of anything else. Spirit, if it means breath or life; mind, if it means the organ of perception and conception; soul, if, like *k*aitanya, it means intelligence in general, all these may be predicated of the Âtman, as manifested in the phenomenal world. But they are never subjects in the sense in which the Âtman is; they have no independent being, apart from Âtman. Thus to translate the beginning of the Aitareya-upanishad, Âtmâ vâ idam eka evâgra âsît, by 'This (world) verily was before (the creation of the world) soul alone' (Röer); or, 'Originally this (universe) was indeed soul only' (Colebrooke), would give us a totally false idea. M. Regnaud in his 'Matériaux pour servir à l'histoire de la philosophie de l'Inde' (vol. ii, p. 24) has evidently felt this, and has kept the word Âtman untranslated, 'Au commencement cet univers n'était que l'âtman.' But while in French it would seem impossible to find any equivalent for âtman, I have ventured to translate in English, as I should have done in German, 'Verily, in the beginning all this was Self, one only.'

Thus again when we read in Sanskrit, 'Know the Self by the self,' âtmânam âtmanâ pa*s*ya, tempting as it may seem, it would be entirely wrong to render it by the Greek γνῶθι σεαυτόν. The Brahman called upon his young pupil to know not himself, but his Self, that is, to know his individual self as a merely temporary reflex of the Eternal Self. Were we to translate this so-called âtmavidyâ, this self-knowledge, by knowledge of the soul, we should not be altogether wrong, but we should nevertheless lose all that distinguishes Indian from Greek thought. It may not be good English to say to know his self, still less to know our selfs, but it would be bad Sanskrit to say to know himself, to know ourselves; or, at all events, such a rendering would deprive us of the greatest advantage in the study of Indian philosophy, the opportunity of seeing in how many different ways man has tried to solve the riddles of the world and of his soul.

I have thought it best therefore to keep as close as possible to the Sanskrit original, and where I could not find an adequate term in English, I have often retained the Sanskrit word rather than use a misleading substitute in English. It is impossible, for instance, to find an English equivalent for so simple a word as Sat, τὸ ὄν. We cannot render the Greek τὸ ὄν and τὸ μὴ ὄν by Being or Not-being, for both are abstract nouns; nor by 'the Being,' for this would almost always convey a wrong impression. In German it is easy to distinguish between das Sein, i.e. being, in the abstract, and das Seiende, τὸ ὄν. In the same way the Sanskrit sat can easily be rendered in Greek by τὸ ὄν, in German by das Seiende, but in English, unless we say 'that which is,' we are driven to retain the original Sat.

From this Sat was derived in Sanskrit Sat-ya, meaning originally 'endowed with being,' then 'true.' This is an adjective; but the same word, as a neuter, is also used in the sense of truth, as an abstract; and in translating it is very necessary always to distinguish between Satyam, the true, frequently the same as Sat, τὸ ὄν, and Satyam, truth, veracity. One example will suffice to show how much the clearness of a translation depends on the right rendering of such words as âtman, sat, and satyam.

In a dialogue between Uddâlaka and his son *S*vetaketu, in which the father tries to open his son's mind, and to make him see man's true relation to the Highest Self (*Kh*ândogya-upanishad VI), the father first explains how the Sat produced what we should call the three elements[10], viz. fire, water, and earth, which he calls heat, water, and food. Having produced them (VI, 2, 4), the Sat entered into them, but not with its real nature, but only with its 'living self' (VI, 3, which is a reflection (âbhâsamâtram) of the real Sat, as the sun in the water is a reflection of the real sun. By this apparent union of the Sat with the three elements, every form (rûpa) and every name (nâman) in the world was produced; and therefore he who knows the three elements is supposed to know everything in this world, nearly in the same manner in which the Greeks imagined that through a knowledge of the elements, everything else became known (VI, 4, 7). The same three elements are shown to be also the constituent elements of man (VI, 5). Food or the earthy element is supposed to produce not only flesh, but also mind; water, not only blood, but also breath; heat, not only bone,

[10] Devatâs, literally deities, but frequently to be translated by powers or beings. Mahadeva Moreshvar Kunte, the learned editor of the Vedânta-sûtras, ought not (p. 70) to have rendered devâta, in Kh. Up. I, 11, 5, by goddess.

but also speech. This is more or less fanciful; the important point, however, is this, that, from the Brahmanic point of view, breath, speech, and mind are purely elemental, or external instruments, and require the support of the living self, the *g*îvâtman, before they can act.

Having explained how the Sat produces progressively heat, how heat leads to water, water to earth, and how, by a peculiar mixture of the three, speech, breath, and mind are produced, the teacher afterwards shows how in death, speech returns to mind, mind to breath, breath to heat, and heat to the Sat (VI, 8, 6). This Sat, the root of everything, is called parâ devatâ, the highest deity, not in the ordinary sense of the word deity, but as expressing the highest abstraction of the human mind. We must therefore translate it by the Highest Being, in the same manner as we translate devatâ, when applied to heat, water, and earth, not by deity, but by substance or element.

The same Sat, as the root or highest essence of all material existence, is called a*n*iman, from a*n*u, small, subtile, infinitesimal, atom. It is an abstract word, and I have translated it by subtile essence.

The father then goes on explaining in various ways that this Sat is underlying all existence, and that we must learn to recognise it as the root, not only of all the objective, but likewise of our own subjective existence. 'Bring the fruit of a Nyagrodha tree,' he says, 'break it, and what do you find?' 'The seeds,' the son replies, 'almost infinitesimal.' 'Break one of them, and tell me what you see.' 'Nothing,' the son replies. Then the father continues: 'My son, that subtile essence which you do not see there, of that very essence this great Nyagrodha tree exists.'

After that follows this sentence: 'Etadâtmyam ida*m* sarvam, tat satyam, sa âtmâ, tat tvam asi *S*vetaketu.'

This sentence has been rendered by Rajendralal Mitra in the following way: 'All this universe has the (Supreme) Deity for its life. That Deity is Truth. He is the Universal Soul. Thou art He, O Svetaketu[11].'

This translation is quite correct, as far as the words go, but I doubt whether we can connect any definite thoughts with these words. In spite of the division adopted in the text, I believe it will be necessary to join this sentence with the last words of the preceding paragraph. This is clear from the commentary, and from later paragraphs, where this sentence is repeated, VI, 9, 4, &c. The division in the printed text (VI, 8, 6) is wrong, and VI, 8, 7 should begin with sa ya esho '*n*imâ, i.e. that which is the subtile essence.

The question then is, what is further to be said about this subtile essence. I have ventured to translate the passage in the following way:

[11] Anquetil Duperron translates: 'Ipso hoc modo (ens) illud est subtile: et hoc omne, unus âtma est: et id verum et rectum est, O Sopatkit, tatoumes, id est, ille âtma tu as.'

'That which is the subtile essence (the Sat, the root of everything), in it all that exists has its self, or more literally, its self-hood. It is the True (not the Truth in the abstract, but that which truly and really exists). It is the Self, i.e. the Sat is what is called the Self of everything[12].' Lastly, he sums up, and tells Svetaketu that, not only the whole world, but he too himself is that Self, that Satya, that Sat.

No doubt this translation sounds strange to English ears, but as the thoughts contained in the Upanishads are strange, it would be wrong to smoothe down their strangeness by clothing them in language familiar to us, which, because it is familiar, will fail to startle us, and because it fails to startle us, will fail also to set us thinking.

To know oneself to be the Sat, to know that all that is real and eternal in us is the Sat, that all came from it and will, through knowledge, return to it, requires an independent effort of speculative thought. We must realise, as well as we can, the thoughts of the ancient Rishis, before we can hope to translate them. It is not enough simply to read the half-religious, half-philosophical utterances which we find in the Sacred Books of the East, and to say that they are strange, or obscure, or mystic. Plato is strange, till we know him; Berkeley is mystic, till for a time we have identified ourselves with him. So it is with these ancient sages, who have become the founders of the great religions of antiquity. They can never be judged from without, they must be judged from within. We need not become Brahmans or Buddhists or Taosze altogether, but we must for a time, if we wish to understand, and still more, if we are bold enough to undertake to translate their doctrines. Whoever shrinks from that effort, will see hardly anything in these sacred books or their translations but matter to wonder at or to laugh at; possibly something to make him thankful that he is not as other men. But to the patient reader these same books will, in spite of many drawbacks, open a new view of the history of the human race, of that one race to which we all belong, with all the fibres of our flesh, with all the fears and hopes of our soul. We cannot separate ourselves from those who believed in these sacred books. There is no specific difference between ourselves and the Brahmans, the Buddhists, the Zoroastrians, or the Taosze. Our powers of perceiving, of reasoning, and of believing may be more highly developed, but we cannot claim the possession of any verifying power or of any power of belief which they did not possess as well. Shall we say then that they were forsaken of God, while we are His chosen people? God forbid! There is much, no doubt, in their sacred books which we should tolerate no longer, though we must not forget that

---

[12] The change of gender in sa for tad is idiomatic. One could not say in Sanskrit tad âtmâ, it is the Self, but sa âtmâ. By sa, he, the Sat, that which is, is meant. The commentary explains sa âtmâ by tat sat, and continues tat sat tat tvam asi (p.443).

there are portions in our own sacred books, too, which many of us would wish to be absent, which, from the earliest ages of Christianity, have been regretted by theologians of undoubted piety, and which often prove a stumbling block to those who have been won over by our missionaries to the simple faith of Christ. But that is not the question. The question is, whether there is or whether there is not, hidden in every one of the sacred books, something that could lift up the human heart from this earth to a higher world, something that could make man feel the omnipresence of a higher Power, something that could make him shrink from evil and incline to good, something to sustain him in the short journey through life, with its bright moments of happiness, and its long hours of terrible distress.

If some of those who read and mark these translations learn how to discover some such precious grains in the sacred books of other nations, though hidden under heaps of rubbish, our labour will not have been in vain, for there is no lesson which at the present time seems more important than to learn that in every religion there are such precious grains; that we must draw in every religion a broad distinction between what is essential and what is not, between the eternal and the temporary, between the divine and the human; and that though the non-essential may fill many volumes, the essential can often be comprehended in a few words, but words on which 'hang all the law and the prophets.'

Program of a Translation of the Sacred Books of the East

I here subjoin the program in which I first put forward the idea of a translation of the Sacred Books of the East, and through which I invited the co-operation of Oriental scholars in this undertaking. The difficulty of finding translators, both willing and competent to take a part in it, proved far greater than I had anticipated. Even when I had secured the assistance of a number of excellent scholars, and had received their promises of prompt co-operation, illness, domestic affliction, and even death asserted their control over all human affairs. Professor Childers, who had shown the warmest interest in our work, and on whom I chiefly depended for the Pali literature of the Buddhists, was taken from us, an irreparable loss to Oriental scholarship in general, and to our undertaking in particular. Among native scholars, whose co-operation I had been particularly desired to secure, Rajendralal Mitra, who had promised a translation of the Vâyu-purâ*n*a, was prevented by serious illness from fulfilling his engagement. In other cases sorrow and sickness have caused, at all events, serious delay in the translation of the very books which were to have inaugurated this Series. However, new offers of assistance have come, and I hope that more may still come from Oriental scholars both in India and England, so that the limit of time which had been originally assigned to the publication of twenty-four volumes may not, I hope, be much exceeded.

THE SACRED BOOKS OF THE EAST, TRANSLATED, WITH INTRODUCTIONS AND NOTES, BY VARIOUS ORIENTAL SCHOLARS, AND EDITED BY F. MAX MULLER.

Apart from the interest which the Sacred Books of all religions possess in the eyes of the theologian, and, more particularly, of the missionary, to whom an accurate knowledge of them is as indispensable as a knowledge of the enemy's country is to a general, these works have of late assumed a new importance, as viewed in the character of ancient historical documents. In every country where Sacred Books have been preserved, whether by oral tradition or by writing, they are the oldest records, and mark the beginning of what may be called documentary, in opposition to purely traditional, history.

There is nothing more ancient in India than the Vedas; and, if we except the Vedas and the literature connected with them, there is again no literary work in India which, so far as we know at present, can with certainty be referred to an earlier date than that of the Sacred Canon of the Buddhists. Whatever age we may assign to the various portions of the Avesta and to their final arrangement, there is no book in the Persian language of greater antiquity than the Sacred Books of the followers of Zarathustra, nay, even than their translation in Pehlevi. There may have been an extensive ancient literature in China long before Khung-fû-ȝze and Lâo-ȝze, but among all that was rescued and preserved of it, the five King and the four Shû claim again the highest antiquity. As to the Koran, it is known to be the fountain-head both of the religion and of the literature of the Arabs.

This being the case, it was but natural that the attention of the historian should of late have been more strongly attracted by these Sacred Books, as likely to afford most valuable information, not only on the religion, but also on the moral sentiments, the social institutions, the legal maxims of some of the most important nations of antiquity. There are not many nations that have preserved sacred writings, and many of those that have been preserved have but lately become accessible to us in their original form, through the rapid advance of Oriental scholarship in Europe. Neither Greeks, nor Romans, nor Germans, nor Celts, nor Slaves have left us anything that deserves the name of Sacred Books. The Homeric Poems are national Epics, like the Râmâya*n*a, and the Nibelunge, and the Homeric Hymns have never received that general recognition or sanction which alone can impart to the poetical effusions of personal piety the sacred or canonical character which is the distinguishing feature of the Vedic Hymns. The sacred literature of the early inhabitants of Italy seems to have been of a liturgical rather than of a purely religious kind, and whatever the Celts, the Germans, the Slaves may have possessed of sacred traditions about their gods and heroes, having been handed down by oral tradition chiefly, has perished beyond all hope of recovery. Some portions of the Eddas alone give us an idea of what the religious and heroic poetry of the Scandinavians may have been. The Egyptians possessed Sacred Books, and some of them, such as the Book of the Dead, have come down to us in various forms. There is a translation of the Book of the Dead by Dr. Birch, published in the fifth volume of Bunsen's Egypt, and a new edition and translation of this important work may be expected from the combined labours of Birch, Chabas, Lepsius, and Naville, In Babylon and Assyria, too, important fragments of what may be called a Sacred Literature have lately come to light. The interpretation, however, of these Hieroglyphic and Cuneiform texts is as yet so difficult that, for the present, they are of interest to the scholar only, and hardly available for historical purposes.

Leaving out of consideration the Jewish and Christian Scriptures, it appears that the only great and original religions which profess to be founded on Sacred Books[13], and have preserved them in manuscript, are:—

1. The religion of the Brahmans.
2. The religion of the followers of Buddha.
3. The religion of the followers of Zarathustra.
4. The religion of the followers of Khung-fû-ʒze.
5. The religion of the followers of Lâo-ʒze.
6. The religion of the followers of Mohammed.

A desire for a trustworthy translation of the Sacred Books of these six Eastern religions has often been expressed. Several have been translated into English, French, German, or Latin, but in some cases these translations are difficult to procure, in others they are loaded with notes and commentaries, which are intended for students by profession only. Oriental scholars have been blamed for not having as yet supplied a want so generally felt, and so frequently expressed, as a complete, trustworthy, and readable translation of the principal Sacred Books of the Eastern Religions. The reasons, however, why hitherto they have shrunk from such an undertaking are clear enough. The difficulties in many cases of giving complete translations, and not selections only, are very great. There is still much work to be done in a critical restoration of the original texts, in an examination of their grammar and metres, and in determining the exact meaning of many words and passages.

---

[13] Introduction to the Science of Religion, by F. Max Müller (Longmans, 1873), p.104.

That kind of work is naturally far more attractive to scholars than a mere translation, particularly when they cannot but feel that, with the progress of our knowledge, many a passage which now seems clear and easy, may, on being re-examined, assume a new import. Thus while scholars who are most competent to undertake a translation, prefer to devote their time to more special researches, the work of a complete translation is deferred to the future, and historians are left under the impression that Oriental scholarship is still in so unsatisfactory a state as to make any reliance on translations of the Veda, the Avesta, or the Tâo-te King extremely hazardous.

It is clear, therefore, that a translation of the principal Sacred Books of the East can be carried out only at a certain sacrifice. Scholars must leave for a time their own special researches in order to render the general results already obtained accessible to the public at large. And even then, really useful results can be achieved viribus unitis only. If four of the best Egyptologists have to combine in order to produce a satisfactory edition and translation of one of the Sacred Books of ancient Egypt, a much larger number of Oriental scholars will be required for translating the Sacred Books of the Brahmans, the Buddhists, the Zoroastrians, the followers of Khung-fû-ʒze, Lâo-ʒze, and Mohammed.

Lastly, there was the most serious difficulty of all, a difficulty which no scholar could remove, viz. the difficulty of finding the funds necessary for carrying out so large an undertaking. No doubt there exists at present a very keen interest in questions connected with the origin, the growth, and decay of religion. But much of that interest is theoretic rather than historical. How people might or could or should have elaborated religious ideas, is a topic most warmly discussed among psychologists and theologians, but a study of the documents, in which alone the actual growth of religious thought can be traced, is much neglected. A faithful, unvarnished prose translation of the Sacred Books of India, Persia, China, and Arabia, though it may interest careful students, will never, I fear, excite a widespread interest, or command a circulation large enough to make it a matter of private enterprise and commercial speculation.

No doubt there is much in these old books that is startling by its very simplicity and truth, much that is elevated and elevating, much that is beautiful and sublime; but people who have vague ideas of primeval wisdom and the splendour of Eastern poetry will soon find themselves grievously disappointed. It cannot be too strongly stated, that the chief, and, in many cases, the only interest of the Sacred Books of the East is historical; that much in them is extremely childish, tedious, if not repulsive; and that no one but the historian will be able to understand the important lessons which they teach. It would have been impossible to undertake a translation even of the most important only of the Sacred Books of the East, without the support of an Academy or a University which recognises the necessity of rendering these works more generally accessible, on the same grounds on which it recognises the duty of collecting and exhibiting in Museums the petrifactions of bygone ages, little concerned whether the public admires the beauty of fossilised plants and broken skeletons, as long as hard-working students find there some light for reading once more the darker pages in the history of the earth.

Having been so fortunate as to secure that support, having also received promises of assistance from some of the best Oriental scholars in England and India, I hope I shall be able, after the necessary preparations are completed, to publish about three volumes of translations every year, selecting from the stores of the six so-called 'Book-religions' those works which at present can be translated, and which are most likely to prove useful. All translations will be made from the original texts, and where good translations exist already, they will be carefully revised by competent scholars. Such is the bulk of the religious literature of the Brahmans and the Buddhists, that to attempt a complete translation would be far beyond the powers of one generation of scholars. Still, if the interest in the work itself should continue, there is no reason why this series of translations should not be carried on, even after those who commenced it shall have ceased from their labours.

What I contemplate at present and I am afraid at my time of life even this may seem too sanguine, is no more than a Series of twenty-four volumes, the publication of which will probably extend over eight years. In this Series I hope to comprehend the following books, though I do not pledge myself to adhere strictly to this outline:—

1. From among the Sacred Books of the Brahmans I hope to give a translation of the Hymns of the Rig-veda. While I shall continue my translation of selected hymns of that Veda, a traduction raisonnée which is intended for Sanskrit scholars only, on the same principles which I have followed in the first volume[14], explaining every word and sentence that seems to require elucidation, and carefully examining the opinions of previous commentators, both native and European, I intend to contribute a freer translation of the hymns to this Series, with a few explanatory notes only, such as are absolutely necessary to enable readers who are unacquainted with Sanskrit to understand the thoughts of the Vedic poets. The translation of perhaps another Sa*m*hitâ, one or two of the Brâhma*n*as, or portions of them, will have to be included in our Series, as well as the principal Upanishads, theosophic treatises of great interest and beauty. There is every prospect of an early

[14] Rig-veda-sanhitâ, The Sacred Hymns of the Brahmans, translated and explained by F. Max Müller. Vol. i. Hymns to the Maruts or the Storm-Gods. London, 1869.

appearance of a translation of the Bhagavad-gîtâ, of the most important among the sacred Law-books, and of one at least of the Purânas. I should have wished to include a translation of some of the *G*ain books, of the Granth of the Sikhs, and of similar works illustrative of the later developments of religion in India, but there is hardly room for them at present.

2. The Sacred Books of the Buddhists will be translated chiefly from the two original collections, the Southern in Pali, the Northern in Sanskrit. Here the selection will, no doubt, be most difficult. Among the first books to be published will be, I hope, Sûtras from the Dîgha Nikâya, a part of the Vinaya-pi*t*aka, the Dhammapada, the Divyâvadâna, the Lalita-vistara, or legendary life of Buddha.

3. The Sacred Books of the Zoroastrians lie within a smaller compass, but they will require fuller notes and commentaries in order to make a translation intelligible and useful.

4. The books which enjoy the highest authority with the followers of Khung-fû-ȝze are the King and the Shû. Of the former the Shû King or Book of History; the Odes of the Temple and the Altar, and other pieces illustrating the ancient religious views and practices of the Chinese, in the Shih King or Book of Poetry; the Yî King; the Lî *K*î; and the Hsiâo King or Classic of Filial Piety, will all be given, it is hoped, entire. Of the latter, the Series will contain the *K*ung Yung or Doctrine of the Mean; the Tâ Hsio or Great Learning; all Confucius' utterances in the Lun Yü or Confucian Analects, which are of a religious nature, and refer to the principles of his moral system; and Mang-ȝze's Doctrine of the Goodness of Human Nature.

5. For the system of Lâo-ȝze we require only a translation of the Tâo-teh King with some of its commentaries, and, it may be, an authoritative work to illustrate the actual operation of its principles.

6. For Islam, all that is essential is a trustworthy translation of the Koran.

It will be my endeavour to divide the twenty-four volumes which are contemplated in this Series as equally as possible among the six religions. But much must depend on the assistance which I receive from Oriental scholars, and also on the interest and the wishes of the public.

F. MAX MÜLLER.

OXFORD, October, 1876.

The following distinguished scholars, all of them occupying the foremost rank in their own special departments of Oriental literature, are at present engaged in preparing translations of some of the Sacred Books of the East: S. Beal, R. G. Bhandarkar, G. Bühler, A. Burnell, E. B. Cowell, J. Darmesteter, T. W. Rhys Davids, J. Eggeling, V. Fausböll, H. Jacobi, J. Jolly, H. Kern, F. Kielhorn, J. Legge, H. Oldenberg, E. H. Palmer, R. Pischel, K. T. Telang, E. W. West.

The works which for the present have been selected for translation are the following:

I. ANCIENT VEDIC RELIGION.

Hymns of the *Ri*g-veda.
The *S*atapatha-brâhma*n*a.
The Upanishads.
The G*ri*hya-sûtras of Hira*n*yake*s*in and others.

II. LAW-BOOKS IN PROSE.

The Sûtras of Âpastamba, Gautama, Baudhâyana, Vasishtha, Vishnu, &c.

III. LAW-BOOKS IN VERSE.

The Laws of Manu, Yâgñavalkya, &c.

IV. LATER BRAHMANISM.

The Bhagavad-gîtâ.
The Vâyu-purâ*n*a.

V. BUDDHISM.

1. Pali Documents.

The Mahâparinibbâna Sutta, the Tevigga Sutta, the Mahasudassana Sutta, the Dhamma*k*akkappavattana Sutta; the Suttanipâta; the Mahâvagga, the *K*ullavagga, and the Pâtimokkha.

2. Sanskrit Documents.

The Divyâvadâna and Saddharmapu*nd*arîka.

3. Chinese Documents.

The Phû-yâo King, or life of Buddha.

4. Prakrit *G*aina Documents.

The Â*k*ârâṅga Sûtra, Da*s*avaikâlika Sûtra, Sûtrak*ri*tâṅga, and Uttarâdhyayana Sûtra.

VI. PARSI RELIGION.

1. Zend Documents.

The Vendîdâd.

2. Pehlevi and Parsi Documents.

The Bundahi*s*, Bahman Yasht, Shâyast-lâ-shâyast, Dâdistâni Dînî, Mainyôi Khard.

VII. MOHAMMEDANISM.

The Koran.

VIII. CHINESE RELIGION.

1. Confucianism.

The Shû King, Shih King, Hsiâo King, Yî King, Lî *K*î, Lun Yü, and Măng-ȝze.

2. Tâoism.

The Tâo-teh King, Kwang-ȝze, and Kan Ying Phien.

Transliteration of Oriental Alphabets

The system of transcribing Oriental words with Roman types, adopted by the translators of the Sacred Books of the East, is, on the whole, the same which I first laid down in my Proposals for a Missionary Alphabet, 1854, and which afterwards I shortly described in my Lectures on the Science of Language, Second Series, p. 169 (ninth edition). That system allows of great freedom in its application to different languages, and has, therefore, recommended itself to many scholars, even if they had long been accustomed to use their own system of transliteration.

It rests in fact on a few principles only, which may be applied to individual languages according to the views which each student has formed for himself of the character and the pronunciation of the vowels and consonants of any given alphabet.

It does not differ essentially from the Standard Alphabet proposed by Professor Lepsius. It only endeavours to realise, by means of the ordinary types which are found in every printing office, what my learned friend has been enabled to achieve, it may be in a more perfect manner, by means of a number of new types with diacritical marks, cast expressly for him by the Berlin Academy.

The general principles of what, on account of its easy application to all languages, I have called the Missionary Alphabet, are these:

1. No letters are to be used which do not exist in ordinary founts.

2. The same Roman type is always to represent the same foreign letter, and the same foreign letter is always to be represented by the same Roman type.

3. Simple letters are, as a rule, to be represented by simple, compound by compound types.

4. It is not attempted to indicate the pronunciation of foreign languages, but only to represent foreign letters by Roman types, leaving the pronunciation to be learnt, as it is now, from grammars or from conversation with natives.

5. The foundation of every system of transliteration must consist of a classification of the typical sounds of human speech. Such classification may be more or less perfect, more or less minute, according to the objects in view. For ordinary purposes the classification in vowels and consonants, and of consonants again in gutturals, dentals, and labials suffices. In these three classes we distinguish hard (not-voiced) and sonant (voiced) consonants, each being liable to aspiration; nasals, sibilants, and semivowels, some of these also, being either voiced or not-voiced.

6. After having settled the typical sounds, we assign to them, as much as possible, the ordinary Roman types of the first class.

7. We then arrange in every language which possesses a richer alphabet, all remaining letters, according to their affinities, as modifications of the nearest typical letters, or as letters of the second and third class. Thus linguals in Sanskrit are treated as nearest to dentals, palatals to gutturals.

8. The manner of expressing such modifications is uniform throughout. While all typical letters of the first class are expressed by Roman types, modified letters of the second class are expressed by italics, modified letters of the third class by small capitals. Only in extreme cases, where another class of modified types is wanted, are we compelled to have recourse either to diacritical marks, or to a different fount of types.

9. Which letters in each language are to be considered as primary, secondary, or tertiary may, to a certain extent, be left to the discretion of individual scholars.

10. As it has been found quite impossible to devise any practical alphabet that should accurately represent the pronunciation of words, the Missionary Alphabet, by not attempting to indicate minute shades of pronunciation, has at all events the advantage of not misleading readers in their pronunciation of foreign words. An italic *t*, for instance, or a small capital T, serves simply as a warning that this is not the ordinary t, though it has some affinity with it. How it is to be pronounced must be learnt for each language, as it now is, from a grammar or otherwise. Thus *t* in Sanskrit is the lingual *t*. How that is to be pronounced, we must learn from the Prâtisâkhvas, or from the mouth of a highly educated *S*rotriya. We shall then learn that its pronunciation is really that of what we call the ordinary dental t, as in town, while the ordinary dental t in Sanskrit has a pronunciation of its own, extremely difficult to acquire for Europeans.

11. Words or sentences which used to be printed in italics are spaced.

TRANSLITERATION OF ORIENTAL ALPHABETS ADOPTED FOR THE TRANSLATIONS OF THE SACRED BOOKS OF THE EAST.

CONSONANTS.	MISSIONARY ALPHABET.			Sanskrit.	Zend.	Pehlevi.	Persian.	Arabic.	Hebrew.	Chinese.
	I Class.	II Class.	III Class.							
Gutturales.										
1 Tenuis	k	...	....	क	𐬐	[illegible]	ك	ك	כּ	k
2 „ aspirata	kh	...	....	ख	𐬑	[illegible]	...	...	כ	kh
3 Media	g	...	....	ग	𐬔	[illegible]	گ	...	גּ	...
4 „ aspirata	gh	...	....	घ	𐬖	[illegible]	...	...	ג	...
5 Gutturo-labialis	q	...	....	...	....	...	ق	ق	ק	...
6 Nasalis	ṅ (ng)	...	....	ङ	{ 𐬣 (ng) / 𐬧 (N) }	...	...	...	...	...
7 Spiritus asper	h	...	....	ह	𐬵 (𐬓 *hv*)	[illegible]	ه	ه	ה	h, hs
8 „ lenis	’	...	....	...	....	...	ا	ا	א	...
9 „ asper faucalis	‘h	...	....	...	....	...	ح	ح	ח	...
10 „ lenis faucalis	’h	...	....	...	....	...	ع	ع	ע	...
11 „ asper fricatus	...	*‘h*	....	...	....	...	غ	غ	ה	...
12 „ lenis fricatus	...	*’h*	....	...	....	...	...	...	...	...
Gutturales modificatae (palatales, &c.)										
13 Tenuis	...	*k*	....	च	𐬗	[illegible]	چ	...	...	*k*
14 „ aspirata	...	*kh*	....	छ	....	...	...	...	...	*kh*
15 Media	...	*g*	....	ज	𐬘	[illegible]	ج	ج	...	...
16 „ aspirata	...	*gh*	....	झ	....	...	غ	غ	...	...
17 „ Nasalis	ñ	...	....	ञ	....	...	...	...	...	...

CONSONANTS (*continued*).	MISSIONARY ALPHABET. I Class.	II Class.	III Class.	Sanskrit.	Zend.	Pehlevi.	Persian.	Arabic.	Hebrew.	Chinese.
18 Semivocalis	y	...	...	य	[illegible] init. [illegible]	[illegible]	ي	ي	י	y
19 Spiritus asper	...	(y̔)	...	...	...	...	...	...	...	...
20 ,, lenis	...	(y̓)	...	...	...	...	...	...	...	...
21 ,, asper assibilatus	...	*s*	...	श	[illegible]	[illegible]	ش	ش	...	...
22 ,, lenis assibilatus	...	*z*	...	...	[illegible]	[illegible]	ژ	...	...	*z*
Dentales.										
23 Tenuis	t	...	...	त	[illegible]	[illegible]	ت	ت	תּ	t
24 ,, aspirata	th	...	...	थ	[illegible]	...	...	...	ת	th
25 ,, assibilata	...	...	TH	...	...	...	ث	ث	...	...
26 Media	d	...	...	द	[illegible]	[illegible]	د	د	דּ	...
27 ,, aspirata	dh	...	...	ध	[illegible]	...	...	...	ד	...
28 ,, assibilata	...	...	DH	...	...	...	ذ	ذ	...	...
29 Nasalis	n	...	...	न	[illegible]	[illegible]	ن	ن	נ	n
30 Semivocalis	l	...	...	ल	...	[illegible]	ل	ل	ל	l
31 ,, mollis 1	...	*l*	...	ळ	...	...	...	...	...	...
32 ,, mollis 2	...	...	L	...	...	...	...	...	...	...
33 Spiritus asper 1	s	...	...	स	[illegible]	[illegible]	س(ث)	س	שׂ	s
34 ,, asper 2	...	...	s (ʃ)	...	...	...	...	...	ס	...
35 ,, lenis	z	...	...	...	[illegible]	[illegible]	ز (ذ)	ز	ז	z
36 ,, asperrimus 1	...	...	z (ʒ)	...	...	...	ص	ص	צ	ʒ, ʒh
37 ,, asperrimus 2	...	...	ẓ (ʒ̣)	...	...	...	ض	...	...	...

Dentales modificatae (linguales, &c.)										
38 Tenuis	...	*t*	....	ट	....	...	ط	ط	ט	...
39 „ aspirata	...	*th*	....	ठ	....	...	ظ	ظ	...	...
40 Media	...	*d*	....	ड	[illegible]	[illegible]	...	...	...	...
41 „ aspirata	...	*dh*	....	ढ	....	...	...	ض	...	...
42 Nasalis	...	*n*	....	ण	[illegible]	...	...	...	...	...
43 Semivocalis	r	...	....	र	[illegible]	[illegible]	ر	ر	ר	...
44 „ fricata	...	*r*	....	...	....	...	...	...	...	*r*
45 „ diacritica	...	...	R	...	....	...	...	...	...	...
46 Spiritus asper	sh	...	....	ष	[illegible]	[illegible]	...	...	...	sh
47 „ lenis	zh	...	....	...	....	...	...	...	...	...
Labiales.										
48 Tenuis	p	...	....	प	[illegible]	[illegible]	پ	...	פּ	p
49 „ aspirata	ph	...	....	फ	....	...	...	...	פ	ph
50 Media	b	...	....	ब	[illegible]	[illegible]	ب	ب	בּ	...
51 „ aspirata	bh	...	....	भ	....	...	...	...	ב	...
52 Tenuissima	...	*p*	....	...	....	...	...	...	...	...
53 Nasalis	m	...	....	म	[illegible]	[illegible]	م	م	מ	m
54 Semivocalis	w	...	....	...	[illegible]	...	...	...	...	w
55 „ aspirata	hw	...	....	...	....	...	...	...	...	...
56 Spiritus asper	f	...	....	...	[illegible]	[illegible]	ف	ف	...	f
57 „ lenis	v	...	....	व	»	[illegible]	و	و	ו	...
58 Anusvâra	...	*m*	....	अं	[illegible] ã	...	...	...	...	...
59 Visarga	...	*h*	....	अः	....	...	...	...	...	...

VOWELS.	MISSIONARY ALPHABET. I Class.	II Class.	III Class.	Sanskrit.	Zend.	Pehlevi.	Persian.	Arabic.	Hebrew.	Chinese.
1 Neutralis	0	...	....	...	....	...	...	...	◌ֲ	ă
2 Laryngo-palatalis	ĕ	...	....	...	....	...	...	...	...	...
3 „ labialis	ŏ	...	....	...	....	𐭠 fin.	...	...	...	...
4 Gutturalis brevis	a	...	....	अ	𐬀	𐭠 init	◌َ	◌َ	◌ַ	a
5 „ longa	â	(*a*)	....	आ	𐬁	𐭠	◌َا	◌َا	◌ָ	â
6 Palatalis brevis	i	...	....	इ	𐬌	...	◌ِ	◌ِ	◌ִ	i
7 „ longa	î	(*i*)	....	ई	𐬍	𐭩	◌ِي	◌ِي	◌ִי	î
8 Dentalis brevis	*li*	...	....	ऌ	....	...	...	...	...	...
9 „ longa	*lî*	...	....	ॡ	....	...	...	...	...	...
10 Lingualis brevis	*ri*	...	....	ऋ	....	...	...	...	...	...
11 „ longa	*rî*	...	....	ॠ	....	...	...	...	...	...
12 Labialis brevis	u	...	....	उ	𐬎	...	◌ُ	◌ُ	◌ֻ	u
13 „ longa	û	(*u*)	....	ऊ	𐬏	𐭥	◌ُو	◌ُو	וּ	û
14 Gutturo-palatalis brevis	e	...	....	...	𐬈(e) 𐬉(*e*)	...	...	...	◌ֶ	e
15 „ longa	ê (ai)	(*e*)	....	ए	𐬀𐬉, 𐬀𐬌	𐭩	...	...	◌ֵ	ê
16 Diphthongus gutturo-palatalis	âi	(*ai*)	....	ऐ	....	...	◌َيْ	◌َيْ	...	âi
17 „ „	ei (ĕi)	...	....	...	....	...	...	...	...	ei, êi
18 „ „	oi (ŏu)	...	....	...	....	...	...	...	...	...
19 Gutturo-labialis brevis	o	...	....	...	𐬊	...	...	...	◌ָ	o
20 „ longa	ô (au)	(*o*)	....	ओ	𐬋	𐭥	...	...	וֹ	...
21 Diphthongus gutturo-labialis	âu	(*au*)	....	औ	𐬁𐬎 (*au*)	...	◌َوْ	◌َوْ	...	âu
22 „ „	eu (ĕu)	...	....	...	....	...	...	...	...	...
23 „ „	ou (ŏu)	...	....	...	....	...	...	...	...	...
24 Gutturalis fracta	ä	...	....	...	....	...	...	...	...	...
25 Palatalis fracta	ï	...	....	...	....	...	...	...	...	...
26 Labialis fracta	ü	...	....	...	....	...	...	...	...	ü
27 Gutturo-labialis fracta	ö	...	....	...	....	...	...	...	...	...

Approximate Pronunciation of the Roman Letters as representing the Sanskrit Alphabet.

Vowels.

a	अ	as in	sam
â	आ	,,	psalm
i	इ	,,	knit
î	ई	,,	neat
ri	ऋ	,,	fiery
rî	ॠ	,,	—
li	ऌ	,,	friendly
lî	ॡ	,,	—
u	उ	,,	full
û	ऊ	,,	fool
e	ए	,,	date
ai	ऐ	,,	aisle
o	ओ	,,	note
au	औ	,,	proud

Consonants.

Gutturals.

k	क	as in	kite
kh	ख	,,	inkhorn
g	ग	,,	gate
gh	घ	,,	springhead
ṅ (ng)	ङ	,,	sing
h	ह	,,	hear

Palatals.

k	च	as in	church
kh	छ	,,	church-history
g	ज	,,	jolly
gh	झ	,,	bridge-house
ñ	ञ	as in	new
y	य	,,	yet
s	श	,,	sharp

Dentals.

t	त	as in	tin (tip of tongue striking the bone of the teeth)
th	थ	,,	lanthorn
d	द	,,	din
dh	ध	,,	landholder
n	न	,,	nay
l	ल	,,	let
l	ळ	,,	—
s	स	,,	grass

Linguals.

t	ट	as in	town (tip of tongue striking alveolar region)
th	ठ	,,	outhouse
d	ड	,,	done
dh	ढ	,,	rodhook
n	ण	,,	no
r	र	,,	red
sh	ष	,,	shun

Labials.

p	प	as in	pan
ph	फ	,,	topheavy
b	ब	,,	bed
bh	भ	,,	clubhouse
m	म	,,	mill
v	व	,,	live
m	अं	,,	Anusvâra (slight nasal)
h	अः	,,	Visarga (slight breathing)

Introduction to the Upanishads

FIRST TRANSLATION OF THE UPANISHADS.

DÂRÂ SHUKOH, ANQUETIL DUPERRON, SCHOPENHAUER.

The ancient Vedic literature, the foundation of the whole literature of India, which has been handed down in that country in an unbroken succession from the earliest times within the recollection of man to the present day, became known for the first time beyond the frontiers of India through the Upanishads. The Upanishads were translated from Sanskrit into Persian by, or, it may be, for Dârâ Shukoh, the eldest son of Shâh Jehân, an enlightened prince, who openly professed the liberal religious tenets of the great Emperor Akbar, and even wrote a book intended to reconcile the religious doctrines of Hindus and Mohammedans. He seems first to have heard of the Upanishads during his stay in Kashmir in 1640. He afterwards invited several Pandits from Benares to Delhi, who were to assist him in the work of translation. The translation was finished in 1657. Three years after the accomplishment of this work, in 1659, the prince was put to death by his brother Aurangzib[15], in reality, no doubt, because he was the eldest son and legitimate successor of Shâh Jehân, but under the pretext that he was an infidel, and dangerous to the established religion of the empire.

When the Upanishads had once been translated from Sanskrit into Persian, at that time the most widely read language of the East and understood likewise by many European scholars, they became generally accessible to all who took an interest in the religious literature of India. It is true that under Akbar's reign (1556-1586) similar translations had been prepared[16], but neither those nor the translations of Dârâ Shukoh attracted the attention of European scholars till the year 1775. In that year Anquetil Duperron, the famous traveller and discoverer of the Zend-avesta, received one MS. of the Persian translation of the Upanishads, sent to him by M. Gentil, the French resident at the court of Shuja ud daula, and brought to France by M. Bernier. After receiving another MS., Anquetil Duperron collated the two, and translated the Persian translation[17] into French (not published),

---

[15] Elphinstone, History of India, ed. Cowell, p. 610.

[16] M. M., Introduction to the Science of Religion, p. 79.

[17] Several other MSS. of this translation have since come to light; one at Oxford, Codices Wilsoniani, 399 and 400. Anquetil Duperron gives the following title of the Persian translation: 'Hanc interpretationem τῶν Oupnekhathai quorumvis quatuor librorum Beid, quod, designatum cum secreto magno (per secretum magnum) est, et integram cognitionem luminis luminum, hic Fakir sine tristitia (Sultan) Mohammed Dara Schakoh ipse, cum significatione recta, cum sinceritate, in tempore sex mensium (postremo die, secundo τοῦ Schonbeh, vigesimo) sexto mensis τοῦ Ramazzan, anno 1067

and into Latin. That Latin translation was published in 1801 and 1802, under the title of 'Oupnek'hat, id est, Secretum tegendum: opus ipsa in India rarissimum, continens antiquam et arcanam, seu theologicam et philosophicam doctrinam, e quatuor sacris Indorum libris Rak baid, Djedjer baid, Sam baid, Athrban baid excerptam; ad verbum, e Persico idiomate, Samkreticis vocabulis intermixto, in Latinum conversum: Dissertationibus et Annotationibus difficiliora explanantibus, illustratum: studio et opera Anquetil Duperron, Indicopleustæ. Argentorati, typis et impensis fratrum Levrault, vol. i, 1801; vol. ii, 1802[18].'

This translation, though it attracted considerable interest among scholars, was written in so utterly unintelligible a style, that it required the lynxlike perspicacity of an intrepid philosopher, such as Schopenhauer, to discover a thread through such a labyrinth. Schopenhauer, however, not only found and followed such a thread, but he had the courage to proclaim to an incredulous age the vast treasures of thought which were lying buried beneath that fearful jargon.

As Anquetil Duperron's volumes have become scarce, I shall here give a short specimen of his translation, which corresponds to the first sentences of my translation of the *Kh*ândogya-upanishad:—'Oum hoc verbum (esse) adkit ut sciveris, sic τὸ maschghouli fac (de co meditare), quod ipsum hoc verbum aodkit est; propter illud quod hoc (verbum) oum, in Sam Beid, cum voce altâ, cum harmoniâ pronunciatum fiat.

'Adkiteh porro cremor (optimum, selectissimum) est: quemadmodum ex (præ) omni quieto (non moto), et moto, pulvis (terra) cremor (optimum) est; et e (præ) terra aqua cremor est; et ex aqua, comedendum (victus) cremor est; (et) e comedendo, comedens cremor est; et e comedente, loquela (id quod dicitur) cremor est; et e loquela, aïet τοῦ Beid, et ex aïet, τὸ siam, id est, cum harmonia (pronunciatum); et e Sam, τὸ adkit, cremor est; id est, oum, voce alta, cum harmonia pronunciare, aokit, cremor cremorum (optimum optimorum) est. Major, ex (præ) adkit, cremor alter non est.'

Schopenhauer not only read this translation carefully, but he makes no secret of it, that his own philosophy is powerfully impregnated by the fundamental doctrines of the Upanishads. He dwells on it again and again, and it seems both fair to Schopenhauer's memory and highly important for a true appreciation of the philosophical value of the Upanishads, to put together what that vigorous thinker has written on

---

τοῦ Hedjri (Christi, 1657) in urbe Delhi, in mansione nakhe noudeh, cum absolutione ad finem fecit pervenire.' The MS. was copied by Âtma Ram in the year 1767 A.D. Anquetil Duperron adds: 'Absolutum est hoc Apographum versionis Latinæ τῶν quinquaginta Oupnekhatha, ad verbum, e Persico idiomate, Samskreticis vocabulis intermixto, factæ, die 9 Octobris, 1796, 18 Brumaire, anni 4, Reipublic. Gall. Parisiis.'

[18] M. M., History of Ancient Sanskrit Literature, second edition, p. 325.

those ancient rhapsodies of truth.

In his 'Welt als Wille und Vorstellung,' he writes, in the preface to the first edition, p. xiii:

'If the reader has also received the benefit of the Vedas, the access to which by means of the Upanishads is in my eyes the greatest privilege which this still young century (1818) may claim before all previous centuries, (for I anticipate that the influence of Sanskrit literature will not be less profound than the revival of Greek in the fourteenth century,)—if then the reader, I say, has received his initiation in primeval Indian wisdom, and received it with an open heart, he will be prepared in the very best way for hearing what I have to tell him. It will not sound to him strange, as to many others, much less disagreeable; for I might, if it did not sound conceited, contend that every one of the detached statements which constitute the Upanishads, may be deduced as a necessary result from the fundamental thoughts which I have to enunciate, though those deductions themselves are by no means to be found there.'

And again[19]:

'If I consider how difficult it is, even with the assistance of the best and carefully educated teachers, and with all the excellent philological appliances collected in the course of this century, to arrive at a really correct, accurate, and living understanding of Greek and Roman authors, whose language was after all the language of our own predecessors in Europe, and the mother of our own, while Sanskrit, on the contrary, was spoken thousands of years ago in distant India, and can be learnt only with appliances which are as yet very imperfect;—if I add to this the impression which the translations of Sanskrit works by European scholars, with very few exceptions, produce on my mind, I cannot resist a certain suspicion that our Sanskrit scholars do not understand their texts much better than the higher class of schoolboys their Greek. Of course, as they are not boys, but men of knowledge and understanding, they put together, out of what they do understand, something like what the general meaning may have been, but much probably creeps in ex ingenio. It is still worse with the Chinese of our European Sinologues.

'If then I consider, on the other hand, that Sultan Mohammed Dârâ Shukoh, the brother of Aurangzib, was born and bred in India, was a learned, thoughtful, and enquiring man, and therefore probably understood his Sanskrit about as well as we our Latin, that moreover he was assisted by a number of the most learned Pandits, all this together gives me at once a very high opinion of his translation of the Vedic Upanishads into Persian. If, besides this, I see with what profound and quite appropriate reverence Anquetil Duperron has treated that Persian

[19] Schopenhauer, Parerga, third edition, II, p.426.

translation, rendering it in Latin word by word, retaining, in spite of Latin grammar, the Persian syntax, and all the Sanskrit words which the Sultan himself had left untranslated, though explaining them in a glossary, I feel the most perfect confidence in reading that translation, and that confidence soon receives its most perfect justification. For how entirely does the Oupnekhat breathe throughout the holy spirit of the Vedas! How is every one who by a diligent study of its Persian Latin has become familiar with that incomparable book, stirred by that spirit to the very depth of his soul! How does every line display its firm, definite, and throughout harmonious meaning! From every sentence deep, original, and sublime thoughts arise, and the whole is pervaded by a high and holy and earnest spirit. Indian air surrounds us, and original thoughts of kindred spirits. And oh, how thoroughly is the mind here washed clean of all early engrafted Jewish superstitions, and of all philosophy that cringes before those superstitions! In the whole world there is no study, except that of the originals, so beneficial and so elevating as that of the Oupnekhat. It has been the solace of my life, it will be the solace of my death!

'Though[20] I feel the highest regard for the religious and philosophical works of Sanskrit literature, I have not been able to derive much pleasure from their poetical compositions. Nay, they seem to me sometimes as tasteless and monstrous as the sculpture of India.

'In[21] most of the pagan philosophical writers of the first Christian centuries we see the Jewish theism, which, as Christianity, was soon to become the faith of the people, shining through, much as at present we may perceive shining through in the writings of the learned, the native pantheism of India, which is destined sooner or later to become the faith of the people. Ex oriente lux.'

This may seem strong language, and, in some respects, too strong. But I thought it right to quote it here, because, whatever may be urged against Schopenhauer, he was a thoroughly honest thinker and honest speaker, and no one would suspect him of any predilection for what has been so readily called Indian mysticism. That Schelling and his school should use rapturous language about the Upanishads, might carry little weight with that large class of philosophers by whom everything beyond the clouds of their own horizon is labelled mysticism. But that Schopenhauer should have spoken of the Upanishads as 'products of the highest wisdom' (Ausgeburt der höchsten Weisheit)[22], that he should have placed the pantheism there taught high above the pantheism of Bruno, Malebranche, Spinoza, and Scotus Erigena, as brought to light again at Oxford in 1681[23], may perhaps secure a more

[20] Loc. cit. II, pp. 425.
[21] Loc. cit. I, p. 59.
[22] Loc. cit. II, p. 428.
[23] Loc. cit. I, p. 6. These passages were pointed out to me by Professor Noiré.

considerate reception for these relics of ancient wisdom than anything that I could say in their favour.

RAMMOHUN ROY.

Greater, however, than the influence exercised on the philosophical thought of modern Europe, has been the impulse which these same Upanishads have imparted to the religious life of modern India. In about the same year (1774 or 1775) when the first MS. of the Persian translation of the Upanishads was received by Anquetil Duperron, Rammohun Roy[24] was born in India, the reformer and reviver of the ancient religion of the Brahmans. A man who in his youth could write a book 'Against the Idolatry of all Religions,' and who afterwards expressed in so many exact words his 'belief in the divine authority of Christ'[25] was not likely to retain anything of the sacred literature of his own religion, unless he had perceived in it the same divine authority which he recognised in the teaching of Christ. He rejected the Purâ*n*as, he would not have been swayed in his convictions by the authority of the Laws of Manu, or even by the sacredness of the Vedas. He was above all that. But he discovered in the Upanishads and in the so-called Vedânta something different from all the rest, something that ought not to be thrown away, something that, if rightly understood, might supply the right native soil in which alone the seeds of true religion, aye, of true Christianity, might spring up again and prosper in India, as they had once sprung up and prospered from out the philosophies of Origen or Synesius. European scholars have often wondered that Rammohun Roy, in his defence of the Veda, should have put aside the Sa*m*hitâs and the Brâhma*n*as, and laid his finger on the Upanishads only, as the true kernel of the whole Veda. Historically, no doubt, he was wrong, for the Upanishads presuppose both the hymns and the liturgical books of the Veda. But as the ancient philosophers distinguished in the Veda between the Karma-kâ*nd*a and the *G*ñâna-kâ*nd*a, between works and knowledge; as they themselves pointed to the learning of the sacred hymns and the performance of sacrifices as a preparation only for that enlightenment which was reserved as the highest reward for the faithful performance of all previous duties[26], Rammohun Roy, like Buddha and other enlightened men before him, perceived that the time for insisting on all that previous discipline with its minute prescriptions and superstitious observances was gone, while the knowledge conveyed in the Upanishads or the Vedânta, enveloped though it may be in strange coverings, should henceforth form the foundation of a new religious

---

[24] Born 1774, died at 2.30 A.M., on Friday, 28th September, 1833.
[25] Last Days of Rammohun Roy, by Mary Carpenter, 1866, p. 135.
[26] M. M., History of Ancient Sanskrit Literature, p. 319.

life[27]. He would tolerate nothing idolatrous, not even in his mother, poor woman, who after joining his most bitter opponents, confessed to her son, before she set out on her last pilgrimage to Juggernaut, where she died, that 'he was right, but that she was a weak woman, and grown too old to give up the observances which were a comfort to her.' It was not therefore from any regard of their antiquity or their sacred character that Rammohun Roy clung to the Upanishads, that he translated them into Bengali, Hindi, and English, and published them at his own expense. It was because he recognised in them seeds of eternal truth, and was bold enough to distinguish between what was essential in them and what was not,—a distinction, as he often remarked with great perplexity, which Christian teachers seemed either unable or unwilling to make[28].

The death of that really great and good man during his stay in England in 1833, was one of the severest blows that have fallen on the prospects of India. But his work has not been in vain. Like a tree whose first shoot has been killed by one winter frost, it has broken out again in a number of new and more vigorous shoots, for whatever the outward differences may be between the Âdi Brahmo Samâj of Debendranath Tagore, or the Brahmo Samâj of India of Keshub Chunder Sen, or the Sadharan Brahmo Samâj, the common root of them all is the work done, once for all, by Rammohun Roy. That work may have disappeared from sight for a time, and its present manifestations may seem to many observers who are too near, not very promising. But in one form or another, under one name or another, I feel convinced that work will live. 'In India,' Schopenhauer writes, 'our religion will now and never strike root: the primitive wisdom of the human race will never be pushed aside there by the events of Galilee. On the contrary, Indian wisdom will flow back upon Europe, and produce a thorough change in our knowing and thinking.' Here, again, the great philosopher seems to me to have allowed himself to be carried away too far by his enthusiasm for the less known. He is blind for the dark sides of the Upanishads, and he wilfully shuts his eyes against the bright rays of eternal truth in the Gospels, which even Rammohun Roy was quick enough to perceive behind the mists and clouds of tradition that gather so quickly round the sunrise of every religion.

POSITION OF THE UPANISHADS IN VEDIC LITERATURE.

If now we ask what has been thought of the Upanishads by

---

[27] 'The adoration of the invisible Supreme Being is exclusively prescribed by the Upanishads or the principal parts of the Vedas and also by the Vedant.' Rammohun Roy, Translation of the Kena-upanishad, Calcutta, 1816, p. 6. M. M., History of Ancient Sanskrit Literature, p. 320.

[28] Last Days, p. 11.

Sanskrit scholars or by Oriental scholars in general, it must be confessed that hitherto they have not received at their hands that treatment which in the eyes of philosophers and theologians they seem so fully to deserve. When the first enthusiasm for such works as *S*akuntalâ and Gîta-Govinda had somewhat subsided, and Sanskrit scholars had recognised that a truly scholarlike study of Indian literature must begin with the beginning, the exclusively historical interest prevailed to so large an extent that the hymns of the Veda, the Brâhma*n*as, and the Sûtras absorbed all interest, while the Upanishads were put aside for a time as of doubtful antiquity, and therefore of minor importance.

My real love for Sanskrit literature was first kindled by the Upanishads. It was in the year 1844, when attending Schelling's lectures at Berlin, that my attention was drawn to those ancient theosophic treatises, and I still possess my collations of the Sanskrit MSS. which had then just arrived at Berlin, the Chambers collection, and my copies of commentaries, and commentaries on commentaries, which I made at that time. Some of my translations which I left with Schelling, I have never been able to recover, though to judge from others which I still possess, the loss of them is of small consequence. Soon after leaving Berlin, when continuing my Sanskrit studies at Paris under Burnouf, I put aside the Upanishads, convinced that for a true appreciation of them it was necessary to study, first of all, the earlier periods of Vedic literature, as represented by the hymns and the Brâhma*n*as of the Vedas.

In returning, after more than thirty years, to these favourite studies, I find that my interest in them, though it has changed in character, has by no means diminished.

It is true, no doubt, that the stratum of literature which contains the Upanishads is later than the Sa*m*hitâs, and later than the Brâhma*n*as, but the first germs of Upanishad doctrines go back at least as far as the Mantra period, which provisionally has been fixed between 1000 and 800 B.C. Conceptions corresponding to the general teaching of the Upanishads occur in certain hymns of the Rig-veda-sa*m*hitâ, they must have existed therefore before that collection was finally closed. One hymn in the Sa*m*hitâ of the Rig-veda (I, 191) was designated by Kâtyâyana, the author of the Sarvânukrama*n*ikâ, as an Upanishad. Here, however, upanishad means rather a secret charm than a philosophical doctrine. Verses of the hymns have often been incorporated in the Upanishads, and among the Oupnekhats translated into Persian by Dârâ Shukoh we actually find the Purusha-sûkta, the 90th hymn of the tenth book of the Rig-veda[29], forming the greater portion of the Bark'heh Soukt. In the Sa*m*hitâ of the Yagur-veda,

---

[29] See Weber. Indische Studien, IX, p. 1 seq.

however, in the Vâgasaneyi*s*âkhâ, we meet with a real Upanishad, the famous Î*s*â or Î*s*âvâsya-upanishad, while the Sivasa*m*kalpa, too, forms part of its thirty-fourth book[30]. In the Brâhma*n*as several Upanishads occur, even in portions which are not classed as Âra*n*yakas, as, for instance, the well-known Kena or Talavakâra upanishad. The recognised place, however, for the ancient Upanishads is in the Âra*n*yakas, or forest-books, which, as a rule, form an appendix to the Brâhma*n*as, but are sometimes included also under the general name of Brâhma*n*a. Brâhma*n*a, in fact, meaning originally the sayings of Brahmans, whether in the general sense of priests, or in the more special of Brahman-priest, is a name applicable not only to the books, properly so called, but to all old prose traditions, whether contained in the Sa*m*hitâs, such as the Taittirîya-sa*m*hitâ, the Brâhma*n*as, the Âra*n*yakas, the Upanishads, and even, in certain cases, in the Sûtras. We shall see in the introduction to the Aitareya-âra*n*yaka, that that Âra*n*yaka is in the beginning a Brâhma*n*a, a mere continuation of the Aitareya-brâhma*n*a, explaining the Mahâvrata ceremony, while its last book contains the Sûtras or short technical rules explaining the same ceremony which in the first book had been treated in the style peculiar to the Brâhma*n*as. In the same Aitareya-âra*n*yaka, III, 2, 6, 6, a passage of the Upanishad is spoken of as a Brâhma*n*a, possibly as something like a Brâhma*n*a, while something very like an Upanishad occurs in the Âpastamba-sûtras, and might be quoted therefore as a Sûtra[31]. At all events the Upanishads, like the Âra*n*yakas, belong to what Hindu theologians call Sruti, or revealed literature, in opposition to Sm*ri*ti, or traditional literature, which is supposed to be founded on the former, and allowed to claim a secondary authority only; and the earliest of these philosophical treatises will always, I believe, maintain a place in the literature of the world, among the most astounding productions of the human mind in any age and in any country.

DIFFERENT CLASSES OF UPANISHADS.

The ancient Upanishads, i.e. those which occupy a place in the Sa*m*hitâs, Brâhma*n*as, and Âra*n*yakas, must be, if we follow the chronology which at present is commonly, though, it may be, provisionally only, received by Sanskrit scholars, older than 600 B.C., i.e. anterior to the rise of Buddhism. As to other Upanishads, and their number is very large, which either stand by themselves, or which are ascribed to the Atharva-veda, it is extremely difficult to fix their age. Some of them arc, no doubt, quite modern, for mention is made even of an Allah-upanishad; but others may claim a far higher antiquity than is

[30] See M. M., History of Ancient Sanskrit Literature, p. 317.

[31] Âpastamba, translated by Bühler, Sacred Books of the East, vol. ii, p. 75.

generally assigned to them on internal evidence. I shall only mention that the name of Atharva*s*iras, an Upanishad generally assigned to a very modern date, is quoted in the Sûtras of Gautama and Baudhâyana[32]; that the *S*vetâ*s*vatara-upanishad, or the *S*vetâ*s*vatara*n*âm Mantropanishad, though bearing many notes of later periods of thought, is quoted by *S*aṅkara in his commentary on the Vedânta-sûtras[33]; while the N*ri*si*m*hottaratâpanîya-upanishad forms part of the twelve Upanishads explained by Vidyâra*n*ya in his Sarvopanishad-arthânubhûti-prakâ*s*a. The Upanishads comprehended in that work are:

1. Aitareya-upanishad.
2. Taittirîya-upanishad.
3. *Kh*ândogya-upanishad.
4. Mu*nd*aka-upanishad.
5. Pra*s*na-upanishad.
6. Kaushîtaki-upanishad.
7. Maitrâya*n*îya-upanishad.
8. Ka*th*avallî-upanishad.
9. *S*vetâ*s*vatara-upanishad.
10. B*ri*had-âra*n*yaka-upanishad.
11. Talavakâra (Kena)-upanishad.
12. N*ri*si*m*hottaratâpanîya-upanishad[34].

The number of Upanishads translated by Dârâ Shukoh amounts to 50; their number, as given in the Mahâvâkyamuktâvalî and in the Muktikâ-upanishad, is 108[35]. Professor Weber thinks that their number, so far as we know at present, may be reckoned at 235[36]. In order, however, to arrive at so high a number, every title of an Upanishad would have to be counted separately, while in several cases it is clearly the same Upanishad which is quoted under different names. In an alphabetical list which I published in 1855 (Zeitschrift der Deutschen Morgenländischen Gesellschaft XIX, 137-158), the number of real Upanishads reached 149. To that number Dr. Burnell[37] in his Catalogue (p. 59) added 5, Professor Haug (Brahma und die Brahmanen) 16,

---

[32] Gautama, translated by Bühler, Sacred Books of the East, vol. ii, p. 272, and Introduction, p. lvi.

[33] Vedânta-sûtras I, I, II.

[34] One misses the Î*s*â or Î*s*âvâsya-upanishad in this list. The Upanishads chiefly studied in Bengal are the B*ri*had-âra*n*yaka, Aitareya, *Kh*ândogya, Taittirîya, Î*s*â, Kena, Ka*th*a, Pra*s*na, Mu*nd*aka, and Mâ*nd*ûkya, to which should be added the *S*vetâ*s*vatara. M*M*., History of Ancient Sanskrit Literature, p. 325.

[35] Dr. Burnell thinks that this is an artificial computation, 108 being a sacred number in Southern India. See Kielhorn in Gough's Papers on Ancient Sanskrit Literature, p. 193.

[36] Weber, History of Sanskrit Literature, p. 155 note.

[37] Indian Antiquary, II, 267.

making a sum total of 170. New names, however, are constantly being added in the catalogues of MSS. published by Bühler, Kielhorn, Burnell, Rajendralal Mitra, and others, and I shall reserve therefore a more complete list of Upanishads for a later volume.

Though it is easy to see that these Upanishads belong to very different periods of Indian thought, any attempt to fix their relative age seems to me for the present almost hopeless. No one can doubt that the Upanishads which have had a place assigned to them in the Sa*m*hitâs, Brâhma*n*as, and Âra*n*yakas are the oldest. Next to these we can draw a line to include the Upanishads clearly referred to in the Vedânta-sûtras, or explained and quoted by *S*aṅkara, by Sâya*n*a, and other more modern commentators. We can distinguish Upanishads in prose from Upanishads in mixed prose and verse, and again Upanishads in archaic verse from Upanishads in regular and continuous Anush*t*ubh Slokas. We can also class them according to their subjects, and, at last, according to the sects to which they belong. But beyond this it is hardly safe to venture at present. Attempts have been made by Professor Weber and M. Regnaud to fix in each class the relative age of certain Upanishads, and I do not deny to their arguments, even where they conflict with each other, considerable weight in forming a preliminary judgment. But I know of hardy any argument which is really convincing, or which could not be met by counter arguments equally strong. Simplicity may be a sign of antiquity, but it is not so always, for what seems simple, may be the result of abbreviation. One Upanishad may give the correct, another an evidently corrupt reading, yet it does not follow that the correct reading may not be the result of an emendation. It is quite clear that a large mass of traditional Upanishads must have existed before they assumed their present form. Where two or three or four Upanishads contain the same story, told almost in the same words, they are not always copied from one another, but they have been settled independently, in different localities, by different teachers, it may be, for different purposes. Lastly, the influence of *S*âkhâs or schools may have told more or less on certain Upanishads. Thus the Maitrâya*n*îya-upanishad, as we now possess it, shows a number of irregular forms which even the commentator can account for only as peculiarities of the Maitrâya*n*îya-sâkhâ[38]. That Upanishad, as it has come down to us, is full of what we should call clear indications of a modern and corrupt age. It contains in VI, 37, a *s*loka from the Mânava-dharma-*s*âstra, which startled even the commentator, but is explained away by him as possibly found in another *S*âkhâ, and borrowed from there by Manu. It contains corruptions of easy words

[38] They are generally explained as *kh*ândasa, but in one place (Maitr. Up. II, 4) the commentator treats such irregularities as eta*kkh*âkhâsaṅketapâ*th*a*h*, a reading peculiar to the Maitrâyanîya school. Some learned remarks on this point may be seen in an article by Dr. L. Schroeder, Über die Maitrâya*n*î Sa*m*hitâ.

which one would have thought must have been familiar to every student. Thus instead of the passage as found in the *Kh*ândogya-upanishad VIII, 7, 1, ya âtmâpahatapâpmâ vigaro vimr*i*tyur vi*s*oko 'vigighatso 'pipâsa*h*, &c., the text of the Maitrâyanîya-upanishad (VII, 7) reads, âtmâpahatapâpmâ vigaro vimr*i*tyur vi*s*oko 'vi*k*ikitso 'vipâsa*h*. But here again the commentator explains that another *S*âkhâ reads 'vigighatsa, and that avipâ*s*a is to be explained by means of a change of letters as apipâsa. Corruptions, therefore, or modern elements which are found in one Upanishad, as handed down in one Sâkhâ, do not prove that the same existed in other *S*âkhâs, or that they were found in the original text.

All these questions have to be taken into account before we can venture to give a final judgment on the relative age of Upanishads which belong to one and the same class. I know of no problem which offers so many similarities with the one before us as that of the relative age of the four Gospels. All the difficulties which occur in the Upanishads occur here, and no critical student who knows the difficulties that have to be encountered in determining the relative age of the four Gospels, will feel inclined, in the present state of Vedic scholarship, to speak with confidence on the relative age of the ancient Upanishads.

CRITICAL TREATMENT OF THE TEXT OF THE UPANISHADS.

With regard to a critical restoration of the text of the Upanishads, I have but seldom relied on the authority of new MSS., but have endeavoured throughout to follow that text which is presupposed by the commentaries, whether they are the work of the old *S*aṅkarâ*k*ârya, or of the more modern *S*aṅkarânanda, or *S*âya*n*a, or others. Though there still prevails some uncertainty as to the date of *S*aṅkarâ*k*ârya, commonly assigned to the eighth century A.D., yet I doubt whether any MSS. of the Upanishads could now be found prior to 1000 A.D. The text, therefore, which *S*aṅkara had before his eyes, or, it may be, his ears, commands, I think, a higher authority than that of any MSS. likely to be recovered at present.

It may be objected that *S*aṅkara's text belonged to one locality only, and that different readings and different recensions may have existed in other parts of India. That is perfectly true. We possess various recensions of several Upanishads, as handed down in different *S*âkhâs of different Vedas, and we know of various readings recorded by the commentators. These, where they are of importance for our purposes, have been carefully taken into account.

It has also been supposed that *S*aṅkara, who, in writing his commentaries on the Upanishad, was chiefly guided by philosophical considerations, his chief object being to use the Upanishads as a sacred foundation for the Vedânta philosophy, may now and then have taken liberties with the text. That may be so, but no stringent proof of it has as yet been brought forward, and I therefore hold that when we succeed in establishing throughout that text which served as the basis of *S*aṅkara's commentaries, we have done enough for the present, and have fulfilled at all events the first and indispensable task in a critical treatment of the text of the Upanishads.

But in the same manner as it is easy to see that the text of the Rig-veda, which is presupposed by *S*âya*n*a's commentary and even by earlier works, is in many places palpably corrupt, we cannot resist the same conviction with regard to the text of the Upanishads. In some cases the metre, in others grammar, in others again the collation of analogous passages enable us to detect errors, and probably very ancient errors, that had crept into the text long before *S*aṅkara composed his commentaries.

Some questions connected with the metres of the Upanishads have been very learnedly treated by Professor Gildemeister in his essay, 'Zur Theorie des *S*loka.' The lesson to be derived from that essay, and from a study of the Upanishads, is certainly to abstain for the present from conjectural emendations. In the old Upanishads the same metrical freedom prevails as in the hymns; in the later Upanishads, much may be tolerated as the result of conscious or unconscious imitation. The metrical emendations that suggest themselves are generally so easy and so obvious that, for that very reason, we should hesitate before correcting what native scholars would have corrected long ago, if they had thought that there was any real necessity for correction.

It is easy to suggest, for instance, that in the Vâgasaneyi-sa*m*hitâ-upanishad, verse 5, instead of tad antar asya sarvasya, tadu sarvasyâsya bâhyata*h*, the original text may have been tad antar asya sarvasya tadu sarvasya bâhyata*h*; yet *S*aṅkara evidently read sarvasyâsya, and as the same reading is found in the text of the Vâgasaneyi-sa*m*hitâ, who would venture to correct so old a mistake?

Again, if in verse 8, we left out yâthâtathyata*h*, we should get a much more regular metre,

> Kavir manîshî paribhû*h* svyambhû*h*
> arthân vyădăhâ*k kh*âsvătîbhyai sămâbhya*h*.

Here vyădă forms one syllable by what I have proposed to call synizesis[39], which is allowed in the Upanishads as well as in the hymns. All would then seem right, except that it is difficult to explain how so rare a word as yâthâtathyata*h* could have been introduced into the text.

In verse 10 one feels tempted to propose the omission of eva in

---

[39] Rig-veda, translated by M. M., vol. i, Preface, p. cxliii.

anyad âhur avidyayâ, while in verse 11, an eva inserted after vidyâ*m* ka would certainly improve the metre.

In verse 15 the expression satyadharmâya d*ri*sh*t*aye is archaic, but perfectly legitimate in the sense of 'that we may see the nature of the True,' or 'that we see him whose nature is true.' When this verse is repeated in the Maitr. Up. VI, 35, we find instead, satyadharmâya vish*n*ave, 'for the true Vish*n*u.' But here, again, no sound critic would venture to correct a mistake, intentional or unintentional, which is sanctioned both by the MSS. of the text and by the commentary.

Such instances, where every reader feels tempted at once to correct the textus receptus, occur again and again, and when they seem of any interest they have been mentioned in the notes. It may happen, however, that the correction, though at first sight plausible, has to be surrendered on more mature consideration. Thus in the Vâgasaneyi-sa*m*hitâ-upanishad, verse 2, one feels certainly inclined to write evam tve nânyatheto 'sti, instead of eva*m* tvayi nânyatheto 'sti. But tve, if it were used here, would probably itself have to be pronounced dissyllabically, while tvayi, though it never occurs in the Rig-veda, may well keep its place here, in the last book of the Vâgasaneyi-sa*m*hitâ, provided we pronounce it by synizesis, i.e. as one syllable.

Attempts have been made sometimes to go beyond *S*aṅkara, and to restore the text, as it ought to have been originally, but as it was no longer in *S*aṅkara's time. It is one thing to decline to follow *S*aṅkara in every one of his interpretations, it is quite another to decline to accept the text which he interprets. The former is inevitable, the latter is always very precarious.

Thus I see, for instance, that M. Regnaud, in the Errata to the second volume of his excellent work on the Upanishads (Matériaux pour servir à l'histoire de la philosophie de l'Inde, 1878) proposes to read in the B*ri*had-âra*n*yaka upanishad IV, 3, 1-8, sam anena vadishya iti, instead of sa mene na vadishya iti. *S*aṅkara adopted the latter reading, and explained accordingly, that Yâgñavalkya went to king *G*anaka, but made up his mind not to speak. M. Regnaud, reading sam anena vadishya iti, takes the very opposite view, namely, that Yâgñavalkya went to king *G*anaka, having made up his mind to have a conversation with him. As M. Regnaud does not rest this emendation on the authority of any new MSS., we may examine it as an ingenious conjecture; but in that case it seems to me clear that, if we adopted it, we should have at the same time to omit the whole sentence which follows. *S*aṅkara saw clearly that what had to be accounted or explained was why the king should address the Brahman first, samrâ*d* eva pûrvam papra*kkh*a; whereas if Yâgñavalkya had come with the intention of having a conversation with the king, he, the Brahman, should have spoken first. This irregularity is explained by the intervening sentence, in which we are reminded that on a former occasion, when *G*anaka and Yâgñavalkya had a disputation on the Agnihotra, Yâgñavalkya granted *G*anaka a boon to choose, and he chose as his boon the right of asking questions according to his pleasure. Having received that boon, *G*anaka was at liberty to question Yâgñavalkya, even though he did not like it, and hence *G*anaka is introduced here as the first to ask a question.

All this hangs well together, while if we assume that Yâgñavalkya came for the purpose of having a conversation with *G*anaka, the whole sentence from 'atha ha ya*g* *g*anaka*s* *k*a' to 'pûrvam papra*kkh*a' would be useless, nor would there be any excuse for *G*anaka beginning the conversation, when Yâgñavalkya came himself on purpose to question him.

It is necessary, even when we feel obliged to reject an interpretation of *S*aṅkara's, without at the same time altering the text, to remember that *S*aṅkara, where he is not blinded by philosophical predilections, commands the highest respect as an interpreter. I cannot help thinking therefore that M. Regnaud (vol. i, p. 59) was right in translating the passage in the *Kh*ând. Up. V, 3, 7, tasmâd u sarveshu lokeshu kshattrasyaiva pra*s*âsanam abhût, by 'que le kshatriya seul l'a enseignée dans tous les mondes.' For when he proposes in the 'Errata' to translate instead, 'ç'est pourquoi l'empire dans tous les mondes fut attribué au kshatriya seulement,' he forgets that such an idea is foreign to the ordinary atmosphere in which the Upanishads move. It is not on account of the philosophical knowledge possessed by a few Kshatriyas, such as *G*anaka or Pravâha*n*a, that the privilege of government belongs everywhere to the second class. That rests on a totally different basis. Such exceptional knowledge, as is displayed by a few kings, might be an excuse for their claiming the privileges belonging to the Brahmans, but it would never, in the eyes of the ancient Indian Âryas, be considered as an argument for their claiming kingly power. Therefore, although I am well aware that pra*s*âs is most frequently used in the sense of ruling, I have no doubt that *S*aṅkara likewise was fully aware of that, and that if he nevertheless explained pra*s*âsana here in the sense of pra*s*âst*ri*tva*m* *s*ishyâ*n*âm, he did so because this meaning too was admissible, particularly here, where we may actually translate it by proclaiming, while the other meaning, that of ruling, would simply be impossible in the concatenation of ideas, which is placed before us in the Upanishad.

It seems, no doubt, extremely strange that neither the last redactors of the text of the Upanishads, nor the commentators, who probably knew the principal Upanishads by heart, should have perceived how certain passages in one Upanishad represented the same or nearly the same text which is found in another Upanishad, only occasionally with the most palpable corruptions.

Thus when the ceremony of offering a mantha or mash is

described, we read in the *Kh*ândogya-upanishad V, 2, 6, that it is to be accompanied by certain words which on the whole are intelligible. But when the same passage occurs again in the B*ri*had-âra*n*yaka, those words have been changed to such a degree, and in two different ways in the two *S*âkhâs of the Mâdhyandinas and Kâ*n*vas, that, though the commentator explains them, they are almost unintelligible. I shall place the three passages together in three parallel lines:

I. *Kh*ândogya-upanishad V, 2, 6 :
II. B*ri*had-âra*n*yaka, Mâdhyandina-*s*âkhâ, XIV, 9, 3, 10 :
III. B*ri*had-âra*n*yaka-upanishad, Kâ*n*va-*s*âkhâ, VI, 3, 5 :

I.	Amo nâmâsy amâ	hi te sarvam ida*m*	sa hi *g*yesh*th*a*h*
II.	âmo 'sy	âma*m* hi te mayi	sa hi
III.	âma*m*sy	âma*m*hi te mahi	sa hi
I.	*s*resh*th*o râ*g*âdhipati*h*	sa mâ *g*yaish*th*ya*m*	*s*rai-
II.	râ*g*e*s*âno 'dhipati*h*	sa mâ râ*g*e*s*âno	
III.	ra*g*e*s*âno		
I.	sh*th*ya*m* râ*g*yam âdhipatya*m*	gamayatv aham eveda*m*	
II.	'dhipati*m*	karotv iti.	
III.	'dhipati*m*	karotv iti.	
I.	sarvam asânîti.		
II.			
III.			

The text in the *Kh*ândogya-upanishad yields a certain sense, viz. 'Thou art Ama by name, for all this together exists in thee. He is the oldest and best, the king, the sovereign. May he make me the oldest, the best, the king, the sovereign. May I be all this.' This, according to the commentator, is addressed to Prâ*n*a, and Ama, though a purely artificial word, is used in the sense of Prâ*n*a, or breath, in another passage also, viz. B*ri*had-âra*n*yaka-up. I, 3, 22. If therefore we accept this meaning of Ama, the rest is easy and intelligible.

But if we proceed to the B*ri*had-âra*n*yaka, in the Mâdhyandina-*s*âkhâ, we find the commentator proposing the following interpretation: 'O Mantha, thou art a full knower, complete knowledge of me belongs to thee.' This meaning is obtained by deriving âma*h* from â + man, in the sense of knower, and then taking âmam, as a neuter, in the sense of knowledge, derivations which are simply impossible.

Lastly, if we come to the text of the Kâ*n*va-sâkhâ, the grammatical interpretation becomes bolder still. *S*aṅkara does not explain the passage at all, which is strange, but Ânandagiri interprets âma*m*si tvam by 'Thou knowest (all),' and âma*m*hi te mahi, by 'we know thy great (shape),' which are again impossible forms.

But although there can be little doubt here that the reading of the *Kh*ândogya-upanishad gives us the original text, or a text nearest to the original, no sound critic would venture to correct the readings of the B*ri*had-âra*n*yaka. They are corruptions, but even as corruptions they possess authority, at all events up to a certain point, and it is the fixing of those certain points or chronological limits, which alone can impart a scientific character to our criticism of ancient texts.

In the Kaushîtaki-brâhma*n*a-upanishad Professor Cowell has pointed out a passage to me, where we must go beyond the text as it stood when commented on by the *S*aṅkarânanda. In the beginning of the fourth adhyâya all MSS. of the text read savasan, and this is the reading which the commentator seems anxious to explain, though not very successfully. I thought that possibly the commentator might have had before him the reading sa vasan, or so 'vasan, but both would be very unusual. Professor Cowell in his Various Readings, p. xii, conjectured sa*m*vasan, which would be liable to the same objection. He now, however, informs me that, as B. has sa*m*tvan, and C. satvan, he believes the original text to have been Satvan-Matsyeshu. This seems to me quite convincing, and is borne out by the reading of the Berlin MS., so far as it can be made out from Professor Weber's essay on the Upanishads, Indische Studien I, p. 419. I see that Boehtlingk and Roth in their Sanskrit Dictionary, s*v*. satvat, suggest the same emendation.

The more we study the nature of Sanskrit MSS., the more, I believe, we shall feel convinced that their proper arrangement is one by locality rather than by time. I have frequently dwelt on this subject in the introductions to the successive volumes of my edition of the Rig-veda and its commentary by Sâya*n*â*k*ârya, and my convictions on this point have become stronger ever since. A MS., however modern, from the south of India or from the north, is more important as a check on the textus receptus of any Sanskrit work, as prevalent in Bengal or Bombay, than ever so many MSS., even if of greater antiquity, from the same locality. When therefore I was informed by my friend Dr. Bühler that he had discovered in Kashmir a MS. of the Aitareya-upanishad, I certainly expected some real help from such a treasure. The MS. is described by its discoverer in the last number of the journal of the Bombay Asiatic Society, p. 34[40], and has since been sent to me by the Indian Government. It is written on birch bark (bhûrga), and in the alphabet commonly called *S*âradâ. The leaves are very much injured on the margin and it is almost impossible to handle them without some injury. In many places the bark has shrunk, probably on being moistened, and the letters have become illegible. Apart from these

[40] Journal of the Bombay Branch of the Royal Asiatic Society, 1877. Extra Number, containing the Detailed Report of a Tour in search of Sanskrit MSS., made in Kásmír, Rajputana, and Central India, by G. Bühler.

drawbacks, there remain the difficulties inherent in the *S*âradâ alphabet which, owing to its numerous combinations, is extremely difficult to read, and very trying to eyes which are growing weak. However, I collated the Upanishad from the Aitareya-âra*n*yaka, which turned out to be the last portion only, viz. the Sa*m*hitâ-upanishad (Ait. Âr. III, 1-2), or, as it is called here, Sa*m*hitâra*n*ya, and I am sorry to say my expectations have been disappointed. The MS. shows certain graphic peculiarities which Dr. Bühler has pointed out. It is particularly careful in the use of the sibilants, replacing the Visarga by sibilants, writing s + s and *s* + *s* instead of *h* + s and *h* + *s*; distinguishing also the *G*ihvâmûlîya and Upadhmanîya. If therefore the MS. writes antastha, we may be sure that it really meant to write so, and not anta*h*stha, or, as it would have written, antasstha. It shows equal care in the use of the nasals, and generally carries on the sandhi between different paragraphs. Here and there I met with better readings than those given in Rajendralal Mitra's edition, but in most cases the commentary would have been sufficient to restore the right reading. A few various readings, which seemed to deserve being mentioned, will be found in the notes. The MS., though carefully written, is not free from the ordinary blunders. At first one feels inclined to attribute some importance to every peculiarity of a new MS., but very soon one finds out that what seems peculiar, is in reality carelessness. Thus Ait. Âr. III, I, 5, 2, the Kashmir MS. has pûrvam akshara*m* rûpam, instead of what alone can be right, pûrvarûpam. Instead of pragayâ pa*s*ubhi*h* it writes repeatedly pragaya pa*s*ubhi*h*, which is impossible. In III, 2, 2, it leaves out again and again manomaya between *kh*andomaya and vâṅmaya; but that this is a mere accident we learn later on, where in the same sentence manomayo, is found in its right place. Such cases reduce this MS. to its proper level, and make us look with suspicion on any accidental variations, such as I have noticed in my translation.

The additional paragraph, noticed by Dr. Bühler, is very indistinct, and contains, so far as I am able to find out, sânti verses only.

I have no doubt that the discovery of new MSS. of the Upanishads and their commentaries will throw new light on the very numerous difficulties with which a translator of the Upanishads, particularly in attempting a complete and faithful translation, has at present to grapple. Some of the difficulties, which existed thirty years ago, have been removed since by the general progress of Vedic scholarship, and by the editions of texts and commentaries and translations of Upanishads, many of which were known at that time in manuscript only. But I fully agree with M. Regnaud as to the difficultés considérables que les meilleures traductions laissent subsister, and which can be solved only by a continued study of the Upanishads, the Âra*n*yakas, the Brâhma*n*as, and the Vedânta-sûtras.

MEANING OF THE WORD UPANISHAD.

How Upanishad became the recognised name of the philosophical treatises contained in the Veda is difficult to explain. Most European scholars are agreed in deriving upa-ni-shad from the root sad, to sit down, preceded by the two prepositions ni, down, and upa, near, so that it would express the idea of session, or assembly of pupils sitting down near their teacher to listen to his instruction. In the Trikâ*nd*a*s*esha, upanishad is explained by samîpasadana, sitting down near a person[41].

Such a word, however, would have been applicable, it would seem, to any other portion of the Veda as well as to the chapters called Upanishad, and it has never been explained how its meaning came thus to be restricted. It is still more strange that upanishad, in the sense of session or assembly, has never, so far as I am aware, been met with. Whenever the word occurs, it has the meaning of doctrine, secret doctrine, or is simply used as the title of the philosophic treatises which constitute the *g*ñânakâ*nd*a, the knowledge portion, as opposed to the karmakâ*nd*a, the work or ceremonial portion, of the Veda.

Native philosophers seem never to have thought of deriving upanishad from sad, to sit down. They derive it either from the root sad, in the sense of destruction, supposing these ancient treatises to have received their name because they were intended to destroy passion and ignorance by means of divine revelation[42], or from the root sad, in the sense of approaching, because a knowledge of Brahman comes near to us by means of the Upanishads, or because we approach Brahman by their help. Another explanation proposed by *S*ankara in his commentary on the Taittirîya-upanishad II, 9, is that the highest bliss is contained in the Upanishad (para*m* *s*reyo 'syâ*m* nisha*nn*am).

These explanations seem so wilfully perverse that it is difficult to understand the unanimity of native scholars. We ought to take into account, however, that very general tendency among half-educated people, to acquiesce in any etymology which accounts for the most prevalent meaning of a word. The Âra*n*yakas abound in such etymologies, which probably were never intended as real etymologies, in our sense of the word, but simply as plays on words, helping to account somehow for their meaning. The Upanishads, no doubt, were meant to destroy ignorance and passion, and nothing seemed more natural therefore than that their etymological meaning should be that of destroyers[43].

---

[41] Pânini I, 4, 79, has upanishatk*ri*tya.

[42] M. M., History of Ancient Sanskrit Literature, p. 318; Colebrooke, Essays, I, 92; Regnaud, Matériaux, p. 7.

[43] The distinction between possible and real etymologies is as modern as that between legend and history.

The history and the genius of the Sanskrit language leave little doubt that upanishad meant originally session, particularly a session consisting of pupils, assembled at a respectful distance round their teacher.

With upa alone, sad occurs as early as the hymns of the Rig-veda, in the sense of approaching respectfully[44]:—

Rig-veda IX, 11, 6. Námasâ ít úpa sîdata, 'approach him with praise.' See also Rig-veda X, 73, II; I, 65, I.

In the *Kh*ândogya-upanishad VI, 13, I, a teacher says to his pupil, atha mâ prâtar upasîdathâ*h*, 'come to me (for advice) to-morrow morning.'

In the same Upanishad VII, 8, I, a distinction is made between those who serve their teachers (pari*k*aritâ), and those who are admitted to their more intimate society (upasattâ, comm. samîpaga*h*, antaraṅga*h*, priya*h*).

Again, in the *Kh*ândogya-upanishad VII, I, we read of a pupil approaching his teacher (upâsasâda or upasasâda), and of the teacher telling him to approach with what he knows, i.e. to tell him first what he has learnt already (yad vettha tena mopasîda[45]).

In the Sûtras (Gobhilîya G*ri*hya-sûtra II, 10, 38) upasad is the recognised term for the position assumed by a pupil with his hands folded and his eyes looking up to the teacher who is to instruct him.

It should be stated, however, that no passage has yet been met with in which upa-ni-sad is used in the sense of pupils approaching and listening to their teacher. In the only passage in which upanishasâda occurs (Ait. Âr. II, 2, 1), it is used of Indra sitting down by the side of Vi*s*vâmitra, and it is curious to observe that both MSS. and commentaries give here upanishasasâda, an entirely irregular form.

The same is the case with two other roots which are used almost synonymously with sad, viz. âs and vi*s*. We find upa + âs used to express the position which the pupil occupies when listening to his teacher, eg. Pâ*n*. III, 4, 72, upâsito gurum bhavân, 'thou hast approached the Guru,' or upâsito gurur bhavatâ, 'the Guru has been approached by thee.' We find pari + upa + âs used with regard to relations assembled round the bed of a dying friend, *Kh*ând. Up. VI, 15; or of hungry children sitting round their mother, and likened to people performing the Agnihotra sacrifice (*Kh*ând. Up. V, 24, 5). But I have never met with upa-ni-as in that sense.

We likewise find upa-vis used in the sense of sitting down to a discussion (*Kh*ând. Up. I, 8, 2), but I have never found upa + ni + vis as applied to a pupil listening to his teacher.

The two prepositions upa and ni occur, however, with pat, to fly, in

[44] See M. M.'s History of Ancient Sanskrit Literature, p. 318.

[45] See also *Kh*and. Up. VI, 7, 2.

the sense of flying down and settling near a person, *Kh*ând. Up. IV, 7, 2; IV, 8, 2. And the same prepositions joined to the verb *s*ri, impart to it the meaning of sitting down beneath a person, so as to show him respect: B*ri*h. Âr. I, 4, II. 'Although a king is exalted, he sits down at the end of the sacrifice below the Brahman,' brahmaivântata upani*s*rayati.

Sad, with upa and ni, occurs in upanishâdin only, and has there the meaning of subject, eg. Satap. Brâhm. IX, 4, 3, 3, kshatrâya tad vi*s*am adhastâd upanishâdinî*m* karoti, 'he thus makes the Vi*s* (citizen) below, subject to the Kshatriya.'

Sometimes nishad is used by the side of upanishad, and so far as we can judge, without any difference of meaning[46].

All we can say therefore, for the present, is that upanishad, besides being the recognised title of certain philosophical treatises, occurs also in the sense of doctrine and of secret doctrine, and that it seems to have assumed this meaning from having been used originally in the sense of session or assembly in which one or more pupils receive instruction from a teacher.

Thus we find the word upanishad used in the Upanishads themselves in the following meanings:

1. Secret or esoteric explanation, whether true or false.
2. Knowledge derived from such explanation.
3. Special rules or observances incumbent on those who have received such knowledge.
4. Title of the books containing such knowledge.

I. Ait. Âr. III, 1, 6, 3. 'For this Upanishad, i.e. in order to obtain the information about the true meaning of Sa*m*hitâ, Târukshya served as a cowherd for a whole year.'

Taitt. Up. 1, 3. 'We shall now explain the Upanishad of the Sa*m*hitâ.'

Ait. Âr. III, 2, 5, 1. 'Next follows this Upanishad of the whole speech. True, all these are Upanishads of the whole speech, but this they declare especially.'

Talav. Up. IV, 7. 'As you have asked me to tell you the Upanishad, the Upanishad has now been told you. We have told you the Brâhmî Upanishad,' i.e. the true meaning of Brahman.

In the *Kh*ând. Up. III, II, 3, after the meaning of Brahman has been explained, the text says: 'To him who thus knows this Brahma upanishad (the secret doctrine of Brahman) the sun does not rise and does not set.' In the next paragraph brahma itself is used, meaning either Brahman as the object taught in the Upanishad, or, by a slight change of meaning, the Upanishad itself.

*Kh*ând. Up. I, 13, 4. 'Speech yields its milk to him who knows this

---

[46] Mahâbhârata, *S*ântiparva, 1613.

Upanishad (secret doctrine) of the Sâmans in this wise.'

*Kh*ând. Up. VIII, 8, 4. When Indra and Virokana had both misunderstood the teaching of Pragâpati, he says: 'They both go away without having perceived and without having known the Self, and whoever of these two, whether Devas or Asuras, will follow this doctrine (upanishad), will perish.'

II. In the *Kh*ând. Up. I, i, after the deeper meaning of the Udgîtha or Om has been described, the advantage of knowing that deeper meaning is put forward, and it is said that the sacrifice which a man performs with knowledge, with faith, and with the Upanishad, i.e. with an understanding of its deeper meaning, is more powerful.

III. In the Taittirîya-upanishad, at the end of the second chapter, called the Brahmânandavallî, and again at the end of the tenth chapter, the text itself says: Ity upanishad, this is the Upanishad, the true doctrine.'

IV. In the Kaushîtaki-upanishad II, I; 2, we read: 'Let him not beg, this is the Upanishad for him who knows this.' Here upanishad stands for vrata or rahasya-vrata, rule.

WORKS ON THE UPANISHADS.

Anquetil Duperron, Oupnek'hat, 1801, 1802. See page clii.

Rammohun Roy, Translation of Several Principal Books, Passages, and Texts of the Veds. Second edition. London, 1832.

Translation of the Moonduk-Ooptinishud of the Uthurvu Ved, p. 23.

Translation of the Céna Upanishad, one of the Chapters of the Sáma Véda, p. 41.

Translation of the Kut'h-Oopunishud of the Ujoor-Ved, p. 55.

Translation of the Ishopanishad, one of the Chapters of the Yajur Véda, p. 81.

H. T. Colebrooke, Miscellaneous Essays, in three volumes, 1873.

K. J. H. Windischmann, Die Philosophie im Fortgange der Weltgeschichte, 1827-34.

F. W. Windischmann, Sancara, seu de theologumenis Vedanticorum, 1833.

E. Röer, The Taittirîya, Aitareya, Svetâsvatara, Kena Îsâ, Katha, Prasna, Mu*nd*aka, and Mâ*nd*ûkya Upanishads translated; Bibliotheca, Indica. Calcutta, 1853.

Rajendralal Mitra, The *Kh*ândogya Upanishad, with extracts from the commentary of *S*aṅkara; Bibliotheca Indica. Calcutta, 1862.

E. B. Cowell, The Kaushîtaki-brâhma*n*a-upanishad, edited with an English translation; Bibliotheca Indica. Calcutta, 1861.

E. B. Cowell, The Maitri Upanishad, edited with an English translation; Bibliotheca Indica. Calcutta, 1870.

A. Weber, Die Vagrasû*k*î des A*s*vaghosha. Berlin, 1860.

A. Weber, Die Râma-tâpanîya Upanishad. Berlin, 1864.

A. Weber, Analyse der in Anquetil du Perron's Übersetzung enthalten Upanishad; Indische Studien, vol. i, p. 247 et seq.

A. E. Gough, The Philosophy of the Upanishads; Calcutta Review, CXXXI.

P. Regnaud, Matériaux pour servir à l'histoire de la Philosophic de l'Inde. Paris, 1876.

Editions of the Upanishads, their commentaries and glosses have been published in the Tattvabodhinî patrikâ, and by Poley (who has also translated several Upanishads into French), by Röer, Cowell, Rajendralal Mitra, Hara*k*andra Vidyâbhûsha*n*a, Vi*s*vanâtha *S*âstrî, Râmamaya Tarkaratna, and others. For fuller titles see Gildemeister, Bibliotheca Sanscrita, and E. Haas, Catalogue of Sanskrit and Pali Books in the British Museum, s. v. Upanishads.

I. THE KHÂNDOGYA-UPANISHAD.

The *Kh*ândogya-upanishad belongs to the Sâma-veda. Together with the B*ri*had-âra*n*yaka, which belongs to the Yagur-veda, it has contributed the most important materials to what may be called the orthodox philosophy of India, the Vedânta[47], i.e. the end, the purpose, the highest object of the Veda. It consists of eight adhyâyas or lectures, and formed part of a *Kh*ândogya-brâhma*n*a, in which it was preceded by two other adhyâyas. While MSS. of the *Kh*ândogya-upanishad and its commentary are frequent, no MSS. of the whole Brâhma*n*a has been met with in Europe. Several scholars had actually doubted its existence, but Rajendralal Mitra[48], in the Introduction to his translation of the *Kh*ândogya-upanishad, states that in India 'MSS. of the work are easily available, though as yet he has seen no commentary attached to the Brâhma*n*a portion of any one of them.' 'According to general acceptation,' he adds, 'the work embraces ten chapters, of which the first two are reckoned to be the Brâhma*n*a, and the rest is known under the name of *Kh*ândogya-upanishad. In their arrangement and style the two portions differ greatly, and judged by them they appear to be productions of very different ages, though both are evidently relics of pretty remote antiquity. Of the two chapters of the *Kh*ândogya-brâhma*n*a[49], the first includes eight sûktas (hymns) on the ceremony of marriage, and the rites necessary to be observed at the birth of a child. The first sûktas is intended to be recited when offering an oblation to

---

[47] Vedânta, as a technical term, did not mean originally the last portions of the Veda, or chapters placed, as it were, at the end of a volume of Vedic literature, but the end, i.e. the object, the highest purpose of the Veda. There are, of course, passages, like the one in the Taittirîya-âra*n*yaka (ed. Rajendralal Mitra, p. 820), which have been misunderstood both by native and European scholars, and where vedânta means simply the end of the Veda:—yo vedâdau svara*h* prokto vedânte ka pratish*th*ita*h*, 'the Om which is pronounced at the beginning of the Veda, and has its place also at the end of the Veda.' Here vedânta stands simply in opposition to vedâdau, and it is impossible to translate it, as Sâya*n*a does, by Vedânta or Upanishad. Vedânta, in the sense of philosophy, occurs in the Taittirîya-âra*n*yaka (p. 817), in a verse of the Narâya*n*îya-upanishad, repeated in the Mundaka-upanishad III, 2, 6, and elsewhere, vedântavigñânasuni*sk*itârâ*h*, 'those who have well understood the object of the knowledge arising from the Vedânta,' not 'from the last books of the Veda;' and Svetâsvatara-up. VI, 22, vedânte parama*m* guhyam, 'the highest mystery in the Vedânta.' Afterwards it is used in the plural also, e.g. Kshurikopanishad, 10 (Bibl. Ind. p. 210), pu*nd*arîketi vedânteshu nigadyate, 'it is called pu*nd*arîka in the Vedântas,' i.e. in the *Kh*ândogya and other Upanishads, as the commentator says, but not in the last books of each Veda. A curious passage is found in the Gautama-sûtras XIX, 12, where a distinction seems to be made between Upanishad and Vedânta. Sacred Books, vol. ii, p. 272.

[48] *Kh*ândogya-upanishad, translated by Rajendralal Mitra, Calcutta, 1862, Introduction, p. 17.

[49] It begins, Om, deva savita*h*, pra Suva yagñam pra suva yagñapatim bhagâya. The second begins, ya*h* prâkyâ*m* di*s*i sarparâga esha te bali*h*.

Agni on the occasion of a marriage, and its object is to pray for prosperity in behalf of the married couple. The second prays for long life, kind relatives, and a numerous progeny. The third is the marriage pledge by which the contracting parties bind themselves to each other. Its spirit may be guessed from a single verse. In talking of the unanimity with which they will dwell, the bridegroom addresses his bride, "That heart of thine shall be mine, and this heart of mine shall be thine[50]." The fourth and the fifth invoke Agni, Vâyu, *K*andramas, and Sûrya to bless the couple and ensure healthful progeny. The sixth is a mantra for offering an oblation on the birth of a child; and the seventh and the eighth are prayers for its being healthy, wealthy, and powerful, not weak, poor, or mute, and to ensure a profusion of wealth and milch-cows. The first sûkta of the second chapter is addressed to the Earth, Agni, and Indra, with a prayer for wealth, health, and prosperity; the second, third, fourth, fifth, and sixth are mantras for offering oblations to cattle, the manes, Sûrya, and divers minor deities. The seventh is a curse upon worms, insects, flies, and other nuisances, and the last, the concluding mantra of the marriage ceremony, in which a general blessing is invoked for all concerned.'

After this statement there can be but little doubt that this Upanishad originally formed part of a Brâhma*n*a. This may have been called either by a general name, the Brâhma*n*a of the *Kh*andogas, the followers of the Sâma-veda, or, on account of the prominent place occupied in it by the Upanishad, the Upanishad-brâhma*n*a[51]. In that case it would be one of the eight Brâhma*n*as of the Sâma-veda, enumerated by Kumârila Bha*tt*a and others[52], and called simply Upanishad, scil. Brâhma*n*a.

The text of the Upanishad with the commentary of *S*aṅkara and the gloss of Ânandagiri has been published in the Bibliotheca Indica. The edition can only claim the character of a manuscript, and of a manuscript not always very correctly read.

A translation of the Upanishad was published, likewise in the Bibliotheca Indica, by Rajendralal Mitra.

It is one of the Upanishads that was translated into Persian under the auspices of Dârâ Shukoh[53], and from Persian into French by Anquetil Duperron, in his Oupnekhat, i.e. Secretum Tegendum. Portions of it were translated into English by Colebrooke in his

---

[50] Yad etad dh*r*idaya*m* tava tad astu h*r*idayam mama, Yad ida*m* h*r*idayam mama tad astu h*r*idayam tava.

[51] The same name seems, however, to be given to the adhyâya of the Talavakâra-brâhma*n*a, which contains the Kena-upanishad.

[52] M. M., History of Ancient Sanskrit Literature, p. 348. Most valuable information on the literature of the Sâma-veda may be found in Dr. Burnell's editions of the smaller Brâhma*n*as of that Veda.

[53] M. M., History of Ancient Sanskrit Literature, p. 325.

Miscellaneous Essays, into Latin and German by F. W. Windischmann, in his *S*añkara, seu de theologumenis Vedanticorum. (Bonn, 1833), and in a work published by his father, K. J. H. Windischmann, Die Philosophie im Fortgang der Weltgeschichte (Bonn, 1827-34). Professor A. Weber has treated of this Upanishad in his Indische Studien I, 254; likewise M. P. Regnaud in his Matériaux pour servir à l'histoire dc la philosophie de l'Inde (Paris, 1876) and Mr. Gough in several articles on 'the Philosophy of the Upanishads,' in the Calcutta Review, No. CXXXI.

I have consulted my predecessors whenever there was a serious difficulty to solve in the translation of these ancient texts. These difficulties are very numerous, as those know best who have attempted to give complete translations of these ancient texts. It will be seen that my translation differs sometimes very considerably from those of my predecessors. Though I have but seldom entered into any controversy with them, they may rest assured that I have not deviated from them without careful reflection.

II. THE TALAVAKÂRA-UPANISHAD.

This Upanishad is best known by the name of Kena-upanishad, from its first word. The name of brâhmî-upanishad (IV, 7) can hardly be considered as a title. It means 'the teaching of Brahman,' and is used with reference to other Upanishads also[54]. *S*añkara, in his commentary, tells us that this Upanishad forms the ninth adhyâya of a Brâhma*n*a, or, if we take his words quite literally, he says, 'the beginning of the ninth adhyâya is "the Upanishad beginning with the words Keneshitam, and treating of the Highest Brahman has to be taught."' In the eight preceeding adhyâyas, he tells us, all the sacred rites or sacrifices had been fully explained, and likewise the meditations (upâsana) on the prâ*n*a (vital breath) which belongs to all these sacrifices, and those meditations also which have reference to the fivefold and sevenfold Sâmans. After that followed Gâyatra-sâman and the Va*ms*a, the genealogical list. All this would naturally form the subject of a Sâma-veda-brâhma*n*a, and we find portions corresponding to the description given by *S*añkara in the *Kh*ândogya-upanishad, eg. the fivefold Sâman, II, 2; the sevenfold Sâman, II, 8; the Gâyatra-sâman, III, 12, I.

Ânandagñâna tells us that our Upanishad belonged to the Sâkhâ of the Talavakâras.

All this had formerly to be taken on trust, because no Brâhma*n*a was known containing the Upanishad. Dr. Burnell, however, has lately discovered a Brâhma*n*a of the Sâma-veda which comes very near the description given by *S*añkara. In a letter dated Tanjore, 8th Dec. 1878,

---

[54] See before, p. 56.

he writes: 'It appears to me that you would be glad to know the following about the Kena-upanishad, as it occurs in my MS. of the Talavakâra-brâhma*n*a.

'The last book but one of this Brâhma*n*a is termed Upanishad-brâhma*n*a. It consists of 145 khandas treating of the Gâyatra-sâman, and the 134th is a Vamsa. The Kena-upanishad comprises the 135-145 khandas, or the tenth anuvâka of a chapter. The 139th section begins: âsâ vâ idam agra âsit, &c.

'My MS. of the Talavakâra-brâhma*n*a agrees, as regards the contents, exactly with what *S*aṅkara says, but not in the divisions. He says that the Kena-upanishad begins the ninth adhyâya, but that is not so in my MS. Neither the beginning nor the end of this Upanishad is noticed particularly.

'The last book of this Brâhma*n*a is the Ârsheya-brâhma*n*a, which I printed last February.

'Among the teachers quoted in the Brâhma*n*a I have noticed both Tândya and *S*â*t*yâyani. I should not be surprised to find in it the difficult quotations which are incorrectly given in the MSS. of Sâya*n*a's commentary on the Rig-veda. The story of Apâlâ, quoted by Sâya*n*a in his commentary on the Rig-veda, VIII, 80, as from the *S*â*t*yâyanaka, is found word for word, except some trivial var. lectiones, in sections 220-221 of the Agnish*t*oma book of the Talavakâra-brâhma*n*a. The *S*â*t*yâyanins seem to be closely connected with the Talavakâra-*s*âkhâ.'

From a communication made by Dr. Burnell to the Academy (1 Feb. 79), I gather that this Talavakâra-brâhma*n*a is called by those who study it '*G*aiminîya-brâhma*n*a,' after the *S*âkhâ of the Sâma-veda which they follow. The account given in the Academy differs on some particulars slightly from that given in Dr. Burnell's letter to me. He writes: 'The largest part of the Brâhma*n*a treats of the sacrifices and the Sâmans used at them. The first chapter is on the Agnihotra, and the Agnish*t*oma and other rites follow at great length. Then comes a book termed Upanishad-brâhma*n*a. This contains 145 sections in four chapters. It begins with speculations on the Gâyatra-sâman, followed by a Va*m*sa; next, some similar matter and another Va*m*sa. Then (§§ 135-138) comes the Kena-upanishad (Talavakâra). The last book is the Ârsheya. The Upanishad forms the tenth anuvâka of the fourth chapter, not the beginning of a ninth chapter, as *S*aṅkara remarks.'

The Kena-upanishad has been frequently published and translated. It forms part of Dârâ Shukoh's Persian, and Anquetil Duperron's Latin translations. It was several times published in English by Rammohun Roy (Translations of Several Principal Books, Passages, and Texts of the Veda, London, 1832, p. 41), in German by Windischmann, Poley, and others. It has been more or less fully discussed by Colebrooke, Windischmann, Poley, Weber, Röer, Gough, and Regnaud in the books mentioned before,

Besides the text of this Upanishad contained in the Brâhma*n*a of the Sâma-veda, there is another text, slightly differing, belonging to the Atharva-veda, and there are commentaries on both texts (Colebrooke, Misc. Essays, 1873, II, p. 80).

III. THE AITAREYA-ÂRA*N*YAKA.

In giving a translation of the Aitareya-upanishad, I found it necessary to give at the same time a translation of that portion of the Aitareya-âra*n*yaka which precedes the Upanishad. The Âra*n*yakas seem to have been from the beginning the proper repositories of the ancient Upanishads, though it is difficult at first sight to find out in what relation the Upanishads stood to the Âra*n*yakas. The Âra*n*yakas are to be read and studied, not in the village (grâme), but in the forest, and so are the Upanishads. But the subjects treated in the Upanishads belong to a very different order from those treated in the other portions of the Âra*n*yakas, the former being philosophical, the latter liturgical.

The liturgical chapters of the Âra*n*yakas might quite as well have formed part of the Brâhma*n*as, and but for the restriction that they are to be read in the forest, it is difficult to distinguish between them and the Brâhma*n*as. The first chapter of the Aitareya-âra*n*yaka is a mere continuation of the Aitareya-brâhma*n*a, and gives the description of the Mahâvrata, the last day but one of the Gavâmayana, a sattra or sacrifice which is supposed to last a whole year. The duties which are to be performed by the Hot*ri* priests are described in the Aitareya-âra*n*yaka; not all, however, but those only which are peculiar to the Mahâvrata day. The general rules for the performance of the Mahâvrata are to be taken over from other sacrifices, such as the Vi*s*vagit, Katurvi*m*sa, &c., which form the type (prak*ri*ti) of the Mahâvrata. Thus the two *s*astras or recitations, called âgya-praüga, are taken over from the Vi*s*vagit, the *s*astras of the Hotrakas from the Katurvi*ms*a. The Mahâvrata is treated here as belonging to the Gavâmayana sattra, which is described in a different *S*âkhâ, see Taittirîya Sa*m*hitâ VII, 5, 8, and partly in other Vedas. It is the day preceding the udayanîya, the last day of the sattra. It can be celebrated, however, by itself also, as an ekâha or ahîna sacrifice, and in the latter case it is the tenth day of the Ekada*s*arâtra (eleven nights sacrifice) called Pu*nd*arîka.

Sâyana does not hesitate to speak of the Aitareya-Âra*n*yaka as a part of the Brâhma*n*a[55]; and a still earlier authority, *S*aṅkara, by calling the Aitareya-upanishad by the name of Bahvrika-brâhma*n*a-

---

[55] Aitareyabrâhma*n*e 'sti kâ*nd*am âra*n*yakâbhidham (introduction), a remark which he repeats in the fifth Âra*n*yaka. He also speaks of the Âra*n*yaka-vratarûpam brâhma*n*am; see p. cxiv, l. 24.

upanishad[56], seems to imply that both the Upanishad and the Âra*n*yaka may be classed as Brâhma*n*a.

The Aitareya-Âra*n*yaka appears at first sight a miscellaneous work, consisting of liturgical treatises in the first, fourth, and fifth Âra*n*yakas, and of three Upanishads, in the second and third Âra*n*yakas. This, however, is not the case. The first Âra*n*yaka is purely liturgical, giving a description of the Mahâvrata, so far as it concerns the Hot*ri* priest. It is written in the ordinary Brâhma*n*a style. Then follows the first Upanishad, Âra*n*yaka II, 1-3, showing how certain portions of the Mahâvrata, as described in the first Âra*n*yaka, can be made to suggest a deeper meaning, and ought to lead the mind of the sacrificer away from the purely outward ceremonial to meditation on higher subjects. Without a knowledge of the first Âra*n*yaka therefore the first Upanishad would be almost unintelligible, and though its translation was extremely tedious, it could not well have been omitted.

The second and third Upanishads are not connected with the ceremonial of the Mahâvrata, but in the fourth and fifth Âra*n*yakas the Mahâvrata forms again the principal subject, treated, however, not as before in the style of the Brâhma*n*as, but in the style of Sûtras. The fourth Âra*n*yaka contains nothing but a list of the Mahânâmnî hymns[57], but the fifth describes the Mahâvrata again, so that if the first Âra*n*yaka may be looked upon as a portion of the Aitareya-brâhma*n*as, the fifth could best be classed with the Sûtras of Â*s*valâyana.

To a certain extent this fact, the composite character of the Aitareya-Âra*n*yaka, is recognised even by native scholars, who generally do not trouble themselves much on such questions. They look both on the Aitareya-brâhma*n*a and on the greater portion of Aitareya-Âra*n*yaka as the works of an inspired Rishi, Mahidâsa Aitareya[58], but they consider the fourth and fifth books of the Âra*n*yaka as contributed by purely human authors, such as Â*s*valâyana and Saunaka, who, like other Sûtrakâras, took in verses belonging to other *S*âkhâs, and did not confine their rules to their own *S*âkhâ only.

There are many legends about Mahidâsa, the reputed author of the Aitareya-brâhma*n*a and Âra*n*yaka. He is quoted several times as Mahidâsa Aitareya in the Âra*n*yaka itself, though not in the Brâhma*n*a.

---

[56] In the same manner the Kaushîtaki-upanishad is properly called Kaushîtaki-brâhma*n*a-upanishad, though occurring in the Âra*n*yaka; see Kaushîtaki-brâhma*n*a-upanishad, ed. Cowell, p. 30.

[57] See Boehtlingk and Roth, s*v*. 'Neun Vedische Verse die in ihrem vollständigen Wortlaut aber noch nachtnachgewiesen sind.' Weber Indische Studien VIII, 68. How these hymns are to be employed we learn from the Âsvalâyana-sûtras VII, 12, 10, where we are told that if the Udgâtris sing the Sâkvara Sâman as the Prishthastotra, the nine verses beginning with Vidâ maghavan, and known by the name of Mahânâmnî, are to be joined in a peculiar manner. The only excuse given, why these Mahânâmnîs are mentioned here, and not in the Brâhma*n*a, is that they are to be studied in the forest.

[58] M. M., History of Ancient Sanskrit Literature, pp. 177, 335.

We also meet his name in the *Kh*ândogya-upanishad (III, 16, 7), where we are told that he lived to an age of 116 years[59]. All this, however, would only prove that, at the time of the composition or collection of these Âra*n*yakas and Upanishads, a sage was known of the name of Mahidâsa Aitareya, descended possibly from Itara or Itarâ. and that one text of the Brâhma*n*as and the Âra*n*yakas of the Bahvrikas was handed down in the family of the Aitareyins.

Not content with this apparently very obvious explanation, later theologians tried to discover their own reasons for the name of Aitareya. Thus Sâyana, in his introduction to the Aitareya-brâhma*n*a[60], tells us that there was once a Rishi who had many wives. One of them was called Itarâ, and she had a son called Mahidâsa. His father preferred the sons of his other wives to Mahidâsa, and once he insulted him in the sacrificial hall, by placing his other sons on his lap, but not Mahidâsa. Mahidâsa's mother, seeing her son with tears in his eyes, prayed to her tutelary goddess, the Earth (svîyakuladevatâ Bhûmi*h*), and the goddess in her heavenly form appeared in the midst of the assembly, placed Mahidâsa on a throne, and on account of his learning, gave him the gift of knowing the Brâhma*n*a, consisting of forty adhyâyas, and, as Sâyana calls it, another Brâhma*n*a, 'treating of the Âra*n*yaka duties' (âra*n*yakavratarûpam brâhma*n*am).

Without attaching much value to the legend of Itarâ, we see at all events that Sâyana considered what we call the Aitareyâra*n*yaka as a kind of Brâhma*n*a, not however the whole of it, but only the first, second, and third Âra*n*yakas (atha mahâvratam îtyâdikam â*k*âryâ â*k*âryâ ityantam). How easy it was for Hindu theologians to invent such legends we see from another account of Mahidâsa, given by Ânandatîrtha in his notes on the Aitareya-upanishad. He, as Colebrooke was the first to point out, takes Mahidâsa 'to be an incarnation of Nârâya*n*a, proceeding from Vi*s*âla, son of Abga,' and he adds, that on the sudden appearance of this deity at a solemn celebration, the whole assembly of gods and priests (suraviprasaṅgha) fainted, but at the intercession of Brahmâ, they were revived, and after making their obeisance, they were instructed in holy science. This avatâra was called Mahidâsa, because those venerable personages (mahin) declared themselves to be his slaves (dâsa)[61].

In order properly to understand this legend, we must remember that Ânandatîrtha, or rather Vi*s*ve*s*varatîrtha, whose commentary he explains, treated the whole of the Mahaitareya-upanishad from a Vaish*n*ava point of view, and that his object was to identify Mahidâsa

[59] Not 1600 years, as I printed by mistake; for 24 + 44 + 48 make 116 years. Rajendralal Mitra should not have corrected his right rendering 116 into 1600. Ait. Âr. Introduction, p. 3.

[60] M. M., History of Ancient Sanskrit Literature, p. 336.

[61] Colebrooke, Miscellaneous Essays, 1873, II, p. 42.

with Nârâyana. He therefore represents Nârâyana or Hari as the avatâra of Visâla, the son of Brahman (abgasuta), who appeared at a sacrifice, as described before, who received then and there the name of Mahidâsa (or Mahîdâsa), and who taught this Upanishad. Any other person besides Mahidâsa would have been identified with the same ease by Visvesvaratîrtha with Vishnu or Bhagavat.

A third legend has been made up out of these two by European scholars who represent Mahidâsa as the son of Visâla and Itarâ, two persons who probably never met before, for even the Vaishnava commentator does not attempt to take liberties with the name of Aitareya, but simply states that the Upanishad was called Aitareyî, from Aitareya.

Leaving these legends for what they are worth, we may at all events retain the fact that, whoever was the author of the Aitareya-brâhmana and the first three books of the Aitareya-Âranyaka, was not the author of the two concluding Âranyakas. And this is confirmed in different ways. Sâyana, when quoting in his commentary on the Rig-veda from the last books, constantly calls it a Sûtra of Saunaka, while the fourth Âranyaka is specially ascribed to Âsvalâyana, the pupil and successor of Saunaka[62]. These two names of Saunaka and Âsvalâyana are frequently intermixed. If, however, in certain MSS. the whole of the Aitareya-âranyaka is sometimes ascribed either to Âsvalâyana or Saunaka, this is more probably due to the colophon of the fourth and fifth Âranyakas having been mistaken for the title of the whole work than to the fact that such MSS. represent the text of the Âranyaka, as adopted by the school of Âsvalâyana.

The Aitareya-âranyaka consists of the following five Âranyakas:

[62] M. M., History of Ancient Sanskrit Literature, p. 235.

The first Âra*n*yaka has five Adhyâyas :

1. First Adhyâya, Atha mahâvratam, has four Kha*n*das, 1–4.
2. Second Adhyâya, Â tvâ ratham, has four Kha*n*das, 5–8.
3. Third Adhyâya, Hiṅkâre*n*a, has eight[2] Kha*n*das, 9–16.
4. Fourth Adhyâya, Atha sûdadohâ*h*, has three Kha*n*das, 17–19.
5. Fifth Adhyâya, Vasa*m* sa*m*sati, has three Kha*n*das, 20–22.

The second Âra*n*yaka has seven Adhyâyas :

[Bahv*ri*ka-upanishad: Adhyâyas 6–14; Aitareya-upanishad: Adhyâyas 9–11]

6. First Adhyâya, Eshâ panthâ*h*, has eight Kha*n*das, 1–8.
7. Second Adhyâya, Esha ima*m* lokam, has four Kha*n*das, 9–12.
8. Third Adhyâya, Yo ha vâ âtmânam, has eight (not three) Kha*n*das, 13–20.
9. Fourth Adhyâya, Âtmâ vâ idam, has three Kha*n*das, 21–23.
10. Fifth Adhyâya, Purushe ha vâ, has one Kha*n*da, 24.
11. Sixth Adhyâya, Ko 'yam âtmeti, has one Kha*n*da, 25.
12. Seventh Adhyâya, Vâṅ me manasi, has one Kha*n*da, 26.

The third Âra*n*yaka has two Adhyâyas :

13. First Adhyâya, Athâta*h* sa*m*hitâyâ upanishat, has six Kha*n*das, 1–6.
14. Second Adhyâya, Prâ*n*o va*m*sa iti sthavira*h* *S*âkalya*h*, has six Kha*n*das, 7–12.

The fourth Âra*n*yaka has one Adhyâya :

15. First Adhyâya, Vidâ maghavan, has one Kha*n*da (the Mahânâmnî's).

The fifth Âra*n*yaka has three Adhyâyas :

16. First Adhyâya, Mahâvratasya paṅ*k*avi*m*satim, has six Kha*n*das, 1–6.
17. Second Adhyâya, (Grîvâ*h*) Yasyedam, has five Kha*n*das, 7–11.
18. Third Adhyâya, (Ûrû) Indrâgnî, has four Kha*n*das, 11–14.

With regard to the Upanishad, we must distinguish between the Aitareya-upanishad, properly so-called, which fills the fourth, fifth, and sixth adhyâyas of the second Âra*n*yaka, and the Mahaitareya-upanishad[63], also called by a more general name Bahv*rik*a-upanishad, which comprises the whole of the second and third Âra*n*yakas.

The Persian translator seems to have confined himself to the second Âra*n*yaka[64], to which he gives various titles, Sarbsar, Asarbeh, Antrteheh. That Antrteheh انترته is a misreading of ايتريه was pointed out long ago by Burnouf, and the same explanation applies probably to

[63] This may have been the origin of a Rishi Mahaitareya, by the side of the Rishi Aitareya, mentioned in the Âsvalâyana Grihya-sûtras III, 4 (ed. Stenzler). Professor Weber takes Aitareya and Mahaitareya here as names of works, but he admits that in the Sâṅkhâyana G*ri*hya-sûtras they are clearly names of *R*ishis (Ind. Stud. I, p. 389).

[64] He translates II, I-II, 3, 4, leaving out the rest of the third adhyâya afterwards II, 4-II, 7.

اسربه, asarbeh, and if to that, then to Sarbsar also. No explanation has ever been given why the Aitareya-upanishad should have been called Sarvasâra, which Professor Weber thinks was corrupted into Sarbsar. At all events the Aitareya-upanishad is not the Sarvasâra-upanishad, the Oupnek'hat Sarb, more correctly called Sarvopanishatsâra, and ascribed either to the Taittirîyaka or to the Atharva-veda[65].

The Aitareya-upanishad, properly so called, has been edited and translated in the Bibliotheca Indica by Dr. Röer. The whole of the Aitareya-âra*n*yaka with Sâyana's commentary was published in the same series by Rajendralal Mitra.

Though I have had several MSS. of the text and commentary at my disposal, I have derived little aid from them, but have throughout endeavoured to restore that text which *S*ankara (the pupil of Govinda) and Sâyana had before them. Sâyana, for the Upanishad portion, follows *S*ankara's commentary, of which we have a gloss by Ânandagñâna.

Colebrooke in his Essays (vol. ii, p. 42) says that he possessed one gloss by Nârâya*n*endra on *S*ankara's commentary, and another by Ânandatîrtha on a different gloss for the entire Upanishad. The gloss by Nârâya*n*endra[66], however, is, so Dr. Rost informs me, the same as that of Ânandagñâna, while, so far as I can see, the gloss contained in MS. E. I. H. 2386 (also MS. Wilson 401), to which Colebrooke refers, is not a gloss by Ânandatîrtha at all, but a gloss by Visvesvaratîrtha on a commentary by Ânandatîrthabhagavatpâdâ*k*ârya, also called Pûr*n*apragñâkârya, who explained the whole of the Mahaitareya-upanishad from a Vaish*n*ava point of view.

IV. THE KAUSHÎTAKI-BRÂHMA*N*A-UPANISHAD.

The Kaushîtaki-upanishad, or, as it is more properly called, the Kaushîtaki-brâhma*n*a-upanishad, belongs, like the Aitareya-upanishad, to the followers of the Rig-veda. It was translated into Persian under the title of Kokhenk, and has been published in the Bibliotheca Indica, with *S*ankarânanda's commentary and an excellent translation by Professor Cowell.

Though it is called the Kaushîtaki-brâhma*n*a-upanishad, it does not form part of the Kaushîtaki-brâhma*n*a in 30 adhyâyas which we possess, and we must therefore account for its name by admitting that the Âra*n*yaka, of which it formed a portion, could be reckoned as part

---

[65] Bibliotheca Indica, the Atharva*n*a-upanishads, p. 394.

[66] A MS. in the Notices of Sanskrit MSS., vol. ii, p. 133, ascribed to Abhinavanârâya*n*endra, called Âtmasha*t*kabhâshya*t*îkâ, begins like the gloss edited by Dr. Röer, and ends like Sâyana's commentary on the seventh adhyâya, as edited by Rajendralal Mitra. The same name is given in MS. Wilson 94, *S*rîmatkaivalyendrasarasvatîpûgyapâda*s*ishya-*s*rîmadabhinavanârâya*n*endrasarasvatî.

of the Brâhma*n*a literature of the Rig-veda (see Aitareya-âra*n*yaka, Introduction), and that hence the Upanishad might be called the Upanishad of the Brâhma*n*a of the Kaushîtakins[67].

From a commentary discovered by Professor Cowell it appears that the four adhyâyas of this Upanishad were followed by five other adhyâyas, answering, so far as we can judge from a few extracts, to some of the adhyâyas of the Aitareya-âra*n*yaka, while an imperfect MS. of an Âra*n*yaka in the Royal Library at Berlin (Weber, Catalogue, p.20) begins, like the Aitareya-âra*n*yaka, with a description of the Mahâvrata, followed by discussions on the uktha in the second adhyâya; and then proceeds in the third adhyâya to give the story of *K*itra Gâṅgyâyani in the same words as the Kaushîtaki-upanishad in the first adhyâya. Other MSS. again adopt different divisions. In one MS. of the commentary (MS. A), the four adhyâyas of the Upanishad are counted as sixth, seventh, eighth, and ninth (ending with ityâra*n*yake navamo 'dhyâya*h*); in another (MS. P) the third and fourth adhyâyas of the Upanishad are quoted as the fifth and sixth of the Kaushîtakyâra*n*yaka, possibly agreeing therefore, to a certain extent, with the Berlin MS. In a MS. of the *S*âṅkhâyana Âra*n*yaka in the Royal Library at Berlin, there are 15 adhyâyas, 1 and 2 corresponding to Ait. Âr. 1 and 5; 3-6 containing the Kaushîtaki-upanishad; 7 and 8 corresponding to Ait. Âr. 3[68]. Poley seems to have known a MS. in which the four adhyâyas of the Upanishad formed the first, seventh, eighth, and ninth adhyâyas of a Kaushîtaki-brâhma*n*a.

As there were various recensions of the Kaushîtaki-brâhma*n*a (the *S*âṅkhâyana, Kauthuma, &c.), the Upanishad also exists in at least two texts. The commentator, in some of its MSS., refers to the various readings of the *S*âkhâs, explaining them, whenever there seems to be occasion for it. I have generally followed the text which is presupposed by *S*aṅkarânanda's Dîpikâ, and contained in MSS. F, G (Cowell, Preface, p. v), so far as regards the third and fourth adhyâyas. According to Professor Cowell, Vidyâranya in his Sarvopanishadarthânubhûtiprakâ*s*a followed the text of the commentary, while Sankarâkârya, if we may trust to extracts in his commentary on the Vedânta-sûtras, followed the other text, contained in MS. A (Cowell, Preface, p. v).

The style of the commentator differs in so marked a manner from that of *S*aṅkarâ*k*ârya, that even without the fact that the author of the commentary on the Kaushîtaki-upanishad is called *S*aṅkarânanda, it would have been difficult to ascribe it, as has been done by some scholars, to the famous *S*aṅkarânanda. *S*aṅkarânanda is called the teacher of Mâdhavâ*k*ârya (Hall, Index, p. 98), and the disciple of

[67] A Mahâ-kaushîtaki-brâhma*n*a is quoted, but has not yet been met with.

[68] See Weber, History of Sanskrit Literature, p. 50.

Ânandâtma Muni (Hall, Index, p. 116).

I have had the great advantage of being able to consult for the Kaushîtaki-upanishad, not only the text and commentary as edited by Professor Cowell, but also his excellent translation. If I differ from him in some points, this is but natural, considering the character of the text and the many difficulties that have still to be solved, before we can hope to arrive at a full understanding of these ancient philosophical treatises.

V. THE VÂGASANEYI-SAMHITÂ-UPANISHAD.

The Vâgasaneyi-sa*m*hitâ-upanishad, commonly called from its beginning, Îsâ or Îsâvâsya, forms the fortieth and concluding chapter of the Sa*m*hitâ of the White Yagur-veda. If the Sa*m*hitâs are presupposed by the Brâhma*n*as, at least in that form in which we possess them, then this Upanishad, being the only one that forms part of a Sa*m*hitâ, might claim a very early age. The Sa*m*hitâ of the White Yagur-veda, however, is acknowledged to be of modern origin, as compared with the Sa*m*hitâ of the Black Yagur-veda, and it would not be safe therefore to ascribe to this Upanishad a much higher antiquity than to those which have found a place in the older Brâhma*n*as and Âra*n*yakas.

There are differences between the text, as contained in the Yagur-veda-sa*m*hitâ, and the text of the Upanishad by itself. Those which are of some interest have been mentioned in the notes.

In some notes appended to the translation of this Upanishad I have called attention to what seems to me its peculiar character, namely, the recognition of the necessity of works as a preparation for the reception of the highest knowledge. This agrees well with the position occupied by this Upanishad at the end of the Sa*m*hitâ, in which the sacrificial works and the hymns that are to accompany them are contained. The doctrine that the moment a man is enlightened, he becomes free, as taught in other Upanishads, led to a rejection of all discipline and a condemnation of all sacrifices, which could hardly have been tolerated in the last chapter of the Yagur-veda-sa*m*hitâ, the liturgical Veda par excellence.

Other peculiarities of this Upanishad are the name Î*s*, lord, a far more personal name for the highest Being than Brahman; the asurya (demoniacal) or asûrya (sunless) worlds to which all go who have lost their self; Mâtari*s*van, used in the sense of prâ*n*a or spirit; asnâviram, without muscles, in the sense of incorporeal; and the distinction between sambhûti and asambhûti in verses 12-14.

The editions of the text, commentaries, and glosses, and the earlier translations may be seen in the works quoted before (Works on the Upanishads).

Volume I

*KH*ÂNDOGYA-UPANISHAD.

FIRST PRAPÂ*TH*AKA.

FIRST KH*A*N*D*A[69].

1. Let a man meditate on the syllable[70] Om, called the udgîtha; for the udgîtha (a portion of the Sâma-veda) is sung, beginning with Om.

The full account, however, of Om is this:—

2. The essence[71] of all beings is the earth, the essence of the earth is water, the essence of water the plants, the essence of plants man, the essence of man speech, the essence of speech the Rig-veda, the essence of the Rig-veda the Sâma-veda[72], the essence of the Sâma-veda the udgîtha (which is Om).

3. That udgîtha (Om) is the best of all essences, the highest, deserving the highest place[73], the eighth.

4. What then is the *Rik*? What is the Sâman? What is the udgîtha? This is the question.

5. The *Rik* indeed is speech, Sâman is breath, the udgîtha is the syllable Om. Now speech and breath, or *Rik* and Sâman, form one couple.

6. And that couple is joined together in the syllable Om. When two people come together, they fulfil each other's desire.

7. Thus he who knowing this, meditates on the syllable (Om), the udgîtha, becomes indeed a fulfiller of desires.

8. That syllable is a syllable of permission, for whenever we permit

---

[69] The *Kh*ândogya-upanishad begins with recommending meditation on the syllable Om, a sacred syllable that had to be pronounced at the beginning of each Veda and of every recitation of Vedic hymns. As connected with the Sâma-veda, that syllable Om is called udgîtha. Its more usual name is pra*n*ava. The object of the Upanishad is to explain the various meanings which the syllable Om may assume in the mind of a devotee, some of them being extremely artificial and senseless, till at last the highest meaning of Om is reached, viz. Brahman, the intelligent cause of the universe.

[70] Akshara means both syllable and the imperishable, i.e. Brahman.

[71] Essence, rasa, is explained in different ways, as origin, support, end, cause, and effect. Rasa means originally the sap of trees. That sap may be conceived either as the essence extracted from the tree, or as what gives vigour and life to a tree. In the former case it might be transferred to the conception of effect, in the latter to that of cause. In our sentence it has sometimes the one, sometimes the other meaning. Earth is the support of all beings, water pervades the earth, plants arise from water, man lives by plants, speech is the best part of man, the Rig-veda the best part of speech, the Sâma-veda the best extract from the *Rik*, udgîtha, or the syllable Om, the crown of the Sâma-veda.

[72] Because most of the hymns of the Sâma-veda are taken from the Rig-veda.

[73] Parârdhya is here derived from para, highest, and ardha, place. The eighth means the eighth or East in the series of essences.

anything, we say Om, yes. Now permission is gratification. He who knowing this meditates on the syllable (Om), the udgîtha, becomes indeed a gratifier of desires.

9. By that syllable does the threefold knowledge (the sacrifice, more particularly the Soma-sacrifice, as founded on the three Vedas) proceed. When the Adhvaryu priest gives an order, he says Om. When the Hot*ri* priest recites, he says Om. When the Udgât*ri* priest sings, he says Om,—all for the glory of that syllable. The threefold knowledge (the sacrifice) proceeds by the greatness of that syllable (the vital breaths), and by its essence (the oblations)[74].

10. Now therefore it would seem to follow, that both he who knows this (the true meaning of the syllable Om), and he who does not, perform the same sacrifice[75]. But this is not so, for knowledge and ignorance are different. The sacrifice which a man performs with knowledge, faith, and the Upanishad[76] is more powerful. This is the full account of the syllable Om.

SECOND KHA*ND*A[77].

1. When the Devas and Asuras[78] struggled together, both of the race of Pragâpati, the Devas took the udgîtha[79] (Om), thinking they

---

[74] These are allusions to sacrificial technicalities, all intended to show the importance of the syllable Om, partly as a mere word, used at the sacrifices, partly as the mysterious name of the Highest Self. As every priest at the Soma-sacrifices, in which three classes of priests are always engaged, has to begin his part of the ceremonial with Om, therefore the whole sacrifice is said to be dependent on the syllable Om, and to be for the glory of that syllable, as an emblem of the Highest Self, a knowledge of whom is the indirect result of all sacrifices. The greatness of the syllable Om is explained by the vital breaths of the priest, the sacrificer, and his wife; its essence by rice, corn, &c., which constitute the oblations. Why breath and food are due to the syllable Om is explained by the sacrifice, which is dependent on that syllable, ascending to the sun, the sun sending rain, rain producing food, and food producing breath and life.

[75] He who simply pronounces the syllable Om as part of his recitation at a sacrifice, and he who knows the hidden meaning of that syllable, both may perform the same sacrifice. But that performed by the latter is more powerful, because knowledge is better than ignorance. This is, as usual, explained by some comparisons. It is true that both he who knows the quality of the harîtakî and he who does not, are purged alike if they take it. But on the other hand, if a jeweller and a mere clod sell a precious stone, the knowledge of the former bears better fruit than the ignorance of the latter.

[76] Upanishad is here explained by yoga, and yoga by devatâdivishayam upâsanam, meditation directed to certain deities, More likely, however, it refers to this very upanishad, i.e. to the udgîthavidyâ, the doctrine of the secret meaning of Om, as here explained.

[77] A very similar story is told in the B*ri*had-âranyaka I, 1, 3, 1. But though the coincidences between the two are considerable, amounting sometimes to verbal identity, the purport of the two seems to be different. See Vedânta-sûtra III, 3, 6.

[78] Devas and Asuras, gods and demons, are here explained by the commentator as the good and evil inclinations of man; Pragâpati as man in general.

[79] Udgîtha stands, according to the commentator, for the sacrificial act to be performed by the Udgât*ri*, the Sâma-veda priest, with the udgîtha hymns; and as these

would vanquish the Asuras with it.

2. They meditated on the udgîtha[79] (Om) as the breath (scent) in the nose[80], but the Asuras pierced it (the breath) with evil. Therefore we smell by the breath in the nose both what is good-smelling and what is bad-smelling. For the breath was pierced by evil.

3. Then they meditated on the udgîtha (Om) as speech, but the Asuras pierced it with evil. Therefore we speak both truth and falsehood. For speech is pierced by evil.

4. Then they meditated on the udgîtha (Om) as the eye, but the Asuras pierced it with evil. Therefore we see both what is sightly and unsightly. For the eye is pierced by evil.

5. Then they meditated on the udgîtha (Om) as the ear, but the Asuras pierced it with evil. Therefore we hear both what should be heard and what should not be heard. For the car is pierced by evil.

6. Then they meditated on the udgîtha (Om) as the mind, but the Asuras pierced it with evil. Therefore we conceive both what should be conceived and what should not be conceived. For the mind is pierced by evil.

7. Then comes this breath (of life) in the mouth[81]. They meditated on the udgîtha (Om) as that breath. When the Asuras came to it, they were scattered, as (a ball of earth) would be scattered when hitting a solid stone.

8. Thus, as a ball of earth is scattered when hitting on a solid stone, will he be scattered who wishes evil to one who knows this, or who persecutes him; for he is a solid stone.

9. By it (the breath in the mouth) he distinguishes neither what is good nor what is bad-smelling, for that breath is free from evil. What we eat and drink with it supports the other vital breaths (i.e. the senses, such as smell, &c.) When at the time of death he[82] does not find that breath (in the mouth, through which he eats and drinks and lives), then he departs. He opens the mouth at the time of death (as if wishing to eat).

10. Aṅgiras[83] meditated on the udgîtha (Om) as that breath, and

---

sacrificial acts always form part of the *G*yotish*t*oma &c., these great Soma-sacrifices are really intended. In the second place, however, the commentator takes udgîtha in the sense of Udgât*ri*, the performer of the udgîtha, which is or was by the Devas thought to be the breath in the nose. I have preferred to take udgîtha in the sense of Om, and all that is implied by it.

[80] They asked that breath should recite the udgîtha. Comm.

[81] Mukhya prâ*n*a is used in two senses, the principal or vital breath, also called sresh*th*a, and the breath in the mouth, also called âsanya.

[82] According to the commentator, the assemblage of the other vital breaths or senses is here meant. They depart when the breath of the mouth, sometimes called sarvambhari, all-supporting, does no longer, by eating and drinking, support them.

[83] The paragraphs from 10 to 14 are differently explained by Indian commentators. By treating the nominatives aṅgirâs, b*ri*haspatis, and ayâsyas (here the printed text reads ayâsyam) as accusatives, or by admitting the omission of an iti after them, they connect

people hold it to be Aṅgiras, i.e. the essence of the members (angânâ*m* rasa*h*);

11. Therefore B*ri*haspati meditated on udgîtha (Om) as that breath, and people hold it to be B*ri*haspati, for speech is b*ri*hatî, and he (that breath) is the lord (pati) of speech;

12. Therefore Ayâsya meditated on the udgîtha (Om) as that breath, and people hold it to be Ayâsya, because it comes (ayati) from the mouth (âsya);

13. Therefore Vaka Dâlbhya knew it. He was the Udgât*ri* (singer) of the Naimishîya-sacrificers, and by singing he obtained for them their wishes.

14. He who knows this, and meditates on the syllable Om (the imperishable udgîtha) as the breath of life in the mouth, he obtains all wishes by singing. So much for the udgîtha (Om) as meditated on with reference to the body[84].

THIRD KHA*ND*A.

1. Now follows the meditation on the udgîtha with reference to the gods. Let a man meditate on the udgîtha (Om) as he who sends warmth (the sun in the sky). When the sun rises it sings as Udgât*ri* for the sake of all creatures. When it rises it destroys the fear of darkness. He who knows this, is able to destroy the fear of darkness (ignorance).

2. This (the breath in the mouth) and that (the sun) are the same. This is hot and that is hot. This they call svara (sound), and that they call pratyâsvara[85] (reflected sound). Therefore let a man meditate on the udgîtha (Om) as this and that (as breath and as sun).

3. Then let a man meditate on the udgîtha (Om) as vyâna indeed. If we breathe up, that is prâ*n*a, the up-breathing. If we breathe down, that is apâna, the down-breathing. The combination of prâ*n*a and apâna is vyâna, back-breathing or holding in of the breath. This vyâna is speech. Therefore when we utter speech, we neither breathe up nor down.

---

paragraphs 9, 10, and 11 with paragraph 12, and thus gain the meaning that Vaka Dâlbhya meditated on the breath in the mouth as Aṅgiras, B*ri*haspati, and Ayâsya, instead of those saints having themselves thus meditated; and that he, knowing the secret names and qualities of the breath, obtained, when acting as Udgât*ri* priest, the wishes of those for whom he sacrificed. Tena is difficult to explain, unless we take it in the sense of tenânu*s*ish*t*ah, taught by him.

[84] Adhyâtma means with reference to the body, not with reference to the self or the soul. Having explained the symbolical meaning of Om as applied to the body and its organs of sense, he now explains its symbolical meaning adhidaivatam, i.e. as applied to divine beings.

[85] As applied to breath, svara is explained by the commentator in the sense of moving, going out; pratyâsvara, as applied to the sun, is explained as returning every day. More likely, however, svara as applied to breath means sound, Om itself being called svara (*Kh.* Up. I, 4, 3), and prasvâra in the Rig-veda-prâti*s*âkhya, 882. As applied to the sun, svara and pratyâsvara were probably taken in the sense of light and reflected light.

4. Speech is *Rik*, and therefore when a man utters a *Rik* verse he neither breathes up nor down.

Rik is Sâman, and therefore when a man utters a Sâman verse he neither breathes up nor down.

Sâman is udgîtha, and therefore when a man sings (the udgîtha, Om) he neither breathes up nor down.

5. And other works also which require strength, such as the production of fire by rubbing, running a race, stringing a strong bow, are performed without breathing up or down. Therefore let a man meditate on the udgîtha (Om) as vyâna.

6. Let a man meditate on the syllables of the udgîtha, i.e. of the word udgîtha. Ut is breath (prâ*n*a), for by means of breath a man rises (uttish*th*ati). Gî is speech, for speeches are called gira*h*. Tha is food, for by means of food all subsists (sthita).

7. Ut is heaven, gî the sky, tha the earth. Ut is the sun, gî the air, tha the fire. Ut is the Sâma-veda, gî the Yagur-veda, tha the Rig-veda[86].

---

[86] The commentator supplies explanations to all these fanciful etymologies. The heaven is ut, because it is high; the sky is gî, because it gives out all the worlds (gira*n*ât); earth is tha, because it is the place (sthâna) of living beings. The sun is ut, because it is high. The wind is gî, because it gives out fire, &c. (gira*n*ât); fire is tha, because it is the place (sthâna) of the sacrifice. The Sâma-veda is ut, because it is praised as svarga; the Yagur-veda is gî, because the gods take the oblation offered with a Yagus; the Rig-veda is tha, because the Sâma verses stand in it. All this is very childish, and worse than childish, but it is interesting as a phase of human folly which is not restricted to the Brahmans of India. I take the following passage from an interesting article, 'On the Ogam Beithluisnin and on Scythian Letters,' by Dr. Charles Graves, Bishop of Limerick. 'An Irish antiquary,' he says, 'writing several hundred years ago, proposes to give an account of the origin of the names of the notes in the musical scale.

'"It is asked here, according to Saint Augustine, What is chanting, or why is it so called? Answer. From this word *cantalena*; and *cantalena* is the same thing as *lenis cantus*, i.e. a soft, sweet chant to God, and to the Virgin Mary, and to all the Saints. And the reason why the word *puinec* (*puncta*) is so called is because the points (or musical notes) *ut*, *re*, *mi*, *fa*, *sol*, *la*, hurt the devil and puncture him. And it is thus that these points are to be understood: viz. When Moses the son of Amram, with his people in their Exodus was crossing the Red Sea, and Pharaoh and his host were following him, this was the chant which Moses had to protect him from Pharaoh and his host—these six points in praise of the Lord:—

'"The first point of these, i.e. *ut*: and *ut* in the Greek is the same as *liberat* in the Latin; and that is the same as *saer* in the Gaelic; i.e. O God, said Moses, deliver us from the harm of the devil.

'"The second point of them, i.e. *re*: and *re* is the same as *saer*; i.e. O God, deliver us from everything hurtful and malignant.

'"The third point, i.e. *mi*: and *mi* in the Greek is the same as *militum* in the Latin; and that is the same as *ridere* (a knight) in the Gaelic; i.e. O God, said Moses, deliver us from those knights who are pursuing us.

'"The fourth point, i.e. *fa*: and *fa* in the Greek is the same as *famulus* in the Latin; and that is the same as *mug* (slave) in the Gaelic; i.e. O God, said Moses, deliver us from those slaves who are pursuing us.

'"The fifth point, i.e. *sol*: and *sol* is the same as *grian* (sun); and that is the same as righteousness; because righteousness and Christ are not different; i.e. O Christ, said Moses, deliver us.

Speech yields the milk, which is the milk of speech itself[87], to him who thus knowing meditates on those syllables of the name of udgîtha, he becomes rich in food and able to eat food.

8. Next follows the fulfilment of prayers. Let a man thus meditate on the Upasara*n*as, i.e. the objects which have to be approached by meditation: Let him (the Udgât*ri*) quickly reflect on the Sâman with which he is going to praise;

9. Let him quickly reflect on the *Rik* in which that Sâman occurs; on the *R*ishi (poet) by whom it was seen or composed; on the Devatâ (object) which he is going to praise;

10. On the metre in which he is going to praise; on the tune with which he is going to sing for himself;

11. On the quarter of the world which he is going to praise. Lastly, having approached himself (his name, family, &c.) by meditation, let him sing the hymn of praise, reflecting on his desire, and avoiding all mistakes in pronunciation, &c. Quickly[88] will the desire be then fulfilled to him, for the sake of which he may have offered his hymn of praise, yea, for which he may have offered his hymn of praise[89].

'"The sixth point, i.e. *la*, is the same as *lav*; and that is the same as *indail* (wash); i.e. O God, said Moses, wash away our sins from us.

'"And on the singing of that laud Pharaoh and his host were drowned.

'"Understand, O man, that in whatever place this laud, i.e. this chant, is sung, the devil is bound by it, and his power is extirpated thence, and the power of God is called in."

'We have been taught that the names of the first six notes in the gamut were suggested by the initial syllables of the first six hemistichs in one of the stanzas of a hymn to St. John:

Ut queant laxis
*Re*sonare fibris
*Mi*ra gestorum
*Fa*muli tuorum,
*So*lve polluti
*La*bii reatum,
*S*ancte *I*oannes.'

[87] The milk of speech consists in rewards to be obtained by the Rig-veda, &c. Or we may translate, Speech yields its milk to him who is able to milk speech.

[88] Abhyâ*s*o ha yat, lit. depend on it that it will be fulfilled, but always explained by quickly. See *Kh*. Up. II, 1, 4; III, 19, 4; V, 10, 7. Frequently, but wrongly, written with a dental s.

[89] The repetition of the last sentence is always an indication that a chapter is finished. This old division into chapters is of great importance for a proper study of the Upanishads.

FOURTH KHA*ND*A.

1. Let a man meditate on the syllable Om, for the udgîtha is sung beginning with Om. And this is the full account of the syllable Om—

2. The Devas, being afraid of death, entered upon (the performance of the sacrifice prescribed in) the threefold knowledge (the three Vedas). They covered themselves with the metrical hymns. Because they covered (*kh*ad) themselves with the hymns, therefore the hymns are called *kh*andas.

3. Then, as a fisherman might observe a fish in the water, Death observed the Devas in the *Rik*, Yagus, and Sâman-(sacrifices). And the Devas seeing this, rose from the *Rik*, Yagus, and Sâman-sacrifices, and entered the Svara[90], i.e. the Om (they meditated on the Om).

4. When a man has mastered the Rig-veda, he says quite loud Om; the same, when he has mastered the Sâman and the Yagus. This Svara is the imperishable (syllable), the immortal, free from fear. Because the Devas entered it, therefore they became immortal, and free from fear.

5. He who knowing this loudly pronounces (pra*n*auti)[91]—that syllable, enters the same (imperishable) syllable, the Svara, the immortal, free from fear, and having entered it, becomes immortal, as the Devas are immortal.

FIFTH KHA*ND*A.

1. The udgîtha is the pra*n*ava[92], the pra*n*ava is the udgîtha. And as the udgîtha is the sun[93], So is the pra*n*ava, for he (the sun) goes sounding Om.

2. 'Him I sang praises to, therefore art thou my only one,' thus said Kaushîtaki to his son. 'Do thou revolve his rays, then thou wilt have many sons.' So much in reference to the Devas.

3. Now with reference to the body. Let a man meditate on the udgîtha as the breath (in the mouth), for he goes sounding Om[94].

4. 'Him I sang praises to, therefore art thou my only son,' thus said Kaushîtaki to his son. 'Do thou therefore sing praises to the breath as manifold, if thou wishest to have many sons.'

5. He who knows that the udgîtha is the pra*n*ava, and the pra*n*ava

---

[90] Cf. I, 3, 2.

[91] Pra*n*auti, he lauds, i.e. he meditates on. Comm.

[92] Pranava is the name used chiefly by the followers of the Rig-veda, udgîtha the name used by the followers of the Sâma-veda. Both words are intended for the syllable Om.

[93] Cf. *Kh*. Up. I, 3, 1.

[94] The breath in the mouth, or the chief breath, says Om, i.e. gives permission to the five senses to act, just as the sun, by saying Om, gives permission to all living beings to move about.

the udgîtha, rectifies from the seat of the Hot*ri* priest any mistake committed by the Udgât*ri* priest in performing the udgîtha, yea, in performing the udgîtha.

SIXTH KHA*ND*A.

1. The *Rik* (veda) is this earth, the Sâman (veda) is fire. This Sâman (fire) rests on that *Rik* (earth)[95]. Therefore the Sâman is sung as resting on the *Rik*. Sâ is this earth, ama is fire, and that makes Sâma.

2. The *Rik* is the sky, the Sâman air. This Sâman (air) rests on that *Rik* (sky). Therefore the Sâman is sung as resting on the *Rik*. Sâ is the sky, ama the air, and that makes Sâma.

3. *Rik* is heaven, Sâman the sun. This Sâman (sun) rests on that *Rik* (heaven). Therefore the Sâman is sung as resting on the *Rik*. Sâ is heaven, ama the sun, and that makes Sâma.

4. *Rik* is the stars, Sâman the moon. This Sâman (moon) rests on that *Rik* (stars). Therefore the Sâman is sung as resting on the *Rik*. Sâ is the stars, ama the moon, and that makes Sâma.

5. *Rik* is the white light of the sun, Sâman the blue exceeding darkness[96] (in the sun). This Sâman (darkness) rests on that *Rik* (brightness). Therefore the Sâman is sung as resting on the *Rik*.

6. Sâ is the white light of the sun, ama the blue exceeding darkness, and that makes Sâma.

Now that golden[97] person, who is seen within the sun, with golden beard and golden hair, golden altogether to the very tips of his nails,

7. Whose eyes are like blue lotus's[98], his name is ut, for he has risen (udita) above all evil. He also who knows this, rises above all evil.

8. *Rik* and Sâman are his joints, and therefore he is udgîtha. And therefore he who praises him (the ut) is called the Ud-gât*ri*[99] (the out-singer). He (the golden person, called ut) is lord of the worlds beyond that (sun), and of all the wishes of the Devas (inhabiting those worlds). So much with reference to the Devas.

SEVENTH KHA*ND*A.

1. Now with reference to the body. *Rik* is speech, Sâman breath[100]. This Sâman (breath) rests on that *Rik* (speech). Therefore the Sâman is sung as resting on the *Rik*. Sâ is speech, ama is breath, and that makes

---

[95] The Sâma verses are mostly taken from the Rig-veda.

[96] The darkness which is seen by those who can concentrate their sight on the sun.

[97] Bright as gold.

[98] The colour of the lotus is described by a comparison with the Kapyâsa, the seat of the monkey (kapip*r*ish*th*ânto yena upavi*s*ati), It was probably a botanical name.

[99] Name of the principal priest of the Sâma-veda.

[100] Breath in the nose, sense of smelling. Comm.

Sâma.

2. *Rik* is the eye, Sâman the self[101]. This Sâman (shadow) rests on that *Rik* (eye). Therefore the Sâman is sung as resting on the *Rik*. Sâ is the eye, ama the self, and that makes Sâma.

3. *Rik* is the ear, Sâman the mind. This Sâman (mind) rests on that *Rik* (ear). Therefore the Sâman is sung as resting on the *Rik*. Sâ is the ear, ama the mind, and that makes Sâma.

4. *Rik* is the white light of the eye, Sâman the blue exceeding darkness. This Sâman (darkness) rests on the *Rik* (brightness). Therefore the Sâman is sung as resting on the *Rik*. Sâ is the white light of the eye, ama the blue exceeding darkness, and that makes Sâma.

5. Now the person who is seen in the eye, he is *Rik*, he is Sâman, Uktha[102], Yagus, Brahman. The form of that person (in the eye) is the same[103] as the form of the other person (in the sun), the joints of the one (*Rik* and Sâman) are the joints of the other, the name of the one (ut) is the name of the other.

6. He is lord of the worlds beneath that (the self in the eye), and of all the wishes of men. Therefore all who sing to the vî*n*â (lyre), sing him, and from him also they obtain wealth.

7. He who knowing this sings a Sâman, sings to both (the adhidaivata and adhyâtma self, the person in the sun and the person in the eye, as one and the same person). He obtains through the one, yea, he obtains the worlds beyond that, and the wishes of the Devas;

8. And he obtains through the other the worlds beneath that, and the wishes of men.

Therefore an Udgât*ri* priest who knows this, may say (to the sacrificer for whom he officiates);

9. 'What wish shall I obtain for you by my songs?' For he who knowing this sings a Sâman is able to obtain wishes through his song, yea, through his song.

EIGHTH KHA*ND*A.

1. There were once three men, well-versed in udgîtha[104], *S*ilaka *S*âlâvatya, *K*aikitâyana, Dâlbhya, and Pravâha*n*a *G*aivali. They said: 'We are well-versed in udgîtha. Let us have a discussion on udgîtha.'

2. They all agreed and sat down. Then Pravâha*n*a *G*aivali[105] said:

---

[101] The shadow-self, the likeness or image thrown upon the eye; see *Kh*. Up. VIII, 9, x.

[102] A set of hymns to be recited, whereas the Sâman is sung, and the Yagus muttered.

[103] Cf. *Kh*. Up. I, 6, 6.

[104] Cognisant of the deeper meanings of udgîtha, i.e. Om.

[105] He, though not being a Brâhma*n*a, turns out to be the only one who knows the true meaning of udgîtha, i.e. the Highest Brahman.

'Sirs, do you both speak first, for I wish to hear what two Brâhma*n*as[106] have to say.'

3. Then *S*ilaka *S*âlâvatya said to *K*aikitâyana Dâlbhya: 'Let me ask you.'

'Ask,' he replied.

4. 'What is the origin of the Sâman?' 'Tone (svara),' he replied.

'What is the origin of tone?' 'Breath,' he replied.

'What is the origin of breath?' 'Food,' he replied.

'What is the origin of food?' 'Water,' he replied.

5. 'What is the origin of water?' 'That world (heaven),' he replied.

'And what is the origin of that world?'—

He replied: 'Let no man carry the Sâman beyond the world of svarga (heaven). We place (recognise) the Sâman in the world of svarga, for the Sâman is extolled as svarga (heaven).'

6. Then said Silaka Sâlâvatya to *K*aikitâyana Dâlbhya: 'O Dâlbhya, thy Sâman is not firmly established. And if any one were to say, Your head shall fall off (if you be wrong), surely your head would now fall.'

7. 'Well then, let me know this from you, Sir,' said Dâlbhya.

'Know it,' replied Silaka Sâlâvatya.

'What is the origin of that world (heaven)?' 'This world,' he replied.

'And what is the origin of this world?'—

He replied: 'Let no man carry the Sâman beyond this world as its rest. We place the Sâman in this world as its rest, for the Sâman is extolled as rest.'

8. Then said Pravâha*n*a *G*aivali to *S*ilaka *S*âlâvatya: 'Your Sâman (the earth), O *S*âlâvatya, has an end. And if any one were to say, Your head shall fall off (if you be wrong), surely your head would now fall.'

'Well then, let me know this from you, Sir,' said Sâlâvatya.

'Know it,' replied *G*aivali.

NINTH KHA*ND*A.

1. 'What is the origin of this world?' 'Ether[107],' he replied. For all these beings take their rise from the ether, and return into the ether. Ether is older than these, ether is their rest.

2. He is indeed the udgîtha (Om = Brahman), greater than great (parovarîyas), he is without end.

He who knowing this meditates on the udgîtha, the greater than great, obtains what is greater than great, he conquers the worlds which are greater than great.

---

[106] In V, 3, 5, Pravâhana Gaivali is distinctly called a râganyabandhu.

[107] Ether, or we might translate it by space, both being intended, however, as names or symbols of the Highest Brahman. See Vedânta-sûtra I, 1, 22.

3. Atidhanvan *S*aunaka, having taught this udgîtha to Udara-sâ*nd*ilya, said: 'As long as they will know in your family this udgîtha, their life in this world will be greater than great.

4. 'And thus also will be their state in the other world.' He who thus knows the udgîtha, and meditates on it thus, his life in this world will be greater than great, and also his state in the other world, yea, in the other world.

TENTH KHA*ND*A.

1. When the Kurus had been destroyed by (hail) stones[108], Ushasti *K*âkrâya*n*a lived as a beggar with his virgin[109] wife at Ibhyagrâma.

2. Seeing a chief eating beans, he begged of him. The chief said: 'I have no more, except those which are put away for me here.'

3. Ushasti said: 'Give me to eat of them.' He gave him the beans, and said: 'There is something to drink also!' Then said Ushasti: 'If I drank of it, I should have drunk what was left by another, and is therefore unclean.'

4. The chief said: 'Were not those beans also left over and therefore unclean?'

'No,' he replied; 'for I should not have lived, if I had not eaten them, but the drinking of water would be mere pleasure[110].'

5. Having eaten himself, Ushasti gave the remaining beans to his wife. But she, having eaten before, took them and put them away.

6. Rising the next morning, Ushasti said to her: 'Alas, if we could only get some food, we might gain a little wealth. The king here is going to offer a sacrifice, he should choose me for all the priestly offices.'

7. His wife said to him: 'Look, here are those beans of yours.' Having eaten them, he went to the sacrifice which was being performed.

8. He went and sat down on the orchestra near the Udgât*ri*s, who were going to sing their hymns of praise. And he said to the Prastot*ri* (the leader):

9. 'Prastot*ri*, if you, without knowing[111] the deity which belongs to

---

[108] When they had been killed either by stone weapons, or by a shower of stones, which produced a famine in the land. Comm.

[109] Â*t*ikî is not the name of the wife of Ushasti, nor does it mean strong enough to travel. *S*aṅkara explains it as anupagâtapayodhâridistrîvyañganâ, and Ânandagiri adds, Svairasa*m*kâre 'pi na vyabhikâra*s*aṅketi dar*s*ayitum â*t*ikyeti vi*s*esha*n*am. She was so young that she was allowed to run about freely, without exciting any suspicion. Another commentator says, G*ri*hâd bahirgantumarhâ anupagâtapayodharâ.

[110] Or, according to the commentator, 'water I can get whenever I like.'

[111] The commentator is at great pains to show that a priest may officiate without knowing the secret meanings here assigned to certain parts of the sacrifice, and without

the prastâva (the hymns &c. of the Prastot*ri*), are going to sing it, your head will fall off.'

10. In the same manner he addressed the Udgât*ri*: 'Udgât*ri*, if you, without knowing the deity which belongs to the udgîtha (the hymns of the Udgât*ri*), are going to sing it, your head will fall off.'

11. In the same manner he addressed the Pratihart*ri*: 'Pratihart*ri*, if you, without knowing the deity which belongs to the pratihâra (the hymns of the Pratihart*ri*), are going to sing it, your head will fall off.'

They stopped, and sat down in silence.

ELEVENTH KHA*ND*A.

1. Then the sacrificer said to him: 'I should like to know who you are, Sir.' He replied: 'I am Ushasti *K*âkrâya*n*a.'

2. He said: 'I looked for you, Sir, for all these sacrificial offices, but not finding you[112], I chose others.'

3. 'But now, Sir, take all the sacrificial offices.'

Ushasti said: 'Very well; but let those, with my permission, perform the hymns of praise. Only as much wealth as you give to them, so much give to me also.'

The sacrificer assented.

4. Then the Prastot*ri* approached him, saying: 'Sir, you said to me, "Prastot*ri*, if you, without knowing the deity which belongs to the prastâva, are going to sing it, your head will fall off,"—which then is that deity?'

5. He said: 'Breath (prâ*n*a). For all these beings merge into breath alone, and from breath they arise. This is the deity belonging to the prastâva. If, without knowing that deity, you had sung forth your hymns, your head would have fallen off, after you had been warned by me.'

6. Then the Udgât*ri* approached him, saying: 'Sir, you said to me, "Udgât*ri*, if you, without knowing the deity which belongs to the udgîtha, are going to sing it, your head will fall off,"—which then is that deity?'

7. He said: 'The sun (âditya). For all these beings praise the sun when it stands on high. This is the deity belonging to the udgîtha. If, without knowing that deity, you had sung out your hymns, your head would have fallen off, after you had been warned by me.'

8. Then the Pratihart*ri* approached him, saying: 'Sir, you said to me, "Pratihart*ri*, if you, without knowing the deity belonging to the pratihâra, are going to sing it, your head will fall off,"—Which then is

---

running any risk of punishment. Only, if another priest is present, who is initiated, then the uninitiated, taking his place, is in danger of losing his head.

[112] Should it be avittvâ, as in I, 2, 9?

that deity?'

9. He said: 'Food (anna). For all these beings live when they partake of food. This is the deity belonging to the pratihâra. If, without knowing that deity, you had sung your hymns, your head would have fallen off, after you had been warned by me[113].'

TWELFTH KHA*ND*A.

1. Now follows the udgîtha of the dogs. Vaka Dâlbhya, or, as he was also called, Glâva Maitreya, went out to repeat the Veda (in a quiet place).

2. A white (dog) appeared before him, and other dogs gathering round him, said to him: 'Sir, sing and get us food, we are hungry.'

3. The white dog said to them: 'Come to me to-morrow morning.' Vaka Dâlbhya, or, as he was also called, Glâva Maitreya, watched.

4. The dogs came on, holding together, each dog keeping the tail of the preceding dog in his mouth, as the priests do when they are going to sing praises with the Vahishpavamâna hymn[114]. After they had settled down, they began to say Hiṅ.

5. 'Om, let us eat! Om, let us drink! Om, may the divine Varu*n*a, Pragâpati, Savit*ri*[115] bring us food! Lord of food, bring hither food, bring it, Om!'

THIRTEENTH KHA*ND*A[116].

1. The syllable Hâu[117] is this world (the earth), the syllable Hâi[118] the air, the syllable Atha the moon, the syllable Iha the self, the syllable Î[119] is Agni, fire.

2. The syllable Û is the sun, the syllable E is the Nihava or invocation, the syllable Auhoi[120] is the Vi*s*ve Devas, the syllable Hiṅ is

---

[113] There are certain etymological fancies for assigning each deity to a certain portion of the Sâma-veda ceremonial. Thus prâ*n*a is assigned to the prastâva, because both words begin with pra. Âditya is assigned to the udgîtha, because the sun is ut. Anna, food, is assigned to the pratihâra, because food is taken, pratih*ri*yate, &c.

[114] This alludes to a ceremony where the priests have to walk in procession, each priest holding the gown of the preceding priest.

[115] The commentator explains Varu*n*a and Pragâpati as epithets of Savit*ri*, or the sun, meaning rain-giver and man-protector.

[116] The syllables here mentioned are the so-called stobhâksharas, sounds used in the musical recitation of the Sâman hymns, probably to fill out the intervals in the music for which there were no words in the hymns. These syllables are marked in the MSS. of the Sâma-veda, but their exact character and purpose are not quite clear.

[117] A stobha syllable used in the Rathantara Sâman.

[118] Used in the Vâmadevya Sâman.

[119] The Sâman addressed to Agni takes the syllable î as nidhana.

[120] The stobha syllables used in the Sâman addressed to the Vi*s*ve Devas.

Pragâpati, Svara[121] (tone) is breath (prâ*n*a), the syllable Yâ is food, the syllable Vâg[122] is Virâg.

3. The thirteenth stobha syllable, viz. the indistinct syllable Huṅ, is the Undefinable (the Highest Brahman).

4. Speech yields the milk, which is the milk of speech itself to him who knows this Upanishad (secret doctrine) of the Sâmans in this wise. He becomes rich in food, and able to eat food[123],—yea, able to eat food.

SECOND PRAPÂTHAKA.

FIRST KHA*ND*A.

1. Meditation on the whole[124] of the Sâman is good, and people, when anything is good, say it is Sâman; when it is not good, it is not Sâman.

2. Thus they also say, he approached him with Sâman, i.e. becomingly; and he approached him without Sâman, i.e. unbecomingly.

:3. And they also say, truly this is Sâman for us, i.e. it is good for us, when it is good; and truly that is not Sâman for us, i.e. it is not good for us, when it is not good.

4. If any one knowing this meditates on the Sâman as good, depend upon it all good qualities will approach quickly, aye, they will become his own[125].

SECOND KHA*ND*A.

1. Let a man meditate on the fivefold Sâman[126] as the five worlds. The hiṅkâra is, the earth, the prastâva the fire, the udgîtha the sky, the pratihâra the sun, the nidhana heaven; so in an ascending line.

2. In a descending line, the hiṅkâra is heaven, the prastâva the sun, the udgîtha the sky, the pratihâra the fire, the nidhana the earth.

3. The worlds in an ascending and in a descending line belong to him who knowing this meditates on the fivefold Sâman as the worlds[127].

---

[121] See *Kh*. Up. I, 4, 4.

[122] The commentator takes vâg as a stobha, as a syllable occurring in hymns addressed to Virâg, and as implying either the deity Virâg or food.

[123] wealthy and healthy.

[124] Hitherto meditation on certain portions only of the Sâma-veda and the Sâma-sacrifice had been enjoined, and their deeper meaning explained. Now the same is done for the whole of the Sâman.

[125] Cf. *Kh*. Up. III, 19, 4.

[126] The five forms in which the Sâman is used for sacrificial purposes. The Sâman is always to be under-stood as the Good, as Dharma, and as Brahman.

[127] The commentator supplies some fanciful reasons why each of the five Sâmans is identified with certain objects. Earth is said to be the hiṅkâra, because both always come

THIRD KHA*ND*A.

1. Let a man meditate on the fivefold Sâman as rain. The hiṅkâra is wind (that brings the rain); the prastâva is, 'the cloud is come;' the udgîtha is, 'it rains;' the pratihâra, 'it flashes, it thunders;'

2. The nidhana is, 'it stops.' There is rain for him, and he brings rain for others who thus knowing meditates on the fivefold Sâman as rain.

FOURTH KHA*ND*A.

1. Let a man meditate on the fivefold Sâman in all waters. When the clouds gather, that is the hiṅkâra; when it rains, that is the prastâva that which flows in the east[128], that is the udgîtha that which flows in the west[129], that is the pratihâra the sea is the nidhana.

2. He does not die in water[130], nay, he is rich in water who knowing this meditates on the fivefold Sâman as all waters.

FIFTH KHA*ND*A.

1. Let a man meditate on the fivefold Sâman as the seasons. The hiṅkâra is spring, the prastâva summer (harvest of yava, &c.), the udgîtha the rainy season, the pratihâra autumn, the nidhana winter.

2. The seasons belong to him, nay, he is always in season (successful) who knowing this meditates on the fivefold Sâman as the seasons.

SIXTH KHA*ND*A.

1. Let a man meditate on the fivefold Sâman in animals. The hiṅkâra is goats, the prastâva sheep, the udgîtha cows, the pratihâra horses, the nidhana man.

2. Animals belong to him, nay, he is rich in animals who knowing this meditates on the fivefold Sâman as animals.

---

first. Agni is prastâva, because sacrifices are praised in the fire (prastûyante). The sky is udgîtha, because it is also called gagana, and both words have the letter g in common. The sun is pratihâra, because everybody wishes the sun to come towards him (prati). Heaven is nidhana, because those who depart from here are placed there (nidhîyante), &c.

[128] The Ganges, &c. Comm.

[129] The Narmadâ, &c. Comm.

[130] The commentator adds, 'unless he wishes to die in the Ganges.'

SEVENTH KHA*ND*A.

1. Let a man meditate on the fivefold Sâman, which is greater than great, as the prâ*n*as (senses). The hiṅkâra is smell[131] (nose), the prastâva speech (tongue), the udgîtha sight (eye), the pratihâra hearing (ear), the nidhana mind. These are one greater than the other.

2. What is greater than great belongs to him, nay, he conquers the worlds which are greater than great, who knowing this meditates on the fivefold Sâman, which is greater than great, as the prâ*n*as (senses).

EIGHTH KHA*ND*A.

1. Next for the sevenfold Sâman. Let a man meditate on the sevenfold Sâman in speech. Whenever there is in speech the syllable huṅ[132], that is hiṅkâra, pra is the prastâva, â is the âdi, the first, i.e. Om,

2. Ud is the udgîtha, pra the pratihâra, upa the upadrava, ni the nidhana.

3. Speech yields the milk, which is the milk of speech itself, to him who knowing this meditates on the sevenfold Sâman in speech. He becomes rich in food, and able to eat food.

NINTH KHA*ND*A.

1. Let a man meditate on the sevenfold Sâman as the sun. The sun is Sâman, because he is always the same (sama); he is Sâman because he is the same, everybody thinking he looks towards me, he looks towards me[133].

2. Let him know that all beings are dependent on him (the sun). What he is before his rising, that is the hiṅkâra. On it animals are dependent. Therefore animals say hiṅ (before sunrise), for they share the hiṅkâra of that Sâman (the sun).

3. What he is when first risen, that is the prastâva. On it men are dependent. Therefore men love praise (prastuti) and celebrity, for they share the prastâva of that Sâman.

4. What he is at the time of the saṅgava[134], that is the âdi, the first, the Om. On it birds are dependent. Therefore birds fly about in the sky

---

[131] Prâ*n*a is explained by ghrâ*n*a, smell; possibly ghrâ*n*a may have been the original reading. Anyhow, it cannot be the mukhya prâ*n*a here, because it is distinctly represented as the lowest sense.

[132] These are again the stobhâksharas, or musical syllables used in the performance of the Sâman hymns; see p. 83.

[133] Cf. *Kh*. Up. II, 2, 2. Comm.

[134] When the sun puts forth his rays, and when the cows are together with their calves, i.e. as Rajendralal Mitra says, after the cows have been milked and are allowed by the cowherds to suckle their young.

without support, holding themselves, for they share the âdi[135] (the Om) of that Sâman.

5. What he is just at noon, that is the udgîtha. On it the Devas are dependent (because they are brilliant). Therefore they are the best of all the descendants of Pragâpati, for they share the udgîtha of that Sâman.

6. What he is after midday and before afternoon, that is the pratihâra. On it all germs are dependent. Therefore these, having been conceived (pratih*ri*ta), do not fall, for they share the pratihâra of that Sâman.

7. What he is after the afternoon and before sunset, that is the upadrava. On it the animals of the forest are dependent. Therefore, when they see a man, they run (upadravanti) to the forest as a safe hiding-place, for they share the upadrava of that Sâman.

8. What he is when he first sets, that is the nidhana. On it the fathers are dependent. Therefore they put them[136] down (nidadhati), for they share the nidhana of that Sâman. Thus a man meditates on the sevenfold Sâman as the sun.

TENTH KHA*ND*A.

1. Next let a man meditate on the sevenfold Sâman which is uniform in itself[137] and leads beyond death. The word hiṅkâra has three syllables, the word prastâva has three syllables: that is equal (sama).

2. The word âdi (first, Om) has two syllables, the word pratihâra has four syllables. Taking one syllable from that over, that is equal (sama).

3. The word udgîtha has three syllables, the word upadrava has four syllables. With three and three syllables it should be equal. One syllable being left over, it becomes trisyllabic. Hence it is equal.

4. The word nidhana has three syllables, therefore it is equal. These make twenty-two syllables.

5. With twenty-one syllables a man reaches the sun (and death), for the sun is the twenty-first[138] from here; with the twenty-second he conquers what is beyond the sun: that is blessedness, that is freedom from grief.

6. He obtains here the victory over the sun (death), and there is a higher victory than the victory over the sun for him, who knowing this meditates on the sevenfold Sâman as uniform in itself, which leads

---

[135] The tertium comparationis is here the â of âdi and the â of âdâya, i.e. holding. The d might have been added.

[136] The cakes for the ancestral spirits, or the spirits themselves.

[137] Âtmasammita is explained by the commentator either as having the same number of syllables in the names of the different Sâmans, or as equal to the Highest Self.

[138] There are twelve months, five seasons, three worlds, then follows the sun as the twenty-first. Comm.

beyond death, yea, which leads beyond death.

ELEVENTH KHA*ND*A[139].

1. The hiṅkâra is mind, the prastâva speech, the udgîtha sight, the pratihâra hearing, the nidhana breath. That is the Gâyatra Sâman, as interwoven in the (five) prâ*n*as[140].

2. He who thus knows this Gâyatra interwoven in the prâ*n*as, keeps his senses, reaches the full life, he lives long[141], becomes great with children and cattle, great by fame. The rule of him who thus meditates on the Gâyatra is, 'Be not high-minded.'

TWELFTH KHA*ND*A.

1. The hiṅkâra is, he rubs (the fire-stick); the prastâva, smoke rises; the udgîtha, it burns; the pratihâra, there are glowing coals; the nidhana, it goes down; the nidhana, it is gone out. This is the Rathantara Sâman as interwoven in fire[142].

2. He who thus knows this Rathantara interwoven in fire, becomes radiant[143] and strong. He reaches the full life, he lives long, becomes great with children and cattle, great by fame. The rule is, 'Do not rinse the mouth or spit before the fire.'

THIRTEENTH KHA*ND*A.

1, 2. Next follows the Vâmadevya as interwoven in generation[144].

---

[139] After having explained the secret meaning of the whole Sâma-veda ceremonial, as it is to be understood by meditation only (dhyâna),he proceeds to explain the secret meaning of the same ceremonial, giving to each its proper name in proper succession (gâyatra, rathantara, &c.), and showing the hidden purport of those names.

[140] Cf. *Kh*. Up. II, 7, 1, where prâ*n*a is explained differently. The Gâyatrî itself is sometimes called prâ*n*a.

[141] The commentator generally takes gyok in the sense of bright.

[142] The Rathantara is used for the ceremony of producing fire.

[143] Brahmavar*k*asa is the 'glory of countenance' produced by higher knowledge, an inspired look. Annâda, lit. able to eat, healthy, strong.

[144] Upamantrayate sa hiṅkâro, gñapayate sa prastâva*h*, striyâ saha *s*ete sa udgîtha*h*, pratistrî saha sete sa pratihâra*h*, kâlam ga*kkh*ati tan nidhanam, pâra*m* ga*kkh*ati tan nidhanam. Etad vâmadevyam mithune protam. 2. Sa ya evam etad vâmadevyam mithune prota*m* veda, mithunî bhavati, mithunân mithunât pragâyate, sarvam âyur eti, gyog gîvati, mahân pragayâ pa*s*ubhir bhavati, mahân kîrttyâ. Na kâ*m*kana pariharet tad vratam.

FOURTEENTH KHA*N*D*A*.

1. Rising, the sun is the hiṅkâra, risen, he is the prastâva, at noon he is the udgîtha, in the afternoon he is the pratihâra, setting, he is the nidhana. That is the B*ri*hat Sâman as interwoven in the sun[145].

2. He who thus knows the B*ri*hat as interwoven in the sun, becomes refulgent[146] and strong, he reaches the full life, he lives long, becomes great with children and cattle, great by fame. His rule is, 'Never complain of the heat of the sun.'

FIFTEENTH KHA*N*D*A*.

1. The mists gather, that is the hiṅkâra; the cloud has risen, that is the prastâva; it rains, that is the udgîtha; it flashes and thunders, that is the pratihâra; it stops, that is the nidhana. That is the Vairûpa Sâman, as interwoven in Parganya, the god of rain.

2. He who thus knows the Vairûpa as interwoven in Parganya, obtains all kinds of cattle (virûpa), he reaches the full life, he lives long, becomes great with children and cattle, great by fame. His rule is, 'Never complain of the rain.'

SIXTEENTH KHA*N*D*A*.

1. The hiṅkâra is spring, the prastâva summer, the udgîtha the rainy season, the pratihâra autumn, the nidhana winter. That is the Vairâga Sâman, as interwoven in the seasons.

2. He who thus knows the Vairâga, as interwoven in the seasons, shines (virâgati) through children, cattle, and glory of countenance. He reaches the full life, he lives long, becomes great with children and cattle, great by fame. His rule is, 'Never complain of the seasons.'

SEVENTEENTH KHA*N*D*A*.

1. The hiṅkâra is the earth, the prastâva the sky, the udgîtha heaven, the pratihâra the regions, the nidhana the sea. These are the *S*akvarî Sâmans, as interwoven in the worlds[147].

2. He who thus knows the *S*akvarîs, as interwoven in the worlds, becomes possessed of the worlds, he reaches the full life, he lives long, becomes great with children and cattle, great by fame. His rule is,

---

[145] The sun is b*ri*hat. The B*ri*hat Sâman is to be looked upon as the sun, or the B*ri*hat has Âditya for its deity.

[146] The same as brahmavar*k*asin.

[147] The *S*akvarîs are sung with the Mahânâmnîs. These are said to be water, and the worlds are said to rest on water.

'Never complain of the worlds.'

EIGHTEENTH KHA*ND*A.

1. The hiṅkâra is goats, the prastâva sheep, the udgîtha cows, the pratihâra horses, the nidhana man. These are the Revatî Sâmans, as interwoven in animals.

2. He who thus knows these Revatîs, as interwoven in animals, becomes rich in animals[148], he reaches the full life, he lives long, becomes great with children and cattle, great by fame. His rule is, 'Never complain of animals.'

NINETEENTH KHA*ND*A.

1. The hiṅkâra is hair, the prastâva skin, the udgîtha flesh, the pratihâra bone, the nidhana marrow. That is the Yagñâyagñîya Sâman, as interwoven in the members of the body.

2. He who thus knows the Yagñâyagñîya, as interwoven in the members of the body, becomes possessed of strong limbs, he is not crippled in any limb, he reaches the full life, he lives long, becomes great with children and cattle, great by fame. His rule is, 'Do not eat marrow for a year,' or 'Do not eat marrow at all.'

TWENTIETH KHA*ND*A.

1. The hiṅkâra is fire, the prastâva air, the udgîtha the sun, the pratihâra the stars, the nidhana the moon. That is the Râgana Sâman, as interwoven in the deities.

2. He who thus knows the Râgana, as interwoven in the deities, obtains the same world, the same happiness, the same company as the gods, he reaches the full life, he lives long, becomes great with children and cattle, great by fame. His rule is, 'Do not speak evil of the Brâhma*n*as.'

TWENTY-FIRST KHA*ND*A.

1. The hiṅkâra is the threefold knowledge, the prastâva these three worlds, the udgîtha Agni (fire), Vâyu (air), and Âditya (sun), the pratihâra the stars, the birds, and the rays, the nidhana the serpents, Gandharvas, and fathers. That is the Sâman, as interwoven in everything.

2. He who thus knows this Sâman, as interwoven in everything, he becomes everything.

---

[148] Revat means rich.

3. And thus it is said in the following verse: There are the fivefold three (the three kinds of sacrificial knowledge, the three worlds &c. in their fivefold form, i.e. as identified with the hiṅkâra, the prastâva, &c.), and the other forms of the Sâman. Greater than these there is nothing else besides.'

4. He who knows this, knows everything. All regions offer him gifts. His rule is, 'Let him meditate (on the Sâman), knowing that he is. everything, yea, that he is everything[149].'

TWENTY-SECOND KHA*ND*A[150].

1. The udgîtha, of which a poet said, I choose the deep sounding note of the Sâman as good for cattle, belongs to Agni; the indefinite note belongs to Pragâpati, the definite note to Soma, the soft and smooth note to Vâyu, the smooth and strong note to Indra, the heron-like note to B*ri*haspati, the dull note to Varu*n*a. Let a man cultivate all of these, avoiding, however, that of Varu*n*a.

2. Let a man sing[151], wishing to obtain by his song immortality for the Devas. 'May I obtain by my song oblations (svadhâ) for the fathers, hope for men, fodder and water for animals, heaven for the sacrificer, food for myself,' thus reflecting on these in his mind, let a man (Udgât*ri* priest) sing praises, without making mistakes in pronunciation, &c.

3. All vowels (svara) belong to Indra, all sibilants (ûshman) to Pragâpati, all consonants (spar*s*a) to M*ri*tyu (death). If somebody should reprove him for his vowels, let him say, 'I went to Indra as my refuge (when pronouncing my vowels): he will answer thee.'

4. And if somebody should reprove him for his sibilants, let him say, 'I went to Pragâpati as my refuge: he will smash thee.' And if somebody should reprove him for his consonants, let him say, 'I went to M*ri*tyu as my refuge: he will reduce thee to ashes.'

5. All vowels are to be pronounced with voice (ghosha) and strength (bala), so that the Udgât*ri* may give strength to Indra. All sibilants are to be pronounced, neither as if swallowed (agrasta)[152], nor as if thrown out (nirasta)[153], but well opened[154] (viv*ri*ta), so that the

---

149 Here ends the Sâmopâsana.

150 These are lucubrations on the different tones employed in singing the Sâman hymns, and their names, such as vinardi, anirukta, nirukta, m*ri*du *s*laksh*n*a, *s*laksh*n*a balavad, krauñ*k*a, apadhvânta.

151 It would be better if the first ity âgâyet could be left out. The commentator ignores these words.

152 Grâsa, according to the Rig-veda-prâti*s*âkhya 766, is the stiffening of the root of the tongue in pronunciation.

153 Nirâsa, according to the Rig-veda-prâti*s*âkhya 760, is the withdrawing of the active from the passive organ in pronunciation.

Udgât*ri* may give himself to Pragâpati. All consonants are to be pronounced slowly, and without crowding them together[155], so that the Udgât*ri* may withdraw himself from M*ri*tyu.

TWENTY-THIRD KHA*ND*A.

1. There are three branches of the law. Sacrifice, study, and charity are the first[156],

2. Austerity the second, and to dwell as a Brahma*k*ârin in the house of a tutor, always mortifying the body in the house of a tutor, is the third. All these obtain the worlds of the blessed; but the Brahmasa*m*stha alone (he who is firmly grounded in Brahman) obtains immortality.

3. Pragâpati brooded on the worlds. From them, thus brooded on, the threefold knowledge (sacrifice) issued forth. He brooded on it, and from it, thus brooded on, issued the three syllables, Bhû*h*, Bhuva*h*, Sva*h*.

4. He brooded on them, and from them, thus brooded on, issued the Om. As all leaves are attached to a stalk, so is all speech (all words) attached to the Om (Brahman). Om is all this, yea, Om is all this.

TWENTY-FOURTH KHA*ND*A.

1. The teachers of Brahman (Veda) declare, as the Prâta*h*-savana (morning-oblation) belongs to the Vasus, the Mâdhyandina-savana (noon-libation) to the Rudras, the third Savana (evening-libation) to the Âdityas and the Vi*s*ve Devas,

2. Where then is the world of the sacrificer? He who does not know this, how can he perform the sacrifice? He only who knows, should perform it[157].

---

154 The opening, viv*ri*ta, may mean two things, either the opening of the vocal chords (kha), which imparts to the ûshmans their surd character (Rig. Prât. 709), or the opening of the organs of pronunciation (kara*n*a), which for the ûshmans is asp*ri*sh*t*am sthitam (Rig. Prât. 719), or viv*ri*ta (Ath. Prât. I, 31; Taitt. Prât. 5).

155 Anabhinihita, for thus the commentaries give the reading, is explained by anabhinikshipta. On the real abhinidhâna, see Rig. Prât. 393. The translation does not follow the commentary. The genitive pragâpate*h* is governed by paridadâni.

156 Not the first in rank or succession, but only in enumerating the three branches of the law. This first branch corresponds to the second stage, the â*s*rama of the householder. Austerity is meant for the Vânaprastha, the third â*s*rama, while the third is intended for the Brahma*k*ârin, the student, only that the naish*th*ika or perpetual Brahma*k*ârin here takes the place of the ordinary student. The Brahmasa*m*stha would represent the fourth â*s*rama, that of the Sannyâsin or parivrâg, who has ceased to perform any works, even the tapas or austerities of the Vânaprastha.

157 The commentator is always very anxious to explain that though it is better that a priest should know the hidden meaning of the sacrificial acts which he has to perform, yet there is nothing to prevent a priest, who has not yet arrived at this stage of knowledge, from performing his duties.

3. Before the beginning of the Prâtaranuvâka, (matin-chant), the sacrificer, sitting down behind the household altar (gârhapatya), and looking towards the north, sings the Sâman, addressed to the Vasus:

4. 'Open the door of the world (the earth), let us see thee, that we may rule (on earth).'

5. Then he sacrifices, saying: 'Adoration to Agni, who dwells on the earth, who dwells in the world! Obtain that world for me, the sacrificer! That is the world for the sacrificer!'

6. 'I (the sacrificer) shall go thither, when this life is over. Take this! (he says, in offering the libation.) Cast back the bolt!' Having said this, he rises. For him the Vasus fulfil the morning-oblation.

7. Before the beginning of the Mâdhyandina-savana, the noon-oblation, the sacrificer, sitting down behind the Âgnidhrîya altar, and looking towards the north, sings the Sâman, addressed to the Rudras:

8. 'Open the door of the world (the sky), let us see thee, that we may rule wide (in the sky).'

9. Then he sacrifices, saying: 'Adoration to Vâyu (air), who dwells in the sky, who dwells in the world. Obtain that world for me, the sacrificer! That is the world for the sacrificer!'

10. 'I (the sacrificer) shall go thither, when this life is over. Take this! Cast back the bolt!' Having said this, he rises. For him the Rudras fulfil the noon-oblation.

11. Before the beginning of the third oblation, the sacrificer, sitting down behind the Âhavanîya altar, and looking towards the north, sings the Sâman, addressed to the Âdityas and Vi*s*ve Devas:

12. 'Open the door of the world (the heaven), let us see thee, that we may rule supreme (in heaven).' This is addressed to the Âdityas.

13. Next the Sâman addressed to the Vi*s*ve Devas: 'Open the door of the world (heaven), let us see thee, that we may rule supreme (in heaven).'

14. Then he sacrifices, saying: 'Adoration to the Âdityas and to the Vi*s*ve Devas, who dwell in heaven, who dwell in the world. Obtain that world for me, the sacrificer!'

15. 'That is the world for the sacrificer! I (the sacrificer) shall go thither, when this life is over. Take this! Cast back the bolt!' Having said this, he rises.

16. For him the Âdityas and the Vi*s*ve Devas fulfil the third oblation. He who knows this, knows the full measure of the sacrifice, yea, he knows it.

THIRD PRAPÂ*TH*AKA.

FIRST KHA*ND*A[158].

1. The sun is indeed the honey[159] of the Devas. The heaven is the cross-beam (from which) the sky (hangs as) a hive, and the bright vapours are the eggs of the bees[160].

2. The eastern rays of the sun are the honey-cells in front. The *Rik* verses are the bees, the Rig-veda (sacrifice) is the flower, the water (of the sacrificial libations) is the nectar (of the flower).

3. Those very *Rik* verses then (as bees) brooded over the Rig-veda sacrifice (the flower); and from it, thus brooded on, sprang as its (nectar) essence, fame, glory of countenance, vigour, strength, and health[161].

4. That (essence) flowed forth and went towards the sun[162]. And that forms what we call the red (rohita) light of the rising sun.

SECOND KHA*ND*A.

1. The southern rays of the sun are the honey-cells on the right. The Yagus verses are the bees, the Yagur-veda sacrifice is the flower, the water (of the sacrificial libations) is the nectar (of the flower).

2. Those very Yagus verses (as bees) brooded over the Yagur-veda sacrifice (the flower); and from it, thus brooded on, sprang as its (nectar) essence, fame, glory of countenance, vigour, strength, and health.

3. That flowed forth and went towards the sun. And that forms what we call the white (*s*ukla) light of the sun.

---

[158] After the various meditations on the Sâma-veda sacrifice, the sun is next to be meditated on, as essential to the performance of all sacrifices.

[159] Everybody delights in the sun, as the highest reward of all sacrifices.

[160] I am not certain whether this passage is rightly translated. Rajendralal Mitra speaks of an arched bamboo, whence the atmosphere hangs pendant like a hive, in which the vapours are the eggs. Apûpa means a cake, and may mean a hive. In order to understand the simile, we ought to have a clearer idea of the construction of the ancient bee-hive.

[161] Annâdya, explained as food, but more likely meaning power to eat, appetite, health. See III, 13, 1.

[162] The commentator explains: The *Rik* verses, on becoming part of the ceremonial, perform the sacrifice. The sacrifice (the flower), when surrounded by the *Rik* verses (bees), yields its essence, the nectar. That essence consists in all the rewards to be obtained through sacrifice, and as these rewards are to be enjoyed in the next world and in the sun, therefore that essence or nectar is said to ascend to the sun.

THIRD KHA*ND*A.

1. The western rays of the sun are the honey-cells behind. The Sâman verses are the bees, the Sâma-veda sacrifice is the flower, the water is the nectar.

2. Those very Sâman verses (as bees) brooded over the Sâma-veda sacrifice; and from it, thus brooded on, sprang as its (nectar) essence, fame, glory of countenance, vigour, strength, and health.

3. That flowed forth and went towards the sun. And that forms what we call the dark (k*r*ish*n*a) light of the sun.

FOURTH KHA*ND*A.

1. The northern rays of the sun are the honey-cells on the left. The (hymns of the) Atharvâṅgiras are the bees, the Itihâsa-purâ*n*a[163] (the reading of the old stories) is the flower, the water is the nectar.

2. Those very hymns of the Atharvâṅgiras (as bees) brooded over the Itihâsa-purâ*n*a; and from it, thus brooded on, sprang as its (nectar) essence, fame, glory of countenance, vigour, strength, and health.

3. That flowed forth, and went towards the sun. And that forms what we call the extreme dark (para*h* k*r*ish*n*am) light of the sun.

FIFTH KHA*ND*A.

1. The upward rays of the sun are the honey cells above. The secret doctrines are the bees, Brahman (the Om) is the flower, the water is the nectar.

2. Those secret doctrines (as bees) brooded over Brahman (the Om); and from it, thus brooded on, sprang as its (nectar) essence, fame, glory of countenance, brightness, vigour, strength, and health.

3. That flowed forth, and went towards the sun. And that forms what seems to stir in the centre of the sun.

4. These (the different colours in the sun) are the essences of the essences. For the Vedas are essences (the best things in the world); and of them (after they have assumed the form of sacrifice) these (the colours rising to the sun) are again the essences. They are the nectar of the nectar. For the Vedas are nectar (immortal), and of them these are

---

[163] As there is no Atharva-veda sacrifice, properly so called, we have corresponding to the Atharva-veda hymns the so-called fifth Veda, the Itihâsa-purâ*n*a. This may mean the collection of legends and traditions, or the old book of traditions. At all events it is taken as one Purâ*n*a, not as many. These ancient stories were repeated at the A*s*vamedha sacrifice during the so-called Pariplava nights. Many of them have been preserved in the Brâhma*n*as; others, in a more modern form, in the Mahâbhârata. See Weber, Indische Studien, I, p. 258, note.

the nectar.

SIXTH KHA*ND*A.

1. On the first of these nectars (the red light, which represents fame, glory of countenance, vigour, strength, health) the Vasus live, with Agni at their head. True, the Devas do not eat or drink, but they enjoy by seeing the nectar.

2. They enter into that (red) colour, and they rise from that colour[164].

3. He who thus knows this nectar, becomes one of the Vasus, with Agni at their head, he sees the nectar and rejoices. And he, too, having entered that colour, rises again from that colour.

4. So long as the sun rises in the east and sets in the west[165], so long does he follow the sovereign supremacy of the Vasus.

SEVENTH KHA*ND*A.

1. On the second of these nectars the Rudras live, with Indra at their head. True, the Devas do not eat or drink, but they enjoy by seeing the nectar.

2. They enter into that white colour, and they rise from that colour.

3. He who thus knows this nectar, becomes one of the Rudras, with Indra at their head, he sees the nectar and rejoices. And he, having entered that colour, rises again from that colour.

4. So long as the sun rises in the east and sets in the west, twice as long does it rise in the south and set in the north; and so long does he follow the sovereign supremacy of the Rudras.

EIGHTH KHA*ND*A.

1. On the third of these nectars the Âdityas live, with Varu*n*a at their head. True, the Devas do not eat or drink, but they enjoy by seeing the nectar.

2. They enter into that (dark) colour, and they rise from that colour.

3. He who thus knows this nectar, becomes one of the Âdityas, with Varu*n*a at their head, he sees the nectar and rejoices. And he, having entered that colour, rises again from that colour.

---

[164] This is differently explained by the commentator. He takes it to mean that, when the Vasus have gone to the sun, and see that there is no opportunity for enjoying that colour, they rest; but when they see that there is an opportunity for enjoying it, they exert themselves for it. I think the colour is here taken for the colour of the morning, which the Vasus enter, and from which they go forth again.

[165] 1. East: Vasus: red: Agni. 2. South: Rudras: white: Indra. 3. West: Âditya: dark: Varu*n*a. 4. North: Marut: very dark: Soma. 5. Upward: Sâdhya: centre: Brahman.

4. So long as the sun rises in the south and sets in the north, twice as long does it rise in the west and set in the east; and so long does he follow the sovereign supremacy of the Âdityas.

NINTH KHA*ND*A.

1. On the fourth of these nectars the Maruts live, with Soma at their head. True, the Devas do not eat or drink, but they enjoy by seeing the nectar.

2. They enter in that (very dark) colour, and they rise from that colour.

3. He who thus knows this nectar, becomes one of the Maruts, with Soma at their head, he sees the nectar and rejoices. And he, having entered that colour, rises again from that colour.

4. So long as the sun rises in the west and sets in the east, twice as long does it rise in the north and set in the south; and so long does he follow the sovereign supremacy of the Maruts.

TENTH KHA*ND*A.

1. On the fifth of these nectars the Sâdhyas live, with Brahman at their head. True, the Devas do not eat or drink, but they enjoy by seeing the nectar.

2. They enter into that colour, and they rise from that colour.

3. He who thus knows this nectar, becomes one of the Sâdhyas, with Brahman at their head; he sees the nectar and rejoices. And he, having entered that colour, rises again from that colour.

4. So long as the sun rises in the north and sets in the south, twice as long does it rise above, and set below; and so long does he follow the sovereign power of the Sâdhyas[166].

---

[166] The meaning of the five Khandas from 6 to 10 is clear, in so far as they are intended to show that he who knows or meditates on the sacrifices as described before, enjoys his reward in different worlds with the Vasus, Rudras, &c. for certain periods of time, till at last he reaches the true Brahman. Of these periods each succeeding one is supposed to be double the length of the preceding one. This is expressed by imagining a migration of the sun from east to south, west, north, and zenith. Each change of the sun marks a new world, and the duration of each successive world is computed as double the duration of the preceding world. Similar ideas have been more fully developed in the Purâ*n*as, and the commentator is at great pains to remove apparent contradictions between the Paurâ*n*ik and Vaidik accounts, following, as Ânandagñânagiri remarks, the Dravi*d*â*k*ârya (p. 173, l. 13).

ELEVENTH KHA*ND*A.

1. When from thence he has risen upwards, he neither rises nor sets. He is alone, standing in the centre. And on this there is this verse:

2. 'Yonder he neither rises nor sets at any time. If this is not true, ye gods, may I lose Brahman.'

3. And indeed to him who thus knows this Brahma-upanishad (the secret doctrine: of the Veda) the sun does not rise and does not set. For him there is day, once and for all[167].

4. This doctrine (beginning with III, 1, 1) Brahman (m. Hira*n*yagarbha) told to Pragâpati (Virâ*g*), Pragâpati to Manu, Manu to his offspring (Ikshvâku, &c.) And the father told that (doctrine of) Brahman (n.) to Uddâlaka Âru*n*i.

5. A father may therefore tell that doctrine of Brahman to his eldest son[168], or to a worthy pupil.

But no one should tell it to anybody else, even if he gave him the whole sea-girt earth, full of treasure, for this doctrine is worth more than that, yea, it is worth more.

TWELFTH KHA*ND*A.

1. The Gâyatrî[169] (verse) is everything whatsoever here exists. Gâyatrî indeed is speech, for speech sings forth (gâya-ti) and protects (trâya-te) everything that here exists.

2. That Gâyatrî is also the earth, for everything that here exists rests on the earth, and does not go beyond.

3. That earth again is the body in man, for in it the vital airs (prâ*n*as[170], which are everything) rest, and do not go beyond.

4. That body again in man is the heart within man, for in it the prâ*n*as (which are everything) rest, and do not go beyond.

5. That Gâyatrî has four feet[171] and is sixfold[172]. And this is also

---

[167] Cf. *Kh*. Up. VIII, 4, 2.

[168] This was the old, not the present custom, says Ânandagiri. Not the father, but an â*k*ârya, has now to teach his pupils.

[169] The Gâyatrî is one of the sacred metres, and is here to be meditated on as Brahman. It is used in the sense of verse, and as the name of a famous hymn. The Gâyatrî is often praised as the most powerful metre, and whatever can be obtained by means of the recitation of Gâyatrî verses is described as the achievement of the Gâyatrî. The etymology of gâyatrî from gai and trâ is, of course, fanciful.

[170] The prâ*n*as may be meant for the five senses, as explained in *Kh*. I, 2, 1; II, 7, 1; or for the five breathings, as explained immediately afterwards in III, 13, 1. The commentator sees in them everything that here exists (*Kh*. Up. III, 15, 4), and thus establishes the likeness between the body and the Gâyatrî. As Gâyatrî is the earth, and the earth the body, and the body the heart, Gâyatrî is in the end to be considered as the heart.

[171] The four feet are explained as the four quarters of the Gâyatrî metre, of six syllables each. The Gâyatrî really consists of three feet of eight syllables each.

declared by a *Rik* verse (Rig-Veda X, 90, 3):—

6. 'Such is the greatness of it (of Brahman, under the disguise of Gâyatrî[173]); greater than it is the Person[174] (purusha). His feet are all things. The immortal with three feet is in heaven (i.e. in himself).'

7. The Brahman which has been thus described (as immortal with three feet in heaven, and as Gâyatrî) is the same as the ether which is around us;

8. And the ether which is around us, is the same as the ether which is within us. And the ether which is within us,

9. That is the ether within the heart. That ether in the heart (as Brahman) is omnipresent and unchanging. He who knows this obtains omnipresent and unchangeable happiness.

THIRTEENTH KHA*ND*A[175].

1. For that heart there are five gates belonging to the Devas (the senses). The eastern gate is the Prâ*n*a (up-breathing), that is the eye, that is Âditya (the sun). Let a man meditate on that as brightness (glory of countenance) and health. He who knows this, becomes bright and healthy.

2. The southern gate is the Vyâna (back-breathing), that is the ear, that is the moon. Let a man meditate on that as happiness and fame. He who knows this, becomes happy and famous.

3. The western gate is the Apâna (down-breathing), that is speech, that is Agni (fire). Let a man meditate on that as glory of countenance and health. He who knows this, becomes glorious and healthy.

4. The northern gate is the Samâna (on-breathing), that is mind, that is Parganya (rain). Let a man meditate on that as celebrity and beauty. He who knows this, becomes celebrated and beautiful.

5. The upper gate is the Udâna (out-breathing), that is air, that is ether. Let a man meditate on that as strength and greatness. He who knows this, becomes strong and great.

6. These are the five men of Brahman, the doorkeepers of the Svarga (heaven) world. He who knows these five men of Brahman, the door-keepers of the Svarga world, in his family a strong son is born. He who thus knows these five men of Brahman, as the door-keepers of the Svarga world, enters himself the Svarga world.

---

[172] The Gâyatrî has been identified with all beings, with speech, earth, body, heart, and the vital airs, and is therefore called sixfold. This, at least, is the way in which the commentator accounts for the epithet 'sixfold.'

[173] Of Brahman modified as Gâyatrî, having four feet, and being sixfold.

[174] The real Brahman, unmodified by form and name.

[175] The meditation on the five gates and the five gate-keepers of the heart is meant to be subservient to the meditation on Brahman, as the ether in the heart, which, as it is said at the end, is actually seen and heard by the senses as being within the heart.

7. Now that light which shines above this heaven, higher than all, higher than everything, in the highest world, beyond which there are no other worlds, that is the same light which is within man. And of this we have this visible proof[176]:

8. Namely, when we thus perceive by touch the warmth here in the body[177]. And of it we have this audible proof: Namely, when we thus, after stopping our ears, listen to what is like the rolling of a carriage, or the bellowing of an ox, or the sound of a burning fire[178] (within the ears). Let a man meditate on this as the (Brahman) which is seen and heard. He, who knows this, becomes conspicuous and celebrated, yea, he becomes celebrated.

FOURTEENTH KHA*ND*A.

1. All this is Brahman (n.) Let a man meditate on that (visible world) as beginning, ending, and breathing[179] in it (the Brahman).

Now man is a creature of will. According to what his will is in this world, so will he be when he has departed this life. Let him therefore have this will and belief:

2. The intelligent, whose body is spirit, whose form is light, whose thoughts are true, whose nature is like ether (omnipresent and invisible), from whom all works, all desires, all sweet odours and tastes proceed; he who embraces all this, who never speaks, and is never surprised,

3. He is my self within the heart, smaller than a corn of rice, smaller than a corn of barley, smaller than a mustard seed, smaller than a canary seed or the kernel of a canary seed. He also is my self within the heart, greater than the earth, greater than the sky, greater than heaven, greater than all these worlds.

4. He from whom all works, all desires, all sweet odours and tastes proceed, who embraces all this, who never speaks and who is never surprised, he, my self within the heart, is that Brahman (n.) When I shall have departed from hence, I shall obtain him (that Self). He who has this faith[180] has no doubt; thus said *S*â*nd*ilya[181], yea, thus he said.

---

[176] The presence of Brahman in the heart of man is not to rest on the testimony of revelation only, but is here to be established by the evidence of the senses. Childish as the argument may seem to us, it shows at all events how intently the old Brahmans thought on the problem of the evidence of the invisible.

[177] That warmth must come from something, just as smoke comes from fire, and this something is supposed to be Brahman in the heart.

[178] Cf. Ait. Âr. III, 2, 4, 11-13.

[179] *G*alân is explained by *g*a, born, la, absorbed, and an, breathing. It is an artificial term, but fully recognised by the Vedânta school, and always explained in this manner.

[180] Or he who has faith and no doubt, will obtain this.

[181] This chapter is frequently quoted as the *S*â*nd*ilya-vidyâ, Vedântasâra, init; Vedânta-sûtra III, 3, 31.

FIFTEENTH KHA*ND*A[182].

1. The chest which has the sky for its circumference and the earth for its bottom, does not decay, for the quarters are its sides, and heaven its lid above. That chest is a treasury, and all things are within it.

2. Its eastern quarter is called *G*uhû, its southern Sahamânâ, its western Râgñî, its northern Subhûtâ[183]. The child of those quarters is Vâyu, the air, and he who knows that the air is indeed the child of the quarters, never weeps for his sons. 'I know the wind to be the child of the quarters, may I never weep for my sons.'

3. 'I turn to the imperishable chest with such and such and such[184].' 'I turn to the Prâ*n*a (life) with such and such and such.' 'I turn to Bhû*h* with such and such and such.' 'I turn to Bhuva*h* with such and such and such.' 'I turn to Sva*h* with such and such and such.'

4. 'When I said, I turn to Prâ*n*a, then Prâ*n*a means all whatever exists here—to that I turn.'

5. 'When I said, I turn to Bhû*h*, what I said is, I turn to the earth, the sky, and heaven.'

6. 'When I said, I turn to Bhuva*h*, what I said is, I turn to Agni (fire), Vâyu (air), Âditya (sun).'

7. 'When I said, I turn to Sva*h*, what I said is, I turn to the *Rig*-veda, Yagur-veda, and Sâma-veda. That is what I said, yea, that is what I said.'

SIXTEENTH KHA*ND*A[185].

1. Man is sacrifice. His (first) twenty-four years are the morning-libation. The Gâyatrî has twenty-four syllables, the morning-libation is offered with Gâyatrî hymns. The Vasus are connected with that part of the sacrifice. The Prâ*n*as (the five senses) are the Vasus, for they make all this to abide (vâsayanti).

2. If anything ails him in that (early) age, let him say: 'Ye Prâ*n*as, ye Vasus, extend this my morning-libation unto the midday-libation, that I, the sacrificer, may not perish in the midst of the Prâ*n*as or Vasus.' Thus he recovers from his illness, and becomes whole.

---

[182] The object of this section, the Ko*s*avigñâna, is to show how the promise made in III, 13, 6, 'that a strong son should be born in a man's family,' is to be fulfilled.

[183] These names are explained by the commentator as follows: Because people offer libations (guhvati), turning to the east, therefore it is called *G*uhû. Because evil doers suffer (sahante) in the town of Yama, which is in the south, therefore it is called Sahamânâ. The western quarter is called Râgñî, either because it is sacred to king Varu*n*a (râgan), or on account of the red colour (râga) of the twilight. The north is called Subhûtâ, because wealthy beings (bhûtimat), like Kuvera &c., reside there.

[184] Here the names of the sons are to be pronounced.

[185] The object of this Kha*nd*a is to show how to obtain long life, as promised before.

3. The next forty-four years are the midday-libation. The Trish*t*ubh has forty-four syllables, the midday-libation is offered with Trish*t*ubh hymns. The Rudras are connected with that part of it. The Prâ*n*as are the Rudras, for they make all this to cry (rodayanti).

4. If anything ails him in that (second) age, let him say: 'Ye Prâ*n*as, ye Rudras, extend this my midday-libation unto the third libation, that I, the sacrificer, may not perish in the midst of the Prâ*n*as or Rudras.' Thus he recovers from his illness, and becomes whole.

5. The next forty-eight years are the third libation. The *G*agatî has forty-eight syllables, the third libation is offered with *G*agatî hymns. The Âdityas are connected with that part of it. The Prâ*n*as are the Âdityas, for they take up all this (âdadate).

6. If anything ails him in that (third) age, let him say: 'Ye Prâ*n*as, ye Âdityas, extend this my third libation unto the full age, that I, the sacrificer, may not perish in the midst of the Prâ*n*as or Âdityas.' Thus he recovers from his illness, and becomes whole.

7. Mahidâsa Aitareya (the son of Itarâ), who knew this, said (addressing a disease): 'Why dost thou afflict me, as I shall not die by it?' He lived a hundred and sixteen years (i.e. 24 + 44 + 48). He, too, who knows this lives on to a hundred and sixteen years.

SEVENTEENTH KHA*ND*A[186].

1. When a man (who is the sacrificer) hungers, thirsts, and abstains from pleasures, that is the Dîkshâ (initiatory rite).

2. When a man eats, drinks, and enjoys pleasures, he does it with the Upasadas (the sacrificial days on which the sacrificer is allowed to partake of food).

3. When a man laughs, eats, and delights himself, he does it with the Stuta-*s*astras (hymns sung and recited at the sacrifices).

4. Penance, liberality, righteousness, kindness, truthfulness, these form his Dakshi*n*âs (gifts bestowed on priests, &c.)

5. Therefore when they say, 'There will be a birth,' and 'there has been a birth' (words used at the Soma-sacrifice, and really meaning, 'He will pour out the Soma-juice,' and 'he has poured out the Soma-juice'), that is his new birth. His death is the Avabh*r*itha ceremony (when the sacrificial Vessels are carried away to be cleansed).

6. Ghora Âṅgirasa, after having communicated this (view of the sacrifice) to K*r*ish*n*a, the son of Devăkî[187]—and he never thirsted again

---

[186] Here we have a representation of the sacrifice as performed without any ceremonial, and as it is often represented when performed in thought only by a man living in the forest.

[187] The curious coincidence between K*r*ish*n*a Devakîputra, here mentioned as a pupil of Ghora Âṅgirasa, and the famous K*r*ish*n*a, the son of Devakî, was first pointed out by Colebrooke, Miscell. Essays, II, 177. Whether it is more than a coincidence, is

(after other knowledge)—said: 'Let a man, when his end approaches, take refuge with this Triad[188]: "Thou art the imperishable," "Thou art the unchangeable," "Thou art the edge of Prâ*n*a."' On this subject there are two *Rik* verses (Rig-veda VIII, 6, 30):—

7. 'Then they see (within themselves) the ever-present light of the old seed (of the world, the Sat), the highest, which is lighted in the brilliant (Brahman).' Rig-veda I, 50, 10:—

'Perceiving above the darkness (of ignorance) the higher light (in the sun), as the higher light within the heart, the bright source (of light and life) among the gods, we have reached the highest light, yea, the highest light[189].'

EIGHTEENTH KHA*ND*A[190].

1. Let a man meditate on mind as Brahman (n.), this is said with reference to the body. Let a man meditate on the ether as Brahman (n.), this is said with reference to the Devas. Thus both the meditation which has reference to the body, and the meditation which has reference to the Devas, has been taught.

2. That Brahman (mind) has four feet (quarters). Speech is one foot, breath is one foot, the eye is one foot, the car is one foot-so much

---

difficult to say. Certainly we can build no other conclusions on it than those indicated by Colebrooke, that new fables may have been constructed elevating this personage to the rank of a god. We know absolutely nothing of the old K*r*ish*n*a Devakîputra except his having been a pupil of Ghora Âṅgirasa, nor does there seem to have been any attempt made by later Brahmans to connect their divine K*r*ish*n*a, the son of Vasudeva, with the K*r*ish*n*a Devakîputra of our Upanishad. This is all the more remarkable because the author of the Sâ*nd*ilya-sûtras, for instance, who is very anxious to find a *s*rauta authority for the worship of K*r*ish*n*a Vâsudeva as the supreme deity, had to be satisfied with quoting such modern compilations as the Nârâya*n*opanishad, Atharva*s*iras, VI, 9, brahma*n*yo devakîputro, brahmanyo madhusûdana*h* (see Sâ*nd*ilya-sûtras, ed. Ballantyne, p. 36, translated by Cowell, p. 51), without venturing to refer to the K*r*ish*n*a Devakîputra of the Khândogya-upanishad. The occurrence of such names as K*r*ish*n*a, Vâsudeva, Madhusûdanah stamps Upanishads, like the Âtmabodha-upanishad, as modern (Colebrooke, Essays, 1, 101), and the same remark applies, as Weber has shown, to the Gopâlatâpanî-upanishad (Bibliotheca Indica, No. 183), where we actually find such names as *S*rîk*r*ish*n*a Govinda, Gopîganavallabha, Devakyâm gâtâ*h* (p. 38), &c. Professor Weber has treated these questions very fully, but it is not quite clear to me whether he wishes to go beyond Colebrooke and to admit more than a similarity of name between the pupil of Ghora Âṅgirasa and the friend of the Gopîs.

[188] Let him recite these three verses.

[189] Both these verses had to be translated here according to their scholastic interpretation, but they had originally a totally different meaning. Even the text was altered, divâ being changed to divi, sva*h* to sve. The first is taken from a hymn addressed to Indra, who after conquering the dark clouds brings back the light of the sun. When he does that, then the people see again, as the poet says, the daily light of the old seed (from which the sun rises) which is lighted in heaven. The other verse belongs to a hymn addressed to the sun. Its simple meaning. is: 'Seeing above the darkness (of the night) the rising light, the Sun, bright among the bright, we came towards the highest light.'

[190] This is a further elucidation of *Kh*. Up. III, 14, 2.

with reference to the body. Then with reference to the gods, Agni (fire) is one foot, Vâyu (air) is one foot, Âditya (sun) is one foot, the quarters are one foot. Thus both the worship which has reference to the body, and the worship which has reference to the Devas, has been taught.

3. Speech is indeed the fourth foot of Brahman. That foot shines with Agni (fire) as its light, and warms. He who knows this, shines and warms through his celebrity, fame, and glory of countenance.

4. Breath is indeed the fourth foot of Brahman. That foot shines with Vâyu (air) as its light, and warms. He who knows this, shines and warms through his celebrity, fame, and glory of countenance.

5. The eye is indeed the fourth foot of Brahman. That foot shines with Âditya (sun) as its light, and warms. He who knows this, shines and warms through his celebrity, fame, and glory of countenance.

6. The ear is indeed the fourth foot of Brahman. That foot shines with the quarters as its light, and warms. He who knows this, shines and warms through his celebrity, fame, and glory of countenance.

NINETEENTH KHA*ND*A.

1. Âditya (the sun[191]) is Brahman, this is the doctrine, and this is the fuller account of it:—

In the beginning this was non-existent[192]. It became existent, it grew. It turned into an egg[193]. The egg lay for the time of a year. The egg broke open. The two halves were one of silver, the other of gold.

2. The silver one became this earth, the golden one the sky, the thick membrane (of the white) the mountains, the thin membrane (of the yoke) the mist with the clouds, the small veins the rivers, the fluid the sea.

3. And what was born from it that was Âditya, the sun. When he was born shouts of hurrah arose, and all beings arose, and all things which they desired. Therefore whenever the sun rises and sets, shouts of hurrah arise, and all beings arise, and all things which they desire.

4. If any one knowing this meditates on the sun as Brahman, pleasant shouts will approach him and will continue, yea, they will continue.

---

[191] Âditya, or the sun, had before been represented as one of the four feet of Brahman. He is now represented as Brahman, or as to be meditated on as such.

[192] Not yet existing, not yet developed in form and name, and therefore as if not existing.

[193] Â*nd*a instead of a*nd*a is explained as a Vedic irregularity. A similar cosmogony is given in Manu's Law Book, I, 12 seq. See Kellgren, Mythus de ovo mundano, Helsingfors, 1849.

FOURTH PRAPÂ*TH*AKA.

FIRST KHA*ND*A[194].

1. There lived once upon a time *G*ânas*r*uti Pautrâya*n*a (the great-grandson of *G*anas*r*uta), who was a pious giver, bestowing much wealth upon the people, and always keeping open house. He built places of refuge everywhere, wishing that people should everywhere eat of his food.

2. Once in the night some Ha*m*sas (flamingoes) flew over his house, and one flamingo said to another: 'Hey, Bhallâksha, Bhallâksha (short-sighted friend). The light (glory) of *G*ânas*r*uti Pautrâya*n*a has spread like the sky. Do not go near, that it may not burn thee.'

3. The other answered him: 'How can you speak of him, being what he is (a râganya, noble), as if he were like Raikva with the car[195]?'

4. The first replied: 'How is it with this Raikva with the car of whom thou speakest?'

The other answered: 'As (in a game of dice) all the lower casts[196] belong to him who has conquered with the K*r*ita cast, so whatever good deeds other people perform, belong to that Raikva. He who knows what he knows, he is thus spoken of by me.'

5. *G*ânas*r*uti Pautrâya*n*a overheard this conversation, and as soon as he had risen in the morning, he said to his. door-keeper (kshatt*ri*): 'Friend, dost thou speak of (me, as if I were) Raikva with the car?'

He replied: 'How is it with this Raikva, with the car?'

6. The king said: 'As (in a game of dice), all the lower casts belong to him who has conquered with the K*r*ita cast, so whatever good deeds other people perform, belong to that Raikva. He who knows what he knows, he is thus spoken of by me.'

7. The door-keeper went to look for Raikva, but returned saying, 'I found him not.' Then the king said: 'Alas! where a Brâhma*n*a should be searched for (in the solitude of the forest), there go for him.'

8. The door-keeper came to a man who was lying beneath a car and scratching his sores[197]. He addressed him, and said: 'Sir, are you

---

[194] Vâyu (air) and Prâ*n*a (breath) had before been represented as feet of Brahman, as the second pair. Now they are represented as Brahman, and as to be meditated on as such. This is the teaching of Raikva. The language of this chapter is very obscure, and I am not satisfied with the translation.

[195] Sayugvan is explained as possessed of a car with yoked horses or oxen. Could it have meant originally, 'yoke-fellow, equal,' as in Rig-veda X, 130, 4? Anquetil renders it by 'semper cum se ipso camelum solutum habens.'

[196] Instead of adhareyâ*h*, we must read adhare 'yâ*h*.

[197] It is curious that in a hymn of the Atharva-veda (V, 22, 5, 8) takman, apparently a disease of the skin, is relegated to the Mahâv*ri*shas, where Raikva dwelt. Roth, Zur Literatur des Veda, p. 36.

Raikva with the car?'

He answered: 'Here I am.'

Then the door-keeper returned, and said: 'I have found him.'

SECOND KHA*N*DA.

1. Then *G*ânas*r*uti Pautrâya*n*a took six hundred cows, a necklace, and a carriage with mules, went to Raikva and said:

2. 'Raikva, here are six hundred cows, a necklace, and a carriage with mules; teach me the deity which you worship.'

3. The other replied: 'Fie, necklace and carriage be thine, O *S*ûdra, together with the cows.'

Then *G*ânas*r*uti Pautrâya*n*a took again a thousand cows, a necklace, a carriage with mules, and his own daughter, and went to him.

4. He said to him: 'Raikva, there are a thousand cows, a necklace, a carriage with mules, this wife, and this village in which thou dwellest. Sir, teach me!'

5. He, opening her mouth[198], said: 'You have brought these (cows and other presents), O *S*ûdra, but only by that mouth did you make me speak.'

These are the Raikva-par*n*a villages in the country of the Mahâv*ri*shas (mahâpu*n*yas) where Raikva dwelt under him[199]. And he said to him:

THIRD KHA*N*DA.

1. 'Air (vâyu) is indeed the end of all[200]. For when fire goes out, it goes into air. When the sun goes down, it goes into air. When the moon goes down, it goes into air.

2. 'When water dries up, it goes into air. Air indeed consumes them all. So much with reference to the Devas.

3. 'Now with reference to the body. Breath (prâ*n*a) is indeed the end of all. When a man sleeps, speech goes into breath, so do sight, hearing, and mind. Breath indeed consumes them all.

4. 'These are the two ends, air among the Devas, breath among the senses (prâ*n*âh).'

---

[198] To find out her age. The commentator translates, 'Raikva, knowing her mouth to be the door of knowledge, i.e. knowing that for her he might impart his knowledge to *G*ânas*r*uti, and that *G*ânas*r*uti by bringing such rich gifts had become a proper receiver of knowledge, consented to do what he had before refused.'

[199] The commentator supplies adât, the king gave the villages to him.

[200] Sa*m*varga, absorption, whence sa*m*vargavidyâ, not sa*m*sarga. It is explained by sa*m*vargana, sa*m*graha*n*a, and sa*m*grasana, in the text itself by adana, eating.

5. Once while *S*aunaka Kâpeya and Abhipratârin Kâkshaseni were being waited on at their meal, a religious student begged of them. They gave him nothing.

6. He said: 'One god—who is he?—swallowed the four great ones[201], he, the guardian of the world. O Kâpeya, mortals see him not, O Abhipratârin, though he dwells in many places. He to whom this food belongs, to him it has not been given[202].'

7. *S*aunaka Kâpeya, pondering on that speech, went to the student and said: 'He is the self of the Devas, the creator of all beings, with golden tusks, the eater, not without intelligence. His greatness is said to be great indeed, because, without being eaten, he eats even what is not food[203]. Thus do we, O Brahma*k*ârin, meditate on that Being.' Then he said: 'give him food.'

8. They gave him food. Now these five (the eater Vâyu (air), and his food, Agni (fire), Âditya (sun), *K*andramas (moon), Ap (water)) and the other five (the eater Prâ*n*a (breath), and his food, speech, sight, hearing, mind) make ten, and that is the K*ri*ta (the highest[204]) cast (representing the ten, the eaters and the food). Therefore in all quarters those ten are food (and) K*ri*ta (the highest cast). These are again the Virâg[205] (of ten syllables) which eats the food. Through this all this becomes seen. He who knows this sees all this and becomes an eater of food, yea, he becomes an eater of food.

FOURTH KHA*ND*A[206].

1. Satyakâma, the son of *G*abâlâ, addressed his mother and said: 'I wish to become a Brahma*k*ârin (religious student), mother. Of what family am I?'

2. She said to him: 'I do not know, my child, of what family thou art. In my youth when I had to move about much as a servant (waiting

---

[201] This must refer to Vâyu and Prâ*n*a swallowing the four, as explained in IV, 3, 2, and IV, 3, 3. The commentator explains it by Pragâpati, who is sometimes called Ka. In one sense it would be Brahman, as represented by Vâyu and Prâ*n*a.

[202] The food which you have refused to me, you have really refused to Brahman.

[203] *S*aunaka wishes the student to understand that though I mortals see him not,' he sees and knows him, viz. the god who, as Vâyu, swallows all the gods, but produces them again, and who, as prâ*n*a, swallows during sleep all senses, but produces them again at the time of waking.

[204] The words are obscure, and the commentator does not throw much light on them. He explains, however, the four casts of the dice, the K*ri*ta = 4, the Tretâ = 3, the Dvâpara = 2, the Kali = 1, making together 10, the K*ri*ta cast absorbing the other casts, and thus counting ten.

[205] Virâg, name of a metre of ten syllables, and also a name of food. One expects, 'which is the food and eats the food.'

[206] This carries on the explanation of the four feet of Brahman, as first mentioned in III, 18, x. Each foot or quarter of Brahman is represented as fourfold, and the knowledge of these sixteen parts is called the Sho*d*a*s*akalâvidyâ.

on the guests in my father's house), I conceived thee. I do not know of what family thou art. I am *G*abâlâ by name, thou art Satyakâma (Philalethes). Say that thou art Satyakâma *G*âbâlâ.'

3. He going to Gautama Hâridrumata said to him, 'I wish to become a Brahma*k*ârin with you, Sir. May I come to you, Sir?'

4. He said to him: 'Of what family are you, my friend?' He replied: 'I do not know, Sir, of what family I am. I asked my mother, and she answered: "In my youth when I had to move about much as a servant, I conceived thee. I do not know of what family thou art. I am *G*abâlâ by name, thou art Satyakâma," I am therefore Satyakâma *G*âbâlâ, Sir.'

5. He said to him: 'No one but a true Brâhma*n*a would thus speak out. Go and fetch fuel, friend, I shall initiate you. You have not swerved from the truth.'

Having initiated him, he chose four hundred lean and weak cows, and said: 'Tend these, friend.'

He drove them out and said to himself, 'I shall not return unless I bring back a thousand.' He dwelt a number of years (in the forest), and when the cows had become a thousand,

FIFTH KHA*ND*A.

1. The bull of the herd (meant for Vâyu) said to him: 'Satyakâma!' He replied: 'Sir!' The bull said: 'We have become a thousand, lead us to the house of the teacher;

2. 'And I will declare to you one foot of Brahman.'

'Declare it, Sir,' he replied.

He said to him: 'The eastern region is one quarter, the western region is one quarter, the southern region is one quarter, the northern region is one quarter. This is a foot of Brahman, consisting of the four quarters, and called Prakâ*s*avat (endowed with splendour).

3. 'He who knows this and meditates on the foot of Brahman, consisting of four quarters, by the name of Prakâ*s*avat, becomes endowed with splendour in this world. He conquers the resplendent worlds, whoever knows this and meditates on the foot of Brahman, consisting of the four quarters, by the name of Prakâ*s*avat.

SIXTH KHA*ND*A.

1. 'Agni will declare to you another foot of Brahman.'

(After these words of the bull), Satyakâma, on the morrow, drove the cows (toward the house of the teacher). And when they came towards the evening, he lighted a fire, penned the cows, laid wood on the fire, and sat down behind the fire, looking to the east.

2. Then Agni (the fire) said to him: 'Satyakâma!' He replied: 'Sir.'

3. Agni said: 'Friend, I will declare unto you one foot of

Brahman.'

'Declare it, Sir,' he replied.

He said to him: 'The earth is one quarter, the sky is one quarter, the heaven is one quarter, the ocean is one quarter. This is a foot of Brahman, consisting of four quarters, and called Anantavat (endless).'

4. 'He who knows this and meditates on the foot of Brahman, consisting of four quarters, by the name of Anantavat, becomes endless in this world. He conquers the endless worlds, whoever knows this and meditates on the foot of Brahman, consisting of four quarters, by the name of Anantavat.

SEVENTH KHA*ND*A.

1. 'A Ha*m*sa (flamingo, meant for the sun) will declare to you another foot of Brahman.'

(After these words of Agni), Satyakâma, on the morrow, drove the cows onward. And when they came towards the evening, he lighted a fire, penned the cows, laid wood on the fire, and sat down behind the fire, looking toward the east.

2. Then a Ha*m*sa flew near and said to him 'Satyakâma.' He replied: 'Sir.'

3. The Ha*m*sa said: 'Friend, I will declare unto you one foot of Brahman.'

'Declare it, Sir,' he replied.

He said to him: 'Fire is one quarter, the sun is one quarter, the moon is one quarter, lightning is one quarter. This is a foot of Brahman, consisting of four quarters, and called *G*yotishmat (full of light).

4. 'He who knows this and meditates on the foot of Brahman, consisting of four quarters, by the name of *G*yotishmat, becomes full of light in this world. He conquers the worlds which are full of light, whoever knows this and meditates on the foot of Brahman, consisting of four quarters, by the name of *G*yotishmat.

EIGHTH KHA*ND*A.

1. 'A diver-bird (Madgu, meant for Prâ*n*a) will declare to you another foot of Brahman.'

(After these words of the Ha*m*sa), Satyakâma, on the morrow, drove the cows onward. And when they came towards the evening, he lighted a fire, penned the cows, laid wood on the fire, and sat down behind the fire, looking toward the east.

2. Then a diver flew near and said to him 'Satyakâma.' He replied: 'Sir.'

3. The diver said: 'Friend, I will declare unto you one foot of Brahman.'

'Declare it, Sir,' he replied.

He said to him: 'Breath is one quarter, the eye is one quarter, the ear is one quarter, the mind is one quarter. This is a foot of Brahman, consisting of four quarters, and called Âyatanavat (having a home).

'He who knows this and meditates on the foot of Brahman, consisting of four quarters, by the name of Âyatanavat, becomes possessed of a home in this world. He conquers the worlds which offer a home, whoever knows this and meditates on the foot of Brahman, consisting of four quarters, by the name of Âyatanavat.'

NINTH KHA*ND*A.

1. Thus he reached the house of his teacher. The teacher said to him: 'Satyakâma.' He replied: 'Sir.'

2. The teacher said: 'Friend, you shine like one who knows Brahman. Who then has taught you[207]?' He replied: 'Not men. But you only, Sir, I wish, should teach me[208];

3. 'For I have heard from men like you, Sir, that only knowledge which is learnt from a teacher (Â*k*ârya), leads to real good.' Then he taught him the same knowledge. Nothing was left out, Yea, nothing was left out.

TENTH KHA*ND*A[209].

1. Upako*s*ala Kâmalâyana dwelt as a Brahma*k*ârin (religious student) in the house of Satyakâma *G*âbâla. He tended his fires for twelve years. But the teacher, though he allowed other pupils (after they had learnt the sacred books) to depart to their own homes, did not allow Upakosala to depart.

2. Then his wife said to him: 'This student, who is quite exhausted (with austerities), has carefully tended your fires. Let not the fires themselves blame you, but teach him.' The teacher, however, went away on a journey without having taught him.

The student from sorrow was not able to eat. Then the wife of the teacher said to him: 'Student, eat! Why do you not eat?' He said: 'There are many desires in this man here, which lose themselves in different directions. I am full of sorrows, and shall take no food.'

4. Thereupon the fires said among themselves: 'This student, who is quite exhausted, has carefully tended us. Well, let us teach him.'

---

[207] It would have been a great offence if Satyakâma had accepted instruction from any man, except his recognised teacher.

[208] The text should be, bhagavâ*m*s tv eva me kâme brûyât (me kâme = mame*kkh*âyâm).

[209] The Upako*s*ala-vidyâ teaches first Brahman as the cause, and then in its various forms, and is therefore called âtmavidyâ and agnividyâ.

They said to him:

5. 'Breath is Brahman, Ka (pleasure) is Brahman, Kha (ether) is Brahman.'

He said: 'I understand that breath is Brahman, but I do not understand Ka or Kha[210].'

They said: 'What is Ka is Kha, what is Kha is Ka[211].' They therefore taught him Brahman as breath, and as the ether (in the heart)[212].

ELEVENTH KHA*ND*A.

1. After that the Gârhapatya fire[213] taught him Earth, fire, food, and the sun (these are my forms, or forms of Brahman). The person that is seen in the sun, I am he, I am he indeed[214].

2. 'He who knowing this meditates on him, destroys sin, obtains the world (of Agni Gârhapatya), reaches his full age, and lives long; his descendants do not perish. We guard him in this world and in the other, whosoever knowing this meditates on him.'

TWELFTH KHA*ND*A.

1. Then the Anvâhârya fire[215] taught him: Water, the quarters, the stars, the moon (these are my forms). The person that is seen in the moon, I am he, I am he indeed.

2. 'He who knowing this meditates on him, destroys sin, obtains the world (of Agni Anvâhârya), reaches his full age, and lives long; his descendants do not perish. We guard him in this world and in the other, whosoever knowing this meditates on him.'

---

[210] I do not understand, he means, how Ka, which means pleasure, and is non-eternal, and how Kha, which means ether, and is not intelligent, can be Brahman.

[211] The commentator explains as follows:—Ka is pleasure, and Kha is ether, but these two words are to determine each other mutually, and thus to form one idea. Ka therefore does not mean ordinary pleasures, but pleasures such as belong to Kha, the ether. And Kha does not signify the ordinary outward ether, but the ether in the heart, which alone is capable of pleasure. What is meant by Ka and Kha is therefore the sentient ether in the heart, and that is Brahman, while Prâ*n*a, breath, is Brahman, in so far as it is united with the ether in the heart.

[212] And as its ether, i.e. as the ether in the heart, the Brahman, with which prâ*n*a is connected. Comm.

[213] The household altar.

[214] Fanciful similarities and relations between the fires of the three altars and their various forms and manifestations are pointed out by the commentator. Thus earth and food are represented as warmed and boiled by the fire. The sun is said to give warmth and light like the fire of the altar. The chief point, however, is that in all of them Brahman is manifested.

[215] The altar on the right. Anvâhârya is a sacrificial oblation, chiefly one intended for the manes.

THIRTEENTH KHA*ND*A.

1. Then the Âhavanîya[216] fire taught him: 'Breath, ether, heaven, and lightning (these are my forms). The person that is seen in the lightning, I am he, I am he indeed.

2. 'He who knowing this meditates on him, destroys sin, obtains the world (of Agni Âhavanîya), reaches his full age, and lives long; his descendants do not perish. We guard him in this world and in the other, whosoever knowing this meditates on him.'

FOURTEENTH KHA*ND*A.

1. Then they all said: 'Upakosala, this is our knowledge, our friend, and the knowledge of the Self, but the teacher will tell you the way (to another life).'

2. In time his teacher came back, and said to him: 'Upakosala.' He answered: 'Sir.' The teacher said: 'Friend, your face shines like that of one who knows Brahman. Who has taught you?'

'Who should teach me, Sir?' he said. He denies, as it were. And he said (pointing) to the fires: 'Are these fires other than fires?'

The teacher said: 'What, my friend, have these fires told you?'

3. He answered: 'This' (repeating some of what they had told him).

The teacher said: 'My friend, they have taught you about the worlds, but I shall tell you this; and as water does not cling to a lotus leaf, so no evil deed clings to one who knows it.' He said: 'Sir, tell it me.'

FIFTEENTH KHA*ND*A.

1. He said: 'The person that is seen in the eye, that is the Self. This is the immortal, the fearless, this is Brahman[217]. Even though they drop melted butter or water on him, it runs away on both sides[218].

2. 'They call him Sa*m*yadvâma, for all blessings (vâma) go towards him (sa*m*yanti). All blessings go towards him who knows this.

3. 'He is also Vâmanî, for he leads (nayati) all blessings (vâma). He leads all blessings who knows this.

4. 'He is also Bhâmanî, for he shines (bhâti) in all worlds. He who knows this, shines in all worlds.

5. 'Now (if one who knows this, dies), whether people perform

---

[216] The Âhavanîya altar is the altar on the eastern side of the sacrificial ground.

[217] This is also the teaching of Pragâpati in VIII, 7, 4.

[218] It does so in the eye, and likewise with the person in the eye, who is not affected by anything. Cf. *Kh*. Up. IV, 14, 3.

obsequies for him or no, he goes to light (ar*k*is)[219], from light to day, from day to the light half of the moon, from the light half of the moon to the six months during which the sun goes to the north, from the months to the year, from the year to the sun, from the sun to the moon, from the moon to the lightning. There is a person not human,

6. 'He leads them to Brahman. This is the path of the Devas, the path that leads to Brahman. Those who proceed on that path, do not return to the life of man, yea, they do not return.'

SIXTEENTH KHA*ND*A[220].

1. Verily, he who purifies (Vâyu) is the sacrifice, for he (the air) moving along purifies everything. Because moving along he purifies everything, therefore he is the sacrifice. Of that sacrifice there are two ways, by mind and by speech.

2. The Brahman priest performs one of them in his mind[221], the Hot*ri*, Adhvaryu, and Udgât*ri* priests perform the other by words. When the Brahman priest, after the Prâtaranuvâka ceremony has begun, but before the recitation of the Paridhânîyâ hymn, has (to break his silence and) to speak,

3. He performs perfectly the one way only (that by words), but the other is injured. As a man walking on one foot, or a carriage going on one wheel, is injured, his sacrifice is injured, and with the injured sacrifice the sacrificer is injured; yes, having sacrificed, he becomes worse.

4. But when after the Prâtaranuvâka ceremony has begun, and before the recitation of the Paridhânîyâ hymn, the Brahman priest has not (to break his silence and) to speak, they perform both ways perfectly, and neither of them is injured.

5. As a man walking on two legs and a carriage going on two wheels gets on, so his sacrifice gets on, and with the successful sacrifice the sacrificer gets on; yes, having sacrificed, he becomes better.

---

[219] The commentator takes light, day, &c. as persons, or devatâs. Cf. *Kh*. Up. V, 10, 1.

[220] If any mistakes happen during the performance of a sacrifice, as described before, they are remedied by certain interjectional syllables (vyâh*ri*ti), the nature of which is next described. All this is supposed to take place in the forest.

[221] While the other priests perform the sacrifice, the Brahman priest has to remain silent, following the whole sacrifice in his mind, and watching that no mistake be committed. If a mistake is committed, he has to correct it, and for that purpose certain corrective penances (prâya*sk*itta) are enjoined. The performance of the Brahman priest resembles the meditations of the sages in the forest, and therefore this chapter is here inserted.

SEVENTEENTH KHA*ND*A.

1. Pragâpati brooded over the worlds, and from them thus brooded on he squeezed out the essences, Agni (fire) from the earth, Vâyu (air) from the sky, Âditya (the sun) from heaven.

2. He brooded over these three deities, and from them thus brooded on he squeezed out the essences, the *Rik* verses from Agni, the Yagus verses from Vâyu, the Sâman verses from Âditya.

3. He brooded over the threefold knowledge (the three Vedas), and from it thus brooded on he squeezed out the essences, the sacred interjection Bhûs from the *Rik* verses, the sacred interjection Bhuvas from the Yagus verses, the sacred interjection Svar from the Sâman verses.

4. If the sacrifice is injured from the Rig-Veda side, let him offer a libation in the Gârhapatya fire, saying, Bhû*h*, Svâha! Thus does he bind together and heal, by means of the essence and the power of the *Rik* verses themselves, whatever break the *Rik* sacrifice may have suffered.

5. If the sacrifice is injured from the Yagur-veda side, let him offer a libation in the Dakshi*n*a fire, saying, Bhuva*h*, Svâhâ! Thus does he bind together and heal, by means of the essence and the power of the Yagus verses themselves, whatever break the Yagus sacrifice may have suffered.

6. If the sacrifice is injured by the Sâma-veda side, let him offer a libation in the Âhavanîya fire, saying, Sva*h*, Svâhâ! Thus does he bind together and heal, by means of the essence and the power of the Sâman verses themselves, whatever break the Sâman sacrifice may have suffered.

7. As one binds (softens) gold by means of lava*n*a[222] (borax), and silver by means of gold, and tin by means of silver, and lead by means of tin, and iron (loha) by means of lead, and wood by means of iron, or also by means of leather,

8. Thus does one bind together and heal any break in the sacrifice by means of (the Vyâh*ri*tis or sacrificial interjections which are) the essence and strength of the three worlds, of the deities, and of the threefold knowledge. That sacrifice is healed[223] in which there is a Brahman priest who knows this.

9. That sacrifice is inclined towards the north (in the right way) in which there is a Brahman priest who knows this. And with regard to

---

[222] Lava*n*a, a kind of salt, explained by kshâra and *t*aṅka or *t*aṅkana. It is evidently borax, which is still imported from the East Indies under the name of tincal, and used as a flux in chemical processes.

[223] Bheshagak*ri*ta, explained by bheshagena 'iva k*ri*ta*h* sa*m*sk*ri*ta*h*, and also by *k*ikitsakena su*s*ikshitena 'esha yagño bhavati,' which looks as if the commentator had taken it as a genitive of bheshagak*ri*t.

such a Brahman priest there is the following Gâthâ[224]: 'Whereever it falls back, thither the man[225] goes,'—viz. the Brahman only, as one of the *Ri*tvig priests. 'He saves the Kurus as a mare' (viz. a Brahman priest who knows this, saves the sacrifice, the sacrificer, and all the other priests). Therefore let a man make him who knows this his Brahman priest, not one who does not know it, who does not know it.

FIFTH PRAPÂTHAKA[226].

FIRST KHA*ND*A.

1. He who knows the oldest and the best becomes himself the oldest and the best. Breath indeed is the oldest and the best.

2. He who knows the richest, becomes himself the richest. Speech indeed is the richest.

3. He who knows the firm rest, becomes himself firm in this world and in the next. The eye indeed is the firm rest.

4. He who knows success, his wishes succeed, both his divine and human wishes. The ear indeed is success.

5. He who knows the home, becomes a home of his people. The mind indeed is the home.

6. The five senses quarrelled together[227], who was the best, saying, I am better, I am better.

7. They went to their father Pragâpati and said: 'Sir, who is the best of us?' He replied: 'He by whose departure the body seems worse than worst, he is the best of you.'

8. The tongue (speech) departed, and having been absent for a year, it came round and said: 'How have you been able to live without me?' They replied: 'Like mute people, not speaking, but breathing with

---

[224] This Gâthâ (or, according to *S*aṅkara, Anugâthâ) is probably a Gâyatrî, though Ânandagiri says that it is not in the Gâyatrî or any other definite metre. It may have been originally 'yato yata âvartate, tattad ga*kkh*ati mânava*h*, kurûn a*s*vâbhirakshati.' This might be taken from an old epic ballad, 'Wherever the army fell back, thither the man went; the mare (mares being preferred to stallions in war) saves the Kurus.' That verse was applied to the Brahman priest succouring the sacrifice, whenever it seemed to waver, and protecting the Kurus, i.e. the performers of the sacrifice.

[225] Mânava, explained from mauna, or manana, but possibly originally, a descendant of Manu.

[226] The chief object is to show the different ways on which people proceed after death. One of these ways, the Devapatha that leads to Brahman and from which there is no return, has been described, IV, 15. The other ways for those who on earth know the conditioned Brahman only, have to be discussed now.

[227] The same fable, the prâ*n*asa*m*vâda or prâ*n*avidyâ, is told in the B*ri*hadâra*n*yaka VI, 1, 1-14, the Aitareya Âr. II, 4, the Kaush. Up. III, 3, and the Pra*s*na Up. II, 3. The last is the simplest version of all, but it does not follow therefore that it is the oldest. It would be difficult to find two fables apparently more alike, yet in reality differing from each other more characteristically than this fable and the fable told to the plebeians by Menenius Agrippa.

the breath, seeing with the eye, hearing with the ear, thinking with the mind. Thus we lived.' Then speech went back.

9. The eye (sight) departed, and having been absent for a year, it came round and said: 'How have you been able to live without me?' They replied: 'Like blind people, not seeing, but breathing with the breath, speaking with the tongue, hearing with the ear, thinking with the mind. Thus we lived.' Then the eye went back.

10. The ear (hearing) departed, and having been absent for a year, it came round and said: 'How have you been able to live without me?' They replied: 'Like deaf people, not hearing, but breathing with the breath, speaking with the tongue, thinking with the mind. Thus we lived.' Then the ear went back.

11. The mind departed, and having been absent for a year, it came round and said: 'How have you been able to live without me?' They replied: 'Like children whose mind is not yet formed, but breathing with the breath, speaking with the tongue, seeing with the eye, hearing with the ear. Thus we lived.' Then the mind went back.

12. The breath, when on the point of departing, tore up the other senses, as a horse, going to start, might tear up the pegs to which he is tethered[228]. They came to him and said: 'Sir, be thou (our lord); thou art the best among us. Do not depart from us!'

13. Then the tongue said to him: 'If I am the richest, thou art the richest.' The eye said to him: 'If I am the firm rest, thou art the firm rest[229].'

14. The ear said to him: 'If I am success, thou art success.' The mind said to him: 'If I am the home, thou art the home.'

15. And people do not call them, the tongues, the eyes, the ears, the minds, but the breaths (prâ*n*a, the senses). For breath are all these.

SECOND KHA*ND*A.

1. Breath said: 'What shall be my food?' They answered: 'Whatever there is, even unto dogs and birds.' Therefore this is food for Ana (the breather). His name is clearly Ana[230]. To him who knows this there is nothing that is not (proper) food.

2. He said: 'What shall be my dress?' They answered: 'Water. Therefore wise people, when they are going to eat food, surround their food before and after with water[231].' He (prâ*n*a) thus gains a dress, and

---

[228] Pa*d*vî*s*a, fetter, πέδη, pedica, a word now well known, but which Burnouf (Commentaire sur le Yaçna, Notes, CLXXIV) tried in vain to decipher.

[229] Burnouf rightly preferred pratish*th*âsi to pratish*th*o 'si, though the commentary on the corresponding passage of the B*ri*hadâra*n*yaka seems to favour tatpratish*th*o 'si.

[230] Ana, breather, more general than pra-ana = prâ*n*a, forth-breather, and the other more specified names of breath.

[231] They rinse the mouth before and after every meal.

is no longer naked[232]'.

3. Satyakâma *G*âbâla, after he had communicated this to Go*s*ruti Vaiyâghrapadya, said to him: 'If you were to tell this to a dry stick, branches would grow, and leaves spring from it.'

4. If[233] a man wishes to reach greatness, let him perform the Dîkshâ[234] (preparatory rite) on the day of the new moon, and then, on the night of the full moon, let him stir a mash of all kinds of herbs with curds and honey, and let him pour ghee on the fire (âvasathya laukika), saying; 'Svâhâ to the oldest and the best.' After that let him throw all that remains (of the ghee)[235] into the mash.

5. In the same manner let him pour ghee on. the fire, saying, 'Svâhâ to the richest.' After that let him throw all that remains together into the mash.

In the same manner let him pour ghee on the fire, saying, 'Svâhâ to the firm rest.' After that let him throw all that remains together into the mash.

In the same manner let him pour ghee on the fire, saying, 'Svâhâ to success.' After that let him throw all that remains together into the mash.

6. Then going forward and placing the mash in his hands, he recites: 'Thou (Prâ*n*a) art Ama[236] by name, for all this together exists in thee. He is the oldest and best, the king, the sovereign May he make me the oldest, the best, the king, the sovereign. May I be all this.'

7. Then he eats with the following *Rik* verse at every foot: 'We choose that food'—here he swallows—'Of the divine Savit*ri* (prâ*n*a)'—here he swallows—'The best and all-supporting food'—here he swallows—'We meditate on the speed of Bhaga (Savit*ri*, prâ*n*a)'—here he drinks all.

8. Having cleansed the vessel, whether it be a ka*m*sa or a *k*amasa, he sits down behind the fire on a skin or on the bare ground, without speaking or making any other effort. If in his dream he sees a woman, let him know this to be a sign that his sacrifice has succeeded.

9. On this there is a *S*loka: 'If during sacrifices which are to fulfil certain wishes he sees in his dreams a woman, let him know success

---

232 We expect, 'He who knows this' instead of prâ*n*a, but as prâ*n*a may apply to every individual prâ*n*a, the usual finishing sentence was possibly dropt on purpose.

233 The oblation here described is called mantha, a mortar, or what is pounded in a mortar, i.e. barley stirred in some kind of gravy. See *G*aim. N. M. V. p. 406.

234 Not the real dîkshâ, which is a preparatory rite for great sacrifices, but penance, truthfulness, abstinence, which take the place of dîkshâ with those who live in the forest and devote themselves to upâsana, meditative worship.

235 What is here called sampâtam avanayati is the same as sa*m*sravam avanayati in the B*r*ih. Âr. VI, 3, 2. The commentator says: Sruvâvalepanam âgyam mantham sa*m*srâvayati.

236 Cf. B*r*ih. Âr. I, 1, 3, 22.

from this vision in a dream, yea, from this vision in a dream.'

THIRD KHA*ND*A[237].

1. *S*vetaketu Âru*n*eya went to an assembly[238] of the Pañ*k*âlas. Pravâha*n*a *G*aivali[239] said to him: 'Boy, has your father instructed you?' 'Yes, Sir,' he replied.

2. 'Do you know to what place men go from here?' 'No, Sir,' he replied.

'Do you know how they return again?' 'No Sir,' he replied.

'Do you know where the path of Devas and the path of the fathers diverge?' 'No, Sir,' he replied.

3. 'Do you know why that world[240] never becomes full?' 'No, Sir,' he replied.

'Do you know why in the fifth libation water is called Man[241]? No, Sir,' he replied.

4. 'Then why did you say (you had been) instructed? How could anybody who did not know these things say that he had been instructed?' Then the boy went back sorrowful to the place of his father, and said: 'Though you had not instructed me, Sir, you said you had instructed me.

5. 'That fellow of a Râganya, asked me five questions, and I could not answer one of them.' The father said: 'As you have told me these questions of his, I do not know any one of them[242]. If I knew these questions, how should I not have told you[243]?'

6. Then Gautama went to the king's place, and when he had come to him, the king offered him proper respect. In the morning the king went out on his way to the assembly[244]. The king said to him: 'Sir, Gautama, ask a boon of such things as men possess.' He replied: 'Such things as men possess may remain with you. Tell me the speech which you addressed to the boy.'

7. The king was perplexed, and commanded him, saying: 'Stay with me some time.' Then he said: 'As (to what) you have said to me,

---

[237] This story is more fully told in the B*ri*hadâra*n*yaka VI, 2, *S*atapatha-brâhma*n*a XIV, 8, 16.

[238] Samiti, or parishad, as in the B*ri*h. Âr.

[239] He is the same Kshatriya sage who appeared in I, 8, 1, silencing the Brâhmans.

[240] That of the fathers. Comm.

[241] Or, according to others, why the water has a human voice; purushavâ*k*a*h* in B*ri*h. Âr. XIV, 9, 3.

[242] I doubt whether the elliptical construction of these sentences is properly filled out by the commentator. In the B*ri*hadâra*n*yaka the construction is much easier. 'You know me well enough to know that whatever I know, I told you.'

[243] I read avedishyam, though both the text and commentary give avadishyam. Still viditavân asmi points to an original avedishyam, and a parallel passage, VI, 1, 7, confirms this emendation.

[244] Cf. *Kh*. Up. V, II, 5.

Gautama, this knowledge did not go to any Brâhma*n*a before you, and therefore this teaching belonged in all the worlds to the Kshatra class alone.' Then he began:

FOURTH KHA*ND*A[245]

1. 'The altar (on which the sacrifice is supposed to be offered) is that world (heaven), O Gautama; its fuel is the sun itself, the smoke his rays, the light the day, the coals the moon, the sparks the stars.

2. 'On that altar the Devas (or prâ*n*as, represented by Agni, &c.) offer the *s*raddha libation (consisting of water). From that oblation rises Soma, the king[246] (the moon).

FIFTH KHA*ND*A.

1. 'The altar is Parganya (the god of rain), O Gautama; its fuel is the air itself, the smoke the cloud, the light the lightning, the coals. the thunderbolt, the sparks the thunderings[247].

2. 'On that altar the Devas offer Soma, the king (the moon). From that oblation rises rain[248].

SIXTH KHA*ND*A.

1. 'The altar is the earth, O Gautama; its fuel is the year itself, the smoke the ether, the light the night, the coals the quarters, the sparks the intermediate quarters.

2. 'On that altar the Devas (prâ*n*as) offer rain. From that oblation rises food (corn, &c.)

SEVENTH KHA*ND*A.

1. 'The altar is man, O Gautama; its fuel speech itself, the smoke the breath, the light the tongue, the coals the eye, the sparks the ear.

2. 'On that altar the Devas (prâ*n*as) offer food. From that oblation rises seed.

---

245 He answers the last question, why water in the fifth libation is called Man, first.

246 The sacrificers themselves rise through their oblations to heaven, and attain as their reward a Soma-like nature.

247 Hrâduni, generally explained by hail, but here by stanayitnu*s*abdâ*h*, rumblings.

248 The water, which had assumed the nature of Soma, now becomes rain.

EIGHTH KHA*ND*A.

1. 'The altar is woman, O Gautama[249].

2. 'On that altar the Devas (prâ*n*as) offer seed, From that oblation rises the germ.

NINTH KHA*ND*A.

1. 'For this reason is water in the fifth oblation called Man. This germ, covered in the womb, having dwelt there ten months, or more or less, is born.

2. 'When born, he lives whatever the length of his life may be. When he has departed, his friends carry him, as appointed, to the fire (of the funeral pile) from whence he came, from whence he sprang.

TENTH KHA*ND*A.

'Those who know this[250] (even though they still be g*r*ihasthas, householders) and those who in the forest follow faith and austerities (the vânaprasthas, and of the parivrâgakas those who do not yet know the Highest Brahman) go[251] to light (ar*k*is), from light to day, from day to the light half of the moon, from the light half of the moon to the six months when the sun goes to the north, from the six months when the sun goes to the north to the year, from the year to the sun, from the sun to the moon, from the moon to the lightning. There is a person not human[252],—

2. 'He leads them to Brahman (the conditioned Brahman). This is the path of the Devas.

3. 'But they who living in a village practise (a life of) sacrifices, works of public utility, and alms, they go to the smoke, from smoke to night, from night to the dark half of the moon, from the dark half of the moon to the six months when the sun goes to the south. But they do not reach the year.

4. 'From the months they go to the world of the fathers, from the world of the fathers to the ether, from the ether to the moon. That is Soma, the king. Here they are loved (eaten) by the Devas, yes, the

---

[249] Tasyâ upastha eva samid, yad upamantrayate sa dhûmo, yonir ar*k*ir, yad anta*h* karoti te 'ṅgârâ abhinandâ vishphuliṅgâ*h*.

[250] The doctrine of the five fires, and our being born in them, i.e. in heaven, rain, earth, man, and woman.

[251] Cf. *Kh*. Up. IV, 15, 5.

[252] Instead of mânava, human, or amânava, not human, the B*r*ih. Âr. reads mânasa, mental, or created by manas, mind.

Devas love (eat) them[253].

5. 'Having dwelt there, till their (good) works are consumed, they return again that way as they came[254], to the ether, from the ether to the air. Then the sacrificer, having become air, becomes smoke, having become smoke, he becomes mist,

6. 'Having become mist, he becomes a cloud, having become a cloud, he rains down. Then he is born as rice and corn, herbs and trees, sesamum. and beans. From thence the escape is beset with most difficulties. For whoever the persons may be that eat the food, and beget offspring, he henceforth becomes like unto them.

7. 'Those whose conduct has been good, will quickly attain some good birth, the birth of a Brâhma*n*a, or a Kshatriya, or a Vai*s*ya. But those whose conduct has been evil, will quickly attain an evil birth, the birth of a dog, or a hog, or a *Kand*âla.

8. 'On neither of these two ways those small creatures (flies, worms, &c.) are continually returning of whom it may be said, Live and die. Theirs is a third place.

'Therefore that world never becomes full[255] (cf. V, 3, 2).

---

[253] This passage has been translated, 'They are the food of the gods. The gods do eat it.' And this is indeed the literal meaning of the words. But bhag (to enjoy) and bhaksh (to eat) are often used by theosophical writers in India, in the more general sense of cherishing or loving, and anna in the sense of an object of desire, love, and protection. The commentators, however, as the use of bhaksh in this sense is exceptional, or as it has no support in the use of the ancients, warn us here against a possible misunderstanding. If those, they say, who have performed sacrifices enter at last into the essence of Soma, the moon, and are eaten by the Devas, by Indra, &c., what is the use of their good works? No, they reply, they are not really eaten. Food (anna) means only what is helpful and delightful; it is not meant that they are eaten by morsels, but that they form the delight of the Devas. Thus we hear it said that men, women, and cattle are food for kings. And if it is said that women are loved by men, they are, in being loved, themselves loving. Thus these men also, being loved by the Devas, are happy and rejoice with the Devas. Their body, in order to be able to rejoice in the moon, becomes of a watery substance, as it was said before, that the water, called the Sraddha libation, when offered in heaven, as in the fire of the altar, becomes Soma, the king (*Kh*. Up. V, 4, 1). That water becomes, after various changes, the body of those who have performed good works, and when a man is dead and his body burnt (*Kh*. Up. V, 9, 2), the water rises from the body upwards with the smoke, and carries him to the moon, where, in that body, he enjoys the fruits of his good works, as long as they last. When they are consumed, like the oil in a lamp, he has to return to a new round of existences.

[254] But only to a certain point.

[255] In this manner all the five questions have been answered. First, why in the fifth oblation water is called man; secondly, to what place men go after death, some by the path of the Devas, others by the path of the fathers, others again by neither of these paths; thirdly, how they return, some returning to Brahman, others returning to the earth; fourthly, where the paths of the Devas and the fathers diverge, viz. when from the half-year the path of the Devas goes on to the year, while that of the fathers branches off to the world of the fathers; fifthly, why that world, the other world, does never become full, viz. because men either go on to Brahman or return again to this world.

Many questions are raised among Indian philosophers on the exact meaning of certain passages occurring in the preceding paragraphs. First, as to who is admitted to the

'Hence let a man take care to himself[256]! And thus it is said in the following *S*loka[257]:—

9. 'A man who steals gold, who drinks spirits, who dishonours his Guru's bed, who kills a Brahman, these four fall, and as a fifth he who associates with them.

---

path of the Devas? Householders, who know the secret doctrine of the five fires or the five libations of the Agnihotra, as described above, while other householders, who only perform the ordinary sacrifices, without a knowledge of their secret meaning, go by the path of the fathers. Secondly, those who have retired to the forest, and whose worship there consists in faith and austerities, i.e. Vânaprasthas and Parivrâgakas, before they arrive at a knowledge of the true Brahman. The question then arises, whether religious students also enter the path of the Devas? This is affirmed, because Purâ*n*as and Sm*ri*tis assert it, or because our text, if properly understood, does not exclude it. Those, on the contrary, who know not only a conditioned, but the highest unconditioned Brahman, do not proceed on the path of the Devas, but obtain Brahman immediately.

Again, there is much difference of opinion whether, after a man has been in the moon, consuming his works, he can be born again. Birth is the result of former works, and if former works are altogether consumed, there can be no new birth. This, however, is shown to be an erroneous view, because, besides the good sacrificial works, the fruits of which are consumed in the moon, there are other works which have to be enjoyed or expiated, as the case may be, in a new existence.

The great difficulty or danger in the round of transmigration arises when the rain has fructified the earth, and passes into herbs and trees, rice, corn, and beans. For, first of all, some of the rain does not fructify at once, but falls into rivers and into the sea, to be swallowed up by fishes and sea monsters. Then, only after these have been dissolved in the sea, and after the sea water has been attracted by the clouds, the rain falls down again, it may be on desert or stony land. Here it may be swallowed by snakes or deer, and these may be swallowed by other animals, so that the round of existence seems endless. Nor is this all. Some rain may dry up, or be absorbed by bodies that cannot be eaten. Then, if the rain is absorbed by rice, corn, &c., and this be eaten, it may be eaten by children or by men who have renounced marriage, and thus again lose the chance of a new birth.. Lastly, there is the danger arising from the nature of the being; in whom the food, such as rice and corn, becomes a new seed, and likewise from the nature of the mother. All these chances have to be met before a new birth as a Brâhma*n*a, Kshatriya, or Vai*s*ya can be secured.

Another curious distinction is here made by *S*ankara in his commentary. There are some, he says, who assume the form of rice, corn, &c., not in their descent from a higher world, as described in the Upanishad, but as a definite punishment for certain evil deeds they have committed. These remain in that state till the results of their evil deeds are over, and assume then a new body, according to their work, like caterpillars. With them there is also a consciousness of these states, and the acts which caused them to assume this or that body, leave impressions behind, like dreams. This is not the case with those who in their descent from the moon, pass, as we saw, through an existence as rice, corn, &c. They have no consciousness of such existences, at least not in their descent. In their ascent to the moon, they have consciousness, as a man who climbs up a tree knows what he is about. But in their descent, that consciousness is gone, as it is when a man falls down from a tree. Otherwise a man, who by his good works had deserved rewards in the moon, would, while corn is being ground, suffer tortures, as if he were in hell, and the very object of good works, as taught by the Veda, would be defeated. As we see that a man struck by a hammer can be carried away unconscious, so it is in the descent of souls, till they are born again as men, and gain a new start for the attainment of the Highest Brahman.

[256] Let him despise it. Comm.

[257] Evidently an old Trish*t*ubh verse, but irregular in the third line. See Manu XI, 54.

10. 'But he who thus knows the five fires is not defiled by sin even though he associates with them. He who knows this, is pure, clean, and obtains the world of the blessed, yea, he obtains the world of the blessed.'

ELEVENTH KHA*N*DA[258].

1. Prâ*k*îna*s*âla Aupamanyava, Satyayagña Paulushi, Indradyumna Bhâllaveya, *G*ana *S*ârkarâkshya, and Bu*d*ila Â*s*vatara*s*vi, these five great householders and great theologians came once together and held a discussion as to What is our Self, and what is Brahman[259].

2. They reflected and said: 'Sirs, there is that Uddâlaka Âru*n*i, who knows at present that Self, called Vai*s*vânara. Well, let us go to him.' They went to him.

3. But he reflected: 'Those great householders and great theologians will examine me, and I shall not be able to tell them all; therefore I shall recommend another teacher to them.'

4. He said to them: 'Sirs, A*s*vapati Kaikeya knows at present that Self, called Vai*s*vânara. Well, let us go to him.' They went to him.

5. When they arrived (the king) ordered proper presents to be made separately to each of them. And rising the next morning[260] he said: 'In my kingdom there is no thief, no miser, no drunkard, no man without an altar in his house, no ignorant person, no adulterer, much less an adulteress. I[261] am going to perform a sacrifice, Sirs, and as much wealth as I give to each *Ri*tvig priest, I shall give to you, Sirs. Please to stay here.'

6. They replied: 'Every man ought to say for what purpose he comes. You know at present that Vai*s*vânara Self, tell us that.'

7. He said: 'To-morrow I shall give you an answer.' Therefore on the next morning they approached him, carrying fuel in their hands (like students), and he, without first demanding any preparatory rites[262], said to them:

---

[258] The same story is found in the *S*atapatha-brâhma*n*a X, 6, 1,1.

[259] Âtman and Brâhman are to be taken as predicate and subject.

[260] The commentator explains that the king, seeing that they would not accept his presents, and thinking that they did not consider him worthy of bestowing presents on them, made these remarks.

[261] When they still refused his presents, he thought the presents he had offered were too small, and therefore invited them to a sacrifice.

[262] He was satisfied with the humility of the Brahmans, who, being Brahmans, came to him, who was not a Brahman, as pupils. Generally a pupil has first to pass through several initiatory rites before he is admitted to the benefit of his master's teaching.

TWELFTH KHA*ND*A.

1. 'Aupamanyava, whom do you meditate on as the Self?' He replied: 'Heaven only, venerable king.' He said: 'The Self which you meditate on is the Vai*s*vânara Self, called Sutegas (having good light). Therefore every kind of Soma libation is seen in your house[263].

2. 'You eat food, and see your desire (a son, &c.), and whoever thus meditates on that Vai*s*vânara Self, eats food, sees his desire, and has Vedic glory (arising from study and sacrifice) in his house. That, however, is but the head of the Self, and thus your head would have fallen (in a discussion), if you had not come to me.'

THIRTEENTH KHA*ND*A.

1. Then he said to Satyayagña Paulushi: 'O Prâ*k*înayogya, whom do you meditate on as the Self?' He replied: 'The sun only, venerable king.' He said: 'The Self which you meditate on is the Vai*s*vânara Self, called Vi*s*varûpa (multiform). Therefore much and manifold wealth is seen in your house.

2. 'There is a car with mules, full of slaves and jewels. You eat food and see your desire, and whoever thus meditates on that Vai*s*vânara Self, eats food and sees his desire, and has Vedic glory in his house.

'That, however, is but the eye of the Self, and you would have become blind, if you had not come to me.'

FOURTEENTH KHA*ND*A.

1. Then he said to Indradyumna Bhâllaveya: 'O Vaiyâghrapadya, whom do you meditate on as the Self?' He replied: 'Air only, venerable king.' He said: 'The Self which you meditate on is the Vai*s*vânara Self, called P*ri*thagvartman (having various courses). Therefore offerings come to you in various ways, and rows of cars follow you in various ways.

2. 'You eat food and see your desire, and whoever thus meditates on that Vai*s*vânara Self, eats food and sees his desire, and has Vedic glory in his house.

'That, however, is but the breath of the Self, and your breath would have left you, if you had not come to me.'

---

[263] Soma is said to be suta in the Ekâha, prasuta in the Ahîna, âsuta in the Sattra-sacrifices.

FIFTEENTH KHA*N*DA.

1. Then he said to *G*ana *S*ârkarâkshya: 'Whom do you meditate on as the Self?' He replied: 'Ether only, venerable king.' He said: 'The Self which you meditate on is the Vai*s*vânara Self, called Bahula (full). Therefore you are full of offspring and wealth.

2. 'You eat food and see your desire, and whoever thus meditates on that Vai*s*vânara Self, eats food and sees his desire, and has Vedic glory in his house.

'That, however, is but the trunk of the Self, and your trunk would have perished, if you had not come to me.'

SIXTEENTH KHA*N*DA.

1. Then he said to Bu*d*ila Â*s*vatarâ*s*vi, 'O Vaiyâghrapadya, whom do you meditate on as the Self?' He replied: 'Water only, venerable king.' He said; 'The Self which you meditate on is the Vai*s*vânara Self, called Rayi (wealth). Therefore are you wealthy and flourishing.

2. 'You eat food and see your desire, and whoever thus meditates on that Vai*s*vânara Self, eats food and sees his desire, and has Vedic glory in his house.

'That, however, is but the bladder of the Self, and your bladder would have burst, if you had not come to me.'

SEVENTEENTH KHA*N*DA.

1. Then he said to Auddâlaka Âruni: 'O Gautama, whom do you meditate on as the Self?' He replied: 'The earth only, venerable king.' He said: 'The Self which you meditate on is the Vai*s*vânara Self, called Pratish*th*â (firm rest). Therefore you stand firm with offspring and cattle.

2. 'You eat food and see your desire, and whoever thus meditates on that Vai*s*vânara Self, eats food and sees his desire, and has Vedic glory in his house.

'That, however, are but the feet of the Self, and your feet would have given way, if you had not come to me.'

EIGHTEENTH KHA*ND*A.

1. Then he said to them all: 'You eat your food, knowing that Vai*s*vânara Self as if it were many. But he who worships the Vai*s*vânara Self as a span long, and as[264] identical with himself, he eats food in all worlds, in all beings, in all Selfs.

2. 'Of that Vai*s*vânara Self the head is Sutegas (having good light), the eye Vi*s*varûpa (multiform), the breath P*ri*thagvartman (having various courses), the trunk Bahula (full), the bladder Rayi (wealth), the feet the earth, the chest the altar, the hairs the grass on the altar, the heart the Gârhapatya fire, the mind the Anvâhârya fire, the mouth the Âhavanîya fire.

NINETEENTH KHA*ND*A.

1. 'Therefore[265] the first food which a man may take, is in the place of Homa. And he who offers that first oblation, should offer it to Prâ*n*a (up-breathing), saying Svâhâ. Then Prâ*n*a (up-breathing) is satisfied,

2. 'If Prâ*n*a is satisfied, the eye is satisfied, if the eye is satisfied, the sun is satisfied, if the sun is satisfied, heaven is satisfied, if heaven is satisfied, whatever is under heaven and under the sun is satisfied.. And through their satisfaction he (the sacrificer or eater) himself is satisfied with offspring, cattle, health, brightness, and Vedic splendour.

TWENTIETH KHA*ND*A.

1. 'And he who offers the second oblation, should offer it to Vyâna (back-breathing), saying Svâhâ. Then Vyâna is satisfied,

2. 'If Vyâna is satisfied, the ear is satisfied, if the ear is satisfied, the moon is satisfied, if the moon is satisfied, the quarters are satisfied, if the quarters are satisfied, whatever is under the quarters and under the moon is satisfied. And through their *s*atisfaction he (the sacrificer or

---

[264] The two words prâde*s*amâtra and abhivimâna are doubtful. The commentator explains the first in different ways, which are all more or less fanciful. He is measured or known (mâtra) as Self, by means of heaven as his head and the earth as his feet, these being the prâde*s*as; or, in the mouth and the rest, which are instruments, he is known as without action himself; or, he has the length from heaven to earth, heaven and earth being called prâde*s*a, because they are taught. The interpretation, supported by the *G*âbâla*s*ruti, that prâde*s*a is the measure from the forehead to the chin, he rejects. Abhivimâna is taken in the same meaning as abhimâna in the Vedânta, seeing everything in oneself. Vai*s*vânara is taken as the real Self of all beings, and, in the end, of all Selfs, and as thus to be known and worshipped.

[265] The object now is to show that to him who knows the Vai*s*vânara Self, the act of feeding himself is like feeding Vai*s*vânara, and that feeding Vai*s*vânara is the true Agnihotra.

eater) himself is satisfied with offspring, cattle, health, brightness, and Vedic splendour.

TWENTY-FIRST KHA*ND*A.

1. 'And he who offers the third oblation, should offer it to Apâna (down-breathing), saying Svâhâ. Then Apâna is satisfied. If Apâna is satisfied, the tongue is satisfied, if the tongue is satisfied, Agni (fire) is satisfied, if Agni is satisfied, the earth is satisfied, if the earth is satisfied, whatever is under the earth and under fire is satisfied.

2. 'And through their satisfaction he (the sacrificer or eater) himself is satisfied with offspring, cattle, health, brightness, and Vedic splendour.

TWENTY-SECOND KHA*ND*A.

1. 'And he who offers the fourth oblation, should offer it to Samâna (on-breathing), saying Svâhâ. Then Samâna is satisfied,

2. 'If Samâna is satisfied, the mind is satisfied, if the mind is satisfied, Parganya (god of rain) is satisfied, if Parganya is satisfied, lightning is satisfied, if lightning is satisfied, whatever is under Parganya and under lightning is satisfied. And through their satisfaction he (the sacrificer or cater) himself is satisfied with offspring, cattle, health, brightness, and Vedic splendour.

TWENTY-THIRD KHA*ND*A.

1. 'And he who offers the fifth oblation, should offer it to Udâna (out-breathing), saying Svâhâ. Then Udâna is satisfied,

2. 'If Udâna is satisfied, Vâyu (air) is satisfied, if Vâyu is satisfied, ether is satisfied, if ether is satisfied, whatever is under Vâyu, and under the ether is satisfied. And through their satisfaction he (the sacrificer or eater) himself is satisfied with offspring, cattle, health, brightness, and Vedic splendour.

TWENTY-FOURTH KHA*ND*A.

1. 'If, without knowing this, one offers an Agnihotra, it would be as if a man were to remove the live coals and pour his libation on dead ashes.

2. 'But he who offers this Agnihotra with a full knowledge of its true purport, he offers it (i.e. he eats food)[266] in all worlds, in all beings, in all Selfs.

---

[266] Cf. V, 18, 1.

3. 'As the soft fibres of the Ishîkâ reed, when thrown into the fire, are burnt, thus all his sins are burnt whoever offers this Agnihotra with a full knowledge of its true purport.

4. 'Even if he gives what is left of his food to a *Kand*âla, it would be offered in his (the *Kand*âla's) Vai*s*vânara Self. And so it is said in this *S*loka:—

'As hungry children here on earth sit (expectantly) round their mother, so do all beings sit round the Agnihotra, yea, round the Agnihotra.'

SIXTH PRAPÂ*TH*AKA.

FIRST KHA*ND*A.

1. Hari*h*, Om. There lived once *S*vetaketu Âru*n*eya (the grandson of Aru*n*a). To him his father (Uddâlaka, the son of Aru*n*a) said: '*S*vetaketu, go to school; for there is none belonging to our race, darling, who, not having studied (the Veda), is, as it were, a Brâhma*n*a by birth only.'

2. Having begun his apprenticeship (with a teacher) when he was twelve years of age[267], *S*vetaketu returned to his father, when he was twenty-four, having then studied all the Vedas,—conceited, considering himself well-read, and stern.

3. His father said to him: '*S*vetaketu, as you are so conceited, considering yourself so well-read, and so stern, my dear, have you ever asked for that instruction by which we hear what cannot be heard, by which we perceive what cannot be perceived, by which we know what cannot be known?'

4. 'What is that instruction, Sir?' he asked.

The father replied: 'My dear, as by one clod of clay all that is made of clay is known, the difference[268] being only a name, arising from speech, but the truth being that all is clay;

5. 'And as, my dear, by one nugget of gold[269] all that is made of gold is known, the difference being only a name, arising from speech, but the truth being that all is gold?

6. 'And as, my dear, by one pair of nail-scissors all that is made of iron (kârsh*n*âyasam) is known, the difference being only a name, arising from speech, but the truth being that all is iron,—thus, my dear, is that instruction.'

7. The son said: 'Surely those venerable men (my teachers) did not

---

[267] This was rather late, for the son of a Brahman might have begun his studies when he was seven years old. Âpastamba-sûtras I, 1, 18. Twelve years was considered the right time for mastering one of the Vedas.

[268] Vikâra, difference, variety, change, by form and name, development, cf. VI, 3, 3.

[269] The commentator takes lohamani here as suvar*n*apin*d*a.

know that. For if they had known it, why should they not have told it me? Do you, Sir, therefore tell me that.' 'Be it so,' said the father.

SECOND KHA*ND*A[270]

1. 'In the beginning,' my dear, 'there was that only which is (τὸ ὄν), one only, without a second. Others say, in the beginning there was that only which is not (τὸ μὴ ὄν), one only, without a second; and from that which is not, that which is was born.

2. 'But how could it be thus, my dear?' the father continued. 'How could that which is, be born of that which is not? No, my dear, only that which is, was in the beginning, one only, without a second.

3. 'It thought[271], may I be many, may I grow forth. It sent forth fire[272].

'That fire[273] thought, may I be many, may I grow forth. It sent forth water[274].

'And therefore whenever anybody anywhere is hot and perspires, water is produced on him from fire alone.

4. 'Water thought, may I be many, may I grow forth. It sent forth earth[275] (food).

'Therefore whenever it rains anywhere, most food is then produced. From water alone is eatable food produced.

THIRD KHA*ND*A.

1. 'Of all living things there are indeed three origins only[276], that which springs from an egg (oviparous), that which springs from a living being (viviparous), and that which springs from a germ.

2. 'That Being[277] (i.e. that which had produced fire, water, and

---

[270] Cf. Taitt. Up. II, 6.

[271] Literally, it saw. This verb is explained as showing that the Sat is conscious, not unconscious (bewusst, nicht unbewusst).

[272] In other Upanishads the Sat produces first âkâsa, ether, then vâyu, air, and then only tegas, fire. Fire is a better rendering for tegas than light or heat. See Jacobi, Zeitschrift der Deutschen Morgenl. Gesellschaft, XXIX, p. 242. The difficulties, however, of accurately translating tegas are not removed by rendering if by fire, as may be seen immediately afterward in VI, 4, 1, where tegas is said to supply the red colour of agni, the burning fire, not the god of fire. See also VI, 8, 6. In later philosophical treatises the meaning of tegas is more carefully determined than in the Upanishads.

[273] Really the Sat, in the form of fire. Fire is whatever burns, cooks, shines, and is red.

[274] By water is meant all that is fluid, and bright in colour.

[275] By anna, food, is here meant the earth, and all that is heavy, firm, dark in colour.

[276] In the Ait. Up. four are mentioned, a*nd*aga, here â*nd*aga, gâruga (i.e. garâyuga), here gîvaga, svedaga, and udbhigga, svedaga, born from heat, being additional. Cf. Atharva-veda I, 12, 1.

[277] The text has devatâ, deity; here used in a very general sense. The Sat, though it has produced fire, water, and earth, has not yet obtained its wish of becoming many.

earth) thought, let me now enter those three beings[277] (fire, water, earth) with this living Self (gîva âtmâ)[278], and let me then reveal (develop) names and forms.

3. 'Then that Being having said, Let me make each of these three tripartite (so that fire, water, and earth should each have itself for its principal ingredient, besides an admixture of the other two) entered into those three beings (devatâ) with this living self only, and revealed names and forms.

4. 'He made each of these tripartite; and how these three beings become each of them tripartite, that learn from me now, my friend!

FOURTH KHA*ND*A.

1. 'The red colour of burning fire (agni) is the colour of fire, the white colour of fire is the colour of water, the black colour of fire the colour of earth. Thus vanishes what we call fire, as a mere variety, being a name, arising from speech. What is true (satya) are the three colours (or forms).

2. 'The red colour of the sun (âditya) is the colour of fire, the white of water, the black of earth. Thus vanishes what we call the sun, as a mere variety, being a name, arising from speech. What is true are the three colours.

3. 'The red colour of the moon is the colour of fire, the white of water, the black of earth. Thus vanishes what we call the moon, as a mere variety, being a name, arising from speech. What is true are the three colours.

4. 'The red colour of the lightning is the colour of fire, the white of water, the black of earth. Thus vanishes what we call the lightning, as a mere variety, being a name, arising from speech. What is true are the three colours.

5. 'Great householders and great theologians of olden times who knew this, have declared the same, saying, "No one can henceforth mention to us anything which we have not heard, perceived, or known[279]." Out of these (three colours or forms) they knew all.

6. 'Whatever they thought looked red, they knew was the colour of fire. Whatever they thought looked white, they knew was the colour of water. Whatever they thought looked black, they knew was the colour of earth.

7. 'Whatever they thought was altogether unknown, they knew was some combination of those three beings (devatâ).

---

[278] This living self is only a shadow, as it were, of the Highest Self; and as the sun, reflected in the water, does not suffer from the movement of the water, the real Self does not suffer pleasure or pain on earth, but the living self only.

[279] This reminds one of the Aristotelian διὰ γὰρ ταῦτα καὶ ἐκ τούτων τἄλλα γνωρίζεται, ἀλλ' οὐ ταῦτα διὰ τῶν ὑποκειμένων.

'Now learn from me, my friend, how those three beings, when they reach man, become each of them tripartite.

FIFTH KHA*ND*A.

1. 'The earth (food) when eaten becomes threefold; its grossest portion becomes feces, its middle portion flesh, its subtilest portion mind.

2. 'Water when drunk becomes threefold; its grossest portion becomes water, its middle portion blood, its subtilest portion breath.

3. 'Fire (i.e. in oil, butter, &c.) when eaten becomes threefold; its grossest portion becomes bone, its middle portion marrow, its subtilest portion speech[280].

4. 'For truly, my child, mind comes of earth, breath of water, speech of fire.'

'Please, Sir, inform me still more,' said the son.

'Be it so, my child,' the father replied.

SIXTH KHA*ND*A.

1. 'That which is the subtile portion of curds, when churned, rises upwards, and becomes butter.

2. 'In the same manner, my child, the subtile portion of earth (food), when eaten, rises upwards, and becomes mind.

3. 'That which is the subtile portion of water, when drunk, rises upwards, and becomes breath.

4. 'That which is the subtile portion of fire, when consumed, rises upwards, and becomes speech.

5. 'For mind, my child, comes of earth, breath of water, speech of fire.'

'Please, Sir, inform me still more,' said the son.

'Be it so, my child,' the father replied.

SEVENTH KHA*ND*A.

1. 'Man (purusha), my son, consists of sixteen parts. Abstain from food for fifteen days, but drink as much water as you like, for breath comes from water, and will not be cut off, if you drink water.'

2. *S*vetaketu abstained from food for fifteen days. Then he came to his father and said: 'What shall I say?' The father said: 'Repeat the *Rik*, Yagus, and Sâman verses.' He replied: 'They do not occur to me, Sir.'

---

[280] Food, water, and fire are each to be taken as tripartite; hence animals which live on one of the three elements only, still share in some measure the qualities of the other elements also.

3. The father said to him: 'As of a great lighted fire one coal only of the size of a firefly may be left, which would not burn much more than this (i.e. very little), thus, my dear son, one part only of the sixteen parts (of you) is left, and therefore with that one part you do not remember the Vedas. Go and eat!

4. 'Then wilt thou understand me.' Then *S*vetaketu. ate, and afterwards approached his father. And whatever his father asked him, he knew it all by heart. Then his father said to him:

5. 'As of a great lighted fire one coal of the size of a firefly, if left, may be made to blaze up again by putting grass upon it, and will thus burn more than this,

6. 'Thus, my dear son, there was one part of the sixteen parts left to you, and that, lighted up with food, burnt up, and by it you remember now the Vedas.' After that, he understood what his father meant when he said: 'Mind, my son, comes from food, breath from water, speech from fire.' He understood what he said, yea, he understood it[281].

EIGHTH KHA*ND*A.

1. Uddâlaka Âru*n*i said to his son *S*vetaketu: 'Learn from me the true nature of sleep (svapna). When a man sleeps here, then, my dear son, he becomes united with the True[282], he is gone to his own (Self). Therefore they say, svapiti, he sleeps, because he is gone (apîta) to his own (sva)[283].

2. 'As a bird when tied by a string flies first in every direction, and finding no rest anywhere, settles down at last on the very place where it is fastened, exactly in the same manner, my son, that mind (the gîva, or living Self in the mind, see VI, 3, 2), after flying in every direction, and finding no rest anywhere, settles down on breath[284]; for indeed, my son, mind is fastened to breath.

3. 'Learn from me, my son, what are hunger and thirst. When a

---

[281] The repetition shows that the teaching of the Trivr*i*kara*n*a, the tripartite nature of things, is ended.

[282] The deep sushupta sleep is meant, in which personal consciousness is lost, and the self for a time absorbed in the Highest Self. Sleep is produced by fatigue. Speech, mind, and the senses rest, breath only remains awake, and the gîva, the living soul, in order to recover from his fatigue, returns for a while to his true Self (âtmâ). The Sat must be taken as a substance, nay, as the highest substance or subject, the Brahman. The whole purpose of the Upanishad is obscured if we translate sat or satyam by truth, instead of the True, the true one,τὸ ὄντως ὄν.

[283] This is one of the many recognised plays on words in the Upanishads and the Vedânta philosophy. Svapiti, he sleeps, stands for sva (his own), i.e. the self, and apîta, gone to.

[284] The commentator takes prâ*n*a here in the sense of Sat, which it often has elsewhere. If so, this illustration would have the same object as the preceding one. If we took prâ*n*a in the sense of breath, breath being the result of water, this paragraph might be taken to explain the resignation of the living Self to its bondage to breath, while on earth.

man is thus said to be hungry, water is carrying away (digests) what has been eaten by him. Therefore as they speak of a cow-leader (go-nâya), a horse-leader (a*s*va-nâya), a man-leader (purusha-nâya), so they call water (which digests food and causes hunger) food-leader (a*s*a-nâya). Thus (by food digested &c.), my son, know this offshoot (the body) to be brought forth, for this (body) could not be without a root (cause).

4. 'And where could its root be except in food (earth)[285]? And in the same manner, my son, as food (earth) too is an offshoot, seek after its root, viz. water. And as water too is an offshoot, seek after its root, viz. fire. And as fire too is an offshoot, seek after its root, viz. the True. Yes, all these creatures, my son, have their root in the True, they dwell in the True, they rest in the True.

5. 'When a man is thus said to be thirsty, fire carries away what has been drunk by him. Therefore as they speak of a cow-leader (go-nâya), of a horse-leader (a*s*va-nâya), of a man-leader (purusha-nâya), so they call fire udanyâ, thirst, i.e. water-leader. Thus (by water digested &c.), my son, know this offshoot (the body) to be brought forth: this (body) could not be without a root (cause).

6. 'And where could its root be except in water? As water is an offshoot, seek after its root, viz. fire. As fire is an offshoot, seek after its root, viz. the True. Yes, all these creatures, O son, have their root in the True, they dwell in the True, they rest in the True.

'And how these three beings (devatâ), fire, water, earth, O son, when they reach man, become each of them tripartite, has been said before (VI, 4, 7). When a man departs from hence, his speech[286] is merged in his mind, his mind in his breath, his breath in heat (fire), heat in the Highest Being.

7. 'Now that which is that subtile essence (the root of all), in it all that exists has its self. It is the True. It is the Self, and thou, O *S*vetaketu, art it.'

---

[285] That food is the root of the body is shown by the commentator in the following way: Food when softened by water and digested becomes a fluid, blood (*s*onita). From it comes flesh, from flesh fat, from fat bones, from bones marrow, from marrow seed. Food eaten by a woman becomes equally blood (lohita), and from seed and blood combined the new body is produced. We must always have before us the genealogical table:—

Sat, τὸ ὄν.
|
Te*g*as (fire)=Vâ*k* (speech).
|
Ap (water)=Prâ*n*a (breath).
|
Anna (earth)=Manas (mind).

[286] If a man dies, the first thing which his friends say is, He speaks no more. Then, he understands no more. Then, he moves no more. Then, he is cold.

'Please, Sir, inform me still more,' said the son.

'Be it so, my child,' the father replied.

NINTH KHA*ND*A.

1. 'As the bees[287], my son, make honey by collecting the juices of distant trees, and reduce the juice into one form,

2. 'And as these juices have no discrimination, so that they might say, I am the juice of this tree or that, in the same manner, my son, all these creatures, when they have become merged in the True (either in deep sleep or in death), know not that they are merged in the True.

3. 'Whatever these creatures are here, whether a lion, or a wolf, or a boar, or a worm, or a midge, or a gnat, or a musquito, that they become again and again.

4. 'Now that which is that subtile essence, in it all that exists has its self. It is the True. It is the Self, and thou, O *S*vetaketu, art it.'

'Please, Sir, inform me still more,' said the son.

'Be it so, my child,' the father replied.

TENTH KHA*ND*A[288]

1. 'These rivers, my son, run, the eastern (like the Gangâ) toward the east, the western (like the Sindhu) toward the west. They go from sea to sea (i.e. the clouds lift up the water from the sea to the sky, and send it back as rain to the sea). They become indeed sea. And as those rivers, when they are in the sea, do not know, I am this or that river,

2. 'In the same manner, my son, all these creatures, when they have come back from the True, know not that they have come back from the True. Whatever these creatures are here, whether a lion, or a wolf, or a boar, or a worm, or a midge, or a gnat, or a musquito, that they become again and again.

3. 'That which is that subtile essence, in it all that exists has its self. It is the True. It is the Self, and thou, O *S*vetaketu, art it.'

'Please, Sir, inform me still more,' said the son.

'Be it so, my child,' the father replied.

---

[287] At the beginning of each chapter the commentator supplies the question which the son is supposed to have asked his father. The first is: All creatures falling every day into deep sleep (sushupti) obtain thereby the Sat, the true being. How is it then that they do not know that they obtain the Sat every day?

[288] The next question which the son is supposed to have asked is: If a man who has slept in his own house, rises and goes to another village, he. knows that he has come from his own house. Why then do people not know that they have come from the Sat?

ELEVENTH KHA*ND*A[289].

1. 'If some one were to strike at the root of this large tree here, it would bleed, but live. If he were to strike at its stem, it would bleed, but live. If he were to strike at its top, it would bleed, but live. Pervaded by the living Self that tree stands firm, drinking in its nourishment and rejoicing;

2. 'But if the life (the living Self) leaves one of its branches, that branch withers; if it leaves a second, that branch withers; if it leaves a third, that branch withers. If it leaves the whole tree, the whole tree withers[290]. In exactly the same manner, my son, know this.' Thus he spoke:

3. 'This (body) indeed withers and dies when the living Self has left it; the living Self dies not.

'That which is that subtile essence, in it all that exists has its self. It is the True. It is the Self, and thou, *S*vetaketu, art it.'

'Please, Sir, inform me still more,' said the son.

'Be it so, my child,' the father replied.

TWELFTH KHA*ND*A[291].

1. 'Fetch me from thence a fruit of the Nyagrodha tree.'

'Here is one, Sir.'

'Break it.'

---

[289] The next question is: Waves, foam, and bubbles arise from the water, and. when they merge again in the water, they are gone, How is it that living beings, when in sleep or death they are merged again in the Sat, are not destroyed?

[290] The commentator remarks that according to the Veda, trees are conscious, while Buddhists and followers of Ka*n*âda hold them to be unconscious. They live, because one sees how their sap runs and how it dries up, just as one sees the sap in a living body, which, as we saw, was produced by food and water. Therefore the simile holds good. The life, or, more correctly, the liver, the living Self, pervades the tree, as it pervades man, when it has entered the organism which produces breath, mind, and speech. If any accident happens to a branch, the living Self draws himself away from that branch, and then the branch withers. The sap which caused the living Self to remain, goes, and the living Self goes away with it. The same applies to the whole tree. The tree dies when the living Self leaves it, but the living Self does not die; it only leaves an abode which it had before occupied. Some other illustrations, to show that the living Self remains, are added by the commentator: First, with regard to the living Self being the same when it awakes from deep sleep (sushupti), he remarks that we remember quite well that we have left something unfinished before we fell asleep. And then with regard to the living Self being the same when it awakes from death to a new life, he shows that creatures, as soon as they are born take the breast, and exhibit terror, which can only be explained, as he supposes, by their possessing a recollection of a former state of existence.

[291] The question which the son is supposed to have asked is How can this universe which has the form and name of earth &c. be produced from the Sat which is subtile, and has neither form nor name?

'It is broken, Sir.'

'What do you see there?'

'These seeds, almost infinitesimal.'

'Break one of them.'

'It is broken, Sir.'

'What do you see there?'

'Not anything, Sir.'

2. The father said: 'My son, that subtile essence which you do not perceive there, of that very essence this great Nyagrodha tree exists.

3. 'Believe it, my son. That which is the subtile essence, in it all that exists has its self. It is the True. It is the Self, and thou, O *S*vetaketu, art it.'

'Please, Sir, inform me still more,' said the son.

'Be it so, my child,' the father replied.

THIRTEENTH KHA*ND*A[292].

1. 'Place this salt in water, and then wait on me in the morning.'

The son did as he was commanded.

The father said to him: 'Bring me the salt, which you placed in the water last night.'

The son having looked for it, found it not, for, of course, it was melted.

2. The father said: 'Taste it from the surface of the water. How is it?'

The son replied: 'It is salt.'

'Taste it from the middle. How is it?'

The son replied: 'It is salt.'

'Taste it from the bottom. How is it?'

The son replied 'It is salt.'

The father said Throw it away[293] and then wait on me.'

He did so; but salt exists for ever.

Then the father said: 'Here also, in this body, forsooth, you do not perceive the True (Sat), my son; but there indeed it is.

3. 'That which is the subtile essence, in it all that exists has its self. It is the True. It is the Self, and thou, O *S*vetaketu, art it.'

'Please, Sir, inform me still more,' said the son.

'Be it so, my child,' the father replied.

---

[292] The question here is supposed to have been: If the Sat is the root of all that exists, why is it not perceived?

[293] Read abhiprâsya, which is evidently intended by the commentary: abhiprâsya parityagya. See B. R. Sanskrit Dictionary, s. v.

FOURTEENTH KHA*ND*A[294].

1. 'As one might lead a person with his eyes covered away from the Gandhâras[295], and leave him then in a place where there are no human beings; and as that person would turn towards the east, or the north, or the west, and shout, "I have been brought here with my eyes covered, I have been left here with my eyes covered,"

2. 'And as thereupon some one might loose his bandage and say to him, "Go in that direction, it is Gandhâra, go in that direction;" and as thereupon, having been informed and being able to judge for himself, he would by asking his way from village to village arrive at last at Gandhâra,—in exactly the same manner does a man, who meets with a teacher to inform him, obtain the true knowledge[296]. For him there is only delay so long as he is not delivered (from the body); then he will be perfect[297].

---

[294] The question here asked is: The salt, though no longer perceptible by means of sight or touch, could be discovered by taste. Then how can the Sat be discovered, although it is imperceptible by all the senses?

[295] The Gandhâras, but rarely mentioned in the Rig-veda and the Ait. Brâhma*n*a, have left their name in Κάνδαροι and Candahar. The fact of their name being evidently quite familiar to the author of the Upanishad might be used to prove either its antiquity or its Northern origin.

[296] Tedious as the commentator is in general, he is sometimes almost eloquent in bringing out all that is implied or supposed to be implied in the sacred text. He explains the last simile as follows: A man was carried away by robbers from his own country. After his eyes had been covered, he was taken to a forest full of terrors and dangers arising from tigers, robbers, &c. Not knowing where he was, and suffering from hunger and thirst, he began to cry, wishing to be delivered from his bonds. Then a man took pity on him and removed his bonds, and when he had returned to his home, he was happy. Next follows the application. Our real home is the True (Sat), the Self of the world. The forest into which we are driven is the body, made of the three elements, fire, water, earth, consisting of blood, flesh, bones, &c., and liable to cold, heat, and many other evils. The bands with which our eyes are covered are our desires for many things, real or unreal, such as wife children, cattle, &c., while the robbers by whom we are driven into the forest are our good and evil deeds. Then we cry and say: 'I am the son of so and so, these arc my relatives, I am happy, I am miserable, I am foolish, I am wise, I am just, I am born, I am dead, I am old, I am wretched, my son is dead, my fortune is gone, I am undone, how shall I live, where shall I go, who will save me?' These and hundreds and thousands of other evils are the bands which blind us. Then, owing to some supererogatory good works we may have done, we suddenly meet a man who knows the Self of Brahman, whose own bonds have been broken, who takes pity on us and shows us the way to see the evil which attaches to all that we love in this world. We then withdraw ourselves from all worldly pleasures. We learn that we are not mere creatures of the world, the son of so and so, &c., but that we are that which is the True (Sat). The bands of our ignorance and blindness are removed, and, like the man of Gandhâra, we arrive at our own home, the Self, or the True. Then we are happy and blessed.

[297] The last words are really—'for him there is only delay so long as I shall not be delivered; then I shall be perfect.' This requires some explanation. First of all, the change from the third to the first person, is best explained by assuming that at the point where all

3. 'That which is the subtile essence, in it all that exists has its self. It is the True. It is the Self, and thou, O *S*vetaketu, art it.'

'Please, Sir, inform me still more,' said the son.

'Be it so, my child,' the father replied.

FIFTEENTH KHA*ND*A[298].

1. 'If a man is ill, his relatives assemble round him and ask: "Dost thou know me? Dost thou know me?" Now as long as his speech is not merged in his mind, his mind in breath, breath in heat (fire), heat in the Highest Being (devatâ), he knows them.

2. 'But when his speech is merged in his mind, his mind in breath, breath in heat (fire), heat in the Highest Being, then he knows them not.

'That which is the subtile essence, in it all that exists has its self. It is the True. It is the Self, and thou, O *S*vetaketu, art it.'

'Please, Sir, inform me still more,' said the son.'

'Be it so, my child,' the father replied.

---

individuality vanishes, the father, as teacher, identifies himself with the person of whom he is speaking.

The delay (the *k*ira or kshepa) of which he speaks is the time which passes between the attainment of true knowledge and death, or freedom from the effects of actions performed before the attainment of knowledge. The actions which led to our present embodiment must be altogether consumed, before the body can perish, and then only are we free. As to any actions performed after the attainment of knowledge, they do not count; otherwise there would be a new embodiment, and the attainment of even true knowledge would never lead to final deliverance.

[298] The question supposed to be asked is: By what degrees a man, who has been properly instructed in the knowledge of Brahman, obtains the Sat, or returns to the True. To judge from the text both he who knows the True and he who does not, reach, when they die, the Sat, passing from speech to mind and breath and heat (fire). But whereas he who knows, remains in the Sat, they who do not know, return again to a new form of existence. It is important to observe that the commentator denies that he who knows, passes at his death through the artery of the head to the sun, and then to the Sat. He holds that with him who knows there is no further cause for delay, and that as soon as he dies, he returns to the Sat.

SIXTEENTH KHA*ND*A[299].

1. 'My child, they bring a man hither whom they have taken by the hand, and they say: "He has taken something, he has committed a theft." (When he denies, they say), "Heat the hatchet for him." If he committed the theft, then he makes himself to be what he is not. Then the false-minded, having covered his true Self by a falsehood, grasps the heated hatchet—he is burnt, and he is killed.

2. 'But if he did not commit the theft, then he makes himself to be what he is. Then the true-minded, having covered his true Self by truth, grasps the heated hatchet—he is not burnt, and he is delivered.

'As that (truthful) man is not burnt, thus has all that exists its self in That. It is the True. It is the Self, and thou, O *S*vetaketu, art it.' He understood what he said, yea, he understood it.

SEVENTH PRAPÂ*TH*AKA.

FIRST KHA*ND*A.

1. Nârada approached Sanatkumâra and said, 'Teach me, Sir!' Sanatkumâra said to him: 'Please to tell me what you know; afterward I shall tell you what is beyond.'

2. Nârada said: 'I know the Rig-veda, Sir, the Yagur-veda, the Sâma-veda, as the fourth the Âtharva*n*a, as the fifth the Itihâsa-purâ*n*a (the Bhârata); the Veda of the Vedas (grammar); the Pitrya (the rules for the sacrifices for the ancestors); the Râ*s*i (the science of numbers); the Daiva (the science of portents); the Nidhi (the science of time); the Vâkovâkya (logic); the Ekâyana (ethics); the Deva-vidyâ (etymology); the Brahma-vidyâ (pronunciation, *s*ikshâ, ceremonial, kalpa, prosody, *kh*andas); the Bhûta-vidyâ (the science of demons); the Kshatra-vidyâ (the science of weapons); the Nakshatra-vidyâ (astronomy); the Sarpa and Devagana-vidyâ (the science of serpents or poisons, and the sciences of the genii, such as the making of perfumes, dancing, singing,

---

[299] The next question is: Why does he who knows, on obtaining the Sat, not return, while he who does not know, though obtaining the Sat in death, returns? An illustration is chosen which is intended to show how knowledge produces a material effect. The belief in the efficacy of ordeals must have existed at the time, and appealing to that belief, the teacher says that the man who knows himself guilty, is really burnt by the heated iron, while the man who knows himself innocent, is not. In the same manner the man who knows his Self to be the true Self, on approaching after death the true Self, is not repelled and sent back into a new existence, while he who does not know, is sent back into a new round of births and deaths. The man who tells a falsehood about himself, loses his true Self and is burnt; the man who has a false conception about his Self, loses likewise his true Self, and not knowing the true Self, even though approaching it in death, he has to suffer till he acquires some day the true knowledge.

playing, and other fine arts)[300]. All this I know, Sir.

3. 'But, Sir, with all this I know the Mantras only, the sacred books, I do not know the Self. I have heard from men like you, that he who knows the Self overcomes grief. I am in grief. Do, Sir, help me over this grief of mine.'

Sanatkumâra, said to him: 'Whatever you have read, is only a name.

4. 'A name is the Rig-veda, Yagur-veda, Sâma-veda, and as the fourth the Âtharvana, as the fifth the Itihâsa-purâ*n*a, the Veda of the Vedas, the Pitrya, the Râ*s*i, the Daiva, the Nidhi, the Vâkovâkya, the Ekâyana, the Deva-vidyâ, the Brahma-vidyâ, the Bhûta-vidyâ, the Kshatra-vidyâ, the Nakshatra-vidyâ, the Sarpa and Devagana-vidyâ. All these are a name only. Meditate on the name.

5. 'He who meditates on the name as Brahman[301], is, as it were, lord and master as far as the name reaches-he who meditates on the name as Brahman.'

'Sir, is there something better than a name?'

'Yes, there is something better than a name.'

'Sir, tell it me.'

SECOND KHA*ND*A.

1. 'Speech is better than a name. Speech makes us understand the *R*ig-veda, Yagur-veda, Sâma-veda, and as the fourth the Âtharvana, as the fifth the Itihâsa-purâ*n*a, the Veda of the Vedas, the Pitrya, the Râ*s*i, the Daiva, the Nidhi, the Vâkovâkya, the Ekâyana, the Deva-vidyâ, the Brahma-vidyâ, the Kshatra-vidyâ, the Nakshatra-vidyâ, the Sarpa and Devagana-vidyâ; heaven, earth, air, ether, water, fire, gods, men, cattle, birds, herbs, trees, all beasts down to worms, midges, and ants; what is right and what is wrong; what is true and what is false; what is good and what is bad; what is pleasing and what is not pleasing. For if there were no speech, neither right nor wrong would be known[302], neither the true nor the false, neither the good nor the bad, neither the pleasant nor

---

[300] This passage, exhibiting the sacred literature as known at the time, should be compared with the B*r*ihadâra*n*yaka, II, 4, 10. The explanation of the old titles rests on the authority of *S*añkara, and he is not always consistent. See Colebrooke, Miscellaneous Essays, 1873, 11, p. 10.

[301] Why a man who knows the Veda should not know the Self, while in other places it is said that the Veda teaches the Self, is well illustrated by the commentary. If a royal procession approaches, he says, then, though. we do not see the king, because he is hidden by flags, parasols, &c., yet we say, there is the king. And if we ask who is the king, then again, though we cannot see him and point him out, we can say, at least, that he is different from all that is seen. The Self is hidden in the Veda as a king is hidden in a royal procession.

[302] The commentator explains vyagñâpayishyat by avigñâtam abhavishyat. Possibly h*r*idayagño stands for h*r*idayagñam.

the unpleasant. Speech makes us understand all this. Meditate on speech.

2. 'He who meditates on speech as Brahman, is, as it were, lord and master as far as speech reaches he who meditates on speech as Brahman.'

'Sir, is there something better than speech?'

'Yes, there is something better than speech.'

'Sir, tell it me.'

THIRD KHA*ND*A.

1. 'Mind (manas) is better than speech. For as the closed fist holds two amalaka or two kola or two aksha fruits, thus does mind hold speech and name. For if a man is minded in his mind to read the sacred hymns, he reads them; if he is minded in his mind to perform any actions, he performs them; if he is minded to wish for sons and cattle, he wishes for them; if he is minded to wish for this world and the other, he wishes for them. For mind is indeed the self[303], mind is the world, mind is Brahman. Meditate on the mind.

2. 'He who meditates on the mind as Brahman, is, as it were, lord and master as far as the mind reaches—he who meditates on the mind as Brahman.'

'Sir, is there something better than mind?'

'Yes, there is something better than mind.'

'Sir, tell it me.'

FOURTH KHA*ND*A.

1. 'Will[304] (saṅkalpa) is better than mind. For when a man wills, then he thinks in his mind, then he sends forth speech, and he sends it forth in a name. In a name the sacred hymns are contained, in the sacred hymns all sacrifices.

2. 'All these therefore (beginning with mind and ending in sacrifice) centre in will, consist of will, abide in will. Heaven and earth willed, air and ether willed, water and fire willed. Through the will of heaven and earth &c. rain wills; through the will of rain food wills; through the will of food the vital airs will; through the will of the vital airs the sacred hymns will; through the will of the sacred hymns the sacrifices will; through the will of the sacrifices the world (as their

---

[303] The commentator explains this by saying that, without the instrument of the mind, the Self cannot act or enjoy.

[304] Saṅkalpa is elsewhere defined as a modification of manas. The commentator says that, like thinking, it is an activity of the inner organ. It is difficult to find any English term exactly corresponding to saṅkalpa. Rajendralal Mitra translates it by will, but it implies not only will, but at the same time conception, determination, and desire.

reward) wills; through the will of the world everything wills[305]. This is will. Meditate on will.

3. 'He who meditates on will as Brahman, he, being himself safe, firm, and undistressed, obtains the safe, firm, and undistressed worlds which he has willed; he is, as it were, lord and master as far as will reaches—he who meditates on will as Brahman.'

'Sir, is there something better than will?'

'Yes, there is something better than will.'

'Sir, tell it me.'

FIFTH KHA*ND*A.

1. 'Consideration (*k*itta)[306] is better than will. For when a man considers, then he wills, then he thinks in his mind, then he sends forth speech, and he sends it forth in a name. In a name the sacred hymns are contained, in the sacred hymns all sacrifices.

2. 'All these (beginning with mind and ending in sacrifice) centre in consideration, consist of consideration, abide in consideration. Therefore if a man is inconsiderate, even if he possesses much learning, people say of him, he is nothing, whatever he may know; for, if he were learned, he would not be so inconsiderate. But if a man is considerate, even though he knows but little, to him indeed do people listen gladly. Consideration is the centre, consideration is the self, consideration is the support of all these. Meditate on consideration.

3. 'He who meditates on consideration as Brahman, he, being himself safe, firm, and undistressed, obtains the safe, firm, and undistressed worlds which he has considered; he is, as it were, lord and master as far as consideration reaches—he who meditates on consideration as Brahman.'

'Sir, is there something better than consideration?'

'Yes, there is something better than consideration.'

'Sir, tell it me.'

---

[305] This paragraph is obscure. The text seems doubtful, for instance, in samak*l*ipatâm, samakalpetâm, and samakalpatâm. Then the question is the exact meaning of sa*m*k*l*iptyai, which must be taken as an instrumental case. What is intended is that, without rain, food is impossible &c. or inconceivable; but the text says, 'By the will of rain food wills,' &c. Will seems almost to be taken here in the sense in which modern philosophers use it, as a kind of creative will. By the will of rain food wills, would mean, that first rain wills and exists, and afterwards the vital airs will and exist, &c.

[306] *K*itta, thought, implies here consideration and reflection.

SIXTH KHA*ND*A.

1. 'Reflection (dhyâna)[307] is better than consideration. The earth reflects, as it were, and thus does the sky, the heaven, the water, the mountains, gods and men. Therefore those who among men obtain greatness here on earth, seem to have obtained a part of the object of reflection (because they show a certain repose of manner). Thus while small and vulgar people are always quarrelling, abusive, and slandering, great men seem to have obtained a part of the reward of reflection. Meditate on reflection.

2. 'He who meditates on reflection as Brahman, is lord and master, as it were, as far as reflection reaches—he who meditates on reflection as Brahman.'

'Sir, is there something better than reflection?'

'Yes, there is something better than reflection.'

'Sir, tell it me.'

SEVENTH KHA*ND*A.

1. 'Understanding (vigñâna) is better than reflection. Through understanding we understand the Rig-veda, the Yagur-veda, the Sâma-veda, and as the fourth the Âtharvana, as the fifth the Itihâsa-purâ*n*a[308], the Veda of the Vedas, the Pitrya, the Râ*s*i, the Daiva, the Nidhi, the Vâkovâkya, the Ekâyana, the Deva-vidyâ, the Brahma-vidyâ, the Bhûta-vidyâ, the Kshatra-vidyâ, the Nakshatra-vidyâ, the Sarpa and Devagana-vidyâ, heaven, earth, air, ether, water, fire, gods, men, cattle, birds, herbs, trees, all beasts down to worms, midges, and ants; what is right and what is wrong; what is true and what is false; what is good and what is bad; what is pleasing and what is not pleasing; food and savour, this world and that, all this we understand through understanding. Meditate on understanding.

2. 'He who meditates on understanding as Brahman, reaches the worlds where there is understanding and knowledge[309]; he is, as it were, lord and master as far as understanding reaches—he who meditates on understanding as Brahman.'

'Sir, is there something better than understanding?'

'Yes, there is something better than understanding.'

---

[307] Reflection is concentration of all our thoughts on one object, ekâgratâ. And as a man who reflects and meditates on the highest objects acquires thereby repose, becomes firm and immovable, so the earth is supposed to be in repose and immovable, as it were, by reflection and meditation.

[308] See before, p. 139.

[309] The commentator takes vigñâna here as understanding of sacred books, *g*ñâna as cleverness with regard to other subjects.

'Sir, tell it me.'

EIGHTH KHA*ND*A.

1. 'Power (bala) is better than understanding. One powerful man shakes a hundred men of understanding. If a man is powerful, he becomes a rising man. If he rises, he becomes a man who visits wise people. If he visits, he becomes a follower of wise people. If he follows them, he becomes a seeing, a hearing, a perceiving, a knowing, a doing, an understanding man. By power the earth stands firm, and the sky, and the heaven, and the mountains, gods and men, cattle, birds, herbs, trees, all beasts down to worms, midges, and ants; by power the world stands firm. Meditate on power.

2. 'He who meditates on power as Brahman, is, as it were, lord and master as far as power reaches—he who meditates on power as Brahman.'

'Sir, is there something better than power?'

'Yes, there is something better than power.'

'Sir, tell it me.'

NINTH KHA*ND*A.

1. 'Food (anna) is better than power. Therefore if a man abstain from food for ten days, though he live, he would be unable to see, hear, perceive, think, act, and understand. But when he obtains food, he is able to see, hear, perceive, think, act, and understand. Meditate on food.

2. 'He who meditates on food as Brahman, obtains the worlds rich in food and drink; he is, as it were, lord and master as far as food reaches—he who meditates on food as Brahman.'

'Sir, is there something better than food

'Yes, there is something better than food.'

'Sir, tell it me.'

TENTH KHA*ND*A.

1. 'Water (ap) is better than food. Therefore if there is not sufficient rain, the vital spirits fail from fear that there will be less food. But if there is sufficient rain, the vital spirits rejoice, because there will be much food. This water, on assuming different forms, becomes this earth, this sky, this heaven, the mountains, gods and men, cattle, birds, herbs and trees, all beasts down to worms, midges, and ants. Water indeed assumes all these forms. Meditate on water.

2. 'He who meditates on water as Brahman, obtains all wishes, he becomes satisfied; he is, as it were, lord and master as far as water reaches—he who meditates on water as Brahman.'

'Sir, is there something better than water?'

'Yes, there is something better than water.'

'Sir, tell it me.'

ELEVENTH KHA*ND*A.

1. 'Fire (tegas) is better than water. For fire united with air, warms the ether. Then people say, It is hot, it burns, it will rain. Thus does fire, after showing this sign (itself) first, create water. And thus again thunderclaps come with lightnings, flashing upwards and across the sky. Then people say, There is lightning and thunder, it will rain. Then also does fire, after showing this sign first, create water. Meditate on fire.

2. 'He who meditates on fire as Brahman, obtains, resplendent himself, resplendent worlds, full of light and free of darkness; he is, as it were, lord and master as far as fire reaches—he who meditates on fire as Brahman.'

'Sir, is there something better than fire?'

'Yes, there is something better than fire.'

'Sir, tell it me.'

TWELFTH KHA*ND*A.

1. 'Ether (or space) is better than fire. For in the ether exist both sun and moon, the lightning, stars, and fire (agni). Through the ether we call, through the ether we hear, through the ether we answer[310]. In the ether or space we rejoice (when we are together), and rejoice not (when we are separated). In the ether everything is born, and towards the ether everything tends when it is born[311]. Meditate on ether.

2. 'He who meditates on ether as Brahman, obtains the worlds of ether and of light, which are free from pressure and pain, wide and spacious[312]; he is, as it were, lord and master as far as ether reaches—he who meditates on ether as Brahman.'

'Sir, is there something better than ether?'

Yes, there is something better than ether.'

'Sir, tell it me.'

---

[310] Cf. *Kh*. Up. IV, 5, 2.

[311] The seed grows upwards towards the ether; not downwards.

[312] Cf. Kâ*th*. Up. II, 11.

THIRTEENTH KHA*ND*A.

1. 'Memory[313] (smara) is better than ether. Therefore where many are assembled together, if they have no memory, they would hear no one, they would not perceive, they would not understand. Through memory we know our sons, through memory our cattle. Meditate on memory.

2. 'He who meditates on memory as Brahman, is, as it were, lord and master as far as memory reaches;—he who meditates on memory as Brahman.'

'Sir, is there something better than memory?'

'Yes, there is something better than memory.'

'Sir, tell it me.'

FOURTEENTH KHA*ND*A.

1. 'Hope (âsâ) is better than memory. Fired by hope does memory read the sacred hymns, perform sacrifices, desire sons and cattle, desire this world and the other. Meditate on hope.

2. 'He who meditates on hope as Brahman, all his desires are fulfilled by hope, his prayers are not in vain; he is, as it were, lord and master as far as hope reaches—he who meditates on hope as Brahman.'

'Sir, is there something better than hope?'

'Yes, there is something better than hope.'

'Sir, tell it me.'

FIFTEENTH KHA*ND*A.

1. 'Spirit[314] (prâ*n*a) is better than hope. As the spokes of a wheel hold to the nave[315], so does all this (beginning with names and ending in hope) hold to spirit. That spirit moves by the spirit, it gives spirit to the spirit. Father means spirit, mother is spirit, brother is spirit, sister is spirit, tutor is spirit, Brâhma*n*a is spirit.

2. 'For if one says anything unbecoming to a father, mother, brother, sister, tutor or Brâhma*n*a, then people say, Shame on thee! thou hast offended thy father, mother, brother, sister, tutor, or a Brâhma*n*a.

---

313 The apparent distance between ether and memory is bridged over by the commentator pointing out that without memory everything would be as if it were not, so far as we are concerned.

314 Prâ*n*a is used here in a technical sense. It does not mean simply breath, but the spirit, the conscious self (pragñâtman) which, as we saw, enters the body in order to reveal the whole variety of forms and names. It is in one sense the mukhya prâ*n*a.

315 The commentary carries the simile Still further. The felloe he says, holds to the spokes, the spokes to the nave. So do the bhûtamâtrâs hold to the pragñâmâtrâs, and these to the prâ*n*a.

3. 'But, if after the spirit has departed from them, one shoves them together with a poker, and burns them to pieces, no one would say, Thou offendest thy father, mother, brother, sister, tutor or a Brâhma*n*a.

4. 'Spirit then is all this. He who sees this, perceives this, and understands this, becomes an ativâdin[316]. If people say to such a man, Thou art an ativâdin, he may say, I am an ativâdin; he need not deny it.'

SIXTEENTH KHA*ND*A[317].

1. 'But in reality he is an ativâdin who declares the Highest Being to be the True (Satya, τὸ ὄντως ὄν).'

'Sir, may I become an ativâdin by the True?'

'But we must desire to know the True.'

'Sir, I desire to know the True.'

SEVENTEENTH KHA*ND*A.

1. 'When one understands the True, then one declares the True. One who does not understand it, does not declare the True[318]. Only he who understands it, declares the True. This understanding, however, we must desire to understand.'

'Sir, I desire to understand it.'

EIGHTEENTH KHA*ND*A.

1. 'When one perceives, then one understands. One who does not perceive, does not understand. Only he who perceives, understands. This perception, however, we must desire to understand.'

'Sir, I desire to understand it.'

---

[316] One who declares something that goes beyond all the declarations made before, beginning with the declaration that names are Brahman, and ending with the declaration that hope is Brahman;—one who knows that prâ*n*a, spirit, the conscious self, is Brahman. This declaration represents the highest point reached by ordinary people, but Nârada wishes to go beyond. In the Mu*nd*aka, III, 1, 4, an ativâdin is contrasted with one who really knows the highest truth.

[317] As Nârada asks no further, whether there is anything better, higher, truer than prâ*n*a, he is supposed to be satisfied with his belief that prâ*n*a is the Highest Being. Sanatkumâra, however, wishes to lead him on to a still higher view; hence the paragraphs which follow from 16 to 26.

[318] He would, for instance, call fire real, not knowing that fire is only a mixture of the three elements (cf. VI, 4), the rûpatraya, a mere variety (vikâra), and name (nâman).

NINETEENTH KHA*ND*A.

1. 'When one believes, then one perceives. One who does not believe, does not perceive. Only he who believes, perceives. This belief, however, we must desire to understand.'

'Sir, I desire to understand it.'

TWENTIETH KHA*ND*A.

1. 'When one attends on a tutor (spiritual guide), then one believes. One who does not attend on a tutor, does not believe. Only he who attends, believes. This attention on a tutor, however, we must desire to understand.'

'Sir, I desire to understand it.'

TWENTY-FIRST KHA*ND*A.

1. 'When one performs all sacred duties[319], then one attends really on a tutor. One who does not perform his duties, does not really attend on a tutor. Only he who performs his duties, attends on his tutor. This performance of duties, however, we must desire to understand.'

'Sir, I desire to understand it.'

TWENTY-SECOND KHA*ND*A.

1. 'When one obtains bliss (in oneself), then one performs duties. One who does not obtain bliss, does not perform duties. Only he who obtains bliss, performs duties. This bliss, however, we must desire to understand.'

'Sir, I desire to understand it.'

TWENTY-THIRD KHA*ND*A.

1. 'The Infinite (bhûman)[320] is bliss. There is no bliss in anything finite. Infinity only is bliss. This Infinity, however, we must desire to understand.'

'Sir, I desire to understand it.'

---

[319] The duties of a student, such as restraint of the senses, concentration of the mind, &c.

[320] Bhûman is sometimes translated by grandeur, the superlative, the akme. It is the highest point that can be reached, the infinitc and the true.

TWENTY-FOURTH KHA*ND*A.

1. 'Where one sees nothing else, hears nothing else, understands nothing else, that is the Infinite. Where one sees something else, hears something else, understands something else, that is the finite. The Infinite is immortal, the finite is mortal.'

'Sir, in what does the Infinite rest?'

'In its own greatness—or not even in greatness[321].'

2. 'In the world they call cows and horses, elephants and gold, slaves, wives, fields and houses greatness. I do not mean this,' thus he spoke; 'for in that case one being (the possessor) rests in something else, (but the Infinite cannot rest in something different from itself.)

TWENTY-FIFTH KHA*ND*A.

1. 'The Infinite indeed is below, above, behind, before, right and left—it is indeed all this.

'Now follows the explanation of the Infinite as the I: I am below, I am above, I am behind, before, right and left—I am all this.

2. 'Next follows the explanation of the Infinite as the Self: Self is below, above, behind, before, right and left—Self is all this.

'He who sees, perceives, and understands this, loves the Self, delights in the Self, revels in the Self, rejoices in the Self—he becomes a Svarâg, (an autocrat or self-ruler); he is lord and master in all the worlds.

'But those who think differently from this, live in perishable worlds, and have other beings for their rulers.

TWENTY-SIXTH KHA*ND*A.

1. 'To him who sees, perceives, and understands this[322], the spirit (prâ*n*a) springs from the Self, hope springs from the Self, memory springs from the Self; so do ether, fire, water, appearance and disappearance[323], food, power, understanding, reflection, consideration, will, Mind, speech, names, sacred hymns, and sacrifices—aye, all this

---

[321] This phrase reminds one of the last verse in the No sad âsîd hymn, where, likewise, the expression of the highest certainty is followed by a misgiving that after all it may be otherwise. The commentator takes yadi vâ in the sense of, if you ask in the highest sense, then I say no; for the Infinite cannot rest in anything, not even in greatness.

[322] Before the acquirement of true knowledge, all that has been mentioned before, spirit, hope, memory, &c., on to names, was supposed to spring from the Sat, as something different from oneself. Now he is to know that the Sat is the Self.

[323] In the preceding paragraphs appearance and disappearance (birth and death) are not mentioned. This shows how easy it was in these treatises either to omit or to add anything that seemed important.

springs from the Self.

2. 'There is this verse, "He who sees this, does not see death, nor illness, nor pain; he who sees this, sees everything, and obtains everything everywhere.

'"He is one (before creation), he becomes three (fire, water, earth), he becomes five, he becomes seven, he becomes nine; then again he is called the eleventh, and hundred and ten and one thousand and twenty[324]."

'When the intellectual aliment has been purified, the whole nature becomes purified. When the whole nature has been purified, the memory becomes firm. And when the memory (of the Highest Self) remains firm, then all the ties (which bind us to a belief in anything but the Self) are loosened.

'The venerable Sanatkumâra showed to Nârada, after his faults had been rubbed out, the other side of darkness. They call Sanatkumâra Skanda, yea, Skanda they call him.'

EIGHTH PRAPÂ*TH*AKA.

FIRST KHANDA[325].

1. Hari*h*, Om. There is this city of Brahman (the body), and in it the palace, the small lotus (of the heart), and in it that small ether. Now what exists within that small ether, that is to be sought for, that is to be understood.

2. And if they should say to him: 'Now with regard to that city of Brahman, and the palace in it, i.e. the small lotus of the heart, and the small ether within the heart, what is there within it that deserves to be sought for, or that is to be understood?'

3. Then he should say: 'As large as this ether (all space) is, so large

---

[324] This too is meant as a verse. The commentary says that the various numbers are intended to show the endless variety of form on the Self after creation. Cf. Mait. Up. V, 2.

[325] The eighth Prapâthaka seems to form a kind of appendix to the Upanishad. The highest point that can be reached by speculation had been reached in the seventh Prapâthaka, the identity of our self and of everything else with the Highest Self. This speculative effort, however, is too much for ordinary people. They cannot conceive the Sat or Brahman as out of space and time, as free from all qualities, and in order to help them, they are taught to adore the Brahman, as it appears in space and time, an object endowed with certain qualities, living in nature and in the human heart. The Highest Brahman, besides which there is nothing, and which can neither be reached as an object, nor be considered as an effect, seems to ordinary minds like a thing which is not. Therefore while the true philosopher, after acquiring the knowledge of the Highest Sat, becomes identified with it suddenly, like lightning, the ordinary mortal must reach it by slow degrees, and as a preparation for that higher knowledge which is to follow, the eighth Prapâthaka, particularly the first portion of it, has been added to the teaching contained in the earlier books.

is that ether within the heart. Both heaven and earth are contained within it, both fire and air, both sun and moon, both lightning and stars; and whatever there is of him (the Self) here in the world, and whatever is not (i.e. whatever has been or will be), all that is contained within it[326].'

4. And if they should say to him: 'If everything that exists is contained in that city of Brahman, all beings and all desires (whatever can be imagined or desired), then what is left of it, when old age reaches it and scatters it, or when it falls to pieces?'

5. Then he should say: 'By the old age of the body, that (the ether, or Brahman within it) does not age; by the death of the body, that (the ether, or Brahman within it) is not killed. That (the Brahman) is the true Brahma-city (not the body[327]). In it all desires are contained. It is the Self, free from sin, free from old age, from death and grief, from hunger and thirst, which desires nothing but what it ought to desire, and imagines nothing but what it ought to imagine. Now as here on earth people follow as they are commanded, and depend on the object which they are attached to, be it a country or a piece of land,

6. 'And as here on earth, whatever has been acquired by exertion, perishes, so perishes whatever is acquired for the next world by sacrifices and other good actions performed on earth. Those who depart from hence without having discovered the Self and those true desires, for them there is no freedom in all the worlds. But those who depart from hence, after having discovered the Self and those true desires[328], for them there is freedom in all the worlds.

SECOND KHA*ND*A.

1. 'Thus he who desires the world[329] of the fathers, by his mere will the fathers come to receive him, and having obtained the world of the fathers, he is happy.

2. 'And he who desires the world of the mothers, by his mere will the mothers come to receive him, and having obtained the world of the mothers, he is happy.

3. 'And he who desires the world of the brothers, by his mere will the brothers come to receive him, and having obtained the world of the

---

[326] The ether in the heart is really a name of Brahman. He is there, and therefore all that comes of him when he assumes bodily shapes, both what is and what is not, i.e. what is no longer or not yet; for the absolute nothing is not intended here.

[327] I translate this somewhat differently from the commentator, though the argument remains the same.

[328] True desires are those which we ought to desire, and the fulfilment of which depends on ourselves, supposing that we have acquired the knowledge which enables us to fulfil them.

[329] World is the nearest approach to loka: it means life with the fathers, or enjoying the company of the fathers.

brothers, he is happy.

4. 'And he who desires the world of the sisters, by his mere will the sisters come to receive him, and having obtained the world of the sisters, he is happy.

5. 'And he who desires the world of the friends, by his mere will the friends come to receive him, and having obtained the world of the friends, he is happy.

6. 'And he who desires the world of perfumes and garlands (gandhamâlya), by his mere will perfumes and garlands come to him, and having obtained the world of perfumes and garlands, he is happy.

7. 'And he who desires the world of food and drink, by his mere will food and drink come to him, and having obtained the world of food and drink, he is happy.

8. 'And he who desires the world of song and music, by his mere will song and music come to him, and having obtained the world of song and music, he is happy.

9. 'And he who desires the world of women, by his mere will women come to receive him, and having obtained the world of women, he is happy.

'Whatever object he is attached to, whatever object he desires, by his mere will it comes to him, and having obtained it, he is happy.

THIRD KHA*ND*A.

1. 'These true desires, however, are hidden by what is false; though the desires be true, they have a covering which is false. Thus, whoever belonging to us has departed this life, him we cannot gain back, so that we should see him with our eyes.

2. 'Those who belong to us, whether living or departed, and whatever else there is which we wish for and do not obtain, all that we find there (if we descend into our heart, where Brahman dwells, in the ether of the heart), There are all our true desires, but hidden by what is false[330]. As people who do not know the country, walk again and again over a gold treasure that has been hidden somewhere in the earth and do not discover it, thus do all these creatures day after day go into the Brahma-world (they are merged in Brahman, while asleep), and yet do not discover it, because they are carried away by untruth (they do not come to themselves, i.e. they do not discover the true Self in Brahman, dwelling in the heart).

3. 'That Self abides in the heart. And this is the etymological explanation. The heart is called h*ri*d-ayam, instead of h*ri*dy-ayam, i.e.

---

[330] All the desires mentioned before are fulfilled, if we find their fulfilment in our Self, in the city of Brahman within our heart. There we always can possess those whom we have loved, only we must not wish to see them with our eyes; that would be a false covering to a true desire.

He who is in the heart. He who knows this, that He is in the heart, goes day by day (when in sushupti, deep sleep) into heaven (svarga), i.e. into the: Brahman of the heart.

4. 'Now that serene being[331] which, after having risen from out this earthly body, and having reached the highest light (self-knowledge), appears in its true form, that is the Self,' thus he spoke (when asked by his pupils). This is the immortal, the fearless, this is Brahman. And of that Brahman the name is the True, Satyam,

5. This name Sattyam consists of three syllables, sat-tî-yam[332]. Sat signifies the immortal, t, the mortal, and with yam he binds both. Because he binds both, the immortal and the mortal, therefore it is yam. He who knows this goes day by day into heaven (svarga).

FOURTH KHA*ND*A.

1. That Self is a bank[333], a boundary, so that these worlds may not be confounded. Day and night do not pass that bank, nor old age, death, and grief; neither good nor evil deeds. All evil-doers turn back from it, for the world of Brahman is free from all evil.

2. Therefore he who has crossed that bank, if blind, ceases to be blind; if wounded, ceases to be wounded; if afflicted, ceases to be afflicted. Therefore when that bank has been crossed, night becomes day indeed, for the world of Brahman is lighted up once for all[334].

3. And that world of Brahman belongs to those only who find it by abstinence—for them there is freedom in all the worlds.

FIFTH KHA*ND*A.

1. What people call sacrifice (yagña), that is really abstinence (brahma*k*arya). For he who knows, obtains that (world of Brahman, which others obtain by sacrifice), by means of abstinence.

What people call sacrifice (ish*t*a), that is really abstinence, for by abstinence, having searched (ish*t*vâ), he obtains the Self.

2. What people call sacrifice (sattrâya*n*a), that is really abstinence, for by abstinence he obtains from the Sat (the true), the safety (trâ*n*a) of the Self.

---

331 Cf. *Kh*. Up. VIII, 12, 3.

332 We ought probably to read Sattyam, and then Sat-tî-yam. The î in tî would then be the dual of an anubandha ĭ. Instead of yaddhi, I conjecture yatti. See Ait. Âra*n*yaka II, 5, 5.

333 Setu, generally translated by bridge, was originally a bank of earth (m*ri*dâdimaya), thrown up to serve as a pathway (pons) through water or a swamp. Such banks exist still in many places, and they serve at the same time as boundaries (maryâdâ) between fields belonging to different properties. Cf. Mait. Up. VII, 7; Kâ*th* Up. III, 2; Talav. Up. comm. p. 59; Mu*nd*. Up. II, 2, 5.

334 *Kh*. Up. III, 1, 3.

What people call the vow of silence (mauna), that is really abstinence, for he who by abstinence has found out the Self, meditates (manute).

3. What people call fasting (anâ*s*akâyana), that is really abstinence, for that Self does not perish (na na*s*yati), which we find out by abstinence.

What people call a hermit's life (ara*n*yâyana), that is really abstinence. Ara[335] and *N*ya are two lakes in the world of Brahman, in the third heaven from hence; and there is the lake Airanimadîya, and the A*s*vattha tree, showering down Soma, and the city of Brahman (Hira*n*yagarbha) Aparâgitâ[336], and the golden Prabhuvimita (the hall built by Prabhu, Brahman).

Now that world of Brahman belongs to those who find the lakes Ara and *N*ya in the world of Brahman by means of abstinence; for them there is freedom in all the worlds[337].

---

[335] In the Kaush. Br. Up. I, 3, the lake is called Ara, at least according to the commentator.

[336] In the Kaush. Br. Up. Aparâgita is not pû*h*, but âyatanam.

[337] The fifth kha*nd*a is chiefly meant to recommend brahma*k*arya or abstinence from all worldly enjoyments, enjoined on the brahma*k*ârin, the student, as a means of obtaining a knowledge of Brahman. But instead of showing that such abstinence is indispensable for a proper concentration of our intellectual faculties, we are told that abstinence is the same as certain sacrifices; and this is shown, not by arguments, but by a number of very far-fetched plays on words. These it is impossible to render in any translation, nay, they hardly deserve being translated. Thus abstinence is said to be identical with sacrifice, yag*ñ*a, because yo g*ñ*âtâ, 'he who knows,' has a certain similarity with yag*ñ*a. Ish*t*a, another kind of sacrifice, is compared with esha*n*â, search; sattrâya*n*a with Sat, the True, the Brahman, and trâya*n*a, protection; mauna, silence, with manana, meditating (which may be right); anâ*s*akâyana, fasting, with na*s*, to perish, and ara*n*yâgana, a hermit's life, with ara, *n*ya, and ayana, going to the two lakes Ara and *N*ya, which are believed to exist in the legendary world of Brahman. Nothing can be more absurd. Having once struck the note of Brahmanic legends, such as we find it, for instance, in the Kaushîtaki-brâhma*n*a-upanishad, the author goes on. Besides the lakes Ara and *N*ya (in the Kaushîtaki-brâhma*n*a-upanishad we have only one lake, called Âra), he mentions the Airammadîya lake, and explains it as aira (irâ annam, tanmaya airo ma*nd*as, tena pûr*n*am airam) and madîya, delightful. The Asvattha tree, which pours down Soma, is not tortured into anything else, except that Soma is explained as the immortal, or nectar. Aparâgita becomes the city of Brahman, because it can be conquered by no one except those who have practised abstinence. And the hall which elsewhere is called Vibhu-pramita becomes Prabhu-vimitam, or Prabhu-vinirmita, made by Prabhu, i.e. Brahman. All the fulfilled desires, as enumerated in kha*nd*as 2-5, whether the finding again of our fathers and mothers, or entering the Brahmaloka with its lakes and palaces, must be taken, not as material (sthûla), but as mental only (mânasa). On that account, however, they are by no means considered as false or unreal, as little as dreams are. Dreams are false and unreal, relatively only, i.e. relatively to what we see, when we awake; but not in themselves. Whatever we see in waking, also, has been shown to be false; because it consists of forms and names only; yet these forms and names have a true element in them, viz. the Sat. Before we know that Sat, all the objects we see in waking seem true; as dreams seem true in dreaming. But when once we awake from our waking by true knowledge, we see that nothing is true but the Sat. When we imagine we see a serpent, and then discover that it is a rope, the serpent disappears as false, but what was true in it, the rope, remains true.

SIXTH KHA*ND*A.

1. Now those arteries of the heart consist of a brown substance, of a white, blue, yellow, and red substance, and so is the sun brown, white, blue, yellow, and red.

2. As a very long highway goes to two places, to one at the beginning, and to another at the end, so do the rays of the sun go to both worlds, to this one and to the other. They start from the sun, and enter into those arteries; they start from those arteries, and enter into the sun.

3. And when a man is asleep, reposing, and at perfect rest, so that he sees no dream[338], then he has entered into those arteries. Then no evil touches him, for he has obtained the light (of the sun).

4. And when a man falls ill, then those who sit round him, say, 'Do you know me? Do you know me?' As long as he has not departed from this body, he knows them.

5. But when he departs from this body, then he departs upwards by those very rays (towards the worlds which he has gained by merit, not by knowledge); or he goes out while meditating on Om[339] (and thus securing an entrance into the Brahmaloka). And while his mind is failing, he is going to the sun. For the sun is the door of the world (of Brahman). Those who know, walk in; those who do not know, are shut out. There is this verse[340]: 'There are a hundred and one arteries of the heart; one of them penetrates the crown of the head; moving upwards by it a man reaches the immortal; the others serve for departing in different directions, yea, in different directions[341].'

---

[338] Svapna in Sanskrit is both somnus and somnium. Hence one might translate also, 'so that he is not aware that he is asleep,' which in some respects would seem even more appropriate in our passage; cf. VIII, 11, 1.

[339] According to the explanation given of the Om in the Upanishads, and more particularly in the Dahara-vidyâ contained in this Prapâ*th*aka.

[340] Prasna Up. II, 1.

[341] The same verse occurs in the Ka*th*a 6, 16, and is frequently quoted elsewhere, for instance, Mait. comm. p. 164. For vishvaṅṅ, the right reading would seem to be vishvak. In the Mait. Up. VI, 30, the Trish*t*ubh are reduced to Anush*t*ubh verses. See also Prasna Up. III, 6-7; Mu*nd*. Up. II, 2.

SEVENTH KHA*ND*A[342].

1. Pragâpati said: 'The Self which is free from sin, free from old age, from death and grief, from hunger and thirst, which desires nothing but what it ought to desire, and imagines nothing but what it ought to imagine, that it is which we must search out, that it is which we must try to understand. He who has searched out that Self and understands it, obtains all worlds and all desires.'

2. The Devas (gods) and Asuras (demons) both heard these words, and said: 'Well, let us search for that Self by which, if one has searched it out, all worlds and all desires are obtained.'

Thus saying Indra went from the Devas, Viro*k*ana from the Asuras, and both, without having communicated with each other, approached Pragâpati, holding fuel in their hands, as is the custom for pupils approaching their master.

3. They dwelt there as pupils for thirty-two years. Then Pragâpati asked them: 'For what purpose have you both dwelt here?'

They replied: 'A saying of yours is being repeated, viz. "the Self which is free from sin, free from old age, from death and grief, from hunger and thirst, which desires nothing but what it ought to desire, and imagines nothing but what it ought to imagine, that it is which we must search out, that it is which we must try to understand. He who has searched out that Self and understands it, obtains all worlds and all desires." Now we both have dwelt here because we wish for that Self.'

Pragâpati said to them: 'The person that is seen in the eye[343], that is the Self. This is what I have said. This is the immortal, the fearless, this is Brahman.'

They asked: 'Sir, he who is perceived in the water, and he who is perceived in a mirror, who is he?'

He replied: 'He himself indeed is seen in all these[344].'

---

[342] Here the highest problem is treated again, the knowledge of the true Self, which leads beyond the world of Brahmâ (masc.), and enables the individual self to return into the Highest Self.

[343] The commentator explains this rightly. Pragâpati means by the person that is seen in the eye, the real agent of seeing, who is seen by sages only, even with their eyes shut. His pupils, however, misunderstand him. They think of the person that is seen, not of the person that sees (Yoga-sûtras II, 6). The person seen in the eye is to them the small figure imaged in the eye, and they go on therefore to ask, whether the image in the water or in a mirror is not the Self.

[344] The commentators are at great pains to explain that Pragâpati told no falsehood. He meant by purusha the personal element in the highest sense, and it was not his fault that his pupils took purusha for man or body.

EIGHTH KHA*ND*A.

1. 'Look at your Self in a pan of water, and whatever you do not understand of your Self[345], come and tell me.'

They looked in the water-pan. Then Pragâpati said to them: 'What do you see?'

They said: 'We both see the self thus altogether, a picture even to the very hairs and nails.'

2. Pragâpati said to them: 'After you have adorned yourselves, have put on your best clothes and cleaned yourselves, look again into the water-pan.

They, after having adorned themselves, having put on their best clothes and cleaned themselves, looked into the water-pan.

Pragâpati said: 'What do you see?'

3. They said: 'Just as we are, well adorned, with our best clothes and clean, thus we are both there, Sir, well adorned, with our best clothes and clean.'

Pragâpati said: 'That is the Self, this is the immortal, the fearless, this is Brahman.'

Then both went away satisfied in their hearts.

4. And Pragâpati, looking after them, said: 'They both go away without having perceived and without having known the Self, and whoever of these two[346], whether Devas or Asuras, will follow this doctrine (upanishad), will perish.'

Now Virokana, satisfied in his heart, went to the Asuras and preached that doctrine to them, that the self (the body) alone is to be worshipped, that the self (the body) alone is to be served, and that he who worships the self and serves the self, gains both worlds, this and the next.

5. Therefore they call even now a man who does not give alms here, who has no faith, and offers no sacrifices, an Âsura, for this is the doctrine (upanishad) of the Asuras. They deck out the body of the dead with perfumes, flowers, and fine raiment by way of ornament, and think they will thus conquer that world[347].

---

[345] I take âtmana*h* as a genitive, governed by yad, not as an accusative plural.

[346] The commentator reads yatare for yata*h*.

[347] This evidently refers to the customs and teaching of tribes not entirely conforming to the Brahmanic system. Whether the adorning of the dead body implies burial instead of burning, seems doubtful.

NINTH KHA*N*DA.

1. But Indra, before he had returned to the Devas, saw this difficulty. As this self (the shadow in the water)[348] is well adorned, when the body is well adorned, well dressed, when the body is well dressed, well cleaned, if the body is well cleaned, that self will also be blind, if the body is blind, lame, if the body is lame[349], crippled, if the body is crippled, and will perish in fact as soon as the body perishes. Therefore I see no good in this (doctrine).

2. Taking fuel in his hand he came again as a pupil to Pragâpati. Pragâpati said to him: 'Maghavat (Indra), as you went away with Virokana, satisfied in your heart, for what purpose did you come back?'

He said: 'Sir, as this self (the shadow) is well adorned, when the body is well adorned, well dressed, when the body is well dressed, well cleaned, if the body is well cleaned, that self will also be blind, if the body is blind, lame, if the body is lame, crippled, if the body is crippled, and will perish in fact as soon as the body perishes. Therefore I see no good in this (doctrine).'

3. 'So it is indeed, Maghavat,' replied Pragâpati; 'but I shall explain him (the true Self) further to you. Live with me another thirty-two years.'

He lived with him another thirty-two years, and then Pragâpati said:

TENTH KHA*N*DA.

1. 'He who moves about happy in dreams, he is the Self, this is the immortal, the fearless, this is Brahman.'

Then Indra went away satisfied in his heart. But before he had returned to the Devas, he saw this difficulty. Although it is true that that self is not blind, even if the body is blind, nor lame, if the body is lame, though it is true that that self is not rendered faulty by the faults of it (the body),

2. Nor struck when it (the body) is struck, nor lamed when it is lamed, yet it is as if they struck him (the self) in dreams, as if they chased him[350]. He becomes even conscious, as it were, of pain, and

---

[348] The commentator remarks that though both Indra and Viro*k*ana had mistaken the true import of what Pragâpati said, yet while Viro*k*ana took the body to be the Self, Indra thought that the Self was the shadow of the body.

[349] Srâma, lame, is explained by the commentator as one-eyed, ekanetra.

[350] I have adopted the reading vi*kkh*âyayanti, because it is the most difficult, and therefore explains most easily the various corruptions, or it may be emendations, that have crept into the text. *S*aṅkara explains vi*kkh*âdayanti by vidrâvayanti, and this shows that he too must have read vi*kkh*âyayanti, for he could not have explained vi*kkh*âdayanti, which means they uncover or they deprive of their clothing, by vidrâvayanti, they drive

sheds tears. Therefore I see no good in this.

3. Taking fuel in his hands, he went again as a pupil to Pragâpati. Pragâpati said to him: 'Maghavat, as you went away satisfied in your heart, for what purpose did you come back?'

He said: 'Sir, although it is true that that self is not blind even if the body is blind, nor lame, if the body is lame, though it is true that that self is not rendered faulty by the faults of it (the body),

4. Nor struck when it (the body) is struck, nor lamed when it is lamed, yet it is as if they struck him (the self) in dreams, as if they chased him. He becomes even conscious, as it were, of pain, and sheds tears. Therefore I see no good in this.'

'So it is indeed, Maghavat,' replied Pragâpati; 'but I shall explain him (the true Self) further to you. Live with me another thirty-two years.'

He lived with him another thirty-two years. Then Pragâpati said:

ELEVENTH KHA*ND*A.

1. 'When a man being asleep, reposing, and at perfect rest[351], sees no dreams, that is the Self, this is the immortal, the fearless, this is Brahman.'

Then Indra went away satisfied in his heart. But before he had returned to the Devas, he saw this difficulty. In truth he thus does not know himself (his self) that he is I, nor does he know anything that exists. He is gone to utter annihilation. I see no good in this.

2. Taking fuel in his hand he went again as a pupil to Pragâpati. Pragâpati said to him: 'Maghavat, as you went away satisfied in your heart, for what purpose did you come back?'

He said: 'Sir, in that way he does not know himself (his self) that he is I, nor does he know anything that exists. He is gone to utter annihilation. I see no good in this!

3. 'So it is indeed, Maghavat,' replied Pragâpati; 'but I shall

---

away. It is true that vi*kkh*âyayanti may be explained in two ways; it may be the causative of *kh*â, to cut, but this meaning is not very appropriate here, and quite inadmissible in another passage where vi*kkh*âyayanti occurs, whereas, if derived from vi*kh* (οἴχομαι) in a causative sense, *S*aṅkara could hardly have chosen a better explanation than vidrâvayanti, they make run away. The root vi*kh*, vi*kkh*âyayati is recognised in Pâ*n*ini III, 1, 28, and in the Dhâtupâ*th*a 28, 129, but it has hitherto been met with in this passage only, and in B*ri*hadâra*n*yaka, Up. IV, 3, 20. Here also the author speaks of a man who imagines that people kill him or do him violence, or that an elephant chases him or that he falls into a pit. Here we have hastîva vi*kkh*âyayati, and *S*aṅkara, at least as printed by Dr. Roer, explains this by vi*kkh*âpayati, vi*kkh*âdayati, vidrâvayati; dhâvatîty artha*h*. Much better is Dvivedaganga's commentary, as published by Dr. Weber, Satap. Brâhm. p. 1145, Kadâ*k*id ena*m* hastî vi*kkh*âyayatîva vidrâvayatîva; vi*kh*a gatau, gupûdhûpavi*kh*ipa*n*ipanibhya âya iti (Pâ*n*. III, 1, 28) svârtha âyapratyaya*h*. In the Dictionary of Boehtlingk and Roth the derivation from *kh*â, to cut, is preferred; see Nachträge, s. v. *kh*â.

[351] See *Kh*. Up. VIII, 6, 3.

explain him (the true Self) further to you, and nothing more than this[352]. Live here other five years.'

He lived there other five years. This made in all one hundred and one years, and therefore it is said that Indra Maghavat lived one hundred and one years as a pupil with Pragâpati. Pragâpati said to him:

TWELFTH KHA*ND*A.

1. 'Maghavat, this body is mortal and always held by death. It is the abode of that Self which is immortal and without body[353]. When in the body (by thinking this body is I and I am this body) the Self is held by pleasure and pain. So long as he is in the body, he cannot get free from pleasure and pain. But when he is free of the body (when he knows himself different from the body), then neither pleasure nor pain touches him[354].

2. 'The wind is without body, the cloud, lightning, and thunder are without body (without hands, feet, &c.) Now as these, arising from this heavenly ether (space), appear in their own form, as soon as they have approached the highest light,

3. 'Thus does that serene being, arising from this body, appear in its own form, as soon as it has approached the highest light (the knowledge of Self[355]) He (in that state) is the highest person (uttama pûrusha). He moves about there laughing (or eating), playing, and rejoicing (in his mind), be it with women, carriages, or relatives, never minding that body into which he was born[356].

'Like as a horse attached to a cart, so is the spirit[357] (prâ*n*a, pragñâtman) attached to this body.

---

[352] *S*aṅkara explains this as meaning the real Self, not anything different from the Self.

[353] According to some, the body is the result of the Self, the elements of the body, fire, water, and earth springing from the Self, and the Self afterwards entering them.

[354] Ordinary, worldly pleasure. Comm.

[355] The simile is not so striking as most of those old similes are. The wind is compared with the Self, on account of its being for a time lost in the ether (space), as the Self is in the body, and then rising again out of the ether and assuming its own form as wind. The chief stress is laid on the highest light, which in the one case is the sun of summer, in the other the light of knowledge.

[356] These are pleasures which seem hardly compatible with the state of perfect peace which the Self is supposed to have attained. The passage may be interpolated, or put in on purpose to show that the Self enjoys such pleasures as an inward spectator only, without identifying himself with either pleasure or pain. He sees them, as he says afterwards, with his divine eye. The Self perceives in all things his Self only, nothing else. In his commentary on the Taittîrya Upanishad (p. 324) *S*aṅkara refers this passage to Brahman as an effect, not to Brahman as a cause.

[357] The spirit, the conscious self, is not identical with the body, but only joined to it, like a horse, or driving it, like a charioteer. In other passages the senses are the horses; buddhi, reason, the charioteer; manas, mind, the reins. The spirit is attached to the cart by the *k*etana; cf. Ânandagñânagiri.

4. 'Now where the sight has entered into the void (the open space, the black pupil of the eye), there is the person of the eye, the eye itself is the instrument of seeing. He who knows, let me smell this, he is the Self, the nose is the instrument of smelling. He who knows, let me say this, he is the Self, the tongue is the instrument of saying. He who knows, let me hear this, he is the Self, the ear is the instrument of hearing.

5. 'He who knows, let me think this, he is the Self, the mind is his divine eye[358]. He, the Self, seeing these pleasures (which to others are hidden like a buried treasure of gold) through his divine eye, i.e. the mind, rejoices.

'The Devas who are in the world of Brahman meditate on that Self (as taught by Pragâpati to Indra, and by Indra to the Devas). Therefore all worlds belong to them, and all desires. He who knows that Self and understands it, obtains all worlds and all desires.' Thus said Pragâpati, yea, thus said Pragâpati.

THIRTEENTH KHA*ND*A[359].

1. From the dark (the Brahman of the heart) I come to the nebulous (the world of Brahman), from the nebulous to the dark, shaking off all evil, as a horse shakes his hairs, and as the moon frees herself from the mouth of Râhu[360]. Having shaken off the body, I obtain, self made and satisfied, the uncreated world of Brahman, yea, I obtain it.

FOURTEENTH KHA*ND*A.

1. He who is called ether[361] (âkâ*s*a) is the revealer of all forms and names. That within which these forms and names are contained is the Brahman, the Immortal, the Self.

I come to the hall of Pragâpati, to the house; I am the glorious among Brahmans, glorious among princes, glorious among men[362]. I obtained that glory, I am glorious among the glorious. May I never go

[358] Because it perceives not only what is present, but also what is past and future.

[359] This chapter is supposed to contain a hymn of triumph.

[360] Râhu, in later times a monster, supposed to swallow the sun and moon at every solar or lunar eclipse. At first we only hear of the mouth or head of Râhu. In later times a body was assigned to him, but it had to be destroyed again by Vishnu, so that nothing remained of him but his head. Râhu seems derived from rah, to separate, to remove. From it raksh, to wish or strive to remove, to keep off, to protect, and in a different application rákshas, a tearing away, violence, rakshás, a robber, an evil spirit.

[361] Âkâ*s*a, ether or space, is a name of Brahman, because, like ether, Brahman has no body and is infinitely small.

[362] Here the three classes, commonly called castes, are clearly marked by the names of brâhma*n*a, râgan, and vi*s*.

to the white, toothless, yet devouring, white abode[363]; may I never go to it.

FIFTEENTH KHA*ND*A.

1. Brahmâ (Hira*n*yagarbha or Parame*s*vara) told this to Pragâpati (Ka*s*yapa), Pragâpati to Manu (his son), Manu to mankind. He who has learnt the Veda from a family of teachers, according to the sacred rule, in the leisure time left from the duties to be performed for the Guru, who, after receiving his discharge, has settled in his own house, keeping up the memory of what he has learnt by repeating it regularly in some sacred spot, who has begotten virtuous sons, and concentrated all his senses on the Self, never giving pain to any creature, except at the tîrthas[364] (sacrifices, &c.), he who behaves thus all his life, reaches the world of Brahman, and does not return, yea, he does not return.

TALAVAKÂRA OR KENA-UPANISHAD.

FIRST KHA*ND*A.

1. The Pupil asks: 'At whose wish does the mind sent forth proceed on its errand? At whose command does the first breath go forth? At whose wish do we utter this speech? What god directs the eye, or the ear?'

2. The Teacher replies: 'It is the ear of the ear, the mind of the mind, the speech of speech, the breath of breath, and the eye of the eye. When freed (from the senses) the wise, on departing from this world, become immortal[365].

3. 'The eye does not go thither, nor speech, nor mind. We do not know, we do not understand, how any one can teach it.

4. 'It is different from the known, it is also above the unknown, thus we have heard from those of old, who taught us this[366].

5. 'That which is not expressed by speech and by which speech is expressed, that alone know as Brahman, not that which people here

---

[363] Yoni*s*abditam praganan endriyam.

[364] The commentator says that even travelling about as a mendicant causes pain, but that a mendicant is allowed to importune people for alms at tîrthas, or sacred places. Others explain this differently.

[365] This verse admits of various translations, and still more various explanations. Instead of taking vâka*m*, like all the other words, as a nominative, we might take them all as accusatives, governed by atimu*k*ya, and sa u prâ*n*asya prâ*n*a*h* as a parenthetical sentence. What is meant by the ear of the ear is very fully explained by the commentator, but the simplest acceptation would seem to take it as an answer to the preceding questions, so that the car of the ear should be taken for him who directs the ear, i.e. the Self, or Brahman. This will become clearer as we proceed.

[366] Cf. Î*s*a Up. II; 13.

adore.

6. 'That which does not think by mind, and by which, they say, mind is thought[367], that alone know as Brahman, not that which people here adore.

7. 'That which does not see by the eye, and by which one sees (the work of) the eyes, that alone know as Brahman, not that which people here adore.

8. 'That which does not hear by the ear, and by which the ear is heard, that alone know as Brahman, not that which people here adore.

9. 'That which does not breathe by breath, and by which breath is drawn, that alone know as Brahman, not that which people here adore.'

SECOND KHA*ND*A.

1. The Teacher says: 'If thou thinkest I know it well, then thou knowest surely but little, what is that form of Brahman known, it may be, to thee[368]?'

2. The Pupil says: 'I do not think I know it well, nor do I know that I do not know it. He among us who knows this, he knows it, nor does he know that he does not know it[369].

3. 'He by whom it (Brahman) is not thought, by him it is thought; he by whom it is thought, knows it not. It is not understood by those who understand it, it is understood by those who do not understand it.

4. 'It is thought to be known (as if) by awakening, and (then) we obtain immortality indeed. By the Self we obtain strength, by knowledge we obtain immortality.

5. 'If a man know this here, that is the true (end of life); if he does not know this here, then there is great destruction (new births). The wise who have thought on all things (and recognised the Self in them) become immortal, when they have departed from this world.'

---

[367] The varia lectio manaso matam (supported also by the commentary) is metrically and grammatically easier, but it may be, for that very reason, an emendation.

[368] In order to obtain a verse, we must leave out the words tvam yad asya deveshv atha nu mîmâ*m*syam eva. They were probably inserted, as an excuse for the third kha*nd*a treating of the relation of Brahman to the Devas. There is considerable variety in the text, as handed down in the Sâma-veda and in the Atharva-veda, which shows that it has been tampered with. Daharam for dabhram may be the older reading, as synezesis occurs again and again in the Upanishads.

[369] This verse has again been variously explained. I think the train of thought is this: We cannot know Brahman, as we know other objects, by referring them to a class and pointing out their differences. But, on the other hand, we do not know that we know him not, i.e. no one can assert that we know him not, for we want Brahman in order to know anything. He, therefore, who knows this double peculiarity of the knowledge of Brahman, he knows Brahman, as much as it can be known; and he does not know, nor can anybody prove it to him, that he does not know Brahman.

THIRD KHA*ND*A[370].

1. Brahman obtained the victory for the Devas. The Devas became elated by the victory of Brahman, and they thought, this victory is ours only, this greatness is ours only.

2. Brahman perceived this and appeared to them. But they did not know it, and said: 'What sprite (yaksha or yakshya) is this?'

3. They said to Agni (fire): 'O *G*âtavedas, find out what sprite this is.' 'Yes,' he said.

4. He ran toward it, and Brahman said to him: 'Who are you?' He replied: 'I am Agni, I am *G*âtavedas.'

5. Brahman said: 'What power is in you?' Agni replied: 'I could burn all whatever there is on earth.'

6. Brahman put a straw before him, saying: 'Burn this.' He went towards it with all his might, but he could not burn it. Then he returned thence and said: 'I could not find out what sprite this is.'

7. Then they said to Vâyu (air): 'O Vâyu, find out what sprite this is.' 'Yes,' he said.

8. He ran toward it, and Brahman said to him: 'Who are you?' He replied: 'I am Vâyu, I am Mâtari*s*van.'

9. Brahman said: 'What power is in you?' Vâyu replied: 'I could take up all whatever there is on earth.'

10. Brahman put a straw before him, saying: 'Take it up.' He went towards it with all his might, but he could not take it up. Then he returned thence and said: 'I could not find out what sprite this is.'

11. Then they said to Indra: 'O Maghavan, find out what sprite this is.' He went towards it, but it disappeared from before him.

12. Then in the same space (ether) he came towards a woman, highly adorned: it was Umâ, the daughter of Himavat[371]. He said to her: 'Who is that sprite?'

---

[370] This kha*nd*a is generally represented as a later addition, but its prose style has more of a Brâhma*n*a character than the verses in the preceding kha*nd*as, although their metrical structure is irregular, and may be taken as a sign of antiquity.

[371] Umâ may here be taken as the wife of *S*iva, daughter of Himavat, better known by her earlier name, Pârvatî, the daughter of the mountains. Originally she was, not the daughter of the mountains or of the Himâlaya, but the daughter of the cloud, just as Rudra was originally, not the lord of the mountains, girî*s*a, but the lord of the clouds. We are, however, moving here in a secondary period of Indian thought, in whi.ch we see, as among Semitic nations, the manifested powers, and particularly the knowledge and wisdom of the gods, represented by their wives. Umâ means originally flax, from vâ, to weave, and the same word may have been an old name of wife, she who weaves (cf. duhit*ri*; spinster, and possibly wife itself, if O. H. G. wîb is connected with O. H. G. wĕban). It is used almost synonymously with ambikâ, Taitt. Âr. p. 839. If we wished to take liberties, we might translate umâ haimavatî by an old woman coming from the Himavat mountains; but I decline all responsibility for such an interpretation.

FOURTH KHA*N*D*A*.

1. She replied: 'It is Brahman. It is through the victory of Brahman that you have thus become great.' After that he knew that it was Brahman.

2. Therefore these Devas, viz. Agni, Vâyu, and Indra, are, as it were, above the other gods, for they touched it (the Brahman) nearest[372].

3. And therefore Indra is, as it were, above the other gods, for he touched it nearest, he first knew it.

4. This is the teaching of Brahman, with regard to the gods (mythological): It is that which now flashes forth in the lightning, and now vanishes again.

5. And this is the teaching of Brahman, with regard to the body (psychological): It is that which seems to move as mind, and by it imagination remembers again and again[373].

6. That Brahman is called Tadvana[374], by the name of Tadvana it is to be meditated on. All beings have a desire for him who knows this.

7. The Teacher: 'As you have asked me to tell you the Upanishad, the Upanishad has now been told you. We have told you the Brâhmî Upanishad.

8. 'The feet on which that Upanishad stands are penance, restraint,

---

[372] The next phrase was borrowed from § 3, without even changing the singular to the plural. As Indra only found out that it was Brahman, the original distinction between Indra and the other gods, who only came near to it, was quite justified. Still it might be better to adopt the var. lect. sa hy etat in § 2.

[373] I have translated these paragraphs very differently from *S*aṅkara and other interpreters. The wording is extremely brief, and we can only guess the original intention of the Upanishad by a reference to other passages. Now the first teaching of Brahman, by means of a comparison with the gods or heavenly things in general, seems to be that Brahman is what shines forth suddenly like lightning. Sometimes the relation between the phenomenal world and Brahman is illustrated by the relation between bubbles and the sea, or lightning and the unseen heavenly light (Mait. Up. V 1, 35). In another passage, *Kh*. Up. VIII, 12, 2, lightning, when no longer seen, is to facilitate the conception of the reality of things, as distinct from their perceptibility. I think, therefore, that the first simile, taken from the phenomenal world, was meant to show that Brahman is that which appears for a moment in the lightning, and then vanishes from our sight.

The next illustration is purely psychological. Brahman is proved to exist, because our mind moves towards things, because there is something in us which moves and perceives, and because there is something in us which holds our perceptions together (saṅkalpa), and revives them again by memory.

I give my translation as hypothetical only, for certainty is extremely difficult to attain, when we have to deal with these enigmatical sayings which, when they were first delivered, were necessarily accompanied by oral explanations.

[374] Tadvana, as a name of Brahman, is explained by 'the desire of it,' and derived from van, to desire, the same as vâñ*kh*.

sacrifice; the Vedas are all its limbs[375], the True is its abode.

9. 'He who knows this Upanishad, and has shaken off all evil, stands in the endless, unconquerable[376] world of heaven, yea, in the world of heaven.'

AITAREYA-ÂRA*N*YAKA.

FIRST ÂRA*N*YAKA.

FIRST ADHYÂYA.

FIRST KHA*ND*A.

1. Now follows the Mahâvrata ceremony.

2. After having killed V*ri*tra, Indra became great. When he became great, then there was the Mahâvrata (the great work). This is why the Mahâvrata ceremony is called Mahâvrata.

3. Some people say: 'Let the priest make two (recitations with the offering of the) âgya (ghee) on that day,' but the right thing is one[377].

4. He who desires prosperity should use the hymn, pra vo devâyâgnaye (Rv. III, 13, 1).

5. He who desires increase should use the hymn, vi*s*o vi*s*o atithim (Rv. VIII, 74, 1).

6. The people (visa*h*) indeed are increase[378], and therefore he (the sacrificer) becomes increased.

7. But (some say), there is the word atithim (in that hymn, which means a guest or stranger, asking for food). Let him not therefore take that hymn. Verily, the atithi (stranger) is able[379] to go begging.

8. 'No,' he said, 'let him take that hymn.

9. 'For he who follows the good road and obtains distinction, he is

---

[375] It is impossible to adopt *S*aṅkara's first rendering, 'the Vedas and all the Aṅgas,' i.e. the six subsidiary doctrines. He sees himself that sarvâṅgâni stands in opposition to pratish*th*â and âyatana, but seeing Veda and Aṅga together, no Brahman could help thinking of the Vedâṅgas.

[376] Might we read agyeye for *g*yeye? cf. Satap. Brâhm. XI, 5, 7, 1.

[377] That it should be one only is proved from the types, i.e. from other sacrifices, that have to be followed in the performance of the Mahâvrata. The first type is the Agnish*t*oma, where one *s*astra is enjoined as âgya*s*astra, viz. pra vo devâyâgnaye. In the Vi*s*vagit, which has to follow the Agnish*t*oma, another hymn is put in its place, viz. agni*m* naro dîdhitibhi*h*. In the Mahâvrata, which has to follow the Vi*s*vagit, some people recommend the use of both these hymns. But that is wrong, for there must be in the sacrifices which follow the Agnish*t*oma twelve *s*astras altogether; and if there were two here, instead of one, we should get a total of thirteen.

[378] The word visa*h*, which occurs in the hymn, means people. The commentator says that because the Vai*s*yas or tradespeople increase their capital, therefore they are called increase.

[379] Able, or liable; cf. Ait. Âr. II, 3, 5, 7.

an atithi (guest)[380].

10. 'They do not consider him who is not so, worthy to be (called) an atithi (guest).

11. 'Therefore let him by all means take that hymn.'

12. If he takes that hymn, let him place the (second) tristich, âganma v*ri*trahantamam, 'we came near to the victorious,' first.

13. For people worship the whole year (performing the Gavâmayana sacrifice) wishing for this day (the last but one)—they do come near.

14. The (next following) three tristichs begin with an Anush*t*ubh[381]. Now Brahman is Gâyatrî, speech is Anush*t*ubh. He thus joins speech with Brahman.

15. He who desires glory should use the hymn, abodhy agni*h* samidhâ ganânâm (Rv. V, 1, 1).

16. He who desires offspring and cattle should use the hymn, hotâganishta *k*etana*h* (Rv. II, 5, 1).

SECOND KHA*ND*A.

1. He who desires proper food[382] should use the hymn, agnim naro dîdhitibhi*h* (Rv. VII, 1, 1)[383].

2. Verily, Agni (fire) is the eater of food.

In the other (recitations accompanying the) offerings of âgya (where Agni is likewise mentioned) the worshippers come more slowly near to Agni (because the name of Agni does not stand at the beginning of the hymn). But here a worshipper obtains proper food at once, he strikes down evil at once.

3. Through the words (occurring in the second foot of the first verse), hasta*k*yuti *g*anayanta, 'they caused the birth of Agni by moving their arms,' the hymn becomes endowed with (the word) birth. Verily, the sacrificer is born from this day of the sacrifice, and therefore the hymn is endowed with (the word) birth.

4. There are four metrical feet (in the Trish*t*ubh verses of this hymn). Verily, cattle have four feet, therefore they serve for the gaining of cattle.

---

[380] Atithi is here explained by yo bhavati, and bhavati is explained as walking on the good road. One expects yo vâ atati. The obtaining of distinction is probably derived from ati, above, in atithi.

[381] In the first and second the Anush*t*ubh is followed by two Gâyatrîs.

[382] Annâdyam is always explained as food, here as annam tad âdya*m* *k*a. It must be so translated here and elsewhere (1, 2, 10), though it is often an abstract of annâda, an eater of food, a healthy man.

[383] This hymn is prescribed in the Vi*s*vagit sacrifice, and taken over to the Mahâvrata, according to rule. It is used, however, both as obligatory and as optional at the same time, i.e. it is an essential part of the sacrifice, and at the same time to be used by those who wish for proper food.

5. There are three metrical feet (in the Virâg, verses of this hymn). Verily, three are these three-fold worlds. Therefore they serve for the conquest of the worlds.

6. These (the Trish*t*ubh and Virâg verses of the hymn) form two metres, which form a support (pratish*th*â). Verily, man is supported by two (feet), cattle by four feet. Therefore this hymn places the sacrificer who stands on two feet among cattle which stand on four.

7. By saying them straight on there are twenty-five verses in this hymn. Man also consists of twenty-five. There are ten fingers on his hands, ten toes on his feet, two legs, two arms, and the trunk (âtman) the twenty-fifth. He adorns that trunk, the twenty-fifth, by this hymn.

8. And then this day (of the sacrifice) consists of twenty-five, and the Stoma hymn of that day consists of twenty-five[384] (verses); it becomes the same through the same. Therefore these two, the day and the hymn, are twenty-five[385].

9. These twenty-five verses, by repeating the first thrice and the last thrice, become thirty less one. This is a Virâg, verse (consisting of thirty syllables), too small by one. Into the small (heart) the vital spirits are placed, into the small stomach food is placed[386], therefore this Virâg, small by one, serves for the obtainment of those desires.

10. He who knows this, obtains those desires.

11. The verses (contained in the hymn agnim naro dîdhitibhi*h*) become the B*r*ihatî[387] metre and the Virâg metre, (they become) the perfection which belongs to that day (the mahâvrata). Then they also become Anush*t*ubh[388], for the offerings of âgya (ghee) dwell in Anush*t*ubhs[389].

---

[384] Cf. Ait. Âr. I, 1, 4, 21; II, 3, 4, 2.

[385] The plural after the dual is explained by the fact that the hymn means the twenty-five verses.

[386] Cf. I, 3, 7, 5.

[387] The hymn consists of eighteen Virâg and seven Trish*t*ubh verses. Therefore the eighteen Virâg verses remain what they are, only that the first is repeated three times, so that we have twenty Virâg verses. The seven Trish*t*ubhs, by repeating the last three times, become nine. We then take eight syllables away from each verse, thus changing them into nine B*r*ihatî verses. The nine times eight syllables, which were taken off, give us seventy-two syllables, and as each B*r*ihatî consists of thirty-six syllables, two B*r*ihatîs.

[388] The change of the first verse, which is a Virâg of thirty-three syllables, into an Anush*t*ubh is produced by a still easier process. The first Virâg consists here of thirty-three syllables, the Anush*t*ubh should have thirty-two. But one or two syllables more or less does not destroy a metre, according to the views of native metricians. The Virâg itself, for instance, should have thirty syllables, and here has thirty-three. Therefore if changed into an Anush*t*ubh, it simply has one syllable over, which is of no consequence. Comm.

[389] Cf. Ait. Âr. I, 1, 1, 4.

THIRD KHA*ND*A[390].

1. Some say: 'Let him take a Gâyatrî hymn for the Pra-uga. Verily, Gâyatrî is brightness and glory of countenance, and thus the sacrificer becomes bright and glorious.'

2. Others say: 'Let him take a Ush*n*ih hymn for the Pra-uga. Verily, Ush*n*ih is life, and thus the sacrificer has a long life.'

Others say: 'Let him take an Ansh*t*ubh hymn for the Pra-uga. Verily, Anush*t*ubh is valour, and it serves for obtaining valour.'

Others say: 'Let him take a B*ri*hatî hymn for the Pra-uga. Verily, B*ri*hatî is fortune, and thus the sacrificer becomes fortunate.'

Others say: 'Let him take a Paṅkti hymn for the Pra-uga. Verily, Paṅkti is food, and thus the sacrificer becomes rich in food.'

Others say: 'Let him take a Trish*t*ubh hymn for the Pra-uga. Verily, Trish*t*ubh is strength, and thus the sacrificer becomes strong.'

Others say: 'Let him take a *G*agatî hymn for the Pra-uga. Verily, cattle is *G*agatî-like, and thus the sacrificer becomes rich in cattle.'

But we say: 'Let him take a Gâyatrî hymn only. Verily, Gâyatrî is Brahman, and that day (the mahâvrata) is (for the attainment of) Brahman. Thus he obtains Brahman by means of Brahman.

4. 'And it must be a Gâyatrî hymn by Madhu*kkh*andas,

5. 'For Madhu*kkh*andas is called Madhu*kkh*andas, because he wishes (*kh*andati) for honey (madhu) for the *R*ishis.

6. 'Now food verily is honey, all is honey, all desires are honey, and thus if he recites the hymn of Madhu*kkh*andas, it serves for the attainment of all desires.

7. 'He who knows this, obtains all desires.'

This (Gâyatrî pra-uga), according to the one-day (ekâha) ceremonial[391], is perfect in form[392]. On that day (the mahâvrata) much is done now and then which has to be hidden[393], and has to be atoned for y recitation of hymns). Atonement (*s*ânti) is rest, the one-day sacrifice. Therefore at the end of the year (on the last day but one of the sacrifice that lasts a whole year) the sacrificers rest on this atonement as their rest.

8. He who knows this rests firm, and they also for whom a Hot*ri*

---

[390] Thus far the hymn which has to be recited by the Hot*ri* priest, after the eating of the *ri*tugrabas, has been considered. What follows next is the so-called Pra-uga hymn, consisting of seven t*rik*as, which the Hot*ri* has to recite after the Vi*s*vedevagraha. Different *S*âkhâs recommend hymns of different metres, our *S*âkhâ fixes on the Gâyatrî.

[391] It is copied from the Vi*s*vagit, and that from the Agnish*t*oma.

[392] Nothing is wanting for its performance, if one only follows the rules given in the Agnish*t*oma.

[393] Dâsîn*ri*tya-bahubhûtamaithuna-brahma*k*âripu*msk*alîsampravâ-dâdikam. See Rajendralal Mitra, Introduction to his edition of the Aitareya-âra*n*yaka, p. 25. It might be better to join ekâha*h* with *s*ântyâm, but even then the argumentation is not quite clear.

priest who knows this, recites this hymn.

FOURTH KHA*N*DA[394].

1. Rv. I, 2, 1-3. Vâyav â yâhi dar*s*ateme somâ ara*m* k*ri*tâ*h*, 'Approach, O Vâyu, conspicuous, these Somas have been made ready.' Because the word ready occurs in these verses, therefore is this day (of the sacrifice) ready (and auspicious) for the sacrificer and for the gods.

2. Yes, this day is ready (and auspicious) to him who knows this, or for whom a Hot*ri* priest who knows this, recites.

3. Rv. I, 2, 4-6. Indravâyû ime sutâ, â yâtam upa nishk*ri*tam, 'Indra and Vâyu, these Somas are prepared, come hither towards what has been prepared.' By nishk*ri*ta, prepared, he means what has been well prepared (sa*m*skr*i*ta).

4. Indra and Vâyu go to what has been prepared by him who knows this, or for whom a Hot*ri* priest who knows this, recites.

5. Rv. I, 2, 7. Mitra*m* huve pûtadaksham, dhiya*m* gh*ri*tâkî*m* sâdhantâ, 'I call Mitra of holy strength; (he and Varu*n*a) they fulfil the prayer accompanied with clarified butter.' Verily, speech is the prayer accompanied with clarified butter.

6. Speech is given to him who knows this, or for whom a Hot*ri* priest who knows this, recites.

7. Rv. I, 3, 1. A*s*vinâ yagvarîr isha*h*, 'O A*s*vinau, (eat) the sacrificial offerings.' Verily, the sacrificial offerings are food, and this serves for the acquirement of food.

8. Rv. I, 3, 3. Â yâta*m* rudravartanî, 'Come hither, ye Rudravartanî.'

9. The Asvinau go to the sacrifice of him who knows this, or for whom a Hot*ri* priest who knows this, recites.

10. Rv. I, 3, 4-6. Indrâ yâhi *k*itrabhâno, indrâ yâhi dhiyeshita*h*, indrâ yâhi tûtugâna, 'Come hither, Indra, of bright splendour, Come hither, Indra, called by prayer, Come hither, Indra, quickly!' Thus he recites, Come hither, come hither!

11. Indra comes to the sacrifice of him who knows this, or for whom a Hot*ri* priest who knows this, recites.

12. Rv. I, 3, 7. Omâsa*s* *k*arsha*n*îdh*ri*to vi*s*ve devâsa â gata, 'Vi*s*ve Devas, protectors, supporters of men, come hither!'

13. Verily, the Vi*s*ve Devas come to the call of him who knows this, or for whom a Hot*ri* priest who knows this, recites.

14. Rv. I, 3, 7. Dâsvâ*m*so dâ*s*usha*h* sutam, 'Come ye givers to the libation of the giver!' By dâ*s*usha*h* he means dadusha*h*, i.e. to the libation of every one that gives.

---

[394] Next follows a list of the verses which form the seven t*rik*as (groups of three verses) of the Pra-uga hymn, with occasional remarks on certain words.

15. The gods fulfil his wish, with whatever wish he recites this verse,

16. (The wish of him) who knows this, or for whom a Hot*ri* priest who knows this, recites.

17. Rv. I, 3, 10. Pâvakâ na*h* sarasvatî yagña*m* vash*t*u dhiyâvasu*h*, 'May the holy Sarasvatî accept our sacrifice, rich in prayer!' Speech is meant by 'rich in prayer.'

18. Speech is given to him who knows this, or for whom a Hot*ri* priest who knows this, recites.

19. And when he says, 'May she accept our sacrifice!' what he means is, 'May she carry off our sacrifice!'

20. If these verses are recited straight on, they are twenty-one. Man also consists of twenty-one. There are ten fingers on his hands, ten toes on his feet, and the trunk the twenty-first. He adorns that trunk, the twenty-first, by this hymn[395].

21. By repeating the first and the last verses thrice, they become twenty-five. The trunk is the twenty-fifth, and Pragâpati is the twenty-fifth. There are ten fingers on his hands, ten toes on his feet, two legs, two arms, and the trunk the twenty-fifth. He adorns that trunk, the twenty-fifth, by this hymn'.

Now this day consists of twenty-five, and the Stoma hymn of that day consists of twenty-five: it becomes the same through the same. Therefore these two, the day and the hymn, are twenty-five, yea, twenty-five.

SECOND ADHYÂYA.

FIRST KHA*ND*A[396].

1. The two *trik*as, Rv. VIII, 68, 1-3, â tvâ ratha*m* yathotaye, and Rv. VIII, 2, 1-3, ida*m* vaso sutam andha*h*, form the first (pratipad) and the second (anu*k*ara) of the Marutvatîya hymn.

2. Both, as belonging to the one-day ceremonial[397], are perfect in form. On that day much is done now and then which has to be hidden, and has to be atoned for. Atonement is rest, the one-day sacrifice. Therefore at the end of the year the sacrificers rest on this atonement as their rest. He who knows this rests firm, and they also for whom a Hot*ri* priest who knows this, recites this hymn[398].

---

395 Cf. I, 1, 2, 7; I, 3, 5, 7.

396 In the first adhyâya the two hymns to be recited by the Hot*ri* priest at the morning-libation (the âgya and pra-uga *s*astra) have been considered. Now follows the Marutvatîya hymn, to be recited by the Hot*ri* priest at the noon-libation.

397 Taken from the Agnish*t*oma.

398 Cf. I, 1, 3, 7-8.

3. In the second verse of (the Pragâtha[399]), indra nedîya ed ihi, pra sû tirâ sa*k*îbhir ye ta ukthina*h* (Rv. VIII, 53, 5, 6), there occurs the word ukthina*h*, reciters of hymns[400]. Verily, this day (the mahâvrata) is an uktha (hymn), and as endowed with an uktha, the form of this day is perfect.

4. In the first verse (of another Pragâtha) the word vîra, strong, occurs (Rv. I, 40, 3), and as endowed with the word vîra, strong, the form of this day is perfect.

5. In the second verse (of another Pragâtha) the word suvîryam, strength, occurs (Rv. I. 40, 1), and as endowed with the word suvîrya, strength, the form of this day is perfect.

6. In the first verse (of another Pragâtha) the word ukthyam, to be hymned, occurs (Rv. I, 40, 5). Verily, this day is an uktha, and as endowed with an uktha, the form of this day is perfect.

7. In the (Dhayyâ) verse agnir netâ (Rv. III, 2 0, 4) the word v*ri*trahâ, killer of V*ri*tra, occurs. The killing of V*ri*tra is a form (character) of Indra, this day (the mahâvrata) belongs to Indra, and this is the (perfect) form of that day.

8. In the (Dhayyâ) verse tva*m* soma kratubhi*h* sukratur bhû*h* (Rv. I, 91, 2) the word v*ri*shâ[401], powerful, occurs. Powerful is a form (character) of Indra, this day belongs to Indra, and this is the (perfect) form of that day.

9. In the (Dhayyâ) verse pinvanty apa*h* (Rv. I, 64, 6) the word vâginam, endowed with food, occurs. Endowed with food is a form (character) of Indra, this day belongs to Indra, and this is the (perfect) form of that day.

10. In the same verse the word stanayantam, thundering, occurs. Endowed with thundering is a form (character) of Indra, this day belongs to Indra, and this is the (perfect) form of that day.

11. In (the Pragâtha) pra va indrâya b*ri*hate (Rv. VIII, 89, 3) (the word b*ri*hat occurs). Verily, b*ri*hat is mahat (great), and as endowed with mahat, great, the form of this day (mahâvrata) is perfect.

12. In (the Pragâtha) b*ri*had indrâya gâyata (Rv. VIII, 89, 1) (the word b*ri*hat occurs). Verily, b*ri*hat is mahat (great), and as endowed with mahat, the form of this day is perfect.

13. In (the Pragâtha) naki*h* sudâso ratham pary âsa na rîramad (Rv. VII, 32, 10) the words paryâsa (he moved round) and na rîramad (he did not enjoy) occur, and as endowed with the words paryasta and rânti the form of this day is perfect[402].

---

[399] All these Pragâthas consist of two verses expanded into a t*rik*a.

[400] Hotrâdaya ukthina*h* sastri*n*ah.

[401] Cf. I, 2, 2, 14.

[402] Because the performance of the Mahâvrata sacrifice moves the worshipper round to another world and gives him enjoyment. Comm. It is difficult to surpass the absurdity of these explanations. Na rîramat means no one stopped the chariot of Sudâs. But even if

He recites all (these) Pragâthas, in order to obtain all the days (of the sacrifice), all the Ukthas[403], all the P*r*ish*th*as[404], all the *S*astras[405], all the Pra-ugas[406], and all the Savanas (libations).

SECOND KHA*ND*A[407].

1. He recites the hymn, asat su me *g*arita*h* sâbhivega*h* (Rv. X, 27, 1), (and in. it the word) satyadhv*ri*tam, the destroyer of truth. Verily, that day is truth, and as endowed with the word satya, truth, the form of this day is perfect[408].

2. That hymn is composed by Vasukra. Verily, Vasukra is Brahman, and that day is Brahman. Thus he obtains Brahman by means of Brahman[409].

3. Here they say: ‘Why then is that Marutvatîya, hymn completed by the hymn of Vasukra?’ Surely because no other *R*ishi but Vasukra brought out a Marutvatîya hymn, or divided it properly[410]. Therefore that Marutvatîya hymn is completed by the hymn of Vasukra.

4. That hymn, asat su me, is not definitely addressed to any deity, and is therefore supposed to be addressed to Pra*g*âpati. Verily, Pra*g*âpati is indefinite, and therefore the hymn serves to win Pra*g*âpati.

5. Once in the hymn (Rv. X, 27, 22) he defines Indra (indrâya sunvat); therefore it does not fall off from its form, as connected with Indra.

6. He recites the hymn (Rv. VI, 17, 1) pibâ somam abhi yam ugra tarda*h*.

7. In the verse ûrvam gavyam mahi g*rin*âna indra the word mahi, great, occurs. Endowed with the word mahat, the form of this day is perfect.

8. That hymn is composed by Bharadvâ*g*a, and Bharadvâ*g*a was he

---

it meant that no one rejoiced through the chariot of Sudâs, it would be difficult to see how the negative of enjoyment, mentioned in the hymn, could contribute to the perfection of a sacrifice which is to confer positive enjoyment on the worshipper.

403 The stotras following after the Yagñâyagñîya Sâman, serving for the ukthya-kratus.

404 The stotras of the noon-libation, to be performed with the Rathantara, B*ri*hat, and other Sâmans.

405 The *s*astras, recitations, accompanying the oblations of âgya.

406 The pra-ugas, a division of *s*astras, described above.

407 The type after which the Marutvatîya-*s*astra is to be performed is the *K*aturvi*m*sa day. Hitherto (from â tvâ ratham to naki*h* sudâsa*h*), all that is taken over from the type to the modification, i.e. the Marutvatîya, has been explained. Now follow the verses which are new and peculiar to the Marutvatîya of the Mahâvrata.

408 The commentator endeavours to make the meaning more natural by taking in the word prahantâ, he who kills the destroyer of truth. But considering the general character of these remarks, this is hardly necessary.

409 Cf. I, 1, 3, 3.

410 By separating the first t*rik*a from the second, and so forth.

who knew most, who lived longest, and performed the greatest austerities among the *Ri*shis, and by this hymn he drove away evil. Therefore if he recites the hymn of Bharadvâga, then, after having driven away evil, he becomes learned, long-lived, and full of austerities.

9. He recites the hymn kayâ subhâ savayasa*h* sanîlâ*h* (Rv. I, 165, 1).

10. In the verse â *s*âsate prati haryanty ukthâ (Rv. I, 165, 4) the word uktha occurs. Verily, that day (the mahâvrata) is uktha (hymn). Endowed with the word uktha, the form of this day becomes perfect.

11. That hymn is called Kayâ*s*ubhîya[411]. Verily, that hymn, which is called Kayâ*s*ubhîya, is mutual understanding and it is lasting. By means of it Indra, Agastya, and the Maruts came to a mutual understanding. Therefore, if he recites the Kayâ*s*ubhîya hymn, it serves for mutual understanding.

12. The same hymn is also long life. Therefore, if the sacrificer is dear to the Hot*ri*, let him recite the Kayâ*s*ubhîya hymn for him.

13. He recites the hymn marutvâ*n* indra v*ri*shabo ra*n*âya (Rv. III, 47, 1).

14. In it the words indra v*ri*shabha (powerful) occur. Verily, powerful is a form of Indra[412], this day belongs to Indra, and this is the perfect form of that day.

15. That hymn is composed by Vi*s*vâmitra. Verily, Vi*s*vâmitra was the friend (mitra) of all (vi*s*va).

16. Everybody is the friend of him who knows this, and for whom a Hot*ri* priest who knows this, recites this hymn.

17. The next hymn, ganish*th*â ugra*h* sahase turâya (Rv. I, 73, 1), forms a Nividdhâna[413], and, according to the one-day (ekâha) ceremonial, is perfect in form. On that day much is done now and then which has to be hidden, and has to be atoned for (by recitation of hymns). Atonement is rest, the one-day sacrifice. Therefore at the end of the year (on the last day but one of the sacrifice that lasts a whole year) the sacrificers rest on this atonement as their rest.

He who knows this rests firm, and they also for whom a Hot*ri* priest who knows this, recites this hymn[414].

---

[411] Cf. Ait. Brâhm. V, 16.

[412] Cf. Ait. Âr. II, 2, 1, 8.

[413] The hymn consists of eleven verses. In the middle, after the sixth verse, nivids or invocations, such as indro marutvân, are inserted, and therefore it is called a nividdhâna hymn.

[414] With this hymn the Marutvatîya-*s*astra is finished. All the hymns from â tvâ ratham to asat su me garitar are simply taken over from the *K*aturvi*m*sa ceremonial, the rest are peculiar to the Mahâvrata day, the day preceding the Udayanîya or final day of the Gavâmayana sattra. All this is more fully described in the fifth Âra*n*yaka (V, 1, 1, 8), containing the Sûtras or rules of *S*aunaka, while the earlier Âra*n*yakas are reckoned as

18. These, if recited straight on, are ninety-seven verses[415]. The ninety are three Virâg, each consisting of thirty, and then the seven verses which are over. Whatever is the praise of the seven, is the praise of ninety also.

19. By repeating the first and last verses three times each, they become one hundred and one verses.

20. There are five fingers, of four joints each, two pits (in the elbow and the arm), the arm, the eye, the shoulder-blade; this makes twenty-five. The other three parts have likewise twenty-five each[416]. That makes a hundred, and the trunk is the one hundred and first.

21. Hundred is life, health, strength, brightness. The sacrificer as the one hundred and first rests in life, health, strength, and brightness.

22. These verses become Trish*t*ubh[417], for the noonday-libation consists of Trish*t*ubh verses.

THIRD KHA*ND*A[418].

1. They say: 'What is the meaning of preṅkha, swing?' Verily, he is the swing, who blows (the wind). He indeed goes forward (pra + iṅkhate) in these worlds, and that is why the swing is called preṅkha.

2. Some say, that there should be one plank, because the wind blows in one way, and it should be like the wind.

3. That is not to be regarded.

Brâhma*n*as, and are therefore mixed up with matters not actually required for the performance of the sacrifice.

415

The first Stotriya and Ânurûpa tri*k*as =	6 (I, 2, 1, 1).
The six Pragâthas, each of 2 verses raised to 3 (but the text gives seven Pragâthas) =	18 (I, 2, 1, 3; 4; 5; 6; 11; 12; 13).
Three Dhâyyâs =	3 (I, 2, 1, 7; 8; 9).
Asat su =	24 (I, 2, 2, 1).
Pibâ somam =	15 (I, 2, 2, 6).
Kayâ *s*ubhâ =	15 (I, 2, 2, 9).
Marutvâ*n* indra =	5 (I, 2, 2, 13).
*G*anish*th*â ugra*h* =	11 (I, 2, 2, 17).
	97

416 The left side as well as the right, and then the left and right side of the lower body. Thus we have twenty joints of the five toes, a thigh, a leg, and three joints, making twenty-five on each side.

417 Approach the Trish*t*ubh metre of the last hymn. Comm.

418 After having considered the Marutvatîya, he proceeds to consider the Nishkevalya. This has to be recited by the Hot*ri* while sitting on a swing.

4. Some say, there should be three planks, because there are these three threefold worlds, and it should be like them.

5. That is not to be regarded.

6. Let there be two, for these two worlds (the earth and heaven) are seen as if most real, while the ether (space) between the two is the sky (antariksha). Therefore let there be two planks.

7. Let them be made of Udumbara wood. Verily, the Udumbara tree is sap and eatable food, and thus it serves to obtain sap and eatable food.

8. Let them be elevated in the middle (between the earth and the cross-beam). Food, if placed in the middle, delights man, and thus he places the sacrificer in the middle of eatable food.

9. There are two kinds of rope, twisted towards the right and twisted towards the left. The right ropes serve for some animals, the left ropes for others. If there are both kinds of rope, they serve for the attainment of both kinds of cattle.

10. Let them be made of Darbha (Ku*s*a grass), for among plants Darbha is free from evil, therefore they should be made of Darbha grass.

FOURTH KHA*ND*A.

1. Some say: 'Let the swing be one ell (aratni) above the ground, for by that measure verily the Svarga worlds are measured.' That is not to be regarded.

2. Others say: 'Let it be one span (prâde*s*a), for by that measure verily the vital airs were measured.' That is not to be regarded[419].

3. Let it be one fist (mush*t*i), for by that measure verily all eatable food is made, and by that measure all eatable food is taken; therefore let it be one fist above the ground.

4. They say: 'Let him mount the swing from east to west, like he who shines; for the sun mounts these worlds from east to west.' That is not to be regarded.

5. Others say: 'Let him mount the swing sideways, for people mount a horse sideways[420], thinking that thus they will obtain all desires.' That is not to be regarded.

6. They say: 'Let him mount the swing[421] from behind, for people mount a ship from behind, and this swing is a ship in which to go to heaven.' Therefore let him mount it from behind.

7. Let him touch the swing with his chin (*kh*ubuka). The parrot (*s*uka) thus mounts a tree, and he is of all birds the one who eats most

---

[419] They rise one span above the heart, and they proceed one span from out the mouth. Comm.

[420] Here we have clearly riding on horseback.

[421] While the swing points to the east, let him stand west, and thus mount.

food. Therefore let him touch it with his chin.

8. Let him mount the swing with his arms[422]. The hawk swoops thus on birds and on trees, and he is of all birds the strongest. Therefore let him mount with his arms.

9. Let him not withdraw one foot (the right or left) from the earth, for fear that he may lose his hold.

10. The Hot*ri* mounts the swing, the Udgât*ri* the seat made of Udumbara wood. The swing is masculine, the seat feminine, and they form a union. Thus he makes a union at the beginning of the uktha in order to get offspring.

He who knows this, gets offspring and cattle.

12. Next the swing is food, the seat fortune. Thus he mounts and obtains food and fortune.

13. The Hotrakas (the Prasâst*ri*, Brâhma*n*â*kkh*a*m*sin, Pot*ri*, Nesh*t*ri, Agnâdhra, and A*kkh*âvâka) together with the Brahman sit down on cushions made of grass, reeds, leaves, &c.

14. Plants and trees, after they have grown up, bear fruit. Thus if the priests mount on that day altogether (on their seats), they mount on solid and fluid as their proper food. Therefore this serves for the attainment of solid as proper food[423].

15. Some say: 'Let him descend after saying vasha*t* [424].' That is not to be regarded. For, verily, that respect is not shown which is shown to one who does not see it[425].

16. Others say: 'Let him descend after he has taken the food in his hand.' That is not to be regarded. For, verily, that respect is not shown which is shown to one after he has approached quite close.

17. Let him descend after he has seen the food. For, verily, that is real respect which is shown to one when he sees it. Only after having actually seen the food (that is brought to the sacrifice), let him descend from the swing.

18. Let him descend turning towards the east, for in the east the seed of the gods springs up[426]. Therefore let him rise turning towards the east, yea, turning towards the east.

---

[422] The fore-arms, from the elbow to the end, the aratnî. Comm.

[423] One expects isha*h* before ûrga*h*, but it is wanting in both text and commentary, and in other MSS. also.

[424] The word by which the Hot*ri* invites the Adhvaryu to offer the oblation to the gods. The descending from the swing belongs, of course, to a later part of the sacrifice.

[425] It is supposed that the Hot*ri* rises from the swing to show respect to the sacrificial food, when it is brought near. But as it is not brought near, immediately after the Hot*ri* has finished his part with the word vasha*t*, the food could not see the Hot*ri* rise, and this mark of respect, intended for the food, would thus be lost.

[426] Should it be devareta*h* sampragâyate, or devaretasam pragâyate?

THIRD ADHYÂYA.

FIRST KHA*ND*A.

1. Let him begin this day[427] with singing 'Him,' thus they say.

2. Verily, the sound Him is Brahman, that day also is Brahman. He who knows this, obtains Brahman even by Brahman.

3. As he begins with the sound Him, surely that masculine sound of Him and the feminine *Rik* (the verse) make a couple. Thus he makes a couple at the beginning of the hymn in order to get offspring[428]. He who knows this, gets cattle and offspring.

4. Or, as he begins with the sound Him, surely like a wooden spade, so the sound Him serves to dig up Brahman (the sap of the Veda). And as a man wishes to dig up any, even the hardest soil, with a spade, thus he digs up Brahman.

5. He who knows this digs up, by means of the sound Him, everything he may desire.

6. If he begins with the sound Him, that sound is the holding apart of divine and human speech.

Therefore, he who begins, after having uttered the sound Him, holds apart divine and human speech[429].

SECOND KHA*ND*A.

1. And here they ask: 'What is the beginning of this day?' Let him say: 'Mind and speech[430].'

2. All desires dwell in the one (mind), the other yields all desires.

3. All desires dwell in the mind, for with the mind he conceives all desires.

4. All desires come to him who knows this.

5. Speech yields all desires, for with speech he declares all his desires.

6. Speech yields all desires to him who knows this.

7. Here they say: 'Let him not begin this day with a *Rik*, a Yagus, or a Sâman verse (divine speech), for it is said, he should not start with a *Rik*, a Yagus, or a Sâman[431].'

---

[427] The Nishkevalya-*s*astra, of the noon-libation; Cf. I, 2, 2, 1.

[428] Cf. I, 2, 4, 10.

[429] Human speech is the ordinary speech, divine speech that of the Veda. Thus between the hymns, or the divine speech, and the ordinary language of conversation the sound Him is interposed as a barrier.

[430] Mind, to think about the hymns which have to be recited; speech, to recite them without a flaw.

[431] It is doubtful whether neyâd *ri*ka*h* and apaga*kkh*et can have this meaning. However, what is intended is clear, viz. that the priest, even after having uttered the

8. Therefore, let him say these Vyâh*ri*tis (sacred interjections) first.

9. These interjections Bhûs, Bhuvas, Svar are the three Vedas, Bhûs the *Rig*-veda, Bhuvas the Yagur-veda, Svar the Sâma-veda. Therefore (by intercalating these) he does not begin simply with a *Rik*, Yagus, or Sâman verse, he does not start with a *Rik*, Yagus, or Sâman verse.

THIRD KHA*ND*A.

1. He begins with tad, this, (the first word of the first hymn, tad id âsa). Verily 'this, this' is food, and thus he obtains food.

2. Pragâpati indeed uttered this as the first word, consisting of one or two syllables, viz. tata and tâta (or tat)[432]. And thus does a child, as soon as he begins to speak, utter the word, consisting of one or two syllables, viz. tata and tâta (or tat). With this very word, consisting of tat or tatta, he begins.

3. This has been said by a *Ri*shi (Rv. X, 71, 1)[433]:—

4. 'O B*ri*haspati, the first point of speech;'—for this is the first and highest point of speech.

5. 'That which you have uttered, making it a name;'—for names are made by speech.

6. 'That (name) which was the best and without a flaw;'—for this is the best and without a flaw.

7. 'That which was hidden by their love, is made manifest;'—for this was hidden in the body, viz. those deities (which enter the body, Agni as voice, entering the mouth, &c.); and that was manifest among the gods in heaven. This is what was intended by the verse.

---

sound Him, should not immediately begin with verses from the Vedas, but should intercalate the three syllables bhûr bhuva*h* svar, or, if taken singly, bhûs, bhuvas, svar.

[432] Tata and tâta are used both by children in addressing their parents, and by parents in addressing their children. If tat is called the very same word, eva is used in the sense of iva.

[433] The verse is cited to confirm the meaning of tat, the first word of the first hymn (tad id âsa), as explained before. It was said that tat was the first name applied to a child. Now, according to Â*s*valâyana G*ri*hya-sûtra I, 16, 8, a name is given to a child at the time of its birth, a name which no one knows except father and mother, till the time when he is initiated by a Guru. This is called the abhivadanîya name. In allusion to this custom it is said here that tata is the secret name of the child, which becomes publicly known at a later time only. Of course the interpretation of the verse in that sense is unnatural, but quite in keeping with the general character of the Âra*n*yaka. I doubt whether even the commentator understood what was intended by the author, and whether the gods who enter the body are supposed to know the name, or whether the name refers to these gods, or, it may be, to tad, the Brahman.

FOURTH KHA*ND*A[434].

1. He begins with: 'That indeed was the oldest in the worlds[435];'—for that (the Brahman) is verily the oldest in the worlds.

2. 'Whence was born the fierce one, endowed with brilliant force;'—for from it was born the fierce one, who is endowed with brilliant force.

3. 'When born he at once destroys the enemies;'—for he at once when born struck down the evil one.

4. 'He after whom all friends rejoice;'—verily all friends are the creatures, and they rejoice after him, saying, 'He has risen, he has risen[436].'

5. 'Growing by strength, the almighty[437];'—for he (the sun) does grow by strength, the almighty.

6. 'He, as enemy, causes fear to the slave;'—for everything is afraid of him.

7. 'Taking the breathing and the not-breathing;'—this means the living and the lifeless.

8. 'Whatever has been offered at feasts came to thee;'—this means everything is in thy power.

9. 'All turn their thought also on thee[438];'—this means all these beings, all minds, all thoughts also turn to thee.

10. 'When these two become three protectors;'—i.e. when these two united beget offspring.

11. He who knows this, gets offspring and cattle.

12. 'Join what is sweeter than sweet (offspring) with the sweet (the parents);'—for the couple (father and mother) is sweet, the offspring is sweet, and he thus joins the offspring with the couple.

13. 'And this (the son, when married) being very sweet, conquered through the sweet;'—i.e. the couple is sweet, the offspring is sweet, and thus through the couple he conquers offspring[439].

14. This is declared by a *R*ishi[440]: 'Because he (Pragâpati) raised his body (the hymn tad id âsa or the Veda in general) in the body (of the sacrificer)' (therefore that Nishkevalya hymn is praised);—i.e. this body, consisting of the Veda, in that corporeal form (of the sacrificer).

15. 'Then let this body indeed be the medicine of that body;'—i.e. this body, consisting of the Veda, of that corporeal form (of the

---

[434] He now explains the first hymn of the Nishkevalya, which is called the Râgana.

[435] Rv. X, 120, 1.

[436] The sun and the fire.

[437] Rv. X, 120, 2.

[438] Rv. X, 120, 3.

[439] All these are purely fanciful interpretations.

[440] Not to be found in our *S*âkhâ of the Rig-veda.

sacrificer).

16. Of this (the first foot of Rv. X, 120, 1) the eight syllables are Gâyatrî, the eleven syllables are Trish*t*ubh, the twelve syllables are *G*agatî, the ten syllables are Virâ*g*. The Virâ*g*, consisting of ten syllables, rests in these three metres[441].

17. The word purusha, consisting of three syllables, that indeed goes into the Virâ*g*[442].

18. Verily, these are all metres, these (Gâyatrî, Trish*t*ubh, Gagatî) having the Virâ*g* as the fourth. In this manner this day is complete in all metres to him who knows this.

FIFTH KHA*ND*A.

1. He extends these (verses) by (interpolating) the sound[443]. Verily, the sound is purusha, man. Therefore every man when he speaks, sounds loud, as it were.

2. At the end of each foot of the first verse of the hymn tad id âsa, he inserts one foot of the second verse of hymn Rv. VIII, 69, nada*m* va odatînâm, &c. Thus the verse is to be recited as follows:

Tad id âsa bhuvaneshu *g*yesh*th*am pu
  nada*m* va odatînâm,
Yato *g*agña ugras tveshan*r*im*n*o ru
  nada*m* yoyuvatînâm,
Sadyo gagñâno ni ri*n*âti *s*atrûn
  pati*m* vo aghnyânâm,
Anu yam vi*s*ve madanti ûmâ*h* sho
  dhenûnâm ishudhyasi.

---

[441] These metres are obtained by a purely arbitrary counting of syllables in the hymn tadidâsa, which really consists of Trish*t*ubh verses.

[442] If we simply count syllables, the first and second feet of the first verse consist of ten syllables only, the fourth of nine or ten. In order to bring them to the right number, the word purusha is to be added to what is a Virâ*g*, i.e. to the first, the second, and fourth feet. We thus get:

tad id âsa bhuvaneshu *g*yesh*th*am pu
yato *g*agña ugras tveshan*r*im*n*o ru
sadyo gagñâno ni ri*n*âti *s*atrûn
anu ya*m* vi*s*ve madanti ûmâ*h* sha*h*.

Cf. Ait. Âr. V, 1, 6.

[443] The sound, nada, is really a verse beginning with nadam, and which is interpolated after the syllables pu ru sha*h*.

In nada*m* va odatînâm (Rv. VIII, 69, 2), odati[444] are the waters in heaven, for they water all this; and they are the waters in the mouth, for they water all good food.

3. In nada*m* yoyuvatînâm (Rv. VIII, 69, 2), yoyuvatî are the waters in the sky, for they seem to inundate; and they are the waters of perspiration, for they seem to run continually.

4. In pati*m* vo aghnyânâm (Rv. VIII, 69, 2), aghnyâ are the waters which spring from the smoke of fire, and they are the waters which spring from the organ.

5. In dhenûnâm ishudhyasi (Rv. VIII, 69, 2), the dhenu (cows) are the waters, for they delight all this; and ishudhyasi means, thou art food.

6. He extends a Trish*t*ubh and an Anush*t*ubh[445]. Trish*t*ubh is the man, Anush*t*ubh the wife, and they make a couple. Therefore does a man, after having found a wife, consider himself a more perfect man.

7. These verses, by repeating the first three times, become twenty-five. The trunk is the twenty-fifth, and Pragâpati is the twenty-fifth[446]. There are ten fingers on his hands, ten toes on his feet, two legs, two arms, and the trunk the twenty-fifth. He adorns that trunk as the twenty-fifth. Now this day consists of twenty-five, and the Stoma hymn of that day consists of twenty-five: it becomes the same through the same. Therefore the two, the day and the hymn, are twenty-five[447].

SIXTH KHA*ND*A.

This is an exact repetition of the third kha*nd*a. According to the commentator, the third kha*nd*a was intended for the glory of the first word tad, while the sixth is intended for the glory of the whole hymn.

---

[444] The nasal pluta on iti is explained as pâdapratîkagraha*n*e 'tyantamâdarârtha*h*. Cf. Ait. Âr. II, 1, 4, 3.

[445] Tad id âsa is a Trish*t*ubh, nada*m* va*h* an Anush*t*ubh.

[446] Cf. I, 1, 2, 7; I, 1, 4, 21.

[447] The number is obtained as follows:

1. Tad id âsa (Rv. X, 120)= . .	9 verses
2. Tâ*m* su te kîrtim (Rv. X, 54)= .	6 "
3. Bhûya id vav*ri*dhe (Rv. VI, 30)= .	5 "
4. N*ri*nâm u tvâ (Rv. I, 51, 4)= . .	3 "
	23 + 2 = 25

SEVENTH KHA*ND*A.

1. He begins with the hymn, Tad id âsa, bhuvaneshu gyesh*th*am (Rv. X, 120). Verily, gyesh*th*a, the oldest, is mahat, great. Endowed with mahat the form of this day is perfect.

2. Then follows the hymn, Tâ*m* su te kîrtim maghavan mahitvâ (Rv. X, 54), with the auspicious word mahitvâ.

3. Then follows the hymn, Bhûya id vav*ri*dhe vîryâya (Rv. VI, 30), with the auspicious word vîrya.

4. Then follows the hymn, N*ri*n*â*m u tvâ n*ri*ta*mam* gobhir ukthai*h* (Rv. I, 51, 4), with the auspicious word uktha.

5. He extends the first two pâdas, which are too small, by one syllable (Rv. X, 120, 1 a, and Rv. VIII, 69, 2 a)[448]. Into the small heart the vital spirits are placed, into the small stomach food is placed. It serves for the attainment of these desires. He who knows this, obtains these desires.

6. The two feet, each consisting of ten syllables (Rv. X, 120, 1 a, b), serve for the gaining of both kinds of food[449], of what has feet (animal food), and what has no feet (vegetable food).

7. They come to be of eighteen syllables each[450]. Of those which are ten, nine are the prâ*n*as (openings of the body)[451], the tenth is the (vital) self. This is the perfection of the (vital) self; Eight syllables remain in each. He who knows them, obtains whatever he desires.

EIGHTH KHA*ND*A.

1. He extends (these verses) by (interpolating) the sound[452]. Verily, breath (prâ*n*a) is sound. Therefore every breath when it sounds, sounds loud, as it were.

2. The verse (VIII, 69, 2) nada*m* va odatînâm, &c., is by its syllables an Ush*n*ih[453], by its feet an Anush*t*ubh[454]. Ush*n*ih is life,

---

[448] Cf. I, 1, 2, 9.

[449] Because Virâg, a foot of ten syllables, is food.

[450]

Rv. X, 120, 1 a= . .	10
Rv. VIII, 69, 2 a= .	7
Syllable pu= . .	1
	18

[451] Seven in the head and two in the body; sapta vai sirsha*n*yâ*h* prâ*n*â dvâv avâñ*k*âv iti.

[452] Cf. I, 3, 5, 1.

[453] Each pâda has seven syllables, the third only six; but a seventh syllable is gained by pronouncing the y as i. Comm.

[454] Because it has four pâdas.

Anush*t*ubh, speech. He thus places life and speech in him (the sacrificer.)

3. By repeating the first verse three times, they become twenty-five. The trunk is the twenty-fifth, and Pragâpati is the twenty-fifth. There are ten fingers on his hands, ten toes on his feet, two legs, two arms, and the trunk the twenty-fifth. He adorns that trunk as the twenty-fifth. Now this day consists of twenty-five, and the Stoma hymn of that day consists of twenty-five: it becomes the same through the same. Therefore the two, the day and the hymn, are twenty-five. This is the twenty-fifth with regard to the body.

4. Next, with regard to the deities: The eye, the ear, the mind, speech, and breath, these five deities (powers) have entered into that person (purusha), and that person entered into the five deities. He is wholly pervaded there with his limbs to the very hairs and nails. Therefore all beings to the very insects are born as pervaded (by the deities or senses)[455].

5. This has been declared by a *R*ishi (Rv. X, 4, 8):—

6. 'A thousandfold are these fifteen hymns;'—for five arise from ten[456].

7. 'As large as heaven and earth, so large is it;'—verily, the self (gîvâtman) is as large as heaven and earth.

8. 'A thousandfold are the thousand powers[457];'—by saying this the poet pleases the hymns (the senses), and magnifies them.

9. 'As far as Brahman reaches, so far reaches speech;'—wherever there is Brahman, there is a word; and wherever there is a word, there is Brahman, this was intended.

10. The first of the hymns among all those hymns has nine verses. Verily, there are nine prâ*n*as (openings), and it serves for their benefit.

11. Then follows a hymn of six verses. Verily, the seasons are six, and it serves to obtain them.

12. Then follows a hymn of five verses. Verily' the Paṅkti consists of five feet. Verily, Paṅkti is food, and it serves for the gaining of proper food.

13. Then follows a tristich. Three are these threefold worlds, and it serves to conquer them.

14. These verses become B*r*ihatîs[458], that metre being immortal,

---

[455] The commentator takes this in a different sense, explaining atra, there, as the body pervaded by the person, yet afterwards stating that all beings are born, pervaded by the senses.

[456] The commentator explains ukthâ, hymns, as members or organs. They are the five, and they spring from the ten, i.e. from the five elements (earth, water, fire, wind, and ether), forming part of the father and mother each, and therefore called ten, or a decade. Da*s*ata*h* is explained by bhûtada*s*akât.

[457] The application of the senses to a thousand different objects.

[458] Each foot of the Trish*t*ubh has eleven syllables, to which seven are added from the Nada hymn. This gives eighteen syllables for each pâda. Two pâdas therefore give

leading to the world of the Devas. That body of verses is the trunk (of the bird represented by the whole *s*astra), and thus it is. He who knows this comes by this way (by making the verses the trunk of the bird) near to the immortal Self, yea, to the immortal Self[459].

FOURTH ADHYÂYA.

FIRST KHA*ND*A.

1. Next comes the Sûdadohas[460] verse. Sûdadohas is breath, and thereby he joins all joints with breath.

2. Next follow the neck verses. They recite them as Ush*n*ih, according to their metre[461].

3. Next comes (again) the Sûdadohas verse. Sûdadohas is breath, and thereby he joins all joints with breath.

4. Next follows the head. That is in Gâyatrî verses. The Gâyatrî is the beginning of all metres[462]; the head the first of all members. It is in Arkavat verses (Rv. I, 7, 1-9)[463]. Arka is Agni. They are nine verses. The head consists of nine pieces. He recites the tenth verse, and that is the skin and the hairs on the head. It serves for reciting one verse more than (the nine verses contained in) the Stoma[464]. These form the Trivrit Stoma and the Gâyatrî metre, and whatever there exists, all this is produced after the production of this Stoma and this metre. Therefore the recitation of these head-hymns serves for production.

5. He who knows this, gets offspring and cattle.

6. Next comes the Sûdadohas verse. Verily, Sûdadohas is breath, and thereby he joins all joints with breath.

7. Next follow the vertebrae[465] (of the bird). These verses are Virâg

---

thirty-six syllables, and this is a B*r*ihatî. In this manner the twenty-three verses of the hymns yield forty-six B*r*ihatîs. Comm.

[459] He obtains a birth among the gods by means of this Mahâvrata ceremonial, if performed with meditation and a right understanding of its hidden meaning.

[460] The Nishkevalya-*s*astra is represented in the shape of a bird, consisting of trunk, neck, head, vertebrae, wings, tail, and stomach. Before describing the hymns which form the neck, another hymn has to be mentioned, called Sûdadohas, which has to be recited at the end of the hymns, described before, which form the trunk. Sûdadohas is explained as 'yielding milk,' and because that word occurs in the verse, the verse is called Sûdadohas. It follows on the Nada verse, Rv. VIII, 69, 3. Cf. Ait. Âr. I, 5, 1, 7.

[461] They occur in another *s*âkhâ, and are to be recited such as they are, without any insertions. They are given by *S*aunaka, Ait. Âr. V, 2, 1.

[462] It was created from the mouth of Pragâpati.

[463] They are called so, because the word arka occurs in them.

[464] The chanters of the Sâma-veda make a Triv*r*it Stoma of this hymn, without any repetitions, leaving out the tenth verse. The reciters of the Rig-veda excel them therefore by reciting a tenth verse. This is called ati*s*a*m*sanam (or -nâ).

[465] Vigavas may be a singular, and the commentator seems to take it as such in his first explanation. The text, tâ virâgo bhavanti, proves nothing, because it could not be sa virâgo bhavanti, nor even sa virâ*d* bhavati. Possibly the word may occur in both forms,

(shining). Therefore man says to man, 'Thou shinest above us;' or to a stiff and proud man, 'Thou carriest thy neck stiff.' Or because the (vertebrae of the neck) run close together, they are taken to be the best food. For Virâg, is food, and food is strength.

8. Next comes the Sûdadohas verse. Sûdadohas is breath, and thereby he joins all joints with breath.

SECOND KHA*ND*A.

1. Next follows the right wing. It is this world (the earth), it is this Agni, it is speech, it is the Rathantara[466], it is Vasish*th*a, it is a hundred[467]. These are the six powers (of the right wing)[468]. The Sampâta hymn (Rv. IV, 20) serves indeed for obtaining desires and for firmness. The Pańkti verse (Rv. I, 80, 1) serves for proper food.

---

vigu, plural vigava*h*, and vigava*h*. In a somewhat similar way we find grîvâ and grîvâ*h*, folia and la feuille. On p. 109, the commentator speaks of vigavabhâga, and again, p. 110, pakshamûlarûpâ vigavâ abhihitâ*h*. He, however, explains its meaning rightly, as the root of the wings, or rather the lower bones of the neck. Grîvâ*h*, plural, were originally the vertebrae of the neck. The paragraph, though very empty, contains at least some interesting forms of language. First vigu, vertebrae, then the participles duta and sambâ*lh*atama, and lastly the verb pratya*k*, the last probably used in the sense of to bring near, to represent, with the superlative adverb annatamâm (Pâ*n*. V, 4, 11), i.e. they are represented as if they brought the best food.

[466] Rathantara is the name of the whole number of hymns to be recited at this part of the sacrifice. It was made by Vasish*th*a, and consists of one hundred verses.

[467]

1.	Stotriya, abhi tvâ *s*ûra nonuma*h* (Rv. VII, 32, 22)	2 (3)
2.	Anurûpa, abhi tvâ pûrvapîtaye (Rv. VIII, 3, 7)	2 (3)
3.	Indrasya nu (Rv. I, 32)	15
4.	Tve ha (Rv. VII, 18, 1–15)	15
5.	Yas tigma (Rv. VII, 19)	11
6.	Ugro *g*a*g*ñe (Rv. VII, 20)	10
7.	Ud u (Rv. VII, 23)	6
8.	Â te maha*h* (Rv. VII, 25)	6
9.	Na soma*h* (Rv. VII, 26)	5
10.	Indra*m* nara*h* (Rv. VII, 27)	5
11.	Brahmâ *nah* (Rv. VII, 28)	5
12.	Aya*m* soma*h* (Rv. VII, 29)	5
13.	Â na indra*h* (Rv. IV, 20)	11
		98 (100)
14.	Itthâ hi (Rv. I, 80, 1)	1
		99 (101)

These hymns and verses are given Ait. Âr. V, 2, 2, 1. Here we also learn that hymn Rv. IV, 20, is called Sampâta, and that the last verse is a Pańkti.

[468] The six powers are earth, Agni, speech, Rathantara, Vasish*th*a, and a hundred.

2. Next comes the Sûdadohas verse. Sûdadohas is breath, thereby he joins all joints with breath.

3. Next follows the left wing. It is that world (heaven), it is that sun, it is mind, it is the Brihat, it a, it is a hundred[469]. These are the six powers (of the left wing). The Sampâta hymn (Rv. IV, 23) serves indeed for obtaining desires and for firmness. The Pankti verse (Rv. I, 81, 1) serves for proper food.

4. These two (the right and the left wings) are deficient and excessive[470]. The Brihat (the left wing) is man, the Rathantara (the right wing) is woman. The excess belongs to the man, the deficiency to the woman. Therefore they are deficient and excessive.

5. Now the left wing of a bird is verily by one feather better, therefore the left wing is larger by one verse.

6. Next comes the Sûdadohas verse. Sûdadohas is breath, and thereby he joins all joints with breath.

7. Next follows the tail. They are twenty-one Dvipadâ verses[471].

---

[469] The hundred verses are given Ait. Âr. V, 2, 2, 5.

1.	Stotriya, tvâm id dhi (Rv. VI, 46, 1)	2 (3)
2.	Anurûpa, tva*m* hy ehi (Rv. VIII, 61, 7)	2 (3)
3.	Tam u sh*t*uhi (Rv. VI, 18)	15
4.	Suta it tvam (Rv. VI, 23)	10
5.	V*ri*shâ mada*h* (Rv. VI, 24)	10
6.	Yâ ta ûti*h* (Rv. VI, 25)	9
7.	Abhûr eka*h* (Rv. VI, 31)	5
8.	Apûrvyâ (Rv. VI, 32)	5
9.	Ya ogish*th*a*h* (Rv. VI, 33)	5
10.	Sa*m* *k*a tve (Rv. VI, 34)	5
11.	Kadâ bhuvan (Rv. VI, 35)	5
12.	Satrâ madâsa*h* (Rv. VI, 36)	5
13.	Arvâg ratham (Rv. VI, 37)	5
14.	Apâd (Rv. VI, 38)	5
15.	Kathâ mahân (Rv. IV, 23)	11
		99 (101)
16.	Indro madâya (Rv. I, 81, 1)	1
		100 (102)

Though there are said to be 100 verses before the Pankti (No. 16), I can get only 99 or 101. See the following note.

[470] The right wing, is deficient by one verse, the left wing exceeds by one verse. I count 99 or 101 verses in the right, and 100 or 102 in the left wing.

[471] These verses are given Ait. Âr. V, 2, 2, 9.

For there are twenty-one backward feathers in a bird.

8. Then the Ekavi*m*sa is the support of all Stomas, and the tail the support of all birds[472].

9. He recites a twenty-second verse. This is made the form of two supports. Therefore all birds support themselves on their tail, and having supported themselves on their tail, they fly up. For the tail is a support.

10. He (the bird and the hymn) is supported by two decades which are Virâg. The man (the sacrificer) is supported by the two Dvipadâs, the twenty first and twenty-second. That which forms the bird serves for the attainment of all desires; that which forms the man, serves for his happiness, glory, proper food, and honour.

11. Next comes a Sûdadohas verse, then a Dhayyâ, then a Sûdadohas verse. The Sûdadohas is a man, the Dhayyâ a woman, therefore he recites the Dhayyâ as embraced on both sides by the Sûdadohas. Therefore does the seed of both, when it is effused, obtain oneness, and this with regard to the woman only. Hence birth takes place in and from the woman. Therefore he recites that Dhayyâ in that place[473].

THIRD KHA*ND*A.

1. He recites the eighty tristichs of Gâyatrîs[474]. Verily, the eighty Gâyatrî tristichs are this world (earth). Whatever there is in this world of glory, greatness, wives, food, and honour, may I obtain it, may I win it, may it be mine.

2. Next comes the Sûdadohas verse. Sûdadohas verily is breath. He joins this world with breath.

3. He recites the eighty tristichs of B*ri*hatîs. Verily, the eighty B*ri*hatî tristichs are the world of the sky. Whatever there is in the world of the sky of glory, greatness, wives, food, and honour, may I obtain it, may I win it, may it be mine.

4. Next comes the Sûdadohas verse. Sûdadohas verily is breath. He joins the world of the sky with breath.

1.	Imâ nu kam (Rv. X, 157)	5
2.	Â yâhi (Rv. X, 172)	4
3.	Pra va indrâya &c. (not in the *S*âkalya-sa*m*hitâ)	9
4.	Esha brahmâ &c. (not in the *S*âkalya-sa*m*hitâ)	3
		21

[472] The other Stomas of the Agnish*t*oma are the Triv*ri*t, Pañ*k*ada*s*a, Saptada*s*a, the Ekavi*ms*a being the highest. Cf. I, 5, 1, 3.

[473] Asmin vigavabhâge. Comm.

[474] These and the following verses form the food of the bird. Comm. The verses themselves are given by *S*aunaka in the fifth Âra*n*yaka.

5. He recites the eighty tristichs of Ush*n*ih. Verily, the eighty Ush*n*ih tristichs are that world, the heaven. Whatever there is in that world of glory, greatness, wives, food, and honour, also the divine being of the Devas (Brahman), may I obtain it, may I win it, may it be mine.

6. Next comes the Sûdadohas verse. Sûdadohas verily is the breath. He joins that world with breath, yea, with breath.

FIFTH ADHYÂYA.

FIRST KHA*ND*A.

1. He recites the Va*s*a hymn[475], wishing, May everything be in my power.

2. They (its verses) are twenty-one[476], for twenty-one are the parts (the lungs, spleen, &c.) in the belly.

3. Then the Ekavi*m*sa is verily the support of all Stomas, and the belly the support of all food.

4. They consist of different metres. Verily, the intestines are confused, some small, some large.

5. He recites them with the pra*n*ava[477], according to the metre[478], and according to rule[479]. Verily, the intestines are according to rule, as it were; some shorter, some longer.

6. Next comes the Sûdadohas verse. Sûdadohas verily is breath. He joins the joints; with breath.

7. After having recited that verse twelve times he leaves it off there. These prâ*n*as are verily twelvefold, seven in the head, two on the breast, three below. In these twelve places the prâ*n*as are contained, there they are perfect. Therefore he leaves it off there[480].

8. The hymn indrâgnî yuva*m* su nah (Rv. VIII, 40) forms the two thighs (of the bird) belonging to Indra and Agni, the two supports with broad bones.

---

475 Having recited the verses which form the body, neck, head, wings, and tail of the bird, also the food intended for the bird, he now describes the Va*s*a hymn, i.e. the hymn composed by Va*s*a, Rv. VIII, 46. That hymn takes the place of the stomach which receives the food intended for the bird. Cf. Ait. Âr. V, 2, 5. In I, 5, 2, 4 it is called a Nivid.

476 Verses 1-20 of the Vasa hymn, and one Sûdadohas.

477 Pra*n*âvam means 'with pra*n*ava,' i.e. inserting Om in the proper places.

478 According as the metres of the different verses are fixed by *S*aunaka, Ait. Âr. V, 2, 5, who says that verse 15 is Dvipadâ, and that the last four words, nûnam atha, form an Ekapadâ.

479 According to rule, i.e. so that they should come right as Â*s*valâyana has prescribed the recitation of Dvipadâ and Ekapadâ verses. In a Dvipadâ there should be a stop after the first foot, and Om at the end of the second. Ira an Ekapadâ there should be Om at the beginning and at the end.

480 He repeats the Sûdadohas verse no more. Comm.

9. These (verses) consist of six feet, so that they may stand firm. Man stands firm on two feet, animals on four. He thus places man (the sacrificer), standing on two feet, among four-footed cattle.

10. The second verse has seven feet, and he makes it into a Gâyatrî and Anush*t*ubh. Gâyatrî is Brahman, Anush*t*ubh is speech; and he thus puts together speech with Brahman.

11. He recites a Trish*t*ubh at the end. Trish*t*ubh is strength, and thus does he come round animals by strength. Therefore animals come near where there is strength (of command, &c.); they come to be roused and to rise up, (they obey the commands of a strong shepherd.)

SECOND KHA*ND*A.

1. When he recites the Nishkevalya hymn addressed to Indra (Rv. X, 50), pra vo mahe, he inserts a Nivid[481] (between the fourth and fifth verses). Thus he clearly places strength in himself (in the *s*astra, in the bird, in himself).

2. They are Trish*t*ubhs and *G*agatîs.

3. There they say: 'Why does he insert a Nivid among mixed Trish*t*ubhs and *G*agatîs[482]?' But surely one metre would never support the Nivid of this day, nor fill it: therefore he inserts the Nivid among mixed Trish*t*ubhs and *G*agatîs.

4. Let him know that this day has three Nivids: the Vasa hymn is a Nivid, the Vâlakhilyas[483] are a Nivid, and the Nivid itself is a Nivid. Thus let him know that day as having three Nivids.

5. Then follow the hymns vane na vâ (Rv. X, 29) and yo *g*âta eva (Rv. II, 12). In the fourth verse of the former hymn occur the words anne samasya yad asan manîshâ*h*, and they serve for the winning of proper food.

6. Then comes an insertion. As many Trish*t*ubh and *G*agatî verses[484], taken from the ten Ma*nd*alas and addressed to Indra, as they insert (between the two above-mentioned hymns), after changing them into B*ri*hatîs, so many years do they live beyond the (usual) age (of one hundred years). By this insertion age is obtained.

7. After that he recites the Saganîya hymn, wishing that cattle may always come to his offspring.

8. Then he recites the Târkshya hymn[485]. Târkshya is verily welfare, and the hymn leads to welfare. Thus (by reciting the hymn) he

---

[481] Sentences like indro deva*h* somam pibatu.

[482] According to the Prak*ri*ti of the Agnish*t*oma they ought to be all Trish*t*ubhs. Comm.

[483] These hymns occur in the eighty B*ri*hatî tristichs.

[484] From the Sa*m*hitâ, which consists of ten thousand verses. Comm.

[485] Rv. X, 178. Târksha Garu*d*a being the deity of the hymn, it is called Târkshya.

fares well[486].

9. Then he recites the Ekapadâ (indro vi*s*va*m* vi râgati), wishing, May I be everything at once, and may I thus finish the whole work of metres[487].

10. In reciting the hymn indra*m* vi*s*vâ aviv*ri*dhan (Rv. I, 11) he intertwines the first seven verses by intertwining their feet[488]. There are seven prâ*n*as (openings) in the head, and he thus places seven prâ*n*as in the head. The eighth verse (half-verse) he does not intertwine[489]. The eighth is speech, and he thinks, May my speech never be intertwined with the other prâ*n*as. Speech therefore, though dwelling in the same abode as the other prâ*n*as, is not intertwined with them.

11. He recites the Virâ*g* verses[490]. Verily, Virâ*g* verses are food, and they thus serve for the gaining of food.

12. He ends with the hymn of Vasish*th*a[491], wishing, May I be Vasish*th*a!

13. But let him end with the fifth verse, esha stomo maha ugrâya vâhe, which, possessing the word mahat, is auspicious.

14. In the second foot of the fifth verse the word dhuri occurs. Verily, dhu*h* (the place where the horse is fastened to the car) is the end (of the car). This day also is the end (of the sacrifice which lasts a whole year)[492]. Thus the verse is fit for the day.

15. In the third foot the word arka is auspicious.

16. The last foot is: 'Make our glory high as heaven over heaven.' Thus wherever Brahmanic speech is uttered, there his glory will be, when he who knows this finishes with that verse. Therefore let a man who knows this, finish (the Nishkevalya) with that verse.

THIRD KHA*ND*A[493].

1. Tat savitur v*rin*îmahe (Rv. V, 82, 1-3) and adyâ no deva savitar (Rv. V, 82, 4-6) are the beginning (pratipad) and the next step (anu*k*ara) of the Vai*s*vadeva hymn, taken from the Ekâha ceremonial and therefore proper[494].

---

486 Cf. I, 5, 3, 13.

487 The Ekapadâ forms the last metre in this ceremony.

488 The first and last half-verses of the hymn are not to be intertwined. Of the remaining fourteen half-verses he joins, for instance, the fourth foot of the first verse with the second foot of the second verse, and so on. Comm.

489 Because nothing more follows. Comm.

490 Rv. VII, 22, 1-6.

491 Rv. VII, 24.

492 The last day is the udayanîyâtirâtra. Comm.

493 After finishing the Nishkevalya of the noon-libation, he explains the vai*s*vadeva*s*astra of the third libation.

494 The norm of the Mahâvrata is the Vi*s*vagit, and the norm of that, the Agnish*t*oma Ekâha. The verses to be used for the Vaisvadeva hymn are prescribed in those normal sacrifices, and are here adopted.

2. On that day[495] much is done now and then which has to be hidden, and has to be atoned for. Atonement is rest, the one-day sacrifice. Therefore at the end of the year the sacrificers; rest on this atonement as their rest. He who knows this rests firm, and they also for whom a Hot*ri* priest who knows this, recites this hymn.

3. Then (follows) the hymn addressed to Savit*ri*, tad devasya savitur vâryam mahat (Rv. IV, 53). Verily, mahat, great, (in this foot) is the end[496]. This day too is the end. Thus the verse is fit for the day.

4. The hymn katarâ pûrvâ katarâ parâyo*h* (Rv. I, 185), addressed to Dyâvâp*ri*thivî, is one in which many verses have the same ending. Verily, this day also (the mahâvrata) is one in which many receive the same reward[497]. Thus it is fit for the day.

5. The hymn ana*s*vo *g*âto anabhî*s*ur ukthya*h* (Rv. IV, 36) is addressed to the *Ri*bhus.

6. In the first verse the word tri (*k*akra*h*) occurs, and trivat[498] is verily the end. This day also is the end (of the sacrifice). Thus the verse is fit for the day.

7. The hymn asya vâmasya palitasya hotu*h* (Rv. I, 164), addressed to the Vi*s*vedevas, is multiform. This day also is multiform[499]. Thus the verse is fit for the day.

8. He recites the end of it, beginning with gaurîr mimâya (Rv. I, 164, 41).

9. The hymn â no bhadrâ*h* kratavo yantu vi*s*vata*h* (Rv. I, 89), addressed to the Vi*s*vedevas, forms the Nividdhâna, taken from the Ekâha ceremonial, and therefore proper.

10. On that day much is done now and then which has to be hidden, and has to be atoned for. Atonement is rest, the one-day sacrifice. Therefore at the end of the year the sacrificers rest on this atonement as their rest. He who knows this rests firm, and they also for whom a Hot*ri* priest who knows this, recites this hymn.

11. The hymn vai*s*vânarâya dhisha*n*âm *ri*tav*ri*dhe (Rv. III, 2) forms the beginning of the Âgnimâruta. Dhisha*n*â, thought, is verily the end, this day also is the end. Thus it is fit for the day.

12. The hymn prayagyavo maruto bhrâgad*ri*sh*t*aya*h* (Rv. V, 55), addressed to the Maruts, is one in which many verses have the same ending. Verily, this day also is one in which many receive the same reward. Thus it is fit for the day[500].

13. He recites the verse *g*âtavedase sunavâma somam (Rv. I, 99,

---

[495] Cf. Ait. Âr. I, 2, 1, 2.

[496] Nothing higher than the great can be wished for or obtained. Comm.

[497] All who perform the ceremony obtain Brahman. Cf. § 12.

[498] The third wheel, in addition to the usual two wheels, forms the end of a carriage, as before the dhuh, Cf. I, 5, 2, 14. This day also is the end.

[499] Consisting of Vedic hymns and dances, &c. Comm.

[500] Cf. § 4.

1), addressed to *G*âtavedas, before the (next following) hymn. That verse addressed to *G*âtavedas is verily welfare, and leads to welfare. Thus (by reciting it) he fares well[501].

14. The hymn ima*m* stomam arhate *g*âtavedase (Rv. I, 94), addressed to *G*âtavedas, is one in which many verses have the same ending. Verily, this day also (the mahâvrata) is one in which many receive the same reward. Thus it is fit for the day, yea, it is fit for the day.

SECOND ÂRANYAKA.

FIRST ADHYÂYA.

FIRST KHA*ND*A.

With the second Âra*n*yaka the Upanishad begins. It comprises the second and third Âra*n*yakas, and may be said to consist of three divisions, or three Upanishads. Their general title is Bahv*rik*a-upanishad, sometimes Mahaitareya-upanishad, while the Upanishad generally known as, Aitareya-upanishad comprises the 4th, 5th, and 6th adhyâyas only of the second Âra*n*yaka.

The character of the three component portions of the Upanishad can best be described in *S*aṅkara's own words (Âr. III, 1, I, Introd. p. 306): 'There are three classes of men who want to acquire knowledge. The highest consists of those who have turned away from the world, whose minds are fixed on one subject and collected, and who yearn to be free at once. For these a knowledge of Brahman is intended, as taught in the Ait. Âr. II, 4-6. The middle class are those who wish to become free gradually by attaining to the world of Hira*n*yagarbha. For them the knowledge and worship of Prâ*n*a (breath and life) is intended, as explained in the Ait. Âr. II, 1-3. The lowest class consists of those who do not care either for immediate or gradual freedom, but who desire nothing but offspring, cattle, &c. For these the meditative worship of the Sa*m*hitâ is intended, as explained in the third Âra*n*yaka. They cling too strongly to the letter of the sacred text to be able to surrender it for a knowledge either of Prâ*n*a (life) or of Brahman.'

The connexion between the Upanishad or rather the three Upanishads and the first Âra*n*yaka seems at first sight very slight. Still we soon perceive that it would be impossible to understand the first Upanishad, without a previous knowledge of the Mahâvrata ceremony as described in the first Âra*n*yaka.

On this point too there are some pertinent remarks in *S*aṅkara's commentary on the Âra*n*yaka II, 1, 2. 'Our first duty,' he says, 'consists

---

[501] Cf. I, 5, 2, 8.

in performing sacrifices, such as are described in the first portion of the Veda,, the Sa*m*hitâs, Brâhma*n*as, and, to a certain extent, in the Âra*n*yakas also. Afterwards arises a desire for knowledge, which cannot be satisfied except a man has first attained complete concentration of thought (êkâgratâ). In order to acquire that concentration, the performance of certain upâsanas or meditations is enjoined, such as we find described in our Upanishad, viz. in Âr. II, I-V.'

This meditation or, as it is sometimes translated, worship is of two kinds, either brahmopâsana or pratîkopâsana. Brahmopâsana or meditation on Brahman consists in thinking of him as distinguished by certain qualities. Pratîkopâsana or meditation on symbols consists in looking upon certain worldly objects as if they were Brahman, in order thus to withdraw the mind from the too powerful influence of external objects.

These objects, thus lifted up into symbols of Brahman, are of two kinds, either connected with sacrifice or not. In our Upanishad we have to deal with the former class only, viz. with certain portions of the Mahâvrata, as described in the first Âra*n*yaka. In order that the mind may not be entirely absorbed by the sacrifice, it is lifted up during the performance from the consideration of these sacrificial objects to a meditation on higher objects, leading up at last to Brahman as prâ*n*a or life.

This meditation is to be performed by the priests, and while they meditate they may meditate on a hymn or on a single word of it as meaning something else, such as the sun, the earth, or the sky, but not vice versâ. And if in one *S*âkhâ, as in that of the Aitareyins, for instance, a certain hymn has been symbolically explained, the same explanation may be adopted by another *S*âkhâ also, such as that of the Kaushîtakins. It is not necessary, however, that every part of the sacrifice should be accompanied by meditation, but it is left optional to the priest in what particular meditation he wishes to engage, nor is even the time of the sacrifice the only right time for him to engage in these meditations.

1. This is the path: this sacrifice, and this Brahman. This is the true[502].

2. Let no man swerve from it, let no man transgress it.

3. For the old (sages) did not transgress it, and those who did transgress, became lost.

4. This has been declared by a *R*ishi (Rv. VIII, 101, 14): 'Three (classes of) people transgressed, others settled down round about the

---

[502] Comm. The path is twofold, consisting of works and knowledge. Works or sacrifices have been described in the Sa*m*hitâ, the Brâhma*n*a, and the first Âra*n*yaka. Knowledge of Brahman forms the subject of the second and third Âra*n*yakas. The true path is that of knowledge.

venerable (Agni, fire); the great (sun) stood in the midst of the worlds, the blowing (Vâyu, air) entered the Harits (the dawns, or the ends of the earth).'

5. When he says: 'Three (classes of) people transgressed,' the three (classes of) people who transgressed are what we see here (on earth, born again) as birds, trees, herbs, and serpents[503].

6. When he says: 'Others settled down round about the venerable,' he means those who now sit down to worship Agni (fire).

7. When he says: 'The great stood in the midst of the worlds,' the great one in the midst of the world is meant for this Âditya, the sun.

8. When he says: 'The blowing entered the Harits,' he means that Vâyu, the air, the purifier, entered all the corners of the earth[504].

SECOND KHA*ND*A.

1. People say: 'Uktha, uktha,' hymns, hymns! (without knowing what uktha, hymn[505], means.) The hymn is truly (to be considered as) the earth, for from it all whatsoever exists arises.

2. The object of its praise is Agni (fire), and the eighty verses (of the hymn) are food, for by means of food one obtains everything.

3. The hymn is truly the sky, for the birds fly along the sky, and men drive following the sky. The object of its praise is Vâyu (air), and the eighty verses (of the hymn) are food, for by means of food one obtains everything.

4. The hymn is truly the heaven, for from its gift (rain) all whatsoever exists arises. The object of its praise is Âditya (the sun), and the eighty verses are food, for by means of food one obtains everything.

5. So much with reference to the gods (mythological); now with reference to man (physiological).

6. The hymn is truly man. He is great, he is Pragâpati. Let him think, I am the hymn.

7. The hymn is his mouth, as before in the case of the earth.

8. The object of its praise is speech, and the eighty verses (of the hymn) are food, for by means of food he obtains everything.

---

[503] Vaṅgâ*h* is explained by vanagatâ v*ri*kshâ*h*; avagadhâ*h* is explained by vrîhiyavâdyâ oshadhaya*h*; îrapâdâ*h* is explained by ura*h*pâdâ*h* sarpâ*h*. Possibly they are all old ethnic names, like Vaṅga, *K*era, &c. In Ânandatîrtha's commentary vayâ*m*si are explained by Pi*s*â*k*a, Vaṅâvagadhas by Râkshasa, and Îrapâdas by Asuras.

[504] Three classes of men go to Naraka (hell); the fourth class, full of faith and desirous of reaching the highest world, worships Agni, Vâyu, and other gods. Comm.

[505] The Comm. explains uktha as that from whence the favour of the gods arises, uttish*th*aty anena devatâprasâda iti vyutpatte*h*. The object is now to show that the uktha or hymn used at the Mahâvrata ceremony has a deeper meaning than it seems to have, and that its highest aim is Brahman; not, however, the highest Brahman, but Brahman considered as life (prâ*n*a).

9. The hymn is the nostrils, as before in the case of the sky.

10. The object of its praise is breath, and the eighty verses (of the hymn) are food, for by means of food he obtains everything.

11. The slight bent (at the root) of the nose is, as it were, the place of the brilliant (Âditya, the sun).

12. The hymn is the forehead, as before in the case of heaven. The object of its praise is the eye, and the eighty verses (of the hymn) are food, for by means of food he obtains everything.

13. The eighty verses (of the hymn) are alike food with reference to the gods as well as with reference to man. For all these beings breathe and live by means of food indeed. By food (given in alms, &c.) he conquers this world, by food (given in sacrifice) he conquers the other. Therefore the eighty verses (of the hymn) are alike food, with reference to the gods as well as with reference to man.

14. All this that is food, and all this that consumes food, is only the earth, for from the earth arises all whatever there is.

115. And all that goes hence (dies on earth), heaven consumes it all; and all that goes thence (returns from heaven to a new life) the earth consumes it all.

16. That earth is thus both food and consumer.

He also (the true worshipper who meditates on himself as being the uktha) is both consumer and consumed (subject and object[506]). No one possesses that which he does not eat, or the things which do not eat him[507].

---

[506] As a master who lives by his servants, while his servants live by him. Comm.

[507] I have translated these paragraphs, as much as possible, according to the commentator. I doubt whether, either in the original or in the interpretation of the commentator, they yield any very definite sense. They are vague speculations, vague, at least, to us, though intended by the Brahmans to give a deeper meaning to certain ceremonial observances connected with the Mahâvrata. The uktha, or hymn, which is to be meditated on, as connected with the sacrifice, is part of the Mahâvrata, an important ceremony, to be performed on the last day but one (the twenty-fourth) of the Gavâmayana sacrifice. That sacrifice lasts a whole year, and its performance has been fully described in the Brâhma*n*as and Âra*n*yakas. But while the ordinary performer of the Mahâvrata has simply to recite the uktha or nishkevalya-*s*astra, consisting of eighty verses (t*rik*a) in the Gâyatrî, B*ri*hatî, and Ush*n*ih metres, the more advanced worshipper (or priest) is to know that this uktha has a deeper meaning, and is to meditate on it as being the earth, sky, heaven, also as the human body, mouth, nostrils, and forehead. The worshipper is in fact to identify himself by meditation with the uktha in all its senses, and thus to become the universal spirit or Hira*n*yagarbha. By this process he becomes the consumer and consumed, the subject and object, of everything, while another sacrificer, not knowing this, remains in his limited individual sphere, or, as the text expresses it, does not possess what he cannot eat (perceive), or what cannot eat him (perceive him). The last sentence is explained differently by the commentator, but in connexion with the whole passage it seems to me to become more intelligible, if interpreted as I have proposed to interpret it.

THIRD KHA*N*DA.

1. Next follows the origin of seed. The seed of Pragâpati are the Devas (gods). The seed of the Devas is rain. The seed of rain are herbs. The seed of herbs is food. The seed of food is seed. The seed of seed are creatures. The seed of creatures is the heart. The seed of the heart is the mind. The seed of the mind is speech (Veda). The seed of speech is action (sacrifice). The action done (in a former state) is this man, the abode of Brahman.

2. He (man) consists of food (irâ), and because he consists of food (irâmaya), he consists of gold (hira*n*maya[508]). He who knows this becomes golden in the other world, and is seen as golden (as the sun) for the benefit of all beings.

FOURTH KHA*N*DA.

1. Brahman (in the shape of prâ*n*a, breath) entered into that man by the tips of his feet, and because Brahman entered (prâpadyata) into that man by the tips of his feet, therefore people call them the tips of the feet (prapada), but hoofs and claws in other animals.

2. Then Brahman crept up higher, and therefore they were (called)[509] the thighs (ûrû).

3. Then he said: 'Grasp wide,' and that was (called) the belly (udara).

4. Then he said: 'Make room for me,' and that was (called) the chest (uras).

5. The *S*ârkarâkshyas meditate on the belly as Brahman, the Âru*n*is on the heart[510]. Both (these places) are Brahman indeed[511].

6. But Brahman crept upwards and came to the head, and because he came to the head, therefore the head is called head[512].

7. Then these delights alighted in the head, sight, hearing, mind, speech, breath.

8. Delights alight on him who thus knows, why the head is called head.

9. These (five delights or senses) strove together, saying: 'I am the uktha (hymn), I am the uktha[513].' 'Well,' they said, 'let us all go out

---

[508] Play on words. Comm.

[509] These are all plays on words. Comm.

[510] This does not appear to be the case either in the *Kh*. Up. V, 15; 17, or in the *S*atapatha-brâhma*n*a X, 6, 1.

[511] The pluti in tâʒi is explained as *s*âstrîyaprasiddhyarthâ.

[512] All puns, as if we were to say, because he hied up to the head, therefore the head was called head.

[513] Each wished to be identified with the uktha, as it was said before that the human body, mouth, nostrils, forehead were to be identified with the uktha. Cf. Kaush. Up. III, 3.

from this body; then on whose departure this body shall fall, he shall be the uktha among us[514].'

10. Speech went out, yet the body without speaking remained, eating and drinking.

Sight went out, yet the body without seeing remained, eating and drinking.

Hearing went out, yet the body without hearing remained, eating and drinking.

Mind went out, yet the body, as if blinking, remained, eating and drinking.

Breath went out, then when breath was gone out, the body fell.

11. It was decayed, and because people said, it decayed, therefore it was (called) body (*s*arîra). That is the reason of its name.

12. If a man knows this, then the evil enemy who hates him decays, or the evil enemy who hates him is defeated.

13. They strove again, saying: 'I am the uktha, I am the uktha.' 'Well,' they said, 'let us enter that body again; then on whose entrance this body shall rise again, he shall be the uktha among us.'

14. Speech entered, but the body lay still. Sight entered, but the body lay still. Hearing entered, but the body lay still. Mind entered, but the body lay still. Breath entered, and when breath had entered, the body rose, and it became the uktha.

15. Therefore breath alone is the uktha.

16. Let people know that breath is the uktha indeed.

17. The Devas (the other senses) said to breath: 'Thou art the uktha, thou art all this, we are thine, thou art ours.'

18. This has also been said by a *R*ishi (Rv. VIII, 92, 32): 'Thou art ours, we are thine.'

FIFTH KHA*ND*A.

Then the Devas carried him (the breath) forth, and being carried forth, he was stretched out, and when people said, 'He was stretched out,' then it was in the morning; when they said, 'He is gone to rest,' then it was in the evening. Day, therefore, is the breathing up, night the breathing down[515].

2. Speech is Agni, sight that Âditya (sun), mind the moon, hearing the Di*s* (quarters): this is the prahitâ*m* sa*m*yoga[516], the union of the

---

[514] Cf. *Kh*. Up. V, 1; B*ri*h. Up. VI, 1; Kaush. Up. II, 12-14; III, 2; Prasna Up. II, 1.

[515] All these are plays on words, prâtar being derived from prâtâyi, sâyam from samâgât. The real object, however, is to show that breath, which is the uktha, which is the worshipper, is endowed with certain qualities, viz. time, speech, &c.

[516] The meaning is, that the four deities, Agni, Âditya, Moon, and the Di*s* proceed from their own places to dwell together in the body of man, and that this is called the prahitâ*m* sa*m*yoga*h*. Prahit is explained as prahita, placed, sent. It is probably formed

deities as sent forth. These deities (Agni, &c.) are thus in the body, but their (phenomenal) appearance yonder is among the deities—this was intended.

3. And Hira*n*yadat Vaida also, who knew this (and who by his knowledge had become Hira*n*yagarbha or the universal spirit), said: 'Whatever they do not give to me, they do not possess themselves.' I know the prahitâ*m* sa*m*yoga, the union of the deities, as entered into the body[517]. This is it.

4. To him who knows this all creatures, without being constrained, offer gifts.

5. That breath is (to be called) sattya (the true), for sat is breath, ti is food, yam is the sun[518]. This is threefold, and threefold the eye also may be called, it being white, dark, and the pupil. He who knows why true is true (why sattya is sattya), even if he should speak falsely, yet what he says is true.

SIXTH KHA*ND*A.

1. Speech is his (the breath's) rope, the names the knots[519]. Thus by his speech as by a rope, and by his names as by knots, all this is bound. For all this are names indeed, and with speech he calls everything.

2. People carry him who knows this, as if they were bound by a rope.

3. Of the body of the breath thus meditated on, the Ush*n*ih verse forms the hairs, the Gâyatrî the skin, the Trish*t*ubh the flesh, the Anush*t*ubh the muscles, the *G*agatî the bone, the Paṅkti the marrow, the B*ri*hatî the breath[520] (prâ*n*a). He is covered with the verses (kha*nd*as, metres). Because he is thus covered with verses, therefore they call them kha*nd*as (coverings, metres).

4. If a man knows the reason why kha*nd*as are called kha*nd*as, the verses cover him in whatever place he likes against any evil deed.

5. This is said by a *Ri*shi (Rv. I, 164, 13):—

6. 'I saw (the breath) as a guardian, never tiring, coming and going on his ways (the arteries). That breath (in the body, being identified with the sun among the Devas), illuminating the principal and

---

from hi, not from dhâ. Prahito*h* sa*m*yoganam is the name of a Sâman, Ind. Stud. III, 225. As Devas or gods they appear each in its own place. The whole passage is very obscure.

[517] All this is extremely obscure, possibly incorrect. For yam, unless it refers to some other word, we expect yan. For dadyu*h* one expects dadyât. What is intended is that Hira*n*yadat had through meditation acquired identity with the universal spirit, and that therefore he might say that whatever was not surrendered to him did not really belong to anybody. On Hiranyadat, see Ait. Brâhm. III, 6.

[518] Cf. *Kh*. Up. VIII, 3, 5.

[519] The rope is supposed to be the chief rope to which various smaller ropes are attached for fastening animals.

[520] Here conceived as the air breathed, not as the deity. Comm.

intermediate quarters of the sky, is returning constantly in the midst of the worlds.'

He says: 'I saw a guardian,' because he, the breath, is a guardian, for he guards everything.

7. He says: 'Never tiring,' because the breath never rests.

8. He says: 'Coming and going on his ways,' because the breath comes and goes on his ways.

9. He says: 'Illuminating the principal and intermediate,' because he illuminates these only, the principal and intermediate quarters of the sky.

10. He says. 'He is returning constantly in the midst of the worlds,' because he returns indeed constantly in the midst of the worlds.

11. And then, there is another verse (Rv. I, 55, 81): 'They are covered like caves by those who make them,'

12. For all this is covered indeed by breath.

13. This ether is supported by breath as B*ri*hatî, and as this ether is supported by breath as B*ri*hatî, so one should know that all things, not excepting ants, are supported by breath as B*ri*hatî.

SEVENTH KHA*ND*A.

1. Next follow the powers of that Person[521].

2. By his speech earth and fire were created. Herbs are produced on the earth, and Agni (fire) makes them ripe and sweet. 'Take this, take this,' thus saying do earth and fire serve their parent, speech.

3. As far as the earth reaches, as far as fire reaches, so far does his world extend, and as long as the world of the earth and fire does not decay, so long does his world not decay who thus knows this power of speech.

4. By breath (in the nose) the sky and the air were created. People follow the sky, and hear along the sky, while the air carries along pure scent. Thus do sky and air serve their parent, the breath.

As far as the sky reaches, as far as the air reaches, so far does his world extend, and as long as the world of the sky and the air does not decay, so long does his world not decay who thus knows this power of breath.

5. By his eye heaven and the sun were created. Heaven gives him rain and food, while the sun causes his light to shine. Thus do the heaven and the sun serve their parent, the eye.

As far as heaven reaches and as far as the sun reaches, so far does his world extend, and as long as the world of heaven and the sun does

[521] The purusha, as described before in the second chapter, is the Pragâpati or universal spirit with whom the worshipper is to identify himself by meditation. The manifestations of his power consist in creating the earth, fire, the sky, the air, heaven, the sun.

not decay, so long does his world not decay who thus knows the power of the eye.

6. By his ear the quarters and the moon were created. From all the quarters they come to him, and from all the quarters he hears, while the moon produces for him the bright and the dark halves for the sake of sacrificial work. Thus do the quarters and the moon serve their parent, the ear.

As far as the quarters reach and as far as the moon reaches, so far does his world extend, and as long as the world of the quarters and the moon does not decay, so long does his world not decay who thus knows the power of the ear.

7. By his mind the water and Varu*n*a were created. Water yields to him faith (being used for sacred acts), Varu*n*a keeps his offspring within the law. Thus do water and Varu*n*a serve their parent, the mind.

As far as water reaches and as far as Varu*n*a reaches, so far does his world extend, and as long as the world of water and Varu*n*a does not decay, so long does his world not decay who thus knows the power of the mind.

EIGHTH KHA*ND*A[522]

1. Was it water really? Was it water? Yes, all this was water indeed. This (water) was the root (cause), that (the world) was the shoot (effect). He (the person) is the father, they (earth, fire, &c.) are the sons. Whatever there is belonging to the son, belongs to the father; whatever there is belonging to the father, belongs to the son. This was intended[523].

2. Mahidâsa Aitareya, who knew this, said: 'I know myself (reaching) as far as the gods, and I know the gods (reaching) as far as me. For these gods receive their gifts from hence, and are supported from hence.'

3. This is the mountain[524], viz. eye, ear, mind, speech, and breath. They call it the mountain of Brahman.

4. He who knows this, throws down the evil enemy who hates him; the evil enemy who hates him is defeated.

---

[522] Having described how Prâ*n*a, the breath, and his companions or servants created the world, he now discusses the question of the material cause of the world out of which it was created. Water, which is said to be the material of the world, is explained by the commentator to mean here the five elements.

[523] Cause and effect are not entirely separated, therefore water, as the elementary cause, and earth, fire, &c., as its effect, are one; likewise the worshipper, as the father, and the earth, fire, &c. as his sons, as described above. Mûla and tûla, root and shoot, are evidently chosen for the sake of the rhyme, to signify cause and effect.

[524] Prâ*n*a is called the giri*h*, because it is swallowed or hidden by the other senses (gira*n*ât). Again a mere play of words, intended to show that Brahman under the form of Prâ*n*a, or life, is to be meditated on.

5. He (the Prâ*n*a, identified with Brahman) is the life, the breath; he is being (while the *g*îvâtman remains), and not-being (when the *g*îvâtman departs).

6. The Devas (speech, &c.) worshipped him (prâ*n*a) as Bhûti or being, and thus they became great beings. And therefore even now a man who sleeps, breathes like bhûrbhu*h*.

7. The Asuras worshipped him as Abhûti or not being, and thus they were defeated.

8. He who knows this, becomes great by himself, while the evil enemy who hates him, is defeated.

9. He (the breath) is death (when he departs), and immortality (while he abides).

10. And this has been said by a *R*ishi (Rv. I, 164, 38):—

11. 'Downwards and upwards he (the wind of the breath) goes, held by food;'—for this up-breathing, being held back by the down-breathing, does not move forward (and leave the body altogether).

12. 'The immortal dwells with the mortal;'—for through him (the breath) all this dwells together, the bodies being clearly mortal, but this being (the breath), being immortal.

13. 'These two (body and breath) go for ever in different directions (the breath moving the senses of the body, the body supporting the senses of the breath: the former going upwards to another world, the body dying and remaining on earth). They increase the one (the body), but they do not increase the other,' i.e. they increase these bodies (by food), but this being (breath) is immortal.

14. He who knows this becomes immortal in that world (having become united with Hira*n*yagarbha), and is seen as immortal (in the sun) by all beings, yea, by all beings.

SECOND ADHYÂYA[525].

FIRST KHA*N*DA.

1. He (the sun), who shines, honoured this world (the body of the worshipper, by entering into it), in the form of man[526] (the worshipper who meditates on breath). For he who shines (the sun) is (the same as) the breath. He honoured this (body of the worshipper) during a hundred

[525] In the first adhyâya various forms of meditating on Uktha, conceived as Prâ*n*a (life), have been declared. In the second some other forms of meditation, all extremely fanciful, are added. They are of interest, however, as showing the existence of the hymns of the Rig-veda, divided and arranged as we now possess them, at the time when this Âra*n*yaka was composed.

[526] The identity of the sun and of breath as living in man has been established before. It is the same power in both, conceived either adhidaivatam (mythological) or adhyâtmam (physiological).

years, therefore there are a hundred years in the life of a man. Because he honoured him during a hundred years, therefore there are (the poets of the first Ma*nd*ala of the Rig-veda, called) the Satar*k*in, (having honour for a hundred years.) Therefore people call him who is really Prâ*n*a (breath), the Satar*k*in poets[527].

2. He (breath) placed himself in the midst of all whatsoever exists. Because he placed himself in the midst of all whatsoever exists, therefore there are (the poets of the second to the ninth Ma*nd*ala of the Rig-veda, called) the Mâdhyamas. Therefore people call him who is really Prâ*n*a (breath), the Mâdhyama poets.

3. He as up-breathing is the swallower (g*ri*tsa), as down-breathing he is delight (mada). Because as up-breathing he is swallower (g*ri*tsa) and as down-breathing delight (mada), therefore there is (the poet of the second Ma*nd*ala of the Rig-veda, called) G*ri*tsamada. Therefore people call him who is really Prâ*n*a (breath), Gritsamada.

4. Of him. (breath) all this whatsoever was a friend. Because of him all (vi*s*vam) this whatsoever was a friend (mitram), therefore there is (the poet of the third Ma*nd*ala of the Rig-veda, called) Vi*s*vâmitra. Therefore people call him who is really Prâ*n*a (breath), Vi*s*vâmitra.

5. The Devas (speech, &c.) said to him (the breath): 'He is to be loved by all of us.' Because the Devas said of him, that he was to be loved (vâma) by all of them, therefore there is (the poet of the fourth Ma*nd*ala of the Rig-veda, called) Vâmadeva. Therefore people call him who is really Prâ*n*a (breath), Vâmadeva.

6. He (breath) guarded all this whatsoever from evil. Because he guarded (atrâyata) all this whatsoever from evil, therefore there are (the poets of the fifth Ma*nd*ala of the Rig-veda, called) Atraya*h*. Therefore people call him who is really Prâ*n*a (breath), Atraya*h*.

SECOND KHA*ND*A.

1. He (breath) is likewise a Bibhradvâga (bringer of offspring). Offspring is vâga, and he (breath) supports offspring. Because he supports it, therefore there is (the poet of the sixth Ma*nd*ala of the Rig-veda, called) Bharadvâga. Therefore people call him who is really Prâ*n*a (breath), Bharadvâga.

2. The Devas (speech, &c.) said to him: 'He it is who chiefly causes us to dwell on earth.' Because the Devas said of him, that he chiefly caused them to dwell on earth, therefore there is (the poet of the seventh Ma*nd*ala of the Rig-veda, called) Vasish*th*a. Therefore people

---

[527] The real ground for the name is that the poets of the first Ma*nd*ala composed on an average each about a hundred *Rik*, verses.

call him who is really Prâ*n*a (breath), Vasish*th*a[528].

3. He (breath) went forth towards[529] all this whatsoever. Because he went forth toward all this whatsoever, therefore there are (the poets of the eighth Ma*nd*ala of the Rig-veda, called) the Pragâthas. Therefore people call him who is really Prâ*n*a (breath), the Pragâthas.

4. He (breath) purified all this whatsoever. Because he purified all this whatsoever, therefore there are (the hymns and also the poets[530] of the ninth Ma*nd*ala of the Rig-veda, called) the Pavamânîs. Therefore people called him who is really Prâ*n*a (breath), the Pavamânîs.

5. He (breath) said: 'Let me be everything whatsoever, small (kshudra) and great (mahat), and this became the Kshudrasûktas and Mahâsûktas.' Therefore there were (the hymns and also the poets of the tenth Ma*nd*ala of the Rig-veda, called) the Kshudrasûktas (and Mahâsûktas). Therefore people call him who is really Prâ*n*a (breath), the Kshudrasûktas (and Mahâsûktas).

6. He (breath) said once: 'You have said what is well said (su-ukta) indeed. This became a Sûkta (hymn).' Therefore there was the Sûkta. Therefore people call him who is really Prâ*n*a (breath), Sûkta[531].

7. He (breath) is a *Rik* (verse), for he did honour[532] to all beings (by entering into them). Because he did honour to all beings, therefore there was the *Rik* verse. Therefore people call him who is really Prâ*n*a (breath), *Rik*.

8. He (breath) is an Ardhar*k*a (half-verse), for he did honour to all places (ardha)[533]. Because he did honour to all places, therefore there was the Ardhar*k*a. Therefore people call him who is really Prâ*n*a (breath), Ardhar*k*a.

9. He (breath) is a Pada (word)[534], for he got into all these beings. Because he got (pâdi) into all these beings, therefore there was the Pada (word). Therefore people call him who is really Prâ*n*a (breath), Pada.

10. He (breath) is an Akshara (syllable), for he pours out (ksharati) gifts to all these beings, and without him no one can pour out (atiksharati) gifts. Therefore there was the Akshara (syllable). Therefore people call him who is really Prâ*n*a (breath), Akshara[535].

---

[528] I translate in accordance with the commentator, and probably with the intention of the author. The same etymology is repeated in the commentary on II, 2, 4, 2. It would be more natural to take vasish*th*a in the sense of the richest.

[529] This is the interpretation of the commentator, and the preposition abhi seems to show that the author too took that view of the etymology of pragâtha.

[530] It seems, indeed, as if in the technical language of the Brahmans, the poets of the ninth Ma*nd*ala were sometimes called Pavamânîs, and the hymns of the tenth Ma*nd*ala Kshudrasûktas and Mahâsûktas (masc.) Cf. Ârsheya-brâhma*n*a, ed. Burnell, p. 42.

[531] The poet also is called Sûkta, taddrash*t*âpi sûktanâmako 'bhût. Comm.

[532] I translate according to the commentator.

[533] Ardha means both half and place.

[534] It may also be intended for pâda, foot of a verse.

[535] The Prâ*n*a (breath) is to be meditated on as all hymns, all poets, all words, &c. Comm.

11. Thus all these *Rik* verses, all Vedas, all sounds[536] are one word, viz. Prâ*n*a (breath). Let him know that Prâ*n*a is all *Rik* verses.

THIRD KHA*ND*A.

1. While Vi*s*vâmitra was going to repeat the hymns of this day (the mahâvrata), Indra sat down near him[537]. Vi*s*vâmitra (guessing that Indra wanted food) said to him, 'This (the verses of the hymn) is food,' and repeated the thousand B*ri*hatî verses[538] By means of this he went to the delightful home of Indra (Svarga).

2. Indra said to him: '*Ri*shi, thou hast come to my delightful home. *Ri*shi, repeat a second hymn[539].' Vi*s*vâmitra (guessing that Indra wanted food) said to him, 'This (the verses of the hymn) is food,' and repeated the thousand B*ri*hatî verses. By means of this he went to the delightful home of Indra (Svarga).

3. Indra said to him: '*Ri*shi, thou hast come to my delightful home. *Ri*shi, repeat a third hymn.' Vi*s*vâmitra (guessing that Indra wanted food) said to him, 'This (the verses of the hymn) is food,' and repeated the thousand B*ri*hatî verses. By means of this he went to the delightful home of Indra (Svarga).

4. Indra said to him: '*Ri*shi, thou hast come to my delightful home. I grant thee a boon.' Vi*s*vâmitra said: 'May I know thee.' Indra said: 'I am Prâ*n*a (breath), O *Ri*shi, thou art Prâ*n*a, all things are Prâ*n*a. For it is Prâ*n*a who shines as the sun, and I here pervade all regions under that form. This food of mine (the hymn) is my friend and my support (dakshi*n*a). This is the food prepared by Visvâmitra. I am verily he who shines (the sun).'

---

[536] All aspirated sonant consonants. Comm.

[537] Upanishasasâda, instead of upanishasâda. The mistake is probably due to a correction, sa for sha; the commentator, however, considers it as a Vedic license. Skâro 'dhika*s* *kh*ândasa*h*.

[538] These are meant for the Nishkevalya hymn recited at the noon-libation of the Mahâvrata. That hymn consists of ten parts, corresponding, as we saw, to ten parts of a bird, viz. its body, neck, head, root of wings, right wing, left wing, tail, belly, chest, and thighs. The verses corresponding to these ten parts, beginning with tad id asa bhuvaneshu gyesh*th*am, are given in the first Âra*n*yaka, and more fully in the fifth Âra*n*yaka by *S*aunaka. Though they consist of many metres, yet, when one counts the syllables, they give a thousand B*ri*hatî verses, each consisting of thirty-six syllables.

[539] Although the Nishkevalya is but one hymn, consisting of eighty t*rik*as, yet as these eighty t*rik*as were represented as three kinds of food (see Ait. Âr. II, 1, 2, 2-4), the hymn is represented as three hymns, first as eighty Gâyatrî t*rik*as, then as eighty B*ri*hatî t*rik*as, lastly as eighty Ush*n*ih t*rik*as.

FOURTH KHA*N*DA.

1. This then becomes perfect as a thousand of B*ri*hatî verses. Its consonants[540] form its body, its voice[541] (vowels) the Soul[542], its sibilants[543] the air of the breath.

2. He who knew this became Vasish*th*a, he took this name from thence[544].

3. Indra verily declared this to Vi*s*vâmitra, and Indra verily declared this to Bharadvâga. Therefore Indra is invoked by him as a friend[545].

4. This becomes perfect as a thousand of B*ri*hatî verses[546], and of that hymn perfect with a thousand Brihad verses, there are 36,000 syllables[547]. So many are also the thousands of days of a hundred years (36,000). With the consonants they fill the nights, with the vowels the days.

5. This becomes perfect as a thousand of B*ri*hatî verses. He who knows this, after this thousand of B*ri*hatîs thus accomplished, becomes full of knowledge, full of the gods, full of Brahman, full of the immortal, and then goes also to the gods.

6. What I am (the worshipper), that is he (sun); what he is, that am I.

7. This has been said by a *Ri*shi (Rv. I, 115, 1): 'The sun is the self of all that moves and rests.'

8. Let him look to that, let him look to that!

---

540 Vyañganâni, explained by kâdini.

541 Ghosha, explained by aspirated sonant consonants.

542 Âtmâ, explained by madhya*s*arîram.

543 Sashasahâ*h*. Comm.

544 He became Prâ*n*a, and because Prâ*n*a causes all to dwell, or covers all (vâsayati), therefore the *Ri*shi was called Vasish*th*a. Comm. Cf. Ait. Âr. II, 2, 2, 2.

545 At the Subrahma*n*yâ ceremony in the Soma sacrifices, the invocations are, Indra â ga*kkh*a, hariva â ga*kkh*a.

546 Cf. Ait. Âr. II, 3, 8, 8.

547 Each B*ri*hatî has thirty-six syllables.

THIRD ADHYÂYA[548].

FIRST KHA*ND*A.

1. He who knows himself as the fivefold hymn (uktha), the emblem of Prâ*n*a (breath), from whence all this springs[549], he is clever. These five are the earth, air, ether, water, and fire (*g*yotis). This is the self, the fivefold uktha. For from him all this springs, and into him it enters again (at the dissolution of the world). He who knows this, becomes the refuge of his friends.

2. And to him who knows the food (object) and the feeder (subject) in that uktha, a strong son is born, and food is never wanting. Water and earth are food, for all food consists of these two. Fire and air are the feeder, for by means of them[550] man eats all food. Ether is the bowl, for all this is poured into the ether. He who knows this, becomes the bowl or support of his friends.

3. To him who knows the food and the feeder in that uktha, a strong son is born, and food is never wanting. Herbs and trees are food, animals the feeder, for animals eat herbs and trees.

4. Of them again those who have teeth above and below, shaped after the likeness of man, are feeders, the other animals are food. Therefore these overcome the other animals, for the eater is over the food.

5. He who knows this is over his friends.

SECOND KHA*ND*A[551].

1. He who knows the gradual development of the self in him (the man conceived as the uktha), obtains himself more development.

2. There are herbs and trees and all that is animated, and he knows the self gradually developing in them. For in herbs and trees sap only is seen[552], but thought (*k*itta) in animated beings.

Among animated beings again the self develops gradually, for in some sap (blood) is seen (as well as thought), but in others thought is not seen.

4. And in man again the self develops gradually, for he is most

---

548 In this adhyâya some more qualities are explained belonging to the Mahâvrata ceremonial and the hymns employed at it, which can be meditated on as referring to Prâ*n*a, life.

549 Because the world is the result or reward for performing a meditation on the uktha. Comm.

550 The digestive fire is lighted by the air of the breath. Comm.

551 This treats of the gradual development of life in man, particularly of the development of a thinking soul (*k*aitanya).

552 In stones there is not even sap, but only being, sattâ. Comm.

endowed with knowledge. He says what he has known, he sees what he has known[553]. He knows what is to happen to-morrow, he knows heaven and hell. By means of the mortal he desires the immortal—thus is he endowed.

5. With regard to the other animals hunger and thirst only are a kind of understanding. But they do not say what they have known, nor do they see what they have known. They do not know what is to happen to-morrow, nor heaven and hell. They go so far and no further, for they are born according to their knowledge (in a former life).

THIRD KHA*ND*A.

1. That man (conceived as uktha) is the sea, rising beyond the whole world[554]. Whatever he reaches, he wishes to go beyond[555]. If he reaches the sky, he wishes to go beyond.

2. If he should reach that (heavenly) world, he would wish to go beyond.

3. That man is fivefold. The heat in him is fire; the apertures (of the senses) are ether; blood, mucus, and seed are water; the body is earth; breath is air.

4. That air is fivefold, viz. up-breathing, down-breathing, back-breathing, out-breathing, on-breathing. The other powers (devatâs), viz. sight, hearing, mind, and speech, are comprised under up-breathing and down-breathing. For when breath departs, they also depart with it.

5. That man (conceived as uktha) is the sacrifice, which is a succession now of speech and now of thought. That sacrifice is fivefold, viz. the Agnihotra, the new and full moon sacrifices, the four-monthly sacrifices, the animal sacrifice, the Soma sacrifice. The Soma sacrifice is the most perfect of sacrifices, for in it these five kinds of ceremonies are seen: the first which precedes the libations (the Dîkshâ, &c.), then three libations, and what follows (the Avabh*ri*tha, &c.) is the fifth.

FOURTH KHA*ND*A.

1. He who knows one sacrifice above another, one day above another, one deity above the others, he is clever. Now this great uktha (the nishkevalya-*s*astra) is the sacrifice above another, the day above

[553] What he has known yesterday he remembers, and is able to say before men, I know this. And when he has known a thing he remembers it, and goes to the same place to see it again. Comm.

[554] Bhûloka. Comm.

[555] Should it not be aty enan manyate?

another, the deity above others[556].

2. This uktha is fivefold. With regard to its being performed as a Stoma (chorus), it is Triv*ri*t, Pañ*k*ada*s*a, Saptada*s*a, Ekavi*m*sa, and Pañ*k*avi*m*sa. With regard to its being performed as a Sâman (song), it is Gâyatra, Rathantara, B*ri*hat, Bhadra, and Râgana. With regard to metre, it is Gâyatrî, Ush*n*ih, B*ri*hatî, Trish*t*ubh, and Dvipadâ. And the explanation (given before in the Âra*n*yaka) is that it is the head, the right wing, the left wing, the tail, and the body of the bird[557].

In each hymn. This, is the first round. He then sings the three middle verses in each hymn. This is the second round. He lastly sings the last three verses in each hymn. This is the third round. This song is called Udyatî.

The Pañ*k*ada*s*a stoma is formed out of one Sûkta only, consisting of three verses. In the first round he sings the first verse three times, the second and third once. In the second round he sings the middle verse three times, in the third round he sings the last verse three times. This song is called Vish*t*uti.

The Saptadasa stoma is formed in the same manner, only that in the first round he sings the first verse three times, in the second the middle verse three times, in the third round the middle and last verses three times. This song is called Da*s*asapta.

The Ekavi*m*sa stoma is formed in the same manner, only that in the first round he sings the last verse once, in the second the first verse once, in the third the middle verse once, while the other verses are each repeated three times. This song is called Saptasaptinî.

The Pañ*k*avi*ms*a stoma is formed in the same manner, only that in the first round he sings the first verse three times, the second four times, the last once; in the second round the first once, the second three times, the third four times; in the third round the first five times, the second once, the last three times; or he sings in the third round the first verse four times, the second twice, the last three times.

Sâya*n*a in his commentary on the Ait. Âr. takes the Triv*ri*t stoma to be formed out of three hymns, each consisting of three verses, while he says that the other stomas are formed out of one hymn only. B. and R., s*v*. triv*ri*t, state that this stoma consists of verses 1, 4, 7; 2, 5, 8; and 3,

---

[556] The uktha is to be conceived as prâ*n*a, breath or life, and this prâ*n*a was shown to be above the other powers (devatâs), speech, hearing, seeing, mind. The uktha belongs to the Mahâvrata day, and that is the most important day of the Soma sacrifice. The Soma sacrifice, lastly, is above all other sacrifices.

[557] All these are technicalities connected with the singing and reciting of the uktha. The commentator says: The stoma is a collection of single *Rik* verses occurring in the t*rik*as which have to be sung. The Triv*ri*t stoma, as explained in the Sâma-brâhma*n*a, is as follows: There are three Sûktas, each consisting of three verses, the first being upâsmai gâyata, S. V. Uttarâr*k*ika I, 1, 1 = Rv. IX, 11. The Udgât*ri* first sings the first three verses.*

* Hiṅk*ri* with dative is explained as gai with accusative.

6, 9 of the Rig-veda hymn IX, 11, but, according to Sâya*n*a, the stoma consists (1) of the first verses of the three Sûktas, upâsmai gâyata, davidyutatyâ, and pavamânasya at the beginning of the Sâma-veda-Uttarâr*k*ika, (2) of the second, (3) Of the third verses of the same three hymns. Mahîdhâra (Yv. X, 9) takes the same view, though the MSS. seem to have left out the description of the second paryâya, while Sâya*n*a in his commentary to the Tâ*nd*ya-brâhma*n*a seems to support the opinion of B. and R. There is an omission, however, in the printed text of the commentary, which makes it difficult to see the exact meaning of Sâya*n*a.

The Pañ*k*ada*s*a stoma is well described by Sâya*n*a, Tâ*nd*ya Br. II, 4. Taking the Sûkta agna â yâhi (Uttarâr*k*ika I, 1, 4 = Rv. VI, 16, 10-12), he shows the stoma to consist of (1) verse 1 × 3, 2, 3 (2) verse 1, 2 × 3, 3; (3) verse 1, 2, 3 × 3.

The five Sâmans are explained by the commentator. The Gâyatra is formed out of the *Rik* (III, 62, 10) tat savitur vare*n*yam. The Rathantara is formed out of the *Rik* (VII, 32, 22) abhi tvâ *s*ûra nonuma. The B*ri*hat is formed out of the *Rik* (VI, 46, 1) tvâm id dhi havâmahe. The Bhadra is formed out of the *Rik* (X, 57, 1) imâ nu kam. The Râgana is formed out of the *Rik* (VII, 27, 1) indram naro nemadhitâ.

The metres require no explanation.

In identifying certain portions of the Nishkevalya hymn with a bird, the head of the bird corresponds to the hymns indram id gâthina*h*, &c.; the right wing to the hymns abhi tvâ *s*ûra, &c.; the left wing to the hymns tvâm id dhi, &c.; the tail to the hymns imâ nu kam, &c.; the body to the hymns tad id âsa, &c. All this was explained in the first Âra*n*yaka.

3. He performs the Prastâva in five ways, he performs the Udgîtha in five ways, he performs the Pratihâra in five ways, he performs the Upadrava in five ways, he performs the Nidhana in five ways[558]. All this together forms one thousand Stobhas, or musical syllables[559].

4. Thus also are the *Rik* verses, contained in the Nishkevalya, recited (by the Hot*ri*) in five orders. What precedes the eighty t*rik*as, that is one order, then follow the three sets of eighty t*rik*as each, and what comes after is the fifth order[560].

---

[558] The Sâmagas sing the Râgana at the Mahâvrata, and in that Sâman there are, as usual, five parts, the Prastâva, Udgîtha, pratihâra, Upadrava, and Nidhana. The Prastot*ri*, when singing the Prastâva portions, sings them five times. The Udgât*ri* and Pratihart*ri* sing their portions, the Udgîtha and Pratihâra, five times. The Udgât*ri* again sings the Upadrava five times. And all the Udgât*ri*s together sing the Nidhana five times.

[559] The Stobha syllables are syllables without any meaning, added when verses have to be sung, in order to have a support for the music. See *Kh*. Up. I, 13. In singing the five Sâmans, each five times, one thousand of such Stobha syllables are required.

[560] There are in the Nishkevalya hymn, which the Hot*ri* has to recite, three sets of eighty t*rik*as each. The first, consisting of Gâyatrîs, begins with mahâ*n* indro ya ogasâ. The second, consisting of B*ri*hatîs, begins with ya *k*id anyad. The third, consisting of

5. This (the hymns of this Sastra) as a whole (if properly counted with the Stobha syllables) comes to one thousand (of B*ri*hatî verses). That (thousand) is the whole, and ten, ten is called the whole. For number is such (measured by ten). Ten tens are a hundred, ten hundreds are a thousand, and that is the whole. These are the three metres (the tens, pervading everything). And this food also (the three sets of hymns being represented as food) is threefold, eating, drinking, and chewing. He obtains that food by those (three numbers, ten, hundred, and thousand, or by the three sets of eighty t*rik*as).

FIFTH KHA*ND*A.

1. This (nishkevalya-*s*astra) becomes perfect as a thousand of B*ri*hatî verses.

2. Some teachers (belonging to a different Sâkhâ) recognise a thousand of different metres (not of B*ri*hatîs only). They say: 'Is another thousand (a thousand of other verses) good? Let us say it is good.'

3. Some say, a thousand of Trish*t*ubh verses, others a thousand of *G*agatî verses, others a thousand of Anush*t*ubh verses.

4. This has been said by a *Ri*shi (Rv. X, 124, 9):—

5. 'Poets through their understanding discovered Indra dancing an Anush*t*ubh.' This is meant to say: They discovered (and meditated) in speech (called Anush*t*ubh)—at that time (when they worshipped the uktha)—the Prâ*n*a (breath) connected with Indra.

6. He (who takes the recited verses as Anush*t*ubhs) is able to become celebrated and of good report.

7. No! he says; rather is such a man liable to die before his time. For that self (consisting of Anush*t*ubhs) is incomplete. For if a man confines himself to speech, not to breath, then driven by his mind, he does not succeed with speech[561].

Ush*n*ihs, begins with ya indra somapâtama. These three sets form the food of the bird, as the emblem of the *s*astra. The hymns which precede these, form the body, head, and wings of the bird. This is one order. Then follow the three sets of eighty t*rik*as each; and lastly, the fifth order, consisting of the hymns which form the belly and the legs of the bird.

[561] This passage is obscure, and probably corrupt. I have followed the commentator as much as possible. He says: 'If the Hot*ri* priest proceeds with reciting the *s*astra, looking to the Anush*t*ubh, which is speech, and not to the thousand of B*ri*hatîs which are breath, then, neglecting the B*ri*hatî (breath), and driven by his mind to the Anush*t*ubh (speech), he does not by his speech obtain that *s*astra. For in speech without breath the Hot*ri* cannot, through the mere wish of the mind, say the *s*astra, the activity of all the senses being dependent on breath.' The commentator therefore takes vâgabhi for vâ*k*am abhi, or for some old locative case formed by abhi. He also would seem to have read prâ*n*e na. One might attempt another construction, though it is very doubtful. One might translate, 'For that self, which is speech, is incomplete, because he understands if driven to the mind by breath, not (if driven) by speech.'

8. Let him work towards the B*ri*hatî, for the B*ri*hatî (breath) is the complete self.

9. That self (gîvâtman) is surrounded on all sides by members. And as that self is on all sides surrounded by members, the B*ri*hatî also is on all sides surrounded by metres[562].

10. For the self (in the heart) is the middle of these members, and the B*ri*hatî is the middle of the metres.

11. 'He is able to become celebrated and of good report, but (the other) able to die before his time,' thus he said. For the B*ri*hatî is the complete self, therefore let him work towards the B*ri*hatî (let him reckon the *s*astra recitation as a thousand B*ri*hatîs).

SIXTH KHA*ND*A.

1. This (nishkevalya-*s*astra) becomes perfect as a thousand of B*ri*hatî verses. In this thousand of B*ri*hatîs there are one thousand one hundred and twenty-five Anush*t*ubhs. For the smaller is contained in the larger.

2. This has been said by a *Ri*shi (Rv. VIII, 76, 12):—

3. 'A speech of eight feet;'—because there are eight feet of four syllables each in the Anush*t*ubh.

4. 'Of nine corners;'—because the B*ri*hatî becomes nine-cornered (having nine feet of four syllables each).

5. 'Touching the truth;'—because speech (Anush*t*ubh) is truth, touched by the verse (B*ri*hatî)[563].

6. 'He (the Hot*ri*) makes the body out of Indra;'—for out of this thousand of B*ri*hatî verses turned into Anush*t*ubhs, and therefore out of Prâ*n*a as connected with Indra[564], and out of the B*ri*hatî (which is Prâ*n*a), he makes speech, that is Anush*t*ubh, as a body[565].

7. This Mahaduktha is the highest development of speech, and it is fivefold, viz. measured, not measured, music, true, and untrue.

8. A *Rik* verse, a gâthâ[566], a kumbyâ[567] are measured (metrical). A Yagus line, an invocation, and general remarks[568], these are not

---

[562] Either in the *s*astra, or in the list of metres, there being some that have more, others that have less syllables.

[563] Vâ*k*, speech, taking the form of Anush*t*ubh, and being joined with the *Rik*, or the B*ri*hatî, touches the true, i.e. Prâ*n*a, breath, which is to be meditated on under the form of the B*ri*hatî. Comm.

[564] Cf. Ait. Âr. II, 2, 3, 4.

[565] Because the Anush*t*ubh is made out of the B*ri*hatî, the B*ri*hatî being breath, therefore the Anush*t*ubh is called its body.

[566] A gâthâ is likewise in verse, for instance, prâta*h* prâtar an*ri*ta*m* te vadanti.

[567] A kumbyâ is a metrical precept, such as, brahma*k*âryasyâpo*s*âna*m* karma kuru, divi ma svâpsî*h*, &c.

[568] Such as arthavâdas, explanatory passages, also gossip, such as is common in the king's palace, laughing at people, &c.

measured (they are in prose). A Sâman, or any portion (parvan) of it, is music. Om is true, Na is untrue.

9. What is true (Om) is the flower and fruit of speech. He is able to become celebrated and of good report, for he speaks the true (Om), the flower and fruit of speech.

10. Now the untrue is the root[569] of speech, and as a tree whose root is exposed dries up and perishes, thus a man who says what is untrue exposes his root, dries up and perishes. Therefore one should not say what is untrue, but guard oneself from it.

11. That syllable Om (yes) goes forward (to the first cause of the world) and is empty. Therefore if a man says Om (yes) to everything, then that (which he gives away) is wanting to him here[570]. If he says Om (yes) to everything, then he would empty himself, and would not be capable of any enjoyments.

12. That syllable Na (no) is full for oneself[571]. If a man says No to everything, then his reputation would become evil, and that would ruin him even here.

13. Therefore let a man give at the proper time only, not at the wrong time. Thus he unites the true and the untrue, and from the union of those two he grows, and becomes greater and greater.

14. He who knows this speech of which this (the mahaduktha) is a development, he is clever. A is the whole of speech, and manifested through different kinds of contact (mutes) and of wind (sibilants), it becomes manifold and different.

15. Speech if uttered in a whisper is breath, if spoken aloud, it is body. Therefore (if whispered) it is almost hidden, for what is incorporeal is almost hidden, and breath is incorporeal. But if spoken aloud, it is body, and therefore it is perceptible, for body is perceptible.

SEVENTH KHA*N*DA.

1. This (nishkevalya-*s*astra) becomes perfect as a thousand of B*ri*hatîs. It is glory (the glorious Brahman, not the absolute Brahman), it is Indra. Indra is the lord of all beings. He who thus knows Indra as the lord of all beings, departs from this world by loosening the bonds of life[572]—so said Mahidâsa Aitareya. Having departed he becomes Indra

---

[569] As diametrically opposed to the flowers and fruits which represent the true. Comm.

[570] Then that man is left empty here on earth for that enjoyment. Comm.

[571] He who always says No, keeps everything to himself.

[572] The commentator explains visrasâ by 'merging his manhood in the identity with all,' and doing this while still alive. Visras is the gradual loosening of the body, the decay of old age, but here it has the meaning of vairâgya rather, the shaking off of all that ties the Self to this body or this life.

(or Hira*n*yagarbha) and shines in those worlds[573].

2. And with regard to this they say: 'If a man obtains the other world in this form (by meditating on the prâ*n*a, breath, which is the uktha, the hymn of the mahâvrata), then in what form does he obtain this world[574]?'

3. Here the blood of the woman is a form of Agni (fire); therefore no one should despise it. And the seed of the man is a form of Âditya (sun); therefore no one should despise it. This self (the woman) gives her self (skin, blood, and flesh) to that self (fat, bone, and marrow), and that self (man) gives his self (fat, bone, and marrow) to this self (skin, blood, and flesh). Thus[575] these two grow together. In this form (belonging to the woman and to fire) he goes to that world (belonging to the man and the sun), and in that form (belonging to man and the sun) he goes to this world (belonging to the woman and to fire[576]).

EIGHTH KHA*ND*A.

1. Here (with regard to obtaining Hira*n*yagarbha) there are these *S*lokas:

2. The fivefold body into which the indestructible (prâ*n*a, breath) enters, that body which the harnessed horses (the senses) draw about, that body where the true of the true (the highest Brahman) follows after, in that body (of the worshipper) all gods[577] become one.

3. That body into which goes the indestructible (the breath) which we have joined (in meditation), proceeding from the indestructible (the highest Brahman), that body which the harnessed horses (the senses) draw about, that body where the true of the true follows after, in that body all gods become one.

4. After separating themselves from the Yes and No of language, and of all that is hard and cruel, poets have discovered (what they sought for); dependent on names they rejoiced in what had been

---

573 The fourteen worlds in the egg of Brahman. Comm. Some hold that he who enters on this path, and becomes deity, does not arrive at final liberation. Others, however, show that this identification with the uktha, and through it with the prâ*n*a (breath) and Hira*n*yagarbha, is provisional only, and intended to prepare the mind of the worshipper for the reception of the highest knowledge of Brahman.

574 The last line on page 223 should, I think, be the penultimate line of page 224.

575 The body consists of six elements, and is hence called shâ*t*kau*s*ika. Of these, three having a white appearance (fat, bone, and marrow), come from the sun and from man; three having a. red appearance, come from fire and from the woman.

576 It is well therefore to shake off this body, and by meditating on the uktha to obtain identity with Hira*n*yagarbha. Comm.

577 The worshipper identifies himself by meditation with prâ*n*a, breath, which comprehends all gods. These gods (Agni and the rest) appear in the forms of speech, &c. Comm.

revealed[578].

5. That in which the poets rejoiced (the revealed nature of prâ*n*a, breath), in it the gods exist all joined together. Having driven away evil by means of that Brahman (which is hidden in prâ*n*a), the enlightened man goes to the Svarga world (becomes one with Hira*n*yagarbha[579], the universal spirit).

6. No one wishing to describe him (prâ*n*a, breath) by speech, describes him by calling him 'woman,' 'neither woman nor man,' or 'man' (all such names applying only to the material body, and not to prâ*n*a or breath).

7. Brahman (as hidden beneath prâ*n*a) is called the A; and the I (ego) is gone there (the worshipper should know that he is uktha and prâ*n*a).

8. This becomes perfect as a thousand of B*ri*hatî verses, and of that hymn, perfect with a thousand Brihad verses, there are 36,000 syllables. So many are also the thousands of days of human life[580]. By means of the syllable of life (the a) alone (which is contained in that thousand of hymns) does a man obtain the day of life (the mahâvrata day, which completes the number of the days in the Gavâmayana, sacrifice), and by means of the day of life (he obtains) the syllable of life.

9. Now there is a chariot of the god (prâ*n*a) destroying all desires (for the worlds of Indra, the moon, the earth, all of which lie below the place of Hira*n*yagarbha). Its front part (the point of the two shafts of the carriage where the yoke is fastened) is speech, its wheels the cars, the horses the eyes, the driver the mind. Prâ*n*a (breath) mounts that chariot (and on it, i.e. by means of meditating on Prâ*n*a, he reaches Hira*n*yagarbha).

10. This has been said by a *Ri*shi (Rv. X, 39, 12):—

11. 'Come hither on that which is quicker than mind,' and (Rv. VIII, 73, 2) 'Come hither on that which is quicker than the twinkling of an eye,' yea, the twinkling of an eye[581].

---

578 The prâ*n*a, breath, and their identity with it through meditation or worship. Comm.

579 Sarvâhammânî hira*n*yagarbha iti *s*ruteh. Comm.

580 Cf. 11, 2, 4, 4.

581 The commentator remarks that the worship and meditation on the uktha as prâ*n*a, as here taught, is different from the prâ*n*avidyâ, the knowledge of prâ*n*a, taught in the *Kh*ândogya, the B*ri*hadâra*n*yaka, &c., where prâ*n*a or life is represented as the object of meditation, without any reference to the uktha or other portions of the Mahâvrata ceremony. He enjoins that the meditation on the uktha as prâ*n*a should be continued till the desired result, the identification of the worshipper with prâ*n*a, is realised, and that it should afterwards be repeated until death, because otherwise the impression might vanish, and the reward of becoming a god, and going to the gods, be lost. Nor is the worship to be confined to the time of the sacrifice, the Mahâvrata, only, but it has to be repeated mentally during life. There are neither certain postures required for it, nor certain times and places. At the time of death, however, he who has become perfect in

FOURTH ADHYÂYA.

FIRST KHA*ND*A.

With this adhyâya begins the real Upanishad, best known under the name of the Aitareya-upanishad, and often separately edited, commented on, and translated. If treated separately, what we call the fourth adhyâya of the second Âra*n*yaka, becomes the first adhyâya of the Upanishad, sometimes also, by counting all adhyâya from the beginning of the Aitareya-âranyaka, the ninth. The divisions adopted by Sâya*n*a, who explains the Upanishad as part of the Âra*n*yaka, and by *S*aṅkara, who explains it independently, vary, though Sâya*n*a states that he follows in his commentary on the Upanishad the earlier commentary of *S*aṅkara. I have given the divisions adopted by Sâya*n*a, and have marked those of *S*aṅkara's by figures in parentheses, placed at the end of each paragraph. The difference between this Upanishad and the three preceding adhyâyas is easily perceived. Hitherto the answer to the question, Whence this world? had been, From Prâ*n*a, prâ*n*a meaning breath and life, which was looked upon for a time as a sufficient explanation of all that is. From a psychological point of view this prâ*n*a is the conscious self (pragñâtman); in a more mythological form it appears as Hira*n*yagarbha, 'the golden germ,' sometimes even as Indra. It is one of the chief objects of the prâ*n*avidyâ, or life-knowledge, to show that the living principle in us is the same as the living principle in the sun, and that by a recognition of their identity and of the true nature of prâ*n*a, the devotee, or he who has rightly meditated on prâ*n*a during his life, enters after death into the world of Hira*n*yagarbha.

This is well expressed in the Kaushîtaki-upanishad III, 2, where

---

this meditation on uktha, as the emblem of prâ*n*a, will have his reward. Up to a certain point his fate will be the same as that of other people. The activity of the senses will be absorbed in the mind, the activity of the mind in breath, breath in the activity of life, life with breath in the five elements, fire, &c., and these five elements will be absorbed up to their seed in the Paramâtman or Highest Self. This ends the old birth. But then the subtile body, having been absorbed in the Highest Self, rises again in the lotus of the heart, and passing out by the channel of the head, reaches a ray of the sun, whether by day or by night, and goes at the northern or southern course of the sun to the road of Ar*k*is or light. That Ar*k*is, light, and other powers carry him on, and led by these he reaches the Brahma-loka, where he creates to himself every kind of enjoyment, according to his wish. He may create for himself a material body and enjoy all sorts of pleasures, as if in a state of waking, or he may, without such a body, enjoy all pleasures in mind only, as if in a dream. And as he creates these various bodies according to his wish, he creates also living souls in each, endowed with the internal organs of mind, and moves about in them, as he pleases. In fact this world is the same for the devotee (yogin) and for the Highest Self, except that creative power belongs truly to the latter only. At last the devotee gains the highest knowledge, that of the Highest Self in himself, and then, at the dissolution of the Brahma-loka, he obtains complete freedom with Brahman.

Indra says to Pratardana: 'I am Prâ*n*a; meditate on me as the conscious self (pragñâtman), as life, as immortality. Life is prâ*n*a, prâ*n*a is life. Immortality is prâ*n*a, prâ*n*a is immortality. By prâ*n*a he obtains immortality in the other world, by knowledge (pragñâ) true conception. Prâ*n*a is consciousness (pragñâ), consciousness is prâ*n*a.'

This, however, though it may have satisfied the mind of the Brahmans for a time, was not a final solution. That final solution of the problem not simply of life, but of existence, is given in the Upanishad which teaches that Âtman, the Self, and not Prâ*n*a, Life, is the last and only cause of everything. In some places this doctrine is laid down in all its simplicity. Our true self, it is said, has its true being in the Highest Self only. In other passages, however, and nearly in the whole of this Upanishad, this simple doctrine is mixed up with much that is mythological, fanciful, and absurd, arthavâda, as the commentators call it, but as it might often be more truly called, anarthavâda, and it is only towards the end that the identity of the self-conscious self with the Highest Self or Brahman is clearly enuntiated.

Adoration to the Highest Self. Hari, Om!

1. Verily, in the beginning[582] all this was Self, one only; there was nothing else blinking[583] whatsoever.

2. He thought: 'Shall I send forth worlds?' (1) He sent forth these worlds,

3. Ambhas (water), Marî*k*i (light), Mara (mortal), and Ap (water).

4. That Ambhas (water) is above the heaven, and it is heaven, the support. The Marî*k*is (the lights) are the sky. The Mara (mortal) is the earth, and the waters under the earth are the Ap world[584]. (2)

5. He thought: 'There are these worlds; shall I send forth guardians of the worlds?'

He then formed the Purusha (the person)[585], taking him forth from

---

[582] Before the creation. Comm.

[583] Blinking, mishat, i.e. living; cf. Rv. X, 190, 2, vi*s*vasya mishato va*s*î, the lord of all living. Sâya*n*a seems to take mishat as a 3rd pers. sing.

[584] The names of the four worlds are peculiar. Ambhas means water, and is the name given to the highest world, the waters above the heaven, and heaven itself. Marî*k*is are rays, here used as a name of the sky, antariksha. Mara means dying, and the earth is called so, because all creatures living there must die. Ap is water, here explained as the waters under the earth. The usual division of the world is threefold, earth, sky, and heaven. Here it is fourfold, the fourth division being the water round the earth, or, as the commentator says, under the earth. Ambhas was probably intended for the highest heaven (dyaus), and was then explained both as what is above the heaven and as heaven itself, the support. If we translate, like *S*aṅkara and Colebrooke, I the water is the region above the heaven which heaven upholds,' we should lose heaven altogether, yet heaven, as the third with sky and earth, is essential in the Indian view of the world.

[585] Purusha; an embodied being, Colebrooke; a being of human shape, Röer; purushâkâram virâ*t*pi*nd*am, Sâya*n*a.

the water[586]. (3)

6. He brooded on him[587], and when that person had thus been brooded on, a mouth burst forth[588] like an egg. From the mouth proceeded speech, from speech Agni (fire)[589].

Nostrils burst forth. From the nostrils proceeded scent (prâ*n*a)[590], from scent Vâyu (air).

Eyes burst forth. From the eyes proceeded sight, from sight Âditya (sun).

Ears burst forth. From the ears proceeded hearing, from hearing the Di*s* (quarters of the world),

Skin burst forth. From the skin proceeded hairs (sense of touch), from the hairs shrubs and trees.

The heart burst forth. From the heart proceeded mind, from mind *K*andramas (moon).

The navel burst forth. From the navel proceeded the Apâna (the down-breathing)[591], from Apâna death.

The generative organ burst forth. From the organ proceeded seed, from seed water. (4)

SECOND KHA*ND*A.

1. Those deities (devatâ), Agni and the rest, after they had been sent forth, fell into this great ocean[592].

Then he (the Self) besieged him, (the person) with hunger and thirst.

2. The deities then (tormented by hunger and thirst) spoke to him (the Self): 'Allow us a place in which we may rest and eat food[593].' (1)

He led a cow towards them (the deities). They said: 'This is not enough.' He led a horse towards them. They said: 'This is not enough.'

---

586 According to the commentator, from the five elements, beginning with water. That person is meant for the Virâ*g*.

587 Tap, as the commentator observes, does not mean here and in similar passages to perform austerities (tapas), such as the K*rikkh*ra, the *K*ândrâya*n*a, &c., but to conceive and to will and to create by mere will. I have translated it by brooding, though this expresses a part only of the meaning expressed by tap.

588 Literally, was opened.

589 Three things are always distinguished here—the place of each sense, the instrument of the sense, and the presiding deity of the sense.

590 Prâ*n*a, i.e. ghrâ*n*endriya, must be distinguished from the prâ*n*a, the up-breathing, one of the five prâ*n*as, and likewise from the prâ*n*a as the principle of life.

591 The Apâna, down-breathing, is generally one of the five vital airs which are supposed to keep the body alive. in our place, however, apâna is deglutition and digestion, as we shall see in II, 4, 3, 10.

592 They fell back into that universal being from whence they had sprung, the first created person, the Virâ*g*. Or they fell into the world, the last cause of which is ignorance.

593 To eat food is explained to mean to perceive the objects which correspond to the senses, presided over by the various deities.

(2)

He led man[594] towards them. Then they said: 'Well done[595], indeed.' Therefore man is well done.

3. He said to them: 'Enter, each according to his place.' (3)

4. Then Agni (fire), having become speech, entered the mouth. Vâyu (air), having become scent, entered the nostrils. Âditya (sun), having become sight, entered the eyes. The Di*s* (regions), having become hearing, entered the ears. The shrubs and trees, having become hairs, entered the skin. *K*andramas (the moon), having become mind, entered the heart. Death, having become down-breathing, entered the navel. The waters, having become seed, entered the generative organ. (4)

5. Then Hunger and Thirst spoke to him (the Self): 'Allow us two (a place).' He said to them: 'I assign you to those very deities there, I make you co-partners with them.' Therefore to whatever deity an oblation is offered, hunger and thirst are co-partners in it. (5)

THIRD KHA*ND*A.

1. He thought: 'There are these worlds and the guardians of the worlds. Let me send forth food for them.' (1)

He brooded over the water[596]. From the water thus brooded on, matter[597] (mûrti) was born. And that matter which was born, that verily was food[598]. (2)

2. When this food (the object matter) had thus been sent forth, it wished to flee[599], crying and turning away. He (the subject) tried to grasp it by speech. He could not grasp it by speech. If he had grasped it by speech, man would be satisfied by naming food. (3)

He tried to grasp it by scent (breath). He could not grasp it by scent. If he had grasped it by scent, man would be satisfied by smelling food. (4)

He tried to grasp it by the eye. He could not grasp it by the eye. If he had grasped it by the eye, man would be satisfied by seeing food. (5)

He tried to grasp it by the ear. He could not grasp it by the ear. If he had grasped it by the ear, man would be satisfied by hearing food. (6)

He tried to grasp it by the skin. He could not grasp it by the skin. If

---

[594] Here purusha is different from the first purusha, the universal person. it can only be intended for intelligent man.

[595] Suk*ri*ta, well done, virtue; or, if taken for svak*ri*ta, self-made.

[596] The water, as mentioned before, or the five elements.

[597] Mûrti, for mûrtti, form, Colebrooke; a being of organised form, Röer; vrîhiyavâdirûpâ mûshakâdirûpâ *k*a mûrti*h*, i.e. vegetable food for men, animal food for cats, &c.

[598] Offered food, i.e. objects for the Devatâs and the senses in the body.

[599] Atyagighâ*m*sat, ati*s*ayena hantu*m* gantum ai*kkh*at. Sâya*n*a.

he had grasped it by the skin, man would be satisfied by touching food. (7)

He tried to grasp it by the mind. He could not grasp it by the mind. If he had grasped it by the mind, man would be satisfied by thinking food. (8)

He tried to grasp it by the generative organ. He could not grasp it by the organ. If he had grasped it by the organ, man would be satisfied by sending forth food. (9)

He tried to grasp it by the down-breathing (the breath which helps to swallow food through the mouth and to carry it off through the rectum, the pâyvindriya). He got it.

3. Thus it is Vâyu (the getter[600]) who lays hold of food, and the Vâyu is verily Annâyu (he who gives life or who lives by food). (10)

4. He thought: 'How can all this be without me?'

5. And then he thought: 'By what way shall I get there[601]?'

6. And then he thought: 'If speech names, if scent smells, if the eye sees, if the ear hears, if the skin feels, if the mind thinks, if the off-breathing digests, if the organ sends forth, then what am I?' (11)

7. Then opening the suture of the skull, he got in by that door.

8. That door is called the Vid*ri*ti (tearing asunder), the Nândana (the place of bliss).

9. There are three dwelling-places for him, three dreams; this dwelling-place (the eye), this dwelling-place (the throat), this dwelling-place (the heart)[602]. (12)

10. When born (when the Highest Self had entered the body) he looked through all things, in order to see whether anything wished to proclaim here another (Self). He saw this person only (himself) as the widely spread Brahman. 'I saw it,' thus he said[603]; (13)

---

[600] An attempt to derive vâyu from vî, to get.

[601] Or, by which of the two ways shall I get in, the one way being from the top of the foot (cf. Ait. Âr. II, 1, 4, 1), the other from the skull? Comm.

[602] Passages like this must always have required an oral interpretation, but it is by no means certain that the explanation given in the commentaries represents really the old traditional interpretation. Sâya*n*a explains the three dwelling-places as the right eye, in a state of waking; as the throat, in a state of dreaming; as the heart, in a state of profound sleep. *S*aṅkara explains them as the right eye, the inner mind, and the ether in the heart. Sâya*n*a allows another interpretation of the three dwelling-places being the body of the father, the body of the mother, and one's own body. The three dreams or sleeps he explains by waking, dreaming, and profound sleep, and he remarks that waking too is called a dream as compared with the true awakening, which is the knowledge of Brahman. In the last sentence the speaker, when repeating three times 'this dwelling-place,' is supposed to point to his right eye, the throat, and the heart. This interpretation is supported by a passage in the Brahma-upanishad, Netre *g*âgarita*m* vidyât ka*n*th*e* svapna*m* samâdi*s*et, sushupta*m* h*ri*dayasya tu.

[603] In this passage, which is very obscure, *S*aṅkara fails us, either because, as Ânandagñâna says, he thought the text was too easy to require any explanation, or because the writers of the MSS. left out the passage. Ânandagñâna explains: 'He looked through all creatures, he identified himself with them, and thought he was a man, blind,

Therefore he was Ida*m*-dra (seeing this).

11. Being Ida*m*dra by name, they call him Indra mysteriously. For the Devas love mystery, yea, they love mystery. (14)

FIFTH ADHYÂYA.

FIRST KHA*ND*A.

1. Let the women who are with child move away[604]!

2. Verily, from the beginning he (the self) is in man as a germ, which is called seed.

3. This (seed), which is strength gathered from all the limbs of the body, he (the man) bears as self in his self (body). When he commits the seed to the woman, then he (the father) causes it to be born. That is his first birth. (1)

4. That seed becomes the self of the woman, as if one of her own limbs. Therefore it does not injure her.

5. She nourishes his (her husband's) self (the son) within her. (2) She who nourishes, is to be nourished.

6. The woman bears the germ. He (the father) elevates the child even before the birth, and immediately after[605].

7. When he thus elevates the child both before and after his birth, he really elevates his own self,

8. For the continuation of these worlds (men). For thus are these worlds continued.

9. This is his second birth. (3)

10. He (the son), being his self, is then placed in his stead for (the performance of) all good works.

---

happy, &c.; or, as it is elsewhere expressed, he developed forms and names. And how did this mistake arise? Because he did not see the other, the true Self;' or literally, 'Did he see the other Self?' which is only a figure of speech to convey the meaning that he did not see it. The particle iti is then to be taken in a causal sense, (i.e. he did so, because what else could he have wished to proclaim?) But he allows another explanation, viz. 'He considered all beings, whether they existed by themselves or not, and after having considered, he arrived at the conclusion, What shall I call different from the true Self?' The real difficulties, however, are not removed by these explanations. First of all, we expect vâvadisham before iti, and secondly, unless anyam refers to âtmânam, we expect anyad. My own translation is literal, but I am not certain that it conveys the true meaning. One might understand it as implying that the Self looked about through all things, in order to find out, 'What does wish to proclaim here another Self?' And when he saw there was nothing which did not come from himself, then he recognised that the Purusha, the person he had sent forth, or, as we should say, the person he had created, was the developed Brahman, was the Âtman, was himself. Sâya*n*a explains vâvadishat by vadishyâmi, but before iti the third person cannot well refer to the subject of vyaikshat.

604 Some MSS. begin this adhyâya with the sentence apakrâmantu garbhi*n*ya*h*, may the women who are with child walk away! It is counted as a paragraph.

605 By nourishing the mother, and by performing certain ceremonies both before and after the birth of a child.

11. But his other self (the father), having done all he has to do, and having reached the full measure of his life, departs.

12. And departing from hence he is born again. That is his third birth.

13. And this has been declared by a *R*ishi (Rv. IV, 27, 1): (4)

14. 'While dwelling in the womb, I discovered all the births of these Devas. A hundred iron strongholds kept me, but I escaped quickly down like a falcon.'

15. Vâmadeva, lying in the womb, has thus declared this. (5)

And having this knowledge he stepped forth, after this dissolution of the body, and having obtained all his desires in that heavenly world, became immortal, yea, he became immortal. (6)

SIXTH ADHYÂYA.

FIRST KHA*ND*A.

1. Let the women go back to their place.

2. Who is he whom[606] we meditate on as the Self? Which[607] is the Self?

3. That by which we see (form), that by which we hear (sound), that by which we perceive smells, that by which we utter speech, that by which we distinguish sweet and not sweet, (1) and what comes from the heart and the mind, namely, perception, command, understanding, knowledge, wisdom, seeing, holding, thinking, considering, readiness (or suffering), remembering, conceiving, willing, breathing, loving, desiring?

4. No, all these are various names only of knowledge (the true Self). (2)

5. And that Self, consisting of (knowledge), is Brahman (m.)[608], it is Indra, it is Pragâpati[609]. All these Devas, these five great elements, earth, air, ether, water, fire, these and those which are, as it were, small and mixed[610], and seeds of this kind and that kind, born from eggs, born from the womb., born from heat, born from germs[611], horses, cows, men, elephants, and whatsoever breathes, whether walking or flying, and what is immoveable—all that is led (produced) by knowledge (the Self).

6. It rests on knowledge (the Self). The world is led (produced) by

---

[606] I read ko yam instead of ko 'yam.

[607] Or, Which of the two, the real or the phenomenal, the nirupâdhika or sopâdhika?

[608] Hira*n*yagarbha. Comm.

[609] Virâg. Comm.

[610] Serpents, &c., says the commentary.

[611] Cf. *Kh*. Up. VI, 3, 1, where the svedaga, born from heat or perspiration, are not mentioned.

knowledge (the Self). Knowledge is its cause[612].

7. Knowledge is Brahman. (3)

8. He (Vâmadeva), having by this conscious self stepped forth from this world, and having obtained all desires in that heavenly world, became immortal, yea, he became immortal. Thus it is, Om. (4)

SEVENTH ADHYÂYA[613].

FIRST KHA*ND*A.

1. My speech rests in the mind, my mind rests in speech[614]. Appear to me (thou, the Highest Self)! You (speech and mind) are the two pins[615] (that hold the wheels) of the Veda. May what I have learnt not forsake me[616]. I join day and night with what I have learnt[617]. I shall speak of the real, I shall speak the true. May this protect me, may this protect the teacher! May it protect me, may it protect the teacher, yea, the teacher!

---

[612] We have no words to distinguish between pragñâ, state of knowing, and pragñâna, act of knowing. Both are names of the Highest Brahman, which is the beginning and end (pratish*th*â) of everything that exists or seems to exist.

[613] This seventh adhyâya contains a propitiatory prayer (*s*ântikaro mantra*h*). It is frequently left out in the MSS. which contain the Aitareya-upanishad with *S*aṅkara's commentary, and Dr. Roer has omitted it in his edition. Sâya*n*a explains it in his commentary on the Aitareya-âranyaka; and in one MS. of *S*aṅkara's commentary on the Aitareya-upanishad, which is in my possession, the seventh adhyâya is added with the commentary of Mâdhavâmâtya, the Âgñâpâlaka of Vîrabukka-mahârâga.

[614] The two depend on each other.

[615] Ant, explained by the commentator as ânayanasamartha.

[616] Cf. *Kh*. Up. IV, 2, 5.

[617] I repeat it day and night so that I may not forget it.

THIRD ÂRA*N*YAKA[618].

FIRST ADHYÂYA.

FIRST KHA*ND*A.

1. Next follows the Upanishad of the Sa*m*hitâ[619].

2. The former half is the earth, the latter half the heaven, their union the air[620], thus says Mâ*nd*ukeya; their union is the ether, thus did Mâkshavya teach it.

3. That air is not considered[621] independent[622], therefore I do not agree with his (Mandûka's) son.

4. Verily, the two are the same, therefore air is considered independent, thus says Âgastya. For it is the same, whether they say air or ether[623].

5. So far with reference to deities (mythologically); now with reference to the body (physiologically):

6. The former half is speech, the latter half is mind, their union breath (prâ*n*a), thus says *S*ûravîra[624] Mâ*nd*ukeya.

7. But his eldest son said: The former half is mind, the latter half speech. For we first conceive with the mind indeed[625], and then we utter with speech. Therefore the former half is indeed mind, the latter half speech, but their union is really breath.

8. Verily, it is the same with both, the father (Mâ*nd*ukeya) and the son[626].

9. This (meditation as here described), joined[627] with mind, speech,

---

[618] This last portion of the Upanishad is found in the MS. discovered by Dr. Bühler in Kashmir, and described by him in the journal of the Bombay Branch of the Royal Asiatic Society, 1877, p. 36. I have collated it, so far as it was possible to read it, many lines being either broken off altogether, or almost entirely obliterated.

[619] Sa*m*hitâ is the sacred text in which all letters are closely joined. The joining together of two letters is called their sa*m*hitâ; the first letter of a joined group the pûrvarûpa (n.), the second the uttararûpa. For instance, in agnim î*l*e the m is pûrvarûpa, the î uttararûpa, and mî their sa*m*hitâ or union.

[620] As in worshipping the *S*âlagrâma stone, we really worship Vishnu, so we ought to perceive the earth, the heaven, and the air when we pronounce the first and the second letters of a group, and that group itself.

[621] Mene has here been taken as 3rd pers. sing. perf. passive. The commentator, however, explains it as an active verb, ni*sk*itavân.

[622] Because it is included in the ether, not the ether in the air. Comm.

[623] Both views are tenable, for it is not the actual air and ether which are meditated on, but their names, as declared and explained in this peculiar act of worship. We should read âkâ*s*a*sk*eti, a reading confirmed both by the commentary and by the Kashmir MS.

[624] The man among heroes. Comm.

[625] The Kashmir MS. reads manasaivâgre.

[626] Both views are admissible. Comm.

[627] Prâ*n*asa*m*hitah, Kashmir MS.

and breath, is (like) a chariot drawn by two horses and one horse between them (prash*t*ivâhana).

10. And he who thus knows this union, becomes united with offspring, cattle, fame, glory of countenance, and the world of Svarga. He lives his full age.

11. Now all this comes from the Mâ*nd*ukeyas.

SECOND KHA*ND*A.

1. Next comes the meditation as taught by *S*âkalya.

2. The first half is the earth, the second half heaven, their uniting the rain, the uniter Parganya[628].

3. And so it is when he (Parganya) rains thus strongly, without ceasing, day and night[629],

4. Then they say also (in ordinary language), 'Heaven and earth have come together.'

5. So much with regard to the deities; now with regard to the body:—

6. Every man is indeed like an egg[630]. There are two halves[631] (of him), thus they say: 'This half is the earth, that half heaven.' And there between them is the ether (the space of the mouth), like the ether between heaven and earth. In this ether there (in the mouth) the breath is fixed, as in that other ether the air is fixed. And as there are those three luminaries (in heaven), there are these three luminaries in man.

7. As there is that sun in heaven, there is this eye in the head. As there is that lightning in the sky, there is this heart in the body; as there is that fire on earth, there is this seed in the member.

8. Having thus represented the self (body) as the whole world, *S*âkalya said: This half is the earth, that half heaven.

9. He who thus knows this union, becomes united with offspring, cattle, fame, glory of countenance, and the world of Svarga. He lives his full age.

---

[628] If i is followed by a, the i is changed to y, and both are united as ya. Here a is the cause which changes i into y. Thus Parganya, the god of rain, is the cause which unites earth and heaven into rain. Comm.

[629] When it rains incessantly, heaven and earth seem to be one in rain.

[630] Ândam, a*nd*asadr*is*am. Comm.

[631] The one half from the feet to the lower jaw, the other half from the upper jaw to the skull. Comm.

THIRD KHA*N*DA[632].

1. Next come the reciters of the Nirbhuga[633].

2. Nirbhuga abides on earth, Prat*rinn*a in heaven, the Ubhayamantare*n*a in the sky.

3. Now, if any one should chide him who recites the Nirbhuga, let him answer: 'Thou art fallen from the two lower places[634].' If any one should chide him who recites the Prat*rinn*a, let him answer: 'Thou art fallen from the two higher places[635].' But he who recites the Ubhayamantare*n*a, there is no chiding him.

4. For when he turns out the Sandhi (the union of words), that is the form of Nirbhuga[636]; and when be pronounces two syllables pure (without modification), that is the form of Prat*rinna*[637]. This comes first[638]. By the Ubhayamantara (what is between the two) both are fulfilled (both the sandhi and the pada).

5. Let him who wishes for proper food say the Nirbhuga; let him who wishes for Svarga, say the Prat*rinn*a; let him who wishes for both say the Ubhayamantare*n*a.

6. Now if another man (an enemy) should chide him who says the Nirbhuga, let him say to him: 'Thou hast offended the earth, the deity; the earth, the deity, will strike thee.'

If another man should chide him who says the Prat*rinn*a, let him say to him: 'Thou hast offended heaven, the deity; heaven, the deity, will strike thee.'

If another man should chide him who says the Ubhayamantare*n*a, let him say to him: 'Thou hast offended the sky, the deity; the sky, the deity, will strike thee.'

7. And whatever the reciter shall say to one who speaks to him or does not speak to him, depend upon it, it will come to pass.

8. But to a Brâhma*n*a let him not say anything except what is auspicious.

---

[632] Cf. Rig-veda-prâti*s*âkhya, ed. Max Müller, p. iii, and Nachträge, p. ii.

[633] Nirbhuga(n) is the recitation of the Veda without intervals, therefore the same as Sa*m*hitâ. Prat*rinn*a is the recitation of each word by itself (pada-pâ*th*a); Ubhayamantarena, the between the two, is the intertwining of Sa*m*hitâ and Pada-pâ*th*a, the so-called Krama-pâ*th*a. By reciting the Sa*m*hitâ inattentively, one may use forms which belong to the Pada-text; and by reciting the Pada inattentively, one may use forms which belong to the Sa*m*hitâ-text. But in reciting the Krama both the Sa*m*hitâ and Pada forms are used together, and therefore mistakes are less likely to happen.

[634] From earth and sky. Cf. *Kh*. Up. II, 22, 3.

[635] From the sky and from heaven.

[636] Nirbhuga may mean without arms, as if the arms of the words were taken away, or with two arms stretched out, the two words forming, as it were, two arms to one body.

[637] Prat*rinn*a means cut asunder, every word being separated from the others.

[638] The words were first each separate, before they were united according to the laws of Sandhi.

9. Only he may curse a Brâhma*n*a in excessive wealth[639].

10. Nay, not even in excessive wealth should he curse a Brâhma*n*a, but he should say, 'I bow before Brâhma*n*as,'—thus says *S*ûravîra Mâ*nd*ûkeya.

FOURTH KHA*ND*A.

1. Next follow the imprecations[640].

2. Let him know that breath[641] is the beam (on which the whole house of the body rests).

3. If any one (a Brâhma*n*a or another man) should chide him, who by meditation has become that breath as beam[642], then, if he thinks himself strong, he says: 'I grasped the breath, the beam, well; thou dost not prevail against me who have grasped the breath as the beam.' Let him say to him: 'Breath, the beam, will forsake thee.'

4. But if he thinks himself not strong, let him say to him: 'Thou couldst not grasp him who wishes to grasp the breath as the beam. Breath, the beam, will forsake thee.'

5. And whatever the reciter shall say to one who speaks to him or does not speak to him, depend upon it, it will come to pass. But to a Brâhma*n*a let him not say anything except what is auspicious. Only he may curse a Brâhma*n*a in excessive wealth. Nay, not even in excessive wealth should he curse a Brâhma*n*a, but he should say, 'I bow before Brâhma*n*as,'—thus says *S*ûravîra Mâ*nd*ûkeya.

FIFTH KHA*ND*A.

1. Now those who repeat the Nirbhuga say:

2. 'The former half[643] is the first syllable, the latter half the second syllable, and the space between the first and second halves is the Sa*m*hitâ (union).'

3. He who thus knows this Sa*m*hitâ (union), becomes united with offspring, cattle, fame, glory of countenance, and the world of Svarga. He lives his full age.

4. Now Hrasva Mâ*nd*ûkeya says: 'We reciters of Nirbhuga say, "Yes, the former half is the first syllable, and the latter half the second

---

639 He may curse him, if he is exceeding rich; or he may wish him the curse of excessive wealth; or he may curse him, if something great depends on it.

640 The commentator explains anuvyâhâra, not as imprecations, but as referring to those who leach or use the imprecations, such imprecations being necessary to guard against the loss of the benefits accruing from the meditation and worship here described; such teachers say what follows.

641 Breath, the union of mind and speech, as explained before. This is the opinion of Sthavira *S*âkalya, cf. III, 2, 1, 1.

642 If he should tell him that he did not meditate on breath properly.

643 As spoken of before, III, 1, 1, 1.

syllable, but the Sa*m*hitâ is the space between the first and second halves in so far as by it one turns out the union (sandhi), and knows what is the accent and what is not[644], and distinguishes what is the mora and what is not."'

5. He who thus knows this Sa*m*hitâ (union), becomes united with offspring, cattle, fame, glory of countenance, and the world of Svarga. He lives his full age.

6. Now his middle son, the child of his mother Prâtibodhî[645], says: 'One pronounces these two syllables letter by letter, without entirely separating them, and without entirely uniting them[646]. Then that mora between the first and second halves, which indicates the union, that is the Sâman (evenness, sliding). I therefore hold Sâman only to be the Sa*m*hitâ (union).'

7. This has also been declared by a *R*ishi (Rv. II, 23, 16):—

8. 'O B*r*ihaspati, they know nothing higher than Sâman.'

9. He who thus knows this Sa*m*hitâ (union), becomes united with offspring, cattle, fame, glory of countenance, and the world of Svarga. He lives his full age.

SIXTH KHA*ND*A.

1. Târukshya[647] said: 'The Sa*m*hitâ (union) is formed by means of the B*r*ihat and Rathantara[648] Sâmans.'

2. Verily, the Rathantara Sâman is speech, the B*r*ihat Sâman is breath. By both, by speech and breath, the Sa*m*hitâ is formed[649].

3. For this Upanishad (for acquiring from his teacher the knowledge of this Sa*m*hitâ of speech and breath) Târukshya guards (his teacher's) cows a whole year.

4. For it alone Târukshya guards the cows a whole year.

5. This has also been declared by a *R*ishi (Rv. X, 181, 1; and Rv. X, 181, 2):—

---

[644] In agnim î*l*e, î*l*e by itself has no accent, but as joined by sandhi with agnim, its first syllable becomes svarita, its second pra*k*ita. In tava it, the vowel i is a short mora or mâtrâ; but if joined with va, it vanishes, and becomes long e, tavet. Comm.

[645] Prâtîbodhîputra, the son of Prâtîbodhî, she being probably one out of several wives of Hrasva. Another instance of this metronymic nomenclature occurred in K*r*ish*n*a Devakîputra, *Kh*. Up. III, 7, 6. The Kashmir MS. reads Prâ*k*îbodhî, but Pratibodha is a recognised name in Ga*n*a Vidâdi, and the right reading is probably Prâtibodhî. The same MS. leaves out putra âha.

[646] So that the ê in tavet should neither be one letter e, nor two letters a + i, but something between the two, enabling us to hear a + i in the pronunciation of ê.

[647] The Kashmir MS. reads Târkshya, a name used before as the title of a hymn (Ait. Âr. I, 5, 2, 8). Here Târakshya seems preferable, see Pâ*n*. IV, 1, 105.

[648] See Ait. Âr. I, 4, 2, 1-4.

[649] These two, the B*r*ihat and Rathantara, are required for the P*r*ish*th*astotra in the Agnish*t*oma, and they are to remind the worshipper that speech and breath are required for all actions.

6. 'Vasish*th*a carried hither the Rathantara; Bharadvâga brought hither the B*ri*hat of Agni.'

7. He who thus knows this Sa*m*hitâ (union), becomes united with offspring, cattle, fame, glory of countenance, and the world of Svarga. He lives his full age.

8. Kau*nth*aravya said: 'Speech is united with breath, breath with the blowing air, the blowing air with the Vi*s*vedevas, the Vi*s*vedevas with the heavenly world, the heavenly world with Brahman. That Sa*m*hitâ is called the gradual Sa*m*hitâ.'

9. He who knows this gradual Sa*m*hitâ (union), becomes united with offspring, cattle, fame, glory of countenance, and the world of Svarga, in exactly the same manner as this Sa*m*hitâ, i.e. gradually.

10. If that worshipper, whether for his own sake or for that of another, recites (the Sa*m*hitâ), let him know when he is going to recite, that this Sa*m*hitâ went up to heaven, and that it will be even so with those who by knowing it become Devas. May it always be so!

11. He who thus knows this Sa*m*hitâ (union), becomes united with offspring, cattle, fame, glory of countenance, and the world of Svarga. He lives his full age.

12. Pañ*k*âla*kand*a said: 'The Sa*m*hitâ (union, composition) is speech.'

13. Verily, by speech the Vedas, by speech the metres are composed. Friends unite through speech, all beings unite through speech; therefore speech is everything here[650].

14. With regard to this (view of speech being more than breath), it should be borne in mind that when we thus repeat (the Veda) or speak, breath is (absorbed) in speech; speech swallows breath. And when we are silent or sleep, speech is (absorbed) in breath; breath swallows speech. The two swallow each other. Verily, speech is the mother, breath the son.

15. This has been declared also by a *Ri*shi (Rv. X, 114, 4):—

16. 'There is one bird; (as wind) he has entered the sky; (as breath or living soul) he saw this whole world. With my ripe mind I saw him close to me (in the heart); the mother (licks or) absorbs him (breath), and he absorbs the mother (speech).'

17. He who thus knows this Sa*m*hitâ (union), becomes united with offspring, cattle, fame, glory of countenance, and the world of Svarga. He lives his full age.

18. Next follows the Pragâpati-Sa*m*hitâ.

19. The former half is the wife, the latter half the man; the result of their union the son; the act of their union the begetting; that Sa*m*hitâ is Aditi (indestructible).

20. For Aditi (indestructible) is all this whatever there is, father,

---

[650] Everything can be obtained by speech in this life and in the next. Comm.

mother, son, and begetting.

21. This has also been declared by a *Ri*shi (Rv. I, 189, 10)—

22. 'Aditi is mother, is father, is son.'

23. He who thus knows this Sa*m*hitâ (union), becomes united with offspring, cattle, fame, glory of countenance, and the world of Svarga. He lives his full age.

SECOND ADHYÂYA[651].

FIRST KHA*ND*A.

1. Sthavira *S*âkalya said that breath is the beam[652], and as the other beams rest on the house-beam, thus the eye, the ear, the mind, the speech, the senses, the body, the whole self rests on this[653] breath.

2. Of that self the breathing is like the sibilants, the bones like the mutes, the marrow like the vowels, and the fourth part, flesh, blood, and the rest, like the semivowels[654],—so said Hrasva Mâ*nd*ûkeya.

3. To us it was said to be a triad only[655].

4. Of that triad, viz. bones, marrow, and joints, there are 360 (parts) on this side (the right), and 360 on that side (the left). They make 720 together, and 720[656] are the days and nights of the year. Thus that self which consists of sight, hearing, metre, mind, and speech is like unto the days.

5. He who thus knows this self, which consists of sight, hearing, metre, mind, and speech, as like unto the days, obtains union, likeness, or nearness with the days, has sons and cattle, and lives his full age.

SECOND KHA*ND*A.

1. Next comes Kau*nth*aravya:

2. There are 360 syllables (vowels), 360 sibilants (consonants), 360, groups.

3. What we called syllables are the days, what we called sibilants are the nights, what we called groups are the junctions of days and nights. So far with regard to the gods (the days).

4. Now with regard to the body. The syllables which we explained

---

651 In the first adhyâya meditations suggested by sa*m*hitâ, pada, and krama have been discussed. Now follow meditations suggested by certain classes of letters.

652 Ait. Âr. III, 1, 4.

653 The Kashmir MS. reads etasmin prâ*n*e. The self here is meant for the body, and yet it seems to be different from *s*arîra.

654 The Kashmir MS. writes antastha without visarga, while it is otherwise most careful in writing all sibilants.

655 *S*âkalya, as we saw, told his disciples that there were three classes only, not four. Comm. The Kashmir MS. reads traya*m* tv eva na ityetat proktam.

656 The Kashmir MS, reads sapta vi*ms*ati*s k*a *s*atâni.

mythologically, are physiologically the bones; the sibilants which we explained mythologically, are physiologically the marrow.

5. Marrow is the real breath (life), for marrow is seed, and without breath (life) seed is not sown. Or when it is sown without breath (life), it will decay, it will not grow.

6. The groups which we explained mythologically, are physiologically the joints.

7. Of that triad, viz. bones, marrow, and joints, there are 540 (parts) on this side (the right), and 540 on that side (the left). They make 1080 together, and 1080 are the rays of the sun. They make the B*ri*hatî verses and the day (of the Mahâvrata)[657].

8. Thus that self which consists of sight, hearing, metre, mind, and speech is like unto the syllables.

9. He who knows this self which consists of sight, hearing, metre, mind, and speech, as like unto syllables, obtains union, likeness, or nearness with the syllables, has sons and cattle, and lives his full age.

THIRD KHA*ND*A.

1. Bâdhva[658] says, there are four persons (to be meditated on and worshipped).

2. The person of the body, the person of the metres, the person of the Veda, and the Great person.

3. What we call the person of the body is this corporeal self. Its essence is the incorporeal conscious self.

4. What we call the person of the metres is this collection of letters (the Veda). Its essence is the vowel a.

5. What we call the person of the Veda is (the mind) by which we know the Vedas, the *Ri*g-veda, Yagur-veda, and Sâma-veda. Its essence is Brahman[659] (m.)

6. Therefore let one chose a Brahman-priest who is full of Brahman (the Veda), and is able to see any flaw in the sacrifice.

7. What we call the Great person is the year, which causes some beings to fall together, and causes others to grow up. Its essence is yonder sun.

8. One should know that the incorporeal conscious self and yonder sun are both one and the same. Therefore the sun appears to every man singly (and differently).

9. This has also been declared by a *Ri*shi (Rv. I, 115, 1):—

10. 'The bright face of the gods arose, the eye of Mitra, Varu*n*a,

---

[657] There are in the Mahâvrata eighty tristichs of B*ri*hatîs, and as each B*ri*hatî is decreed to consist of thirty-six syllables, ten would give 360 syllables, and three times ten, 1080. Comm.

[658] Instead of Bâdhya, the commentary and the Kashmir MS. read Bâdhva.

[659] Hira*n*yagarbha, with whom he who knows the Veda becomes identified. Comm.

and Agni; it filled heaven and earth and the sky,—the sun is the self of all that rests and moves.'

11. 'This I think to be the regular Sa*m*hitâ as conceived by me,' thus said Bâdhva.

12. For the Bahv*rik*as consider him (the self) in the great hymn (mahad uktha), the Adhvaryus in the sacrificial fire, the *Kh*andogas in the Mahâvrata ceremony. Him they see in this earth, in heaven, in the air, in the ether, in the water, in herbs, in trees, in the moon, in the stars, in all beings. Him alone they call Brahman.

13. That self which consists of sight, hearing, metre, mind, and speech is like unto the year.

14. He who recites to another that self which consists of sight, hearing, metre, mind, and speech, and is like unto the year,

FOURTH KHA*ND*A.

1. To him the Vedas yield no more milk, he has no luck in what he has learnt (from his Guru); he does not know the path of virtue.

2. This has also been declared by a *R*ishi (Rv. X, 71, 6):—

3. 'He who has forsaken the friend (the Veda), that knows his friends, in his speech there is no luck. Though he hears, he hears in vain, for he does not know the path of virtue.'

4. Here it is clearly said that he has no luck in what he has learnt, and that he does not know the path of virtue.

5. Therefore let no one who knows this, lay the sacrificial fire (belonging to the Mahâvrata) for another, let him not sing the Sâmans of the Mahâvrata for another, let him not recite the Sastras of that day for another.

6. However, let him willingly do this for a father or for an Â*k*ârya; for that is done really for himself.

7. We have said that the incorporeal conscious self and the sun are one[660]. When these two become separated[661], the sun is seen as if it were the moon[662]; no rays spring from it; the sky is red like madder; the patient cannot retain the wind, his head smells bad like a raven's nest:—let him know then that his self (in the body) is gone, and that he will not live very long[663].

8. Then whatever he thinks he has to do,. let him do it, and let him recite the following hymns: Yad anti ya*k k*a dûrake (Rv. IX, 67, 21-27); Ad it pratnasya retasa*h* (Rv. VIII, 6, 30); Yatra brahmâ pavamâna (Rv.

---

[660] Ait. Âr. III, 2, 3, 8.

[661] This separation of the self of the sun and the conscious self within us is taken as a sign of approaching death, and therefore a number of premonitory symptoms are considered in this place.

[662] ἥλιος μηνοειδής Xen. Hist. gr. 4, 3, 10.

[663] The Kashmir MS. reads gîvayishyati.

IX, 113, 6-11); Ud vaya*m* tamasas pari (Rv. I, 50, 10).

9. Next, when the sun is seen pierced, and seems like the nave of a cart-wheel, when he sees his own shadow pierced, let him know then that it is so (as stated before, i.e. that he is going to die soon).

10. Next, when he sees himself in a mirror or in the water with a crooked head, or without a head[664], or when his pupils are seen inverted[665] or not straight, let him know then that it is so.

11. Next, let him cover his eyes and watch, then threads are seen as if falling together[666]. But if he does not see them, let him know then that it is so.

12. Next, let him cover his ears and listen, and there will be a sound as if of a burning fire or of a carriage[667]. But if he does not hear it, let him know then that it is so.

13. Next, when fire looks blue like the neck of a peacock[668], or when he sees lightning in a cloudless sky, or no lightning in a clouded sky, or when he sees as it were bright rays in a dark cloud, let him know then that it is so.

14. Next, when he sees the ground as if it were burning, let him know that it is so.

15. These are the visible signs (from 7-14).

16. Next come the dreams[669].

17. If he sees a black man with black teeth, and that man kills him; or a boar kills him; a monkey jumps on[670] him; the wind carries him along quickly; having swallowed gold he spits it out[671]; he eats honey; he chews stalks; he carries a red lotus; he drives with asses and boars; wearing a wreath of red flowers (naladas) he drives a black cow with a black calf, facing the south[672],

18. If a man sees any one of these (dreams), let him fast, and cook a pot of milk, sacrifice it, accompanying each oblation with a verse of the Râtri hymn (Rv. X, 12 7), and then, after having fed the Brâhma*n*as, with other food (prepared at his house) eat himself the (rest of the) oblation.

19. Let him know that the person within all beings, not heard here[673], not reached, not thought, not subdued, not seen, not understood, not classed, but hearing, thinking, seeing, classing,

---

[664] The Kashmir MS. reads gihma*s*irasa*m* vâ*s*arîram âtmânam.

[665] A white pupil in a black eye-ball. Comm.

[666] The Kashmir MS. reads ba*t*irakâ*n*i sampatantîva.

[667] See *Kh*. Up. III, 13, 8. The Kashmir MS. and the commentary give the words rathasyevopabdis, which are left out in the printed text.

[668] The Kashmir MS. reads mayûragrîvâ ameghe.

[669] The Kashmir MS. reads svapna*h*.

[670] The Kashmir MS. reads âskandati.

[671] The Kashmir MS. reads avagirati.

[672] The commentator separates the last dream, so as to bring their number to ten.

[673] The Kashmir MS. reads sa yata*s s*ruto.

sounding, understanding, knowing, is his Self.

FIFTH KHA*ND*A[674]

1. Now next the Upanishad of the whole speech.

True all these are Upanishads of the whole speech, but this they call so (chiefly).

2. The mute consonants represent the earth, the sibilants the sky, the vowels heaven.

The mute consonants represent Agni (fire), the sibilants air, the vowels the sun.

The mute consonants represent the *Ri*g-veda, the sibilants the Yagur-veda, the vowels the Sâma-veda.

The mute consonants represent the eye, the sibilants the ear, the vowels the mind.

The mute consonants represent the up-breathing, the sibilants the down-breathing, the vowels the back-breathing.

3. Next comes this divine lute (the human body, made by the gods). The lute made by man is an imitation of it.

4. As there is a head of this, so there is a head of that (lute, made by man). As there is a stomach of this, so there is the cavity[675] (In the board) of that. As there is a tongue of this, so there is a tongue[676] in that. As there are fingers of this, so there are strings of that[677]. As there are vowels of this, so there are tones of that. As there are consonants of this, so there are touches of that. As this is endowed with sound and firmly strung, so that is endowed with sound and firmly strung. As this is covered with a hairy skin, so that is covered with a hairy skin.

5. Verily, in former times they covered a lute with a hairy skin.

6. He who knows this lute made by the Devas (and meditates on it), is willingly listened to, his glory fills the earth, and wherever they speak Âryan languages, there they know him.

7. Next follows the verse, called vâgrasa, the essence of speech. When a man reciting or speaking in an assembly does not please, let him say this verse:

8. 'May the queen of all speech, who is covered, as it were, by the lips, surrounded by teeth, as if by spears, who is a thunderbolt, help me to speak well.' This is the vâgrasa, the essence of speech.

---

[674] After having inserted the preceding chapter on omina and the concluding paragraph on the highest knowledge, he now returns to the meditation on the letters.

[675] The Kashmir MS. reads udara evam, &c.

[676] Vâdanam, what makes the instrument speak, hastena. Comm.

[677] Here the order is inverted in the text.

SIXTH KHA*N*DA.

1. Next K*r*ish*n*a-Hârita[678] confided this Brâhma*n*a[679] concerning speech to him (his pupil):

2. Pragâpati, the year, after having sent forth all creatures, burst. He put himself together again by means of *kh*andas (Vedas). Because he put himself together again by means of *kh*andas, therefore (the text of the Veda) is called Sa*m*hitâ (put together).

3. Of that Sa*m*hitâ the letter *n* is the strength, the letter sh the breath and self (Âtman).

4. He who knows the *Rik* verses and the letters *n* and sh for every Sa*m*hitâ, he knows the Sa*m*hitâ with strength and breath. Let him know that this is the life of the Sa*m*hitâ.

5. If the pupil asks, 'Shall I say it with the letter *n* or without it?' let the teacher say, 'With the letter *n*.' And if he asks, 'Shall I say it with the letter sh or without it?' let the teacher say, 'With the letter sh[680].'

6. Hrasva Mâ*nd*ûkeya said: 'If we here recite the verses according to the Sa*m*hitâ (attending to the necessary changes of n and s into *n* and sh[681]), and if we say the adhyâya of Mâ*nd*ûkeya (Ait. Âr. III, 1), then the letters *n* and sh (strength and breath) have by this been obtained for us.'

7. Sthavira Sâkalya said: 'If we recite the verses according to the Sa*m*hitâ, and if we say the adhyâya of Mâ*nd*ûkeya, then the letters *n* and sh have by this been obtained for us.'

8. Here the *R*ishis, the Kâvasheyas[682], knowing this, said: 'Why should we repeat (the Veda), why should we sacrifice? We offer as a sacrifice breath in speech, or speech in breath. What is the beginning (of one), that is the end (of the other).'

9. Let no one tell these Sa*m*hitâs (Ait. Âr. III, 1-III, 2) to one who is not a resident pupil, who has not been with his teacher at least one

---

678 One of the sons of Harita, who was dark. Comm.

679 Brâhma*n*a, in the sense of Upanishad, this secret doctrine or explanation. It forms an appendix, like the svish*t*ak*r*it at the end of a sacrifice. 'Iva,' which the commentator explains as restrictive or useless, may mean, something like a Brâhma*n*a.

680 The letters n and sh refer most likely to the rules of *n*atva and shatva, i.e. the changing of n and s into *n* and sh.

681 If we know whenever n and s should be changed to *n* and sh in the Sa*m*hitâ.

682 The Kâvasheyas said that, after they had arrived at the highest knowledge of Brahman (through the various forms of meditation and worship that lead to it and that have been described in the Upanishad) no further meditation and no further sacrifice could be required. Instead of the morning and evening stoma they offer breath in speech, whenever they speak, or speech in breath, when they are silent or asleep. When speech begins, breathing ceases; when breathing begins, speech ceases.

year, and who is not himself to become an instructor[683]. Thus say the

---

[683] The strict prohibition uttered at the end of the third Âra*n*yaka, not to divulge a knowledge of the Sa*m*hitâ-upanishad (Ait. Âr. III, 1-2), as here explained, is peculiar. It would have seemed self-evident that, like the rest of the *s*ruti or sacred literature, the Âra*n*yaka too, and every portion of it, could have been learnt from the mouth of a teacher only, and according to rule (niyamena), i.e. by a pupil performing all the duties of a student (brahma*k*ârin [Âpastamba-sûtras, translated by Bühler, p. 18.]), so that no one except a regular pupil (antevâsin) could possibly gain access to it. Nor can there be any doubt that we ought to take the words asa*m*vatsaravâsin and apravakt*ri* as limitations, and to translate, 'Let no one tell these Sa*m*hitâs to any pupil who has not at least been a year with his master, and who does not mean to become a teacher in turn.'

That this is the right view is confirmed by similar injunctions given at the end of the fifth Âra*n*yaka. Here we have first some rules as to who is qualified to recite the Mahâvrata. No one is permitted to do so, who has not passed through the Dîkshâ, the initiation for the Agnish*t*oma. If the Mahâvrata is performed as a Sattra, the sacrificer is a Hotri priest, and he naturally has passed through that ceremony. But if the Mahâvrata is performed as an Ekâha or Ahîna ceremony, anybody might be the sacrificer, and therefore it was necessary to say that no one who is adîkshita, uninitiated, should recite it for another person; nor should he do so, when the Mahâvrata is performed without (or with) an altar, or if it does not last one year. In saying, however, that one should not recite the Mahâvrata for another person, parents and teachers are not to be understood as included, because what is done for them, is done for ourselves.

After these restrictions as to the recitation of the Mahâvrata, follow other restrictions as to the teaching of it, and here we read, as at the end of the Upanishad:

4. 'Let no one teach this day, the Mahâvrata, to one who is not a regular pupil (antevâsin), and has been so for one year, certainly not to one who has not been so for one year; nor to one who is not a brahma*k*ârin and does not study the same Veda [See Gautama-sûtras XIV, 21, and Bühler's note.], certainly not to one who does not study the same Veda; nor to one who does not come to him.

5. 'Let the teaching not be more than saying it once or twice, twice only.

6. 'One man should tell it to one man, so says *G*âtukar*n*ya.

7. 'Not to a child, nor to a man in his third stage of life.

8. 'The teacher and pupil should not stand, nor walk, nor lie down, nor sit on a couch; but they should both sit on the ground.

9. 'The pupil should not lean backward while learning, nor lean forward. He should not be covered with too much clothing, nor assume the postures of a devotee, but without using any of the apparel of a devotee, simply elevate his knees. Nor should he learn, when he has eaten flesh, when he has seen blood, or a corpse, or when he has done an unlawful thing [Nâvratyam âkramya is explained by the commentator by u*kkh*ish*t*âdyâkrama*n*a.]; when he has anointed his eyes, oiled or rubbed his body, when he has been shaved or bathed, put colour on, or ornamented himself with flower-wreaths, when he has been writing or effacing his writing [This, if rightly translated, would seem to be the earliest mention of actual writing in Sanskrit literature.].

10. 'Nor should he finish the reading in one day, so says *G*âtukar*n*ya, while according to Gâlava, he should finish it in one day. Âgnive*s*yâyana holds that he should finish all before the Trikâ*s*îtis [See Ait. Âr. I, 4, 3, 1-4.], and then rest in another place finishing it.

11. 'And in the place where he reads this, he should not read anything else, though he may read this (the Mahâvrata) where he has read something else.

12. 'No one should bathe and become a snâtaka [Âpastamba-sûtras, translated by Bühler, p. 92 (I, 2, 30, 4).] who does not read this. Even if he has read many other things, he should not become a snâtaka if he has not read this.

13. 'Nor should he forget it, and even if he should forget anything else, he should not forget this.

14. 'No, he should never forget this.

teachers, yea, thus say the teachers.

KAUSHÎTAKI-BRÂHMA*N*A-UPANISHAD.

KAUSHÎTAKI-UPANISHAD.

FIRST ADHYÂYA.

1. *K*itra Gâṅgyâyani[684], forsooth, wishing to perform a sacrifice, chose Âru*n*i (Uddâlaka[685], to be his chief priest). But Âru*n*i sent his son, *S*vetaketu, and said: 'Perform the sacrifice for him.' When *S*vetaketu[686] had arrived, *K*itra asked him: 'Son of Gautama[687], is there a hidden place in the world where you are able to place me, or is it the other way, and are you going to place me in the world to which it (that other way) leads[688]?'

---

15. 'If he does not forget this, it will be enough for himself (or for acquiring a knowledge of the Self).

16. 'It is enough, let him know this to be true.

17. 'Let him who knows this not communicate, nor dine, nor amuse himself with any one who does not know it.'

Then follow some more rules as to the reading of the Veda in general:

18. 'When the old water that stood round the roots of trees is dried up (after about the month of Pausha, January to February [Âpastamba-sûtras, translated by Bühler, p. 33 (I, 3, 9, 2).]) he should not read; nor (at any time) in the morning or in the afternoon, when the shadows meet (he should begin at sunrise so soon as the shadows divide, and end in the evening before they fall together). Nor should he read [Âpastamba-sûtras, translated by Bühler, p. 44 (I, 3, 11, 31).] when a cloud has risen; and when there is an unseasonable rain (after the months of Srâva*n*a and Bhâdrapada, August and September [Âpastamba-sûtras, translated by Bühler, p. 33 (I, 3, 9, 1).]) he should stop his Vedic reading for three nights. Nor should he at that time tell stories, not even during the night, nor should he glory in his knowledge.

19. 'This (the Veda thus learnt and studied) is the name of that Great Being; and he who thus knows the name of that Great Being, he becomes Brahman, yea, he becomes Brahman.'

[684] It is difficult to determine whether *K*itra's name was Gâṅgyâyani or Gârgyâya*n*i. Professor Weber adopted first Gârgyâya*n*i (Indische Studien 1, p. 395), afterwards Gâṅgyâyani (ibid. II, 395). Professor Cowell adopts Gâṅgyâyani, but he tells us that the Telugu MS. reads Gârgyâya*n*i throughout, and the other MSS. B, C do so occasionally. The commentator explains Gâṅgyâyani as the descendant (yuvâpatyam) of Gâṅgya. I confess a preference for Gârgyâya*n*i, because both Gaṅgâ and Gâṅgya are names of rare occurrence in ancient Vedic literature, but I admit that for that very reason the transition of Gâṅgyâyani into Gârgyâya*n*i is perhaps more intelligible than that of Gârgyâya*n*i into Gâṅgyâyani.

[685] Cf. *Kh*. Up. V, 11, 2; B*r*ih. Âr. VI, 2, 1.

[686] Cf. *Kh*. Up. V, 3; VI, 1.

[687] B*r*ih. Âr. VI, 2, 4.

[688] The question put by *K*itra to *S*vetaketu is very obscure, and was probably from the first intended to be obscure in its very wording. What *K*itra wished to ask we can gather from other passages in the Upanishads, where we see another royal sage, Pravâha*n*a Gaivali (*Kh*. Up. V, 3; B*r*ih. Âr. VI, 2), enlightening *S*vetaketu on the future life. That future life is reached by two roads; one, the Devapatha, leading to the world of

He answered and said: 'I do not know this. But, let me ask the master.' Having approached his father, he asked: 'Thus has *K*itra asked me; how shall I answer?'

Âru*n*i said: 'I also do not know this. Only after having learnt the proper portion of the Veda in *K*itra's own dwelling, shall we obtain what others give us (knowledge). Come, we will both go.'

Having said this he took fuel in his hand (like a pupil), and approached *K*itra Gâṅgyâyani, saying: 'May I come near to you?' He replied: 'You are worthy of Brahman[689], O Gautama, because you were

---

Brahman (the conditioned), beyond which there lies one other stage only, represented by knowledge of and identity with the unconditioned Brahman; the other leading to the world of the fathers, and from thence, after the reward of good works has been consumed, back to a new round of mundane existence. There is a third road for creatures which live and die, worms, insects, and creeping things, but they are of little consequence. Now it is quite clear that the knowledge which king *K*itra possesses, and which *S*vetaketu does not possess, is that of the two roads after death, sometimes called the right and the left, or the southern and northern roads. These roads are fully described in the *Kh*ândogya-upanishad and in the B*ri*had-âra*n*yaka, with certain variations, yet on the whole with the same purpose. The northern or left road, called also the path of the Devas, passes on from light and day to the bright half of the moon; the southern or right road, called also the path of the fathers, passes on from smoke and night to the dark half of the moon. Both roads therefore meet in the moon, but diverge afterwards. While the northern road passes by the six months when the sun moves towards the north, through the sun, (moon,) and the lightning to the world of Brahman, the southern passes by the six months when the sun moves towards the south, to the world of the fathers, the ether, and the moon. The great difference, however, between the two roads is, that while those who travel on the former do not return again to a new life on earth, but reach in the end a true knowledge of the unconditioned Brahman, those who pass on to the world of the fathers and the moon return to earth to be born again and again.

The question therefore which *K*itra addresses to *S*vetaketu can refer to these two roads only, and though the text is very corrupt, and was so evidently even at the time when the commentary was written, we must try to restore it in accordance with the teaching imparted by *K*itra in what follows. I propose to read: Gautamasya putra, asti sa*m*v*ri*ta*m* loke yasmin mâ dhâsyasy anyatamo vâdhvâ tasya (or yasya) mâ loke dhâsyasi, 'Is there a hidden place in the world where you (by your sacrificing and teaching) are able to place me, or is it the other way, and will you place me in the world to which it leads?' Even thus the text is by no means satisfactory, but it is better than anyam aho vâdhvâ, adopted by the commentator and explained by him: Is there a hidden place in that world in which you will place me as another, i.e. as different from the whole world or identical with the whole world, and, if as different, then having bound me (vâdhvâ = baddhvâ) and made me a different person? We may read anyataro for anyatamo vâdhvâ. The commentator sums up the question as referring to a hidden or not hidden place, where *K*itra should be placed as another person or not another person, as bound or not bound; or, as Professor Cowell renders it, 'O son of Gautama, is there any secret place in the world where thou canst set me unconnected, having fixed me there (as wood united with glue); or is there some other place where thou canst set me?' The speculations on the fate of the soul after death seem to have been peculiar to the royal families of India, while the Brahmans dwelt more on what may be called the shorter cut, a knowledge of Brahman as the true Self. To know, with them, was to be, and, after the dissolution of the body, they looked forward to immediate emancipation, without any further wanderings.

[689] Worthy to know Brahman, or, as the commentator, who reads brahmârgha, thinks, to be honoured like Brahman.

not led away by pride. Come hither, I shall make you know clearly.'

2. And *K*itra said: All who depart from this world (or this body) go to the moon[690]. In the former, (the bright) half, the moon delights in their spirits; in the other, (the dark) half, the moon sends them on to be born again[691]. Verily, the moon is the door of the Svarga world (the heavenly world). Now, if a man objects to the moon (if one is not satisfied with life there) the moon sets him free[692]. But if a man does not object, then the moon sends him down as rain upon this earth. And according to his deeds and according to his knowledge he is born again here as a worm, or as an insect, or as a fish, or as a bird, or as a lion, or as a boar, or as a serpent[693], or as a tiger, or as a man, or as something else in different places[694]. When he has thus returned to the earth, some one (a sage) asks: 'Who art thou?' And he should answer: 'From the wise moon, who orders the seasons[695], when it is born consisting of fifteen parts, from the moon who is the home of our ancestors, the seed was brought. This seed, even me, they (the gods mentioned in the Pañ*k*âgnividyâ[696]) gathered up in an active man, and through an active man they brought me to a mother. Then I, growing up to be born, a being living by months, whether twelve or thirteen, was together with my father, who also lived by (years of) twelve or thirteen months, that I might either know it (the true Brahman) or not know it. Therefore, O ye seasons[697], grant that I may attain immortality (knowledge of Brahman). By this my true saying, by this my toil (beginning with the dwelling in the moon and ending with my birth on earth) I am (like) a season, and the child of the seasons.' 'Who art thou?' the sage asks again. 'I am thou,' he replies. Then he sets him free[698] (to proceed

---

690 Both roads lead to the moon, and diverge afterwards.

691 I should like to read aparapakshe praganayati, instead of aparapakshe*n*a, or aparapakshe na. The negative is out of the question, for praganayati, he sends into a new life, is exactly what the moon does to those who do not proceed on the Devapatha to the Brahmaloka. Therefore if the reading aparapakshena must be retained, it should be rendered by 'the moon with the dark half sends them into a new life.'

692 This is supposed to be the hidden place, or rather the way to it, when the departed leave the moon, and pass on to lightning and to the world of Brahman. This is in fact the Devayâna, as opposed to the Pit*ri*yâna, described in the *Kh*ândogya-upanishad.

693 Para*s*vâ, danda*s*ûkavi*s*esha*h*. There is no authority for translating it by dog; cf. Indische Studien I, 396.

694 This might even include naraka or hell.

695 If *ri*tava*h* is here the genitive of *ri*tu, its meaning would be the ordainer of the seasons; cf. Hibbert Lectures, p. 247. Vi*k*aksha*n*a is applied to the moon again, II, 9, and the throne of Brahman also is called vi*k*aksha*n*a, I, 3.

696 *Kh*. Up. V, 4-8.

697 The commentator takes ritavah as an accusative. I take it as a vocative, and as used in a sense analogous to the Zend ratu, an epithet of Ahura. Darmesteter, Ormazd, p. 12, n. 3.

698 If a person fears heaven (svarga) as much as hell, because neither gives final liberation, then he is fit to proceed to a knowledge of Brahman. It would seem that after

onward).

He (at the time of death), having reached the path of the gods, comes to the world of Agni (fire), to the world of Vâyu (air), to the world of Varu*n*a, to the world of Indra, to the world of Pragâpati (Virâg), to the world of Brahman (Hira*n*yagarbha). In that world there is the lake Âra[699], the moments called Yesh*t*iha[700], the river Vigarâ (age-less), the tree Ilya[701], the city Sâlagya, the palace Aparâgita (unconquerable), the door-keepers Indra and Pragâpati, the hall of Brahman, called Vibhu[702] (built by vibhu, egoism), the throne Vi*k*aksha*n*â (buddhi, perception), the couch Amitaugas (endless splendour), and the beloved Mânasî (mind) and her image *K*âkshushî (eye), who, as if taking flowers, are weaving the worlds, and the Apsaras, the Ambâs (sruti, sacred scriptures), and Ambâyavîs (buddhi, understanding), and the rivers Ambayâs (leading to the knowledge of Brahman). To this world he who knows this (who knows the Paryaṅka-vidyâ) approaches. Brahman says to him: 'Run towards him (servants) with such worship as is due to myself. He has reached the river Vigarâ (age-less), he will never age.'

4. Then five hundred Apsaras go towards him, one hundred with garlands in their hands, one hundred with ointments in their hands, one hundred with perfumes in their hands, one hundred with garments in their hands, one hundred with fruit[703] in their hands. They adorn him with an adornment worthy of Brahman, and when thus adorned with the adornment of Brahman, the knower of Brahman moves towards Brahman (neut.)[704] He comes to the lake Âra, and he crosses it by the mind, while those who come to it without knowing the truth[705], are drowned. He comes to the moments called Yesh*t*iha, they flee from him.

He comes to the river Vigarâ, and crosses it by the mind alone, and there shakes off his good and evil deeds. His beloved relatives obtain the good, his unbeloved relatives the evil he has done. And as a man, driving in a chariot, might look at the two wheels (without being touched by them), thus he will look at day and night, thus at good and evil deeds, and at all pairs (at all correlative things, such as light and

---

this, this person is in the same position as the other who, objecting to remain in the moon, was set free at once.

[699] Consisting of ari's, enemies, such as love, anger, &c. In the *Kh*. Up. VIII, 5, 3, it is called Ara.

[700] Explained to mean, killing the sacrifice, which consists in a desire for Brahman.

[701] The same as the a*s*vattha*h* somasavana*h* in *Kh*. Up. VIII, 5, 3.

[702] Vibhunâmakam pramita*m* sabhâsthalam.

[703] Some MSS. read pha*n*ahastâ*h*, and the commentator explains pha*n*a by âbhara*n*a.

[704] Though brahman is used here as a neuter, it refers to the conditioned Brahman.

[705] Samprativid is here explained as brahmavidyâ*s*ûnya, ignorant, while in other places (Ait. Âr. II, 3, 1) it stands for samyagabhigña. If the latter is the true meaning, we might read here tam itvâsamprativido.

darkness, heat and cold, &c.) Being freed from good and freed from evil he, the knower of Brahman (neut.), moves towards Brahman.

5. He approaches the tree Ilya, and the odour of Brahman reaches him. He approaches the city Sâlagya, and the flavour of Brahman reaches him. He approaches the palace Aparâgita, and the splendour of Brahman reaches him. He approaches the door-keepers Indra and Pragâpati, and they run away from him. He approaches the hall Vibhu, and the glory of Brahman reaches him (he thinks, I am Brahman). He approaches the throne Vi*k*aksha*n*â. The Sâman verses, B*ri*had and Rathantara, are the eastern feet of that throne[706]; the Sâman verses, *S*yaita and Naudhasa, its western feet; the Sâman verses, Vairûpa and Vairâga, its sides lengthways (south and north); the Sâman verses, *S*âkvara and Raivata, its sides crossways (east and west). That throne is Pragñâ, knowledge, for by knowledge (self-knowledge) he sees clearly. He approaches the couch Amitaugas. That is Prâ*n*a (speech). The past and the future are its eastern feet; prosperity and earth its western feet; the Sâman verses, Brihad and Rathantara, are the two sides lengthways of the couch (south and north); the Sâman verses, Bhadra and Yagñâyagñîya, are its cross-sides at the head and feet (east and west); the *Rik* and Sâman are the long sheets[707] (east and west); the Yagus the cross-sheets (south and north); the moon-beam the cushion; the Udgîtha the (white) coverlet; prosperity the pillow[708]. On this couch sits Brahman, and he who knows this (who knows himself one with Brahman sitting on the couch) mounts it first with one foot only. Then Brahman says to him: 'Who art thou?' and he shall answer:

6. 'I am (like) a season, and the child of the seasons, sprung from the womb of endless space, from the light (from the luminous Brahman). The light, the origin of the year, which is the past, which is the present, which is all living things, and all elements, is the Self[709]. Thou art the Self. What thou art, that am I.'

Brahman says to him: 'Who am I?' He shall answer: 'That which is, the true' (Sat-tyam).

Brahman asks: 'What is the true?' He says to him: 'What is different from the gods and from the senses (prâ*n*a) that is Sat, but the

---

[706] Cf. Atharva-veda XV; Aufrecht, in Indische Studien I, p. 122.

[707] Sheets or coverings seem more applicable here than mere threads forming the woof and warp; cf. Aufrecht, Indische Studien I, p. 131.

[708] I read udgîtha upa*s*rî*h*, *s*rir upabarha*n*am. The Atharva text has udgîtho 'pa*s*raya*h*.

[709] This passage is corrupt, and the various readings and various interpretations of the commentators do not help us much. One view, which I have followed, as far as possible, is that it had to be explained how the same being could be the child of the seasons, or living from year to year, and, at the same time, born of the light. The answer is, Because light is the seed or cause of the year, and the year the cause of everything else. I take no responsibility for this view, and I see no way of discovering the original reading and the original meaning of these sentences.

gods and the senses are Tyam. Therefore by that name Sattya (true) is called all this whatever there is. All this thou art.'

7. This is also declared by a verse: 'This great *Ri*shi, whose belly is the Yagus, the head the Sâman, the form the *Rik*, is to be known as being imperishable, as being Brahman.'

Brahman says to him: 'How dost thou obtain my male names?' He should answer: 'By breath (prâ*n*a*h*).'

Brahman asks: 'How my female names?' He should answer: 'By speech (vâ*k*).'

Brahman asks: 'How my neuter names?' He should answer: 'By mind (manas).'

'How smells?' 'By the nose.' 'How forms?' 'By the eye.' 'How sounds?' 'By the ear.' 'How flavours of food?' 'By the tongue.' 'How actions?' 'By the hands.' 'How pleasures and pain?' 'By the body.' 'How joy, delight, and offspring?' 'By the organ.' 'How journeyings?' 'By the feet.' 'How thoughts, and what is to be known and desired?' 'By knowledge (pragñâ) alone.'

Brahman says to him: 'Water indeed is this my world[710], the whole Brahman world, and it is thine.'

Whatever victory, whatever might belongs to Brahman, that victory and that might he obtains who knows this, yea, who knows this[711].

SECOND ADHYÂYA.

1. Prâ*n*a (breath)[712] is Brahman, thus says Kaushîtaki. Of this prâ*n*a, which is Brahman, the mind (manas) is the messenger, speech the housekeeper, the eye the guard, the ear the informant. He who knows mind as the messenger of prâ*n*a, which is Brahman, becomes possessed of the messenger. He who knows speech as the housekeeper, becomes possessed of the housekeeper. He who knows the eye as the guard, becomes possessed of the guard. He who knows the ear as the informant, becomes possessed of the informant.

Now to that prâ*n*a, which is Brahman, all these deities (mind, speech, eye, ear) bring an offering, though he asks not for it, and thus to him who knows this all creatures bring an offering, though he asks not for it. For him who knows this, there is this Upanishad (secret vow),

---

[710] It sprang from water and the other elements. Comm. Professor Weber proposes to translate âpa*h* by Erlangungen, acquisitions, with reference to apnoshi, 'how dost thou acquire my names?' in what precedes.

[711] Who knows the conditioned and mythological form of Brahman as here described, sitting on the couch.

[712] In the first chapter it was said, 'He approaches the couch Amitaugas, that is prâ*n*a, breath, spirit, life. Therefore having explained in the first adhyâya the knowledge of the couch (of Brahman), the next subject to be explained is the knowledge of prâ*n*a, the living spirit, taken for a time as Brahman, or the last cause of everything.'

'Beg not!' As a man who has begged through a village and got nothing sits down and says, 'I shall never eat anything given by those people,' and as then those who formerly refused him press him (to accept their alms), thus is the rule for him who begs not, but the charitable will press him and say, 'Let us give to thee.'

2. Prâ*n*a (breath) is Brahman, thus says Paiṅgya. And in that prâ*n*a, which is Brahman, the eye stands firm behind speech, the ear stands firm behind the eye, the mind stands firm behind the car, and the spirit stands firm behind the mind[713]. To that prâ*n*a, which is Brahman, all these deities bring an offering, though he asks not for it, and thus to him who knows this, all creatures bring an offering, though he asks not for it. For him who knows this, there is this Upanishad (secret vow), 'Beg not!' As a man who has begged through a village and got nothing sits down and says, 'I shall never eat anything given by those people,' and as then those who formerly refused him press him (to accept their alms), thus is the rule for him who begs not, but the charitable will press him and say, 'Let us give to thee.'

3. Now follows the attainment of the highest treasure (scil. prâ*n*a, spirit[714]). If a man meditates on that highest treasure, let him on a full moon or a new moon, or in the bright fortnight, under an auspicious Nakshatra, at one of these proper times, bending his right knee, offer oblations of ghee with a ladle (sruva), after having placed the fire, swept the ground[715], strewn the sacred grass, and sprinkled water. Let him say: 'The deity called Speech is the attainer, may it attain this for me from him (who possesses and can bestow what I wish for). Svâhâ to it!'

'The deity called prâ*n*a (breath) is the attainer, may it attain this for me from him. Svâhâ to it!'

'The deity called the eye is the attainer, may it attain this for me from him. Svâhâ to it!'

'The deity called the car is the attainer, may it attain this for me from him. Svâhâ to it!'

'The deity called mind (manas) is the attainer of it, may it attain this for me from him. Svâhâ to it.'

'The deity called pragñâ (knowledge) is the attainer of it, may it attain this for me from him. Svâhâ to it!'

---

[713] I translate vâkparastât, *k*akshu*h*parastât, mana*h*parastât as compounds, and read *s*rotraparastât. The commentator requires this. He says that speech is uncertain, and has to be checked by the eye. The eye is uncertain, taking mother of pearl for silver, and must be checked by the ear. The ear is uncertain, and must be checked by the mind, for unless the mind is attentive, the ear hears not. The mind, lastly, depends on the spirit, for without spirit there is no mind. The commentator is right in reading rundhe or runddhe instead of rundhate.

[714] The vital spirits are called the highest treasure, because a man surrenders everything to preserve his vital spirits or his life.

[715] Cf. Brih. Âr. VI, 3, 1.

Then having inhaled the smell of the smoke, and having rubbed his limbs with the ointment of ghee, walking on in silence, let him declare his wish, or let him send a messenger. He will surely obtain his wish.

4. Now follows the Daiva Smara, the desire to be accomplished by the gods. If a man desires to become dear[716] to any man or woman, or to any men or women, then at one of the (fore-mentioned) proper times he offers, in exactly the same manner (as before), oblations of ghee, saying: 'I offer thy speech in myself, I (this one here[717]), Svâhâ.' 'I offer thy ear in myself, I (this one here), Svâhâ.' 'I offer thy mind in myself, I (this one here), Svâhâ.' 'I offer thy pragñâ (knowledge) in myself, I (this one here), Svâhâ.' Then having inhaled the smell of the smoke, and having rubbed his limbs with the ointment of. ghee, walking on in silence, let him try to come in contact or let him stand speaking in the wind, (so that the wind may carry his words to the person by whom he desires to be loved). Surely he becomes dear, and they think of him.

5. Now follows the restraint (sa*m*yamana) instituted by Pratardana (the son of Divodâsa): they call it the inner Agni-hotra. So long as a man speaks, he cannot breathe, he offers all the while his prâ*n*a (breath) in his speech. And so long as a man breathes, he cannot speak, he offers all the while his speech in his breath. These two endless and immortal oblations he offers always, whether waking or sleeping. Whatever other oblations there are (those, e. g. of the ordinary Agnihotra, consisting of milk and other things), they have an end, for they consist of works (which, like all works, have an end). The ancients, knowing this (the best Agnihotra), did not offer the (ordinary) Agnihotra.

6. Uktha[718] is Brahman, thus said *S*ushkabh*ri*ṅgâra. Let him meditate on it (the uktha) as the same with the *Rik*, and all beings will praise him as the best. Let him meditate on it as the same with the Yagus, and all beings will join before him as the best. Let him meditate on it as the same with the Sâman, and all beings will bow before him as the best[719]. Let him meditate on it as the same with might, let him meditate on it as the same with glory, let him meditate on it as the same

[716] As dear as prâ*n*a or life.

[717] The commentator explains these mysterious utterances by: I offer, I throw, in the fire, which is lit by the fuel of thy indifference or dislike, in myself, being the object of thy love, speech, the organ of speech, of thee, who art going to love me. This one, i.e. I myself, or my love, may prosper. Svâhâ, my speech, may grant approval to the oblation of me, the lover.'

[718] Uktha, a Vedic hymn, has been identified with prâ*n*a, breath, in the Kâ*n*va, and other *S*âkhâs (Brih. Âr. V, 13, 1; Ait. Âr. II, 1, 2). Here uktha, i.e. the prâ*n*a of the uktha, is further identified with Brahman. As uktha (the hymn) is prâ*n*a, and as the sacrifice is performed with hymns, the sacrifice, too, is uktha, and therefore prâ*n*a, and therefore Brahman. Comm.

[719] The verbs ar*k*, yug, and sannam are not used idiomatically, but with reference to the words *rik*, yagus, and sâman.

with splendour. For as the bow is among weapons the mightiest, the most glorious, the most splendid, thus is he who knows this among all beings the mightiest, the most glorious, the most splendid. The Adhvaryu conceives the fire of the altar, which is used for the sacrifice, to be himself. In it he (the Adhvaryu) weaves the Yagus portion of the sacrifice. And in the Yagus portion the Hot*ri* weaves the *Rik* portion of the sacrifice. And in the *Rik* portion the Udgât*ri* weaves the Sâman portion of the sacrifice. He (the Adhvaryu or prâ*n*a) is the self of the threefold knowledge; he indeed is the self of it (of prâ*n*a). He who knows this is the self of it (becomes prâ*n*a[720]).

7. Next follow the three kinds of meditation of the all-conquering (sarvagit) Kaushîtaki. The all-conquering Kaushîtaki adores the sun when rising, having put on the sacrificial cord[721], having brought water, and having thrice sprinkled the water-cup, saying: 'Thou art the deliverer, deliver me from sin.' In the same manner he adores the sun when in the zenith, saying: 'Thou art the highest deliverer, deliver me highly from sin.' In the same manner he adores the sun when setting, saying: 'Thou art the full deliverer, deliver me fully from sin.' Thus he fully removes whatever sin he committed by day and by night. And in the same manner he who knows this, likewise adores the sun, and fully removes whatever sin he committed by day and by night.

8. Then (secondly) let him worship every month (in the year) at the time of the new moon, the moon as it is seen in the west in the same manner (as before described with regard to the sun), or let him send forth his speech toward the moon with two green blades of grass, saying: 'O thou who art mistress of immortal joy, through that gentle heart of mine which abides in the moon, may I never weep for misfortune concerning my children.'

The children of him (who thus adores the moon) do not indeed die before him. Thus it is with a man to whom a son is already born.

Now for one to whom no son is born as yet. He mutters the three *Rik* verses. 'Increase, O Soma! may vigour come to thee' (Rv. I, 91, 16; IX, 31, 4).

---

720 The commentator explains this somewhat differently. He takes it to be the object of the last paragraph to show that the Prâ*n*a-vidyâ can ultimately produce final liberation, and not only temporal rewards. The Adhvaryu priest, he says, takes what is called uktha, and has been identified with *Rik*, Yagus, and Sâman hymns, all contained in the mouth, as being outwardly the sacrificial fire of the altar, because that fire cannot be lighted without such hymns. Thus the self of the Adhvaryu priest becomes identified, not only with the uktha, the hymns, but also with the sacrificial fire, and he meditates on himself as fire, as hymn (uktha), and as breath (prâ*n*a). I read sa esha sarvasyai trayyai vidyâyâ âtmâ, esha u evâsyâtmâ. Etadâtmâ bhavati ya eva*m* veda. But if we read asyâtmâ, we cannot with the commentator explain it by asya uktâyâs trayyâ âtmâ, but must refer asya to prâ*n*a, breath, life, which is here to be identified with Brahman.

721 This is one of the earliest, if not the earliest mention of the yagñopavîta, the sacred cord as worn over the left shoulder for sacrificial purposes; cf. Taitt. Brâhm. III, 10, 19, 12.

'May milk, may food go to thee' (Rv. I, 91, 18); 'That ray which the Âdityas gladden.'

Having muttered these three *Rik* verses, he says: 'Do not increase by our breath (prâ*n*a), by our offspring, by our cattle; he who hates us and whom we hate, increase by his breath, by his offspring, by his cattle. Thus I turn the turn of the god, I return the turn of Âditya[722].' After these words, having raised the right arm (toward Soma), he lets it go again[723].

9. Then (thirdly) let him worship on the day of the full moon the moon as it is seen in the east in the same manner, saying: 'Thou art Soma, the king, the wise, the five-mouthed, the lord of creatures. The Brâhma*n*a is one of thy mouths; with that mouth thou eatest the kings (Kshatriyas); make me an eater of food by that mouth! The king is one of thy mouths; with that mouth thou eatest the people (Vai*s*yas); make me an eater of food by that mouth! The hawk is one of thy mouths; with that mouth thou eatest the birds; make me an eater of food by that mouth! Fire is one of thy mouths; with that mouth thou eatest this world; make me an eater of food by that mouth! In thee there is the fifth mouth; with that mouth thou eatest all beings; make me an eater of food by that mouth! Do not decrease by our life, by our offspring, by our

---

[722] This refers to movements of the arm, following the moon and the sun.

[723] It is extremely difficult to translate the Vedic verses which are quoted in the Upanishads. They are sometimes slightly changed on purpose (see §11), frequently turned from their original purport by the authors of the Upanishads themselves, and then again subjected to the most fanciful interpretations by the various commentators on the Upanishads. In our paragraph (§ 8) the text followed by the commentator differs from the printed text. The commentator seems to have read: Yat te susîma*m* h*ri*dayam adhi *k*andramasi *sri*tam, tenâm*ri*tatvasye*s*âne mâham pautram agha*m* rudam. I have translated according to the commentator, at least up to a certain point, for, as Professor Cowell remarks, there is an undercurrent in the commentator's explanation, implying a comparison between the husband as the sun or fire, and the wife as the moon, which it would be difficult to render in an English translation. The same or a very similar verse occurs in § 10, while other modifications of it may be seen in Â*s*val. G*ri*hya-sûtras I, 13, 7, and elsewhere. The translation of the verses in full, of three of which the Upanishad gives the beginnings only, would be according to the commentator: '(O goddess of the moon) who hast obtained immortal joy through that which is a beautiful (portion of the sun) placed in the moon, and filling thy heart (with pleasure), may I never weep for misfortune concerning my children.'

Rv. I, 91, 16; IX, 31, 4. 'O goddess of the moon, increase! may the vigour from everywhere (from every limb of the fire or the sun) go to thee! Help us in the attainment of food.' Rv. I, 91, 18. 'O goddess of the moon, may the streams of thy milk go well to our sons, those streams of milk which are invigorating, and help to conquer the enemy. O Soma-goddess, increasing for immortal happiness (for the birth of a son), do thou place the highest glory (the streams of thy milk) in the sky.' 'That ray (sushum*n*â) which (as a woman) the Âdityas gladden, that Soma which as imperishable the imperishable Âdityas drink, may the guardian of the world (Pragâpati), B*ri*haspati, and king Varu*n*a gladden us by it.'

The translations are made by the commentator regardless of grammar and sense: yet they command a certain authority, and must be taken into account as throwing light on the latest development of Indian mysticism.

cattle; he who hates us and whom we hate, decrease by his life, by his offspring, by his cattle. Thus I turn the turn of the god, I return the turn of Âditya.' After these words, having raised the right arm, he lets it go again.

10. Next (having addressed these prayers to Soma) when being with his wife, let him stroke her heart, saying: 'O fair one, who hast obtained immortal joy by that which has entered thy heart through Pragâpati, mayest thou never fall into sorrow about thy children[724].' Her children then do not die before her.

11. Next, if a man has been absent and returns home, let him smell (kiss) his son's head, saying: 'Thou springest from every limb, thou art born from the heart, thou, my son, art my self indeed, live thou a hundred harvests.' He gives him his name, saying: 'Be thou a stone, be thou an axe, be thou solid[725] gold; thou, my son, art light indeed, live thou a hundred harvests.' He pronounces his name. Then he embraces him, saying: 'As Pragâpati (the lord of creatures) embraced his creatures for their welfare, thus I embrace thee,' (pronouncing his name.) Then he mutters into his right ear, saying: 'O thou, quick Maghavan, give to him' (Rv. III, 36, 10[726]). 'O Indra, bestow the best wishes' (Rv. II, 21, 6), thus he whispers into his left ear. Let him then thrice smell (kiss) his head, saying: 'Do not cut off (the line of our race), do not suffer. Live a hundred harvests of life; I kiss thy head, O son, with thy name.' He then thrice makes a lowing sound over his head, saying: 'I low over thee with the lowing sound of cows.'

12. Next follows the Daiva Parimara[727], the dying around of the gods (the absorption of the two classes of gods, mentioned before, into prâ*n*a or Brahman). This Brahman shines forth indeed when the fire burns, and it dies when it burns not. Its splendour goes to the sun alone, the life (prâ*n*a, the moving principle) to the air.

This Brahman shines forth indeed when the sun is seen, and it dies when it is not seen. Its splendour goes to the moon alone, the life (prâ*n*a) to the air.

This Brahman shines forth indeed when the moon is seen, and it dies when it is not seen. Its splendour goes to the lightning alone, its life (prâ*n*a) to the air.

This Brahman shines forth indeed when the lightning flashes, and it dies when it flashes not. Its splendour goes to the air, and the life (prâ*n*a) to the air.

Thus all these deities (i.e. fire, sun, moon, lightning), having

---

[724] Cf. Â*s*valâyana G*ri*hya-sûtras I, 13, 7.

[725] Widely scattered, everywhere desired. Comm. Professor Cowell proposes unscattered, hoarded, or unconcealed.

[726] The original has asme, to us, not asmai, to him.

[727] Cf. Taitt. Up. III, 10, 4; Ait. Brâhm. V, 28; Colebrooke, Miscellaneous Essays (1873), II, p. 39.

entered the air, though dead, do not vanish; and out of the very air they rise again. So much with reference to the deities (mythological). Now then with reference to the body (physiological).

13. This Brahman shines forth indeed when one speaks with speech, and it dies when one does not speak. His splendour goes to the eye alone, the life (prâ*n*a) to breath (prâ*n*a).

This Brahman shines forth indeed when one sees with the eye, and it dies when one does not see. Its splendour goes to the ear alone, the life (prâ*n*a) to breath (prâ*n*a).

This Brahman shines forth indeed when one hears with the ear, and it dies when one does not hear. Its splendour goes to the mind alone, the life (prâ*n*a) to breath (prâ*n*a).

This Brahman shines forth indeed when one thinks with the mind, and it dies when one does not think. Its splendour goes to the breath (prâ*n*a) alone, and the life (prâ*n*a) to breath (prâ*n*a).

Thus all these deities (the senses, &c.), having entered breath or life (prâ*n*a) alone, though dead, do not vanish; and out of very breath (prâ*n*a) they rise again. And if two mountains, the southern and northern, were to move forward trying to crush him who knows this, they would not crush him. But those who hate him and those whom he hates, they die around him.

14. Next follows the Ni*hs*reyasâdâna[728] (the accepting of the pre-eminence of prâ*n*a (breath or life) by the other gods). The deities (speech, eye, ear, mind), contending with each for who was the best, went out of this body, and the body lay without breathing, withered, like a log of wood. Then speech went into it, but speaking by speech, it lay still. Then the eye went into it, but speaking by speech, and seeing by the eye, it lay still. Then the ear went into it, but speaking by speech, seeing by the eye, hearing by the car, it lay still. Then mind went into it, but speaking by speech, seeing by the eye, hearing by the ear, thinking by the mind, it lay still. Then breath (prâ*n*a, life) went into it, and thence it rose at once. All these deities, having recognised the pre-eminence in prâ*n*a, and having comprehended prâ*n*a alone as the conscious self (pragñâtman)[729], went out of this body with all these (five different kinds of prâ*n*a), and resting in the air (knowing that prâ*n*a had entered the air), and merged in the ether (âkâ*s*a), they went to heaven. And in the same manner he who knows this, having recognised the pre-eminence in prâ*n*a, and having comprehended prâ*n*a alone as the conscious self (pragñâtman), goes out of this body with all these (does no longer believe in this body), and resting in the air, and merged in the ether, he goes to heaven, he goes to where those gods (speech,

---

[728] For other versions of this story see *Kh*. Up. V, 1, note 2; Ait. Âr. II, 1, 4, 9; Brih. Âr. VI, 1, 1-14; and Kaush. Up. III, 3.

[729] Cf. *Kh*. Up. VII, 15, note.

&c.) are. And having reached this he, who knows this, becomes immortal with that immortality which those gods enjoy.

15. Next follows the father's tradition to the son, and thus they explain it[730]. The father, when going to depart, calls his son, after having strewn the house with fresh grass, and having laid the sacrificial fire, and having placed near it a pot of water with a jug (full of rice), himself covered with a new cloth, and dressed in white. He places himself above his son, touching his organs with his own organs, or he may deliver the tradition to him while he sits before him. Then he delivers it to him. The father says: 'Let me place my speech in thee.' The son says: 'I take thy speech in me.' The father says: 'Let me place my scent (prâ*n*a) in thee.' The son says: 'I take thy scent in me.' The father says: 'Let me place my eye in thee.' The son says: 'I take thy eye in me.' The father says: 'Let me place my ear in thee.' The son says: 'I take thy ear in me.' The father says: 'Let me place my tastes of food in thee.' The son says: 'I take thy tastes of food in me.' The father says: 'Let me place my actions in thee!' The son says: 'I take thy actions in me.' The father says: 'Let me place my pleasure and pain in thee.' The son says: 'I take thy pleasure and pain in me.' The father says: 'Let me place happiness, joy, and offspring in thee.' The son says: 'I take thy happiness, joy, and offspring in me.' The father says: 'Let me place my walking in thee.' The son says: 'I take thy walking in me[731].' The father says: 'Let me place my mind in thee.' The son says: 'I take thy mind in me.' The father says: 'Let me place my knowledge (pragñâ) in thee.' The son says: 'I take thy knowledge in me.' But if the father is very ill, he may say shortly: 'Let me place my spirits (prâ*n*as) in thee,' and the son: 'I take thy spirits in me.'

Then the son walks round his father keeping his right side towards him, and goes away. The father calls after him: 'May fame, glory of countenance, and honour always follow thee.' Then the other looks back over his left shoulder, covering himself with his hand or the hem of his garment, saying: 'Obtain the heavenly worlds (svarga) and all desires.'

If the father recovers, let him be under the authority of his son, or let him wander about (as an ascetic). But if he departs, then let them despatch him, as he ought to be despatched, yea, as he ought to be despatched[732].

---

[730] Cf. B*r*ihad-âra*n*yaka I, 5,17.

[731] Another *s*âkhâ adds here dhiya*h*, the thoughts (active), vigñâtavyam, their object, and kâmâ*h*, desires.

[732] I have taken samâpayati in the sense of performing the last duties towards a dead person, though I confess I know of no parallel passage in which samâpayati occurs in that sense. Professor Cowell translates: 'If he dies, then let them cause the son duly to receive the tradition, as the tradition is to be given.' The text itself varies, for the reading presupposed by the commentator is ena*m* (putram) samâpayati, instead of ena*m* samâpayeyu*h*.

THIRD ADHYÂYA[733].

1. Pratardana, forsooth, the son of Divodâsa (king of Kâ*s*î), came by means of fighting and strength to the beloved abode of Indra. Indra said to him 'Pratardana, let me give you a boon to choose.' And Pratardana answered: 'Do you yourself choose that boon for me which you deem most beneficial for a man.' Indra said to him: 'No one who chooses, chooses for another; choose thyself,' Then Pratardana replied: 'Then that boon to choose is no boon for me.'

Then, however, Indra did not swerve from the truth, for Indra is truth. Indra said to him: 'Know me only; that is what I deem most beneficial for man, that he should know me. I slew the three-headed son of Tvash*tri*; I delivered the Arunmukhas, the devotees, to the wolves (sâlâv*ri*ka); breaking many treaties, I killed the people of Prahlâda in heaven, the people of Puloma in the sky, the people of Kâlakañga on earth[734]. And not one hair of me was harmed there. And he who knows me thus, by no deed of his is his life harmed, not by the murder of his mother, not by the murder of his father, not by theft, not by the killing of a Brahman. If he is going to commit a sin, the bloom[735] does not depart from his face.'

2. Indra said: 'I am prâ*n*a, meditate on me as the conscious self (pragñâtman), as life, as immortality. Life is prâ*n*a, prâ*n*a is life. Immortality is prâ*n*a, prâ*n*a is immortality. As long as prâ*n*a dwells in this body, so long surely there is life. By prâ*n*a he obtains immortality in the other world, by knowledge true conception. He who meditates on me as life and immortality, gains his full life in this world, and obtains in the Svarga world immortality and indestructibility.'

(Pratardana said): 'Some maintain here, that the prâ*n*as become one, for (otherwise) no one could at the same time make known a name by speech, see a form with the eye, hear a sound with the car, think a thought with the mind. After having become one, the prâ*n*as perceive all these together, one by one. While speech speaks, all prâ*n*as speak after it. While the eye sees, all prâ*n*as see after it. While the car hears, all prâ*n*as hear after it. While the mind thinks, all prâ*n*as think after it.

---

[733] The object now is to explain the true Brahma-vidyâ, while the first and second chapters are only introductory, treating of the worship of the couch (paryaṅkopâsanâ) and of the worship of prâ*n*a.

[734] This refers to heroic deeds performed by Indra, as represented in the hymns of the Rig-veda. See Rig-veda V, 34, 4, and Sâya*n*a's commentary; Ait. Brâhm. VII, 28. Weber, Indische Studien I, 410-418, has tried to discover an original physical meaning in the heroic deeds ascribed to Indra. A curious remark is made by the commentator, who says that the skulls of the Arunmukhas were turned into the thorns of the desert (karîra) which remain to this day,—a very common phase in popular tradition.

[735] Professor Cowell compares Taittirîya-Sa*m*hitâ III, 1, 1, nâsya nîta*m* na haro vyeti.

While the prâ*n*a breathes, all prâ*n*as breathe after it.'

'Thus it is indeed,' said Indra, 'but nevertheless there is a pre-eminence among the prâ*n*as[736].'

3. Man lives deprived of speech, for we see dumb people. Man lives deprived of sight, for we see blind people. Man lives deprived of hearing, for we see deaf people. Man lives deprived of mind, for we see infants. Man lives deprived of his arms, deprived of his legs, for we see it thus. But prâ*n*a alone is the conscious self (pragñâtman), and having laid hold of this body, it makes it rise up. Therefore it is said, Let man worship it alone as uktha[737]. What is prâ*n*a, that is pragñâ (self-consciousness); what is pragñâ (self-consciousness), that is prâ*n*a, for together they (pragñâ and prâ*n*a) live in this body, and together they go out of it. Of that, this is the evidence, this is the understanding. When a man, being thus asleep, sees no dream whatever, he becomes one with that prâ*n*a alone[738]. Then speech goes to him (when he is absorbed in prâ*n*a) with all names, the eye with all forms, the ear with all sounds, the mind with all thoughts. And when he awakes, then, as from a burning fire sparks proceed in all directions, thus from that self the prâ*n*âs (speech, &c.) proceed, each towards its place; from the prâ*n*as the gods (Agni, &c.), from the gods the worlds.

Of this, this is the proof, this is the understanding. When a man is thus sick, going to die, falling into weakness and faintness, they say: 'His thought has departed, he hears not, he sees not, he speaks not, he thinks not.' Then he becomes one with that prâ*n*a alone. Then speech goes to him (who is absorbed in prâ*n*a) with all names, the eye with all forms, the ear with all sounds, the mind with all thoughts. And when he departs from this body, he departs together with all these[739].

4. Speech gives up to him (who is absorbed in prâ*n*a) all names, so that by speech he obtains all names. The nose gives up to him all odours, so that by scent he obtains all odours. The eye gives up to him all forms, so that by the eye he obtains all forms. The ear gives up to him all sounds, so that by the ear he obtains all sounds. The mind gives up to him all thoughts, so that by the mind he obtains all thoughts. This is the complete absorption in prâ*n*a. And what is prâ*n*a is pragñâ (self-consciousness), what is pragñâ (self-consciousness) is prâ*n*a. For together do these two live in the body, and together do they depart.

Now we shall explain how all things become one in that pragñâ

---

[736] Prâ*n*âs, in the plural, is supposed to stand for the five senses as modifications of breath. It would be better if we could read prâ*n*asya ni*hs*reyasam. See before, II, 14.

[737] Uktha, hymn, is artificially derived from ut-thâpayati, to raise up, and hence uktha, hymn, is to be meditated on as prâ*n*a, breath, which likewise raises up the body. See Ait. Âr. II, 1, 15.

[738] He is absorbed in prâ*n*a. Or should it be prâ*n*a*h* as nominative?

[739] According to another reading we might translate, 'Speech takes away all names from that body; and prâ*n*a, in which speech is absorbed, thus obtains all names.'

(self-consciousness).

5. Speech is one portion taken out[740] of pragñâ (self-conscious knowledge), the word is its object, placed outside. The nose is one portion taken out of it, the odour is its object, placed outside. The eye is one portion taken out of it, the form is its object, placed outside. The ear is one portion taken out of it, the sound is its object, placed outside. The tongue is one portion taken out of it, the taste of food is its object, placed outside. The two hands are one portion taken out of it, their action is their object, placed outside. The body is one portion taken out of it, its pleasure and pain are its object, placed outside. The organ is one portion taken out of it, happiness, joy, and offspring are its object, placed outside. The two feet are one portion taken out of it, movements are their object, placed outside. Mind is one portion taken out of it, thoughts and desires are its object, placed outside.

6. Having by pragñâ (self-conscious knowledge) taken possession of speech, he obtains by speech all words. Having by pragñâ taken possession of the nose, he obtains all odours. Having by pragñâ taken possession of the eye, he obtains all forms. Having by pragñâ taken possession of the ear, he obtains all sounds. Having by pragñâ taken possession of the tongue, he obtains all tastes of food. Having by pragñâ taken possession of the two hands, he obtains all actions. Having by pragñâ taken possession of the body, he obtains pleasure and pain. Having by pragñâ taken possession of the organ, he obtains happiness, joy, and offspring. Having by pragñâ taken possession of the two feet, he obtains all movements. Having by pragñâ taken possession of mind, he obtains all thoughts.

7. For without pragñâ (self-consciousness) speech does not make known (to the self) any word[741]. 'My mind was absent,' he says, 'I did not perceive that word.' Without pragñâ the nose does not make known any odour. 'My mind was absent,' he says, 'I did not perceive that odour.' Without pragñâ the eye does not make known any form. 'My mind was absent,' he says, 'I did not perceive that form.' Without pragñâ the ear does not make known any sound. 'My mind was absent,'

---

[740] I read udû*lh*am or udû*dh*am, instead of adû*dh*am, explained by the commentator as adûduhat. Professor Cowell translates, 'Speech verily milked one portion thereof,' which may have been the original purport of the writer.

[741] Professor Cowell has translated a passage from the commentary which is interesting as showing that its author and the author of the Upanishad too had a clear conception of the correlative nature of knowledge. 'The organ of sense,' he says, 'cannot exist without pragñâ (self-consciousness), nor the objects of sense be obtained without the organ, therefore—on the principle, that when one thing cannot exist without another, that thing is said to be identical with the other—as the cloth, for instance, being never perceived without the threads, is identical with them, or the (false perception of) silver being never found without the mother of pearl is identical with it, so the objects of sense being never found without the organs are identical with them, and the organs being never found without pragñâ (self-consciousness) are identical with it.'

he says, 'I did not perceive that sound.' Without pragñâ the tongue does not make known any taste. 'My mind was absent,' he says, 'I did not perceive that taste.' Without pragñâ the two hands do not make known any act. 'Our mind was absent,' they say, 'we did not perceive any act.' Without pragñâ the body does not make known pleasure or pain. 'My mind was absent,' he says, 'I did not perceive that pleasure or pain.' Without pragñâ the organ does not make known happiness, joy, or offspring. 'My mind was absent,' he says, 'I did not perceive that happiness, joy, or offspring.' Without pragñâ, the two feet do not make known any movement. 'Our mind was absent,' they say, 'we did not perceive that movement.' Without pragñâ no thought succeeds, nothing can be known that is to be known.

8. Let no man try to find out what speech is, let him know the speaker. Let no man try to find out what odour is, let him know him who smells. Let no man try to find out what form is, let him know the seer. Let no man try to find out what sound is, let him know the hearer. Let no man try to find out the tastes of food, let him know the knower of tastes. Let no man try to find out what action is, let him know the agent. Let no man try to find out what pleasure and pain are, let him know the knower of pleasure and pain. Let no man try to find out what happiness, joy, and offspring are, let him know the knower of happiness, joy, and offspring. Let no man try to find out what movement is, let him know the mover. Let no man try to find out what mind is, let him know the thinker. These ten objects (what is spoken, smelled, seen, &c.) have reference to pragñâ (self-consciousness), the ten subjects (speech, the senses, mind) have reference to objects. If there were no objects, there would be no subjects; and if there were no subjects, there would be no objects. For on either side alone nothing could be achieved. But that (the self of pragñâ, consciousness, and prâ*n*a, life) is not many, (but one.) For as in a car the circumference of a wheel is placed on the spokes, and the spokes on the nave, thus are these objects (circumference) placed on the subjects (spokes), and the subjects on the prâ*n*a. And that prâ*n*a (breath, the living and breathing power) indeed is the self of pragñâ (the self-conscious self), blessed, imperishable, immortal. He does not increase by a good action, nor decrease by a bad action. For he (the self of prâ*n*a and pragñâ) makes him, whom he wishes to lead up from these worlds, do a good deed; and the same makes him, whom he wishes to lead down from these worlds, do a bad deed[742]. And he is the guardian of the world, he is the king of the world, he is the lord of the universe,—and he is my (Indra's) self, thus let it be known, yea, thus let it be known!

[742] The other text says, 'whom he wishes to draw after him; and whom he wishes to draw away from these worlds.' Râmatîrtha, in his commentary on the Mait. Up. 3, 2, quotes the text as translated above.

FOURTH ADHYÂYA[743]

1. There was formerly Gârgya Bâlâki[744], famous as a man of great reading; for it was said of him that he lived among the Us*î*naras, among the Satvat-Matsyas, the Kuru-Pañ*k*âlas, the Kâs*î*-Videhas[745]. Having gone to Ag*â*tas*a*tru, (the king) of Kâs*î*, he said to him: 'Shall I tell you Brahman?' Ag*â*tas*a*tru said to him: 'We give a thousand (cows) for that speech (of yours), for verily all people run away, saying, "*G*anaka (the king of Mithilâ) is our father (patron)."'

---

[743] Prâ*n*a, breath or life, has been explained in the preceding chapter. But this prâ*n*a is not yet the highest point that has to be reached. Prâ*n*a, life, even as united with pragñâ, consciousness, is only a covering of something else, viz. the Self, and this Highest Self has now to be explained.

[744] The same story is told in the B*r*ihad-âra*n*yaka II, 1 seq., but with important variations.

[745] I take iti to depend on sa*m*spash*t*a, and read satvanmatsyeshu, though the commentary seems to have read so 'vasan, or sa vasan, for savasan. See Introduction, p. 52.

2. B*R*IHAD-ÂRA*N*YAKA-UPANISHAD.	KAUSHÎTAKI-BRÂHMA*N*A-UPANISHAD.
i. Âditye purusha*h*. atish*th*â*h* sarveshâm bhûtânâm mûrdhâ râ*g*â.	i. Id. b*ri*hat pâ*nd*aravâsâ (*pânduravâsâ*) atish*th*â*h* sarveshâm bhûtânâm mûrdhâ.
ii. *K*andre purusha*h*. b*ri*hat pâ*nd*aravâsâ*h* somo râ*g*â. (Nâsyânna*m* kshîyate, is the reward.)	ii. *K*andramasi. somo râ*g*â, annasyâtmâ. *Only annasyâtmâ.*
iii. Vidyuti purusha*h*. te*g*asvî.	iii. Id. te*g*asy âtmâ. *satyasyâtmâ.*
	iii[b]. stanayitnau purusha*h*. *s*abdasyâtmâ.
iv. Âkâ*s*e purusha*h*. pûr*n*am apravarti.	iv. Id. (5) pûr*n*am apravarti brahma. *apravritti.*
v. Vâyau purusha*h*. indro vaiku*nth*o 'parâ*g*itâ senâ.	v. Id. (4) Id.
vi. Agnau purusha*h*. vishâsahi*h*.	vi. Id. Id.
vii. Apsu purusha*h*. pratirûpa*h*.	vii. Id. nâmnasyâtmâ. *tegasa âtmâ.*
viii. Âdar*s*e purusha*h*. ro*k*ish*n*u*h*.	viii. Id. pratirûpa*h*.
	viii[b]. prati*s*rutkâyâm purusha*h*. (9) dvitîyo 'napaga*h*. *asuh.* [746]

[746] The second paragraph forms a kind of table of contents for the discussion which is to follow. I have given instead a fuller table of contents, taken from the Brihad-

ix. Yantam pas*k*â*k* *kh*abda*h*.
asu*h*.
x. Dikshu purusha*h*.
dvitîyo 'napaga*h*.
xi. *Kh*âyâmaya*h* purusha*h*.
m*ri*tyu*h*.
xii. Âtmani purusha*h*.
âtmanvî.

ix. Ya*h* *s*abda*h* purusham anveti. (10) *sabde*.
Id. *mrityu*h.
x. Deest.
x. *Kh*âyâpurusha*h*. (8b) kh*âyâyâm*.
Id. *dvitîyo 'napaga*h.
xi. *S*ârîra*h* purusha*h*. (12) *sarîre purusha*h.
pra*g*âpati*h*.
xii. Ya*h* prâ*g*ña âtmâ, yenaitat supta*h* svapnayâ *k*arati.
Yamo râ*g*â. (11) *purusha*h *svapnayâ* k*arati* *yamo râgâ*.
xiii. Dakshi*n*e 'kshan purusha*h*.
nâmna (*vâ*k*a*) âtmâ, agner âtmâ, *g*yotisha âtmâ.
xiv. Savye 'kshan purusha*h*.
satyasyâtmâ, vidyuta âtmâ, te*g*asa âtmâ.

3. Bâlâki said: 'The person that is in the sun, on him I meditate (as Brahman).'

Agâtasatru said to him: 'No, no! do not challenge me (to a disputation) on this[747]. I meditate on him who is called great, clad in

---

âra*n*yaka II, as compared with the Kaushîtaki-upanishad in its two texts. The variations of text A are given in small letters. In text B, the table of contents is given at the end of the discussion, in § 18.

[747] The king means to say that he knows this already, and that he can mention not only the predicates of the person in the sun thus meditated on as Brahman, but also the rewards of such meditation.

white raiment[748], the supreme, the head of all beings. Whoso meditates on him thus, becomes supreme, and the head of all beings.'

4. Bâlâki said: 'The person that is in the moon, on him I meditate.'

Agâta*s*atru said to him: 'Do not challenge me on this. I meditate on him as Soma, the king, the self, (source) of all food. Whoso meditates on him thus, becomes the self, (source) of all food.'

5. Bâlâki said: 'The person that is in the lightning, on him I meditate.'

Agâta*s*atru said to him: 'Do not challenge me on this. I meditate on him as the self in light. Whoso meditates on him thus, becomes the self in light.'

6. Bâlâki said: 'The person that is in the thunder, on him I meditate.'

Agâta*s*atru said to him: 'Do not challenge me on this. I meditate on him as the self of sound[749]. Whoso meditates on him thus, becomes the self of sound.'

7. Bâlâki said: 'The person that is in the ether, on him I meditate.'

Agâta*s*atru said to him: 'Do not challenge me on this. I meditate on him as the full, quiescent Brahman. Whoso meditates on him thus, is filled with offspring and cattle. Neither he himself nor his offspring dies before the time.'

8. Bâlâki said: 'The person that is in the air, on him I meditate.'

Agâta*s*atru said to him: 'Do not challenge me on this. I meditate on him as Indra Vaiku*nth*a, as the unconquerable army. Whoso meditates on him thus, becomes victorious, unconquerable, conquering his enemies.'

9. Bâlâki said: 'The person that is in the fire, on him I meditate.'

Agâta*s*atru said to him: 'Do not challenge me on this. I meditate on him as powerful. Whoso meditates on him thus, becomes powerful among others[750].'

10. Bâlâki said: 'The person that is in the water, on him I meditate.'

Agâta*s*atru said to him: 'Do not challenge me on this. I meditate on him as the self of the name. Whoso meditates on him thus, becomes the self of the name.' So far with regard to deities (mythological); now with regard to the body (physiological).

11. Bâlâki said: 'The person that is in the mirror, on him I meditate.'

Agâta*s*atru said to him: 'Do not challenge me on this. I meditate on him as the likeness. Whoso meditates on him thus, to him a son is born

---

[748] This is properly a predicate of the moon, and used as such in the B*r*ihad-âra*n*yaka-upanishad, in the second paragraph of the dialogue.

[749] This is not mentioned in the B*r*ihad-âra*n*yaka.

[750] Instead of anyeshu, the second text, as printed by Professor Cowell, has anv esha.

in his family who is his likeness, not one who is not his likeness.'

12. Bâlâki said: 'The person that is in the echo, on him I meditate.'

Agâta*s*atru said to him: 'Do not challenge me on this. I meditate on him as the second, who never goes away. Whoso meditates on him thus, he gets a second from his second (his wife), he becomes doubled[751].

Bâlâki said: 'The sound that follows a man, on that I meditate.'

Agâta*s*atru said to him: 'Do not challenge me on this. I meditate on him as life. Whoso meditates on him thus, neither he himself nor his offspring will faint before the time.'

14. Bâlâki said: 'The person that is in the shadow, on him I meditate.'

Agâta*s*atru said to him: 'Do not challenge me on this. I meditate on him as death. Whoso meditates on him thus, neither he himself nor his offspring will die before the time.'

15. Bâlâki said: 'The person that is embodied, on him I meditate.'

Agâta*s*atru said to him: 'Do not challenge me on this. I meditate on him as Lord of creatures. Whose, meditates on him thus, is multiplied in offspring and cattle.'

16. Bâlâki said: 'The Self which is conscious (prâgña), and by whom he who sleeps here, walks about in sleep, on him I meditate.'

Agâta*s*atru said to him: 'Do not challenge me on this. I meditate on him as Yama the king. Whoso meditates on him thus, everything is subdued for his excellencies.'

17. Bâlâki said: 'The person that is in the right eye, on him I meditate.'

Agâta*s*atru said to him: 'Do not challenge me on this. I meditate on him as the self of the name, as the self of fire, as the self of splendour. Whoso meditates on him thus, he becomes the self of these.'

18. Bâlâki said The person that is in the left eye, on him I meditate.'

Agâta*s*atru said to him: 'Do not challenge me on this. I meditate on him as the self of the true, as the self of lightning, as the self of light. Whoso meditates on him thus, he becomes the self of these.'

19. After this Bâlâki became silent. Agâta*s*atru said to him: 'Thus far only (do you know), O Bâlâki?' 'Thus far only,' replied Bâlâki.

Then Agâta*s*atru said to him: 'Vainly did you challenge me,' saying: 'Shall I tell you Brahman? O Bâlâki, he who is the maker of those persons (whom you mentioned), he of whom all this is the work, he alone is to be known.'

Thereupon Bâlâki came, carrying fuel in his hand, saying: 'May I come to you as a pupil?' Agâta*s*atru said to him: 'I deem it improper that a Kshatriya should initiate a Brâhma*n*a. Come, I shall make you

---

[751] This paragraph does not occur in the B*ri*had-âra*n*yaka.

know clearly.' Then taking him by the hand, he went forth. And the two together came to a person who was asleep. And Agâta*s*atru called him, saying: 'Thou great one, clad in white raiment, Soma, King[752].' But he remained lying. Then he pushed him with a stick, and he rose at once. Then said Agâta*s*atru to him: 'Bâlâki, where did this person here sleep? Where was he? Whence came he thus back?' Bâlâki did not know.

20. And Agâta*s*atru said to him: 'Where this person here slept, where he was, whence he thus came back, is this: The arteries of the heart called Hita extend from the heart of the person towards the surrounding body. Small as a hair divided a thousand times, they stand full of a thin fluid of various colours, white, black, yellow, red. In these the person is when sleeping he sees no dream.

'Then he becomes one with that prâ*n*a alone. Then speech goes to him with all names, the eye with all forms, the car with all sounds, the mind with all thoughts. And when he awakes, then, as from a burning fire, sparks proceed in all directions, thus from that self the prâ*n*as (speech, &c.) proceed, each towards its place, from the prâ*n*as the gods, from the gods the worlds. And as a razor might be fitted in a razor-case, or as fire in the fire-place (the ara*n*i on the altar), even thus this conscious self enters the self of the body (considers the body as himself) to the very hairs and nails. And the other selfs (such as speech, &c.) follow that self, as his people follow the master of the house. And as the master feeds with his people, nay, as his people feed on the master, thus does this conscious self feed with the other selfs, as a master with his people, and the other selfs follow him, as his people follow the master. So long as Indra did not understand that self, the Asuras conquered him. When he understood it, he conquered the Asuras and obtained the pre-eminence among all gods, sovereignty, supremacy. And thus also he who knows this obtains pre-eminence among all beings, sovereignty, supremacy,—yea, he who knows this.'

---

[752] See § 3 init.

VÂ*G*ASANEYI-SA*M*HITÂ-UPANISHAD,

SOMETIMES CALLED

ÎSÂVÂSYA OR ÎSÂ-UPANISHAD

VÂ*G*ASANEYI-SA*M*HITÂ-UPANISHAD.

1. All this, whatsoever moves on earth, is to be hidden in the Lord (the Self). When thou hast surrendered all this, then thou mayest enjoy. Do not covet the wealth of any man!

2. Though a man may wish to live a hundred years, performing works, it will be thus with him; but not in any other way: work will thus not cling to a man.

3. There are the worlds of the Asuras[753] covered with blind darkness. Those who have destroyed their self (who perform works, without having arrived at a knowledge of the true Self), go after death to those worlds.

4. That one (the Self), though never stirring, is swifter than thought. The Devas (senses) never reached it, it walked[754] before them. Though standing still, it overtakes the others who are running. Mâtarisvan (the wind, the moving spirit) bestows powers[755] on it.

5. It stirs and it stirs not; it is far, and likewise near[756]. It is inside of all this, and it is outside of all this.

6. And he who beholds all beings in the Self, and the Self in all beings, he never turns away from it[757].

7. When to a man who understands, the Self has become all things, what sorrow, what trouble can there be to him who once beheld that unity?

8. He[758] (the Self) encircled all, bright, incorporeal, scatheless, without muscles, pure, untouched by evil; a seer, wise, omnipresent, self-existent, he disposed all things rightly for eternal years.

---

[753] Asury`â, Vâg. Sa*m*hitâ; asûryâ, Upan. Asuryà in the Upanishads in the sense of belonging to the Asuras, i.e. gods, is exceptional. I should prefer asûryá, sunless, as we find asûryé támasi in the Rig-veda, V, 32, 6.

[754] Pûrvam ar*s*at, Vâg. Sa*m*h.; pûrvam arshat, Upan. Mahîdhara suggests also arsat as a contraction of a-ri*s*at, not perishing.

[755] Apas is explained by karmâ*n*i, acts, in which case it would be meant for ápas, opus. But the Vâg. Sa*m*hitâ accentuates apás, i.e. aquas, and Ânandagiri explains that water stands for acts, because most sacrificial acts are performed with water.

[756] Tad v antike, Vâg. Sa*m*h.; tadvad antike, Upan.

[757] Vi*k*ikitsati, Vâg. Sa*m*h.; vigugupsate, Upan.

[758] *S*aṅkara takes the subject to be the Self, and explains the neuter adjectives as masculines. Mahîdhara takes the subject to be the man who has acquired a knowledge of the Self, and who reaches the bright, incorporeal Brahman, &c. Mahîdhara, however, likewise allows the former explanation.

9. All who worship what is not real knowledge (good works), enter into blind darkness: those who delight in real knowledge, enter, as it were, into greater darkness.

10. One thing, they say, is obtained from real knowledge; another, they say, from what is not knowledge. Thus we have heard from the wise who taught us this[759].

11. He who knows at the same time both knowledge and not-knowledge, overcomes death through not-knowledge, and obtains immortality through knowledge.

12. All who worship what is not the true cause, enter into blind darkness: those who delight in the true cause, enter, as it were, into greater darkness.

13. One thing, they say, is obtained from (knowledge of) the cause; another, they say, from (knowledge of) what is not the cause. Thus we have heard from the wise who taught us this.

14. He who knows at the same time both the cause and the destruction (the perishable body), overcomes death by destruction (the perishable body), and obtains immortality through (knowledge of) the true cause.

15. The door of the True is covered with a golden disk[760]. Open that, O Pûshan, that we may see the nature of the True[761].

16. O Pûshan, only seer, Yama (judge), Sûrya (sun), son of Pragâpati, spread thy rays and gather them! The light which is thy fairest form, I see it. I am what He is (viz. the person in the sun)[762].

17. Breath[763] to air, and to the immortal! Then this my body ends in ashes. Om! Mind, remember! Remember thy deeds! Mind, remember! Remember thy deeds[764]!

18. Agni, lead us on to wealth (beatitude) by a good path, thou, O God, who knowest all things! Keep far from us crooked evil, and we shall offer thee the fullest praise! (Rv. I, 189, 1.)

This Upanishad, though apparently simple and intelligible, is in reality one of the most difficult to understand properly. Coming at the end of the Vâgasaneyi-sa*m*hitâ, in which the sacrifices and the hymns to be used by the officiating priests have been described, it begins by

---

759 Cf. Talavak. Up. I, 4; vidyâya*h*, avidyâyâ*h*, Vâg. Sa*m*h.; vidyayâ, avidyayâ, Upan.

760 Mahîdhara on verse 17: 'The face of the true (purusha in the sun) is covered by a golden disk.'

761 Cf. Maitr. Up. VI, 35.

762 Asau purusha*h* should probably be omitted.

763 These lines are supposed to be uttered by a man in the hour of death.

764 The Vâgasaneyi-sa*m*hitâ reads: Om, krato smara, k*l*ibe smara, k*r*ita*m* smara. Uva*t*a holds that Agni, fire, who has been worshipped in youth and manhood, is here invoked in the form of mind, or that kratu is meant for sacrifice. 'Agni, remember me! Think of the world! Remember my deeds!'

declaring that all has to be surrendered to the Lord. The name is, lord, is peculiar, as having a far more personal colouring than Âtman, Self, or Brahman, the usual names given by the Upanishads to what is the object of the highest knowledge.

Next follows a permission to continue the performance of sacrifices, provided that all desires have been surrendered. And here occurs our first difficulty, which has perplexed ancient as well as modern commentators.

I shall try, first of all, to justify my own translation. I hold that the Upanishad wishes to teach the uselessness by themselves of all good works, whether we call them sacrificial, legal, or moral, and yet, at the same time, to recognise, if not the necessity, at least the harmlessness of good works, provided they are performed without any selfish motives, without any desire of reward, but simply as a preparation for higher knowledge, as a means, in fact, of subduing all passions, and producing that serenity of mind without which man is incapable of receiving the highest knowledge. From that point of view the Upanishad may well say, Let a man wish to live here his appointed time, let him even perform all works. If only he knows that all must be surrendered to the Lord, then the work done by him will not cling to him. It will not work on and produce effect after effect, nor will it involve him in a succession of new births in which to enjoy the reward of his works, but it will leave him free to enjoy the blessings of the highest knowledge. It will have served as a preparation for that higher knowledge which the Upanishad imparts, and which secures freedom from further births.

The expression 'na karma lipyate nare' seems to me to admit of this one explanation only, viz. that work done does not cling to man, provided he has acquired the highest knowledge. Similar expressions occur again and again. Lip was, no doubt, used originally of evil deeds which became, as it were, engrained in man; but afterwards of all work, even of good work, if done with a desire of reward. The doctrine of the Upanishads is throughout that orthodoxy and sacrifice can procure a limited beatitude only, and that they are a hindrance to real salvation, which can be obtained by knowledge alone. In our passage therefore we can recognise one meaning only, viz. that work does not cling to man or stain him, if only he knows, i.e. if he has been enlightened by the Upanishad.

*S*aṅkara, in his commentary on the Vedânta-sûtras III, 4, 7; 13; 14, takes the same view of this passage. The opponent of Bâdarâya*n*a, in this case, *G*aimini himself, maintains that karma, work, is indispensable to knowledge, and among other arguments, he says, III, 4, 7, that it is so 'Niyamât,' 'Because it is so laid down by the law.' The passage here referred to is, according to *S*aṅkara, our very verse, which, he thinks, should be translated as follows: 'Let a man wish to live a hundred years here (in this body) performing works; thus will an evil deed not cling to thee, while thou art a man; there is no other way but this by which to escape the influence of works.' In answer to this, Bâdarâya*n*a says, first of all, III, 4, 13, that this rule may refer to all men in general, and not to one who knows; or, III, 4, 14, if it refers to a man who knows, that then the permission to perform works is only intended to exalt the value of knowledge, the meaning being that even to a man who performs sacrifices all his life, work does not cling, if only he knows;—such being the power of knowledge.

The same *S*ankara, however, who here sees quite clearly that this verse refers to a man who knows, explains it in the Upanishad as referring to a man who does not know (itarasyânâtmag*ñ*atay-âtmagraha*n*â*s*aktasya). It would then mean: 'Let such a one, while performing works here on earth, wish to live a hundred years. In this manner there is no other way for him but this (the performance of sacrifices), so that an evil deed should not be engrained, or so that he should not be stained by such a deed.' The first and second verses of the Upanishad would thus represent the two paths of life, that of knowledge and that of works. and the following verses would explain the rewards assigned to each.

Mahîdhara, in his commentary on the Vâgasaneyi-sa*m*hitâ, steers at first a middle course. He would translate: 'Let one who performs the Agnihotra and other sacrifices, without any desire of reward, wish to live here a hundred years. If thou do so, there will be salvation for thee, not otherwise. There are many roads that, lead to heaven, but one only leading to salvation, namely, performance of good works, without any desire of reward, which produces a pure heart. Work thus done, merely as a preparation for salvation, does not cling to man, i.e. it produces a pure heart, but does not entail any further consequences.' So far he agrees with Uva*t*a's explanation[765]. He allows, however, another explanation also, so that the second line would convey the meaning: 'If a man lives thus (performing good works), then there is no other way by which an evil deed should not be engrained; i.e. in order to escape the power of sin, he must all his life perform sacred acts.'

Next follows a description of the lot of those who, immersed in works, have not arrived at the highest knowledge, and have not recovered their true self in the Highest Self, or Brahman. That Brahman, though the name is not used here, is then described, and salvation is promised to the man who beholds all things in the Self and the Self in all things.

The verses 9-14 are again full of difficulty, not so much in themselves as in their relation to the general system of thought which prevails in the Upanishads, and forms the foundation of the Vedânta

[765] Uva*t*a explains gigîshivishe*h* for gigîvishet as a purushavyataya*h*.

philosophy. The commentators vary considerably in their interpretations. *S*aṅkara explains avidyâ, not-knowledge, by good works, particularly sacrifice, performed with a hope of reward; vidyâ, or knowledge, by a knowledge of the gods, but not, as yet, of the highest Brahman. The former is generally supposed to lead the sacrificer to the pit*ri*loka, the world of the fathers, from whence he returns to a series of new births; the latter to the devaloka, the world of the gods, from whence he may either proceed to Brahman, or enter upon a new round of existences. The question then arises, how in our passage the former could be said to lead to blind darkness, the latter to still greater darkness. But for that statement, I have no doubt that all the commentators would, as usual, have taken vidyâ for the knowledge of the Highest Brahman, and avidyâ for orthodox belief in the gods and good works, the former securing immortality in the sense of freedom from new births, while the reward of the latter is blessedness in heaven for a limited period, but without freedom from new births.

This antithesis between vidyâ and avidyâ seems to me so firmly established that I cannot bring myself to surrender it here. Though this Upanishad has its own very peculiar character, yet its object is, after all, to impart a knowledge of the Highest Self, and not to inculcate merely a difference between faith in the ordinary gods and good works. It was distinctly said before (ver. 3), that those who have destroyed their self, i.e. who perform works only, and have not arrived at a knowledge of the true Self, go to the worlds of the Asuras, which are covered with blind darkness. If then the same blind darkness is said in verse 9 to be the lot of those who worship not-knowledge, this can only mean those who have not discovered the true Self, but are satisfied with the performance of good works. And if those who perform good works are opposed to others who delight in true knowledge, that knowledge can be the knowledge of the true Self only.

The difficulty therefore which has perplexed *S*aṅkara is this, how, while the orthodox believer is said to enter into blind darkness, the true disciple, who has acquired a knowledge of the true Self, could be said to enter into still greater darkness. While *S*aṅkara in this case seems hardly to have caught the drift of the Upanishad, Uva*t*a and Mahîdhara propose an explanation which is far more satisfactory. They perceive that the chief stress must be laid on the words ubhaya*m* saha, 'both together,' in verses 11 and 14. The doctrine of certain Vedânta philosophers was that works, though they cannot by themselves lead to salvation, are useful as a preparation for the highest knowledge, and that those who imagine that they can attain the highest knowledge without such previous preparation, are utterly mistaken. From this point of view therefore the author of the Upanishad might well say that those who give themselves to what is not knowledge, i.e. to sacrificial and other good works, enter into darkness, but that those who delight altogether in knowledge, despising the previous discipline of works, deceive themselves and enter into still greater darkness.

Then follows the next verse, simply stating that, according to the teaching of wise people, the reward of knowledge is one thing, the reward of ignorance, i.e. trust in sacrifice, another. Here Mahîdhara is right again by assigning the pit*ri*loka, the world of the fathers, as the reward of the ignorant; the devaloka, the world of the gods, as the reward of the enlightened, provided that from the world of the gods they pass on to the knowledge of the Highest Self or Brahman.

The third verse contains the strongest confirmation of Mahîdhara's view. Here it is laid down distinctly that he only who knows both together, both what is called ignorance and what is called knowledge, can be saved, because by good works he overcomes death, here explained by natural works, and by knowledge he obtains the Immortal, here explained by oneness with the gods, the last step that leads on to oneness with Brahman.

Uva*t*a, who takes the same view of these verses, explains at once, and even more boldly than Mahîdhara[766], vidyâ, or knowledge, by brahmavigñâna, knowledge of Brahman, which by itself, and if not preceded by works, leads to even greater darkness than what is called ignorance, i.e. sacrifice and orthodoxy without knowledge.

The three corresponding verses, treating of sambhûti and asambhûti instead of vidyâ and avidyâ, stand first in the Vâgasaneyi-sa*m*hitâ. They must necessarily be explained in accordance with our explanation of the former verses, i.e. sambhûti must correspond to vidyâ, it must be meant for the true cause, i.e. for Brahman, while asambhûti must correspond with avidyâ, as a name of what is not real, but phenomenal only and perishable.

Mahîdhara thinks that these verses refer to the Bauddhas, which can hardly be admitted, unless we take Buddhist in a very general sense. Uva*t*a puts the Lokâyatas in their place[767]. It is curious also to observe that Mahîdhara, following Uva*t*a, explains asambhûti at first by the denial of the resurrection of the body, while he takes sambhûti rightly for Brahman. I have chiefly followed Uva*t*a's commentary, except in his first explanation of asambhûti, resurrection[768]. In what follows Uva*t*a explains sambhûti rightly by the only cause of the origin of the whole world, i.e. Brahman[769], while he takes vinâ*s*a, destruction, as a name of the perishable body[770].

---

[766] Mahîdhara decides in the end that vidyâ and am*ri*tam must here be taken in a limited or relative sense, tasmâd vidyopâsanâm*ri*ta*m* *k*âpekshikam iti dik, and so agrees on the whole with *S*aṅkara, pp. 25-27.

[767] Sha*d* anush*t*ubha*h*, lokâyatikâ*h* prastûyante yeshâm etad dar*s*anam.

[768] M*ri*tasya sata*h* puna*h* sambhavo nâsti, ata*h* *s*arîragraha*n*âd asmâkam muktir eva.

[769] Samastasya *g*agata*h* sambhavaikahetu brahma.

[770] Vinâsa*m* vinâ*s*i *k*a vapu*h* *s*arîram.

*S*aṅkara sees much more in these three verses than Uva*t*a. He takes asambhûti as a name of Prakriti, the undeveloped cause, sambhûti as a name of the phenomenal Brahman or Hira*n*yagarbha. From a worship of the latter a man obtains supernatural powers, from devotion to the former, absorption in Prak*ri*ti.

Mahîdhara also takes a similar view, and he allows, like *S*aṅkara, another reading, viz. sambhûtim avinâ*s*a*m* ka, and avinâ*s*ena m*ri*tyum tîrtvâ. In this case the sense would be: 'He who knows the worship both of the developed and the undeveloped, overcomes death, i.e. such evil as sin, passion, &c., through worship of the undeveloped, while he obtains through worship of the developed, i.e. of Hira*n*yagarbha, immortality, absorption in Prak*ri*ti.'

All these forced explanations to which the commentators have recourse, arise from the shifting views held by various authorities with regard to the value of works. Our Upanishad seems to me to propound the doctrine that works, though in themselves useless, or even mischievous, if performed with a view to any present or future rewards, are necessary as a preparatory discipline. This is or was for a long time the orthodox view. Each man was required to pass through the â*s*ramas, or stages of student and householder, before he was admitted to the freedom of a Sannyâsin. As on a ladder, no step was to be skipped. Those who attempted to do so, were considered to have broken the old law, and in some respects they may indeed be looked upon as the true precursors of the Buddhists.

Nevertheless the opposite doctrine, that a man whose mind had become enlightened, might at once drop the fetters of the law, without performing all the tedious duties of student and householder, had strong supporters too among orthodox philosophers. Cases of such rapid conversion occur in the ancient traditions, and Bâdarâya*n*a himself was obliged to admit the possibility of freedom and salvation without works, though maintaining the superiority of the usual course, which led on gradually from works to enlightenment and salvation[771]. It was from an unwillingness to assent to the decided teaching of the Î*s*â-upanishad that *S*aṅkara attempted to explain vidyâ, knowledge, in a limited sense, as knowledge of the gods, and not yet knowledge of Brahman. He would not admit that knowledge without works could lead to darkness, and even to greater darkness than works without knowledge. Our Upanishad seems to have dreaded libertinism, knowledge without works, more even than ritualism, works without knowledge, and its true object was to show that orthodoxy and sacrifice, though useless in themselves, must always form the preparation for higher enlightenment.

How misleading *S*aṅkara's explanation may prove, we can see

[771] Vedânta-sûtras III, 4, 36-39.

from the translation of this Upanishad by Rammohun Roy. He followed *S*aṅkara implicitly, and this is the sense which he drew from the text:—

'9. Those observers of religious rites that perform only the worship of the sacred fire, and oblations to sages, to ancestors, to men, and to other creatures, without regarding the worship of celestial gods, shall enter into the dark region: and those practisers of religious ceremonies who habitually worship the celestial gods only, disregarding the worship of the sacred fire, and oblations to sages, to ancestors, to men, and to other creatures, shall enter into a region still darker than the former.

'10. It is said that adoration of the celestial gods produces one consequence; and that the performance of the worship of sacred fire, and oblations to sages, to ancestors, to men, and to other creatures, produce another: thus have we heard from learned men, who have distinctly explained the subject to us.

'11. Of those observers of ceremonies whosoever, knowing that adoration of celestial gods, as well as the worship of the sacred fire, and oblation to sages, to ancestors, to men, and to other creatures, should be observed alike by the same individual, performs them both, will, by means of the latter, surmount the obstacles presented by natural temptations, and will attain the state of the celestial gods through the practice of the former.

'12. Those observers of religious rites who worship Prak*ri*ti alone (Prak*ri*ti or nature, who, though insensible, influenced by the Supreme Spirit, operates throughout the universe) shall enter into the dark region: and those practisers of religious ceremonies that are devoted to worship solely the prior operating sensitive particle, allegorically called Brahmá, shall enter into a region much more dark than the former.

'13. It is said that one consequence may be attained by the worship of Brahmâ, and another by the adoration of Prak*ri*ti. Thus have we heard from learned men, who have distinctly explained the subject to us.

'14. Of those observers of ceremonies, whatever person, knowing that the adoration of Prak*ri*ti and that of Brahmá should be together observed by the same individual, performs them both, will by means of the latter overcome indigence, and will attain the state of Prak*ri*ti, through the practice of the former.'

Volume II

INTRODUCTION.

This second volume completes the translation of the principal Upanishads to which *S*ankara appeals in his great commentary on the Vedânta-Sûtras,[772] viz.:

1. *Kh*ândogya-upanishad,
2. Talavakâra or Kena-upanishad,
3. Aitareya-upanishad,
4. Kaushîtaki-upanishad,
5. Vâgasaneyi or Î*s*â-upanishad,
6. Ka*th*a-upanishad,
7. Mu*nd*aka-upanishad,
8. Taittirîyaka-upanishad,
9. B*ri*hadâra*n*yaka-upanishad,
10. *S*vetâ*s*vatara-upanishad,
11. Pra*sñ*a-upanishad.

These eleven have sometimes[773] been called the old and genuine Upanishads, though I should be satisfied to call them the eleven classical Upanishads, or the fundamental Upanishads of the Vedânta philosophy.

Vidyâranya,[774] in his 'Elucidation of the meaning of all the Upanishads,' Sarvopanishadarthânubhûti-prakâ*s*a, confines himself likewise to those treatises, dropping, however, the Î*s*â, and adding the Maitrâya*n*a-upanishad, of which I have given a translation in this volume, and the N*ri*si*m*hottara-tapanîya-upanishad, the translation of which had to be reserved for the next volume.

It is more difficult to determine which of the Upanishads were chosen by *S*ankara or deserving the honour of a special commentary. We possess his commentaries on the eleven Upanishads mentioned before,[775] with the exception of the Kaushîtaki[776]-upanishad. We likewise possess his commentary on the Mândûkya-upanishad, but we do not know for certain whether he left commentaries on any of the

---

[772] See Deussen, Vedânta, Einleitung, p. 38. *S*ankara occasionally refers also to the Paingi, Agnirahasya, *G*âbâla, and Narâya*n*îya Upanishads.

[773] Deussen, loc. cit. p. 82.

[774] I state this on the authority of Professor Cowell. See also Fitzedward Hall, Index to the Bibliography of the Indian Philosophical Systems, pp. 116 and 236.

[775] They have been published by Dr. Roer in the Bibliotheca Indica.

[776] Dr. Weber's statement that *S*ankara wrote a commentary on the Kaushîtaki-upanishad has been corrected by Deussen, loc. cit. p. 39.

other Upanishads. Some more or less authoritative statements have been made that he wrote commentaries on some of the minor Upanishads, such as the Atharva*s*iras, Atharva-*s*ikhâ, and the N*ri*si*m*hatâpanî.[777] But as, besides *S*ankarâ*k*ârya, the disciple of Govinda, there is *S*ankarânanda, the disciple of Ânandâtman, another writer of commentaries on the Upanishads, it is possible that the two names may have been confounded by less careful copyists.[778]

With regard to the N*ri*si*m*hatâpanî all uncertainty might seem to be removed, after Professor Râmamaya Tarkaratna has actually published its text with the commentary of *S*ankarâkârya in the Bibliotheca Indica, Calcutta, 1871. But some uncertainty still remains. While at the end of each Khanda of the N*ri*si*m*ha-pûrvatâpanî we read that the Bhâshya was the work of the Paramaha*m*sa-parivrâgakâ*k*ârya *S*rî-*S*ankara, the pupil of Govinda, we have no such information for the N*ri*si*m*ha-uttaratâpanî, but are told on the contrary that the words *S*rî-Govindabhagavat &c. have been added at the end by the editor, because he thought fit to do so. This is, to say the least, very suspicious, and we must wait for further confirmation. There is another commentary on this Upanishad by Nârâya*n*abha*tt*a, the son of Bha*tt*a Ratnâkara,[779] who is well known as the author of Dîpikâs on several Upanishads.

I subjoin a list of thirty of the smaller Upanishads, published by Professor Râmamaya Tarkaratna in the Bibliotheca Indica, with the commentaries of Nârâya*n*abha*tt*a.

---

[777] See Deussen, loc. cit. p. 39.

[778] A long list of works ascribed to *S*ankara may be seen in Regnaud, Philosophie de l'Inde, p. 34, chiefly taken from Fitzedward Hall's Index of Indian Philosophical Systems.

[779] See Tarkaratna's Vigñâpana, p. 3, l. 5.

1. *S*ira-upanishad, pp. 1–10; Dîpikâ by Nârâya*n*a, pp. 42–60.
2. Garbha-upanishad, pp. 11–15; „ pp. 60–73.
3. Nâdavindu-upanishad, pp. 15–17; „ pp. 73–78.
4. Brahmavindu-upanishad, pp. 18–20; „ pp. 78–82.
5. Am*ri*tavindu-upanishad, pp. 21–25; „ pp. 83–101.
6. Dhyânavindu-upanishad, pp. 26–28; „ pp. 102–114.
7. Te*g*ovindu-upanishad, pp. 29–30; „ pp. 114–118.
8. Yoga*s*ikhâ-upanishad, pp. 31–32; „ pp. 118–122.
9. Yogatattva-upanishad, pp. 33–34; „ pp. 122–127.
10. Sannyâsa-upanishad, pp. 35–39; „ pp. 128–184.
11. Âru*n*eya-upanishad, pp. 39–41; „ pp. 184–196.
12. Brahmavidyâ-upanishad, pp. 197–203; „ ibidem.
13. Kshurikâ-upanishad, pp. 203–218; „ „
14. *K*ûlikâ-upanishad, pp. 219–228; „ „
15. Atharva*s*ikhâ-upanishad, pp. 229–238; „ „
16. Brahma-upanishad, pp. 239–259; „ „
17. Prâ*n*âgnihotra-upanishad, pp. 260–271; „ „
18. Nîlarudra-upanishad, pp. 272–280; „ „
19. Ka*nth*a*s*ruti-upanishad, pp. 281–294; „ „
20. Pi*nd*a-upanishad, pp. 295–298; „ „
21. Âtma-upanishad, pp. 299–303; „ „
22. Râmapûrvatâpanîya-upanishad, pp. 304–358; „ „
23. Râmottaratâpanîya-upanishad, pp. 359–384; „ „
24. Hanumadukta-Râma-upanishad, pp. 385–393; „ „
25. Sarvopanishat-sâra*h*, pp. 394–404; „ „
26. Ha*m*sa-upanishad, pp. 404–416; „ „
27. Paramaha*m*sa-upanishad, pp. 417–436; „ „
28. *G*âbâla-upanishad, pp. 437–455; „ „
29. Kaivalya-upanishad, pp. 456–464; „ „
    Kaivalya-upanishad, pp. 465–479; Dîpikâ by *S*a*n*karânanda, „
30. Garu*d*a-upanishad, pp. 480 seq.; Dîpikâ by Nârâya*n*a, „

We owe to the same editor in the earlier numbers of the Bibliotheca the following editions:

N*ri*si*m*hapûrvatâparî-upanishad, with commentary.
N*ri*si*m*hottaratâpanî-upanishad, with commentary.
Sha*tk*akra-upanishad, with commentary by Nârâyana.

Lastly, Hara*k*andra Vidyâbhûsha*n*a and Vi*s*vanâtha *S*âstrî have published in the Bibliotheca Indica an edition of the Gopâlatâpanî-upanishad, with commentary by Vi*s*ve*s*vara.

These editions of the text and commentaries of the Upanishads are no doubt very useful, yet there are many passages where the text is doubtful, still more where the commentaries leave us without any help.

Whatever other scholars may think of the difficulty of translating the Upanishads, I can only repeat what I have said before, that I know of few Sanskrit texts presenting more formidable problems to the translator than these philosophical treatises. It may be said that most of them had been translated before. No doubt they have been, and a careful comparison of my own translation with those of my predecessors will show, I believe, that a small advance, at all events, has now been made towards a truer understanding of these ancient texts. But I know full well how much still remains to be done, both in restoring a correct text, and in discovering the original meaning of the Upanishads; and I have again and again had to translate certain passages tentatively only, or following the commentators, though conscious all the time that the meaning which they extract from the text cannot be the right one.

As to the text, I explained in my preface to the first volume that I attempted no more than to restore the text, such as it must have existed at the time when *S*aṅkara wrote his commentaries. As *S*aṅkara lived during the ninth century A.D.,[780] and as we possess no MSS. of so early a date, all reasonable demands of textual criticism would thereby seem to be satisfied. Yet, this is not quite so. We may draw such a line, and for the present keep within it, but scholars who hereafter take up the study of the Upanishads will probably have to go beyond. Where I had an opportunity of comparing other commentaries, besides those of *S*aṅkara, it became quite clear that they often followed a different text, and when, as in the case of the Maitrâya*n*a-brâhma*n*a-upanishad, I was enabled to collate copies which came from the South of India, the opinion which I have often expressed of the great value of Southern MSS. received fresh confirmation. The study of Grantha and other Southern MSS. will inaugurate, I believe, a new period in the critical treatment of Sanskrit texts, and the text of the Upanishads will, I hope, benefit quite as much as later texts by the treasures still concealed in the libraries of the Dekhan.

---

[780] India, What can it teach us? p. 360.

The rule which I have followed myself, and which I have asked my fellow translators to follow, has been adhered to in this new volume also, viz. whenever a choice has to be made between what is not quite faithful and what is not quite English, to surrender without hesitation the idiom rather than the accuracy of the translation. I know that all true scholars have approved of this, and if some of our critics have been offended by certain unidiomatic expressions occurring in our translations, all I can say is, that we shall always be most grateful if they would suggest translations which are not only faithful, but also idiomatic. For the purpose we have in view, a rugged but faithful translation seems to us more useful than a smooth but misleading one.

However, we have laid ourselves open to another kind of censure also, namely, of having occasionally not been literal enough. It is impossible to argue these questions in general, but every translator knows that in many cases a literal translation may convey an entirely wrong meaning. I shall give at least one instance.

My old friend, Mr. Nehemiah Goreh—at least I hope he will still allow me to call him so—in the 'Occasional Papers on Missionary Subjects,' First Series, No. 6, quotes, on p. 39, a passage from the *Kh*ândogya-upanishad, translates it into English, and then remarks that I had not translated it accurately. But the fault seems to me to lie entirely with him, in attempting to translate a passage without considering the whole chapter of which it forms a part. Mr. Nehemiah Goreh states the beginning of the story rightly when he says that a youth by name Svetaketu went, by the advice of his father, to a teacher to study under him. After spending twelve years, as was customary, with the teacher, when he returned home he appeared rather elated. Then the father asked him:

Uta tam âde*s*am aprâksho[781] yenâ*s*ruta*m* *s*rutam bhavaty amatam matam avig*ñ*âta*m* vig*ñ*âtam iti?

I translated this: 'Have you ever asked for that instruction by which we hear what cannot be heard, by which we perceive what cannot be perceived, by which we know what cannot be known?'

Mr. Nehemiah Goreh translates: 'Hast thou asked (of thy teacher) for that instruction by which what is not heard becomes heard, what is not comprehended becomes comprehended, what is not known becomes known?'

I shall not quarrel with my friend for translating man by to comprehend rather than by to perceive. I prefer my own translation, because manas is one side of the common sensory (anta*h*kara*n*a), buddhi, the other; the original difference between the two being, so far

---

[781] Mr. Nehemiah Goreh writes aprâkshyo, and this is no doubt the reading adopted by Roer in his edition of the *Kh*ândogya-upanishad in the Bibliotheca Indica, p. 384. In *S*aṅkara's commentary also the same form is given. Still grammar requires aprâksho.

as I can see, that the manas originally dealt with percepts, the buddhi with concepts.[782] But the chief difference on which my critic lays stress is that I translated a*s*rutam, amatam, and avig*ñ*âtam not by 'not heard, not comprehended, not known,' but by 'what cannot be heard, what cannot be perceived, what cannot be known.'

Now, before finding fault, why did he not ask himself what possible reason I could have had for deviating from the original, and for translating avigñâta by unknowable or what cannot be known, rather than by unknown, as every one would be inclined to translate these words at first sight? If he had done so, he would have seen in a moment, that without the change which I introduced in the idiom, the translation would not have conveyed the sense of the original, nay, would have conveyed no sense at all. What could Svetaketu have answered, if his father had asked him, whether he had not asked for that instruction by which what is not heard becomes heard, what is not comprehended becomes comprehended, what is not known becomes known? He would have answered, 'Yes, I have asked for it; and from the first day on which I learnt the *S*ikshâ, the A B C, I have every day heard something which I had not heard before, I have comprehended something which I had not comprehended before, I have known something which I had not known before.' Then why does he say in reply, 'What is that instruction?' Surely Mr. Nehemiah Goreh knew that the instruction which the father refers to, is the instruction regarding Brahman, and that in all which follows the father tries to lead his son by slow degrees to a knowledge of Brahman.[783] Now that Brahman is called again and again 'that which cannot be seen, cannot be heard, cannot be perceived, cannot be conceived,' in the ordinary sense of these words; can be learnt, in fact, from the Veda only.[784] It was in order to bring out this meaning that I translated a*s*rutam not by 'not heard,' but by 'not hearable,' or, in better English, by 'what cannot be heard.'[785]

---

[782] The Pa*ñk*adas*î* (I, 20) distinguishes between manas and buddhi, by saying, mano vimar*s*arûpa*m* syâd buddhi*h* syân ni*sk*âyatmikâ, which places the difference between the two rather in the degree of certainty, ascribing deliberation to manas, decision to buddhi.

[783] In the Vedânta-Sara, Sadânanda lays great stress on the fact that in this very chapter of the *Kh*ândogya-upanishad, the principal subject of the whole chapter is mentioned both in the beginning and in the end. Tatra prakara*n*apratipâdyasyarthasya tadâdyantayor upâdânam upakramasa*m*hâram. Yathâ *Kh*ândogyashash*th*aprapâ*th*ake prakara*n*apratipâdyansyadvitîyavastuna ekam evâdvitîyam (VI, 2, 1) ityâdâv aitadâtmyam ida*m* sarvam (VI, 16, 3) ity ante *k*a pratipâdanam. 'The beginning with and ending with' imply that the matter to be declared in any given section is declared both at the beginning and at the end thereof:—as, for instance, in the sixth section of the *Kh*ândogya-upanishad, 'the Real, besides which there is nought else'—which is to be explained in that section—is declared at the outset in the terms, 'One only, without a second,' and at the end in the terms 'All this consists of That.'

[784] Vedânta-Sâra, No. 118, tatraivâdvitîyavastuno mânântarâvishayîkara*n*am.

[785] See Mu*nd*. Up. I, 1, 6, adresyam agrâhyam.

Any classical scholar knows how often we must translate invictus by invincible, and how Latin tolerates even invictissimus, which we could never render in English by 'the most unconquered,' but 'the unconquerable.' English idiom, therefore, and common sense required that avig*ñ*âta should be translated, not by inconceived, but by inconceivable, if the translation was to be faithful, and was to give to the reader a correct idea of the original.

Let us now examine some other translations, to see whether the translators were satisfied with translating literally, or whether they attempted to translate thoughtfully.

Anquetil Duperron's translation, being in Latin, cannot help us much. He translates: 'Non auditum, auditum fiat; et non scitum, scitum; et non cognitum, cognitum.'

Rajendralal Mitra translates: 'Have you enquired of your tutor about that subject which makes the unheard-of heard, the unconsidered considered, and the unsettled settled?'

He evidently knew that Brahman was intended, but his rendering of the three verbs is not exact.

Mr. Gough (p. 43) translates: 'Hast thou asked for that instruction by which the unheard becomes heard, the unthought thought, the unknown known?'

But now let us consult a scholar who, in a very marked degree, always was a thoughtful translator, who felt a real interest in the subject, and therefore was never satisfied with mere words, however plausible. The late Dr. Ballantyne, in his translation of the Vedânta-Sâra,[786] had occasion to translate this passage from the *Kh*ândogya-upanishad, and how did he translate it? 'The eulogizing of the subject is the glorifying of what is set forth in this or that section (of the Veda); as, for example, in that same section, the sixth chapter of the *Kh*ândogya-upanishad, the glorifying of the Real, besides whom there is nought else, in the following terms: "Thou, O disciple, hast asked for that instruction whereby the unheard-of becomes heard, the inconceivable becomes conceived, and the unknowable becomes thoroughly known."'

Dr. Ballantyne therefore felt exactly what I felt, that in our passage a strictly literal translation would be wrong, would convey no meaning, or a wrong meaning; and Mr. Nehemiah Goreh will see that he ought not to express blame, without trying to find out whether those whom he blames for want of exactness, were not in reality more scrupulously exact in their translation than he has proved himself to be.

Mr. Nehemiah Goreh has, no doubt, great advantages in

[786] Lecture on the Vedânta, embracing the text of the Vedânta-Sâra, Allababad, 1851, p. 69. Vedântasâra, with N*ri*si*m*ha-Sarasvatî's Subodhinî and Râmatîrtha's Vidvanmanora*ñ*ginî, Calcutta, 1860, p. 89. Here we find the right reading, aprâksha*h*.

interpreting the Upanishads, and when he writes without any theological bias, his remarks are often very useful. Thus he objects rightly, I think, to my translation of a sentence in the same chapter of the *Kh*ândogya-upanishad, where the father, in answer to his son's question, replies: 'Sad eva, Somya, idam agra âsîd ekam evâdvitîyam.' I had tried several translations of these words, and yet I see now that the one I proposed in the end is liable to be misunderstood. I had translated. 'In the beginning, my dear, there was that only which is, one only, without a second.' The more faithful translation would have been: 'The being alone was this in the beginning.' But 'the being' does not mean in English that which is, τὸ ὄν, and therefore, to avoid any misunderstanding, I translated 'that which is.' I might have said, however, 'The existent, the real, the true (satyam) was this in the beginning,' just as in the Aitareya-upanishad we read: 'The Self was all this, one alone, in the beginning,'[787] But in that case I should have sacrificed the gender, and this in our passage is of great importance, being neuter, and not masculine.

What, however, is far more important, and where Mr. Nehemiah Goreh seems to me to have quite misapprehended the original Sanskrit, is this, that sat, τὸ ὄν, and âtmâ, the Self, are the subjects in these sentences, and not predicates. Now Mr. Nehemiah Goreh translates: 'This was the existent one itself before, one only without a second;' and he explains: 'This universe, before it was developed in the present form, was the existent one, Brahma, itself.' This cannot be. If 'idam,' this, i.e. the visible world, were the subject, how could the Upanishad go on and say, tad aikshata bahu syâm pragâyeyeti tat te*g*o 's*ri*gata, 'that thought, may I be many, may I grow forth. It sent forth fire.' This can be said of the Sat only, that is, the Brahman.[788] Sat, therefore, is the subject, not idam, for a Vedântist may well say that Brahman is the world, or sent forth the world, but not that the world, which is a mere illusion, was, in the beginning, Brahman.

This becomes clearer still in another passage, Maitr. Up. VI, 17, where we read: Brahma ha vâ idam agra âsîd eko 'nanta*h*, 'In the beginning Brahman was all this. He was one, and infinite.' Here the transition from the neuter to the masculine gender shows that Brahman only can be the subject, both in the first and in the second sentence.

In English it may seem to make little difference whether we say, 'Brahman was this,' or 'this was Brahman.' In Sanskrit too we find, Brahma khalv idam vâva sarvam, 'Brahman indeed is all this' (Maitr. Up. IV, 6), and Sarva*m* khalv idam Brahma, 'all this is Brahman indeed' (Khâ*nd*. Up. III, 14, 1). But the logical meaning is always that

---

[787] Âtmâ vâ idam eka evâgra âsît.

[788] *S*aṅkara says (p. 398, l. 5): ekam evâdvitîyam paramârthata idam buddhikâle 'pi tat sad aikshata.

Brahman was all this, i.e. all that we see now, Brahman being the subject, idam the predicate. Brahman becomes idam, not idam Brahman.

Thus the Pa*ñk*adasî, I, 18, says:

Ekâda*s*endriyair yuktyâ *s*âstre*n*âpy avagamyate
Yâvat ki*mk*id bhaved etad ida*ms*abdodita*m* *g*agat,

which Mr. A. Venis (Pandit, V, p. 667) translates: 'Whatever may be apprehended through the eleven organs, by argument and revelation, i.e. the world of phenomena, is expressed by the word idam, this.' The Pa*ñk*adasî then goes on:

Ida*m* sarvam purâ s*r*ish*t*er ekam evâdvitâyakam
Sad evâsîn nâmarûpe nâstâm ity Âru*n*er va*k*a*h*.

This Mr. Venis translates: 'Previous to creation, all this was the existent (sat), one only without a second: name and form were not:—this is the declaration of the son of Aru*n*a.'

This is no doubt a translation grammatically correct, but from the philosophical standpoint of the Vedânta, what is really meant is that before the s*r*ish*t*i (which is not creation, but the sending forth of the world, and the sending forth of it, not as something real, but as a mere illusion), the Real alone, i.e. the Brahman, was, instead of this, i.e. instead of this illusory world. The illusion was not, but the Real, i.e. Brahman, was. What became, or what seemed to change, was Brahman, and therefore the only possible subject, logically, is Brahman, everything else being a predicate, and a phenomenal predicate only.

If I were arguing with a European, not with an Indian scholar, I should venture to go even a step further, and try to prove that the idam, in this and similar sentences, does not mean this, i.e. this world, but that originally it was intended as an adverb, meaning now, or here. This use of idam, unsuspected by native scholars, is very frequent in Vedic literature, and instances may be seen in Boehtlingk's Dictionary. In that case the translation would be: 'The real (τὸ ὄν), O friend, was here in the beginning.' This meaning of idam, however, would apply only to the earliest utterances of ancient Brahmavâdins, while in later times idam was used and understood in the sense of all that is seen, the visible universe, just as iyam by itself is used in the sense of the earth.

However, difficulties of this kind may be overcome, if once we have arrived at a clear conception of the general drift of the Upanishads. The real difficulties are of a very different character. They consist in the extraordinary number of passages which seem to us utterly meaningless and irrational, or, at all events, so far-fetched that we can hardly believe that the same authors who can express the deepest thoughts on religion and philosophy with clearness, nay, with a kind of poetical eloquence, could have uttered in the same breath such utter rubbish. Some of the sacrificial technicalities, and their philosophical interpretations with which the Upanishads abound, may perhaps in time assume a clearer meaning, when we shall have more fully mastered the intricacies of the Vedic ceremonial. But there will always remain in the Upanishads a vast amount of what we can only call meaningless jargon, and for the presence of which in these ancient mines of thought I, for my own part, feel quite unable to account. 'Yes,' a friend of mine wrote to me, after reading some of the Sacred Books of the East, 'you are right, how tremendously ahead of other sacred books is the Bible. The difference strikes one as almost unfairly great.' So it does, no doubt. But some of the most honest believers and admirers of the Bible have expressed a similar disappointment, because they had formed their ideas of what a Sacred Book ought to be, theoretically, not historically. The Rev. J. M. Wilson, in his excellent Lectures on the Theory of Inspiration, p. 32, writes: 'The Bible is so unlike what you would expect; it does not consist of golden sayings and rules of life; give explanations of the philosophical and social problems of the past, the present, and the future; contain teachings immeasurably unlike those of any other book; but it contains history, ritual, legislation, poetry, dialogue, prophecy, memoirs, and letters; it contains much that is foreign to your idea of what a revelation ought to be. But this is not all. There is not only much that is foreign, but much that is opposed, to your preconceptions. The Jews tolerated slavery, polygamy, and other customs and cruelties of imperfect civilisation. There are the vindictive psalms, too, with their bitter hatred against enemies,—psalms which we chant in our churches. How can we do so? There are stories of immorality, of treachery, of crime. How can we read them?' Still the Bible has been and is a truly sacred, because a truly historical book, for there is nothing more sacred in this world than the history of man, in his search after his highest ideals. All ancient books which have once been called sacred by man, will have their lasting place in the history of mankind, and those who possess the courage, the perseverance, and the self-denial of the true miner, and of the true scholar, will find even in the darkest and dustiest shafts what they are seeking for,—real nuggets of thought, and precious jewels of faith and hope.

I. THE KA*TH*A-UPANISHAD.

The Ka*th*a-upanishad is probably more widely known than any other Upanishad. It formed part of the Persian translation, was rendered into English by Râmmohun Roy, and has since been frequently quoted by English, French, and German writers as one of the most perfect specimens of the mystic philosophy and poetry of the ancient Hindus.

It was in the year 1845 that I first copied at Berlin the text of this

Upanishad, the commentary of *S*aṅkara (MS. 127 Chambers[789]), and the gloss of Gopâlayogin (MS. 224 Chambers). The text and commentary of *S*aṅkara and the gloss of Ânandagiri have since been edited by Dr. Roer in the Bibliotheca Indica, with translation and notes. There are other translations, more or less perfect, by Râmmohun Roy, Windischmann, Poley, Weber, Muir, Regnaud, Gough, and others. But there still remained many difficult and obscure portions, and I hope that in some at least of the passages where I differ from my predecessors, not excepting *S*aṅkara, I may have succeeded in rendering the original meaning of the author more intelligible than it has hitherto been.

The text of the Ka*th*a-upanishad is in some MSS. ascribed to the Yagur-veda. In the Chambers MS. of the commentary also it is said to belong to that Veda,[790] and in the Muktikopanishad it stands first among the Upanishads of the Black Yagur-veda. According to Colebrooke (Miscellaneous Essays, 1, 96, note) it is referred to the Sâma-veda also. Generally, however, it is counted as one of the Âtharva*n*a Upanishads.

The reason why it is ascribed to the Yagur-veda, is probably because the legend of Na*k*iketas occurs in the Brâhma*n*a of the Taittirîya Yagur-veda. Here we read (III, 1, 8):

Vâga*s*ravasa, wishing for rewards, sacrificed all his wealth. He had a son, called Na*k*iketas. While he was still a boy, faith entered into him at the time when the cows that were to be given (by his father) as presents to the priests, were brought in. He said: ‘Father, to whom wilt thou give me?’ He said so a second and third time. The father turned round and said to him: ‘To Death, I give thee.’

Then a voice said to the young Gautama, as he stood up: ‘He (thy father) said, Go away to the house of Death, I give thee to Death.’ Go therefore to Death when he is not at home, and dwell in his house for three nights without eating. If he should ask thee, ‘Boy, how many nights hast thou been here?’ say, ‘Three.’ When he asks thee, ‘What didst thou eat the first night?’ say, ‘Thy offspring.’ ‘What didst thou eat the second night?’ say, ‘Thy cattle.’ ‘What didst thou eat the third night?’ say, ‘Thy good works.’

He went to Death, while he was away from home, and lie dwelt in his house for three nights without eating. When Death returned, he asked: ‘Boy, how many nights hast thou been here?’ He answered: ‘Three.’ ‘What didst thou eat the first night?’ ‘Thy offspring.’, ‘What didst thou eat the second night?’ ‘Thy cattle.’ ‘What didst thou eat the third night?’ ‘Thy good works.’

Then he said: ‘My respect to thee, O venerable sir! Choose a boon.’

[789] MS. 133 is a mere copy of MS. 127.

[790] Yagurvede Ka*th*avallîbhâshyam.

'May I return living to my father,' he said.

'Choose a second boon.'

'Tell me how my good works may never perish.'

Then he explained to him this Nâkiketa fire (sacrifice), and hence his good works do not perish.

'Choose a third boon.'

'Tell me the conquest of death again.'

Then he explained to him this (chief) Nâkiketa fire (sacrifice), and hence he conquered death again.[791]

This story, which in the Brâhma*n*a is told in order to explain the name of a certain sacrificial ceremony called Nâkiketa, was used as a peg on which to hang the doctrines of the Upanishad. In its original form it may have constituted one Adhyâya only, and the very fact of its division into two Adhyâyas may show that the compilers of the Upanishad were still aware of its gradual origin. We have no means, however, of determining its original form, nor should we even be justified in maintaining that the first Adhyâya ever existed by itself, and that the second was added at a much later time. Whatever its component elements may have been before it was an Upanishad, when it was an Upanishad it consisted of six Vallîs, neither more nor less.

The name of vallî, lit. creeper, as a subdivision of a Vedic work, is important. It occurs again in the Taittirîya Upanishads. Professor Weber thinks that vallî, creeper, in the sense of chapter, is based on a modern metaphor, and was primarily intended for a creeper, attached to the *s*âkhâs or branches of the Veda.[792] More likely, however, it was used in the same sense as parvan, a joint, a shoot, a branch, i.e. a division.

Various attempts have been made to distinguish the more modern from the more ancient portions of our Upanishad.[793] No doubt there are peculiarities of metre, grammar, language, and thought which indicate the more primitive or the more modern character of certain verses. There are repetitions which offend us, and there are several passages which are clearly taken over from other Upanishads, where they seem to have had their original place. Thirty-five years ago, when I first worked at this Upanishad, I saw no difficulty in re-establishing what I thought the original text of the Upanishad must have been. I now feel that we know so little of the time and the circumstances when these half-prose and half-metrical Upanishads were first put together, that I

---

[791] The commentator explains punar-m*ri*tyu as the death that follows after the present inevitable death.

[792] History of Indian Literature, p. 93, note; p. 157.

[793] Though it would be unfair to hold Professor Weber responsible for his remarks on this and other questions connected with the Upanishads published many years ago (Indische Studien, 1853, p. 197), and though I have hardly ever thought it necessary to criticise them, some of his remarks are not without their value even now.

should hesitate before expunging even the most modern-sounding lines from the original context of these Vedântic essays.[794]

The mention of Dhât*ri*, creator, for instance (Ka*th*. Up. II, 20), is certainly startling, and seems to have given rise to a very early conjectural emendation. But dhât*ri* and vidhât*ri* occur in the hymns of the Rig-veda (X, 82, 2), and in the Upanishads (Maitr. Up. VI, 8); and Dhât*ri*, as almost a personal deity, is invoked with Pragâpati in Rig-veda X, 184, I. Deva, in the sense of God (Ka*th*. Up. II, 12), is equally strange, but occurs in other Upanishads also (Maitr. Up. VI, 23; *S*vetâ*s*v. Up. I, 3). Much might be said about setu, bridge (Ka*th*. Up. III, 2; Mu*nd*. Up. II, 2, 5), âdar*s*a, mirror (Ka*th*. Up. VI, 5), as being characteristic of a later age. But setu is not a bridge, in our sense of the word, but rather a wall, a bank, a barrier, and occurs frequently in other Upanishads (Maitr. Up. VII. 7; Khâ*nd*. Up. VIII, 4; B*ri*h. Up. IV, 4, 22, &c.), while âdar*s*as, or mirrors, are mentioned in the B*ri*hadâra*n*yaka and the Srauta-sûtras. Till we know something more about the date of the first and the last composition or compilation of the Upanishads, how are we to tell what subjects and what ideas the first author or the last collector was familiar with? To attempt the impossible may seem courageous, but it is hardly scholarlike.

With regard to faulty or irregular readings, we can never know whether they are due to the original composers, the compilers, the repeaters, or lastly the writers of the Upanishads. It is easy to say that adre*s*ya (Mu*nd*. Up. I, 1, 6) ought to be ad*ri*sya; but who would venture to correct that form? Whenever that verse is quoted, it is quoted with adresya, not adrisya. The commentators themselves tell us sometimes that certain forms are either Vedic or due to carelessness (pramâdapâ*th*a); but that very fact shows that such a form, for instance, as samîyâta (Khâ*nd*. Up. I, 12, 3) rests on an old authority.

No doubt, if we have the original text of an author, and can prove that his text was corrupted by later compilers or copyists or printers, we have a right to remove those later alterations, whether they be improvements or corruptions. But where, as in our case, we can never hope to gain access to original documents, and where we can only hope, by pointing out what is clearly more modem than the rest or, it may be, faulty, to gain an approximate conception of what the original composer may have had in his mind, before handing his composition over to the safe keeping of oral tradition, it is almost a duty to discourage, as much as lies in our power, the work of reconstructing an old text by so-called conjectural emendations or critical omissions.

I have little doubt, for instance, that the three verses 16-18 in the first Vallî of the Ka*th*a-upanishad are later additions, but I should not

---

[794] See Regnaud, Le Pessimisme Brahmanique, Annales du Musée Guimet, 1880; tom. i, p. 101.

therefore venture to remove them. Death had granted three boons to Na*k*iketas, and no more. In a later portion, however, of the Upanishad (II, 3), the expression s*r*ińkâ vittamayî occurs, which I have translated by 'the road which leads to wealth.' As it is said that Na*k*iketas did not choose that s*r*ińkâ, some reader must have supposed that a s*r*ińkâ was offered him by Death. S*r*ińkâ, however, meant commonly a string or necklace, and hence arose the idea that Death must have offered a necklace as an additional gift to Na*k*iketas. Besides this, there was another honour done to Na*k*iketas by M*r*ityu, namely, his allowing the sacrifice which he had taught him, to be called by his name. This also, it was supposed, ought to have been distinctly mentioned before, and hence the insertion of the three verses 16-18. They are clumsily put in, for after punar evâha, 'he said again,' verse 16 ought not to have commenced by tam abravît, 'he said to him.' They contain nothing new, for the fact that the sacrifice is to be called after Na*k*iketas was sufficiently indicated by verse 19, 'This, O Na*k*iketas, is thy fire which leads to heaven, which thou hast chosen as thy second boon.' But so anxious was the interpolator to impress upon his hearers the fact that the sacrifice should in future go by that name, that, in spite of the metre, he inserted tavaiva, 'of thee alone,' in verse 19.

II. THE MU*ND*AKA-UPANISHAD.

This is an Upanishad of the Atharva-veda. It is a Mantra-upanishad, i.e. it has the form of a Mantra. But, as the commentators observe, though it is written in verse, it is not, like other Mantras, to be used for sacrificial purposes. Its only object is to teach the highest knowledge, the knowledge of Brahman, which cannot be obtained either by sacrifices or by worship (upâsana), but by such teaching only as is imparted in the Upanishad. A man may a hundred times restrain his breath, &c., but without the Upanishad his ignorance does not cease. Nor is it right to continue for ever in the performance of sacrificial and other good works, if one wishes to obtain the highest knowledge of Brahman. The Sannyâsin alone, who has given up everything, is qualified to know and to become Brahman. And though it might seem from Vedic legends that G*r*ihasthas also who continued to live with their families, performing all the duties required of them by law, had been in possession of the highest knowledge, this, we are told, is a mistake. Works and knowledge can be as little together as darkness and light.

This Upanishad too has been often translated since it first appeared in the Persian translation of Dârâ Shukoh. My own copy of the text and *S*ańkara's commentary from the MS. in the Chambers Collection was made in October 1844. Both are now best accessible in the Bibliotheca Indica, where Dr. Roer has published the text, the commentary by

*S*aṅkara, a gloss by Ânandag*ñ*âna, and an English translation with notes.

The title of the Upanishad, Mu*nd*aka, has not yet been explained. The Upanishad is called Mu*nd*aka-upanishad, and its three chapters are each called Mu*nd*akam. Native commentators explain it as the shaving Upanishad, that is, as the Upanishad which cuts off the errors of the mind, like a razor. Another Upanishad also is called Kshurikâ, the razor, a name which is explained in the text itself as meaning an instrument for removing illusion and error. The title is all the more strange because Mu*nd*aka, in its commonest acceptation, is used as a term of reproach for Buddhist mendicants, who are called 'Shavelings,' in opposition to the Brâhmans, who dress their hair carefully, and often display by its peculiar arrangement either their family or their rank. Many doctrines of the Upanishads are, no doubt, pure Buddhism, or rather Buddhism is on many points the consistent carrying out of the principles laid down in the Upanishads. Yet, for that very reason, it seems impossible that this should be the origin of the name, unless we suppose that it was the work of a man who was, in one sense, a Mu*nd*aka, and yet faithful to the Brahmanic law.

III. THE TAITTIRÎYAKA-UPANISHAD.

The Taittirîyaka-upanishad seems to have had its original place in the Taittirîya-Âra*n*yaka. This Âra*n*yaka consists, as Rajendralal Mitra has shown in the Introduction to his edition of the work in the Bibliotheca Indica, of three portions. Out of its ten Prapâ*th*akas, the first six form the Âra*n*yaka proper, or the Karma-kâ*nd*a, as Sâya*n*a writes. Then follow Prapâ*th*akas VII, VIII, and IX, forming the Taittirîyaka-upanishad; and lastly, the tenth Prapâ*th*aka, the Yâg*ñ*ikî or Mahânârâya*n*a-upanishad, which is called a Khila, and was therefore considered by the Brâhmans themselves as a later and supplementary work.

*S*aṅkara, in his commentary on the Taittirîyaka-upanishad, divides his work into three Adhyâyas, and calls the first *S*ikshâ-vallî, the second the Brahmânanda-vallî, while he gives no special name to the Upanishad explained in the third Adhyâya. This, however, may be due to a mere accident, for whenever the division of the Taittirîyaka-upanishad into Vallîs is mentioned, we always have three,[795] the *S*ikshâ-vallî, the Brahmânanda-vallî, and the Bh*r*igu-vallî.[796] Properly, however, it is only the second Anuvâka of the seventh Prapâ*th*aka which deserves and receives in the text itself the name of

[795] *S*aṅkara (ed. Roer, p. 141) himself speaks of two Vallîs, teaching the paramâtmag*ñ*âna (the *S*ikshâ-vallî has nothing to do with this), and Anquetil has Anandbli = Ânanda-vallî, and Bharkbli = Bhrigu-vallî.

[796] The third Vallî ends with Bh*r*igur ity upanishat.

*S*ikshâdhyâya, while the rest of the first Vallî ought to go by the name of Sa*m*hitâ-upanishad,[797] or Sâ*m*hitî-upanishad.

Sâya*n*a,[798] in his commentary on the Taittirîya-âra*n*yaka, explains the seventh chapter, the *S*ikshâdhyâya (twelve anuvâkas), as Sâ*m*hitî-upanishad. His commentary, however, is called *S*ikshâ-bhâshya. The same Sâya*n*a treats the eighth and ninth Prapâ*th*akas as the Vâru*n*y-upanishad.[799]

The Ânanda-vallî and Bh*ri*gu-vallî are quoted among the Upanishads of the Âtharvana.[800]

At the end of each Vallî there is an index of the Anuvâkas which it contains. That at the end of the first Vallî is intelligible. It gives the Pratîkas, i.e. the initial words, of each Anuvâka, and states their number as twelve. At the end of the first Anuvâka, we have the final words 'satyam vadishyâmi,' and pa*ñk*a *k*a, i.e. five short paragraphs at the end. At the end of the second Anuvâka, where we expect the final words, we have the initial, i.e. *s*îkshâm, and then pa*ñk*a, i.e. five sections in the Anuvâka. At the end of the third Anuvâka, we have the final words, but no number of sections. At the end of the fourth Anuvâka, we have the final words of the three sections, followed by one paragraph; at the end of the fifth Anuvâka, three final words, and two paragraphs, though the first paragraph belongs clearly to the third section. In the sixth Anuvâka, we have the final words of the two Anuvâkas, and one paragraph. In the seventh Anuvâka, there is the final word sarvam, and one paragraph added. In the eighth Anuvâka, we have the initial word, and the number of sections, viz. ten. In the ninth Anuvâka, there are the final words of one section, and six paragraphs. In the tenth Anuvâka, there is the initial word, and the number of paragraphs, viz. six. In the eleventh Anuvâka, we have the final words of four sections, and seven paragraphs, the first again forming an integral portion of the last section. The twelfth Anuvâka has one section, and five paragraphs. If five, then the *s*ânti would here have to be included, while, from what is said afterwards, it is clear that as the first word of the Vallî is *s*am na*h*, so the last is vaktâram.

In the second Vallî the index to each Anuvâka is given at the end of the Vallî.

---

797 See Taittirîyaka-upanishad, ed. Roer, p. 12.

798 See M. M., Alphabetisches Verzeichniss der Upanishads, p. 144.

799 The Anukrama*n*î of the Âtreyî school (see Weber, Indische Studien, II, p. 208) of the Taittirîyaka gives likewise the name of Vâru*n*î to the eighth and ninth Prapâ*th*aka, while it calls the seventh Prapâ*th*aka the Sâmhitî, and the tenth Prapâ*th*aka the Yâg*ñ*ki-upanishad. That Anukramanî presupposes, however, a different text, as may be seen both from the number of Anuvâkas, and from the position assigned to the Yâg*ñ*ki as between the Sâmhitî and Vârunî Upanishads.

800 See M. M., Alphabetisches Verzeichniss der Upanishads.

1st Anuvâka: pratîka: brahmavid, and some other catchwords, idam, ayam, idam. Number of sections, 21.
2nd Anuvâka: pratîka: annâd, and other catchwords; last word, pu*kkh*a. Sections, 26.
3rd Anuvâka: pratîka: prânam, and other catchwords; last word, pu*kkh*a. Sections, 22.
4th Anuvâka: pratîka: yata*h*, and other catchwords; last word, pu*kkh*a. Sections, 18.
5th Anuvâka: pratîka: vig*ñ*anam, and other catchwords; last word, pu*kkh*a. Sections, 22.
6th Anuvâka: pratîka: asanneva, then atha (deest in Taitt. Âr. 7). Sections, 28.
7th Anuvâka: pratîka: asat. Sections, 16.
8th Anuvâka: pratîka: bhîshâsmât, and other catchwords; last word, upasaṅkrâmati. Sections, 51.
9th Anuvâka: pratîka: yata*h*—kuta*s**k*ana; then tam (deest in Taitt. Ar.). Sections, 11.

In the third Vallî the Anukramanî stands at the end.

1. The first word, bh*ri*gu*h*, and some other catchwords. Sections, 13.
2. The first word, annam. Sections, 12
3. The first word, prâ*n*am. Sections, 12.
4. The first word, manah. Sections, 12.
5. The first word, vig*ñ*ânam, and some other words. Sections, 12.
6. The first word, ânanda, and some other words. Sections, 10.
7. The first words, anna*m* na nindyât, prâ*n*a*h*, *s*arîram. Sections, 11.
8. The first words, anna*m* na pari*k*akshîta, âpo *g*yoti*h*. Sections, 11.
9. The first words, anna*m* bahu kurvîta p*ri*thivîm âkâ*s*a. Sections, 11.
10. The first words, na ka*ñk*ana. Sections 61. The last words of each section are given for the tenth Anuvâka.

IV. THE BRIHADÂRA*N*YAKA-UPANISHAD.

This Upanishad has been so often edited and discussed that it calls for no special remarks. It forms part of the Satapatha-brâhma*n*a. In the Mâdhyandina-*s*âkhâ of that Brâhma*n*a, which has been edited by Professor Weber, the Upanishad, consisting of six adhyâyas, begins with the fourth adhyâya (or third prapâ*th*aka) of the fourteenth book.

There is a commentary on the B*ri*hadâra*n*yaka-upanishad by Dviveda*s*rînârâya*n*asûnu Dvivedagaṅga, which has been carefully edited by Weber in his great edition of the *S*atapatha-brâhma*n*a from a MS. in the Bodleian Library, formerly belonging to Dr. Mill, in which the Upanishad is called Mâdhyandinîya-brâhma*n*a-upanishad.

In the Kâ*n*va-*s*âkhâ the B*ri*hadâra*n*yaka-upanishad forms the seventeenth book of the *S*atapatha-brâhma*n*a, consisting of six adhyâyas.

As *S*aṅkara's commentary and the gloss of Ânandatîrtha, edited by Dr. Roer in the Bibliotheca Indica, follow the Kâ*n*va-*s*âkhâ, I have followed the same text in my translation.

Besides Dr. Roer's edition of the text, commentary and gloss of this Upanishad, there is Poley's edition of the text. There is also a translation of it by Dr. Roer, with large extracts from *S*aṅkara's commentary.

V. THE *S*VETÂ*S*VATARA-UPANISHAD.

The *S*vetâ*s*vatara-upanishad has been handed down as one of the thirty-three Upanishads of the Taittirîyas, and though this has been doubted, no real argument has ever been brought forward to invalidate the tradition which represents it as belonging to the Taittirîya or Black Yagur-veda.

It is sometimes called *S*vetâ*s*vatarâ*n*âm Mantropanishad (p. 274), and is frequently spoken of in the plural, as *S*vetâ*s*vataropanishada*h*. At the end of the last Adhyâya we read that *S*vetâ*s*vatara told it to the best among the hermits, and that it should be kept secret, and not be taught to any one except to a son or a regular pupil. It is also called *S*vetâ*s*va,[801] though, it would seem, for the sake of the metre only. The *S*vetâ*s*vataras are mentioned as a *S*âkha,[802] subordinate to the *K*arakas; but of the literature belonging to them in particular, nothing is ever mentioned beyond this Upanishad.

*S*vetâ*s*vatara means a white mule, and as mules were known and prized in India from the earliest times, *S*vetâ*s*vatara, as the name of a person, is no more startling than *S*vetâ*s*va, white horse, an epithet of Arguna. Now as no one would be likely to conclude from the name of one of the celebrated Vedic *Ri*shis, *S*yâvâ*s*va, i.e. black horse, that negro influences might be discovered in his hymns, it is hardly necessary to say that all speculations as to Christian influences, or the teaching of white Syro-Christian missionaries, being indicated by the name of *S*vetâ*s*vatara, are groundless.[803]

The *S*vetâ*s*vatara-upanishad holds a very high rank among the Upanishads. Though we cannot say that it is quoted by name by Bâdarâyana in the Vedânta-sûtras, it is distinctly referred to as sruta or revealed.[804] It is one of the twelve Upanishads chosen by Vidyâranya in his Sarvopanishad-arthânabhûtiprakâ*s*a, and it was singled out by *S*aṅkara as worthy of a special commentary.

The *S*vetâ*s*vatara-upanishad seems to me one of the most difficult,

---

[801] Vâ*k*aspatyam, p. 1222.

[802] Catal. Bodl. p. 271 a; p. 222 a.

[803] See Weber, Ind. Stud. I, pp. 400, 421.

[804] See Deussen, Vedânta, p. 24; Ved. Sûtra I, 1, II; I, 4, 8; II, 3, 22.

and at the same time one of the most interesting works of its kind. Whether on that and on other grounds it should be assigned to a more ancient or to a more modern period is what, in the present state of our knowledge, or, to be honest, of our ignorance of minute chronology during the Vedic period, no true scholar would venture to assert. We must be satisfied to know that, as a class, the Upanishads are presupposed by the Kalpa-sûtras, that some of them, called Mantra-upanishads, form part of the more modern Sa*m*hitâs, and that there are portions even in the Rig-veda-sa*m*hitâ[805] for which the name of Upanishad is claimed by the Anukrama*n*îs. We find them most frequent, however, during the Brâhma*n*a-period, in the Brâhma*n*as themselves, and, more especially, in those portions which are called Âra*n*yakas, while a large number of them is referred to the Atharva-veda. That, in imitation of older Upanishads, similar treatises were composed to a comparatively recent time, has, of course, long been known.[806]

But when we approach the question whether among the ancient and genuine Upanishads one may be older than the other, we find that, though we may guess much, we can prove nothing. The Upanishads belonged to Parishads or settlements spread all over India. There is a stock of ideas, even of expressions, common to most of them. Yet, the ideas collected in the Upanishads cannot all have grown tip in one and the same place, still less in regular succession. They must have had an independent growth, determined by individual and local influences, and opinions which in one village might seem far advanced, would in another be looked upon as behind the world. We may admire the ingeniousness of those who sometimes in this, sometimes in that peculiarity see a clear indication of the modern date of an Upanishad, but to a conscientious scholar such arguments are really distasteful for the very sake of their ingeniousness. He knows that they will convince many who do not know the real difficulties; he knows they will have to be got out of the way with no small trouble, and he knows that, even if they should prove true in the end, they will require very different support from what they have hitherto received, before they can be admitted to the narrow circle of scientific facts.

While fully admitting therefore that the *S*vetâ*s*vatara-upanishad has its peculiar features and its peculiar difficulties, I must most strongly maintain that no argument that has as yet been brought forward, seems to me to prove, in any sense of the word, its modern character.

It has been said, for instance, that the *S*vetâ*s*vatara-upanishad is a sectarian Upanishad, because, when speaking of the Highest Self or the Highest Brahman, it applies such names to him as Hara (I, 10), Rudra

[805] See Sacred Books of the East, vol. i, p. lxvi.
[806] Loc. cit. p. lxvii.

(II, 17; III, 2; 4; IV, 12; 21; 22), *S*iva (III, 14; IV, 10), Bhagavat (III, 14), Agni, Âditya, Vâyu, &c. (IV, 2). But here it is simply taken for granted that the idea of the Highest Self was developed first, and, after it had reached its highest purity, was lowered again by an identification with mythological and personal deities. The questions whether the conception of the Highest Self was formed once and once only, whether it was formed after all the personal and mythological deities had first been merged into one Lord (Pragâpati), or whether it was discovered behind the veil of any other name in the mythological pantheon of the past, have never been mooted. Why should not an ancient Rishi have said: What we have hitherto called Rudra, and what we worship as Agni, or *S*iva, is in reality the Highest Self, thus leaving much of the ancient mythological phraseology to be used with a new meaning? Why should we at once conclude that late sectarian worshippers of mythological gods replaced again the Highest Self, after their fathers had discovered it, by their own sectarian names? If we adopt the former view, the Upanishads, which still show these rudera of the ancient temples, would have to be considered as more primitive even than those in which the idea of the Brahman or the Highest Self has reached its utmost purity.

It has been considered a very strong argument in support of the modern and sectarian character of the *S*vetâ*s*vatara-upanishad, that 'it inculcates what is called Bhakti,[807] or implicit reliance on the favour of the deity worshipped.' Now it is quite true that this Upanishad possesses a very distinct character of its own, by the stress which it lays on the personal, and sometimes almost mythical character of the Supreme Spirit; but, so far from inculcating bhakti, in the modern sense of the word, it never mentions that word, except in the very last verse, a verse which, if necessary, certain critics would soon dispose of as a palpable addition. But that verse says no more than this: 'If these truths (of the Upanishad) have been told to a high-minded man, who feels the highest devotion for God, and for his Guru as for God, then they will shine forth indeed.' Does that prove the existence of Bhakti as we find it in the Sâ*nd*ilya-sûtras?[808]

Again, it has been said that the *S*vetâ*s*vatara-upanishad is sectarian in a philosophical sense, that it is in fact an Upanishad of the Sâṅkhya system of philosophy, and not of the Vedânta. Now I am quite willing to admit that, in its origin, the Vedânta philosophy is nearer to the Vedic literature than any other of the six systems of philosophy, and that if we really found doctrines, peculiar to the Sâṅkhya, and opposed to the Vedânta, in the *S*vetâ*s*vatara-upanishad, we might feel inclined to

---

[807] Weber, Ind. Stud. I, 422; and History of Indian Literature, p. 238.

[808] The Aphorisms of Sândilya, or the Hindu Doctrine of Faith, translated by E. B. Cowell, Calcutta, 1879.

assign to our Upanishad a later date. But where is the proof of this?

No doubt there are expressions in this Upanishad which remind us of technical terms used at a later time in the Sâṅkhya system of philosophy, but of Sâṅkhya doctrines, which I had myself formerly suspected in this Upanishad,

I can on closer study find very little. I think it was Mr. Gough who, in his Philosophy of the Upanishads, for the first time made it quite clear that the teaching of our Upanishad is, in the main, the same as that of the other Upanishads. 'The *S*vetâ*s*vatara-upanishad teaches,' as he says, 'the unity of souls in the one and only Self; the unreality of the world as a series of figments of the self-feigning world-fiction; and as the first of the fictitious emanations, the existence of the Demiurgos or universal soul present in every individual soul, the deity that projects the world out of himself, that the migrating souls may find the recompense of their works in former lives.'

I do not quite agree with this view of the Î*s*vara, whom Mr. Gough calls the Demiurgos, but he seems to me perfectly right when he says that the *S*vetâ*s*vatara-upanishad propounds in Sâṅkhya terms the very principles that the Sâṅkhya philosophers make it their business to subvert. One might doubt as to the propriety of calling certain terms 'Sâṅkhya terms' in a work written at a time when a Sâṅkhya philosophy, such as we know it as a system, had as yet no existence, and when the very name Sâṅkhya meant something quite different from the Sâṅkhya system of Kapila. Sâṅkhya is derived from saṅkhyâ, and that meant counting, number, name, corresponding very nearly to the Greek λόγος. Sâṅkhya, as derived from it, meant originally no more than theoretic philosophy, as opposed to yoga, which meant originally practical religious exercises and penances, to restrain the passions and the senses in general. All other interpretations of these words, when they had become technical names, are of later date.

But even in their later forms, whatever we may think of the coincidences and differences between the Sâṅkhya and Vedânta systems of philosophy, there is one point on which they are diametrically opposed. Whatever else the Sâṅkhya may be, it is dualistic; whatever else the Vedânta may be, it is monistic. In the Sâṅkhya, nature, or whatever else we may call it, is independent of the purusha; in the Vedânta it is not. Now the *S*vetâ*s*vatara-upanishad states distinctly that nature, or what in the Sâṅkhya philosophy is intended by Pradhâna, is not an independent power, but a power (*s*akti) forming the very self of the Deva. 'Sages,' we read, 'devoted to meditation and concentration, have seen the power belonging to God himself, hidden in its own qualities.'

What is really peculiar in the *S*vetâ*s*vatara-upanishad is the strong stress which it lays on the personality of the Lord, the Î*s*vara, Deva, in the passage quoted, is perhaps the nearest approach to our own idea of a personal God, though without the background which the Vedânta always retains for it. It is God as creator and ruler of the world, as îsvara, lord, but not as Paramâtman, or the Highest Self. The Paramâtman constitutes, no doubt, his real essence, but creation and creator have a phenomenal character only.[809] The creation is mâyâ, in its original sense of work, then of phenomenal work, then of illusion. The creator is mâyin, in its original sense of worker or maker, but again, in that character, phenomenal only.[810] The Gunas or qualities arise, according to the Vedânta, from prakriti or mâyâ, within, not beside, the Highest Self, and this is the very idea which is here expressed by 'the Self-power of God, hidden in the gunas or determining qualities.' How easily that sakti or power may become an independent being, as Mâyâ, we see in such verses as:

> Sarvabhûteshu sarvâtman yâ *s*aktir aparâbhavâ
> Gu*n*â*s*rayâ namas tasyai *s*a*s*vatâyai pare*s*vara.[811]

But the important point is this, that in the *S*vetâ*s*vatara-upanishad this change has not taken place. Throughout the whole of it we have one Being only, as the cause of everything, never two. Whatever Sâṅkhya philosophers of a later date may have imagined that they could discover in that Upanishad in support of their theories,[812] there is not one passage in it which, if rightly interpreted, not by itself, but in connection with the whole text, could be quoted in support of a dualistic philosophy such as the Sâṅkhya, as a system, decidedly is.

If we want to understand, what seems at first sight contradictory, the existence of a God, a Lord, a Creator, a Ruler, and at the same time the existence of the super-personal Brahman, we must remember that the orthodox view of the Vedânta[813] is not what we should call Evolution, but Illusion. Evolution of the Brahman, or Pari*n*âma, is heterodox, illusion or Vivarta is orthodox Vedânta. Brahman is a concept involving such complete perfection that with it evolution, or a tendency towards higher perfection, is impossible. If therefore there is change, that change can only be illusion, and can never claim the same reality as Brahman. To put it metaphorically, the world, according to the orthodox Vedântin, does not proceed from Brahman as a tree from a germ, but as a mirage from the rays of the sun. The world is, as we express it, phenomenal only, but whatever objective reality there is in it, is Brahman, 'das Ding an sich,' as Kant might call it.

Then what is Î*s*vara, or Deva, the Lord or God? The answers given

---

[809] Prathamam î*s*varâtmanâ mâyirûpe*n*âvatish*th*ate brahma; See p. 280, l. 5.

[810] Mâyî s*r*igate sarvam etat.

[811] See p. 279, l. 5. Sârvatman seems a vocative, like pare*s*vara.

[812] See Sarvadar*s*anasaṅgraha, p. 152.

[813] Vedântaparibhâshâ, in the Pandit, vol. iv, p. 496.

to this question are not very explicit. Historically, no doubt, the idea of the Îsvara, the personal God, the creator and ruler, the omniscient and omnipotent, existed before the idea of the absolute Brahman, and after the idea of the Brahman had been elaborated, the difficulty of effecting a compromise between the two ideas, had to be overcome. Îsvara, the Lord, is Brahman, for what else could he be? But he is Brahman under a semblance, the semblance, namely, of a personal creating and governing God. He is not created, but is the creator, an office too low, it was supposed, for Brahman. The power which enabled Îsvara to create, was a power within him, not independent of him, whether we call it Devâtmasakti, Mâyâ, or Prakriti. That power is really inconceivable, and it has assumed such different forms in the mind of different Vedântists, that in the end Mâyâ herself is represented as the creating power, nay, as having created Îsvara himself. In our Upanishad, however, Îsvara is the creator, and though, philosophically speaking, we should say that be was conceived as phenomenal, yet we must never forget that the phenomenal is the form of the real, and Îsvara therefore an aspect of Brahman.[814] 'This God,' says Pramâda Dâsa Mitra,[815] 'is the spirit conscious of the universe. Whilst an extremely limited portion, and that only of the material universe, enters into my consciousness, the whole of the conscious universe, together, of course, with the material one that hangs upon it, enters into the consciousness of God.' And again, 'Whilst we (the *g*îvâtmans) are subject to Mâyâ, Mâyâ is subject to Îsvara. If we truly know Îsvara, we know him as Brahman; if we truly know ourselves, we know ourselves as Brahman. This being so, we must not be surprised if sometimes we find Îsvara sharply distinguished from Brahman, whilst at other times Îsvara, and Brahman are interchanged.'

Another argument in support of the sectarian character of the *S*vetâ*s*vatara-upanishad is brought forward, not by European students only, but by native scholars, namely, that the very name of Kapila, the reputed founder of the Sâṅkhya philosophy, occurs in it. Now it is quite true that if we read the second verse of the fifth Adhyâya by itself, the occurrence of the word Kapila may seem startling. But if we read it in connection with what precedes and follows, we shall see hardly anything unusual in it. It says:

'It is he who, being one only, rules over every germ (cause), over all forms, and over all germs; it is he who, in the beginning, bears in his thoughts the wise son, the fiery, whom he wished to look on while he was born.'

Now it is quite clear to me that the subject in this verse is the same as in IV, II, where the same words are used, and where yo yoni*m* yonim

---

[814] Savi*s*esham Brahma, or *s*abalam Brahma.

[815] Journal of the Royal Asiatic Society, 1878, p. 40.

adhitish*th*aty eka*h* refers clearly to Brahman. It is equally clear that the prasûta, the son, the offspring of Brahman, in the Vedânta sense, can only be the same person who is elsewhere called Hira*n*yagarbha, the personified Brahman. Thus we read before, III, 4, 'He the creator and supporter of the gods, Rudra, the great seer (maharshi), the lord of all, formerly gave birth to Hira*n*yagarbha;' and in IV, 11, we have the very expression which is used here, namely, 'that he saw Hira*n*yagarbha being born.' Unfortunately, a new adjective is applied in our verse to Hira*n*yagarbha, namely, kapila, and this has called forth interpretations totally at variance with the general tenor of the Upanishad. If, instead of kapilam, reddish, fiery,[816] any other epithet had been used of Hira*n*yagarbha, no one, I believe, would have hesitated for a moment to recognise the fact that our text simply repeats the description of Hira*n*yagarbha in his relation to Brahman, for the other epithet *ri*shim, like maharshim, is too often applied to Brahman himself and to Hira*n*yagarbha to require any explanation.

But it is a well known fact that the Hindus, even as early as the Brâhma*n*a-period, were fond of tracing their various branches of knowledge back to Brahman or to Brahman Svayambhû and then through Pragâpati, who even in the Rig-veda (X, 121, 10) replaces Hira*n*yagarbha, and sometimes through the Devas, such as Mrityu, Vâyu, Indra, Agni,[817] &c., to the various ancestors of their ancient families.

In the beginning of the Mu*nd*akopanishad we are told that Brahman told it to Atharvan, Atharvan to Aṅgir, Aṅgir to Satyavâha Bhâradvâga, Bhâradvâga to Aṅgiras, Aṅgiras to *S*aunaka. Manu, the ancient lawgiver, is called both Haira*n*yagarbha and Svâyambhuva, as descended from Svâyambhu or from Hira*n*yagarbha.[818] Nothing therefore was more natural than that the same tendency should have led some one to assign the authorship of a great philosophical system like the Sâṅkhya to Hira*n*yagarbha, if not to Brahman Svayambhû. And if the name of Hira*n*yagarbha had been used already for the ancestors of other sages, and the inspirers of other systems, what could be more natural than that another name of the same Hira*n*yagarbha should be chosen, such as Kapila. If we are told that Kapila handed his knowledge to Âsuri, Âsuri to Pa*ñk*a*s*ikha, this again is in perfect keeping with the character of literary tradition in India. Âsuri occurs in the Va*m*sas of the *S*atapatha-brâhma*n*a (see above, pp. 407, 431); Pa*ñk*asikha,[819] having five tufts, might be either a general name or a proper name of an ascetic, Buddhist or otherwise. He is quoted in the

[816] Other colours, instead of kapila, are nîla, harita, lohitâksha; see IV, 1; 4.

[817] See Vamsa-brâhma*n*a, ed. Burnell, p. 10; B*ri*hadâra*n*yaka-up. pp. 185, 224.

[818] See M. M., India, p. 372.

[819] For fuller information on Pa*ñk*asikha, Kapila, &c., see F. Hall's Preface to Sâṅkhya-prava*k*ana-bhâshya, p. 9 seq.; Weber, Ind. Stud. I, p. 433.

Sâṅkhya-sûtras, V, 32; VI, 68.

But after all this was settled, after Kapila had been accepted, like Hira*n*yagarbha, as the founder of a great system of philosophy, there came a reaction. People had now learnt to believe in a real Kapila, and when looking out for credentials for him, they found them wherever the word Kapila occurred in old writings. The question whether there ever was a real historical person who took the name of Kapila and taught the Sâṅkhya-sûtras, does not concern us here. I see no evidence for it. What is instructive is this, that our very passage, which may have suggested at first the name of Kapila, as distinct from Hira*n*yagarbha, Kapila, was later on appealed to to prove the primordial existence of a Kapila, the founder of the Sâṅkhya philosophy. However, it requires but a very slight acquaintance with Sanskrit literature and very little reflection in order to see that the author of our verse could never have dreamt of elevating a certain Kapila, known to him as a great philosopher, if there ever was such a man, to a divine rank.[820] Hira*n*yagarbha kapila may have given birth to Kapila, the hero of the Sâṅkhya philosophers, but Kapila, a real human person, was never changed into Hira*n*yagarbha kapila.

Let us see now what the commentators say. *S*aṅkara first explains kapilam by kanaka*m*[821] kapilavar*n*am . . . . Hira*n*yagarbham. Kapilo 'graga iti purâ*n*ava*k*anât. Kapilo Hira*n*yagarbho vâ nirdi*s*yate. But he afterwards quotes some verses in support of the theory that Kapila was a Paramarshi, a portion of Vish*n*u, intended to destroy error in the K*ri*ta Yuga, a teacher of the Sâṅkhya philosophy.

Vigñânâtman explains the verse rightly, and without any reference to Kapila, the Sâṅkhya teacher.

*S*aṅkarânanda goes a step further, and being evidently fully aware of the misuse that had been made of this passage, even in certain passages of the Mahâbhârata (XII, 13254, 13703), and elsewhere, declares distinctly that kapila cannot be meant for the teacher of the Sâṅkhya (na tu sâṅkhyapra*n*etâ kapila*h*, nâmamâtrasâmyena tadgraha*n*e syâd atiprasaṅga*h*). He is fully aware of the true interpretation, viz. avyâk*ri*tasya prathamakâryabhûta*m* kapila*m* vi*k*itravar*nam g*ñânakriyâ*s*aktyâtmaka*m* Hira*n*yagarbham ityarthah, but he yields to another temptation, and seems to prefer another view which makes Kapila Vâsudevasyâvatârabûta*m* Sagaraputrâ*n*â*m* dagdhâram, an Avatâra of Vâsudeva, the burner of the sons of Sagara. What vast conclusions may be drawn from no facts, may be seen in Weber's Indische Studien, vol. i, p. 430, and even in his History of Indian Literature, published in 1878.

---

[820] Weber, Hist. of Indian Literature, p. 236.

[821] This ought to be Kanakavar*n*am, and I hope will not be identified with the name of Buddha in a former existence.

Far more difficult to explain than these supposed allusions to the authors and to the teaching of the Sâṅkhya philosophy are the frequent references in the *S*vetâ*s*vatara-upanishad to definite numbers, which are supposed to point to certain classes of subjects as arranged in the Sâṅkhya and other systems of philosophy. The Sâṅkhya philosophy is fond of counting and arranging, and its very name is sometimes supposed to have been chosen because it numbers (sankhyâ) the subjects of which it treats. It is certainly true that if we meet, as we do in the *S*vetâ*s*vatara-upanishad, with classes of things,[822] numbered as one, two, three, five, eight, sixteen, twenty, forty-eight, fifty and more, and if some of these numbers agree with those recognised in the later Sâṅkhya and Yoga systems, we feel doubtful as to whether these coincidences are accidental, or whether, if not accidental, they are due to borrowing on the part of those later systems, or on the part it impossible to come to a decision on this point. Even so early as the hymns of the Rig-veda we meet with these numbers assigned to days and months and seasons, rivers and countries, sacrifices and deities. They clearly prove the existence of a considerable amount of intellectual labour which had become fixed and traditional before the composition of certain hymns, and they prove the same in the case of certain Upanishads. But beyond this, for the present, I should not like to go; and I must say that the attempts of most of the Indian commentators at explaining such numbers by a reference to later systems of philosophy or cosmology, are generally very forced and unsatisfactory.

One more point I ought to mention as indicating the age of the *S*vetâ*s*vatara-upanishad, and that is the obscurity of many of its verses, which may be due to a corruption of the text, and the number of various readings, recognised as such, by the commentators. Some of them have been mentioned in the notes to my translation.

The text of this Upanishad was printed by Dr. Roer in the Bibliotheca Indica, with *S*aṅkara's commentary. I have consulted besides, the commentary of Vig*ñ*ânâtman, the pupil of Paramaha*m*sa-parivrâgakâ*k*ârya-*s*rîmag-*Gñ*ânotta-mâ*k*ârya, MS. I. O. 1133; and a third commentary, by *S*aṅkarânanda, the pupil of Paramaha*m*sa-parivrâgakâ*k*âryânandâtman, MS. I. O. 1878. These were kindly lent me by Dr. Rost, the learned and liberal librarian of the India Office.

---

[822] See I, 4; 5; VI, 3

VI. PRA*SÑ*A-UPANISHAD.

This Upanishad is called the Pra*sñ*a or Sha*t*-pra*sñ*a-upanishad, and at the end of a chapter we find occasionally iti pra*sñ*aprativa*k*anam, i.e. thus ends the answer to the question. It is ascribed to the Atharva-veda, and occasionally to the Pippalâda-*s*âkhâ, one of the most important *s*âkhâs of that Veda. Pippalâda is mentioned in the Upanishad as the name of the principal teacher.

*S*aṅkara, in the beginning of his commentary, says: Mantroktasyârthasya vistarânuvâdidam Brâhma*n*am ârabhyate, which would mean 'this Brâhma*n*a is commenced as more fully repeating what has been declared in the Mantra.' This, however, does not, I believe, refer to a Mantra or hymn in the Atharva-veda-samhitâ, but to the Mu*nd*aka-upanishad, which, as written in verse, is sometimes spoken of as a Mantra, or Mantropanishad. This is also the opinion of Ânandagiri, who says, I one might think that it was mere repetition (punarukti), if the essence of the Self, which has been explained by the Mantras, were to be taught here again by the Brâhma*n*a.' For he adds, 'by the Mantras "Brahma devânâm," &c.,' and this is evidently meant for the beginning of the Mu*nd*aka-upanishad, 'Brahmâ devânâm.' Ânandagiri refers again to the Mu*nd*aka in order to show that the Pra*sñ*a is not a mere repetition, and if *S*aṅkara calls the beginning of it a Brâhma*n*a, this must be taken in the more general sense of 'what is not Mantra.'[823] Mantropanishad is a name used of several Upanishads which are written in verse, and some of which, like the Î*s*â, have kept their place in the Sa*m*hitâs.

VII. MAITRÂYANA-BRÂHMANA-UPANISHAD.

In the case of this Upanishad we must first of all attempt to settle its right title. Professor Cowell, in his edition and translation of it, calls it Maitri or Maitrâya*n*îya-upanishad, and states that it belongs to the Maitrâya*n*îya-*s*âkhâ of the Black Yagur-veda, and that it formed the concluding portion of a lost Brâhma*n*a of that *S*âkhâ, being preceded by the sacrificial (karma) portion, which consisted of four books.

In his MSS. the title varied between Maitry-upanishad and Maitrî-*s*âkhâ-upanishad. A Poona MS. calls it Maitrâya*n*îya-*s*âkhâ-upanishad, and a MS. copied for Baron von Eckstein, Maitrâya*n*îyopanishad. I myself in the Alphabetical List of the Upanishads, published in the journal of the German Oriental Society, called it, No. 104, Maitrâya*n*a or Maitrî-upanishad, i.e. either the Upanishad of the Maitrâya*n*as, or the

---

823 Mantravyatiriktabhâge tu brâhma*n*asabda*h*, Rig-veda, Sâya*n*a's Introduction, vol. i, p. 23.

Upanishad of Maitrî, the principal teacher.

In a MS. which I received from Dr. Burnell, the title of our Upanishad is Maitrâya*n*î-brâhma*n*a-upanishad, varying with Maitrâya*n*î-brâhma*n*a-upanishad, and Srîyagus*s*âkhâyâm Maitrâya*n*îya-brâhma*n*a-upanishad.

The next question is by what name this Upanishad is quoted by native authorities. Vidyâranya, in his Sarvopanishad-arthânubhûtiprakâ*s*a,[824] v. 1, speaks of the Maitrâya*n*îyanâmnî yâgushî *s*âkhâ, and he mentions Maitra (not Maitrî) as the author of that *S*âkhâ. (vv. 55,150).

In the Muktikâ-upanishad[825] we meet with the name of Maitrâya*n*î as the twenty-fourth Upanishad, with the name of Maitreyî as the twenty-ninth; and again, in the list of the sixteen Upanishads of the Sâma-veda, we find Maitrâya*n*î and Maitreyî as the fourth and fifth.

Looking at all this evidence, I think we should come to the conclusion that our Upanishad derives its name from the *S*âkhâ of the Maitrâya*n*as, and may therefore be called Maitrâya*n*a-upanishad or Maitrâya*n*î Upanishad. Maitrâya*n*a-brâhma*n*a-upanishad seems likewise correct, and Maitrâya*n*i-brâhma*n*a-upanishad, like Kaushîtaki-brâhma*n*a-upanishad and Vâgasaneyi-sa*m*hitopanishad, might be defended, if Maitrâyanîn were known as a further derivative of Maitrâya*n*a. If the name is formed from the teacher Maitrî or Maitra, the title of Maitrî-upanishad would also be correct, but I doubt whether Maitrî-upanishad would admit of any grammatical justification.[826]

Besides this Maitrâya*n*a-brâhma*n*a-upanishad, however, I possess a MS. of what is called the Maitreyopanishad, sent to me likewise by the late Dr. Burnell. It is very short, and contains no more than the substance of the first Prapâ*th*aka of the Maitrâya*n*a-brâhma*n*a-upanishad. I give the text of it, as far as it can be restored from the one MS. in my possession:

Hari*h* Om. B*ri*hadratho vai nâma râgâ vairâgye putra*m* nidhâpayitvedam a*s*â*s*vatam manyamâna*h* sarîra*m* vairâgyam upeto 'ra*n*ya*m* nirgagâma. Sa tatra paramam tapa[827] âdityam udîkshamâ*n*a ûrdhvas tish*th*aty. Ante sahasrasya muner antikam âgagâma.[828] Atha B*ri*hadratho brahmavitpravaram munîndra*m* sampûgya stutvâ bahu*s*a*h* pra*n*âmam akarot. So 'bravîd agnir ivâdhûmakas tegasâ nirdahann ivâtmavid Bhagavâ*n* *kh*âkâyanya, uttish*th*ottish*th*a vara*m* v*rin*îshveti

[824] See Cowell, Maitr: Up. pref. p. iv.

[825] Calcutta, 1791 (1869), p. 4; also as quoted in the Mahâvâkya-ratnâvalî, p. 2b.

[826] Dr. Burnell, in his Tanjore Catalogue, mentions, p. 35a, a Maitrâya*n*î-brâhma*n*opanishad, which can hardly be a right title, and p. 36b a Maitrâya*n*îya and Maitreyîbrâhma*n*a.

[827] One expects âsthâya.

[828] This seems better than the Maitrâya*n*a text. He went near a Muni, viz. *S*âkâyanya.

râgânam abravît.[829] Sa tasmai punar namask*ri*tyovâ*k*a, Bhagavan nâ(ha)mâtmavit tva*m* tattvavi*k* *kh*u*s*rumo vayam; sa tvam no brûhity etad vratam purastâd a*s*akyam mâ pri*kkh*a pra*s*ñam Aikshvâkânyân kâmân v*rin*îshveti Sâkâyanya*h*. *S*arîrasya *s*arîre (sic) *k*ara*n*âv abhim*ris*yamâno râgemâ*m* gâthâ*m* *g*agâda. 1

Bhagavann, asthi*k*armasnâyumaggâmâ*m*sa*s*ukla*s*o*n*ita*s*reshmâ*s*ru-dashikâvi*n*mûtrapittakaphasa*m*ghâte durgandhe ni*h*sâre 'smiñ *kh*arîre ki*m* kâmabhogai*h*. 2

Kâmakrodhalobhamohabhayavishâdershesh*t*aviyogânish*t*asampray ogakshutpipâsâ*g*arâm*ri*tyuroga*s*okâdyair abhihate 'smiñ *kh*arîre ki*m* kâmabhogai*h*. 3

Sarva*m* *k*eda*m* kshayish*n*u pa*s*yâmo yatheme da*m*sama*s*akâdayas t*rin*avan[830] na*s*yata yodbhûtapradhva*m*sina*h*. 4

Atha kim etair vâ pare 'nye dhamartharâ*s* (sic) *k*akravartina*h* Sudyumnabhûridyumnakuvalayâ*s*vayauvanâ*s*vavaddh*ri*yâ*s*vâ*s*vapati*h* *s*a*s*abindur hari*s*kandro '*m*barîsho nanukastvayâtir yayâtir a*n*ara*n*yokshasenâdayo marutabharataprabh*ri*tayo râgâno mishato bandhuvargasya mahatî*m* *s*riya*m* tyaktvâsmâl lokâd amu*m* lokam prayânti. 5.

Atha kim etair vâ pare 'nye gandharvâsurayaksharâksha-sabhûtaga*n*api*s*â*k*oragrahâdinâ*m* nirodhanam pa*s*yâma*h*. 6

Atha kim etair vânyanâ*m* sosha*nam* mahâr*n*avânâ*m* *s*ikhari*n*âm prapatana*m* dhruvasya pra*k*alana*m* vâtarû*n*â*m* nimagganam p*ri*thivyâ*h* sthânâpasara*nam* surâ*n*âm. So 'ham ity etadvidhe 'smin sa*m*sâre ki*m* kâmopabhogair yair evâ*s*ritasya sak*ri*d âvartana*m* d*ris*yata ity uddhartum arhasi tyandodapânabheka ivâham asmin sa*m* Bhagavas tva*m* gatis tva*m* no gatir iti. 7

Ayam[831] agnir vai*s*vânaro yo 'yam anta*h* purushe yenedam annam pa*k*yate yad idam adyate tasyaisha ghosho bhavati yam etat kar*n*âv apidhâya *s*r*in*oti, sa yadotkramishyan[832] bhavati naina*m* ghosha*m* s*rin*oti. 8

Yathâ[833] nirindhano vahni*h* svayonâv upa*s*âmyati. 9[834]

Sa *s*iva*h* so 'nte vai*s*vânaro bhûtvâ sa dagdhvâ sarvâ*n*i bhûtâni p*ri*thivyapsu pralîyate,[835] âpas tegasi lîyante,[836] tego vâyau pralîyate,[837] vâyur âkâ*s*e vilîyate,[838] âkâ*s*am indriyeshv, indriyâ*n*i tanmâtreshu,

---

[829] This seems unnecessary.

[830] There may be an older reading hidden in this, from which arose the reading of the Maitrâyana B. U. t*rin*avanaspatayodbhûtapradhva*m*sina*h*, or yo bhûtapradhva*m*sina*h*.

[831] Maitr. Up. II, 6; p. 32.

[832] kramishyân, m.

[833] Yadhâ, m.

[834] Maitr. Up. VI, 34; p. 178.

[835] lipyate.

[836] lipyante.

[837] lîyyate.

[838] lîyyate.

tanmâtrâ*n*i bhûtâdau vilîyante,[839] bhûtâdi mahati vilîyate,[840] mahân avyakte vilîyate,[841] avyaktam akshare vilîyate[842]], aksharam tamasi vilîyate,[843] tama ekîbhavati parasmin, parastân na[844] san nâsan na sad ityetan nirvâ*n*am anu*s*âsanam iti vedânu*s*âsanam.

We should distinguish therefore between the large Maitrâya*n*a-brâhma*n*a-upanishad and the smaller Maitreyopanishad. The title of Maitreyî-brâhma*n*a has, of course, a totally different origin, and simply means the Brâhma*n*a which tells the story of Maitreyî.[845]

As Professor Cowell, in the Preface to his edition and translation of the Maitrâya*n*a-brâhma*n*a-upanishad, has discussed its peculiar character, I have little to add on that subject. I agree with him in thinking that this Upanishad has grown, and contains several accretions. The Sanskrit commentator himself declares the sixth and seventh chapters to be Khilas or supplementary. Possibly the Maitreya-upanishad, as printed above, contains the earliest framework. Then we have traces of various recensions. Professor Cowell (Preface, p. vi) mentions a MS., copied for Baron Eckstein, apparently from a Telugu original, which contains the first five chapters only, numbered as four. The verses given in VI, 34 (p. 177), beginning with atreme *s*lokâ bhavanti, are placed after IV, 3. In my own MS. these verses are inserted at the beginning of the fifth chapter.[846] Then follows in Baron Eckstein's MS. as IV, 5, what is given in the printed text as V, 1, 2 (pp. 69-76). In my own MS., which likewise comes from the South, the Upanishad does not go beyond VI, 8, which is called the sixth chapter and the end of the Upanishad.

We have in fact in our Upanishad the first specimen of that peculiar Indian style, so common in the later fables and stories, which delights in enclosing one story within another. The kernel of our Upanishad is really the dialogue between the Vâlakhilyas and Pragâpati Kratu. This is called by the commentator (see note 1881) a Vyâkhyâna, i.e. a fuller explanation of the Sûtra which comes before, and which expresses in the few words, 'He is the Self, this is the immortal, the fearless, this is Brahman,' the gist of the whole Upanishad.

This dialogue, or at all events the doctrine which it was meant to illustrate, was communicated by Maitrî (or Maitra) to *S*âkâyanya, and by *S*âkâyanya to King B*ri*hadratha Aikshvâka, also called Marut (II, 1;

---

839 liyante.

840 liyyate.

841 lipyate.

842 liyyate.

843 liyyate.

844 tânasannâ.

845 See Khâ*nd*. Up. p. 623.

846 See note 1775; note 1787; note 1826.

VI, 30). This dialogue might seem to come to an end in VI, 29, and likewise the dialogue between *S*âkâyanya and B*ri*hadratha; but it is carried on again to the end of VI, 30, and followed afterwards by a number of paragraphs which may probably be considered as later additions.

But though admitting all this, I cannot bring myself to follow Professor Cowell in considering, as he does, even the earlier portion of the Upanishad as dating from a late period, while the latter portions are called by him comparatively modern, on account of frequent Vaish*n*ava quotations. What imparts to this Upanishad, according to my opinion, an exceptionally genuine and ancient character, is the preservation in it of that peculiar Sandhi which, thanks to the labours of Dr. von Schroeder, we now know to be characteristic of the Maitrâya*n*a-*s*âkhâ. In that *S*âkhâ final unaccented as and e are changed into â, if the next word begins with an accented vowel, except a. Before initial a, however, e remains unchanged, and as becomes o, and the initial a is sometimes elided, sometimes not. Some of these rules, it must be remembered, run counter to Pâ*n*ini, and we may safely conclude therefore that texts in which they are observed, date from the time before Pâ*n*ini. In some MSS., as, for instance, in my own MS. of the Maitrâya*n*a-brâhma*n*a-upanishad, these rules are not observed, but this makes their strict observation in other MSS. all the more important. Besides, though to Dr. von Schroeder belongs, no doubt, the credit of having, in his edition of the Maitrâya*n*î Samhitâ, first pointed out these phonetic peculiarities, they were known as such to the commentators, who expressly point out these irregular Sandhis as distinctive of the Maitrâya*n*î *s*âkhâ. Thus we read Maitr. Up. II, 3 (p. 18), that tigmategasâ ûrdhvaretaso, instead of tigmategasâ, is eva*m*vidha eta*kkh*âkhâsaṅketapâ*th*as *kh*ândasa*h* sarvatra, i.e. is throughout the Vedic reading indicatory of that particular *S*âkhâ, namely the Maitrâya*n*î.

A still stranger peculiarity of our *S*âkhâ is the change of a final *t* before initial *s* into *ñ*. This also occurs in our Upanishad. In VI, 8, we read *s*vâ*ñ* *s*arîrâd; in VI, 2 7, ya*ñ* *s*arîrasya. Such a change seems phonetically so unnatural, that the tradition must have been very strong to perpetuate it among the Maitrâya*n*as.

Now what is important for our purposes is this, that these phonetic peculiarities run through all the seven chapters of our Upanishad. This will be seen from the following list:

I. Final as changed into â before initial vowel:[847]

II, 3, tigmatega*s*â ûrdhvaretaso (Comm. eta*kkh*âkhâsaṅketapâ*th*as *kh*ândasa*h* sarvatra).

II, 5, vibodhâ evam.

II, 7, avasthitâ iti.

III, 5, etair abhibhûtâ îti.

IV, i, vidyatâ iti.

VI, 4, pra*n*avâ iti; bhâmyâdayâ eko.

VI, 6, âdityâ iti; âhavanîyâ iti; sûryâ iti; ahaṅkârâ iti; vyânâ iti.

VI, 7, bhargâ iti.

VI, 7, sannivish*t*â iti.

VI, 23, devâ oṅkâro.

VI, 30, prâyâtâ iti.

VI, 30, vinirgatâ iti.

II. Final e before initial vowels becomes â. For instance:

I, 4, d*ris*yatâ iti.

II, 2, nishpadyatâ iti.

III, 2, âpadyatâ iti.

III, 2, pushkarâ iti.

IV, i, vidyatâ iti.

VI, 10, bhuṅktâ iti.

VI, 20, a*s*nutâ iti.

VI, 30, ekâ âhur.

Even prag*ri*hya e is changed to â in—

VI, 23, etâ upâsita, i.e. ete uktalaksha*n*e brahma*n*î.

In VI, 31, instead of te etasya, the commentator seems to have read te vâ etasya.

III. Final as before â, u, and au becomes a, and is then contracted. For instance:

I, 4, vanaspatayodbhûta, instead of vanaspataya, udbhûta. (Comm. Sandhi*s kh*ândaso vâ, ukâro vâtra lupto drash*t*avya*h*.)

II, 6, devaush*n*yam, instead of deva aush*n*yam. (Comm. Sandhi*s kh*ândasa*h*.)

VI, 24, atamâvish*t*am, instead of atama-âvish*t*am (Comm. Sandhi*s kh*ândasa*h*); cf. Khâ*nd*. Up. VI, 8, 3, a*s*anâyeti (Comm. visarganîyalopa*h*).

IV. Final e before i becomes a, and is then contracted. For instance:

VI, 7, âtmâ ganîteti for ganîta iti. (Comm. gânite, gânâti.)

---

[847] I have left out the restriction as to the accent of the vowels, because they are disregarded in the Upanishad. It should be observed that this peculiar Sandhi occurs in the Upanishad chiefly before iti.

VI, 28, ava*t*aiva for avata iva. (Comm. Sandhiv*ri*ddhî *kh*ândase.)

V. Final au before initial vowels becomes â. For instance:

II, 6, yena vâ etâ anug*ri*hîtâ iti.

VI, 22, asâ abhidhyâtâ.

On abhibhûyamânay iva, see note 1726.

V, 2, asâ âtmâ (var. lect. asâv âtmâ).

VI. Final o of atho produces elision of initial short a. For instance:

III, 2, atho 'bhibhûatvât. (Comm. Sandhi*s* *kh*ândasa*h*.) Various reading, ato 'bhibhûtatvât.

VI, 1, so antar is explained as sa u.

VII. Other irregularities:

VI, 7, âpo pyâyanât, explained by pyâyanât and âpyâyanât. Might it be, âpo 'py ayanât?

VI, 7, âtmano tmâ netâ.

II, 6, so tmânam abhidhyâtvâ.

VI, 35, dvidharmondharn for dvidharmândham. (Comm. *kh*ândasa.)

VI, 35, tegasendham, i.e. tegasâ-iddhan. (In explaining other irregular compounds, too, as in I, 4, the commentator has recourse to a *kh*ândasa or prâmâdika licence.)

VI, 1, hira*n*yavasthât for hira*n*yâvasthât. Here the dropping of a in avasthât is explained by a reference to Bhâguri (vash*t*i Bhâgurir allopam avâpyor upasargayo*h*). See Vopadeva III, 171.

VIII. Vi*s*lish*t*apâtha:

VII, 2, brahmadhîyâlambana. (Comm. vi*s*lish*t*apâtha*s* *kh*ândasa*h*.)

VI, 35, apyay aṅkurâ for apy aṅkurâ. (Comm. yakâra*h* pramâdapa*th*ita*h*.)

On the contrary VI, 35, vlîyânte for vilîyante.

If on the grounds which we have hitherto. examined there seems good reason to ascribe the Maitrâya*n*a-brâhma*n*a-upanishad to an early rather than to a late period, possibly to an ante-Pâ*n*inean period, we shall hardly be persuaded to change this opinion on account of supposed references to Vaishnava or to Bauddha doctrines which some scholars have tried to discover in it.

As to the worship of Vishnu, as one of the many manifestations of the Highest Spirit, we have seen it alluded to in other Upanishads, and we know from the Brâhma*n*as that the name of Vishnu was connected with many of the earliest Vedic sacrifices.

As to Bauddha doctrines, including the very name of Nirvâ*n*a (p. 297), we must remember, as I have often remarked, that there were Bauddhas before Buddha. B*ri*haspati, who is frequently quoted in later philosophical writings as the author of an heretical philosophy, denying the authority of the Vedas, is mentioned by name in our Upanishad (VII, 9), but we are told that this Brihaspati, having become Sukra, promulgated his erroneous doctrines in order to mislead the Asuras, and thus to insure the safety of Indra, i.e. of the old faith.

The fact that the teacher of King B*ri*hadratha in our Upanishad is called *S*âkâyanya, can never be used in support of the idea that, being a descendant of *S*âka,[848] he must have been, like *S*âkyamuni, a teacher of Buddhist doctrines. He is the very opposite in our Upanishad, and warns his hearers against such doctrines as we should identify with the doctrines of Buddha. As I have pointed out on several occasions, the breaking through the law of the Âsramas is the chief complaint which orthodox Brâhmans make against Buddhists and their predecessors, and this is what *S*âkâyanya condemns. A Brâhman may become a Sannyâsin, which is much the same as a Buddhist Bhikshu, if he has first passed through the three stages of a student, a householder, and a Vânaprastha. But to become a Bhikshu without that previous discipline, was heresy in the eyes of the Brâhmans, and it was exactly that heresy which the Bauddhas preached and practised. That this social laxity was gaining ground at the time when our Upanishad was written is clear (see VII, 8). We hear of people who wear red dresses (like the Buddhists) without having a right to them; we even hear of books, different from the Vedas, against which the true Brâhmans are warned. All this points to times when what we call Buddhism was in the air, say the sixth century B. C., the very time to which I have always assigned the origin of the genuine and classical Upanishads. The Upanishads are to my mind the germs of Buddhism, while Buddhism is in many

---

[848] *S*âkâyanya means a grandson or further descendant of *S*âka; see Ga*n*aratnâvalî (Baroda, 1874), p. 57[a].

respects the doctrine of the Upanishads carried out to its last consequences, and, what is important, employed as the foundation of a new social system. In doctrine the highest goal of the Vedânta, the knowledge of the true Self, is no more than the Buddhist Samyaksambodhi; in practice the Sannyâsin is the Bhikshu, the friar, only emancipated alike from the tedious discipline of the Brâhmanic student, the duties of the Brâhmanic householder, and the yoke of useless penances imposed on the Brâhmanic dweller in the forest. The spiritual freedom of the Sannyâsin becomes in Buddhism the common property of the Saṅgha, the Fraternity, and that Fraternity is open alike to the young and the old, to the Brâhman and the Sûdra, to the rich and the poor, to the wise and the foolish. In fact there is no break between the India of the Veda and the India of the Tripitaka, but there is an historical continuity between the two, and the connecting link between extremes that seem widely separated must be sought in the Upanishads.[849]

F. MAX MÜLLER.

OXFORD, February, 1884.

[849] As there is room left on this page, I subjoin a passage from the Abhidharma-kosha-vyâkhyâ, ascribed to the Bhagavat, but which, as far as style and thought are concerned, might be taken from an Upanishad: Ukta*m* hi Bhagavatâ: P*ri*thivî bho Gautama kutra pratish*th*itâ? P*ri*thivî Brâhma*n*a abma*nd*ale pratish*th*itâ. Abma*nd*alam bho Gautama kva pratish*th*itam? Vâyau pratish*th*itam. Vâyur bho Gautama kva pratish*th*ita*h*? Âkâ*s*e pratish*th*itah. Âkâ*s*am bho Gautama kutra pratish*th*itam? Atisarasi Mahâbrâhma*n*a, atisarasi Mahâbrâhma*n*a. Âkâsam Brâhma*n*âpratish*th*itam, anâlambanam iti vistara*h*. Tasmâd asty âkâsam iti Vaibhâshikâ*h*. (See B*ri*had-Âr. Up. III, 6, 1. Burnouf, Introduction à l'histoire du Buddhisme, p. 449.)

'For it is said by the Bhagavat: "O Gautama, on what does the earth rest?" "The earth, O Brâhma*n*a, rests on the sphere of water." "O Gautama, on what does the sphere of water rest?" "It rests on the air." "O Gautama, on what does the air rest?" "It rests on the ether (âkâsa)." "O Gautama, on what does the ether rest?" "Thou goest too far, great Brâhma*n*a; thou goest too far, great Brâhma*n*a. The ether, O Brâhma*n*a, does not rest. It has no support." Therefore the Vaibhâshikas hold that there is an ether,' &c.

KA*TH*A-UPANISHAD.

FIRST ADHYÂYA.

FIRST VALLÎ

1. Vâga*s*ravasa,[850] desirous (of heavenly rewards), surrendered (at a sacrifice) all that he possessed. He had a son of the name of Na*k*iketas.

2. When the (promised) presents were being given (to the priests), faith entered into the heart of Na*k*iketas, who was still a boy, and he thought:

3. 'Unblessed,[851] surely, are the worlds to which a man goes by giving (as his promised present at a sacrifice) cows which have drunk water, eaten hay, given their milk,[852] and are barren.'

4. He (knowing that his father had promised to give up all that he possessed, and therefore his son also) said to his father: 'Dear father, to whom wilt thou give me?'

He said it a second and a third time. Then the father replied (angrily):

'I shall give thee[853] unto Death.'

(The father, having once said so, though in haste, had to be true to his word and to sacrifice his son.)

5. The son said: 'I go as the first, at the head of many (who have still to die); I go in the midst of many (who are now dying). What will be the work of Yama (the ruler of the departed) which to-day he has to do unto me?[854]

---

[850] Vâga*s*ravasa is called Âru*n*i Auddâlaki Gautama, the father of Na*k*iketas. The father of *S*vetaketu, another enlightened pupil (see *Kh*ând. Up. VI, 1, 1), is also called Âru*n*i (Uddâlaka, comm. Kaush. Up. I, x) Gautama. *S*vetaketu himself is called Âru*n*eya, i.e. the son of Âru*n*i, the grandson of Âru*n*a, and likewise Auddâlaki. Auddâlaki is a son of Uddâlaka, but *S*aṅkara (Kâ*th*. Up. I, 11) takes Auddâlaki as possibly the same as Uddâlaka. See B*r*ih. Âr. Up. III, 6, 1.

[851] As to ănanda, unblessed, see B*r*ih. Âr. Up. IV, 4, 11; Vâgas. Sa*m*h. Up. 3 (Sacred Books of the East, vol. i, p. 310.

[852] Ânandagiri explains that the cows meant here are cows no longer able to drink, to eat, to give milk, and to calve.

[853] Dadâmi, I give, with the meaning of the future. Some MSS. write dâsyâmi.

[854] I translate these verses freely, i.e. independently of the commentator, not that I ever despise the traditional interpretation which the commentators have preserved to us, but because I think that, after having examined it, we have a right to judge for ourselves. *S*aṅkara says that the son, having been addressed by his father full of anger, was sad, and said to himself: 'Among many pupils I am the first, among many middling pupils I am the middlemost, but nowhere am I the last. Yet though I am such a good pupil, my father has said that he will consign me unto death. What duty has he to fulfil toward Yama which he means to fulfil to-day by giving me to him? There may be no duty, he may only have spoken in haste. Yet a father's word must not be broken.' Having considered this,

6. 'Look back how it was with those who came before, look forward how it will be with those who come hereafter. A mortal ripens like corn, like corn he springs up again.'[855]

(Na*k*iketas enters into the abode of Yama Vaivasvata, and there is no one to receive him. Thereupon one of the attendants of Yama is supposed to say:)

7. 'Fire enters into the houses, when a Brâhma*n*a enters as a guest.[856] That fire is quenched by this peace-offering;—bring water, O Vaivasvata![857]

8. 'A Brâhma*n*a that dwells in the house of a foolish man without receiving food to eat, destroys his hopes and expectations, his possessions, his righteousness, his sacred and his good deeds, and all his sons and cattle.'[858]

(Yama, returning to his house after an absence of three nights, during which time Na*k*iketas had received no hospitality from him, says:)

9. 'O Brâhma*n*a, as thou, a venerable guest, hast dwelt in my house three nights without eating, therefore choose now three boons. Hail to thee! and welfare to me!'

10. Na*k*iketas said: 'O Death, as the first of the three boons I choose that Gautama, my father, be pacified, kind, and free from anger towards me; and that he may know me and greet me, when I shall have been dismissed by thee.'

11. Yama said: 'Through my favour Auddâlaki Âru*n*i, thy father,

---

the son comforted his father, and exhorted him to behave like his forefathers, and to keep his word. I do not think this view of *S*aṅkara's could have been the view of the old poet. He might have made the son say that he was the best or one of the best of his father's pupils, but hardly that he was also one of his middling pupils, thus implying that he never was among the worst. That would be out of keeping with the character of Na*k*iketas, as drawn by the poet himself. Na*k*iketas is full of faith and wishes to die, he would be the last to think of excuses why he should not die. The second half of the verse may be more doubtful. It may mean what *S*aṅkara thinks it means, only that we should get thus again an implied complaint of Na*k*iketas against his father, and this is not in keeping with his character. The mind of Na*k*iketas is bent on what is to come, on what he will see after death, and on what Yama will do unto him. 'What has Yama to do,' he asks, 'what can he do, what is it that he will to-day do unto me?' This seems to me consistent with the tenor of the ancient story, while *S*aṅkara's interpretations and interpolations savour too much of the middle ages of India.

[855] Sasyâ, corn rather than grass; εἴα, ἤιον Benfey; Welsh haidd, according to Rhys; different from *s*ash-pa, ces-pes, Benfey.

[856] Cf. Vasish*th*a XI, 13; Sacred Books of the East, vol. xiv, p. 51.

[857] Vaivasvata, a name of Yama, the ruler of the departed. Water is the first gift to be offered to a stranger who claims hospitality.

[858] Here again some words are translated differently from *S*aṅkara. He explains âsâ as asking for a wished-for object, pratikshâ as looking forward with a view to obtaining an unknown object. Saṅgata he takes as reward for intercourse with good people; sûn*ri*tâ, as usual, as good and kind speech; ish*t*a as rewards for sacrifices; pûrta as rewards for public benefits.

will know thee, and be again towards thee as he was before. He shall sleep peacefully through the night, and free from anger, after having seen thee freed from the mouth of death.'

12. Na*k*iketas said: 'In the heaven-world there is no fear; thou art not there, O Death, and no one is afraid on account of old age. Leaving behind both hunger and thirst, and out of the reach of sorrow, all rejoice in the world of heaven.'

13. 'Thou knowest, O Death, the fire-sacrifice which leads us to heaven; tell it to me, for I am full of faith. Those who live in the heaven-world reach immortality,—this I ask as my second boon.'

14. Yama said: 'I tell it thee, learn it from me, and when thou understandest that fire-sacrifice which leads to heaven, know, O Na*k*iketas, that it is the attainment of the endless worlds, and their firm support, hidden in darkness.'[859]

15. Yama then told him that fire-sacrifice, the beginning of all the worlds,[860] and what bricks are required for the altar, and how many, and how they are to be placed. And Na*k*iketas repeated all as it had been told to him. Then M*ri*tyu, being pleased with him, said again:

16. The generous,[861] being satisfied, said to him:

I give thee now another boon; that fire-sacrifice shall be named after thee, take also this many-coloured chain.'[862]

17. 'He who has three times performed this Nâ*k*iketa rite, and has been united with the three (father, mother, and teacher), and has performed the three duties (study, sacrifice, almsgiving) overcomes birth and death. When he has learnt and understood this fire, which knows (or makes us know) all that is born of Brahman,[863] which is venerable and divine, then he obtains everlasting peace.'

18. 'He who knows the three Nâ*k*iketa fires, and knowing the three, piles up the Nâ*k*iketa sacrifice, he, having first thrown off the chains of death, rejoices in the world of heaven, beyond the reach of grief.'

19. 'This, O Na*k*iketas, is thy fire which leads to heaven, and which thou hast chosen as thy second boon. That fire all men will proclaim.[864] Choose now, O Na*k*iketas, thy third boon.'

20. Na*k*iketas said: 'There is that doubt, when a man is dead,—some saying, he is; others, he is not. This I should like to know, taught

---

[859] The commentator translates: 'I tell it thee, attend to me who knows the heavenly fire.' Here the nom. sing. of the participle would be very irregular, as we can hardly refer it to bravîmi. Then, 'Know this fire as a means of obtaining the heavenly world, know that fire as the rest or support of the world, when it assumes the form of Virâg, and as hidden in the heart of men.'

[860] *S*aṅkara: the first embodied, in the shape of Virâg.

[861] Verses 16-18 seem a later addition.

[862] This arises probably from a misunderstanding of verse 11, 3.

[863] *G*âtavedas.

[864] Tavaiva is a later addition, caused by the interpolation of verses 15-18.

by thee; this is the third of my boons.'

21. Death said: 'On this point even the gods have doubted formerly; it is not easy to understand. That subject is subtle. Choose another boon, O Na*k*iketas, do not press me, and let me off that boon.'

22. Na*k*iketas said: 'On this point even the gods have doubted indeed, and thou, Death, hast declared it to be not easy to understand, and another teacher like thee is not to be found:—surely no other boon is like unto this.'

23. Death said: 'Choose sons and grandsons who shall live a hundred years, herds of cattle, elephants, gold, and horses. Choose the wide abode of the earth, and live thyself as many harvests as thou desirest.'

24. 'If you can think of any boon equal to that, choose wealth, and long life. Be (king), Na*k*iketas, on the wide earth.[865] I make thee the enjoyer of all desires.'

25. 'Whatever desires are difficult to attain among mortals, ask for them according to thy wish;—these fair maidens with their chariots and musical instruments,—such are indeed not to be obtained by men,—be waited on by them whom I give to thee, but do not ask me about dying.'

26. Na*k*iketas said: 'These things last till tomorrow, O Death, for they wear out this vigour of all the senses. Even the whole of life is short. Keep thou thy horses, keep dance and song for thyself.'

27. 'No man can be made happy by wealth. Shall we possess wealth, when we see thee? Shall we live, as long as thou rulest? Only that boon (which I have chosen) is to be chosen by me.'

28. 'What mortal, slowly decaying here below, and knowing, after having approached them, the freedom from decay enjoyed by the immortals, would delight in a long life, after he has pondered on the pleasures which arise from beauty and love?'[866]

29. 'No, that on which there is this doubt, O Death, tell us what there is in that great Hereafter. Na*k*iketas does not choose another boon but that which enters into the hidden world.'

---

[865] Mahâbhûmau, on the great earth, has been explained also by mahâ bhûmau, be great on the earth. It is doubtful, however, whether mahi for mahin could be admitted in the Upanishads, and whether it would not be easier to write mahân bhûmau.

[866] A very obscure verse. *S*ankara gives a various reading kva tadâstha*h* for kvadha*h*stha*h*, in the sense of I given to these pleasures,' which looks like an emendation. I have changed agîryatâm into agâryatâm, and take it for an acc. sing., instead of a gen. plur., which could hardly be governed by upetya.

SECOND VALLÎ

1. Death said: 'The good is one thing, the pleasant another; these two, having different objects, chain a man. It is well with him who clings to the good; he who chooses the pleasant, misses his end.'

2. 'The good and the pleasant approach man: the wise goes round about them and distinguishes them. Yea, the wise prefers the good to the pleasant, but the fool chooses the pleasant through greed and avarice.'

3. 'Thou, O Na*k*iketas, after pondering all pleasures that are or seem delightful, hast dismissed them all. Thou hast not gone into the road[867] that leadeth to wealth, in which many men perish.'

4. 'Wide apart and leading to different points are these two, ignorance, and what is known as wisdom. I believe Na*k*iketas to be one who desires knowledge, for even many pleasures did not tear thee away.'[868]

5. 'Fools dwelling in darkness, wise in their own conceit, and puffed up with vain knowledge, go round and round, staggering to and fro, like blind men led by the blind.'[869]

6. 'The Hereafter never rises before the eyes of the careless child, deluded by the delusion of wealth. "This is the world," he thinks, "there is no other;"—thus he falls again and again under my sway.'

7. 'He (the Self) of whom many are not even able to hear, whom many, even when they hear of him, do not comprehend; wonderful is a man, when found, who is able to teach him (the Self); wonderful is he who comprehends him, when taught by an able teacher.'[870]

8. 'That (Self), when taught by an inferior man, is not easy to be known, even though often thought upon;[871] unless it be taught by another, there is no way to it, for it is inconceivably smaller than what is small.'[872]

9. 'That doctrine is not to be obtained[873] by argument, but when it is declared by another, then, O dearest, it is easy to understand. Thou hast obtained it now;[874] thou art truly a man of true resolve. May we

---

[867] Cf. I, 16.

[868] The commentator explains lolupanta*h* by vi*kkh*eda*m* k*ri*tavanta*h*. Some MSS. read lolupante and lolupanti, but one expects either lolupyante or lolupati.

[869] Cf. Mu*nd*. Up. II, 8.

[870] Cf. Bhag. Gîtâ II, 29.

[871] Cf. Mu*nd*. Up. II, 4.

[872] I read a*n*upramâ*n*ât. Other interpretations: If it is taught by one who is identified with the Self, then there is no uncertainty. If it has been taught as identical with ourselves, then there is no perception of anything else. If it has been taught by one who is identified with it, then there is no failure in understanding it (agati).

[873] Âpaneyâ; should it be âpanâya, as afterwards sug*ñ*ânâya?

[874] Because you insist on my teaching it to thee.

have always an inquirer like thee!'[875]

10. Na*k*iketas said: 'I know that what is called a treasure is transient, for that eternal is not obtained by things which are not eternal. Hence the Nâkiketa fire(-sacrifice) has been laid by me (first); then, by means of transient things, I have obtained what is not transient (the teaching of Yama).'[876]

11. Yama said: 'Though thou hadst seen the fulfilment of all desires, the foundation of the world, the endless rewards of good deeds, the shore where there is no fear, that which is magnified by praise, the wide abode, the rest,[877] yet being wise thou hast with firm resolve dismissed it all.'

12. 'The wise who, by means of meditation on his Self, recognises the Ancient, who is difficult to be seen, who has entered into the dark, who is hidden in the cave, who dwells in the abyss, as God, he indeed leaves joy and sorrow far behind.'[878]

13. 'A mortal who has heard this and embraced it, who has separated from it all qualities, and has thus reached the subtle Being, rejoices, because he has obtained what is a cause for rejoicing. The house (of Brahman) is open, I believe, O Na*k*iketas.'

14. Na*k*iketas said: 'That which thou seest as neither this nor that, as neither effect nor cause, as neither past nor future, tell me that.'

15. Yama said: 'That word (or place) which all the Vedas record, which all penances proclaim, which men desire when they live as religious students, that word I tell thee briefly, it is Om.'[879]

16. 'That (imperishable) syllable means Brahman, that syllable means the highest (Brahman); he who knows that syllable, whatever he desires, is his.'

17. 'This is the best support, this is the highest support; he who knows that support is magnified in the world of Brahmâ.'

18. 'The knowing (Self) is not born, it dies not; it sprang from nothing, nothing sprang from it. The Ancient is unborn, eternal, everlasting; he is not killed, though the body is killed.'[880]

19. 'If the killer thinks that he kills, if the killed thinks that he is killed, they do not understand; for this one does not kill, nor is that one killed.'

---

[875] Unless no is negative, for Yama, at first, does not like to communicate his knowledge.

[876] The words in parentheses have been added in order to remove the otherwise contradictory character of the two lines.

[877] Cf. *Kh*ând. Up. VII, 12, 2.

[878] Yama seems here to propound the lower Brahman only, not yet the highest. Deva, God, can only be that as what the Old, i.e. the Self in the heart, is to be recognised. It would therefore mean, he who finds God or the Self in his heart. See afterwards, verse 21.

[879] Cf. *S*vet. Up. IV, 9; Bhag. Gîtâ VIII, 11.

[880] As to verses 18 and 19, see Bhag. Gîtâ II, 19, 20.

20. 'The Self,[881] smaller than small, greater than great, is hidden in the heart of that creature. A man who is free from desires and free from grief, sees the majesty of the Self by the grace of the Creator.'[882]

21. 'Though sitting still, he walks far; though lying down, he goes everywhere.[883] Who, save myself, is able to know that God who rejoices and rejoices not?'

22. 'The wise who knows the Self as bodiless within the bodies, as unchanging among changing things, as great and omnipresent, does never grieve.'

23. 'That Self[884] cannot be gained by the Veda, nor by understanding, nor by much learning. He whom the Self chooses, by him the Self can be gained. The Self chooses him (his body) as his own.'

24. 'But he who has not first turned away from his wickedness, who is not tranquil, and subdued, or whose mind is not at rest, he can never obtain the Self (even) by knowledge.'

25. 'Who then knows where He is, He to whom the Brahmans and Kshatriyas are (as it were) but food,[885] and death itself a condiment?'

THIRD VALLÎ

1. 'There are the two,[886] drinking their reward in the world of their own works, entered into the cave (of the heart), dwelling on the highest summit (the ether in the heart). Those who know Brahman call them shade and light; likewise, those householders who perform the Tri*n*â*k*iketa sacrifice.'

2. 'May we be able to master that Nâ*k*iketa rite which is a bridge for sacrificers; also that which is the highest, imperishable Brahman for those who wish to cross over to the fearless shore.'[887]

3. 'Know the Self to be sitting in the chariot, the body to be the

---

[881] Cf. *S*vet. Up. III, 2 0; Taitt. Âr. X, 12, 1.

[882] The commentator translates 'through the tranquillity of the senses,' i.e. dhâtuprasâdât, taking prasâda in the technical sense of samprasâda. As to kratu, desire, or rather, will, see B*ri*h. Âr. IV, 4; 5.

[883] Cf. Tal. Up, 5.

[884] Cf. I, 7-9; Mu*nd*. Up. III, 2, 3; Bhag. Gîtâ I, 53.

[885] In whom all disappears, and in whom even death is swallowed up.

[886] The two are explained as the higher and lower Brahman, the former being the light, the latter the shadow. *Ri*ta is explained as reward, and connected with suk*ri*ta, lit. good deeds, but frequently used in the sense of svak*ri*ta, one's own good and evil deeds. The difficulty is, how the highest Brahman can be said to drink the reward (*ri*tapa) of former deeds, as it is above all works and above all rewards. The commentator explains it away as a metaphorical expression, as we often speak of many, when we mean one. (Cf. Mu*nd*. Up. III, 1, 1.) I have joined suk*ri*tasya with loke, loka meaning the world, i.e. the state, the environment, which we made to ourselves by our former deeds.

[887] These two verses may be later additions.

chariot, the intellect (buddhi) the charioteer, and the mind the reins.'[888]

4. 'The senses they call the horses, the objects of the senses their roads. When he (the Highest Self) is in union with the body, the senses, and the mind, then wise people call him the Enjoyer.'

5. 'He who has no understanding and whose mind (the reins) is never firmly held, his senses (horses) are unmanageable, like vicious horses of a charioteer.'

6. 'But he who has understanding and whose mind is always firmly held, his senses are under control, like good horses of a charioteer.'

7. 'He who has no understanding, who is unmindful and always impure, never reaches that place, but enters into the round of births.'

8. 'But he who has understanding, who is mindful and always pure, reaches indeed that place, from whence he is not born again.'

9. 'But he who has understanding for his charioteer, and who holds the reins of the mind, he reaches the end of his journey, and that is the highest place of Vish*n*u.'

10. 'Beyond the senses there are the objects, beyond the objects there is the mind, beyond the mind there is the intellect, the Great Self is beyond the intellect.'

11. 'Beyond the Great there is the Undeveloped, beyond the Undeveloped there is the Person (purusha). Beyond the Person there is nothing—this is the goal, the highest road.'

12. 'That Self is hidden in all beings and does not shine forth, but it is seen by subtle seers through their sharp and subtle intellect.'

13. 'A wise man should keep down speech and mind;[889] he should keep them within the Self which is knowledge; he should keep knowledge within the Self which is the Great; and he should keep that (the Great) within the Self which is the Quiet.'

14. 'Rise, awake! having obtained your boons,[890] understand them! The sharp edge of a razor is difficult to pass over; thus the wise say the path (to the Self) is hard.'

15. 'He who has perceived that which is without sound, without touch, without form, without decay, without taste, eternal, without smell, without beginning, without end, beyond the Great, and unchangeable, is freed from the jaws of death.'

16. 'A wise man who has repeated or heard the ancient story of Na*k*iketas told by Death, is magnified in the world of Brahman.'

17. 'And he who repeats this greatest mystery in an assembly of Brâhmans, or full of devotion at the time of the *S*râddha sacrifice,

---

[888] The simile of the chariot has some points of similarity with the well-known passage in Plato's Phædros, but Plato did not borrow this simile from the Brahmans, as little as Xenophon need have consulted our Upanishad (II, 2) in writing his prologue of Prodikos.

[889] *S*a*n*kara interprets, he should keep down speech in the mind.

[890] Comm., excellent teachers.

obtains thereby infinite rewards.'

SECOND ADHYÂYA.

FOURTH VALLÎ.

1. Death said: 'The Self-existent pierced the openings (of the senses) so that they turn forward: therefore man looks forward, not backward into himself. Some wise man, however, with his eyes closed and wishing for immortality, saw the Self behind.'

2. 'Children follow after outward pleasures, and fall into the snare of wide-spread death. Wise men only, knowing the nature of what is immortal, do not look for anything stable here among things unstable.'

3. 'That by which we know form, taste, smell, sounds, and loving touches, by that also we know what exists besides. This is that (which thou hast asked for).'

4. 'The wise, when he knows that that by which he perceives all objects in sleep or in waking is the great omnipresent Self, grieves no more.'

5. 'He who knows this living soul which eats honey (perceives objects) as being the Self, always near, the Lord of the past and the future, henceforward fears no more. This is that.'

6. 'He who (knows) him[891] who was born first from the brooding heat[892] (for he was born before the water), who, entering into the heart, abides therein, and was perceived from the elements. This is that.'

7. '(He who knows) Aditi also, who is one with all deities, who arises with Prâ*n*a (breath or Hira*n*yagarbha), who, entering into the heart, abides therein, and was born from the elements. This is that.'

8. 'There is Agni (fire), the all-seeing, hidden in the two fire-sticks, well-guarded like a child (in the womb) by the mother, day after day to be adored by men when they awake and bring oblations. This is that.'

9. 'And that whence the sun rises, and whither it goes to set, there all the Devas are contained, and no one goes beyond. This is that.'[893]

10. 'What is here (visible in the world), the same is there (invisible in Brahman); and what is there, the same is here. He who sees any difference here (between Brahman and the world), goes from death to death.'

11. 'Even by the mind this (Brahman) is to be obtained, and then

---

[891] The first manifestation of Brahman, commonly called Hira*n*yagarbha, which springs from the tapas of Brahman. Afterwards only water and the rest of the elements become manifested. The text of these verses is abrupt, possibly corrupt. The two accusatives, tish*th*antam and tish*th*antim, seem to me to require veda to be supplied from verse 4.

[892] Cf. s*r*ish*t*ikrama.

[893] Cf. V, 8.

there is no difference whatsoever. He goes from death to death who sees any difference here.'

12. 'The person (purusha), of the size of a thumb,[894] stands in the middle of the Self (body?), as lord of the past and the future, and henceforward fears no more. This is that.'

13. 'That person, of the size of a thumb, is like a light without smoke, lord of the past and the future, he is the same to-day and to-morrow. This is that.'

14. 'As rain-water that has fallen on a mountain-ridge runs down the rocks on all sides, thus does he, who sees a difference between qualities, run after them on all sides.'

15. 'As pure water poured into pure water remains the same, thus, O Gautama, is the Self of a thinker who knows.'

FIFTH VALLÎ.

1. 'There is a town with eleven[895] gates belonging to the Unborn (Brahman), whose thoughts are never crooked. He who approaches it, grieves no more, and liberated (from all bonds of ignorance) becomes free. This is that.'

2. 'He (Brahman)[896] is the swan (sun), dwelling in the bright heaven; he is the Vasu (air), dwelling in the sky; he is the sacrificer (fire), dwelling on the hearth; he is the guest (Soma), dwelling in the sacrificial jar; he dwells in men, in gods (vara), in the sacrifice (*ri*ta), in heaven; he is born in the water, on earth, in the sacrifice (*ri*ta), on the mountains; he is the True and the Great.'

3. 'He (Brahman) it is who sends up the breath (prâ*n*a), and who throws back the breath (apâna). All the Devas (senses) worship him, the adorable (or the dwarf), who sits in the centre.'

4. 'When that incorporated (Brahman), who dwells in the body, is torn away and freed from the body, what remains then? This is that.'

5. 'No mortal lives by the breath that goes up and by the breath that goes down. We live by another, in whom these two repose.'

6. 'Well then, O Gautama, I shall tell thee this mystery, the old Brahman, and what happens to the Self, after reaching death.'

7. 'Some enter the womb in order to have a body, as organic beings, others go into inorganic matter, according to their work and according to their knowledge.'[897]

8. 'He, the highest Person, who is awake in us while we are asleep, shaping one lovely sight after another, that indeed is the Bright, that is

---

[894] *S*vet. Up. III, 13.

[895] Seven apertures in the head, the navel, two below, and the one at the top of the head through which the Self escapes. Cf. *S*vet. Up. III, 18; Bhag. Gîtâ V, 13.

[896] Cf. *Ri*g-veda IV, 40, 5.

[897] Cf. B*ri*h. Âr. II, 2, 13.

Brahman, that alone is called the Immortal. All worlds are contained in it, and no one goes beyond. This is that.'[898]

9. 'As the one fire, after it has entered the world, though one, becomes different according to whatever it burns, thus the one Self within all things becomes different, according to whatever it enters, and exists also without.'[899]

10. 'As the one air, after it has entered the world, though one, becomes different according to whatever it enters, thus the one Self within all things becomes different, according to whatever it enters, and exists also without.'

11. 'As the sun, the eye of the whole world, is not contaminated by the external impurities seen by the eyes, thus the one Self within all things is never contaminated by the misery of the world, being himself without.'[900]

12. 'There is one ruler, the Self within all things, who makes the one form manifold. The wise who perceive him within their Self, to them belongs eternal happiness, not to others.'[901]

13. 'There is one eternal thinker, thinking non-eternal thoughts, who, though one, fulfils the desires of many. The wise who perceive him within their Self, to them belongs eternal peace, not to others.'[902]

14. 'They perceive that highest indescribable pleasure, saying, This is that. How then can I understand it? Has it its own light, or does it reflect light?'

15. 'The sun does not shine there, nor the moon and the stars, nor these lightnings, and much less this fire. When he shines, everything shines after him; by his light all this is lighted.'[903]

SIXTH VALLÎ.

1. 'There is that ancient tree,[904] whose roots grow upward and whose branches grow downward;—that[905] indeed is called the Bright,[906] that is called Brahman, that alone is called the Immortal.[907] All worlds are contained in it, and no one goes beyond. This is that.'

---

[898] Cf. IV, 9; VI, 1.

[899] Cf. B*ri*h. Âr. II, 5, 19.

[900] Cf. Bhag. Gîtâ XIII, 52.

[901] Cf. *S*vet. Up. VI, 12.

[902] Cf. *S*vet. Up. VI, 13.

[903] Cf. *S*vet. Up. VI, 14; Mu*nd*. Up. II, 2, 10; Bhag. Gîtâ XV, 6.

[904] The fig-tree which sends down its branches so that they strike root and form new stems, one tree growing into a complete forest.

[905] Cf. Bhag. Gîtâ XV, 1-3.

[906] Cf. V, 8.

[907] The commentator says that the tree is the world, and its root is Brahman, but there is nothing to support this view in the original, where tree, roots, and branches are taken together as representing the Brahman in its various manifestations.

2. 'Whatever there is, the whole world, when gone forth (from the Brahman), trembles in its breath.[908] That Brahman is a great terror, like a drawn sword. Those who know it become immortal.'

3. 'From terror of Brahman fire burns, from terror the sun burns, from terror Indra and Vâyu, and Death, as the fifth, run away.'[909]

4. 'If a man could not understand it before the falling asunder of his body, then he has to take body again in the worlds of creation.'[910]

5. 'As in a mirror, so (Brahman may be seen clearly) here in this body; as in a dream, in the world of the Fathers; as in the water, he is seen about in the world of the Gandharvas; as in light and shade,[911] in the world of Brahmâ.'

6. 'Having understood that the senses are distinct[912] (from the Âtman), and that their rising and setting (their waking and sleeping) belongs to them in their distinct existence (and not to the Âtman), a wise man grieves no more.'

7. 'Beyond. the senses is the mind, beyond the mind is the highest (created) Being,[913] higher than that Being is the Great Self, higher than the Great, the highest Undeveloped.'

8. 'Beyond the Undeveloped is the Person, the all-pervading and entirely imperceptible. Every creature that knows him is liberated, and obtains immortality.'

9. 'His form is not to be seen, no one beholds him with the eye. He is imagined by the heart, by wisdom, by the mind. Those who know this, are immortal.'[914]

10. 'When the five instruments of knowledge stand still together with the mind, and when the intellect does not move, that is called the highest state.'

11. 'This, the firm holding back of the senses, is what is called Yoga. He must be free from thoughtlessness then, for Yoga comes and goes.'[915]

12. 'He (the Self) cannot be reached by speech, by mind, or by the eye. How can it be apprehended except by him who says: "He is?"'

13. 'By the words "He is," is he to be apprehended, and by

---

[908] According to the commentator, in the highest Brahman.

[909] Cf. Taitt. Up. II, 8, 1.

[910] The commentator translates: 'If a man is able to understand (Brahman), then even before the decay of his body, he is liberated. If he is not able to understand it, then he has to take body again in the created worlds.' I doubt whether it is possible to supply so much, and should prefer to read iha *k*en nâ*s*akad, though I find it difficult to explain how so simple a text should have been misunderstood and corrupted.

[911] Roer: 'As in a picture and in the sunshine.'

[912] They arise from the elements, ether, &c.

[913] Buddhi or intellect, cf. III, 10.

[914] Much better in *S*vet. Up. IV, 20: 'Those who know him by the heart as being in the heart, and by the mind, are immortal.'

[915] *S*ankara explains apyaya by apâya.

(admitting) the reality of both (the invisible Brahman and the visible world, as coming from Brahman). When he has been apprehended by the words "He is," then his reality reveals itself.'

14. 'When all desires that dwell in his heart cease, then the mortal becomes immortal, and obtains Brahman.'

15. 'When all the ties[916] of the heart are severed here on earth, then the mortal becomes immortal—here ends the teaching.'[917]

16. 'There are a hundred and one arteries of the heart,[918] one of them penetrates the crown of the head.[919] Moving upwards by it, a man (at his death) reaches the Immortal;[920] the other arteries serve for departing in different directions.'

17. 'The Person not larger than a thumb, the inner Self, is always settled in the heart of men.[921] Let a man draw that Self forth from his body with steadiness, as one draws the pith from a reed.[922] Let him know that Self as the Bright, as the Immortal; yes, as the Bright, as the Immortal.'[923]

18. Having received this knowledge taught by Death and the whole rule of Yoga (meditation), Nâ*k*iketa became free from passion[924] and death, and obtained Brahman. Thus it will be with another also who knows thus what relates to the Self.

19. May He protect us both! May He enjoy us both! May we acquire Strength together! May our knowledge become bright! May we never quarrel![925] Om! Peace! peace! peace! Harih, Om!

---

[916] Ignorance, passion, &c. Cf. Mu*nd*. Up. II, 11, 10; II, 2, 9.

[917] The teaching of the Vedânta extends so far and no farther. (Cf. Pra*s*na Up. VI, 7.) What follows has reference, according to the commentator, not to him who knows the highest Brahman, for he becomes Brahman at once and migrates no more; but to him who does not know the highest Brahman fully, and therefore migrates to the Brahmaloka, receiving there the reward for his partial knowledge and for his good works.

[918] Cf. *Kh*ând. Up. VIII, 6, 6.

[919] It passes out by the head.

[920] The commentator says: He rises through the sun (Mu*nd*. Up. I, 2, 11) to a world in which he enjoys some kind of immortality.

[921] *S*vet. Up. III. 13.

[922] Roer: 'As from a painter's brush a fibre.'

[923] This repetition marks, as usual, the end of a chapter.

[924] Viraga, free from vice and virtue. It may have been vigara, free from old age. See, however, Mu*nd*. Up. I, 2, 11.

[925] Cf. Taitt. Up. III, 1; III, 10, note.

MU*ND*AKA-UPANISHAD.

FIRST MU*ND*AKA.

FIRST KHA*ND*A.

1. Brahma was the first of the Devas, the maker of the universe, the preserver of the world. He told the knowledge of Brahman, the foundation of all knowledge, to his eldest son Atharva.[926]

2. Whatever Brahmâ told Atharvan, that knowledge of Brahman Atharvan formerly told to Aṅgir; he told it to Satyavâha Bhâradvâ*g*a, and Bhâradvâ*g*a told it in succession to Aṅgiras.

3. *S*aunaka, the great householder, approached Aṅgiras respectfully and asked: 'Sir, what is that through which, if it is known, everything else becomes known?'

4. He said to him: 'Two kinds of knowledge must be known, this is what all who know Brahman tell us, the higher and the lower knowledge.'

5. 'The lower knowledge is the *Ri*g-veda, Ya*g*ur-veda, Sâma-veda, Atharva-veda, *S*ikshâ (phonetics), Kalpa (ceremonial), Vyâkara*n*a (grammar), Nirukta (etymology), *Kh*andas (metre), *G*yotisha (astronomy);[927] but the higher knowledge is that by which the Indestructible (Brahman) is apprehended.'

6. 'That which cannot be seen, nor seized, which has no family and no caste,[928] no eyes nor ears, no hands nor feet, the eternal, the omnipresent (all-pervading), infinitesimal, that which is imperishable, that it is which the wise regard as the source of all beings.'

7. 'As the spider sends forth and draws in its thread, as plants grow on the earth, as from every man hairs spring forth on the head and the body, thus does everything arise here from the Indestructible.'

8. 'The Brahman swells by means of brooding (penance);[929] hence

---

[926] The change between Atharva and Atharvan, like that between Na*k*iketas and Nâ*k*iketa, shows the freedom of the phraseology of the Upanishad, and cannot be used for fixing the date of the constituent elements of the Upanishad.

[927] Other MSS. add here itihâsa-purâ*n*a-nyâya-mîmâ*m*sâ-dharma-*s*âstrâ*n*i.

[928] I translate var*n*a by caste on account of its conjunction with gotra. The commentator translates, 'without origin and without qualities.' We should say that which belongs to no genus or species.

[929] I have translated tapas by brooding, because this is the only word in English which combines the two meanings of warmth and thought. Native authorities actually admit two roots, one tap, to burn, the other tap, to meditate; see commentary on Parâsara-sm*ri*ti, p. 39[b] (MS. Bodl.), Tapa*h* kri*kkh*ra*k*andrâya*n*âdirûpe*n*âhâravarganam. Nanu Vyâsena tapo 'nyathâ smaryate, tapa*h* svadharma-vartitva*m* sau*k*a*m* saṅganibarha*n*am iti; nâya*m* dosha*h*, kri*kkh*râder api svadharmavi*s*eshât. Tapa sa*m*tâpa ity asmâd dhâtor utpannasya tapa*h*-*s*abdasya deha*s*oshan*e* v*ri*ttir mukhyâ. . . . Yat tu tatraivokta*m*, ko 'yam

is produced matter (food); from matter breath,[930] mind, the true,[931] the worlds (seven), and from the works (performed by men in the worlds), the immortal (the eternal effects, rewards, and punishments of works).'

9. 'From him who perceives all and who knows all, whose brooding (penance) consists of knowledge, from him (the highest Brahman) is born that Brahman,[932] name, form,[933] and matter (food).'

SECOND KHA*ND*A.

1. This is the truth:[934] the sacrificial works which they (the poets) saw in the hymns (of the Veda) have been performed in many ways in the Tretâ age.[935] Practise[936] them diligently, ye lovers of truth, this is your path that leads to the world of good works![937]

2. When the fire is lighted and the flame flickers, let a man offer his oblations between the two portions of melted butter, as an offering with faith.

3. If a man's Agnihotra sacrifice[938] is not followed by the new-moon and full-moon sacrifices, by the four-months' sacrifices, and by the harvest sacrifice, if it is unattended by guests, not offered at all, or without the Vaisvadeva ceremony, or not offered according to rule, then it destroys his seven worlds.[939]

---

moksha*h* katha*m* tena sa*m*sâram pratipannavân ity âlo*k*anam arthag*ñ*âs tapa*h* sa*m*santi pa*nd*itâ iti so 'nya eva tapa*hs*abda*h*, tapa âlo*k*ana ity asmâd dhâtor utpanna*h*.

[930] Hira*n*yagarbha, the living world as a whole. Comm.

[931] Satya, if we compare Ka*th*. VI, 7 and III, 10, seems to mean buddhi. Here it is explained by the five elements.

[932] Hira*n*yagarbha. Comm.

[933] Nâmarûpam, a very frequent concept in Buddhistic literature.

[934] In the beginning of the second Kha*nd*a the lower knowledge is first described, referring to the performance of sacrifices and other good deeds. The reward of them is perishable, and therefore a desire is awakened after the higher knowledge.

[935] The Tretâ age is frequently mentioned as the age of sacrifices. I should prefer, however, to take tretâ in the sense of trayî vidyâ, and santata as developed, because the idea that the Tretâ age was distinguished by its sacrifices, seems to me of later origin. Even the theory of the four ages or yugas, though known in the Ait. Brâhma*n*a, is not frequently alluded to in the older Upanishads. See Weber, Ind. Stud. I, p. 283.

[936] The termination tha for ta looks suspiciously Buddhistic; see 'Sanskrit Texts discovered in Japan,' J. R. A. S. 1880, p. 180.

[937] Svak*ri*ta and suk*ri*ta are constantly interchanged. They mean the same, good deeds, or deeds performed by oneself and believed to be good.

[938] At the Agnihotra, the first of all sacrifices, and the type of many others, two portions of âgya are sacrificed on the right and left side of the Âhavanîya altar. The place between the two is called the Âvâpasthâna, and here the oblations to the gods are to be offered. There are. two oblations in the morning to Sûrya and Pragâpati, two in the evening to Agni and Pragâpati. Other sacrifices, such as the Dar*s*a and Pûr*n*amâsa, and those mentioned in verse 3, are connected with the Agnihotra.

[939] The seven worlds form the rewards of a pious sacrificer, the first is Bhu*h*, the last Satya. The seven worlds may also be explained as the worlds of the father, grandfather, and great-grandfather, of the son, the grandson, and great-grandson, and of the sacrificer himself.

4. Kâlî (black), Karâlî (terrific), Manogavâ (swift as thought), Sulohitâ (very red), Sudhûmravar*n*â (purple), Sphuliṅginî (sparkling), and the brilliant Vi*s*varûpî[940] (having all forms), all these playing about are called the seven tongues (of fire).

5. If a man performs his sacred works when these flames are shining, and the oblations follow at the right time, then they lead him as sun-rays to where the one Lord of the Devas dwells.

6. Come hither, come hither! the brilliant oblations say to him, and carry the sacrificer on the rays of the sun, while they utter pleasant speech and praise him, saying: 'This is thy holy Brahma-world (Svarga), gained by thy good works.'

7. But frail, in truth, are those boats, the sacrifices, the eighteen, in which this lower ceremonial has been told.[941] Fools who praise this as the highest good, are subject again and again to old age and death.

8. Fools dwelling in darkness, wise in their own conceit, and puffed up with vain knowledge, go round and round staggering to and fro, like blind men led by the blind.[942]

9. Children, when they have long lived in ignorance, consider themselves happy. Because those who depend on their good works are, owing to their passions, improvident, they fall and become miserable when their life (in the world which they had gained by their good works) is finished.

10. Considering sacrifice and good works as the best, these fools know no higher good, and having enjoyed (their reward) on the height of heaven, gained by good works, they enter again this world or a lower one.

11. But those[943] who practise penance and faith in the forest, tranquil, wise, and living on alms, depart free from passion through the sun to where that immortal Person dwells whose nature is imperishable.[944]

12. Let a Brâhma*n*a, after he has examined all these worlds which

---

[940] Or Vi*s*varu*k*î, if there is any authority for this reading in Mahîdhara's commentary to the Vâgas. Sa*m*hitâ XVII, 79. The Râjah of Besmah's edition has vi*s*varukî, which is also the reading adopted by Rammohun Roy, see Complete Works, vol. i, p. 579.

[941] The commentator takes the eighteen for the sixteen priests, the sacrificer, and his wife. But such an explanation hardly yields a satisfactory meaning, nor does plava mean perishable.

[942] Cf. Ka*th*. Up. II, 5.

[943] According to the commentator, this verse refers to those who know the uselessness of sacrifices and have attained to a knowledge of the qualified Brahman. They live in the forest as Vânaprasthas and Sa*m*nyâsins, practising tapas, i.e. whatever is proper for their state, and *s*raddhâ, i.e. a knowledge of Hira*n*yagarbha. The wise are the learned G*ri*hasthas, while those who live on alms are those who have forsaken their family.

[944] That person is Hira*n*yagarbha. His immortality is relative only, it lasts no longer than the world (sa*m*sâra).

are gained by works, acquire freedom from all desires. Nothing that is eternal (not made) can be gained by what is not eternal (made). Let him, in order to understand this, take fuel in his hand and approach a Guru who is learned and dwells entirely in Brahman.

13. To that pupil who has approached him respectfully, whose thoughts are not troubled by any desires, and who has obtained perfect peace, the wise teacher truly told that knowledge of Brahman through which he knows the eternal and true Person.

SECOND MU*ND*AKA.

FIRST KHA*ND*A.

1. This is the truth. As from a blazing fire sparks, being like unto fire,[945] fly forth a thousandfold, thus are various beings brought forth from the Imperishable, my friend, and return thither also.

2. That heavenly Person is without body, he is both without and within, not produced, without breath and without mind, pure, higher than the high Imperishable.[946]

3. From him (when entering on creation) is born breath, mind, and all organs of sense, ether, air, light, water, and the earth, the support of all.

4. Fire (the sky) is his head, his eyes the sun and the moon, the quarters his ears, his speech the Vedas disclosed, the wind his breath, his heart the universe; from his feet came the earth; he is indeed the inner Self of all things.[947]

5. From him comes Agni (fire),[948] the sun being the fuel; from the moon (Soma) comes rain (Parganya); from the earth herbs; and man gives seed unto the woman. Thus many beings are begotten from the Person (purusha).

6. From him come the *Rik*, the Sâman, the Yagush, the Dîkshâ (initiatory rites), all sacrifices and offerings of animals, and the fees bestowed on priests, the year too, the sacrificer, and the worlds, in which the moon shines brightly and the sun.

7. From him the many Devas too are begotten, the Sâdhyas (genii), men, cattle, birds, the up and down breathings, rice and corn (for sacrifices), penance, faith, truth, abstinence, and law.

8. The seven senses (prâ*n*a) also spring from him, the seven lights (acts of sensation), the seven kinds of fuel (objects by which the senses are lighted), the seven sacrifices (results of sensation), these seven worlds (the places of the senses, the worlds determined by the senses)

---

945 Cf. B*r*ih. Âr. II, 1, 20.

946 The high Imperishable is here the creative, the higher the noncreative Brahman.

947 Called Vish*n*u and Virâ*g* by the commentators.

948 There are five fires, those of heaven, rain, earth, man, and woman. Comm.

in which the senses move, which rest in the cave (of the heart), and are placed there seven and seven.

9. Hence come the seas and all the mountains, from him flow the rivers of every kind; hence come all herbs and the juice through which the inner Self subsists with the elements.

10. The Person is all this, sacrifice, penance, Brahman, the highest immortal; he who knows this hidden in the cave (of the heart), he, O friend, scatters the knot of ignorance here on earth.

SECOND KHA*ND*A.

1. Manifest, near, moving in the cave (of the heart) is the great Being. In it everything is centred which ye know as moving, breathing, and blinking, as being and not-being, as adorable, as the best, that is beyond the understanding of creatures.

2. That which is brilliant, smaller than small, that on which the worlds are founded and their inhabitants, that is the indestructible Brahman, that is the breath, speech, mind; that is the true, that is the immortal. That is to be hit. Hit it, O friend!

3. Having taken the Upanishad as the bow, as the great weapon, let him place on it the arrow, sharpened by devotion! Then having drawn it with a thought directed to that which is, hit the mark, O friend, viz. that which is the Indestructible!

4. Om is the bow, the Self is the arrow, Brahman is called its aim. It is to be hit by a man who is not thoughtless; and then, as the arrow (becomes one with the target), he will become one with Brahman.

5. In him the heaven, the earth, and the sky are woven, the mind also with all the senses. Know him alone as the Self, and leave off other words! He is the bridge of the Immortal.

6. He moves about becoming manifold within the heart where the arteries meet, like spokes fastened to the nave. Meditate on the Self as Om! Hail to you, that you may cross beyond (the sea of) darkness!

7. He who understands all and who knows all, he to whom all this glory in the world belongs, the Self, is placed in the ether, in the heavenly city of Brahman (the heart). He assumes the nature of mind, and becomes the guide of the body of the senses. He subsists in food, in close proximity to the heart. The wise who understand this, behold the Immortal which shines forth full of bliss.

8. The fetter of the heart is broken, all doubts are solved, all his works (and their effects) perish when He has been beheld who is high and low (cause and effect).[949]

9. In the highest golden sheath there is the Brahman without passions and without parts. That is pure, that is the light of lights, that

---

[949] Cf. Ka*th*. Up. VI, 15.

is it which they know who know the Self.

10. The[950] sun does not thine there, nor the moon and the stars, nor these lightnings, and much less this fire. When he shines, everything shines after him; by his light all this is lighted.[951]

11. That immortal Brahman is before, that Brahman is behind, that Brahman is right and left. It has gone forth below and above; Brahman alone is all this, it is the best.

THIRD MU*ND*AKA.

FIRST KHA*ND*A.

1. Two birds, inseparable friends, cling to the same tree. One of them eats the sweet fruit, the other looks on without eating.[952]

2. On the same tree man sits grieving, immersed, bewildered by his own impotence (an-îs*â*). But when he sees the other lord (îs*â*) contented and knows his glory, then his grief passes away.[953]

3. When the seer sees the brilliant maker and lord (of the world) as the Person who has his source in Brahman, then he is wise, and shaking off good and evil, he reaches the highest oneness, free from passions;

4. For he is the Breath shining forth in all beings, and he who understands this becomes truly wise, not a talker only. He revels in the Self, he delights in the Self, and having performed his works (truthfulness, penance, meditation, &c.) he rests, firmly established in Brahman, the best of those who know Brahman.[954]

5. By truthfulness, indeed, by penance, right knowledge, and abstinence must that Self be gained; the Self whom spotless anchorites gain is pure, and like a light within the body.

6. The true prevails, not the untrue; by the true the path is laid out, the way of the gods (devayâna*h*), on which the old sages, satisfied in their desires, proceed to where there is that highest place of the True One.

---

[950] Ka*th*. Up. V, 15.

[951] *S*vet. Up. VI, 14; Bhag. Gîtâ IX, 15, 6.

[952] Cf. Rv. I, 164, 20; Nir. XIV, 30; *S*vet. Up. IV, 6; Ka*th*. Up. III, 1.

[953] Cf. *S*vet. Up. IV, 7.

[954] The commentator states that, besides âtmarati*h* kriyâvân, there was another reading, viz. âtmaratikriyâvân. This probably owed its origin to a difficulty felt in reconciling kriyâvân, performing acts, with the brahmavidâ*m* varish*thah*, the best of those who know Brahman, works being utterly incompatible with a true knowledge of Brahman. Kriyâvân, however, as *S*ankara points out, may mean here simply, having performed meditation and other acts conducive to a knowledge of Brahman. Probably truthfulness, penance, &c., mentioned in the next following verse, are the kriyâs or works intended. For grammatical reasons also this reading is preferable. But the last foot esha brahmavidâ*m* varish*thah* is clearly defective. If we examine the commentary, we see that *S*ankara read brahmanish*thah*, and that he did not read esha, which would give us the correct metre, brahmanish*tho* brahmavidâ*m* varish*thah*.

7. That (true Brahman) shines forth grand, divine., inconceivable, smaller than small; it is far beyond what is far and yet near here, it is hidden in the cave (of the heart) among those who see it even here.

8. He is not apprehended by the eye, nor by speech, nor by the other senses, not by penance or good works.[955] When a man's nature has become purified by the serene light of knowledge, then he sees him, meditating on him as without parts.

9. That subtle Self is to be known by thought (*k*etas) there where breath has entered fivefold, for every thought of men is interwoven with the senses, and when thought is purified, then the Self arises.

10. Whatever state a man, whose nature is purified imagines, and whatever desires he desires (for himself or for others),[956] that state he conquers and those desires he obtains. Therefore let every man who desires happiness worship the man who knows the Self.[957]

SECOND KHA*ND*A.

1. He (the knower of the Self) knows that highest home of Brahman,[958] in which all is contained and shines brightly. The wise who, without desiring happiness, worship that Person,[959] transcend this seed, (they are not born again.)

2. He who forms desires in his mind, is born again through his desires here and there. But to him whose desires are fulfilled and who is conscious of the true Self (within himself) all desires vanish, even here on earth.

3. That Self[960] cannot be gained by the Veda, nor by understanding, nor by much learning. He whom the Self chooses, by him the Self can be gained. The Self chooses him (his body) as his own.

4. Nor is that Self to be gained by one who is destitute of strength, or without earnestness, or without right meditation. But if a wise man strives after it by those means (by strength, earnestness, and right meditation), then his Self enters the home of Brahman.

5. When they have reached him (the Self), the sages become satisfied through knowledge, they are conscious of their Self, their passions have passed away, and they are tranquil. The wise, having reached Him who is omnipresent everywhere, devoted to the Self, enter into him wholly.

---

955 Cf. Ka*th*. Up. VI, 12.

956 Cf. B*ri*h. Âr. I, 4, 15.

957 All this is said by the commentator to refer to a knowledge of the conditioned Brahman only.

958 See verse 4.

959 The commentator refers purusha to the knower of the Self.

960 Ka*th*. Up. II, 23.

6. Having well ascertained the object of the knowledge of the Vedânta,[961] and having purified their nature by the Yoga[962] of renunciation, all anchorites, enjoying the highest immortality, become free at the time of the great end (death) in the worlds of Brahmâ.

7. Their fifteen parts[963] enter into their elements, their Devas (the senses) into their (corresponding) Devas.[964] Their deeds and their Self with all his knowledge become all one in the highest Imperishable.

8. As the flowing rivers disappear in the sea,[965] losing their name and their form, thus a wise man, freed from name and form, goes to the divine Person, who is greater than the great.[966]

9. He who knows that highest Brahman, becomes even Brahman. In his race no one is born ignorant of Brahman. He overcomes grief, he overcomes evil; free from the fetters of the heart, he becomes immortal.

10. And this is declared by the following *Rik*-verse: 'Let a man tell this science of Brahman to those only who have performed all (necessary) acts, who are versed in the Vedas, and firmly established in (the lower) Brahman, who themselves offer as an oblation the one *R*ishi (Agni), full of faith, and by whom the rite of (carrying fire on) the head has been performed, according to the rule (of the Âtharva*n*as).'

11. The *R*ishi Aṅgiras formerly told this true (science[967]); a man who has not performed the (proper) rites, does not read it. Adoration to the highest *R*ishis! Adoration to the highest *R*ishis!

---

[961] Cf. Taitt. Âr. X, 12, 3; *S*vet. Up. VI, 22; Kaiv. Up. 3; see Weber, Ind. Stud. I, p. 288.

[962] By the Yoga system, which, through restraint (yoga), leads a man to true knowledge.

[963] Cf. Pra*s*na Up. VI, 4.

[964] The eye into the sun, &c.

[965] Cf. Pra*s*na Up. VI, 5.

[966] Greater than the conditioned Brahman. Comm.

[967] To *S*aunaka, cf. I, 1, 3

TAITTIRÎYAKA-UPANISHAD.

FIRST VALLÎ,

OR, THE CHAPTER ON *S*ÎKSHÂ (PRONUNCIATION).

FIRST ANUVÂKA.[968]

1. Hari*h*, OM! May Mitra be propitious to us, and Varu*n*a, Aryaman also, Indra, B*ri*haspati, and the wide-striding Vish*n*u.[969]

Adoration to Brahman! Adoration to thee, O Vâyu (air)! Thou indeed art the visible Brahman. I shall proclaim thee alone as the visible Brahman. I shall proclaim the right. I shall proclaim the true (scil. Brahman).

(1-5)[970] May it protect me! May it protect the teacher! yes, may it protect me, and may it protect the teacher! Om! Peace! peace! peace!

SECOND ANUVÂKA.

1. Om![971] Let us explain *S*îkshâ, the doctrine of pronunciation, viz. letter, accent, quantity, effort (in the formation of letters), modulation, and union of letters (sandhi). This is the lecture on *S*îkshâ.

THIRD ANUVÂKA.

1. May glory come to both of us (teacher and pupil) together! May Vedic light belong to both of us!

Now let us explain the Upanishad (the secret meaning) of the union (sa*m*hitâ),[972] under five heads, with regard to the worlds, the heavenly lights, knowledge, offspring, and self (body). People call these the great Sa*m*hitâs.

First, with regard to the worlds. The earth is the former element, heaven the latter, ether their union;

---

968 This invocation is here counted as an Anuvâka; see Taitt. Âr., ed. Rajendralal Mitra, p. 725.

969 This verse is taken from *Ri*g-veda-sa*m*hitâ I, 90, 9. The deities are variously explained by the commentators: Mitra as god of the Prâ*n*a (forth-breathing) and of the day; Varu*n*a as god of the Apâna (off-breathing) and of the night. Aryaman is supposed to represent the eye or the sun; Indra, strength; B*ri*haspati, speech or intellect; Vish*n*u, the feet. Their favour is invoked, because it is only if they grant health that the study of the highest wisdom can proceed without fail.

970 Five short sentences, in addition to the one paragraph. Such sentences occur at the end of other Anuvâkas also, and are counted separately.

971 Cf. Rig-veda-prâti*s*âkhya, ed. M. M., p. iv seq.

972 Cf. Aitareya-âra*n*yaka III, 1, 1 (Sacred Books, vol. i, p. 247).

2. That union takes place through Vâyu (air). So much with regard to the worlds.

Next, with regard to the heavenly lights. Agni (fire) is the former element, Âditya (the sun) the latter, water their union. That union takes place through lightning. So much with regard to the heavenly lights.

Next, with regard to knowledge. The teacher is the former element,

The pupil the latter, knowledge their union. That union takes place through the recitation of the Veda. So much with regard to knowledge.

Next, with regard to offspring. The mother is the former element, the father the latter, offspring their union. That union takes place through procreation. So much with regard to offspring.

4. Next, with regard to the self (body). The lower jaw is the former element, the upper jaw the latter, speech their union. That union takes place through speech. So much with regard to the Self. These are the great Sa*m*hitâs. He who knows these Sa*m*hitâs (unions), as here explained, becomes united with offspring, cattle, Vedic light, food, and with the heavenly world.

FOURTH ANUVÂKA.

1. May he[973] who is the strong bull of the Vedas, assuming all forms, who has risen from the Vedas, from the Immortal, may that Indra (lord) strengthen me with wisdom! May I, O God, become an upholder of the Immortal!

May my body be able, my tongue sweet, may I hear much with my ears! Thou (Om) art the shrine (of Brahman), covered by wisdom. Guard what I have learnt.[974]

She (*S*rî, happiness) brings near and spreads,

2. And makes, without delay, garments for herself, cows, food, and drink at all times; therefore bring that *S*rî (happiness) hither to me, the woolly, with her cattle![975] Svâhâ![976] May the Brahman-students come to me, Svâhâ! May they come from all sides, Svâhâ! May they come forth to me, Svâhâ! May they practise restraint, Svâhâ! May they enjoy peace, Svâhâ!

3. May I be a glory among men, Svâhâ! May I be better than the richest, Svâhâ! May I enter into thee, O treasure (Om), Svâhâ! Thou, O

---

[973] The next verses form the prayer and oblation of those who wish for wisdom and happiness. In the first verse it is supposed that the Om is invoked, the most powerful syllable of the Vedas, the essence extracted from all the Vedas, and in the end a name of Brahman. See *Kh*ând. Up. p. x seq.

[974] Here end the prayers for the attainment of wisdom, to be followed by oblations for the attainment of happiness.

[975] The construction is not right. Woolly, loma*s*â, is explained as 'possessed of woolly sheep.'

[976] With the interjection Svâhâ each oblation is offered.

treasure,[977] enter into me, Svâhâ! In thee, consisting of a thousand branches, in thee, O treasure, I am cleansed, Svâhâ! As water runs downward, as the months go to the year, so, O preserver of the world, may Brahman-students always come to me from all sides, Svâhâ!

(1) Thou art a refuge! Enlighten me! Take possession of me!

FIFTH ANUVÂKA.

1. Bhû, Bhuvas, Suvas,[978] these are the three sacred interjections (vyâh*ri*ti). Mâhâ*k*amasya taught a fourth, viz. Mahas, which is Brahman, which is the Self. The others (devatâs) are its members.

Bhû is this world, Bhuvas is the sky, Suvas is the other world.

2. Mahas is the sun. All the worlds are increased by the sun. Bhû is Agni (fire), Bhuvas is Vâyu (air), Suvas is Âditya (sun). Mahas is the moon. All the heavenly lights are increased by the moon.

Bhû is the *Rik*-verses, Bhuvas is the Sâman-verses, Suvas is the Yagus-verses.

3. Mahas is Brahman. All the Vedas are increased by the Brahman.

(1-2) Bhû is Prâ*n*a (up-breathing), Bhuvas is Apâna, (down-breathing), Suvas is Vyâna (back-breathing). Mahas is food. All breathings are increased by food.

Thus there are these four times four, the four and four sacred interjections. He who knows these,

(1-2) Knows the Brahman. All Devas bring offerings to him.

SIXTH ANUVÂKA.

1. There is the ether within the heart, and in it there is the Person (purusha) consisting of mind, immortal, golden.

Between the two palates there hangs the uvula, like a nipple—that is the starting-point of Indra (the lord).[979] Where the root of the hair divides, there he opens the two sides of the head, and saying Bhû, he enters Agni (the fire); saying Bhuvas, he enters Vâyu (air);

2. Saying Suvas, he enters Âditya (sun); saying Mahas, he enters Brahman. He there obtains lordship, he reaches the lord of the mind. He becomes lord of speech, lord of sight, lord of hearing, lord of knowledge. Nay, more than this. There is the Brahman whose body is ether, whose nature is true, rejoicing in the senses (prâ*n*a), delighted in the mind, perfect in peace, and immortal.

(1) Worship thus, O Prâ*k*înayogya!

---

[977] Bhaga, here explained as bhagavat.

[978] The text varies between Bhû, Bhuvas, Suvas, Mahas, and Bhû, Bhuvar, Suvar, Mahar.

[979] Cf. I, 4, 1.

SEVENTH ANUVÂKA.

1. 'The earth, the sky, heaven, the four quarters, and the intermediate quarters,'—'Agni (fire), Vâyu (air), Âditya (sun), *K*andramas (moon), and the stars,'—'Water, herbs, trees, ether, the universal Self (virâ*g*),'—so much with reference to material objects (bhûta).

Now with reference to the self (the body): 'Prâ*n*a (up-breathing), Apâna (down-breathing), Vyâna (back-breathing), Udâna (out-breathing), and Samâ*n*a (on-breathing),'—'The eye, the ear, mind, speech, and touch,'—'The skin, flesh, muscle, bone, and marrow.' Having dwelt on this (fivefold arrangement of the worlds, the gods, beings, breathings, senses, and elements of the body), a *R*ishi said: 'Whatever exists is fivefold (pâṅkta).'[980]

(1) By means of the one fivefold set (that referring to the body) he completes the other fivefold set.

EIGHTH ANUVÂKA.

1. Om means Brahman. 2. Om means all this. 3. Om means obedience. When they have been told, 'Om, speak,' they speak. 4. After Om they sing Sâmans. 5. After Om they recite hymns. 6. After Om the Adhvaryu gives the response. 7. After Om the Brahman-priest gives orders. 8. After Om he (the sacrificer) allows the performance of the Agnihotra. 9. When a Brâhma*n*a is going to begin his lecture, he says, 10. 'Om, may I acquire Brahman (the Veda).' He thus acquires the Veda.

NINTH ANUVÂKA.[981]

1. (What is necessary?) The night, and learning and practising the Veda. The true, and learning and practising the Veda. Penance, and learning and practising the Veda. Restraint, and learning and practising the Veda. Tranquillity, and learning and practising the Veda. The fires (to be consecrated), and learning and practising the Veda. The Agnihotra sacrifice, and learning and practising the Veda. Guests (to be entertained), and learning and practising the Veda. Man's duty, and learning and practising the Veda. Children, and learning and practising the Veda.

---

[980] Cf. B*ri*h. Âr. Up. I, 4, 17.

[981] This chapter is meant to show that knowledge alone, though it secures the highest object, is not sufficient by itself, but must be preceded by works. The learning of the Veda by heart and the practising of it so as not to forget it again, these two must always have been previously performed.

(1-6) Marriage, and learning and practising the Veda. Children's children, and learning and practising the Veda.

Satyavakas Râthîtara thinks that the true only is necessary. Taponitya Paurasishti thinks that penance only is necessary. Nâka Maudgalya thinks that learning and practising the Veda only are necessary,—for that is penance, that is penance.

TENTH ANUVÂKA.

1. 'I am he who shakes the tree (i.e. the tree of the world, which has to be cut down by knowledge). 2. My glory is like the top of a mountain. 3. I, whose pure light (of knowledge) has risen high, am that which is truly immortal, as it resides in the sun. 4. I am the brightest treasure. 5. I am wise, immortal, imperishable.'[982] 6. This is the teaching of the Veda, by the poet Trisanku.

ELEVENTH ANUVÂKA.

1. After having taught the Veda, the teacher instructs the pupil: 'Say what is true! Do thy duty! Do not neglect the study of the Veda! After having brought to thy teacher his proper reward, do not cut off the line of children! Do not swerve from the truth! Do not swerve from duty! Do not neglect what is useful! Do not neglect greatness! Do not neglect the learning and teaching of the Veda!

2. 'Do not neglect the (sacrificial) works due to the Gods and Fathers! Let thy mother be to thee like unto a god! Let thy father be to thee like unto a god! Let thy teacher be to thee like unto a god! Let thy guest be to thee like unto a god! Whatever actions are blameless, those should be regarded, not others. Whatever good works have been performed by us, those should be observed by thee,—

3. 'Not others. And there are some Brâhmanas better than we. They should be comforted by thee by giving them a seat. Whatever is given should be given with faith, not without faith,—with joy, with modesty, with fear, with kindness. If there should be any doubt in thy mind with regard to any sacred act or with regard to conduct,—

4. 'In that case conduct thyself as Brâhmanas who possess good judgment conduct themselves therein, whether they be appointed or not,[983] as long as they are not too severe, but devoted to duty. And with regard to things that have been spoken against, as Brâhmanas who

---

[982] This verse has been translated as the commentator wishes it to be understood, in praise of that knowledge of Self which is only to be obtained after all other duties, and, more particularly, the study of the Veda, have been performed. The text is probably corrupt, and the interpretation fanciful.

[983] Aparaprayuktâ iti svatantrâh. For other renderings, see Weber, Ind. Stud. II, p. 216.

possess good judgment conduct themselves therein, whether they be appointed or not, as long as they are not too severe, but devoted to duty,

(1-7) Thus conduct thyself 'This is the rule. This is the teaching. This is the true purport (Upanishad) of the Veda. This is the command. Thus should you observe. Thus should this be observed.'

TWELFTH ANUVÂKA.

1. May Mitra be propitious to us, and Varu*n*a, Aryaman also, Indra, B*ri*haspati, and the wide-striding Vish*n*u! Adoration to Brahman! Adoration to thee, O Vâyu! Thou indeed art the visible Brahman. I proclaimed thee alone as the visible Brahman.

(1-5) I proclaimed the right. I proclaimed the true. It protected me. It protected the teacher. Yes, it protected me, it protected the teacher. Om! Peace! peace! peace!

SECOND VALLÎ,

OR, THE CHAPTER ON ÂNANDA (BLISS).

Hari*h*, Om! May it (the Brahman) protect us both (teacher and pupil)! May it enjoy us both! May we acquire strength together! May our knowledge become bright! May we never quarrel! Peace! peace! peace![984]

FIRST ANUVÂKA.

He who knows the Brahman attains the highest (Brahman). On this the following verse is recorded:

'He who knows Brahman, which is (i.e. cause, not effect), which is conscious, which is without end, as hidden in the depth (of the heart), in the highest ether, he enjoys all blessings, at one with the omniscient Brahman.'

From that Self[985] (Brahman) sprang ether (âkâ*s*a, that through which we hear); from ether air (that through which we hear and feel); from air fire (that through which we hear, feel, and see); from fire water (that through which we hear, feel, see, and taste); from water earth (that through which we hear, feel, see, taste, and smell). From earth herbs, from herbs food, from food seed, from seed man. Man thus consists of the essence of food. This is his head, this his right arm, this his left arm,

---

[984] Not counted here as an Anuvâka. The other Anuvâkas are divided into a number of small sentences.

[985] Compare with this s*r*ish*t*ikrama, *Kh*ând. Up. VI, 2; Ait. Âr. II, 4, 1.

this his trunk (Âtman), this the seat (the support).[986]

On this there is also the following *S*loka:

SECOND ANUVÂKA.

'From food[987] are produced all creatures which dwell on earth. Then they live by food, and in the end they return to food. For food is the oldest of all beings, and therefore it is called panacea (sarvaushadha, i.e. consisting of all herbs, or quieting the heat of the body of all beings).'

They who worship food as Brahman,[988] obtain all food. For food is the oldest of all beings, and therefore it is called panacea. From food all creatures are produced; by food, when born, they grow. Because it is fed on, or because it feeds on beings, therefore it is called food (anna).

Different from this, which consists of the essence of food, is the other, the inner Self, which consists of breath. The former is filled by this. It also has the shape of man. Like the human shape of the former is the human shape of the latter. Prâ*n*a (up-breathing) is its head. Vyâna (back-breathing) is its right arm. Apâna (down-breathing) is its left arm. Ether is its trunk. The earth the seat (the support).

On this there is also the following *S*loka:

THIRD ANUVÂKA.

'The Devas breathe after breath (prâ*n*a), so do men and cattle. Breath is the life of beings, therefore it is called sarvâyusha (all-enlivening).'

They who worship breath as Brahman, obtain the full life. For breath is the life of all beings, and therefore it is called sarvâyusha. The embodied Self of this (consisting of breath) is the same as that of the former (consisting of food).

Different from this, which consists of breath, is the other, the inner Self, which consists of mind. The former is filled by this. It also has the shape of man. Like the human shape of the former is the human shape of the latter. Yagus is its head. *Rik* is its right arm. Sâman is its left arm. The doctrine (âde*s*a, i.e. the Brâhma*n*a) is its trunk. The Atharvâṅgiras (Atharva-hymns) the seat (the support).

On this there is also the following *S*loka:

---

[986] The text has 'the tail, which is his support.' But pratish*th*â seems to have been added, the Anuvâka ending originally with pu*kkh*a, which is explained by nâbher adhastâd yad aṅgam. In the Persian translation the different members are taken for members of a bird, which is not unlikely.

[987] Anna is sometimes used in the more general sense of matter.

[988] Worship consisting in the knowledge that they are born of food, live by food, and end in food, which food is Brahman.

FOURTH ANUVÂKA.[989]

'He who knows the bliss of that Brahman, from whence all speech, with the mind, turns away unable to reach it, he never fears.' The embodied Self of this (consisting of mind) is the same as that of the former (consisting of breath).

Different from this, which consists of mind, is the other, the inner Self, which consists of understanding. The former is filled by this. It also has the shape of man. Like the human shape of the former is the human shape of the latter. Faith is its head. What is right is its right arm. What is true is its left arm.

Absorption (yoga) is its trunk. The great (intellect?) is the seat (the support).

On this there is also the following *S*loka:

FIFTH ANUVÂKA.

'Understanding performs the sacrifice, it performs all sacred acts. All Devas worship understanding as Brahman, as the oldest. If a man knows understanding as Brahman, and if he does not swerve from it, he leaves all evils behind in the body, and attains all his wishes.' The embodied Self of this (consisting of understanding) is the same as that of the former (consisting of mind).

Different from this, which consists of understanding, is the other inner Self, which consists of bliss. The former is filled by this. It also has the shape of man. Like the human shape of the former is the human shape of the latter. Joy is its head. Satisfaction its right arm. Great satisfaction is its left arm. Bliss is its trunk. Brahman is the seat (the support).

On this there is also the following *S*loka:

SIXTH ANUVÂKA.

'He who knows the Brahman as non-existing, becomes himself non-existing. He who knows the Brahman as existing, him we know himself as existing.' The embodied Self of this (bliss) is the same as that of the former (understanding).

Thereupon follow the questions of the pupil:

'Does any one who knows not, after he has departed this life, ever go to that world? Or does he who knows, after he has departed, go to

[989] Cf. II, 9.

that world?'[990]

The answer is: He wished, may I be many,[991] may I grow forth. He brooded over himself (like a man performing penance). After he had thus brooded, he sent forth (created) all, whatever there is. Having sent forth, he entered into it. Having entered it, he became sat (what is manifest) and tyat (what is not manifest), defined and undefined, supported and not supported, (endowed with) knowledge and without knowledge (as stones), real and unreal.[992] The Sattya (true) became all this whatsoever, and therefore the wise call it (the Brahman) Sat-tya (the true).

On this there is also this *S*loka:

SEVENTH ANUVÂKA.

'In the beginning this was non-existent (not yet defined by form and name). From it was born what exists. That made itself its Self, therefore it is called the Self-made.'[993] That which is Self-made is a flavour[994] (can be tasted), for only after perceiving a flavour can any one perceive pleasure. Who could breathe, who could breathe forth, if that bliss (Brahman) existed not in the ether (in the heart)? For he alone causes blessedness.

When he finds freedom from fear and rest in that which is invisible, incorporeal, undefined, unsupported, then he has obtained the fearless. For if he makes but the smallest distinction in it, there is fear for him}.[995] But that fear exists only for one who thinks himself wise,[996] (not for the true sage.)

On this there is also this *S*loka:

---

[990] As he who knows and he who knows not, are both sprung from Brahman, the question is supposed to be asked by the pupil, whether both will equally attain Brahman.

[991] In the *Kh*ândogya-upanishad VI, 2, 1, where a similar account of the creation is given, the subject is spoken of as tad, neuter. It is said there: 'In the beginning there was that only which is, one only, without a second. It willed, may I be many,' &c. (Cf. B*ri*h. Âr. Up. Vol. ii, p. 52.)

[992] What appears as real and unreal to the senses, not the really real and unreal.

[993] Cf. Ait. Up. I, 2, 3.

[994] As flavour is the cause of pleasure, so Brahman is the cause of all things. The wise taste the flavour of existence, and know that it proceeds from Brahman, the Self-made. See Kaushîtaki-upanishad I, 5; Sacred Books, vol. i, p. 277.

[995] Fear arises only from what is not ourselves. Therefore, as soon as there is even the smallest distinction made between our Self and the real Self, there is a possibility of fear. The explanation ud = api, aram = alpam is very doubtful, but recognised in the schools. It could hardly be a proverbial expression, 'if he makes another stomach' meaning as much as, 'if he admits another person.' According to the commentator, we should translate, 'for one who knows (a difference), and does not know the oneness.'

[996] I read manvânasya, the commentator amanvânasya.

EIGHTH ANUVÂKA.

(1) 'From terror of it (Brahman) the wind blows, from terror the sun rises; from terror of it Agni and Indra, yea Death runs as the fifth.'[997]

Now this is an examination of (what is meant by) Bliss (ânanda):

Let there be a noble young man, who is well read (in the Veda), very swift, firm, and strong, and let the whole world be full of wealth for him, that is one measure of human bliss.

One hundred times that human bliss (2) is one measure of the bliss of human Gandharvas (genii), and likewise of a great sage (learned in the Vedas) who is free from desires.

One hundred times that bliss of human Gandharvas is one measure of the bliss of divine Gandharvas (genii), and likewise of a great sage who is free from desires.

One hundred times that bliss of divine Gandharvas is one measure of the bliss of the Fathers, enjoying their long estate, and likewise of a great sage who is free from desires.

One hundred times that bliss of the Fathers is one measure of the bliss of the Devas, born in the Âgâna heaven (through the merit of their lawful works), (3) and likewise of a great sage who is free from desires.

One hundred times that bliss of the Devas born in the Âgâna heaven is one measure of the bliss of the sacrificial Devas, who go to the Devas by means of their Vaidik sacrifices, and likewise of a great sage who is free from desires.

One hundred times that bliss of the sacrificial Devas is one measure of the bliss of the (thirty-three) Devas, and likewise of a great sage who is free from desires.

One hundred times that bliss of the (thirty-three) Devas is one measure of the bliss of Indra, (4) and likewise of a great sage who is free from desires.

One hundred times that bliss of Indra is one measure of the bliss of B*ri*haspati, and likewise of a great sage who is free from desires.

One hundred times that bliss of B*ri*haspati is one measure of the bliss of Pragâpati, and likewise of a great sage who is free from desires.

One hundred times that bliss of Pragâpati is one measure of the bliss of Brahman, and likewise of a great sage who is free from desires.

(5) He[998] who is this (Brahman) in man, and he who is that (Brahman) in the sun, both are one.[999]

---

997 Ka*th*. Up. VI, 3.

998 Cf. III, 10, 4.

999 In giving the various degrees of happiness, the author of the Upanishad gives us at the same time the various classes of human and divine beings which we must suppose were recognised in his time. We have Men, human Gandharvas, divine Gandharvas,

Fathers (pitaras *k*iralokalokâ*h*), born Gods (âgânagâ devâ*h*), Gods by merit (karmadevâ*h*), Gods, Indra, B*ri*haspati, Pragâpati, Brahman. Such a list would seem to be the invention of an individual rather than the result of an old tradition, if it did not occur in a very similar form in the *S*atapatha-brâhma*n*a, Mâdhyandina-*s*âkhâ XIV, 7, 1 ,31, Kâ*n*va-*s*âkhâ (B*ri*h. Âr. Up. IV, 3, 32). Here, too, the highest measure of happiness is ascribed to the Brahmaloka, and other beings are supposed to share a certain measure only of its supreme happiness. The scale begins in the Mâdhyandina-*s*âkhâ with men, who are followed by the Fathers (pitaro *g*italokâ*h*), the Gods by merit (karmadevâ*h*), the Gods by birth (âgânadevâ*h*, with whom the *S*rotriya is joined), the world of Gods, the world of Gandharvas, the world of Pragâpati, the world of Brahman. In the B*ri*had-âra*n*yaka-upanishad we have Men, Fathers, Gandharvas, Gods by merit, Gods by birth, Pragâpati, and Brahman. If we place the three lists side by side, we find—

TAITTIRÎYA-UPAN.	*S*ATAPATHA-BRÂH.	B*RI*HADÂRA*N*.-UPAN.
Men	Men	Men
Human Gandharvas (and *S*rotriya)	—	—
Divine Gandharvas	—	—
Fathers (*k*iraloka)	Fathers (*g*italoka)	Fathers (*g*italoka)
	—	Gandharvas
Gods by birth	Gods by merit	Gods by merit
Gods by merit	Gods by birth (and *S*rotriya)	Gods by birth (and *S*rotriya)
Gods	Gods	—
Indra	Gandharvas	—
B*ri*haspati	—	—
Pra*g*âpati	Pra*g*âpati	Pra*g*âpati
Brahman	Brahman	Brahman.

The commentators do not help us much. *S*aṅkara on the Taittirîyaka-upanishad explains the human Gandharvas as men who have become Gandharvas, a kind of fairies; divine Gandharvas, as Gandharvas by birth. The Fathers or Manes are called Kiraloka, because they remain long, though not for ever, in their world. The âgânaga Gods are explained as born in the world of the Devas through their good works (smârta), while the Karmadevas are explained as born there through their sacred works (vaidika). The Gods are the thirty-three, whose lord is Indra, and whose teacher B*ri*haspati. Pragâpati is Virâg, Brahman Hira*n*yagarbha. Dvivedagaṅga, in his commentary on the *S*atapatha-brâhma*n*a, explains the Fathers as those who, proceeding on the Southern path, have conquered their world, more particularly by having themselves offered in their life sacrifices to their Fathers. The Karmadevas, according to him, are those who have become Devas by sacred works (*s*rauta), the Âgânadevas those who were gods before there were men. The Gods are Indra and the rest, while the Gandharvas are not explained. Pragâpati is Virâg, Brahman is Hira*n*yagarbha. Lastly, *S*aṅkara, in his commentary on the B*ri*hadâra*n*yakaupanishad, gives nearly the same explanation as before; only that he makes âgânadevâ*h* still clearer, by explaining them as gods âgânata*h*, i.e. utpattita*h*, from their birth.

The arrangement of these beings and their worlds, one rising above the other, reminds us of the cosmography of the Buddhists, but the elements, though in a less systematic form, existed evidently before. Thus we find in the so-called Gargî-brâhma*n*a (Satapatha-brâhma*n*a XIV, 6, 6, 1) the following succession: Water, air, ether [Deest in Kânva-*s*âkhâ.], the worlds of the sky [Between sky and sun, the Kâ*n*va-*s*âkhâ places the Gandharvaloka (B*ri*h. Âr. Up. III, 6, 1, p. 609).], heaven, sun, moon, stars, gods,

He who knows this, when he has departed this world, reaches and comprehends the Self which consists of food, the Self which consists of breath, the Self which consists of mind, the Self which consists of understanding, the Self which consists of bliss.

On this there is also this *S*loka:

NINTH ANUVÂKA.[1000]

He who knows the bliss of that Brahman, from whence all speech, with the mind, turns away unable to reach it, he fears nothing.'[1001]

He does not distress himself with the thought, Why did I not do what is good? Why did I do what is bad? He who thus knows these two (good and bad), frees himself. He who knows both, frees himself.[1002] This is the Upanishad.[1003]

THIRD VALLÎ,

OR, THE CHAPTER OF BH*RI*GU.

Hari*h*, Om! May it (the Brahman) protect us both! May it enjoy us both! May we acquire strength together! May our knowledge become bright! May we never quarrel! Peace! peace! peace![1004]

FIRST ANUVÂKA.

Bh*ri*gu Vâru*n*i went to his father Varu*n*a, saying:

Sir, teach me Brahman.' He told him this, viz. Food, breath, the eye, the ear, mind, speech.

Then he said again to him: 'That from whence these beings are born, that by which, when born, they live, that into which they enter at their death, try to know that. That is Brahman.'

He performed penance. Having performed penance—

Gandharvas [Instead of Gandharvas, the B*ri*h. Âr. Up. places Indra.], Pragâpati, Brahman. In the Kaushîtaki-upanishad I, 3 (Sacred Books of the East, vol. i, p. 275) there is another series, the worlds of Agni, Vâyu, Varu*n*a, Indra, Pragâpati, and Brahman. See Weber, Ind. Stud. II, p. 224.

[1000] Cf. II, 4.

[1001] Even if there is no fear from anything else, after the knowledge of Self and Brahman has been obtained, it might be thought that fear might still arise from the commission of evil deeds, and the omission of good works. Therefore the next paragraphs have been added.

[1002] The construction of these two sentences is not clear to me.

[1003] Here follows the Anukrama*n*î, and in some MSS. the same invocation with which the next Vallî begins.

[1004] The same paragraph, as before (II, 1), occurs at the end of the Ka*th*a-upanishad, and elsewhere.

SECOND ANUVÂKA.

He perceived that food is Brahman, for from food these beings are produced; by food, when born, they live; and into food they enter at their death.

Having perceived this, he went again to his father Varu*n*a, saying: 'Sir, teach me Brahman.' He said to him: 'Try to know Brahman by penance, for penance is (the means of knowing) Brahman.'

He performed penance. Having performed penance—

THIRD ANUVÂKA.

He perceived that breath[1005] is Brahman, for from breath these beings are born; by breath, when born, they live; into breath they enter at their death.

Having perceived this, he went again to his father Varu*n*a, saying: 'Sir, teach me Brahman.' He said to him: 'Try to know Brahman by penance, for penance is (the means of knowing) Brahman.'

He performed penance. Having performed penance—

FOURTH ANUVÂKA.

He perceived that mind (manas) is Brahman, for from mind these beings are born; by mind, when born, they live; into mind they enter at their death.

Having perceived this, he went again to his father Varu*n*a, saying: 'Sir, teach me Brahman.' He said to him: 'Try to know Brahman by penance, for penance is (the means of knowing) Brahman.'

He performed penance. Having performed penance—

FIFTH ANUVÂKA.

He perceived that understanding (vig*ñ*âna) was Brahman, for from understanding these beings are born; by understanding, when born, they live; into understanding they enter at their death.

Having perceived this, he went again to his father Varu*n*a, saying—'Sir, teach me Brahman.' He said to him: 'Try to know Brahman by penance, for penance is (the means of knowing) Brahman.'

He performed penance. Having performed penance—

[1005] Or life; see B*r*ih. Âr. Up. IV, 1, 3.

SIXTH ANUVÂKA.

He perceived that bliss is Brahman, for from bliss these beings are born; by bliss, when born, they live; into bliss they enter at their death.

This is the knowledge of Bh*ri*gu and Varu*n*a,[1006] exalted in the highest heaven (in the heart). He who knows this becomes exalted, becomes rich in food, and able to eat food (healthy), becomes great by offspring, cattle, and the splendour of his knowledge (of Brahman), great by fame.

SEVENTH ANUVÂKA.

Let him never abuse food, that is the rule.

Breath is food,[1007] the body eats the food. The body rests on breath, breath rests on the body. This is the food resting on food. He who knows this food resting on food,[1008] rests exalted, becomes rich in food, and able to cat food (healthy), becomes great by offspring, cattle, and the splendour of his knowledge (of Brahman), great by fame.

EIGHTH ANUVÂKA.

Let him never shun food, that is the rule. Water is food, the light eats the food. The light rests on water, water rests on light. This is the food resting on food.[1009] He who knows this food resting on food, rests exalted, becomes rich in food, and able to eat food (healthy), becomes great by offspring, cattle, and the splendour of his knowledge (of Brahman), great by fame.

NINTH ANUVÂKA.

Let him acquire much food, that is the rule. Earth is food, the ether eats the food. The ether rests on the earth, the earth rests on the ether. This is the food resting on food. He who knows this food resting on food, rests exalted, becomes rich in food, and able to eat food (healthy), becomes great by offspring, cattle, and the splendour of his knowledge (of Brahman), great by fame.

[1006] Taught by Varu*n*a, learnt by Bh*ri*gu Vâru*n*i.

[1007] Because, like food, it is inside the body.

[1008] The interdependence of food and breath. The object of this discussion is to show (see *S*aṅkara's commentary, p. 135) that the world owes its origin to there being an enjoyer (subject) and what is enjoyed (object), but that this distinction does not exist in the Self.

[1009] The interdependence of water and light.

TENTH ANUVÂKA.

1. Let him never turn away (a stranger) from his house, that is the rule. Therefore a man should by all means acquire much food, for (good) people say (to the stranger): 'There is food ready for him.' If he gives food amply, food is given to him amply. If he gives food fairly, food is given to him fairly. If he gives food meanly, food is given to him meanly.

2. He who knows this, (recognises and worships Brahman[1010]) as possession in speech, as acquisition and possession in up-breathing (prâ*n*a) and down-breathing (apâna); as action in the hands; as walking in the feet; as voiding in the anus. These are the human recognitions (of Brahman as manifested in human actions). Next follow the recognitions (of Brahman) with reference to the Devas, viz. as satisfaction in rain; as power in lightning;

3. As glory in cattle; as light in the stars; as procreation, immortality, and bliss in the member; as everything in the ether. Let him worship that (Brahman) as support, and he becomes supported. Let him worship that (Brahman) as greatness (maha*h*), and he becomes great. Let him worship that (Brahman) as mind, and he becomes endowed with mind.

4. Let him worship that (Brahman) as adoration, and all desires fall down before him in adoration. Let him worship that (Brahman) as Brahman, and he will become possessed of Brahman. Let him worship this as the absorption of the gods[1011] in Brahman, and the enemies who hate him will die all around him, all around him will die the foes whom he does not love.

He[1012] who is this (Brahman) in man, and he who is that (Brahman) in the sun, both are one.

5. He who knows this, when he has departed this world, after reaching and comprehending the Self which consists of food, the Self which consists of breath, the Self which consists of mind, the Self which consists of understanding, the Self which consists of bliss, enters and takes possession of these worlds, and having as much food as he likes, and assuming as many forms as he likes, he sits down singing this Sâman (of Brahman): 'Hâvu, hâvu, hâvu!

6. 'I am food (object), I am food, I am food! I am the eater of food (subject), I am the eater of food, I am the eater of food! I am the poet (who joins the two together), I am the poet, I am the poet! I am the

---

[1010] Brâhma*n*a upâsanaprakâtra*h*.

[1011] Cf. Kaush. Up. II, 12. Here the absorption of the gods of fire, sun, moon, and lightning in the god of the air (vâyu) is described. *S*aṅkara adds the god of rain, and shows that air is identical with ether.

[1012] Cf. II, 8.

first-born of the Right (*ri*ta). Before the Devas I was in the centre of all that is immortal. He who gives me away, he alone preserves me: him who eats food, I eat as food.

'I overcome the whole world, I, endowed with golden light.[1013] He who knows this, (attains all this).' This is the Upanishad.[1014]

B*RI*HADÂRA*N*YAKA-UPANISHAD.

FIRST ADHYÂYA.[1015]

FIRST BRÂHMA*N*A.

1. Verily[1016] the dawn is the head of the horse which is fit for sacrifice, the sun its eye, the wind its breath, the mouth the Vai*s*vânara[1017] fire, the year the body of the sacrificial horse. Heaven is the back, the sky the belly, the earth the chest,[1018] the quarters the two sides, the intermediate quarters the ribs, the members the seasons, the joints the months and half-months, the feet days and nights, the bones the stars, the flesh the clouds. The half-digested food is the sand, the rivers the bowels,[1019] the liver and the lungs[1020] the mountains, the hairs the herbs and trees. As the sun rises, it is the forepart, as it sets, the hindpart of the horse. When the horse shakes itself,[1021] then it lightens; when it kicks, it thunders; when it makes water, it rains; voice[1022] is its voice.

[1013] If we read suvar*n*agyoti*h*. The commentator reads suvar *n*a gyoti*h*. i.e. the light is like the sun.

[1014] After the Anukramanî follows the same invocation as in the beginning of the third Vallî, 'May it protect us both,' &c.

[1015] It is the third Adhyâya of the Âra*n*yaka, but the first of the Upanishad.

[1016] This Brâhma*n*a is found in the Mâdhyandina text of the *S*atapatha, ed. Weber, X, 6, 4. Its object is there explained by the commentary to be the meditative worship of Virâg, as represented metaphorically in the members of the horse. Sâya*n*a dispenses with its explanation, because, as part of the B*r*ihadâra*n*yaka-upanishad, according to the Kâ*n*va-*s*âkhâ, it had been enlarged on by the Vârttikakâra and explained.

[1017] Agni or fire, as pervading everything, as universally present in nature.

[1018] Pâgasya is doubtful. The commentator suggests pâd-asya, the place of the feet, i.e. the hoof The Greek Pēgasos, or ἵπποι πηλοί, throws no light on the word. The meaning of hoof would hardly be appropriate here, and I prefer chest on account of uras in I, 2, 3. Deussen (Vedânta, p. 8) translates, die Erde seiner Füsse Schemel; but we want some part of the horse.

[1019] Guda, being in the plural, is explained by nâ*d*î, channel, and sirâ*h*; for we ought to read sirâ or hirâgraha*n*e for *s*irâ, p. 22, l. 16.

[1020] Klomâna*h* is explained as a plurale tantum (nityam bahuva*k*anam ekasmin), and being described as a lump below the heart, on the opposite side of the liver, it is supposed to be the lungs.

[1021] 'When it yawns.' Ânandagiri.

[1022] Voice is sometimes used as a personified power of thunder and other aerial sounds, and this is identified with the voice of the horse.

2. Verily Day arose after the horse as the (golden) vessel,[1023] called Mahiman (greatness), which (at the sacrifice) is placed before the horse. Its place is in the Eastern sea. The Night arose after the horse as the (silver) vessel, called Mahiman, which (at the sacrifice) is placed behind the horse. Its place is in the Western sea. Verily, these two vessels (or greatnesses) arose to be on each side of the horse.

As a racer he carried the Devas, as a stallion the Gandharvas, as a runner the Asuras, as a horse men. The sea is its kin, the sea is its birthplace.

SECOND BRÂHMA*N*A.[1024]

1. In the beginning there was nothing (to be perceived) here whatsoever. By Death indeed all this was concealed,—by hunger; for death is hunger. Death (the first being) thought, 'Let me have a body.' Then he moved about, worshipping. From him thus worshipping water was produced. And he said: 'Verily, there appeared to me, while I worshipped (ar*k*ate), water (ka).' This is why water is called ar-ka.[1025] Surely there is water (or pleasure) for him who thus knows the reason why water is called arka.

2. Verily water is arka. And what was there as the froth of the water, that was hardened, and became the earth. On that earth he (Death) rested, and from him, thus resting and heated, Agni (Virâ*g*) proceeded, full of light.

3. That being divided itself threefold, Âditya (the sun) as the third, and Vâyu (the air) as the third.[1026] That spirit (prâ*n*a)[1027] became threefold. The head was the Eastern quarter, and the arms this and that quarter (i.e. the N. E. and S. E., on the left and right sides). Then the tail was the Western quarter, and the two legs this and that quarter (i.e.

[1023] Two vessels, to hold the sacrificial libations, are placed at the A*s*vamedha before and behind the horse, the former made of gold, the latter made of silver. They are called Mahiman in the technical language of the ceremonial. The place in which these vessels are set, is called their yoni. Cf. Vâgas. Sa*m*hitâ XXIII, 2.

[1024] Called the Agni-brâhma*n*a, and intended to teach the origin of Agni, the fire, which is here used for the Horse-sacrifice. It is found in the *S*atapatha-brâhma*n*a, Mâdhyandina-*s*âkhâ X, 6, 5, and there explained as a description of Hira*n*yagarbha.

[1025] We ought to read arkasyârkatvam, as in Poley's edition, or ark-kasyârkkatvam, to make the etymology still clearer. The commentator takes arka in the sense of fire, more especially the sacrificial fire employed at the Horse-sacrifice. It may be so, but the more natural interpretation seems to me to take arka here as water, from which indirectly fire is produced. From water springs the earth; on that earth he (Mri*t*yu or Pragâpati) rested, and from him, while resting there, fire (Virâ*g*) was produced. That fire assumed three forms, fire, sun, and air, and in that threefold form it is called prâ*n*a, spirit.

[1026] As Agni, Vâyu, and Âditya.

[1027] Here Agni (Virâ*g*) is taken as representing the fire of the altar at the Horse-sacrifice, which is called Arka. The object of the whole Brâhma*n*a was to show the origin and true character of that fire (arka).

the N. W. and S. W.) The sides were the Southern and Northern quarters, the back heaven, the belly the sky, the dust the earth. Thus he (M*ri*tyu, as arka) stands firm in the water, and he who knows this stands firm wherever he goes.

4. He desired,[1028] 'Let a second body be born of me,' and he (Death or Hunger) embraced Speech in his mind. Then the seed became the year. Before that time there was no year. Speech[1029] bore him so long as a year, and after that time sent him forth. Then when he was born, he (Death) opened his mouth, as if to swallow him. He cried Bhâ*n*! and that became speech.[1030]

5. He thought, 'If I kill him, I shall have but little food.' He therefore brought forth by that speech and by that body (the year) all whatsoever exists, the *Rik*, the Yagus, the Sâman, the metres, the sacrifices, men, and animals.

And whatever he (Death) brought forth, that he resolved to eat (ad). Verily because he eats everything, therefore is Aditi (Death) called Aditi. He who thus knows why Aditi is called Aditi, becomes an eater of everything, and everything becomes his food.[1031]

6. He desired to sacrifice again with a greater sacrifice. He toiled and performed penance. And while he toiled and performed penance, glorious power[1032] went out of him. Verily glorious power means the senses (prâ*n*a). Then when the senses had gone out, the body took to swelling (*s*va-yitum), and mind was in the body.

7. He desired that this body should be fit for sacrifice (medhya), and that he should be embodied by it. Then he became a horse (a*s*va), because it swelled (a*s*vat), and was fit for sacrifice (medhya); and this is why the horse-sacrifice is called A*s*va-medha.

Verily he who knows him thus, knows the A*s*vamedha. Then, letting the horse free, he thought,[1033] and at the end of a year he offered it up for himself, while he gave up the (other) animals to the deities. Therefore the sacrificers offered up the purified horse belonging to Pragâpati, (as dedicated) to all the deities.

Verily the shining sun is the A*s*vamedha-sacrifice, and his body is the year; Agni is the sacrificial fire (arka), and these worlds are his bodies. These two are the sacrificial fire and the A*s*vamedha-sacrifice, and they are again one deity, viz. Death. He (who knows this) overcomes another death, death does not reach him, death is his Self, he

---

[1028] He is the same as what was before called m*ri*tyu, death, who, after becoming self-conscious, produced water, earth, fire, &c. He now wishes for a second body, which is the year, or the annual sacrifice, the year being dependent on the sun (Âditya).

[1029] The commentator understands the father, instead of Speech, the mother.

[1030] The interjectional theory.

[1031] All these are merely fanciful etymologies of a*s*vamedha and arka.

[1032] Or glory (senses) and power. Comm.

[1033] He considered himself as the horse. Roer.

becomes one of those deities.

THIRD BRÂHMA*N*A.[1034]

1. There were two kinds of descendants of Pragâpati, the Devas and the Asuras.[1035] Now the Devas were indeed the younger, the Asuras the elder ones.[1036] The Devas, who were struggling in these worlds, said: 'Well, let us overcome the Asuras at the sacrifices (the *G*yotish*t*oma) by means of the udgîtha.'

2. They said to speech (Vâ*k*): 'Do thou sing out for us (the udgîtha).' 'Yes,' said speech, and sang (the udgîtha). Whatever delight there is in speech, that she obtained for the Devas by singing (the three pavamânas); but that she pronounced well (in the other nine pavamânas), that was for herself. The Asuras knew: 'Verily, through this singer they will overcome us.' They therefore rushed at the singer and pierced her with evil. That evil which consists in saying what is bad, that is that evil.

3. Then they (the Devas) said to breath (scent): 'Do thou sing out for us.' 'Yes,' said breath, and sang. Whatever delight there is in breath (smell), that he obtained for the Devas by singing; but that he smelled well, that was for himself. The Asuras knew: 'Verily, through this singer they will overcome us.' They therefore rushed at the singer, and pierced him with evil. That evil which consists in smelling what is bad, that is that evil.

4. Then they said to the eye: 'Do thou sing out for us.' 'Yes,' said the eye, and sang. Whatever delight there is in the eye, that he obtained for the Devas by singing; but that he saw well, that was for himself The Asuras knew: 'Verily, through this singer they will overcome us.' They therefore rushed at the singer, and pierced him with evil. That evil which consists in seeing what is bad, that is that evil.

5. Then they said to the ear: 'Do thou sing out for us.' 'Yes,' said the ear, and sang. Whatever delight there is in the ear, that he obtained for the Devas by singing; but that he heard well, that was for himself. The Asuras knew: 'Verily, through this singer they will overcome us.' They therefore rushed at the singer, and pierced him with evil. That evil which consists in hearing what is bad, that is that evil.

6. Then they said to the mind: 'Do thou sing out for us.' 'Yes,' said the mind, and sang. Whatever delight there is in the mind, that he

---

[1034] Called the Udgîtha-brâhma*n*a. In the Mâdhyandina-*s*âkhâ, the Upanishad, which consists of six adhyâyas, begins with this Brâhma*n*a (cf. Weber's edition, p. 104 7; Commentary, p. 1109).

[1035] The Devas and Asuras are explained by the commentator as the senses, inclining either to sacred or to worldly objects, to good or evil.

[1036] According to the commentator, the Devas were the less numerous and less strong, the Asuras the more numerous and more powerful.

obtained for the Devas by singing; but that he thought well, that was for himself. The Asuras knew: 'Verily, through this singer they will overcome us.' They therefore rushed at the singer, and pierced him with evil. That evil which consists in thinking what is bad, that is that evil.

Thus they overwhelmed these deities with evils, thus they pierced them with evil.

7. Then they said to the breath in the mouth:[1037] 'Do thou sing for us.' 'Yes,' said the breath, and sang. The Asuras knew: 'Verily, through this singer they will overcome us.' They therefore rushed at him and pierced him with evil. Now as a ball of earth will be scattered when hitting a stone, thus they perished, scattered in all directions. Hence the Devas rose, the Asuras fell. He who knows this, rises by his self, and the enemy who hates him falls.

8. Then they (the Devas) said: 'Where was he then who thus stuck to us?'[1038] It was (the breath) within the mouth (âsye 'ntar[1039]), and therefore called Ayâsya; he was the sap (rasa) of the limbs (aṅga), and therefore called Âṅgirasa.

9. That deity was called Dûr, because Death was far (dûran) from it. From him who knows this, Death is far off.

10. That deity, after having taken away the evil of those deities, viz. death, sent it to where the end of the quarters of the earth is. There he deposited their sins. Therefore let no one go to a man, let no one go to the end (of the quarters of the earth[1040]), that he may not meet there with evil, with death.

11. That deity, after having taken away the evil of those deities, viz. death, carried them beyond death.

12. He carried speech across first. When speech had become freed from death, it became (what it had been before) Agni (fire). That Agni, after having stepped beyond death, shines.

13. Then he carried breath (scent) across. When breath had become freed from death, it became Vâyu (air). That Vâyu, after having stepped beyond death, blows.

14. Then he carried the eye across. When the eye had become freed from death, it became Âditya (the sun). That Âditya, after having stepped beyond death, burns.

15. Then he carried the ear across. When the ear had become freed from death, it became the quarters (space). These are our quarters (space), which have stepped beyond death.

16. Then he carried the mind across. When the mind had become

---

[1037] This is the chief or vital breath, sometimes called mukhya.

[1038] Asakta from sañg, to embrace; cf. Rig-veda I, 33, 3. Here it corresponds to the German anhänglich.

[1039] See Deussen, Vedanta, p. 359.

[1040] To distant people.

freed from death, it became the moon (*K*andramas). That moon, after having stepped beyond death, shines. Thus does that deity carry him, who knows this, across death.

17. Then breath (vital), by singing, obtained for himself eatable food. For whatever food is eaten, is eaten by breath alone, and in it breath rests.[1041]

The Devas said: 'Verily, thus far, whatever food there is, thou hast by singing acquired it for thyself. Now therefore give us a share in that food.' He said: 'You there, enter into me.' They said Yes, and entered all into him. Therefore whatever food is eaten by breath, by it the other senses are satisfied.

18. If a man knows this, then his own relations come to him in the same manner; he becomes their supporter, their chief leader, their strong ruler.[1042] And if ever anyone tries to oppose[1043] one who is possessed of such knowledge among his own relatives, then he will not be able to support his own belongings. But he who follows the man who is possessed of such knowledge, and who with his permission wishes to support those whom he has to support, he indeed will be able to support his own belongings.

19. He was called Ayâsya Âṅgirasa, for he is the sap (rasa) of the limbs (aṅga). Verily, breath is the sap of the limbs. Yes, breath is the sap of the limbs. Therefore from whatever limb breath goes away, that limb withers, for breath verily is the sap of the limbs.

20. He (breath) is also B*ri*haspati, for speech is B*ri*hatî (*Ri*g-veda), and he is her lord; therefore he is B*ri*haspati.

21. He (breath) is also Brahma*n*aspati, for speech is Brahman (Yagur-veda), and he is her lord; therefore he is Brahma*n*aspati.

He (breath) is also Sâman (the Udgîtha), for speech is Sâman (Sama-veda), and that is both speech (sâ) and breath (ama).[1044] This is why Sâman is called Sâman.

22. Or because he is equal (sama) to a grub, equal to a gnat, equal to an elephant, equal to these three worlds, nay, equal to this universe, therefore he is Sâman. He who thus knows this Sâman, obtains union and oneness with Sâman.

23. He (breath) is Udgîtha.[1045] Breath verily is Ut, for by breath this universe is upheld (uttabdha); and speech is Gîthâ, song. And because he is ut and gîthâ, therefore he (breath) is Udgîtha.

[1041] This is done by the last nine Pavamânas, while the first three were used for obtaining the reward common to all the prâ*n*as.

[1042] Here annâda is well explained by anâmayâvin, and vyâdhirahita, free from sickness, strong.

[1043] Read pratiprati*h*; see Poley, and Weber, p. 1180.

[1044] Cf. *Kh*ând. Up. V, 2, 6.

[1045] Not used here in the sense of song or hymn, but as an act of worship connected with the Sâman. Comm.

24. And thus Brahmadatta *K*aikitâneya (the grandson of *K*ikitâna), while taking Soma (râgan), said: 'May this Soma strike my head off, if Ayâsya Âṅgirasa sang another Udgîtha than this. He sang it indeed as speech and breath.'

25. He who knows what is the property of this Sâman, obtains property. Now verily its property is tone only. Therefore let a priest, who is going to perform the sacrificial work of a Sama-singer, desire that his voice may have a good tone, and let him perform the sacrifice with a voice that is in good tone. Therefore people (who want a priest) for a sacrifice, look out for one who possesses a good voice, as for one who possesses property. He who thus knows what is the property of that Sâman, obtains property.

26. He who knows what is the gold of that Sâman, obtains gold. Now verily its gold. is tone only. He who thus knows what is the gold of that Sâman, obtains gold.

27. He who knows what is the support of that Sâman, he is supported. Now verily its support is speech only. For, as supported in speech, that breath is sung as that Sâman. Some say the support is in food.

Next follows the Abhyâroha[1046] (the ascension) of the Pavamâna verses. Verily the Prastot*ri* begins to sing the Sâman, and when he begins, then let him (the sacrificer) recite these (three Yagus-verses):

'Lead me from the unreal to the real! Lead me from darkness to light! Lead me from death to immortality!'

Now when he says, 'Lead me from the unreal to the real,' the unreal is verily death, the real immortality. He therefore says, 'Lead me from death to immortality, make me immortal.'

When he says, 'Lead me from darkness to light,' darkness is verily death, light immortality. He therefore says, 'Lead me from death to immortality, make me immortal.'

When he says, 'Lead me from death to immortality,' there is nothing there, as it were, hidden (obscure, requiring explanation).[1047]

28. Next come the other Stotras with which the priest may obtain food for himself by singing them. Therefore let the sacrificer, while these Stotras are being sung, ask for a boon, whatever desire he may desire. An Udgât*ri* priest who knows this obtains by his singing whatever desire he may desire either for himself or for the sacrificer. This (knowledge) indeed is called the conqueror of the worlds. He who thus knows this Sâman,[1048] for him there is no fear of his not being

---

[1046] The ascension is a ceremony by which the performer reaches the gods, or becomes a god. It consists in the recitation of three Yagus, and is here enjoined to take place when the Prastotri priest begins to sing his hymn.

[1047] See Deussen, Vedânta, p. 86.

[1048] He knows that he is the Prâ*n*a, which Prâ*n*a is the Sâman. That Prâ*n*a cannot be defeated by the Asuras, i.e. by the senses which are addicted to evil; it is pure, and the

admitted to the worlds.[1049]

FOURTH BRÂHMA*N*A.[1050]

1. In the beginning this was Self alone, in the shape of a person (purusha). He looking round saw nothing but his Self. He first said, 'This is I;' therefore he became I by name. Therefore even now, if a man is asked, he first says, 'This is I,' and then pronounces the other name which he may have. And because before (pûrva) all this, he (the Self) burnt down (ush) all evils, therefore he was a person (pur-usha). Verily he who knows this, burns down every one who tries to be before him.

2. He feared, and therefore any one who is lonely fears. He thought, 'As there is nothing but myself, why should I fear?' Thence his fear passed away. For what should he have feared? Verily fear arises from a second only.

3. But he felt no delight. Therefore a man who is lonely feels no delight. He wished for a second. He was so large as man and wife together. He then made this his Self to fall in two (pat), and thence arose husband (pati) and wife (patnî). Therefore Yâ*g*ñavalkya said: 'We two[1051] are thus (each of us) like half a shell.'[1052] Therefore the void which was there, is filled by the wife. He embraced her, and men were born.

4. She thought, 'How can he embrace me, after having produced me from himself? I shall hide myself.'

She then became a cow, the other became a bull and embraced her, and hence cows were born. The one became a mare, the other a stallion; the one a male ass, the other a female ass. He embraced her, and hence one-hoofed animals were born. The one became a she-goat, the other a

---

five senses finding refuge in him, recover there their original nature, fire, &c. The Prâ*n*a is the Self of all things, also of speech (*R*ig-yagu*h*-sâmodgîtha), and of the Sâman that has to be sung and well sung. The Prâ*n*a pervades all creatures, and he who identifies himself with that Prâ*n*a, obtains the rewards mentioned in the Brâhma*n*a. Comm.

[1049] In connection with lokagit, lokyatâ is here explained, and may probably have been intended, as worthiness to be admitted to the highest world. Originally lokyatâ and alokyatâ meant right and wrong. See also I, 5, 17.

[1050] Called Purushavidhabrâhma*n*a (Mâdhyandina-*s*âkhâ, p. 1050). See Muir, Original Sanskrit Texts, vol. i, p. 24.

[1051] The Comm. explains sva*h* by âtmana*h*, of himself. But see Boehtlingk, Sanskrit Chrestomathie, p. 357.

[1052] Roer translates: 'Therefore was this only one half of himself, as a split pea is of a whole.' B*r*igala is a half of anything. Muir (Orig. Sansk. Texts, vol. i, p. 25) translates: 'Yâ*g*ñavalkya has said that this one's self is like the half of a split pea.' I have translated the sentence according to Professor Boehtlingk's conjecture (Chrestomathie, 2nd ed. p. 357), though the singular after the dual (sva*h*) is irregular.

he-goat; the one became a ewe,[1053] the other a ram. He embraced her, and hence goats and sheep were born. And thus he created everything that exists in pairs, down to the ants.

5. He knew, 'I indeed am this creation, for I created all this.' Hence he became the creation, and he who knows this lives in this his creation.

6. Next he thus produced fire by rubbing. From the mouth, as from the fire-hole, and from the hands he created fire.[1054] Therefore both the mouth and the hands are inside without hair, for the fire-hole is inside without hair.

And when they say, 'Sacrifice to this or sacrifice to that god,' each god is but his manifestation, for he is all gods.

Now, whatever there is moist, that he created from seed; this is Soma. So far verily is this universe either food or eater. Soma indeed is food, Agni eater. This is the highest creation of Brahman, when he created the gods from his better part,[1055] and when he, who was (then) mortal,[1056] created the immortals. Therefore it was the highest creation. And he who knows this, lives in this his highest creation.

7. Now all this was then undeveloped. It became developed by form and name, so that one could say, 'He, called so and so, is such a one.'[1057] Therefore at present also all this is developed by name and form, so that one can say, 'He, called so and so, is such a one.'

He (Brahman or the Self) entered thither, to the very tips of the finger-nails, as a razor might be fitted in a razor-case, or as fire in a fire-place.[1058]

He cannot be seen, for, in part only, when breathing, he is breath by name; when speaking, speech by name; when seeing, eye by name; when hearing, ear by name; when thinking, mind by name. All these are but the names of his acts. And he who worships (regards) him as the one or the other, does not know him, for he is apart from this (when qualified) by the one or the other (predicate). Let men worship him as Self, for in the Self all these are one. This Self is the footstep of everything, for through it one knows everything.[1059] And as one can find again by footsteps what was lost, thus he who knows this finds

---

[1053] The reading avir itaro, i.e. itarâ u, is not found in the Kâ*n*va text. See Boehtlingk, Chrestomathie, p. 357.

[1054] He blew with the mouth while he rubbed with the hands.

[1055] Or, when he created the best gods.

[1056] As man and sacrificer. Comm.

[1057] The Comm. takes asau-nâmâ as a compound, instead of ida*m*-nâmâ. I read asau nâma, he is this by name, viz. Devadatta, &c. Dr. Boehtlingk, who in his Chrestomathie (2nd ed. p. 31) had accepted the views of the Commentator, informs me that he has changed his view, and thinks that we should read asaú nâ'ma.

[1058] Cf. Kaush. Br. Up. VI, 19.

[1059] As one finds lost cattle again by following their footsteps, thus one finds everything, if one has found out the Self.' Comm.

glory and praise.

8. This, which is nearer to us than anything, this Self, is dearer than a son, dearer than wealth, dearer than all else.

And if one were to say to one who declares another than the Self dear, that he will lose what is dear to him, very likely it would be so. Let him worship the Self alone as dear. He who worships the Self alone as dear, the object of his love will never perish.[1060]

9. Here they say: 'If men think that by knowledge of Brahman they will become everything, what then did that Brahman know, from whence all this sprang?'

10. Verily in the beginning this was Brahman, that Brahman knew (its) Self only, saying, 'I am Brahman.' From it all this sprang. Thus, whatever Deva was awakened (so as to know Brahman), he indeed became that (Brahman); and the same with *Ri*shis and men. The *Ri*shi Vâmadeva saw and understood it, singing, 'I was Manu (moon), I was the sun.' Therefore now also he who thus knows that he is Brahman, becomes all this, and even the Devas cannot prevent it, for he himself is their Self.

Now if a man worships another deity, thinking the deity is one and he another, he does not know. He is like a beast for the Devas. For verily, as many beasts nourish a man, thus does every man nourish the Devas. If only one beast is taken away, it is not pleasant; how much more when many are taken! Therefore it is not pleasant to the Devas that men should know this.

11. Verily in the beginning this was Brahman, one only. That being one, was not strong enough. It created still further the most excellent Kshatra (power), viz. those Kshatras (powers) among the Devas,—Indra, Varu*n*a, Soma, Rudra, Parganya, Yama, M*ri*tyu, Î*s*âna. Therefore there is nothing beyond the Kshatra, and therefore at the Râgasûya sacrifice the Brâhma*n*a sits down below the Kshatriya. He confers that glory on the Kshatra alone. But Brahman is (nevertheless) the birth-place of the Kshatra. Therefore though a king is exalted, he sits down at the end (of the sacrifice) below the Brahman, as his birth-place. He who injures him, injures his own birth-place. He becomes worse, because he has injured one better than himself.

12. He[1061] was not strong enough. He created the Vi*s* (people), the classes of Devas which in their different orders are called Vasus, Rudras, Âdityas, Vi*s*ve Devas, Maruts.

13. He was not strong enough. He created the *S*ûdra colour (caste), as Pûshan (as nourisher). This earth verily is Pûshan (the nourisher); for the earth nourishes all this whatsoever.

[1060] On rudh, to lose, see Taitt. Sa*m*h. II, 6, 8, 5, pp. 765, 771, as pointed out by Dr. Boehtlingk. On î*s*varo (yat) tathaiva syât, see Boehtlingk, s. v.

[1061] Observe the change from tad, it, to sa, he.

14. He was not strong enough. He created still further the most excellent Law (dharma). Law is the Kshatra (power) of the Kshatra,[1062] therefore there is nothing higher than the Law. Thenceforth even a weak man rules a stronger with the help of the Law, as with the help of a king. Thus the Law is what is called the true. And if a man declares what is true, they say he declares the Law; and if he declares the Law, they say he declares what is true. Thus both are the same.

15. There are then this Brahman, Kshatra, Vis, and *S*ûdra. Among the Devas that Brahman existed as Agni (fire) only, among men as Brâhma*n*a, as Kshatriya through the (divine) Kshatriya, as Vaisya through the (divine) Vaisya, as *S*ûdra through the (divine) *S*ûdra. Therefore people wish for their future state among the Devas through Agni (the sacrificial fire) only; and among men through the Brâhma*n*a, for in these two forms did Brahman exist.

Now if a man departs this life without having seen his true future life (in the Self), then that Self, not being known, does not receive and bless him, as if the Veda had not been read, or as if a good work had not been done. Nay, even if one who does not know that (Self), should perform here on earth some great holy work, it will Perish for him in the end. Let a man worship the Self only as his true state. If a man worships the Self only as his true state, his work does not Perish, for whatever he desires that he gets from that Self.

16. Now verily this Self (of the ignorant man) is the world[1063] of all creatures. In so far as man sacrifices and pours out libations, he is the world of the Devas; in so far as he repeats the hymns, &c., he is the world of the *Ri*shis; in so far as he offers cakes to the Fathers and tries to obtain offspring, he is the world of the Fathers; in so far as he gives shelter and food to men, he is the world of men; in so far as he finds fodder and water for the animals, he is the world of the animals; in so far as quadrupeds, birds, and even ants live in his houses, he is their world. And as every one wishes his own world not to be injured, thus all beings wish that he who knows this should not be injured. Verily this is known and has been well reasoned.

17. In the beginning this was Self alone, one only. He desired, 'Let there be a wife for me that I may have offspring, and let there be wealth for me that I may offer sacrifices.' Verily this is the whole desire, and, even if wishing for more, he would not find it. Therefore now also a lonely person desires, 'Let there be a wife for me that I may have offspring, and let there be wealth for me that I may offer sacrifices.' And so long as he does not obtain either of these things, he thinks he is incomplete. Now his completeness (is made up as follows): mind is his self (husband); speech the wife; breath the child; the eye all worldly

---

[1062] More powerful than the Kshatra or warrior caste. Comm.

[1063] Is enjoyed by them all. Comm.

wealth, for he finds it with the eye; the ear his divine wealth, for he hears it with the ear. The body (âtman) is his work, for with the body he works. This is the fivefold[1064] sacrifice, for fivefold is the animal, fivefold man, fivefold all this whatsoever. He who knows this, obtains all this.

FIFTH BRÂHMA*N*A.[1065]

1. 'When the father (of creation) had produced by knowledge and penance (work) the seven kinds of food, one of his (foods) was common to all beings, two he assigned to the Devas, (1)

'Three he made for himself, one he gave to the animals. In it all rests, whatsoever breathes and breathes not. (2)

'Why then do these not perish, though they are always eaten? He who knows this imperishable one, he eats food with his face. (3)

'He goes even to the Devas, he lives on strength.' (4)

2. When it is said, that 'the father produced by knowledge and penance the seven kinds of food,' it is clear that (it was he who) did so. When it is said, that 'one of his (foods) was common,' then that is that common food of his which is eaten. He who worships (eats) that (common food), is not removed from evil, for verily that food is mixed (property).[1066] When it is said, that 'two he assigned to the Devas,' that is the huta, which is sacrificed in fire, and the prahuta, which is given away at a sacrifice. But they also say, the new-moon and full-moon sacrifices are here intended, and therefore one should not offer them as an ish*t*i or with a wish.

When it is said, that 'one he gave to animals,' that is milk. For in the beginning (in their infancy) both men and animals live on milk. And therefore they either make a new-born child lick gh*ri*ta (butter), or they make it take the breast. And they call a new-born creature 'at*rin*âda,' i.e. not eating herbs. When it is said, that 'in it all rests, whatsoever breathes and breathes not,' we see that all this, whatsoever breathes and breathes not, rests and depends on milk.

And when it is said (in another Brâhma*n*a), that a man who sacrifices with milk a whole year,[1067] overcomes death again, let him not think so. No, on the very day on which he sacrifices, on that day he overcomes death again; for he who knows this, offers to the gods the entire food (viz. milk).

When it is said, 'Why do these not perish, though they are always

[1064] Fivefold, as consisting of mind, speech, breath, eye, and ear. See Taitt. Up. I, 7, 1.

[1065] Mâdhyandina text, p. 1054.

[1066] It belongs to all beings.

[1067] This would imply 360 sacrificial days, each with two oblations, i.e. 720 oblations.

eaten,' we answer, Verily, the Person is the imperishable, and he produces that food again and again.[1068]

When it is said, 'He who knows this imperishable one,' then, verily, the Person is the imperishable one, for he produces this food by repeated thought, and whatever he does not work by his works, that perishes.

When it is said, that 'he eats food with his face,' then face means the mouth, he eats it with his mouth.

When it is said, that 'he goes even to the Devas, he lives on strength,' that is meant as praise.

3. When it is said, that 'he made three for himself,' that means that he made mind, speech, and breath for himself. As people say, 'My mind was elsewhere, I did not see; my mind was elsewhere, I did not hear,' it is clear that a man sees with his mind and hears with his mind.[1069] Desire, representation, doubt, faith, want of faith, memory,[1070] forgetfulness, shame, reflexion, fear, all this is mind. Therefore even if a man is touched on the back, he knows it through the mind.

Whatever sound there is, that is speech. Speech indeed is intended for an end or object, it is nothing by itself.

The up-breathing, the down-breathing, the back-breathing, the out-breathing, the on-breathing, all that is breathing is breath (prâ*n*a) only. Verily that Self consists of it; that Self consists of speech, mind, and breath.

4. These are the three worlds: earth is speech, sky mind, heaven breath.

5. These are the three Vedas: the *Ri*g-veda is speech, the Yagur-veda mind, the Sâma-veda breath.

6. These are the Devas, Fathers, and men: the Devas are speech, the Fathers mind, men breath.

7. These are father, mother, and child: the father is mind, the mother speech, the child breath.

8. These are what is known, what is to be known, and what is unknown.

What is known, has the form of speech, for speech is known. Speech, having become this, protects man.[1071]

9. What is to be known, has the form of mind, for mind is what is to be known. Mind, having become this, protects man.

10. What is unknown, has the form of breath, for breath is unknown. Breath, having become this, protects man.[1072]

[1068] Those who enjoy the food, become themselves creators. Comm.

[1069] See Deussen, Vedânta, p. 358.

[1070] Firmness, strength. Comm.

[1071] 'The food (speech), having become known, can be consumed.' Comm.

[1072] This was adhibhautika, with reference to bhûtas, beings. Next follows the adhidaivika, with reference to the devas, gods. Comm.

11. Of that speech (which is the food of Pragâpati) earth is the body, light the form, viz. this fire. And so far as speech extends, so far extends the earth, so far extends fire.

12. Next, of this mind heaven is the body, light the form, viz. this sun. And so far as this mind extends, so far extends heaven, so far extends the sun. If they (fire and sun) embrace each other, then wind is born, and that is Indra, and he is without a, rival. Verily a second is a rival, and he who knows this, has no rival.

13. Next, of this breath water is the body, light the form, viz. this moon. And so far as this breath extends, so far extends water, so far extends the moon.

These are all alike, all endless. And he who worships them as finite, obtains a finite world, but he who worships them as infinite, obtains an infinite world.

14. That Pragâpati is the year, and he consists of sixteen digits. The nights[1073] indeed are his fifteen digits, the fixed point[1074] his sixteenth digit. He is increased and decreased by the nights. Having on the new-moon night entered with the sixteenth part into everything that has life, he is thence born again in the morning. Therefore let no one cut off the life of any living thing on that night, not even of a lizard, in honour (pûgârtham) of that deity.

15. Now verily that Pragâpati, consisting of sixteen digits, who is the year, is the same as a man who knows this. His wealth constitutes the fifteen digits, his Self the sixteenth digit. He is increased and decreased by that wealth. His Self is the nave, his wealth the felly. Therefore even if he loses everything, if he lives but with his Self, people say, he lost the felly (which can be restored again).

16. Next there are verily three worlds, the world of men, the world of the Fathers, the world of the Devas. The world of men can be gained by a son only, not by any other work. By sacrifice the world of the Fathers, by knowledge the world of the Devas is gained. The world of the Devas is the best of worlds, therefore they praise knowledge.

17. Next follows the handing over. When a man thinks he is going to depart, he says to his son: 'Thou art Brahman (the Veda, so far as acquired by the father); thou art the sacrifice (so far as performed by the father); thou art the world.' The son answers: 'I am Brahman, I am the sacrifice, I am the world.' Whatever has been learnt (by the father) that, taken as one, is Brahman. Whatever sacrifices there are, they, taken as one, are the sacrifice. Whatever worlds there are, they, taken as one, are the world. Verily here ends this (what has to be done by a father, viz. study, sacrifice, &c.) 'He (the son), being all this, preserved

[1073] Meant for nychthemera.

[1074] When he is just invisible at the new moon.

me from this world,'[1075] thus he thinks. Therefore they call a son who is instructed (to do all this), a world-son (lokya), and therefore they instruct him.

When a father who knows this, departs this world, then he enters into his son together with his own spirits (with speech, mind, and breath). If there is anything done amiss by the father, of all that the son delivers him, and therefore he is called Putra, son.[1076] By help of his son the father stands firm in this world.[1077] Then these divine immortal spirits (speech, mind, and breath) enter into him.

18. From the earth and from fire, divine speech enters into him. And verily that is divine speech whereby, whatever he says, comes to be.

19. From heaven and the sun, divine mind enters into him. And verily that is divine mind whereby he becomes joyful, and grieves no more.

20. From water and the moon, divine breath (spirit) enters into him. And verily that is divine breath which, whether moving or not moving, does not tire, and therefore does not perish. He who knows this, becomes the Self of all beings. As that deity (Hira*n*yagarbha) is, so does he become. And as all beings honour that deity (with sacrifice, &c.), so do all beings honour him who knows this.

Whatever grief these creatures suffer, that is all one[1078] (and therefore disappears). Only what is good approaches him; verily, evil does not approach the Devas.

21. Next follows the consideration of the observances[1079] (acts). Pragâpati created the actions (active senses). When they had been created, they strove among themselves. Voice held, I shall speak; the eye held, I shall see; the ear held, I shall hear; and thus the other actions too, each according to its own act. Death, having become weariness, took them and seized them. Having seized them, death held them back (from their work). Therefore speech grows weary, the eye grows weary, the ear grows weary. But death did not seize the central breath. Then the others tried to know him, and said: 'Verily, he is the best of us, he who, whether moving or not, does not tire and does not perish. Well, let all of us assume his form.' Thereupon they all assumed his form, and therefore they are called after him 'breaths' (spirits).

In whatever family there is a man who knows this, they call that

---

[1075] Roer seems to have read sa*m*naya, 'all this multitude.' I read, etan mi sarva*m* sann ayam ito 'bhunagad iti.

[1076] The Comm. derives putra from pu (pûr), to fill, and tra (trâ), to deliver, a deliverer who fills the holes left by the father, a stopgap. Others derive it from put, a hell, and tri, to protect; cf. Manu IX, 138.

[1077] 'The manushya-loka, not the pit*ri*-loka and deva-loka.' Comm.

[1078] 'Individuals suffer, because one causes grief to another. But in the universal soul, where all individuals are one, their sufferings are neutralised.' Comm.

[1079] The upâsana or meditative worship.

family after his name. And he who strives with one who knows this, withers away and finally dies. So far with regard to the body.

22. Now with regard to the deities.

Agni (fire) held, I shall burn; Âditya (the sun) held, I shall warm; *K*andramas (the moon) held, I shall shine; and thus also the other deities, each according to the deity. And as it was with the central breath among the breaths, so it was with Vâyu, the wind among those deities. The other deities fade, not Vâyu. Vâyu is the deity that never sets.

23. And here there is this *S*loka:

'He from whom the sun rises, and into whom it sets' (he verily rises from the breath, and sets in the breath)

'Him the Devas made the law, he only is to-day, and he to-morrow also' (whatever these Devas determined then, that they perform to-day also[1080]).

Therefore let a man perform one observance only, let him breathe up and let him breathe down, that the evil death may not reach him. And when he performs it, let him try to finish it. Then he obtains through it union and oneness with that deity (with prâ*n*a).

SIXTH BRÂHMA*N*A.[1081]

1. Verily this is a triad, name, form, and work. Of these names, that which is called Speech is the Uktha (hymn, supposed to mean also origin), for from it all names arise. It is their Sâman (song, supposed to mean also sameness), for it is the same as all names. It is their Brahman (prayer, supposed to mean also support), for it supports all names.

2. Next, of the forms, that which is called Eye is the Uktha (hymn), for from it all forms arise. It is their Sâman (song), for it is the same as all forms. It is their Brahman (prayer), for it supports all forms.

3. Next, of the works, that which is called Body is the Uktha (hymn), for from it all works arise. It is their Sâman (song), for it is the same as all works. It is their Brahman (prayer), for it supports all works.

That being a triad is one, viz. this Self; and the Self, being one, is that triad. This is the immortal, covered by the true. Verily breath is the immortal, name and form are the true, and by them the immortal is covered.

[1080] The prâ*n*a-vrata and vâyu-vrata. Comm.

[1081] Mâdhyandina text, p. 1058.

SECOND ADHYÂYA.[1082]

FIRST BRÂHMA*N*A.[1083]

1. There[1084] was formerly the proud Gârgya Bâlâki,[1085] a man of great reading. He said to Agâta*s*atru of Kâ*s*i, 'Shall I tell you Brahman?' Agâta*s*atru said: 'We give a thousand (cows) for that speech (of yours), for verily all people run away, saying, *G*anaka (the king of Mithilâ) is our father (patron)[1086].'

2. Gârgya said: 'The person that is in the sun,[1087] that I adore as Brahman.' Agâta*s*atru said to him: 'No, no! Do not speak to me on this. I adore him verily as the supreme, the head of all beings, the king. Whoso adores him thus, becomes Supreme, the head of all beings, a king.'

3. Gârgya said: 'The person that is in the moon (and in the mind), that I adore as Brahman.' Agâta*s*atru said to him: 'No, no! Do not speak to me on this. I adore him verily as the great, clad in white raiment, as Soma, the king.' Whoso adores him thus, Soma is poured out and poured forth for him day by day, and his food does not fail.[1088]

4. Gârgya said: 'The person that is in the lightning (and in the heart), that I adore as Brahman.' Agâta*s*atru said to him: 'No, no! Do not speak to me on this. I adore him verily as the luminous.' Whoso adores him thus, becomes luminous, and his offspring becomes luminous.

5. Gârgya said: 'The person that is in the ether (and in the ether of

---

[1082] Mâdhyandina text, p. 1058.

[1083] Whatever has been taught to the end of the third (according to the counting of the Upanishad, the first) Adhyâya, refers to avidyâ, ignorance. Now, however, vidyâ, the highest knowledge, is to be taught, and this is done, first of all, by a dialogue between Gârgya D*ri*ptabâlâki and king Agâta*s*atru, the former, though a Brâhma*n*a, representing the imperfect, the latter, though a Kshatriya, the perfect knowledge of Brahman. While Gârgya worships the Brahman as the sun, the moon, &c., as limited, as active and passive, Agâta*s*atru knows the Brahman as the Self.

[1084] Compare with this the fourth Adhyâya of the Kaushîtaki-upanishad, Sacred Books of the East, vol. i, p. 300; Gough, Philosophy of the Upanishads, p. 144.

[1085] Son of Balâkâ, of the race of the Gârgyas.

[1086] *G*anaka, known as a wise and liberal king. There is a play on his name, which means father, and is understood in the sense of patron, or of teacher of wisdom. The meaning is obscure; and in the Kaush. Up. IV. i, the construction is still more difficult. What is intended seems to be that Agâta*s*atru is willing to offer any reward to a really wise man, because all the wise men are running after *G*anaka and settling at his court.

[1087] The commentator expatiates on all these answers and brings them more into harmony with Vedanta doctrines. Thus he adds that the person in the sun is at the same time the person in the eye, who is both active and passive in the heart, &c.

[1088] We miss the annasyâtmâ, the Self of food, mentioned in the Kaush. Up., and evidently referred to in the last sentence of our paragraph. Suta and prasuta, poured out and poured forth, are explained as referring to the principal and the secondary sacrifices.

the heart), that I adore as Brahman.' Agâta*s*atru said to him: 'No, no! Do not speak to me on this. I adore him as what is full, and quiescent.' Whoso adores him thus, becomes filled with offspring and cattle, and his offspring does not cease from this world.

6. Gârgya said: 'The person that is in the wind (and in the breath), that I adore as Brahman.' Agâta*s*atru said to him: 'No, no! Do not speak to me on this. I adore him as Indra Vaiku*nth*a, as the unconquerable army (of the Maruts).' Whoso adores him thus, becomes victorious, unconquerable, conquering his enemies.

7. Gârgya said: 'The person that is in the fire (and in the heart), that I adore as Brahman.' Agâta*s*atru said to him: 'No, no! Do not speak to me on this. I adore him as powerful.' Whoso adores him thus, becomes powerful, and his offspring becomes powerful.

8. Gârgya said: 'The person that is in the water (in seed, and in the heart), that I adore as Brahman.' Agâta*s*atru said to him: 'No, no! Do not speak to me on this. I adore him as likeness.' Whoso adores him thus, to him comes what is likely (or proper), not what is improper; what is born from him, is like unto him.[1089]

9. Gârgya said: 'The person that is in the mirror, that I adore as Brahman.' Agâta*s*atru said to him: 'No, no! Do not speak to me on this. I adore him verily as the brilliant.' Whoso adores him thus, he becomes brilliant, his offspring becomes brilliant, and with whomsoever he comes together, he outshines them.

10. Gârgya said: 'The sound that follows a man while he moves, that I adore as Brahman.' Agâta*s*atru said to him: 'No, no! Do not speak to me on this. I adore him verily as life.' Whoso adores him thus, he reaches his full age in this world, breath does not leave him before the time.

11. Gârgya said: 'The person that is in space, that I adore as Brahman.' Agâta*s*atru said to him: 'No, no! Do not speak to me on this. I adore him verily as the second who never leaves us.'

Whoso adores him thus, becomes possessed of a second, his party is not cut off from him,

12. Gârgya said: 'The person that consists of the shadow, that I adore as Brahman.' Agâta*s*atru said to him: 'No, no! Do not speak to me on this. I adore him verily as death.' Whoso adores him thus, he reaches his whole age in this world, death does not approach him before the time.

13. Gârgya said: 'The person that is in the body,[1090] that I adore as Brahman.' Agâta*s*atru said to him: 'No, no! Do not speak to me on this.

[1089] Here the Kaush. Up. has the Self of the name, instead of pratirûpa, likeness. The commentator thinks that they both mean the same thing, because a name is the likeness of a thing. Another text of the Kaush. Up. gives here the Self of light. Pratirûpa in the sense of likeness comes in later in the Kaush. Up., § 11.

[1090] 'In the Âtman, in Pragâpati, in the Buddhi, and in the heart.' Comm.

I adore him verily as embodied.' Whoso adores him thus, becomes embodied, and his offspring becomes embodied.[1091]

Then Gârgya became silent.

14. Agâta*s*atru said: 'Thus far only?' 'Thus far only,' he replied. Agâta*s*atru said: 'This does not suffice to know it (the true Brahman).' Gârgya replied: 'Then let me come to you, as a pupil.'

15. Agâta*s*atru said: 'Verily, it is unnatural that a Brâhma*n*a should come to a Kshatriya, hoping that he should tell him the Brahman. However, I shall make you know him clearly,' thus saying he took him by the hand and rose.

And the two together came to a person who was asleep. He called him by these names, 'Thou, great one, clad in white raiment, Soma, King.'[1092] He did not rise. Then rubbing him with his hand, he woke him, and he arose.

16. Agâta*s*atru said: 'When this man was thus asleep, where was then the person (purusha), the intelligent? and from whence did he thus come back?' Gârgya did not know this?

17. Agâta*s*atru said: 'When this man was thus asleep, then the intelligent person (purusha), having through the intelligence of the senses (prâ*n*as) absorbed within himself all intelligence, lies in the ether, which is in the heart.'[1093] When he takes in these different kinds of intelligence, then it is said that the man sleeps (svapiti).[1094] Then the breath is kept in, speech is kept in, the ear is kept in, the eye is kept in, the mind is kept in.

18. But when he moves about in sleep (and dream), then these are his worlds. He is, as it were, a great king; he is, as it were, a great Brâhma*n*a; he rises, as it were, and he falls. And as a great king might keep in his own subjects, and move about, according to his pleasure, within his own domain, thus does that person (who is endowed with intelligence) keep in the various senses (prâ*n*as) and move about, according to his pleasure, within his own body (while dreaming).

19. Next, when he is in profound sleep, and knows nothing, there are the seventy-two thousand arteries called Hita, which from the heart

---

[1091] It is difficult to know what is meant here by âtman and âtmanvin. In the Kaush. Up. Agâta*s*atru refers to Pragâpati, and the commentator here does the same, adding, however, buddhi and h*ri*d. Gough translates âtmanvin by 'having peace of mind.' Deussen, p. 195, passes it over.

[1092] These names are given here as they occur in the Kaushîtaki-upanishad, not as in the B*ri*hadâra*n*yaka-upanishad, where the first name was atish*th*â*h* sarveshâm bhûtânâm mûrdhâ râgâ. This throws an important light on the composition of the Upanishads.

[1093] The ether in the heart is meant for the real Self. He has come to himself, to his Self, i.e. to the true Brahman.

[1094] Svapiti, he sleeps, is explained as sva, his own Self, and apiti for apyeti, he goes towards, so that 'he sleeps' must be interpreted as meaning 'he comes to his Self.' In another passage it is explained by svam apîto bhavati. See *S*aṅkara's Commentary on the B*ri*h. Âr. Up. vol. i, p. 372.

spread through the body.[1095] Through them he moves forth and rests in the surrounding body. And as a young man, or a great king, or a great Brâhma*n*a, having reached the summit of happiness, might rest, so does he then rest.

20. As the spider comes out with its thread, or as small sparks come forth from fire, thus do all senses, all worlds, all Devas, all beings come forth from that Self. The Upanishad (the true name and doctrine) of that Self is 'the True of the True.' Verily the senses are the true, and he is the true of the true.

SECOND BRÂHMA*N*A.[1096]

1. Verily he who knows the babe[1097] with his place,[1098] his chamber,[1099] his post,[1100] and his rope,[1101] he keeps off the seven relatives[1102] who hate him. Verily by the young is meant the inner life, by his place this (body),[1103] by his chamber this (head), by his post the vital breath, by his rope the food.

2. Then the seven imperishable ones[1104] approach him. There are the red lines in the eye, and by them Rudra clings to him. There is the water in the eye, and by it Parganya clings to him. There is the pupil, and by it Âditya (sun) clings to him, There is the dark iris, and by it Agni clings to him. There is the white eye-ball, and by it Indra, clings to him. With the lower eye-lash the earth, with the upper eye-lash the heaven clings to him. He who knows this, his food does never perish.

3. On this there is this *S*loka:

'There[1105] is a cup having its mouth below and its bottom above. Manifold glory has been placed into it. On its lip sit the seven *Ri*shis, the tongue as the eighth communicates with Brahman.' What is called the cup having its mouth below and its bottom above is this head, for its mouth (the mouth) is below, its bottom (the skull) is above. When it is said that manifold glory has been placed into it, the senses verily are manifold glory, and he therefore means the senses. When he says that the seven *Ri*shis sit on its lip, the *Ri*shis are verily the (active) senses,

---

[1095] 'Not the pericardium only, but the whole body.' Comm.

[1096] Mâdhyandina text, p. 1061.

[1097] The liṅgâtman, or subtle body which has entered this body in five ways. Comm.

[1098] The body.

[1099] The head.

[1100] The vital breath.

[1101] Food, which binds the subtle to the coarse body.

[1102] The seven organs of the head through which man perceives and becomes attached to the world.

[1103] The commentator remarks that while saying this, the body and the head are pointed out by touching them with the hand (pâ*n*ipeshapratibodhanena).

[1104] See before, I, 5, 1, 2. They are called imperishable, because they produce imperishableness by supplying food for the prâ*n*a, here called the babe.

[1105] Cf. Atharva-veda-sa*m*h. X, 8, 9.

and he means the senses. And when he says that the tongue as the eighth communicates with Brahman, it is because the tongue, as the eighth, does communicate with Brahman.

4. These two (the two ears) are the *R*ishis Gautama and Bharadvâga; the right Gautama, the left Bharadvâga. These two (the eyes) are the *R*ishis Vi*s*vâmitra and *G*amadagni; the right Vi*s*vâmitra, the left *G*amadagni. These two (the nostrils) are the *R*ishis Vasish*th*a and Ka*s*yapa; the right Vasish*th*a, the left Ka*s*yapa. The tongue is Atri, for with the tongue food is eaten, and Atri is meant for Atti, eating. He who knows this, becomes an eater of everything, and everything becomes his food.

THIRD BRÂHMA*N*A.[1106]

1. There are two forms of Brahman, the material and the immaterial, the mortal and the immortal, the solid and the fluid, sat (being) and tya (that), (i.e. sat-tya, true).[1107]

2. Everything except air and sky is material, is mortal, is solid, is definite. The essence of that which is material, which is mortal, which is solid, which is definite is the sun that shines, for he is the essence of sat (the definite).

3. But air and sky are immaterial, are immortal, are fluid, are indefinite. The essence of that which is immaterial, which is immortal, which is fluid, which is indefinite is the person in the disk of the sun, for he is the essence of tyad (the indefinite). So far with regard to the Devas.

4. Now with regard to the body. Everything except the breath and the ether within the body is material, is mortal, is solid, is definite. The essence of that which is material, which is mortal, which is solid, which is definite is the Eye, for it is the essence of sat (the definite).

5. But breath and the ether within the body are immaterial, are immortal, are fluid, are indefinite. The essence of that which is immaterial, which is immortal, which is fluid, which is indefinite is the person in the right eye, for he is the essence of tyad (the indefinite).

6. And what is the appearance of that person? Like a saffron-coloured raiment, like white wool, like cochineal, like the flame of fire, like the white lotus, like sudden lightning. He who knows this, his glory is like unto sudden lightning.

Next follows the teaching (of Brahman) by No, no![1108] for there is nothing else higher than this (if one says): 'It is not so.' Then comes the name 'the True of the True,' the senses being the True, and he (the

[1106] Mâdhyandina text, p. 1062.
[1107] Sat is explained by definite, tya or tyad by indefinite.
[1108] See III, 9, 26; IV, 2,4; IV, 4, 22; IV, 5, 15.

Brahman) the True of them.

FOURTH BRÂHMA*N*A.[1109]

1. Now when Yâ*gñ*avalkya was going to enter upon another state, he said: 'Maitreyî,[1110] verily I am going away from this my house (into the forest[1111]). Forsooth, let me make a settlement between thee and that Kâtyâyanî (my other wife).'

2. Maitreyî said: 'My Lord, if this whole earth, full of wealth, belonged to me, tell me, should I be immortal by it?'[1112]

'No,' replied Yâ*gñ*avalkya; 'like the life of rich people will be thy life. But there is no hope of immortality by wealth.'

3. And Maitreyî said: 'What should I do with that by which I do not become immortal? What my Lord knoweth (of immortality), tell that to me.'[1113]

4. Yâ*gñ*avalkya replied: 'Thou who art truly dear to me, thou speakest dear words.[1114] Come, sit down, I will explain it to thee, and mark well what I say.'

5. And he said: 'Verily, a husband is not dear, that you may love the husband; but that you may love the Self, therefore a husband is dear.

'Verily, a wife is not dear, that you may love the wife; but that you may love the Self, therefore a wife is dear.

'Verily, sons are not dear, that you may love the sons; but that you may love the Self, therefore sons are dear.

'Verily, wealth is not dear, that you may love wealth; but that you may love the Self, therefore wealth is dear.[1115]

'Verily, the Brahman-class is not dear, that you may love the Brahman-class; but that you may love the Self, therefore the Brahman-class is dear.

[1109] Mâdhyandina text, p. 1062. To the end of the third Brâhma*n*a of the second Adhyâya, all that has been taught does not yet impart the highest knowledge, the identity of the personal and the true Self, the Brahman. In the fourth Brâhma*n*a, in which the knowledge of the true Brahman is to be set forth, the Sa*m*nyâsa, the retiring from the world, is enjoined, when all desires cease, and no duties are to be performed (Sa*m*nyâsa, pârivâgya). The story is told again with slight variations in the B*ri*hadâra*n*yaka-upanishad IV, 5. The more important variations, occurring in IV, 5, are added here, marked with B. There are besides the various readings of the Mâdhyandina*s*âkhâ of the *S*atapatha-brâhma*n*a. See also Deussen, Vedânta, p. 185.

[1110] In B*ri*h. Up. IV, 5, the story begins: Yâ*gñ*avalkya had two wives, Maitreyî and Kâtyâyanî. Of these Maitreyî was conversant with Brahman, but Kâtyâyanî possessed such knowledge only as women possess.

[1111] Instead of udyâsyan, B. gives pravragishyan, the more technical term.

[1112] Should I be immortal by it, or no? B.

[1113] Tell that clearly to me. B.

[1114] Thou who art dear to me, thou hast increased what is dear (to me in this). B.

[1115] B. adds, Verily, cattle are not dear, &c.

'Verily, the Kshatra-class is not dear, that you may love the Kshatra-class; but that you may love the Self, therefore the Kshatra-class is dear.

'Verily, the worlds are not dear, that you may love the worlds; but that you may love the Self, therefore the worlds are dear.

'Verily, the Devas are not dear, that you may love the Devas; but that you may love the Self, therefore the Devas are dear.[1116]

'Verily, creatures are not dear, that you may love the creatures; but that you may love the Self, therefore are creatures dear.

'Verily, everything is not dear that you may love everything; but that you may love the Self, therefore everything is dear.

'Verily, the Self is to be seen, to be heard, to be perceived, to be marked, O Maitreyî! When we see, hear, perceive, and know the Self,[1117] then all this is known.

6. 'Whosoever looks for the Brahman-class elsewhere than in the Self, was[1118] abandoned by the Brahman-class. Whosoever looks for the Kshatra-class elsewhere than in the Self, was abandoned by the Kshatra-class. Whosoever looks for the worlds elsewhere than in the Self, was abandoned by the worlds. Whosoever looks for the Devas elsewhere than in the Self, was abandoned by the Devas.[1119] Whosoever looks for creatures elsewhere than in the Self, was abandoned by the creatures. Whosoever looks for anything elsewhere than in the Self, was abandoned by everything. This Brahman-class, this Kshatra-class, these worlds, these Devas,[1120] these[1121] creatures, this everything, all is that Self.

7. 'Now as[1122] the sounds of a drum, when beaten, cannot be seized externally (by themselves), but the sound is seized, when the drum is seized or the beater of the drum;

8. 'And as the sounds of a conch-shell, when blown, cannot be seized externally (by themselves), but the sound is seized, when the shell is seized or the blower of the shell;

9. 'And as the sounds of a lute, when played, cannot be seized externally (by themselves), but the sound is seized, when the lute is seized or the player of the lute;

10. 'As clouds of smoke proceed by themselves out of a lighted fire kindled with damp fuel, thus, verily, O Maitreyî, has been breathed forth from this great Being what we have as *Ri*g-veda, Yagur-veda,

---

[1116] B. inserts, Verily, the Vedas are not dear, &c.

[1117] When the Self has been seen, heard, perceived, and known. B.

[1118] The commentator translates, 'should be abandoned.'

[1119] B. inserts, Whosoever looks for the Vedas, &c.

[1120] B. adds, these Vedas.

[1121] B. has, all these creatures.

[1122] I construe sa yathâ with evam vai in § 12, looking upon § 11 as probably a later insertion. The sa is not the pronoun, but a particle, as in sa yadi, sa *k*et, &c.

Sama-veda, Atharvâṅgirasas, Itihâsa (legends), Purâ*n*a (cosmogonies), Vidyâ (knowledge), the Upanishads, *S*lokas (verses), Sûtras (prose rules), Anuvyâkhyânas (glosses), Vyâkhyânas (commentaries).[1123] From him alone all these were breathed forth.

11. 'As all waters find their centre in the sea, all touches in the skin, all tastes in the tongue, all smells in the nose, all colours in the eye, all sounds in the ear, all percepts in the mind, all knowledge in the heart, all actions in the hands, all movements in the feet, and all the Vedas in speech,—

12. 'As a lump of salt,[1124] when thrown into water, becomes dissolved into water, and could not be taken out again, but wherever we taste (the water) it is salt,—thus verily, O Maitreyî, does this great Being, endless, unlimited, consisting of nothing but knowledge,[1125] rise from out these elements, and vanish again in them. When he has departed, there is no more knowledge (name), I say, O Maitreyî.' Thus spoke Yâg*ñ*avalkya.

13. Then Maitreyî said: 'Here thou hast bewildered me, Sir, when thou sayest that having departed, there is no more knowledge.'[1126]

But Yâg*ñ*avalkya replied: 'O Maitreyî, I say nothing that is bewildering. This is enough, O beloved, for wisdom.[1127]

'For when there is as it were duality, then one sees the other, one smells the other, one hears the other,[1128] one salutes the other,[1129] one perceives the other,[1130] one knows the other; but when the Self only is all this, how should he smell another,[1131] how should he see[1132] another,[1133] how should he hear[1134] another, how should he salute[1135] another, how should he perceive another,[1136] how should he know another? How should he know Him by whom he knows all this? How, O beloved, should he know (himself), the Knower?'[1137]

[1123] B. adds, what is sacrificed, what is poured out, food, drink, this world and the other world, and all creatures.

[1124] See *Kh*ând. Up. VI, 13.

[1125] As a mass of salt has neither inside nor outside, but is altogether a mass of taste, thus indeed has that Self neither inside nor outside, but is altogether a mass of knowledge. B.

[1126] 'Here, Sir, thou hast landed me in utter bewilderment. Indeed, I do not understand him.' B.

[1127] Verily, beloved, that Self is imperishable, and of an indestructible nature. B.

[1128] B. inserts, one tastes the other.

[1129] B. inserts, one hears the other.

[1130] B. inserts, one touches the other.

[1131] See, B.

[1132] Smell, B.

[1133] B. inserts taste.

[1134] Salute, B.

[1135] Hear, B.

[1136] B. inserts, how should he touch another?

[1137] Instead of the last line, B. adds (IV, 5, 15): That Self is to be described by No, no! He is incomprehensible, for be cannot be comprehended; he is imperishable, for he

FIFTH BRÂHMA*N*A.[1138]

1. This earth is the honey[1139] (madhu, the effect) of all beings, and all beings are the honey (madhu, the effect) of this earth. Likewise this bright, immortal person in this earth, and that bright immortal person incorporated in the body (both are madhu). He indeed is the same as that Self, that Immortal, that Brahman, that All.

2. This water is the honey of all beings, and all beings are the honey of this water. Likewise this bright, immortal person in this water, and that bright, immortal person, existing as seed in the body (both are madhu). He indeed is the same as that Self, that Immortal, that Brahman, that All.

3. This fire is the honey of all beings, and all beings are the honey of this fire. Likewise this bright, immortal person in this fire, and that bright, immortal person, existing as speech in the body (both are madhu). He indeed is the same as that Self, that Immortal, that Brahman, that All.

4. This air is the honey of all beings, and all beings are the honey of this air. Likewise this bright, immortal person in this air, and that bright, immortal person existing as breath in the body (both are madhu). He indeed is the same as that Self, that Immortal, that Brahman, that All.

5. This sun is the honey of all beings, and all beings are the honey of this sun. Likewise this bright, immortal person in this sun, and that bright, immortal person existing as the eye in the body (both are madhu). He indeed is the same as that Self, that Immortal, that Brahman, that All.

6. This space (disa*h*, the quarters) is the honey of all beings, and all beings are the honey of this space. Likewise this bright, immortal person in this space, and that bright, immortal person existing as the ear in the body (both are madhu). He indeed is the same as that Self, that Immortal, that Brahman, that All.

---

cannot perish; he is unattached, for he does not attach himself; unfettered, he does not suffer, he does not fail. How, O beloved, should he know the Knower? Thus, O Maitreyî, thou hast been instructed. Thus far goes immortality.' Having said so, Yâ*gñ*avalkya went away (into the forest). 15. See also *Kh*ând. Up. VII, 24, 1.

[1138] Mâdhyandina text, p. 1064.

[1139] Madhu, honey, seems to be taken here as an instance of something which is both cause and effect, or rather of things which are mutually dependent on each other, or cannot exist without one other. As the bees make the honey, and the honey makes or supports the bees, bees and honey are both cause and effect, or at all events are mutually dependent on one other. In the same way the earth and all living beings are looked upon as mutually dependent, living beings presupposing the earth, and the earth presupposing living beings. This at all events seems to be the general idea of what is called the Madhuvidyâ, the science of honey, which Dadhya*k* communicated to the A*s*vins.

7. This moon is the honey of all beings, and all beings are the honey of this moon. Likewise this bright, immortal person in this moon, and that bright, immortal person existing as mind in the body (both are madhu). He indeed is the same as that Self, that Immortal, that Brahman, that All.

8. This lightning is the honey of all beings, and all beings are the honey of this lightning. Likewise this bright, immortal person in this lightning, and that bright, immortal person existing as light in the body (both are madhu). He indeed is the same as that Self, that Immortal, that Brahman, that All.

9. This thunder[1140] is the honey of all beings, and all beings are the honey of this thunder. Likewise this bright, immortal person in this thunder, and that bright, immortal person existing as sound and voice in the body (both are madhu). He indeed is the same as that Self, that Immortal, that Brahman, that All.

10. This ether is the honey of all beings, and all beings are the honey of this ether. Likewise this bright, immortal person in this ether, and that bright, immortal person existing as heart-ether in the body (both are madhu). He indeed is the same as that Self, that Immortal, that Brahman, that All.

11. This law (dharma*h*) is the honey of all beings, and all beings are the honey of this law. Likewise this bright, immortal person in this law, and that bright, immortal person existing as law in the body (both are madhu). He indeed is the same as that Self, that Immortal, that Brahman, that All.

12. This true[1141] (satyam) is the honey of all beings, and all beings are the honey of this true. Likewise this bright, immortal person in what is true, and that bright, immortal person existing as the true in the body (both are madhu). He indeed is the same as that Self, that Immortal, that Brahman, that All.

13. This mankind is the honey of all beings, and all beings are the honey of this mankind. Likewise this bright, immortal person in mankind, and that bright, immortal person existing as man in the body (both are madhu). He indeed is the same as that Self, that Immortal, that Brahman, that All.

14. This Self is the honey of all beings, and all beings are the honey of this Self Likewise this bright, immortal person in this Self, and that bright, immortal person, the Self (both are madhu). He indeed is the same as that Self, that Immortal, that Brahman, that All.

15. And verily this Self is the lord of all beings, the king of all beings. And as all spokes are contained in the axle and in the felly of a wheel, all beings, and all those selfs (of the earth, water, &c.) are

---

[1140] Stanayitnu, thunder, is explained by the commentator as Parganya.

[1141] Satyam, the true, the real, not, as it is generally translated, the truth.

contained in that Self.

16. Verily Dadhyak Âtharva*n*a proclaimed this honey (the madhu-vidyâ) to the two A*s*vins, and a *Ri*shi, seeing this, said (Rv. I, 116, 12):

'O ye two heroes (A*s*vins), I make manifest that fearful deed of yours (which you performed) for the sake of gain,[1142] like as thunder[1143] makes manifest the rain. The honey (madhu-vidyâ) which Dadhyak Âtharva*n*a proclaimed to you through the head of a horse,' . . .

17. Verily Dadhyak Âtharva*n*a[1144] proclaimed this honey to the two A*s*vins, and a *Ri*shi, seeing this, said (Rv. I, 117, 22):

'O A*s*vins, you fixed a horse's head on Âtharva*n*a Dadhyak, and he, wishing to be true (to his promise), proclaimed to you the honey, both that of Tvasht*ri*[1145] and that which is to be your secret, O ye strong ones.'

18. Verily Dadhyak Âtharva*n*a proclaimed this honey to the two A*s*vins, and a *Ri*shi, seeing this, said:

'He (the Lord) made bodies with two feet, he made bodies with four feet. Having first become a bird, he entered the bodies as purusha (as the person).' This very purusha is in all bodies the puri*s*aya, i.e. he who lies in the body (and is therefore called purusha). There is nothing that is not covered by him, nothing that is not filled by him.

19. Verily Dadhya*k* Âtharva*n*a proclaimed this honey to the two A*s*vins, and a *Ri*shi, seeing this, said (Rv. VI, 47, 18):

'He (the Lord) became like unto every form,[1146] and this is meant to reveal the (true) form of him (the Âtman). Indra (the Lord) appears multiform through the Mâyâs (appearances), for his horses (senses) are yoked, hundreds and ten.'

This (Âtman) is the horses, this (Âtman) is the ten, and the thousands, many and endless. This is the Brahman, without cause and without effect, without anything inside or outside; this Self is Brahman, omnipresent and omniscient. This is the teaching (of the Upanishads).

[1142] The translation here follows the commentary.

[1143] Tanyatu, here explained as Parganya.

[1144] *S*ankara distinguishes here between Atharva*n*a and Âtharva*n*a, if the text is correct.

[1145] *S*ankara explains Tvasht*ri* as the sun, and the sun as the head of the sacrifice which, having been cut off, was to be replaced by the pravargya rite. The knowledge of this rite forms the honey of Tvasht*ri*. The other honey which is to be kept secret is the knowledge of the Self, as taught before in the Madhu-brâhma*n*a.

[1146] He assumed all forms, and such forms, as two-footed or four-footed animals, remained permanent. Comm.

SIXTH BRÂHMA*N*A.

1. Now follows the stem:[1147]

1. Pautimâshya from Gaupavana,
2. Gaupavana from Pautimâshya,
3. Pautimâshya from Gaupavana,
4. Gaupavana from Kau*s*ika,
5. Kau*s*ika from Kau*nd*inya,
6. Kau*nd*inya from Sâ*nd*ilya,
7. Sâ*nd*ilya from Kau*s*ika and Gautama,
8. Gautama

2. from Âgnive*s*ya,

9. Âgnive*s*ya from Sâ*nd*ilya and Ânabhimlâta,
10. Sâ*nd*ilya and Ânabhimlâta from Ânabhimlâta,
11. Ânabhimlâta from Ânabhimlâta,
12. Ânabhimlâta from Gautama,
13. Gautama from Saitava and Prâ*k*înayogya,
14. Saitava and Prâ*k*înayogya from Pâra*s*arya,
15. Pâra*s*arya from Bhâradvâga,
16. Bhâradvâga from Bhâradvâga and Gautama,
17. Gautama from Bharadvâga,
18. Bharadvâga from Pârâ*s*arya,
19. Pârâ*s*arya from Vaigavâpâyana,
20. Vaigavâpâyana from Kau*s*ikâyani,
21.[1148] Kau*s*ikâyani

3. from Gh*ri*takau*s*ika,

22. Gh*ri*takau*s*ika from Pârâ*s*aryâya*n*a,
23. Pârâ*s*aryâya*n*a from Pârâ*s*arya,
24. Pârâ*s*arya from *G*âtûkar*n*ya,[1149]
25. *G*âtûkar*n*ya from Âsurâya*n*a and Yâska,[1150]
26. Âsurâyana and Yâska from Traiva*n*i,
27. Traiva*n*i from Aupagandhani,

[1147] The line of teachers and pupils by whom the Madhukâ*nd*a (the fourth Brâhma*n*a) was handed down. The Mâdhyandina-*s*âkhâ begins with ourselves, then 1. Saurpa*n*âyya, 2. Gautama, 3. Vâtsya, 4. Vâtsya and Pârâ*s*arya, 5. Sâṅk*ri*tya and Bhâradvâga, 6. Audavâhi and Sâ*nd*ilya, 7. Vaigavâpa and Gautama, 8. Vaigavâpâyana and Vaish*t*apureya, 9. Sâ*nd*ilya and Rauhi*n*âyana, 10. *S*aunaka Âtreya, and Raibhya, 11. Pautimâshyâya*n*a and Kau*nd*inyâyana: 12. Kau*nd*inya, 13. Kau*nd*inya, 14. Kau*nd*inya and Âgnive*s*ya, 15. Saitava, 16. Pârâ*s*arya, 17. *G*âtukar*n*ya, 18. Bhâradvâga, 19. Bhâradvâga, Âsurâya*n*a, and Gautama, 20. Bhâradvâga, 21. Vaigavâpâyana. Then the same as the Kâ*n*vas to *G*âtukar*n*ya, who learns from Bhâradvâga, who learns from Bhâradvâga, Âsurâya*n*a, and Yâska. Then Traiva*n*i &c. as in the Kâ*n*va-va*m*sa.

[1148] From here the Va*m*sa agrees with the Va*m*sa at the end of IV, 6.

[1149] Bhâradvâga, in Mâdhyandina text.

[1150] Bhâradvâga, Âsurâya*n*a, and Yâska, in Mâdhyandina text.

28. Aupagandhani from Âsuri,
29. Âsuri from Bhâradvâga,
30. Bhâradvâga from Âtreya,
31. Âtreya from Mâ*nt*i,
32. Mâ*nt*i from Gautama,
33, Gautama from Gautama,
34. Gautama from Vâtsya,
35. Vâtsya from Sâ*nd*ilya,
36. Sâ*nd*ilya from Kai*s*orya Kâpya,
37. Kai*s*orya Kâpya from Kumâraharita,
38. Kumâraharita from Gâlava,
39. Gâlava from Vidarbhî-kau*nd*inya,
40. Vidarbhî-kau*nd*inya from Vatsanapât Bâbhrava,
41. Vatsanapât Bâbhrava from Pathi Saubhara,
42. Pathi Saubhara from Ayâsya Âṅgirasa,
43. Ayâsya Âṅgirasa from Âbhûti Tvâsh*t*ra,
44. Âbhûti Tvâsh*t*ra from Vi*s*varûpa Tvâsh*t*ra,
45. Vi*s*varûpa Tvâsh*t*ra from A*s*vinau,
46. A*s*vinau from Dadhya*k* Âtharva*n*a,
47. Dadhya*k* Âtharva*n*a from Atharvan Daiva,
48. Atharvan Daiva from M*ri*tyu Prâdhva*m*sana,
49. M*ri*tyu Prâdhva*m*sana from Prâdhva*m*sana,
50. Prâdhva*m*sana from Ekarshi,
51. Ekarshi from Vipra*k*itti,[1151]
52. Vipra*k*itti from Vyash*t*i,
53. Vyash*t*i from Sanâru,
54. Sanâru from Sanâtana,
55. Sanâtana from Sanaga,
56. Sanaga from Paramesh*th*in,
57. Paramesh*th*in from Brahman,
58. Brahman is Svayambhu, self-existent.

Adoration to Brahman.[1152]

THIRD ADHYÂYA.

FIRST BRÂHMA*N*A.[1153]

Adoration to the Highest Self (Paramâtman)!

1. *G*anaka Vaideha (the king of the Videhas) sacrificed with a sacrifice at which many presents were offered to the priests of (the A*s*vamedha). Brâhma*n*as of the Kurus and the Pâ*ñ*kâlas had come

1151 Vipragitti, in Mâdhyandina text.
1152 Similar genealogies are found B*ri*h. Âr. Up. IV, 6, and VI, 5.
1153 Mâdhyandina text, p. 1067.

thither, and *G*anaka Vaideha wished to know, which of those Brâhma*n*as was the best read. So he enclosed a thousand cows, and ten pâdas (of gold)[1154] were fastened to each pair of horns.

2. And *G*anaka spoke to them: 'Ye venerable Brâhma*n*as, he who among you is the wisest, let him drive away these cows.'

Then those Brâhma*n*as durst not, but Yâ*gñ*avalkya said to his pupil: 'Drive them away, my dear.'

He replied: 'O glory of the Sâman'[1155] and drove them away.

The Brâhma*n*as became angry and said: 'How could he call himself the wisest among us?'

Now there was A*s*vala, the Hot*ri* priest of *G*anaka Vaideha. He asked him: 'Are you indeed the wisest among us, O Yâ*gñ*avalkya?' He replied: 'I bow before the wisest (the best knower of Brahman), but I wish indeed to have these cows.'

Then A*s*vala, the Hot*ri* priest, undertook to question him.

1. 'Yâ*gñ*avalkya,' he said, 'everything here (connected with the sacrifice) is reached by death, everything is overcome by death. By what means then is the sacrificer freed beyond the reach of death?'

Yâ*gñ*avalkya said: 'By the Hot*ri* priest, who is Agni (fire), who is speech. For speech is the Hot*ri* of the sacrifice (or the sacrificer), and speech is Agni, and he is the Hot*ri*. This constitutes freedom, and perfect freedom (from death).'

4. 'Yâ*gñ*avalkya,' he said, 'everything here is reached by day and night, everything is overcome by day and night. By what means then is the sacrificer freed beyond the reach of day and night?'

Yâ*gñ*avalkya said: 'By the Adhvaryu priest, who is the eye, who is Âditya (the sun).[1156] For the eye is the Adhvaryu of the sacrifice, and the eye is the sun, and he is the Adhvaryu. This constitutes freedom, and perfect freedom.'

5. 'Yâ*gñ*avalkya,' he said, 'everything here is reached by the waxing and waning of the moon, everything is overcome by the waxing and waning of the moon. By what means then is the sacrificer freed beyond the reach of the waxing and waning of the moon?'

Yâ*gñ*avalkya said: 'By the Udgât*ri* priest, who is Vâyu (the wind), who is the breath. For the breath is the Udgât*ri* of the sacrifice, and the breath is the wind, and he is the Udgât*ri*. This constitutes freedom, and perfect freedom.'

[1154] Pala*k*aturbhâga*h* pâda*h* suvar*n*asya. Comm.

[1155] One expects iti after udaga, but Sâma*s*ravas is applied to Yâ*gñ*avalkya, and not to the pupil. Yâ*gñ*avalkya, as the commentator observes, was properly a teacher of the Yagur-veda, but as the pupil calls him Sâmasravas, he shows that Yâ*gñ*avalkya knew all the four Vedas, because the Sâmans are taken from the *Ri*g-veda, and the Atharva-veda is contained in the other three Vedas. Regnaud, however, refers it to the pupil, and translates, 'Ô toi qui apprends le Sâma-veda.'

[1156] One expects âdityena *k*akshushâ, instead of *k*akshushâdityena, but see § 6.

6. 'Yâg*ñ*avalkya,' he said, 'this sky is, as it were, without an ascent (staircase.) By what approach does the sacrificer approach the Svarga world?'

Yâg*ñ*avalkya said: 'By the Brahman priest, who is the mind (manas), who is the moon. For the mind is the Brahman of the sacrifice, and the mind is the moon, and he is the Brahman. This constitutes freedom, and perfect freedom. These are the complete deliverances (from death).'

Next follow the achievements.

7. 'Yâg*ñ*avalkya,' he said, 'how many *Rik* verses will the Hot*ri* priest employ to-day at this sacrifice?'

'Three,' replied Yâg*ñ*avalkya.

'And what are these three?'

'Those which are called Puronuvâkyâ, Yâgyâ, and, thirdly, *S*asyâ.'[1157]

'What does he gain by them?'

'All whatsoever has breath.'

8. 'Yâg*ñ*avalkya,' he said, 'how many oblations (âhuti) will the Adhvaryu priest employ to-day at this sacrifice?'

'Three,' replied Yâg*ñ*avalkya.

'And what are these three?'

'Those which, when offered, flame up; those which, when offered, make an excessive noise; and those which, when offered, sink down.'[1158]

'What does he gain by them?'

'By those which, when offered, flame up, he gains the Deva (god) world, for the Deva world flames up, as it were. By those which, when offered, make an excessive noise, he gains the Pit*ri* (father) world, for the Pit*ri* world is excessively (noisy).[1159] By those which, when offered, sink down, he gains the Manushya (man) world, for the Manushya world is, as it were, down below.'

9. 'Yâg*ñ*avalkya,' he said, 'with how many deities does the Brahman priest on the right protect to-day this sacrifice?'

'By one,' replied Yâg*ñ*avalkya.

'And which is it?'

'The mind alone; for the mind is endless, and the Vi*s*vedevas are endless, and he thereby gains the endless world.'

10. 'Yâg*ñ*avalkya,' he said, 'how many Stotriyâ hymns will the

---

[1157] The Puronuvâkyâs are hymns employed before the actual sacrifice, the Yâgyâs accompany the sacrifice, the *S*asyâs are used for the *S*astra. All three are called Stotriyâs.

[1158] These oblations are explained as consisting of wood and oil, of flesh, and of milk and Soma. The first, when thrown on the fire, flame up. The second, when thrown on the fire, make a loud hissing noise. The third, consisting of milk, Soma, &c., sink down into the earth.

[1159] On account of the cries of those who wish to be delivered out of it. Comm.

Udgât*ri* priest employ to-day at this sacrifice?'

'Three,' replied Yâg*ñ*avalkya.

'And what are these three?'

'Those which are called Puronuvâkyâ, Yâgyâ, and, thirdly, *S*asyâ.'

'And what are these with regard to the body (adhyâtmam)?'

'The Puronuvâkyâ is Prâ*n*a (up-breathing), the Yâgyâ the Apâ*n*a (down-breathing), the *S*asyâ the Vyâna (back-breathing).'

'What does he gain by them?'

'He gains the earth by the Puronuvâkyâ, the sky by the Yâgyâ, heaven by the *S*asyâ.'

After that A*s*vala held his peace.

SECOND BRÂHMA*N*A.[1160]

1. Then *G*âratkârava Ârtabhâga[1161] asked. 'Yâg*ñ*avalkya,' he said, 'how many Grahas are there, and how many Atigrahas?'[1162]

'Eight Grahas,' he replied, 'and eight Atigrahas.'

'And what are these eight Grahas and eight Atigrahas?'

2. 'Prâ*n*a (breath) is one Graha, and that is seized by Apâna (down-breathing) as the Atigrâha,[1163] for one smells with the Apâna.'

3. 'Speech (vâ*k*) is one Graha, and that is seized by name (nâman) as the Atigrâha, for with speech one pronounces names.

4. 'The tongue is one Graha, and that is seized by taste as the Atigrâha, for with the tongue one perceives tastes.'

5. 'The eye is one Graha, and that is seized by form as the Atigrâha, for with the eye one sees forms.'

6. 'The ear is one Graha, and that is seized by sound as the Atigrâha, for with the ear one hears sounds.'

7. 'The mind is one Graha, and that is seized by desire as the Atigrâha, for with the mind one desires desires.'

8. 'The arms are one Graha, and these are seized by work as the Atigrâha, for with the arms one works work.'

9. 'The skin is one Graha, and that is seized by touch as the Atigrâha, for with the skin one perceives touch. These are the eight Grahas and the eight Atigrahas.'

10. 'Yâg*ñ*avalkya,' he said, 'everything is the food of death. What then is the deity to whom death is food?'

'Fire (agni) is death, and that is the food of water. Death is

---

[1160] Mâdhyandina text, p. 1069.

[1161] A descendant of *Ri*tabhâga of the family of *G*aratkâru.

[1162] Graha is probably meant originally in its usual sacrificial sense, as a vessel for offering oblations. But its secondary meaning, in which it is here taken, is a taker, a grasper, i.e. an organ of sense, while atigraha is intended for that which is grasped, i.e. an object of sense.

[1163] Here the â is long, *kh*ândasatvât.

conquered again.'

11. 'Yâ*gñ*avalkya,' he said, 'when such a person (a sage) dies, do the vital breaths (prâ*n*as) move out of him or no?'

'No,' replied Yâ*gñ*avalkya; 'they are gathered up in him, he swells, he is inflated, and thus inflated the dead lies at rest.'

12. 'Yâ*gñ*avalkya,' he said, 'when such a man dies, what does not leave him?'

'The name,' he replied; 'for the name is endless, the Vi*s*vedevas are endless, and by it he gains the endless world.'

13. 'Yâ*gñ*avalkya,' he said,' when the speech of this dead person enters into the fire,[1164] breath into the air, the eye into the sun, the mind into the moon, the hearing into space, into the earth the body, into the ether the self, into the shrubs the hairs of the body, into the trees the hairs of the head, when the blood and the seed are deposited in the water, where is then that person?'

Yâ*gñ*avalkya said: 'Take my hand, my friend. We two alone shall know of this; let this question of ours not be (discussed) in public.' Then these two went out and argued, and what they said was karman (work), what they praised was karman,[1165] viz. that a man becomes good by good work, and bad by bad work. After that *G*âratkârava Ârtabhâga held his peace.

THIRD BRÂHMA*N*A.[1166]

1. Then Bhugyu Lâhyâyani asked. 'Yâ*gñ*avalkya,' he said, 'we wandered about as students,[1167] and came to the house of Pata*ñk*ala Kâpya.' He had a daughter who was possessed by a Gandharva. We asked him, 'Who art thou?' and he (the Gandharva) replied: 'I am Sudhanvan, the Âṅgirasa.' And when we asked him about the ends of the world, we said to him, 'Where were the Pârikshitas?[1168] Where then were the Pârikshitas, I ask thee, Yâ*gñ*avalkya, where were the Pârikshitas?'

2. Yâ*gñ*avalkya said: 'He said to thee, I suppose, that they went where those go who have performed a horse-sacrifice.'

He said: 'And where do they go who have performed a horse-sacrifice?'

Yâ*gñ*avalkya replied: 'Thirty-two journeys of the car of the sun is

---

[1164] The commentator explains purusha here by asamyagdar*s*in, one who does not know the whole truth. See also Deussen, Vedânta, p. 405, and p. 399, note.

[1165] What is intended is that the sa*m*sâra continues by means of karman, while karman by itself never leads to moksha.

[1166] Mâdhyandina text, p. 1070.

[1167] The commentator explains *k*arakâ*h* as adhyayanârtha*m* vrata*k*ara*n*â*k* *k*arakâ*h*, adhvaryavo vâ. See Professor R. G. Bhandarkar, in Indian Antiquary, 1883, p. 145.

[1168] An old royal race, supposed to have vanished from the earth.

this world. The earth surrounds it on every side, twice as large, and the ocean surrounds this earth on every side, twice as large. Now there is between[1169] them a space as large as the edge of a razor or the wing of a mosquito. Indra, having become a bird, handed them (through the space) to Vâyu (the air), and Vâyu (the air), holding them within himself, conveyed them to where they dwell who have performed a horse-sacrifice. Somewhat in this way did he praise Vâyu indeed. Therefore Vâyu (air) is everything by itself, and Vâyu is all things together. He who knows this, conquers death.' After that Bhugyu Lâhyâyani held his peace.

FOURTH BRÂHMA*N*A.[1170]

1. Then Ushasta Kâkrâya*n*a asked. 'Yâg*ñ*avalkya,' he said, 'tell me the Brahman which is visible, not invisible,[1171] the Self (âtman), who is within all.'

Yâg*ñ*avalkya replied: 'This, thy Self, who is within all.'

'Which Self, O Yâg*ñ*avalkya, is within all?'

Yâg*ñ*avalkya replied: 'He who breathes in the up-breathing, he is thy Self, and within all. He who breathes in the down-breathing, he is thy Self, and within all. He who breathes in the on-breathing, he is thy Self, and within all. He who breathes in the out-breathing, he is thy Self, and within all. This is thy Self, who is within all.'

2. Ushasta Kâkrâya*n*a said: 'As one might say, this is a cow, this is a horse, thus has this been explained by thee. Tell me the Brahman which is visible, not invisible, the Self, who is within all.'

Yâg*ñ*avalkya replied: 'This, thy Self, who is within all.'

'Which Self, O Yâg*ñ*avalkya, is within all?'

Yâg*ñ*avalkya replied: 'Thou couldst not see the (true) seer of sight, thou couldst not hear the (true) hearer of hearing, nor perceive the perceiver of perception, nor know the knower of knowledge. This is thy Self, who is within all. Everything also is of evil.' After that Ushasta Kâkrâya*n*a held his peace.

[1169] The commentator explains that this small space or hole is between the two halves of the mundane egg.

[1170] Mâdhyandina text, p. 1071. It follows after what is here the fifth Brâhma*n*a, treating of Kaho*d*a Kaushîtakeya.

[1171] Deussen, Vedanta, p. 163, translates, 'das immanente, nicht transcendente Brahman,' which is right, but too modern.

FIFTH BRÂHMA*N*A.[1172]

1. Then Kahola Kaushîtakeya asked. 'Yâg*ñ*avalkya,' he said, 'tell me the Brahman which is visible, not invisible, the Self (Âtman), who is within all.'

Yâg*ñ*avalkya replied: 'This, thy Self, who is within all.'

'Which Self, O Yâg*ñ*avalkya, is within all?'

Yâg*ñ*avalkya replied: 'He who overcomes hunger and thirst, sorrow, passion, old age, and death. When Brâhma*n*as know that Self, and have risen above the desire for sons,[1173] wealth, and (new) worlds,[1174] they wander about as mendicants. For a desire for sons is desire for wealth, a desire for wealth is desire for worlds. Both these are indeed desires. Therefore let a Brâhma*n*a, after he has done with learning, wish to stand by real strength;[1175] after he has done with that strength and learning, he becomes a Muni (a Yogin); and after he has done with what is not the knowledge of a Muni, and with what is the knowledge of a Muni, he is a Brâhma*n*a. By whatever means he has become a Brâhma*n*a, he is such indeed.[1176] Everything else is of evil.' After that Kahola Kaushîtakeya held his peace.

SIXTH BRÂHMA*N*A.[1177]

1. Then Gârgî Vâ*k*aknavî asked. 'Yâg*ñ*avalkya,' she said, 'everything here is woven, like warp and woof, in water. What then is that in which water is woven, like warp and woof?'

'In air, O Gârgî,' he replied.

'In what then is air woven, like warp and woof?'

'In the worlds of the sky, O Gârgî,' he replied.

'In what then are the worlds of the sky woven, like warp and woof?'

'In the worlds of the Gandharvas, O Gârgî,' he replied.

[1172] Mâdhyandina text, p. 1071, standing before the fourth Brâhma*n*a.

[1173] See B*r*ih. Âr. Up. IV, 4, 22.

[1174] Life in the world of the Fathers, or in the world of the Gods.

[1175] Knowledge of the Self, which enables us to dispense with all other knowledge.

[1176] Mr. Gough proposes as an alternative rendering: 'Let a Brâhma*n*a renounce learning and become as a child; and after renouncing learning and a childlike mind, let him become a quietist; and when he has made an end of quietism and non-quietism, he shall become a Brâhma*n*a, a Brâhma*n*a indeed.' Deussen takes a similar view, but I doubt whether 'the knowledge of babes' is not a Christian rather than an Indian idea, in spite of *S*aṅkara's remarks on Ved. Sûtra, III, 4, 50, which are strangely at variance with his commentary here. Possibly the text may be corrupt, for tish*th*âset too is a very peculiar form. We might conjecture balyena, as we have abalyam, in IV, 4, 1. In Kaush. Up. III, 3, âbâlyam stands for âbălyam, possibly for ăbâlyam. The construction of kena syâd yena syât tenedr*is*a eva, however, is well known.

[1177] Mâdhyandina text, p. 1072.

'In what then are the worlds of the Gandharvas woven, like warp and woof?'

'In the worlds of Âditya (sun), O Gârgî,' he replied.

'In what then are the worlds of Âditya (sun) woven, like warp and woof?'

'In the worlds of *K*andra (moon), O Gârgî,' he replied.

'In what then are the worlds of *K*andra (moon) woven, like warp and woof?'

'In the worlds of the Nakshatras (stars), O Gârgî,' he replied.

'In what then are the worlds of the Nakshatras (stars) woven, like warp and woof?'

'In the worlds of the Devas (gods), O Gârgî,' he replied.

'In what then are the worlds of the Devas (gods) woven, like warp and woof?'

'In the worlds of Indra, O Gârgî,' he replied.

'In what then are the worlds of Indra woven, like warp and woof?'

'In the worlds of Pragâpati, O Gârgî,' he replied.

'In what then are the worlds of Pragâpati woven, like warp and woof?'

'In the worlds of Brahman, O Gârgî,' he replied.

'In what then are the worlds of Brahman woven, like warp and woof?'

Yâg*ñ*avalkya said: 'O Gârgî, Do not ask too much, lest thy head should fall off. Thou askest too much about a deity about which we are not to ask too much.[1178] Do not ask too much, O Gârgî.' After that Gargî Vâ*k*aknavî held her peace.

SEVENTH BRÂHMA*N*A.[1179]

1. Then Uddâlaka Âruni[1180] asked. 'Yâg*ñ*avalkya,' he said, 'we dwelt among the Madras in the houses of Pata*ñk*ala Kâpya, studying the sacrifice. His wife was possessed of a Gandharva, and we asked him: "Who art thou?" He answered: "I am Kabandha Âtharva*n*a." And he said to Pata*ñk*ala Kâpya and to (us) students: "Dost thou know, Kâpya, that thread by which this world and the other world, and all beings are strung together?" And Pata*ñk*ala Kâpya replied: "I do not know it, Sir." He said again to Pata*ñk*ala Kâpya and to (us) students: "Dost thou know, Kâpya, that puller (ruler) within (antaryâmin), who within pulls (rules) this world and the other world and all beings?" And Pata*ñk*ala Kâpya replied: "I do not know it, Sir." He said again to Pata*ñk*ala Kâpya and to (us) students: "He, O Kâpya, who knows that

[1178] According to the commentator questions about Brahman are to be answered from the Scriptures only, and not to be settled by argument.

[1179] Mâdhyandina text, p. 1072.

[1180] Afterwards addressed as Gautama; see before, p. 1, note.

thread and him who pulls (it) within, he knows Brahman, he knows the worlds, he knows the Devas, he knows the Vedas, he knows the Bhûtas (creatures), he knows the Self, he knows everything." Thus did he (the Gandharva) say to them, and I know it. If thou, O Yâg*ñ*avalkya, without knowing that string and the puller within, drivest away those Brahma-cows (the cows offered as a prize to him who best knows Brahman), thy head will fall off.'

Yâg*ñ*avalkya said: 'O Gautama, I believe I know that thread and the puller within.'

The other said: 'Anybody may say, I know, I know. Tell what thou knowest.'

2. Yâg*ñ*avalkya said: 'Vâyu (air) is that thread, O Gautama. By air, as by a thread, O Gautama, this world and the other world, and all creatures are strung together. Therefore, O Gautama, people say of a dead person that his limbs have become unstrung; for by air, as by a thread, O Gautama, they were strung together.'

The other said: 'So it is, O Yâg*ñ*avalkya. Tell now (who is) the puller within.'

3. Yâg*ñ*avalkya said: 'He who dwells in the earth, and within the earth,[1181] whom the earth does not know, whose body the earth is, and who pulls (rules) the earth within, he is thy Self, the puller (ruler) within, the immortal.'

4. 'He who dwells in the water, and within the water, whom the water does not know, whose body the water is, and who pulls (rules) the water within, he is thy Self, the puller (ruler) within, the immortal.'

5. 'He who dwells in the fire, and within the fire, whom the fire does not know, whose body the fire is, and who pulls (rules) the fire within, he is thy Self, the puller (ruler) within, the immortal.'

6. 'He who dwells in the sky, and within the sky, whom the sky does not know, whose body the sky is, and who pulls (rules) the sky within, he is thy Self, the puller (ruler) within, the immortal.'

7. 'He who dwells in the air (vâyu), and within the air, whom the air does not know, whose body the air is, and who pulls (rules) the air within, he is thy Self, the puller (ruler) within, the immortal.'

8. 'He who dwells in the heaven (dyu), and within the heaven, whom the heaven does not know, whose body the heaven is, and who pulls (rules) the heaven within, he is thy Self, the puller (ruler) within, the immortal.'

9. 'He who dwells in the sun (Âditya), and within the sun, whom the sun does not know, whose body the sun is, and who pulls (rules) the sun within, he is thy Self, the puller (ruler) within, the immortal.'

[1181] I translate antara by 'within,' according to the commentator, who explains it by abhyantara, but I must confess that I should prefer to translate it by 'different from,' as Deussen does, l. c. p. 160, particularly as it governs an ablative.

10. 'He who dwells in the space (disah), and within the space, whom the space does not know, whose body the space is, and who pulls (rules) the space within, he is thy Self, the puller (ruler) within, the immortal.'

11. 'He who dwells in the moon and stars (*k*andra-târakam), and within the moon and stars, whom the moon and stars do not know, whose body the moon and stars are, and who pulls (rules) the moon and stars within, he is thy Self, the puller (ruler) within, the immortal.'

12. 'He who dwells in the ether (âkâsa), and within the ether, whom the ether does not know, whose body the ether is, and who pulls (rules) the ether within, he is thy Self, the puller (ruler) within, the immortal.'

13. 'He who dwells in the darkness (tamas), and within the darkness, whom the darkness does not know, whose body the darkness is, and who pulls (rules) the darkness within, he is thy Self, the puller (ruler) within, the immortal.'

14. 'He who dwells in the light (tegas), and within the light, whom the light does not know, whose body the light is, and who pulls (rules) the light within, he is thy Self, the puller (ruler) within, the immortal.'

So far with respect to the gods (adhidaivatam); now with respect to beings (adhibhûtam).

15. Yâg*ñ*avalkya said: 'He who dwells in all beings, and within all beings, whom all beings do not know, whose body all beings are, and who pulls (rules) all beings within, he is thy Self, the puller (ruler) within, the immortal.'

16. 'He who dwells in the breath (prâ*n*a), and within the breath, whom the breath does not know, whose body the breath is, and who pulls (rules) the breath within, he is thy Self, the puller (ruler) within, the immortal.'

17. 'He who dwells in the tongue (vâ*k*), and within the tongue, whom the tongue does not know, whose body the tongue is, and who pulls (rules) the tongue within, he is thy Self, the puller (ruler) within, the immortal.'

18. 'He who dwells in the eye, and within the eye, whom the eye does not know, whose body the eye is, and who pulls (rules) the eye within, he is thy Self, the puller (ruler) within, the immortal.'

19. 'He who dwells in the ear, and within the ear, whom the ear does not know, whose body the ear is, and who pulls (rules) the ear within, he is thy Self, the puller (ruler) within, the immortal.'

20. 'He who dwells in the mind, and within the mind, whom the mind does not know, whose body the mind is, and who pulls (rules) the mind within, he is thy Self, the puller (ruler) within, the immortal.'

21. 'He who dwells in the skin, and within the skin, whom the skin does not know, whose body the skin is, and who pulls (rules) the skin within, he is thy Self, the puller (ruler) within, the immortal.'

22. 'He who dwells in knowledge,[1182] and within knowledge, whom knowledge does not know, whose body knowledge is, and who pulls (rules) knowledge within, he is thy Self, the puller (ruler) within, the immortal.'

23. 'He who dwells in the seed, and within the seed, whom the seed does not know, whose body the seed is, and who pulls (rules) the seed within, he is thy Self, the puller (ruler) within, the immortal; unseen, but seeing; unheard, but hearing; unperceived, but perceiving; unknown, but knowing. There is no other seer but he, there is no other hearer but he, there is no other perceiver but he, there is no other knower but he. This is thy Self, the ruler within, the immortal. Everything else is of evil.' After that Uddâlaka Âruni held his peace.

EIGHTH BRÂHMA*N*A.[1183]

1. Then Vâ*k*aknavî[1184] said: 'Venerable Brâhma*n*as, I shall ask him two questions. If he will answer them, none of you, I think, will defeat him in any argument concerning Brahman.'

Yâg*ñ*avalkya said: 'Ask, O Gârgî.'

2. She said: 'O Yâg*ñ*avalkya, as the son of a warrior from the Kâ*s*îs or Videhas might string his loosened bow, take two pointed foe-piercing arrows in his hand and rise to do battle, I have risen to fight thee with two questions. Answer me these questions.'

Yâg*ñ*avalkya said: 'Ask, O Gârgî.'

3. She said: 'O Yâg*ñ*avalkya, that of which they say that it is above the heavens, beneath the earth, embracing heaven and earth,[1185] past, present, and future, tell me in what is it woven, like warp and woof?'

4. Yâg*ñ*avalkya said: 'That of which they say that it is above the heavens, beneath the earth, embracing heaven and earth, past, present, and future, that is woven, like warp and woof, in the ether (âkâ*s*a).'

5. She said: 'I bow to thee, O Yâg*ñ*avalkya, who hast solved me that question. Get thee ready for the second.'

Yâg*ñ*avalkya said:[1186] 'Ask, O Gârgî.'

6. She said: 'O Yâg*ñ*avalkya, that of which they say that it is above the heavens, beneath the earth, embracing heaven and earth, past, present, and future, tell me in what is it woven, like warp and woof?'

7. Yâg*ñ*avalkya said: 'That of which they say that it is above the heavens, beneath the earth, embracing heaven and earth, past, present,

---

[1182] Self, i.e. the individual Self, according to the Mâdhyandina school; see Deussen, p. 161.

[1183] Mâdhyandina text, p. 1075.

[1184] Gârgî, not the wife of Yâg*ñ*avalkya.

[1185] Deussen, p. 143, translates, 'between heaven and earth,' but that would be the antariksha.

[1186] This repetition does not occur in the Mâdhyandina text.

and future, that is woven, like warp and woof, in the ether.'

Gârgî said: 'In what then is the ether woven, like warp and woof?'

8. He said: 'O Gârgî, the Brâhma*n*as call this the Akshara (the imperishable). It is neither coarse nor fine, neither short nor long, neither red (like fire) nor fluid (like water); it is without shadow, without darkness, without air, without ether, without attachment,[1187] without taste, without smell, without eyes, without ears, without speech, without mind, without light (vigour), without breath, without a mouth (or door), without measure, having no within and no without, it devours nothing, and no one devours it.'

9. 'By the command of that Akshara (the imperishable), O Gârgî, sun and moon stand apart.[1188] By the command of that Akshara, O Gârgî, heaven and earth stand apart. By the command of that Akshara, O Gârgî, what are called moments (nimesha), hours (muhûrta), days and nights, half-months, months, seasons, years, all stand apart. By the command of that Akshara, O Gârgî, some rivers flow to the East from the white mountains, others to the West, or to any other quarter. By the command of that Akshara, O Gârgî, men praise those who give, the gods follow the sacrificer, the fathers the Darvî-offering.'

10. 'Whosoever, O Gârgî, without knowing that Akshara (the imperishable), offers oblations in this world, sacrifices, and performs penance for a thousand years, his work will have an end. Whosoever, O Gargî, without knowing this Akshara, departs this world, he is miserable (like a slave).[1189] But he, O Gârgî, who departs this world, knowing this Akshara, he is a Brâhma*n*a.'

11. 'That Brahman,' O Gârgî, 'is unseen, but seeing; unheard, but hearing; unperceived, but perceiving; unknown, but knowing. There is nothing that sees but it, nothing that hears but it, nothing that perceives but it, nothing that knows but it. In that Akshara then, O Gârgî, the ether is woven, like warp and woof.'

12. Then said Gargî: 'Venerable Brâhmans, you may consider it a great thing, if you get off by bowing before him. No one, I believe, will defeat him in any argument concerning Brahman.' After that Vâka*k*navî held her peace.

[1187] Not adhering to anything, like lac or gum.

[1188] Each follows its own course.

[1189] He stores up the effects from work, like a miser his riches,' Roer. 'He is helpless,' Gough.

NINTH BRÂHMA*N*A.[1190]

1. Then Vidagdha *S*âkalya asked him:[1191] 'How many gods are there, O Yâg*ñ*avalkya?' He replied with this very Nivid:[1192] 'As many as are mentioned in the Nivid of the hymn of praise addressed to the Vi*s*vedevas, viz. three and three hundred, three and three thousand.'[1193]

'Yes,' he said, and asked again: 'How many gods are there really, O Yâg*ñ*avalkya?'

'Thirty-three,' he said.

'Yes,' he said, and asked again: 'How many gods are there really, O Yâg*ñ*avalkya?'

'Six,' he said.

'Yes,' he said, and asked again: 'How many gods are there really, O Yâg*ñ*avalkya?'

'Three,' he said.

'Yes,' he said, and asked again: 'How many gods are there really, O Yâg*ñ*avalkya?'

'Two,' he said.

'Yes,' he said, and asked again: 'How many gods are there really, O Yâg*ñ*avalkya?'

'One and a half (adhyardha),' he said.

'Yes,' he said, and asked again: 'How many gods are there really, O Yâg*ñ*avalkya?'

'One,' he said.

'Yes,' he said, and asked: 'Who are these three and three hundred, three and three thousand?'

2. Yâg*ñ*avalkya replied: 'They are only the various powers of them, in reality there are only thirty-three gods.'[1194]

He asked: 'Who are those thirty-three?'

Yâg*ñ*avalkya replied: 'The eight Vasus, the eleven Rudras, the twelve Âdityas. They make thirty-one, and Indra and Pragâpati make the thirty-three.'[1195]

[1190] Mâdhyandina text, p. 1076.

[1191] This disputation between Yâg*ñ*avalkya and Vidagdha *S*âkalya occurs in a simpler form in the *S*atapatha-brâhma*n*a, XI, p. 873. He is here represented as the first who defies Yâg*ñ*avalkya, and whom Yâg*ñ*avalkya asks at once, whether the other Brâhmans had made him the ulmukâvakshaya*n*a, the cat's paw, literally one who has to take a burning piece of wood out of the fire (ardha. dagdhakâsh*th*am ulmukam; tasya vahirnirasanam avakshaya*nam* vinâ*s*a*h*). The end, however, is different, for on asking the nature of the one god, the Prâ*n*a, he is told by Yâg*ñ*avalkya that he has asked for what he ought not to ask, and that therefore he will die and thieves will carry away his bones.

[1192] Nivid, old and short invocations of the gods; devatâsaṅkhyâvâ*k*akâni mantrapâdni kâni*k*id vai*s*vadeve *s*astre *s*asyante. *S*aṅkara, and Dvivedagaṅga.

[1193] This would make 3306 devatâs.

[1194] 'The glories of these are three and thirty.' Gough, p. 172.

[1195] Trayastri*ms*au, i.e. trayastri*ms*ata*h* pûra*n*au.

3. He asked: 'Who are the Vasus.'

Yâgñavalkya replied: 'Agni (fire), P*ri*thivî (earth), Vâyu (air), Antariksha (sky), Âditya (sun), Dyu (heaven), *K*andramas (moon), the Nakshatras (stars), these are the Vasus, for in them all that dwells (this world)[1196] rests; and therefore they are called Vasus.'

4. He asked: 'Who are the Rudras?'

Yâgñavalkya replied: 'These ten vital breaths (prâ*n*as, the senses, i.e. the five *gñ*ânendriyas, and the five karmendriyas), and Âtman,[1197] as the eleventh. When they depart from this mortal body, they make us cry (rodayanti), and because they make us cry, they are called Rudras.'

5. He asked: 'Who are the Âdityas?'

Yâgñavalkya replied: 'The twelve months of the year, and they are Âdityas, because they move along (yanti), taking up everything[1198] (âdadânâ*h*). Because they move along, taking up everything, therefore they are called Âdityas.'

6. He asked: 'And who is Indra, and who is Pragâpati?'

Yâgñavalkya replied: 'Indra is thunder, Pragâpati is the sacrifice.'

He asked: 'And what is the thunder?'

Yâgñavalkya replied: 'The thunderbolt.'

He asked: 'And what is the sacrifice?'

Yâgñavalkya replied: 'The (sacrificial) animals.'

7. He asked: 'Who are the six?'

Yâgñavalkya replied: 'Agni (fire), P*ri*thivî (earth), Vâyu (air), Antariksha (sky), Âditya (sun), Dyu (heaven), they are the six, for they are all[1199] this, the six.'

8. He asked: 'Who are the three gods?'

Yâgñavalkya replied: 'These three worlds, for in them all these gods exist.'

He asked: 'Who are the two gods?'

Yâgñavalkya replied: 'Food and breath.'

He asked: 'Who is the one god and a half?'

Yâgñavalkya replied: 'He that blows.'

9. Here they say: 'How is it that he who blows like one only, should be called one and a half (adhyardha)?' And the answer is: 'Because, when the wind was blowing, everything grew (adhyardhnot).'

He asked: 'Who is the one god?'

[1196] The etymological explanation of Vasu is not quite clear, and the commentator hardly explains our text. Perhaps vasu is meant for the world or the dwellers therein. The more usual explanation occurs in the *S*atap. Brâh. p. 1077, ete hîda*m* sarva*m* vâsayante tadyad ida*m* sarva*m* vâsayante tasmâd vasava iti; or on p. 874, where we read te yad ida*m* sarvam &c.

[1197] Âtman is here explained as manas, the common sensory.

[1198] The life of men, and the fruits of their work.

[1199] They are the thirty-three gods.

Yâg*ñ*avalkya replied: 'Breath (prâ*n*a), and he is Brahman (the Sûtrâtman), and they call him That (tyad).'

10. *S*âkalya said:[1200] 'Whosoever knows that person (or god) whose dwelling (body) is the earth, whose sight (world) is fire,[1201] whose mind is light,—the principle of every (living) self, he indeed is a teacher, O Yâg*ñ*avalkya.'

Yâg*ñ*avalkya said: 'I know that person, the principle of every self, of whom thou speakest. This corporeal (material, earthy) person, "he is he." But tell me,[1202] *S*âkalya, who is his devatâ[1203] (deity)?'

*S*âkalya replied: 'The Immortal.'[1204]

11. *S*âkalya said: 'Whosoever knows that person whose dwelling is love (a body capable of sensual love), whose sight is the heart, whose mind is light.—the principle of every self, he indeed is a teacher, O Yâg*ñ*avalkya.'

Yâg*ñ*avalkya replied: 'I know that person, the principle of every self, of whom thou speakest. This love-made (loving) person, he is he." But tell me, *S*âkalya, who is his devatâ?'

*S*âkalya replied: 'The women.'[1205]

12. *S*âkalya said: 'Whosoever knows that person whose dwelling are the colours, whose sight is the eye, whose mind is light,—the principle of every self, he indeed is a teacher, O Yâg*ñ*avalkya.'

Yâg*ñ*avalkya replied: 'I know that person, the principle of every self, of whom thou speakest. That person in the sun, "he is he." But tell me, *S*âkalya, who is his devatâ?'

*S*âkalya replied: 'The True.'[1206]

13. *S*âkalya said: 'Whosoever knows that person whose dwelling is

---

[1200] I prefer to attribute this to *S*âkalya, who is still the questioner, and not Yâg*ñ*avalkya; but I am not quite satisfied that I am right in this, or in the subsequent distribution of the parts, assigned to each speaker. If *S*âkalya is the questioner, then the sentence, veda vâ aha*m* tam purusha*m* sarvasyâtmana*h* parâya*n*am yam âttha, must belong to Yâg*ñ*avalkya, because he refers to the words of another speaker. Lastly, the sentence vadaiva has to be taken as addressed to *S*âkalya. The commentator remarks that, he being the questioner, one expects pri*kkh*a instead of vada. But Yâg*ñ*avalkya may also be supposed to turn round on *S*âkalya and ask him a question in turn, more difficult than the question addressed by *S*âkalya to Yâg*ñ*avalkya, and in that case the last sentence must be taken as an answer, though an imperfect one, of *S*âkalya's. The commentator seems to think that after Yâg*ñ*avalkya told *S*âkalya to ask this question, *S*âkalya was frightened and asked it, and that then Yâg*ñ*avalkya answered in turn.

[1201] The Mâdhyandina text varies considerably. It has the first time, *k*ashur loka*h* for agnir loka*h*. I keep to the same construction throughout, taking mano *g*yoti*h*, not as a compound, but like agnir loko yasya, as a sentence, i.e. mano *g*yotir yasya.

[1202] Ask me. Comm.

[1203] That from which he is produced, that is his devatâ. Comm.

[1204] According to the commentator, the essence of food, which produces blood, from which the germ receives life and becomes an embryo and a living being.

[1205] Because they excite the fire of love. Comm.

[1206] The commentator explains satya, the true, by the eye, because the sun owes its origin to the eye.

ether, whose sight is the ear, whose mind is light,—the principle of every self, he indeed is a teacher, O Yâ*gñ*avalkya.'

Yâ*gñ*avalkya replied: 'I know that person, the principle of every self, of whom thou speakest. The person who hears[1207] and answers, "he is he." But tell me, *S*âkalya, who is his devatâ?'

*S*âkalya replied: 'Space.'

14. *S*âkalya said: 'Whosoever knows that person whose dwelling is darkness, whose sight is the heart, whose mind is light,—the principle of every self, he indeed is a teacher, O Yâ*gñ*avalkya.'

Yâ*gñ*avalkya replied: 'I know that person, the principle of every self, of whom thou speakest. The shadowy[1208] person, "he is he." But tell me, *S*âkalya, who is his devatâ?'

*S*âkalya replied: 'Death.'

15. *S*âkalya said: 'Whosoever knows that person whose dwelling are (bright) colours, whose sight is the eye, whose mind is light,—the principle of every self, he indeed is a teacher, O Yâ*gñ*avalkya.'

Yâ*gñ*avalkya replied: 'I know that person, the principle of every self, of whom thou speakest. The person in the looking-glass, "he is he." But tell me, *S*âkalya, who is his devatâ?'

*S*âkalya replied: 'Vital breath' (asu).

16. *S*âkalya said: 'Whosoever knows that person whose dwelling is water, whose sight is the heart, whose mind is light,—the principle of every self, he indeed is a teacher, O Yâ*gñ*avalkya.'

Yâ*gñ*avalkya replied: 'I know that person, the principle of every self, of whom thou speakest. The person in the water, "he is he." But tell me, *S*âkalya, who is his devatâ?'

*S*âkalya replied: 'Varu*n*a.'

17. *S*âkalya said: 'Whosoever knows that person whose dwelling is seed, whose sight is the heart, whose mind is light,—the principle of every self, he indeed is a teacher, O Yâ*gñ*avalkya.'

Yâ*gñ*avalkya replied: 'I know that person, the principle of every self, of whom thou speakest. The filial person, "he is he." But tell me, *S*âkalya, who is his devatâ?'

*S*âkalya replied: 'Pragâpati.'

18. Yâ*gñ*avalkya said: '*S*âkalya, did those Brâhma*n*as (who themselves shrank from the contest) make thee the victim?'[1209]

[1207] Read *s*rautra instead of *s*rotra; see B*r*ih. Âr. Up. II, 5, 6.

[1208] Shadow, *kh*âyâ, is explained here by a*gñ*âna, ignorance, not by *gñ*âna, knowledge.

[1209] Aṅgârâvakshaya*n*a is explained as a vessel in which coals are extinguished, and Ânandagiri adds that Yâ*gñ*avalkya, in saying that *S*âkalya was made an aṅgârâvakshaya*n*a by his fellow Brâhmans, meant that he was given up by them as a victim, in fact that he was being burnt or consumed by Yâ*gñ*avalkya. I should prefer to take aṅgârâvakshaya*n*a in the sense of ulmukâvakshaya*n*a, an instrument with which one takes burning coals from the fire to extinguish them, a pair of tongs. Read sanda*m*sa

*S*âkalya said: 'Yâ*gñ*avalkya, because thou hast decried the Brâhma*n*as of the Kuru-Pa*ñk*âlas, what[1210] Brahman dost thou know?'

19. Yâ*gñ*avalkya said: 'I know the quarters with their deities and their abodes.'

*S*âkalya said: 'If thou knowest the quarters with their deities and their abodes,

20. 'Which is thy deity in the Eastern quarter?'

Yâ*gñ*avalkya said: 'Âditya (the sun).'

*S*âkalya said: 'In what does that Âditya abide?'

Yâ*gñ*avalkya said: 'In the eye.'

*S*âkalya said: 'In what does the eye abide?'

Yâ*gñ*avalkya said: 'In the colours, for with the eye he sees the colours.'

*S*âkalya said: 'And in what then do the colours abide?'

Yâ*gñ*avalkya said: 'In the heart,[1211] for we know colours by the heart, for colours abide in the heart.'[1212]

*S*âkalya said: 'So it is indeed, O Yâ*gñ*avalkya.'

21. *S*âkalya said: 'Which is thy deity in the Southern quarter?'

Yâ*gñ*avalkya said: 'Yama.'

*S*âkalya said: 'In what does that Yama abide?'

Yâ*gñ*avalkya said: 'In the sacrifice.'

*S*âkalya said: 'In what does the sacrifice abide?'

Yâ*gñ*avalkya said: 'In the Dakshi*n*â (the gifts to be given to the priests).'

*S*âkalya said: 'In what does the Dakshi*n*â abide?'

Yâ*gñ*avalkya said: 'In Sraddhâ (faith), for if a man believes, then he gives Dakshi*n*â, and Dakshi*n*â truly abides in faith.'

*S*âkalya said: 'And in what then does faith abide?'

Yâ*gñ*avalkya said: 'In the heart, for by the heart faith knows, and therefore faith abides in the heart.'

*S*âkalya said: 'So it is indeed, O Yâ*gñ*avalkya.'

22. *S*âkalya said: 'Which is thy deity in the Western quarter?'

Yâ*gñ*avalkya said: 'Varu*n*a.'

*S*âkalya said: 'In what does that Varu*n*a abide?'

Yâ*gñ*avalkya said: 'In the water.'

*S*âkalya said: 'In what does the water abide?'

Yâ*gñ*avalkya said: 'In the seed.'

---

instead of sandesa. Kshi with ava means to remove, to take away. We should call an aṅgârâvakshaya*n*a a cat's paw. The Brâhma*n*as used *S*âkalya as a cat's paw.

[1210] It seems better to take kim as the interrogative pronoun than as an interrogative particle.

[1211] Heart stands here for buddhi and manas together. Comm.

[1212] In the text, published by Dr. Roer in the Bibliotheca Indica, a sentence is left out, viz. h*ri*daya ity uvâ*k*a, h*ri*dayena hi rûpâ*n*i gânâti, h*ri*daye hy eva rûpâ*n*i pratish*th*itâni bhavantîty.

*S*âkalya said: 'And in what does the seed abide?'

Yâg*ñ*avalkya said: 'In the heart. And therefore also they say of a son who is like his father, that he seems as if slipt from his heart, or made from his heart; for the seed abides in the heart.'

*S*âkalya said: 'So it is indeed, O Yâg*ñ*avalkya.'

23. *S*âkalya said: 'Which is thy deity in the Northern quarter?'

Yâg*ñ*avalkya said: 'Soma.'

*S*âkalya said: 'In what does that Soma abide?'

Yâg*ñ*avalkya said: 'In the Dîkshâ[1213].'

*S*âkalya said: 'In what does the Dîkshâ abide?'

Yâg*ñ*avalkya said: 'In the True; and therefore they say to one who has performed the Dîkshâ, Speak what is true, for in the True indeed the Dîkshâ abides.'

*S*âkalya said: 'And in what does the True abide?'

Yâg*ñ*avalkya said: 'In the heart, for with the heart do we know what is true, and in the heart indeed the True abides.'

*S*âkalya said: 'So it is indeed, O Yâg*ñ*avalkya.'

24. *S*âkalya said: 'Which is thy deity in the zenith?'

Yâg*ñ*avalkya said: 'Agni.'

*S*âkalya said: 'In what does that Agni abide.'

Yâg*ñ*avalkya said: 'In speech.'

*S*âkalya said: 'And in what does speech abide?'

Yâg*ñ*avalkya said: 'In the heart.'

*S*âkalya said: 'And in what does the heart abide?'

25. Yâg*ñ*avalkya said: 'O Ahallika,[1214] when you think the heart could be anywhere else away from us, if it were away from us, the dogs might eat it, or the birds tear it.'

26. *S*âkalya said: 'And in what dost thou (thy body) and the Self (thy heart) abide?'

Yâg*ñ*avalkya said: 'In the Prâ*n*a (breath).'

*S*âkalya said: 'In what does the Prâ*n*a abide?'

Yâg*ñ*avalkya said: 'In the Apâna (down-breathing).'[1215]

*S*âkalya said: 'In what does the Apâna abide?'

Yâg*ñ*avalkya said: 'In the Vyâna (back-breathing).'[1216]

*S*âkalya said: 'In what does the Vyâna-abide?'

Yâg*ñ*avalkya said: 'In the Udâna (the out-breathing).'[1217]

[1213] Dîkshâ is the initiatory rite for the Soma sacrifice. Having sacrificed with Soma which has to be bought, the sacrificer becomes endowed with wisdom, and wanders to the North, which is the quarter of Soma.

[1214] A term of reproach, it may be a ghost or preta, because ahani lîyate, it disappears by day.

[1215] Because the prâ*n*a would run away, if it were not held back by the apâna.

[1216] Because the apâna would run down, and the prâ*n*a up, if they were not held back by the vyâna.

[1217] Because all three, the prâ*n*a, apâna, and vyâna, would run away in all directions, if they were not fastened to the udâna.

*S*âkalya said: 'In what does the Udâna abide?'

Yâ*gñ*avalkya said: 'In the Samâna.[1218] That Self (âtman) is to be described by No, no![1219] He is incomprehensible, for he cannot be (is not) comprehended; he is imperishable, for he cannot perish; he is unattached, for he does not attach himself; unfettered, he does not suffer, he does not fail.'

'These are the eight abodes (the earth, &c.), the eight worlds (fire, &c.), the eight gods (the immortal food, &c.), the eight persons (the corporeal, &c.) He who after dividing and uniting these persons,[1220] went beyond (the Samâna), that person, taught in the Upanishads, I now ask thee (to teach me). If thou shalt not explain him to me, thy head will fall.'

*S*âkalya did not know him, and his head fell, nay, thieves took away his bones, mistaking them for something else.

27. Then Yâ*gñ*avalkya said: 'Reverend Brâhma*n*as, whosoever among you desires to do so, may now question me. Or question me, all of you. Or whosoever among you desires it, I shall question him, or I shall question all of you.'

But those Brâhma*n*as durst not (say anything).

28. Then Yâ*gñ*avalkya questioned them with these *S*lokas:

1. 'As a mighty tree in the forest, so in truth is man, his hairs are the leaves, his outer skin is the bark.

2. 'From his skin flows forth blood, sap from the skin (of the tree); and thus from the wounded man[1221] comes forth blood, as from a tree that is struck.

3. 'The lumps of his flesh are (in the tree) the layers of wood, the fibre is strong like the tendons.[1222] The bones are the (hard) wood within, the marrow is made like the marrow of the tree.

4. 'But, while the tree, when felled, grows up again more young from the root, from what root, tell me, does a mortal grow up, after he has been felled by death?

5. 'Do not say, "from seed," for seed is produced from the living;[1223] but a tree, springing from a grain, clearly[1224] rises again after

---

[1218] The Samâna can hardly be meant here for one of the five prâ*n*as, generally mentioned before the udâna, but, as explained by Dvivedagaṅga, stands for the Sûtrâtman. This Sûtrâtman abides in the Antaryâmin, and this in the Brahman (Kû*t*astha), which is therefore described next. Could Samâna be here the same as in IV, 3, 7?

[1219] See before, II, 3, 6; also IV, 2, 4; IV, 4, 22; IV, 5, 115.

[1220] Dividing them according to the different abodes, worlds, and persons, and uniting them at last in the heart.

[1221] In the Mâdhyandina-*s*âkhâ, p. 1080, tasmât tadâtunnât, instead of tasmât tadât*rinn*ât.

[1222] *S*aṅkara seems to have read snâvavat, instead of snâva, tat sthiram, as we read in both *S*âkhâs.

[1223] Here the Mâdhyandinas (p. 1080) add, *g*âta eva na *g*âyate, ko nv ena*m g*anayet puna*h*, which the Kâ*n*vas place later.

[1224] Instead of a*ñg*asâ, the Mâdhyandinas have anyata*h*.

death.[1225]

6. 'If a tree is pulled up with the root, it will not grow again; from what root then, tell me, does a mortal grow up, after he has been felled by death?

7. 'Once born, he is not born (again); for who should create him again?'[1226]

'Brahman, who is knowledge and bliss, he is the principle, both to him who gives gifts,[1227] and also to him who stands firm, and knows.'

FOURTH ADHYÂYA.

FIRST BRÂHMA*N*A.

1. When *G*anaka Vaideha was sitting (to give audience), Yâ*gñ*avalkya approached, and *G*anaka Vaideha said: 'Yâ*gñ*avalkya, for what object did you come, wishing for cattle, or for subtle questions?'[1228]

Yâ*gñ*avalkya replied: 'For both, Your Majesty;

2. 'Let us hear what anybody may have told you.'

*G*anaka Vaideha replied: '*G*itvan *S*ailini told me that speech (vâk) is Brahman.'

Yâ*gñ*avalkya said: 'As one who had (the benefit of a good) father, mother, and teacher might tell, so did Sailini[1229] tell you, that speech is

---

1225 The Mâdhyandinas have dhânâruha u vai, which is better than iva vai, the iva being, according to *S*aṅkara's own confession, useless. The thread of the argument does not seem to have been clearly perceived by the commentators. What the poet wants to say is, that a man, struck down by death, does not come to life again from seed, because human seed comes from the living only, while trees, springing from grain, are seen to come to life after the tree (which yielded the grain or the seed) is dead. Pretya-sambhava like pretya-bhâva, means life after death, and pretyasambhava, as an adjective, means coming to life after death.

1226 This line too is taken in a different sense by the commentator. According to him, it would mean: 'If you say, He has been born (and there is an end of all questioning), I say, No; he is born again, and the question is, How?' This is much too artificial. The order of the verses in the Mâdhyandina-*s*âkhâ is better on the whole, leading up more naturally to the question, 'From what root then does a mortal grow up, after he has been felled by death?' When the Brâhmans cannot answer, Yâ*gñ*avalkya answers, or the *S*ruti declares, that the root from whence a mortal springs again, after death, is Brahman.

1227 *S*aṅkara explains râtir dâtu*h* as râter dâtu*h*, a reading adopted by the Mâdhyandinas. He then arrives at the statement that Brahman is the principle or the last source, also the root of a new life, both for those who practise works and for those who, having relinquished works, stand firm in knowledge. Regnaud (II, p. 138) translates: 'C'est Brahma (qui est) l'intelligence, le bonheur, la richesse, le but suprême de celui qui offre (des sacrifices), et de celui qui réside (en lui), de celui qui connaît.'

1228 A*n*v-anta, formed like Sûtrânta, Siddhânta, and probably Vedânta, means subtle questions.

1229 Roer and Poley give here *S*ailina; Weber also (pp. 1080 and 1081) has twice Sailina (*S*ilinasyâpatyam).

Brahman; for what is the use of a dumb person? But did he tell you the body (âyatana) and the resting-place (pratish*th*â) of that Brahman?'

*G*anaka Vaideha said: 'He did not tell me.'

Yâg*ñ*avalkya said: 'Your Majesty, this (Brahman) stands on one leg only.'[1230]

*G*anaka Vaideha said: 'Then tell me, Yâg*ñ*avalkya.'

Yâg*ñ*avalkya said: 'The tongue is its body, ether its place, and one should worship it as knowledge.'

*G*anaka Vaideha said: 'What is the nature of that knowledge?'

Yâg*ñ*avalkya replied: 'Your Majesty, speech itself (is knowledge). For through speech, Your Majesty, a friend is known (to be a friend), and likewise the *Ri*g-Veda, Yagur-veda, Sâma-veda, the Atharvâṅgirasas, the Itihâsa (tradition), Purâ*n*a-vidyâ (knowledge of the past), the Upanishads, *S*lokas (verses), Sûtras (rules), Anuvyâkhyânas and Vyâkhyânas (commentaries,[1231] &c.); what is sacrificed, what is poured out, what is (to be) eaten and drunk, this world and the other world, and all creatures. By speech alone, Your Majesty, Brahman is known, speech indeed, O King, is the Highest Brahman. Speech does not desert him who worships that (Brahman) with such knowledge, all creatures approach him, and having become a god, he goes to the gods.'

*G*anaka Vaideha said: 'I shall give you (for this) a thousand cows with a bull as big as an elephant.'

Yâg*ñ*avalkya said: 'My father was of opinion that one should not accept a reward without having fully instructed a pupil.'

3. Yâg*ñ*avalkya said: 'Let us hear what anybody may have told you.'

*G*anaka Vaideha replied: 'Udaṅka *S*aulbâyana told me that life (prâ*n*a)[1232] is Brahman.'

Yâg*ñ*avalkya said: 'As one who had (the benefit of a good) father, mother, and teacher might tell, so did Udaṅka *S*aulbâyana tell you that life is Brahman; for what is the use of a person without life? But did he tell you the body and the resting-place of that Brahman?'

*G*anaka Vaideha said: 'He did not tell me.'

Yâg*ñ*avalkya said: 'Your Majesty, this (Brahman) stands on one leg only.'

*G*anaka Vaideha said: 'Then tell me, Yâg*ñ*avalkya.'

Yâg*ñ*avalkya said: 'Breath is its body, ether its place, and one should worship it as what is dear.'

*G*anaka Vaideha said: 'What is the nature of that which is dear?'

[1230] This seems to mean that *G*itvan's explanation of Brahman is lame or imperfect, because there are four pâdas of that Brahman, and he taught one only. The other three are its body, its place, and its form of worship (prag*ñ*etîyam upanishad brahma*n*as *k*aturtha*h* pâda*h*). See also Maitr. Up. VII, p. 221.

[1231] See before, II, 4, 10; and afterwards, IV, 5, 11.

[1232] See Taitt. Up. III, 3.

Yâ*gñ*avalkya replied: 'Your Majesty, life itself (is that which is dear);' because for the sake of life, Your Majesty, a man sacrifices even for him who is unworthy of sacrifice, he accepts presents from him who is not worthy to bestow presents, nay, he goes to a country, even when there is fear of being hurt,[1233] for the sake of life. Life, O King, is the Highest Brahman. Life does not desert him who worships that (Brahman) with such knowledge, all creatures approach him, and having become a god, he goes to the gods.'

*G*anaka Vaideha said: 'I shall give you (for this) a thousand cows with a bull as big as an elephant.'

Yâ*gñ*avalkya said: 'My father was of opinion that one should not accept a reward without having fully instructed a pupil.'

4. Yâ*gñ*avalkya said: 'Let us hear what anybody may have told you.'

*G*anaka Vaideha replied: 'Barku Vârsh*n*a told me that sight (*k*akshus) is Brahman.'

Yâ*gñ*avalkya said: 'As one who had (the benefit of a good) father, mother, and teacher might tell, so did Barku Vârshna tell you that sight is Brahman; for what is the use of a person who cannot see? But did he tell you the body and the resting-place of that Brahman?'

*G*anaka Vaideha said: 'He did not tell me.'

Yâ*gñ*avalkya said: 'Your Majesty, this (Brahman) stands on one leg only.'

*G*anaka Vaideha said: 'Then tell me, Yâ*gñ*avalkya.'

Yâ*gñ*avalkya said: 'The eye is its body, ether its place, and one should worship it as what is true.'

Ganaka Vaideha said: 'What is the nature of that which is true?'

Yâ*gñ*avalkya replied: 'Your Majesty, sight itself (is that which is true); for if they say to a man who sees with his eye, "Didst thou see?" and he says, "I saw," then it is true. Sight, O King, is the Highest Brahman. Sight does not desert him who worships that (Brahman) with such knowledge, all creatures approach him, and having become a god, he goes to the gods.'

*G*anaka Vaideha said: 'I shall give you (for this) a thousand cows with a bull as big as an elephant.'

Yâ*gñ*avalkya said: 'My father was of opinion that one should not accept a reward without having fully instructed a pupil.'

5. Yâ*gñ*avalkya said: 'Let us hear what anybody may have told you.'

*G*anaka Vaideha replied: 'Gardabhîvibhîta Bhâradvâga told me that hearing (*s*ruta) is Brahman.'

Yâ*gñ*avalkya said: 'As one who had (the benefit of a good) father,

---

[1233] Or it may mean, he is afraid of being hurt, to whatever country he goes, for the sake of a livelihood.

mother, and teacher might tell, so did Gardabhîvibhîta Bhâradvâga tell you that hearing is Brahman; for what is the use of a person who cannot hear? But did he tell you the body and the resting-place of that Brahman?'

*G*anaka Vaideha said: 'He did not tell me.'

Yâg*ñ*avalkya said: 'Your Majesty, this (Brahman) stands on one leg only.'

*G*anaka Vaideha said: 'Then tell me, Yâg*ñ*avalkya.'

Yâg*ñ*avalkya said: 'The ear is its body, ether its place, and we should worship it as what is endless.'

*G*anaka Vaideha said: 'What is the nature of that which is endless?'

Yâg*ñ*avalkya, replied: 'Your Majesty, space (disa*h*) itself (is that which is endless), and therefore to whatever space (quarter) he goes, he never comes to the end of it. For space is endless. Space indeed, O King, is hearing,[1234] and hearing indeed, O King, is the Highest Brahman. Hearing does not desert him who worships that (Brahman) with such knowledge, all creatures approach him, and having become a god, he goes to the gods.'

*G*anaka Vaideha said: 'I shall give you (for this) a thousand cows with a bull as big as an elephant.'

Yâg*ñ*avalkya said: 'My father was of opinion that one should not accept a reward without having fully instructed a pupil.'

6. Yâg*ñ*avalkya said: 'Let us hear what anybody may have told you.'

*G*anaka Vaideha replied: 'Satyakâma *G*âbâla told me that mind[1235] (manas) is Brahman.'

Yâg*ñ*avalkya said: 'As one who had (the benefit of a good) father, mother, and teacher might tell, so did Satyakâma *G*âbâla tell you that mind is Brahman; for what is the use of a person without mind? But did he tell you the body and the resting-place of that Brahman?'

*G*anaka Vaideha said: 'He did not tell me.'

Yâg*ñ*avalkya said: 'Your Majesty, this (Brahman) stands on one leg only.'

*G*anaka Vaideha said: 'Then tell me, Yâg*ñ*avalkya.'

Yâg*ñ*avalkya said: 'Mind itself is its body, ether its place, and we should worship it as bliss.'

*G*anaka Vaideha said: 'What is the nature of bliss?'

Yâg*ñ*avalkya replied: 'Your Majesty, mind itself; for with the mind does a man desire a woman, and a like son is born of her, and he is bliss. Mind indeed, O King, is the Highest Brahman. Mind does not

---

[1234] Dvivedagaṅga states, digbhâgo hi pârthivâdhish*th*ânâva*kkh*inna*h s*rotram ity u*k*yate, atas tayor ekatvam.

[1235] See also Taitt. Up. III, 4.

desert him who worships that (Brahman) with such knowledge, all creatures approach him, and having become a god, he goes to the gods.'

*G*anaka Vaideha said: 'I shall give you (for this) a thousand cows with a bull as big as an elephant.'

Yâg*ñ*avalkya said: 'My father was of opinion that one should not accept a reward without having fully instructed a pupil.'

7. Yâg*ñ*avalkya said: 'Let us hear what anybody may have told you.'

*G*anaka Vaideha replied: 'Vidagdha *S*âkalya told me that the heart (hridaya) is Brahman.'

Yâg*ñ*avalkya said: 'As one who had (the benefit of a good) father, mother, and teacher might tell, so did Vidagdha *S*âkalya tell you that the heart is Brahman; for what is the use of a person without a heart? But did he tell you the body and the resting-place of that Brahman?'

*G*anaka Vaideha said: 'He did not tell me.'

Yâg*ñ*avalkya said: 'Your Majesty, this (Brahman) stands on one leg only.'

*G*anaka Vaideha said: 'Then tell me, Yâg*ñ*avalkya.'

Yâg*ñ*avalkya said: 'The heart itself is its body, ether its place, and we should worship it as certainty (sthiti).'

*G*anaka Vaideha said: 'What is the nature of certainty?'

Yâg*ñ*avalkya replied: 'Your Majesty, the heart itself; for the heart indeed, O King, is the body of all things, the heart is the resting-place of all things, for in the heart, O King, all things rest. The heart indeed, O King, is the Highest Brahman. The heart does not desert him who worships that (Brahman) with such knowledge, all creatures approach him, and having become a god, he goes to the gods.'

*G*anaka Vaideha said: 'I shall give you (for this) a thousand cows with a bull as big as an elephant.'

Yâg*ñ*avalkya said: 'My father was of opinion that one should not accept a reward without having fully instructed a pupil.'

SECOND BRÂHMA*N*A.

1. *G*anaka Vaideha, descending from his throne, said: 'I bow to you, O Yâg*ñ*avalkya, teach me.'

Yâg*ñ*avalkya said: 'Your Majesty, as a man who wishes to make a long journey, would furnish himself with a chariot or a ship, thus is your mind well furnished by these Upanishads.[1236] You are honourable, and wealthy, you have learnt the Vedas and been told the Upanishads. Whither then will you go when departing hence?'

[1236] This refers to the preceding doctrines which had been communicated to *G*anaka by other teachers, and particularly to the upâsanas of Brahman as knowledge, dear, true, endless, bliss, and certainty.

*G*anaka Vaideha said: 'Sir, I do not know whither I shall go.'

Yâg*ñ*avalkya said: 'Then I shall tell you this, whither you will go.'

*G*anaka Vaideha said: 'Tell it, Sir.'

2. Yâg*ñ*avalkya said: 'That person who is in the right eye,[1237] he is called Indha, and him who is Indha they call indeed[1238] Indra mysteriously, for the gods love what is mysterious, and dislike what is evident.

3. 'Now that which in the shape of a person is in the right eye, is his wife, Virâg.[1239] Their meeting-place[1240] is the ether within the heart, and their food the red lump within the heart. Again, their covering[1241] is that which is like net-work within the heart, and the road on which they move (from sleep to waking) is the artery that rises upwards from the heart. Like a hair divided into a thousand parts, so are the veins of it, which are called Hita,[1242] placed firmly within the heart. Through these indeed that (food) flows on flowing, and he (the Taigasa) receives as it were purer food[1243] than the corporeal Self (the Vai*s*vânara).

4. 'His (the Taigasa's) Eastern quarter are the prâ*n*as (breath) which go to the East;

'His Southern quarter are the prâ*n*as which go to the South;

'His Western quarter are the prâ*n*as which go to the West;

'His Northern quarter are the prâ*n*as which go to the North;

'His Upper (Zenith) quarter are the prâ*n*as which go upward;

'His Lower (Nadir) quarter are the prâ*n*as which go downward;

'All the quarters are all the prâ*n*as. And he (the Âtman in that state) can only be described by No,[1244] no! He is incomprehensible, for he cannot be comprehended; he is undecaying, for he cannot decay; he is not attached, for he does not attach himself; he is unbound, he does not suffer, he does not perish. O *G*anaka, you have indeed reached fearlessness,'—thus said Yâg*ñ*avalkya.

Then *G*anaka said: 'May that fearlessness come to you also who teachest us fearlessness. I bow to you. Here are the Videhas, and here am I (thy slave).'

[1237] See also Maitr. Up. VII, p. 216.

[1238] The Mâdhyandinas read paroksh*en*eva, but the commentator explains iva by eva. See also Ait. Up. I, 3, 14.

[1239] Indra is called by the commentator Vai*s*vânara, and his wife Virâg. This couple, in a waking state, is Vi*s*va; in sleep, Taigasa.

[1240] Sa*m*stâva, lit. the place where they sing praises together, that is, where they meet.

[1241] Prâvara*n*a may also mean hiding-place, retreat.

[1242] Hita, a name frequently given to these nâ*d*is; see IV, 3, 20; *Kh*ând. Up. VI, 5, 3, comm.; Kaush. Up. IV, 20. See also Ka*th*a Up. VI, 16.

[1243] Dvivedagaṅga explains that food, when it is eaten, is first of all changed into the coarse food, which goes away downward, and into the subtler food. This subtler food is again divided into the middle juice that feeds the body, and the finest, which is called the red lump.

[1244] See B*r*ih. Up. II, 3, 6; IV, 9, 26.

THIRD BRÂHMA*N*A.

1. Yâ*gñ*avalkya came to *G*anaka Vaideha, and he did not mean to speak with him.[1245] But when formerly *G*anaka Vaideha and Yâ*gñ*avalkya had a disputation on the Agnihotra, Yâ*gñ*avalkya had granted him a boon, and he chose (for a boon) that he might be free to ask him any question he liked. Yâ*gñ*avalkya granted it, and thus the King was the first to ask him a question.

2. 'Yâ*gñ*avalkya,' he said, 'what is the light of man?'[1246]

Yâ*gñ*avalkya replied: 'The sun, O King; for, having the sun alone for his light, man sits, moves about, does his work, and returns.'

*G*anaka Vaideha said: 'So indeed it is, O Yâ*gñ*avalkya.'

3. *G*anaka Vaideha said: 'When the sun has set, O Yâ*gñ*avalkya, what is then the light of man?'

Yâ*gñ*avalkya replied: 'The moon indeed is his light; for, having the moon alone for his light, man sits, moves about, does his work, and

---

[1245] The introduction to this Brâhma*n*a has a very peculiar interest, as showing the close coherence of the different portions which together form the historical groundwork of the Upanishads. *G*anaka Vaideha and Yâ*gñ*avalkya are leading characters in the B*ri*hadâranyaka-upanishad, and whenever they meet they seem to converse quite freely, though each retains his own character, and Yâ*gñ*avalkya honours *G*anaka as king quite as much as *G*anaka honours Yâ*gñ*avalkya as a Brâhma*n*a. Now in our chapter we read that Yâ*gñ*avalkya did not wish to enter on a discussion, but that *G*anaka was the first to address him (pûrvam papra*kkh*a). This was evidently considered not quite correct, and an explanation is given, that *G*anaka took this liberty because on a former occasion Yâ*gñ*avalkya had granted him permission to address questions to him, whenever he liked. It might be objected that such an explanation looks very much like an after-thought, and we find indeed that in India itself some of the later commentators tried to avoid the difficulty by dividing the words sa mene na vadishya iti, into sam enena vadishya iti, so that we should have to translate, 'Yâ*gñ*avalkya came to *G*anaka intending to speak with him.' (See Dvivedagaṅga's Comm. p. 1141.) This is, no doubt, a very ingenious conjecture, which might well rouse the envy of European scholars. But it is no more. The accents decide nothing, because they are changed by different writers, according to their different views of what the Pada text ought to be. What made me prefer the reading which is supported by *S*aṅkara and Dvivedagaṅga, though the latter alludes to the other pada*kkh*eda, is that the tmesis, sam enena vadishye, does not occur again, while sa mene is a common phrase. But the most interesting point, as I remarked before, is that this former disputation between *G*anaka and Yâ*gñ*avalkya and the permission granted to the King to ask any question he liked, is not a mere invention to account for the apparent rudeness by which Yâ*gñ*avalkya is forced to enter on a discussion against his will, but actually occurs in a former chapter. In *S*atap. Br. XI, 6, 2, 10, we read: tasmai ha Yâ*gñ*avalkyo vara*m* dadau; sa hovâ*k*a, kâmapra*s*na eva me tvayi Yâ*gñ*avalkyâsad iti, tato brahmâ *G*anaka âsa. This would show that *G*anaka was considered almost like a Brâhma*n*a, or at all events enjoyed certain privileges which were supposed to belong to the first caste only. See, for a different view, Deussen, Vedânta, p. 203; Regnaud (Matériaux pour servir à l'histoire de la philosophie de l'Inde), Errata; and Sacred Books of the East, vol. i, p. lxxiii.

[1246] Read ki*mg*yotir as a Bahuvrîhi. Purusha is difficult to translate. It means man, but also the true essence of man, the soul, as we should say, or something more abstract still, the person, as I generally translate it, though a person beyond the Ego.

returns.'

*G*anaka Vaideha said: 'So indeed it is, O Yâg*ñ*avalkya.'

4. *G*anaka Vaideha said: 'When the sun has set, O Yâg*ñ*avalkya, and the moon has set, what is the light of man?'

Yâg*ñ*avalkya replied: 'Fire indeed is his light; for, having fire alone for his light, man sits, moves about, does his work, and returns.'

5. *G*anaka Vaideha said: 'When the sun has set, O Yâg*ñ*avalkya, and the moon has set, and the fire is gone out, what is then the light of man?'

Yâg*ñ*avalkya replied: 'Sound indeed is his light; for, having sound alone for his light, man sits, moves about, does his work, and returns. Therefore, O King, when one cannot see even one's own hand, yet when a sound is raised, one goes towards it.'

*G*anaka Vaideha said: 'So indeed it is, O Yâg*ñ*avalkya.'

6. *G*anaka Vaideha said: 'When the sun has set, O Yâg*ñ*avalkya, and the moon has set, and the fire is gone out, and the sound hushed, what is then the light of man?'

Yâg*ñ*avalkya said: 'The Self indeed is his light; for, having the Self alone as his light, man sits, moves about, does his work, and returns.'

7. *G*anaka Vaideha said: 'Who is that Self?'

Yâg*ñ*avalkya replied: 'He who is within the heart, surrounded by the Prâ*n*as[1247] (senses), the person of light, consisting of knowledge. He, remaining the same, wanders along the two worlds,[1248] as if[1249] thinking, as if moving. During sleep (in dream) he transcends this world and all the forms of death (all that falls under the sway of death, all that is perishable).

8. 'On being born that person, assuming his body, becomes united with all evils; when he departs and dies, he leaves all evils behind.

9. 'And there are two states for that person, the one here in this world, the other in the other world, and as a third[1250] an intermediate state, the state of sleep. When in that intermediate state, he sees both those states together, the one here in this world, and the other in the other world. Now whatever his admission to the other world may be, having gained that admission, he sees both the evils and the

---

[1247] Sâmîpyalaksha*n*â saptamî, Dvivedagaṅga. See B*r*ih. Up. IV, 4, 22.

[1248] In this world, while awake or dreaming; in the other world, while in deep sleep.

[1249] The world thinks that he thinks, but in reality he does not, he only witnesses the acts of buddhi, or thought.

[1250] There are really two sthânas or states only; the place where they meet, like the place where two villages meet, belongs to both, but it may be distinguished as a third. Dvivedagaṅga (p. 1141) uses a curious argument in support of the existence of another world. In early childhood, he says, our dreams consist of the impressions of a former world, later on they are filled with the impressions of our senses, and in old age they contain visions of a world to come.

blessings.[1251]

'And when he falls asleep, then after having taken away with him the material from the whole world, destroying[1252] and building it up again, he sleeps (dreams) by his own light. In that state the person is self-illuminated.

10. 'There are no (real) chariots in that state, no horses, no roads, but he himself sends forth (creates) chariots, horses, and roads. There are no blessings there, no happiness, no joys, but he himself sends forth (creates) blessings, happiness, and joys. There are no tanks there, no lakes, no rivers, but he himself sends forth (creates) tanks, lakes, and rivers. He indeed is the maker.

11. 'On this there are these verses:

'After having subdued by sleep all that belongs to the body, he, not asleep himself, looks down upon the sleeping (senses). Having assumed light, he goes again to his place, the golden person,[1253] the lonely bird. (1)

12. 'Guarding with the breath (prâ*n*a, life) the lower nest, the immortal moves away from the nest; that immortal one goes wherever he likes, the golden person, the lonely bird. (2)

13. 'Going up and down in his dream, the god makes manifold shapes for himself, either rejoicing together with women, or laughing (with his friends), or seeing terrible sights. (3)

14. 'People may see his playground[1254] but himself no one ever sees. Therefore they say, Let no one wake a man suddenly, for it is not easy to remedy, if he does not get back (rightly to his body)."

'Here some people (object and) say: "No, this (sleep) is the same as the place of waking, for what he sees while awake, that only he sees when asleep."[1255] No, here (in sleep) the person is self-illuminated (as

---

[1251] By works, by knowledge, and by remembrance of former things; see B*ri*h. Up. IV, 4, 2.

[1252] Dividing and separating the material, i.e. the impressions received from this world. The commentator explains mâtrâ as a portion of the impressions which are taken away into sleep. 'Destroying' he refers to the body, which in sleep becomes senseless, and 'building up' to the imaginations of dreams.

[1253] The Mâdhyandinas read paurusha, as an adjective to ekaha*m*sa, but Dvivedagaṅga explains paurusha as a synonym of purusha, which is the reading of the Kâ*n*vas.

[1254] Cf. Su*s*ruta III, 7, 1.

[1255] I have translated this according to the commentator, who says: 'Therefore the Self is self-illuminated during sleep. But others say the state of waking is indeed the same for him as sleep; there is no other intermediate place, different from this and from the other world.... And if sleep is the same as the state of waking, then is this Self not separate, not cause and effect, but mixed with them, and the Self therefore not self-illuminated. What he means is that others, in order to disprove the self-illumination, say that this sleep is the same as the state of waking, giving as their reason that we see in sleep or in dreams exactly what we see in waking. But this is wrong, because the senses have stopped, and only when the senses have stopped does one see dreams. Therefore there is no necessity for admitting another light in sleep, but only the light inherent in the

we explained before).'

*G*anaka Vaideha said: 'I give you, Sir, a thousand. Speak on for the sake of (my) emancipation.'

15. Yâ*gñ*avalkya said: 'That (person) having enjoyed himself in that state of bliss (samprasâda, deep sleep), having moved about and seen both good and evil, hastens back again as he came, to the place from which he started (the place of sleep), to dream.[1256] And whatever he may have seen there, he is not followed (affected) by it, for that person is not attached to anything.'

*G*anaka Vaideha said: 'So it is indeed, Yâ*gñ*avalkya. I give you, Sir, a thousand. Speak on for the sake of emancipation.'

16. Yâ*gñ*avalkya said: 'That (person) having enjoyed himself in that sleep (dream), having moved about and seen both good and evil, hastens back again as he came, to the place from which he started, to be awake. And whatever he may have seen there, he is not followed (affected) by it, for that person is not attached to anything.'

*G*anaka Vaideha said: 'So it is indeed, Yâ*gñ*avalkya. I give you, Sir, a thousand. Speak on for the sake of emancipation.'

17. Yâ*gñ*avalkya said: 'That (person) having enjoyed himself in that state of waking, having moved about and seen both good and evil, hastens back again as he came, to the place from which he started, to the state of sleeping (dream).

18. 'In fact, as a large fish moves along the two banks of a river, the right and the left, so does that person move along these two states, the state of sleeping and the state of waking.

19. 'And as a falcon, or any other (swift) bird, after he has roamed about here in the air, becomes tired, and folding his wings is carried to his nest, so does that person hasten to that state where, when asleep, he desires no more desires, and dreams no more dreams.

20. 'There are in his body the veins called Hitâ, which are as small as a hair divided a thousandfold, full of white, blue, yellow, green, and

---

Self. This has been proved by all that went before.' Dr. Roer takes the same view in his translation, but Deussen (Vedânta, p. 205) takes an independent view, and translates: I Therefore it is said: It (sleep) is to him a place of waking only, for what he sees waking, the same he sees in sleep. Thus this spirit serves there for his own light.' Though the interpretations of *S*aṅkara and Dvivedagaṅga sound artificial, still Dr. Deussen's version does not remove all difficulties. If the purusha saw in sleep no more than what he had seen before in waking, then the whole argument in favour of the independent action, or the independent light of the purusha, would go; anyhow it would be no argument on Yâ*gñ*avalkya's side. See also note to paragraph 9, before.

[1256] The Mâdhyandinas speak only of his return from svapnânta to buddhânta, from sleep to waking, instead of his going from sainprasâda (deep sleep) to svapnâ (dream), from svapnâ to buddhânta, and from buddhânta again to svapnânta, as the Kâ*n*vas have it. In § 18 the Kâ*n*vas also mention svapnânta and buddhânta only, but the next paragraph refers to sushupti.

red.[1257] Now when, as it were, they kill him, when, as it were they overcome him, when, as it were, an elephant chases him, when, as it were, he falls into a well, he fancies, through ignorance, that danger which he (commonly) sees in waking. But when he fancies that he is, as it were, a god, or that he is, as it were, a king,[1258] or "I am this altogether," that is his highest world.[1259]

21. 'This indeed is his (true) form, free from desires, free from evil, free from fear.[1260] Now as a man, when embraced by a beloved wife, knows nothing that is without, nothing that is within, thus this person, when embraced by the intelligent (prâg*ñ*a) Self, knows nothing that is without, nothing that is within. This indeed is his (true) form, in which his wishes are fulfilled, in which the Self (only) is his wish, in which no wish is left,—free from any sorrow.[1261]

22. 'Then a father is not a father, a mother not a mother, the worlds not worlds, the gods not gods, the Vedas not Vedas. Then a thief is not a thief, a murderer not a murderer,[1262] a *Kând*âla[1263] not a *Kând*âla, a Paulkasa[1264] not a Paulkasa, a *S*rama*n*a[1265] not a *S*rama*n*a, a Tâpasa[1266] not a Tâpasa. He is not followed by good, not followed by evil, for he

---

[1257] Dvivedagaṅga explains that if phlegm predominates, qualified by wind and bile, the juice in the veins is white; if wind predominates, qualified by phlegm and bile, it is blue; if bile predominates, qualified by wind and phlegm, it is yellow; if wind and phlegm predominate, with little bile only, it is green; and if the three elements are equal, it is red. See also Ânandagiri's gloss, where Su*s*ruta is quoted. Why this should be inserted here, is not quite clear, except that in sleep the purusha is supposed to, move about in the veins.

[1258] Here, again, the commentator seems to be right, but his interpretation does violence to the context. The dangers which a man sees in his sleep are represented as mere imaginations, so is his idea of being of god or a king, while the idea that he is all this (aham eveda*m* sarva*h*, i.e. ida*m* sarvam, see *S*aṅkara, p. 873, l. 11) is represented as the highest and real state. But it is impossible to begin a new sentence with aham evedam sarvam, and though it is true that all the preceding fancies are qualified by iva, I prefer to take deva and râgan as steps leading to the sarvâtmatva.

[1259] The Mâdhyandinas repeat here the sentence from yatra supto to pa*s*yati, from the end of § 19.

[1260] The Kâ*n*va text reads ati*kkh*andâ apahatapâpmâ. *S*aṅkara explains ati*kkh*andâ by ati*kkh*andam, and excuses it as svâdhyâyadharma*h* pâ*th*a*h*. The Mâdhyandinas read ati*kkh*ando, but place the whole sentence where the Kâ*n*vas put âptakâmam &c., at the end of § 21.

[1261] The Kâ*n*vas read *s*okântaram, the Mâdhyandinas a*s*okântaram, but the commentators arrive at the same result, namely, that it means *s*oka*s*ûnyam, free from grief *S*aṅkara says: *s*okântara*m* soka*kkh*idra*m* *s*oka*s*ûnyam ityeta*k*, *kh*okamadhyaman iti vi; sarvathâpy a*s*okam. Dvivedagaṅga says: na vidyate *s*oko 'ntare madhye yasya tad asokântara*m* (ra, Weber) *s*oka*s*ûnyam.

[1262] Bhrû*n*ahan, varish*th*abrabmahantâ.

[1263] The son of a *S*ûdra father and a Brâhma*n*a mother.

[1264] The son of a *S*ûdra father and a Kshatriya mother.

[1265] A mendicant.

[1266] A Vânaprastha, who performs penances.

has then overcome all the sorrows of the heart.[1267]

23. 'And when (it is said that) there (in the Sushupti) he does not see, yet he is seeing, though he does not see.[1268] For sight is inseparable from the seer, because it cannot perish. But there is then no second, nothing else different from him that he could see.

24. 'And when (it is said that) there (in the Sushupti) he does not smell, yet he is smelling, though he does not smell. For smelling is inseparable from the smeller, because it cannot perish. But there is then no second, nothing else different from him that he could smell.

25. 'And when (it is said that) there (in the Sushupti) he does not taste, yet he is tasting, though he does not taste. For tasting is inseparable from the taster, because it cannot perish. But there is then no second, nothing else different from him that he could taste.

26. 'And when (it is said that) there (in the Sushupti) he does not speak, yet he is speaking, though he does not speak. For speaking is inseparable from the speaker, because it cannot perish. But there is then no second, nothing else different from him that he could speak.

27. 'And when (it is said that) there (in the Sushupti) he does not hear, yet he is hearing, though he does not hear. For hearing is inseparable from the hearer, because it cannot perish. But. there is then no second, nothing else different from him that he could hear.

28. 'And when (it is said that) there (in the Sushupti) he does not think, yet he is thinking, though he does not think. For thinking is inseparable from the thinker, because it cannot perish. But there is then no second, nothing else different from him that he could think.

29. 'And when (it is said that) there (in the Sushupti) he does not touch, yet he is touching, though he does not touch. For touching is inseparable from the toucher, because it cannot perish. But there is then no second, nothing else different from him that he could think.

30. 'And when (it is said that) there (in the Sushupti) he does not know, yet he is knowing, though he does not know. For knowing is inseparable from the knower, because it cannot perish. But there is then no second, nothing else different from him that he could know.

[1267] I have translated as if the text were ananvâgata*h* pu*n*yena ananvâgata*h* pâpena. We find anvâgata used in a similar way in §§ 15, 16, &c. But the Kâ*n*vas read ananvâgata*m* pu*n*yena ananvâgatam pâpena, and *S*aṅkara explains the neuter by referring it to rûpam (rûpaparatvân napu*m*sakaliṅgam). The Mâdhyandinas, if we may trust Weber's edition, read ananvâgata*h* pu*n*yenânvâgata*h* pâpena. The second anvâgata*h* may be a mere misprint, but Dvivedagaṅga seems to have read ananvâgatam, like the Kâ*n*vas, for he says: ananvâgatam iti rûpavishayo napu*m*sakanirde*s*a*h*.

[1268] This is the old Upanishad argument that the true sense is the Self, and not the eye. Although therefore in the state of profound sleep, where the eye and the other senses rest, it might be said that the purusha does not see, yet he is a seer all the time, though he does not see with the eye. The seer cannot lose his character of seeing, as little as the fire can lose its character of burning, so long as it is fire. The Self sees by its own light, like the sun, even where there is no second, no object but the Self, that could be seen.

31. 'When (in waking and dreaming) there is, as it were, another, then can one see the other, then can one smell the other, then can one speak to the other, then can one hear the other, then can one think the other, then can one touch the other, then can one know the other.

32. 'An ocean[1269] is that one seer, without any duality; this is the Brahma-world,[1270] O King.' Thus did Yâg*ñ*avalkya teach him. This is his highest goal, this is his highest Success, this is his highest world, this is his highest bliss. All other creatures live on a small portion of that bliss.

33. 'If a man is healthy, wealthy, and lord of others, surrounded by all human enjoyments, that is the highest blessing of men. Now a hundred of these human blessings make one blessing of the fathers who have conquered the world (of the fathers). A hundred blessings of the fathers who have conquered this world make one blessing in the Gandharva world. A hundred blessings in the Gandharva world make one blessing of the Devas by merit (work, sacrifice), who obtain their godhead by merit. A hundred blessings of the Devas by merit make one blessing of the Devas by birth, also (of) a *S*rotriya[1271] who is without sin, and not overcome by desire. A hundred blessings of the Devas by birth make one blessing in the world of Pragâpati, also (of) a *S*rotriya who is without sin, and not overcome. by desire. A hundred blessings in the world of Pragâpati make one blessing in the world of Brahman, also (of) a *S*rotriya who is without sin, and not overcome by desire. And this is the highest blessing.[1272]

'This is the Brahma-world, O king,' thus spake Yâg*ñ*avalkya.

*G*anaka Vaideha said: 'I give you, Sir, a thousand. Speak on for the sake of (my) emancipation.'

Then Yâg*ñ*avalkya was afraid lest the King, having become full of understanding, should drive him from all his positions.[1273]

34. And Yâg*ñ*avalkya said: 'That (person), having enjoyed himself in that state of sleeping (dream), having moved about and seen both good and bad, hastens back again as he came, to the place from which he started, to the state of waking.[1274]

35. 'Now as a heavy-laden carriage moves along groaning, thus does this corporeal Self, mounted by the intelligent Self, move along

---

[1269] Salila is explained as salilavat, like the ocean, the seer being one like the ocean, which is one only. Dr. Deussen takes salila as a locative, and translates it 'In dem Gewoge,' referring to *S*vetâsvatara-upanishad VI, 15.

[1270] Or this seer is the Brahma-world, dwells in Brahman, or is Brahman.

[1271] An accomplished student of the Veda.

[1272] See Taitt. Up. II, 8, p. 59; *Kh*ând. Up. VIII, 2, 1-10; Kaush. Up. I, 3-5; Regnaud, II, p. 33 seq.

[1273] *S*aṅkara explains that Yâg*ñ*avalkya was not afraid that his own knowledge might prove imperfect, but that the king, having the right to ask him any question he liked, might get all his knowledge from him.

[1274] See § 17, before.

groaning, when a man is thus going to expire.[1275]

36. 'And when (the body) grows weak through old age, or becomes weak through illness, at that time that person, after separating himself from his members, as an Amra (mango), or Udumbara (fig), or Pippala-fruit is separated from the stalk, hastens back again as be came, to the place from which he started, to (new) life.

37. 'And as policemen, magistrates, equerries, and governors wait for a king who is coming back, with food and drink, saying, "He comes back, he approaches," thus do all the elements wait on him who knows this, saying, "That Brahman comes, that Brahman approaches."

38. 'And as policemen, magistrates, equerries, and governors gather round a king who is departing, thus do all the senses (prâ*n*as) gather round the Self at the time of death, when a man is thus going to expire.'

FOURTH BRÂHMA*N*A.

1. Yâ*gñ*avalkya continued: 'Now when that Self, having sunk into weakness,[1276] sinks, as it were, into unconsciousness, then gather those senses (prâ*n*as) around him, and he, taking with him those elements of light, descends into the heart When that person in the eye[1277] turns away, then he ceases to know any forms.

2. '"He has become one," they say, "he does not see."[1278] "He has become one," they say, "he does not smell." "He has become one," they say, "he does not taste." "He has become one," they say, "he does not speak." "He has become one," they say, "he does not hear." "He has become one," they say, "he does not think." "He has become one," they say, "he does not touch." "He has become one," they say, "he does not know." The point of his heart[1279] becomes lighted up, and by that light the Self departs, either through the eye,[1280] or through the skull,[1281] or through other places of the body. And when he thus departs, life (the chief prâ*n*a) departs after him, and when life thus departs, all the other vital spirits (prâ*n*as) depart after it. He is conscious, and being

---

1275 *S*aṅkara seems to take ukkhvâsî as a noun. He writes: yatraitad bhavati; etad iti kriyâvi*s*esha*n*am ûrdhvô*kkh*vâsî yatrordhvo*kkh*vâsitvam asya bhavatîtyartha*h*.

1276 In the Kaush. Up. III, 3, we read yatraitat purusha ârto marishyan âbâlyam etya sammohati. Here âbâlyam should certainly be âbâlyam, as in the commentary; but should it not be ăbălyam, as here. See also B*ri*h. Up. III, 5, 1, note.

1277 *K*âkshusha purusha is explained as that portion of the sun which is in the eye, while it is active, but which, at the time of death, returns to the sun.

1278 Ekîbhavati is probably a familiar expression for dying, but it is here explained by *S*aṅkara, and probably was so intended, as meaning that the organs of the body have become one with the Self (liṅgâtman). The same thoughts are found in the Kaush. Up. III, 3, prâ*n*a ekadhâ bhavati.

1279 The point where the nâ*d*îs or veins go out from the heart.

1280 When his knowledge and deeds qualify him to proceed to the sun. *S*aṅkara.

1281 When his knowledge and deeds qualify him to proceed to the Brahma-world.

conscious he follows[1282] and departs.

'Then both his knowledge and his work take hold of him, and his acquaintance with former things.'[1283]

3. 'And as a caterpillar, after having reached the end of a blade of grass, and after having made another approach (to another blade),[1284] draws itself together towards it, thus does this Self, after having thrown off this body[1285] and dispelled all ignorance, and after making another approach (to another body), draw himself together towards it.

4. 'And as a goldsmith, taking a piece of gold, turns it into another, newer and more beautiful shape, so does this Self, after having thrown off this body and dispelled all ignorance, make unto himself another, newer and more beautiful shape, whether it be like the Fathers, or like the Gandharvas, or like the Devas, or like Pragâpati, or like Brahman, or like other beings.

5. 'That Self is indeed Brahman, consisting of knowledge, mind, life, sight, hearing, earth, water, wind, ether, light and no light, desire and no desire, anger and no anger, right or wrong, and all things. Now as a man is like this or like that,[1286] according as he acts and according as he behaves, so will he be:—a man of good acts will become good, a man of bad acts, bad. He becomes pure by pure deeds, bad by bad deeds.

'And here they say that a person consists of desires. And as is his desire, so is his will; and as is his will, so is his deed; and whatever deed he does, that he will reap.

6. 'And here there is this verse: "To whatever object a man's own mind is attached, to that he goes strenuously together with his deed; and

[1282] This is an obscure passage, and the different text of the Mâdhyandinas shows that the obscurity was felt at an early time. The Mâdhyandinas read: Sa*mgñ*ânam anvavakrâmati sa esha *gñah* savi*gñ*âno bhavati. This would mean, 'Consciousness departs after. He the knowing (Self) is self-conscious.' The Kâ*n*vas read: Savi*gñ*âno bhavati, savi*gñ*ânam evânvavakrâmati. Roer translates: 'It is endowed with knowledge, endowed with knowledge it departs;' and he explains, with *S*aṅkara, that the knowledge here intended is such knowledge as one has in a dream, a knowledge of impressions referring to their respective objects, a knowledge which is the effect of actions, and not inherent in the self. Deussen translates: 'Sie (die Seele) ist von Erkenntnissart, und was von Erkenntnissart ist, ziehet ihr nach.' The Persian translator evidently thought that self-consciousness was implied, for he writes: 'Cum quovis corpore addictionem sumat . . . . in illo corpore aham est, id est, ego sum.'

[1283] This acquaintance with former things is necessary to explain the peculiar talents or deficiencies which we observe in children. The three words vidyâ, karman, and pûrvapra*gñ*â often go together (see *S*aṅkara on B*r*ih. Up. IV, 3, 9). Deussen's conjecture, apûrvapra*gñ*â, is not called for.

[1284] See B*r*ih. Up. IV, 3, 9, a passage which shows how difficult it would be always to translate the same Sanskrit words by the same words in English; see also Brahmopanishad, p. 245.

[1285] See B*r*ih. Up. IV, 3, 9, and IV, 3, 13.

[1286] The iti after adomaya is not clear to me, but it is quite clear that a new sentence begins with tadyadetat, which Regnaud, II, p. 101 and p. 139, has not observed.

having obtained the end (the last results) of whatever deed he does here on earth, he returns again from that world (which is the temporary reward of his deed) to this world of action."

'So much for the man who desires. But as to the man who does not desire, who, not desiring, freed from desires, is satisfied in his desires, or desires the Self only, his vital spirits do not depart elsewhere,—being Brahman, he goes to Brahman.

7. 'On this there is this verse: "When all desires which once entered his heart are undone, then does the mortal become immortal, then he obtains Brahman.

'And as the slough of a snake lies on an ant-hill, dead and cast away, thus lies this body; but that disembodied immortal spirit (prâ*n*a, life) is Brahman only, is only light.'

*G*anaka Vaideha said: 'Sir, I give you a thousand.'

8.[1287] 'On this there are these verses:

'The small, old path stretching far away[1288] has been found by me. On it sages who know Brahman move on to the Svarga-loka (heaven), and thence higher on, as entirely free.[1289]

9. 'On that path they say that there is white, or blue, or yellow, or green, or red;[1290] that path was found by Brahman, and on it goes whoever knows Brahman, and who has done good, and obtained splendour.

10. 'All who worship what is not knowledge (avidyâ) enter into blind darkness: those who delight in knowledge, enter, as it were, into greater darkness.[1291]

11. 'There are[1292] indeed those unblessed worlds, covered with blind darkness. Men who are ignorant and not enlightened go after death to those worlds.

12. 'If a man understands the Self, saying, "I am He," what could he wish or desire that he should pine after the body.[1293]

13. 'Whoever has found and understood the Self that has entered

---

[1287] This may be independent matter, or may be placed again into the mouth of Yâgñavalkya.

[1288] Instead of vitata*h*, which perhaps seemed to be in contradiction with anu there is a Mâdhyandina reading vitara, probably intended originally to mean leading across. The other adjective mâm̐sp*ri*sh*t*a I cannot explain. *S*ankara explains it by mâ*m* sp*ri*sh*t*a*h*, mayâ labdha*h*.

[1289] That this is the true meaning, is indicated by the various readings of the Mâdhyandinas, tena dhîrâ apiyanti brahmavida utkramya svarga*m* lokam ito vimuktâ*h*. The road is not to lead to Svarga only, but beyond.

[1290] See the colours of the veins as given before, IV, 3, 20.

[1291] See Vâg. Up. 9. *S*ankara in our place explains avidyâ by works, and vidyâ by the Veda, excepting the Upanishads.

[1292] See Vâg. Up. 3; Ka*th*a Up. I. 3.

[1293] That he should be willing to suffer once more the pains inherent in the body. The Mâdhyandinas read *s*arîram anu sa*m*karet, instead of sa*ñ*gvaret.

into this patched-together hiding-place,[1294] he indeed is the creator, for he is the maker of everything, his is the world, and he is the world itself.[1295]

14. 'While we are here, we may know this; if not, I am ignorant,[1296] and there is great destruction. Those who know it, become immortal, but others suffer pain indeed.

15. 'If a man clearly beholds this Self as God, and as the lord of all that is and will be, then he is no more afraid.

16. 'He behind whom the year revolves with the days, him the gods worship as the light of lights, as immortal time.

17. 'He in whom the five beings[1297] and the ether rest, him alone I believe to be the Self,—I who know, believe him to be Brahman; I who am immortal, believe him to be immortal.

18. 'They who know the life of life, the eye of the eye, the ear of the ear, the mind of the mind, they have comprehended the ancient, primeval Brahman.[1298]

19. 'By the mind alone it is to be perceived,[1299] there is in it no diversity. He who perceives therein any diversity, goes from death to death.

20. 'This eternal being that can never be proved, is to be perceived in one way only; it is spotless, beyond the ether, the unborn Self, great and eternal.

21. 'Let a wise Brâhma*n*a, after he has discovered him, practise wisdom.[1300] Let him not seek after many words, for that is mere weariness of the tongue.

22. 'And he is that great unborn Self, who consists of knowledge, is surrounded by the Prâ*n*as, the ether within the heart.[1301] In it there reposes the ruler of all, the lord of all, the king of all. He does not become greater by good works, nor smaller by evil works. He is the lord of all, the king of all things, the protector of all things. He is a bank[1302] and a boundary, so that these worlds may not be confounded. Brâhma*n*as seek to know him by the study of the Veda, by sacrifice, by gifts, by penance, by fasting, and he who knows him, becomes a Muni.

[1294] The body is meant, and is called deha from the root dih, to knead together. Roer gives sa*m*dehye gahane, which *S*aṅkara explains by sa*m*dehe. Poley has sa*m*deghe, which is the right Kâ*n*va reading. The Mâdhyandinas read sa*m*dehe. Gahane might be taken as an adjective also, referring to sa*m*dehe.

[1295] *S*aṅkara takes loka, world, for âtmâ, self.

[1296] I have followed *S*aṅkara in translating avedi*h* by ignorant, but the text seems corrupt.

[1297] The five ganas, i.e. the Gandharvas, Pit*r*is, Devas, Asuras, and Rakshas; or the four castes with the Nishâdas; or breath, eye, ear, food, and mind.

[1298] See Talavak. Up. I, 2.

[1299] See Ka*th*a Up. IV, 10-11.

[1300] Let him practise abstinence, patience, &c., which are the means of knowledge.

[1301] See B*r*ih. Up. IV, 3, 7.

[1302] See *Kh*ând. Up. VIII, 4.

Wishing for that world (for Brahman) only, mendicants leave their homes.

'Knowing this, the people of old did not wish for offspring. What shall we do with offspring, they said, we who have this Self and this world (of Brahman)?[1303] And they, having risen above the desire for sons, wealth, and new worlds, wander about as mendicants. For desire for sons is desire for wealth, and desire for wealth is desire for worlds. Both these are indeed desires only. He, the Self, is to be described by No, no![1304] He is incomprehensible, for he cannot be comprehended; he is imperishable, for he cannot perish; he is unattached, for he does not attach himself; unfettered, he does not suffer, he does not fail. Him (who knows), these two do not overcome, whether he says that for some reason he has done evil, or for some reason he has done good—he overcomes both, and neither what he has done, nor what he has omitted to do, burns (affects) him.

23. 'This has been told by a verse (*Rik*): "This eternal greatness of the Brâhma*n*a does not grow larger by work, nor does it grow smaller. Let man try to find (know) its trace, for having found (known) it, he is not sullied by any evil deed."

'He therefore that knows it, after having become quiet, subdued, satisfied, patient, and collected,[1305] sees self in Self, sees all as Self. Evil does not overcome him, he overcomes all evil. Evil does not burn him, he burns all evil. Free from evil, free from spots, free from doubt, he becomes a (true) Brâhma*n*a; this is the Brahma-world, O King,'—thus spoke Yâg*ñ*avalkya.

*G*anaka Vaideha said: 'Sir, I give you the Videhas, and also myself, to be together your slaves.'

24. This[1306] indeed is the great, the unborn Self, the strong,[1307] the giver of wealth. He who knows this obtains wealth.

25. This great, unborn Self, undecaying, undying, immortal, fearless, is indeed Brahman. Fearless is Brahman, and he who knows this becomes verily the fearless Brahman.

FIFTH BRÂHMANA[1308].

1. Yâg*ñ*avalkya had two wives, Maitreyî and Kâtyâyanî. Of these Maitreyî was conversant with Brahman, but Kâtyâyanî possessed such knowledge only as women possess. And Yâg*ñ*avalkya, when he wished

---

[1303] Cf. B*r*ih. Up. III, 5, 1.

[1304] See B*r*ih. Up. III, 9, 26; IV, 2, 4.

[1305] See Deussen, Vedânta, p. 85.

[1306] As described in the dialogue between *G*anaka and Yâg*ñ*avalkya.

[1307] Annâda is here explained as 'dwelling in all beings, and eating all food which they eat.'

[1308] See before, II, 4.

to get ready for another state of life (when he wished to give up the state of a householder, and retire into the forest),

2. Said, 'Maitreyî, verily I am going away from this my house (into the forest). Forsooth, let me make a settlement between thee and that Kâtyâyanî.'

3. Maitreyî said: 'My Lord, if this whole earth, full of wealth, belonged to me, tell me, should I be immortal by it, or no?'

'No,' replied Yâgñavalkya, 'like the life of rich people will be thy life. But there is no hope of immortality by wealth.'

4. And Maitreyî said: 'What should I do with that by which I do not become immortal? What my Lord knoweth[1309] (of immortality), tell that clearly to me.'

5. Yâgñavalkya replied: 'Thou who art truly dear to me, thou hast increased what is dear (to me in thee).[1310] Therefore, if you like, Lady, I will explain it to thee, and mark well what I say.'

6. And he said: 'Verily, a husband is not dear, that you may love the husband; but that you may love the Self, therefore a husband is dear.

'Verily, a wife is not dear, that you may love the wife; but that you may love the Self, therefore a wife is dear.

'Verily, sons are not dear, that you may love the sons; but that you may love the Self, therefore sons are dear.

'Verily, wealth is not dear, that you may love wealth; but that you may love the Self, therefore wealth is dear.

'Verily, cattle[1311] are not dear, that you may love cattle; but that you may love the Self, therefore cattle are dear.

'Verily, the Brahman-class is not dear, that you may love the Brahman-class; but that you may love the Self, therefore the Brahman-class is dear.

'Verily, the Kshatra-class is not dear, that you may love the Kshatra-class; but that you may love the Self, therefore the Kshatra-class is dear.

'Verily, the worlds are not dear, that you may love the worlds; but that you may love the Self, therefore the worlds are dear.

'Verily, the Devas are not dear, that you may love the Devas; but that you may love the Self, therefore the Devas are dear.

'Verily, the Vedas are not dear, that you may love the Vedas; but that you may love the Self, therefore the Vedas are dear.

'Verily, creatures are not dear, that you may love the creatures; but that you may love the Self, therefore are creatures dear.

1309 The Kâ*n*va text has vettha instead of veda.

1310 The Kâ*n*va text has av*ri*dhat, which *S*aṅkara explains by vardhitavatî nirdhâritavaty asi. The Mâdhyandinas read av*ri*tat, which the commentator explains by avartayat, vartitavaty asi.

1311 Though this is added here, it is not included in the summing up in § 6.

'Verily, everything is not dear, that you may love everything; but that you may love the Self, therefore everything is dear.

'Verily, the Self is to be seen, to be heard, to be perceived, to be marked, O Maitreyî! When the Self has been seen, heard, perceived, and known, then all this is known!

7. 'Whosoever looks for the Brahman-class elsewhere than in the Self, was abandoned by the Brahman-class. Whosoever looks for the Kshatra-class elsewhere than in the Self, was abandoned by the Kshatra-class. Whosoever looks for the worlds elsewhere than in the Self, was abandoned by the worlds. Whosoever looks for the Devas elsewhere than in the Self, was abandoned by the Devas. Whosoever looks for the Vedas elsewhere than in the Self, was abandoned by the Vedas. Whosoever looks for the creatures elsewhere than in the Self, was abandoned by the creatures. Whosoever looks for anything elsewhere than in the Self, was abandoned by anything.

'This Brahman-class, this Kshatra-class, these worlds, these Devas, these Vedas, all these beings, this everything, all is that Self.

8. 'Now as the sounds of a drum, when beaten, cannot be seized externally (by themselves), but the sound is seized, when the drum is seized, or the beater of the drum;

9. 'And as the sounds of a conch-shell, when blown, cannot be seized externally (by themselves), but the sound is seized, when the shell is seized, or the blower of the shell;

10. 'And as the sounds of a lute, when played, cannot be seized externally (by themselves), but the sound is seized, when the lute is seized, or the player of the lute;

11. 'As clouds of smoke proceed by themselves out of lighted fire kindled with damp fuel, thus verily, O Maitreyî, has been breathed forth from this great Being what we have as *Ri*g-veda, Yagur-veda, Sâma-veda, Atharvâṅgirasas, Itihâsa, Purâ*n*a, Vidyâ, the Upanishads, *S*lokas, Sûtras, Anuvyâkhyânas, Vyâkhyânas, what is sacrificed, what is poured out, food, drink,[1312] this world and the other world, and all creatures. From him alone all these were breathed forth.

12. 'As all waters find their centre in the sea, all touches in the skin, all tastes in the tongue, all smells in the nose, all colours in the eye, all sounds in the ear, all percepts in the mind, all- knowledge in the heart, all actions in the hands, all movements in the feet, and all the Vedas in speech,—

13. 'As a mass of salt has neither inside nor outside, but is altogether a mass of taste, thus indeed has that Self neither inside nor outside, but is altogether a mass of knowledge; and having risen from out these elements, vanishes again in them. When he has departed,

[1312] Explained by annadânanimittam and peyadânanimitta*m* dharmagâtam. See before, IV, 1, 2.

there is no more knowledge (name), I say, O Maitreyî,'—thus spoke Yâg*ñ*avalkya.

14. Then Maitreyî said: 'Here, Sir, thou hast landed me in utter bewilderment. Indeed, I do not understand him.'

But he replied: 'O Maitreyî, I say nothing that is bewildering. Verily, beloved, that Self is imperishable, and of an indestructible nature.

15. 'For when there is as it were duality, then one sees the other, one smells the other, one tastes the other, one salutes the other, one hears the other, one perceives the other, one touches the other, one knows the other; but when the Self only is all this, how should he see another, how should he smell another, how should he taste another, how should he salute another, how should he hear another, how should he touch another, how should he know another? How should he know Him by whom he knows all this? That Self is to be described by No, no![1313] He is incomprehensible, for he cannot be comprehended; he is imperishable, for he cannot perish; he is unattached, for he does not attach himself; unfettered, he does not suffer, he does not fail. How, O beloved, should he know the Knower? Thus, O Maitreyî, thou hast been instructed. Thus far goes immortality.' Having said so, Yâg*ñ*avalkya went away (into the forest).

SIXTH BRÂHMA*N*A.

1. Now follows the stem[1314]:

1. (We) from Pautimâshya,
2. Pautimâshya, from Gaupavana,
3. Gaupavana from Pautimâshya,
4. Pautimâshya from Gaupavana,
5. Gaupavana from Kau*s*ika,
6. Kau*s*ika from Kau*nd*inya,
7. Kau*nd*inya from Sâ*nd*ilya,
8. Sâ*nd*ilya from Kau*s*ika and Gautama,
9. Gautama

2. from Âgnive*s*ya,

[1313] See B*ri*h. Up. III, 9, 26; IV, 2, 4; IV, 4, 22.

[1314] The line of teachers and pupils by whom the Yâg*ñ*avalkya-kâ*nd*a was handed down. From 1-10 the Va*ms*a agrees with the Va*ms*a at the end of II, 6.

The Mâdhyandina text begins with vayam, we, and proceeds to 1. Saurpa*n*âyya, 2. Gautama, 3. Vâtsya, 4. Pâra*s*arya, &c., as in the Madhukâ*nd*a, p. 118, except in 10, where it gives *G*aivantâyana for Âtreya. Then after 12. Kau*nd*inyâyana, it gives 13. 14. the two Kau*nd*inyas, 15. the Aur*n*avâbhas, 16. Kau*nd*inya, 17. Kau*nd*inya, 18. Kau*nd*inya and Âgnivesya, 19. Saitava, 20. Pârâ*s*arya, 2 1. *G*âtukar*n*ya, 22. Bhâradvâga, 2 3. Bhâradvâga, Âsurâya*n*a, and Gautama, 24. Bhâradvâga, 25. Valâkâkau*s*ika, 26. Kâshâya*n*a, 27. Saukarâya*n*a, 28. Traiva*n*i, 29. Aupagandhani, 30. Sâyakâyana, p. Kau*s*ikâyani, &c., as in the Kâ*n*va text, from No. 22 to Brahman.

10. Âgnive*s*ya from Gârgya,
11. Gârgya from Gârgya,
12. Gârgya from Gautama,
13. Gautama from Saitava,
14. Saitava from Pârâ*s*aryâya*n*a,
15. Pârâ*s*aryâya*n*a from Gârgyâya*n*a,
16. Gârgyâya*n*a from Uddâlakâyana,
17. Uddâlakâyana from *G*âbâlâyana,
18. *G*âbâlâyana from Mâdhyandânayana,
19. Mâdhyandânayana from Saukarâya*n*a,
20. Saukarâya*n*a from Kâshâya*n*a,
21. Kâshâya*n*a from Sâyakâyana,
22. Sâyakâyana from Kau*s*ikâyani,[1315]
23. Kau*s*ikâyani

3. from Gh*ri*takau*s*ika,

24. Gh*ri*takau*s*ika from Pârâ*s*aryâya*n*a,
25. Pârâ*s*aryâya*n*a from Pârâ*s*arya,
26. Pârâ*s*arya from *G*âtukar*n*ya,
27. *G*âtukar*n*ya from Âsurâya*n*a and Yâska,[1316]
28. Âsurâya*n*a from Trava*n*i,
29. Trava*n*i from Aupagandhani,
30. Aupagandhani from Âsuri,
31. Âsuri from Bhâradvâga,
32. Bhâradvâga from Âtreya,
33. Âtreya from Mâ*nt*i,
34. Mâ*nt*i from Gautama,
35. Gautama from Gautama,
36. Gautama from Vâtsya,
37. Vâtsya from Sâ*nd*ilya,
38. Sâ*nd*ilya from Kai*s*orya Kâpya,
39. Kai*s*orya Kâpya from Kumârahârita,
40. Kumârahârita from Gâlava,
41. Gâlava from Vidarbhî-kau*nd*inya,
42. Vidarbhî-kau*nd*inya from Vatsanapât Bâbhrava,
43. Vatsanapât Bâbhrava from Pathi Saubhara,
44. Pathi Saubhara from Ayâsya Âṅgirasa,
45. Ayâsya Âṅgirasa from Âbhûti Tvâsh*t*ra,
46. Âbhûti Tvâsh*t*ra from Vi*s*varûpa Tvâsh*t*ra,
47. Vi*s*varûpa Tvâsh*t*ra from A*s*vinau,
48. A*s*vinau from Dadhya*k* Âtharva*n*a,
49. Dadhya*k* Âtharva*n*a from Atharvan Daiva,

[1315] From here the Va*ms*a agrees again with that given at the end of II, 6.

[1316] The Mâdhyandina text has, 1. Bhâradvâga, 2. Bhâradvâga, Âsurâya*n*a, and Yâska.

50. Atharvan Daiva from M*ri*tyu Prâdhva*m*sana,
51. M*ri*tyu Prâdhva*m*sana from Prâdhva*m*sana,
52. Prâdhva*m*sana from Ekarshi,
53. Ekarshi from Vipra*k*itti,[1317]
54. Vipra*k*itti from Vyash*t*i,
55. Vyash*t*i from Sanâru,
56. Sanâru from Sanâtana,
57. Sanâtana from Sanaga,
58. Sanaga from Paramesh*th*in,
59. Paramesh*th*in from Brahman,
60. Brahman is Svayambhu, self-existent.
Adoration to Brahman.

FIFTH ADHYÂYA.

FIRST BRÂHMA*N*A[1318].

1. That (the invisible Brahman) is full, this (the visible Brahman) is full}.[1319] This full (visible Brahman) proceeds from that full (invisible Brahman). On grasping the fulness of this full (visible Brahman) there is left that full (invisible Brahman).[1320]

Om (is) ether, (is) Brahman.[1321] 'There is the old ether (the invisible), and the (visible) ether of the atmosphere,' thus said Kauravyâya*n*îputra. This (the Om) is the Veda (the means of knowledge), thus the Brâhma*n*as know. One knows through it all that has to be known.

SECOND BRÂHMA*N*A.

1. The threefold descendants of Pragâpati, gods, men, and Asuras (evil spirits), dwelt as; Brahma*k*ârins (students) with their father

Pragâpati. Having finished their studentship the gods said: 'Tell us (something), Sir.' He told them the syllable Da. Then he said: 'Did you understand?' They said: 'We did understand. You told us "Dâmyata," Be subdued.' 'Yes,' he said, 'you have understood.'

2. Then the men said to him: 'Tell us something, Sir.' He told them the same syllable Da. Then he said: 'Did you understand?' They said:

[1317] Vipragitti, Mâdhyandina text.

[1318] This is called a Khila, or supplementary chapter, treating of various auxiliary means of arriving at a knowledge of Brahman.

[1319] Full and filling, infinite.

[1320] On perceiving the true nature of the visible world., there remains, i.e. there is perceived at once, as underlying it, or as being it, the invisible world or Brahman. This and the following paragraph are called Mantras.

[1321] This is explained by *S*aṅkara as meaning, Brahman is Kha, the ether, and called Om, i.e. Om and Kha are predicates of Brahman.

'We did understand. You told us, "Datta," Give.' 'Yes,' he said, 'you have understood.'

3. Then the Asuras said to him: 'Tell us something, Sir.' He told them the same syllable Da. Then he said: 'Did you understand?' They said: 'We did understand. You told us, "Dayadham," Be merciful.' 'Yes,' he said, 'you have understood.'

The divine voice of thunder repeats the same, Da Da Da, that is, Be subdued, Give, Be merciful. Therefore let that triad be taught, Subduing, Giving, and Mercy.

THIRD BRÂHMA*N*A.

1. Pragâpati is the heart, is this Brahman, is all this. The heart, h*ri*daya, consists of three syllables. One syllable is h*ri*, and to him who knows this, his own people and others bring offerings.[1322] One syllable is da, and to him who knows this, his own people and others bring gifts. One syllable is yam, and he who knows this, goes to heaven (svarga) as his world.

FOURTH BRÂHMA*N*A.

1. This (heart) indeed is even that, it was indeed the true[1323] (Brahman). And whosoever knows this great glorious first-born as the true Brahman, he conquers these worlds, and conquered likewise may that (enemy) be![1324] yes, whosoever knows this great glorious first-born as the true Brahman; for Brahman is the true.

FIFTH BRÂHMA*N*A.

1. In the beginning this (world) was water. Water produced the true,[1325] and the true is Brahman. Brahman produced Pragâpati,[1326] Pragâpati the Devas (gods). The Devas adore the true (satyam) alone. This satyam consists of three syllables. One syllable is sa, another t(i), the third[1327] yam. The first and last syllables are true, in the middle

---

[1322] *S*aṅkara explains that with regard to the heart, i.e. buddhi, the senses are 'its own people,' and the objects of the senses 'the others.'

[1323] The true, not the truth; the truly existing. The commentator explains it as it was explained in II, 3, 1, as sat and tya, containing both sides of the Brahman.

[1324] An elliptical expression, as explained by the commentator: May that one (his enemy) be conquered, just as that one was conquered by Brahman. If he conquers the world, how much more his enemy 1' It would be better, however, if we could take gita in the sense of vas̀îk*ri*ta or dânta, because we could then go on with ya eva*m* veda.

[1325] Here explained by the commentator as Pûtrâtmaka Hira*n*yagarbha.

[1326] Here explained as Virâg.

[1327] Satyam is often pronounced satiam, as trisyllabic. *S*aṅkara, however, takes the second syllable as t only, and explains the i after it as an anubandha. The Kâ*n*va text

there is the untrue.[1328] This untrue is on both sides enclosed by the true, and thus the true preponderates. The untrue does not hurt him who knows this.

2. Now what is the true, that is the Âditya (the sun), the person that dwells in yonder orb, and the person in the right eye. These two rest on each other, the former resting with his rays in the latter, the latter with his prâ*n*as (senses) in the former. When the latter is on the point of departing this life, he sees that orb as white only, and those rays (of the sun) do not return to him.

3. Now of the person in that (solar) orb Bhû*h* is the head, for the head is one, and that syllable is one; Bhuva*h* the two arms, for the arms are two, and these syllables are two; Svar the foot, for the feet are two, and these syllables are two.[1329] Its secret name is Ahar (day), and he who knows this destroys (hanti) evil and leaves (*g*ahâti) it.

4. Of the person in the right eye Bhû*h* is the head, for the head is one, and that syllable is one; Bhuva*h* the two arms, for the arms are two, and these syllables are two; Svar the foot, for the feet are two, and these syllables are two. Its secret name is Aham (ego), and he who knows this, destroys (hanti) evil and leaves (*g*ahâti) it.

SIXTH BRÂHMA*N*A.

1. That person, under the form of mind (manas), being light indeed,[1330] is within the heart, small like a grain of rice or barley. He is the ruler of all, the lord of all—he rules all this, whatsoever exists.

SEVENTH BRÂHMANA.

1. They say that lightning is Brahman, because lightning (vidyut) is called so from cutting off (vidânât).[1331] Whosoever knows this, that lightning is Brahman, him (that Brahman) cuts off from evil, for lightning indeed is Brahman.

---

gives the three syllables as sa, ti, am, which seems preferable; cf. *Kh*ând. Up. VIII, 3, 5; Taitt. Up. II, 6.

[1328] This is explained by a mere play on the letters, sa and ya having nothing in common with m*ri*tyu, death, whereas t occurs in m*ri*tyu and an*ri*ta. Dvivedagaṅga takes sa and am as true, because they occur in satya and am*ri*ta, and not in m*ri*tyu, while ti is untrue, because the t occurs in m*ri*tyu and am*ri*ta.

[1329] Svar has to be pronounced suvar.

[1330] Bhâ*h*satya must be taken as one word, as the commentator says, bhâ eva satya*m* sadbhâva*h* svarûpa*m* yasya so 'yam bhâ*h*satyo bhâsvara*h*.

[1331] From do, avakha*nd*ane, to cut; the lightning cutting through the darkness of the clouds, as Brahman, when known, cuts through the darkness of ignorance.

EIGHTH BRÂHMA*N*A.

1. Let him meditate on speech as a cow. Her four udders are the words Svâhâ, Vasha*t*, Hanta, and Svadhâ.[1332] The gods live on two of her udders, the Svâhâ and the Vasha*t*, men on the Hanta, the fathers on the Svadhâ. The bull of that cow is breath (prâ*n*a), the calf the mind.

NINTH BRÂHMA*N*A.

1. Agni Vai*s*vânara, is the fire within man by which the food that is eaten is cooked, i.e. digested. Its noise is that which one hears, if one covers one's ears. When he is on the point of departing this life, he does not hear that noise.

TENTH BRÂHMA*N*A.

1. When the person goes away from this world, he comes to the wind. Then the wind makes room for him, like the hole of a carriage wheel, and through it he mounts higher. He comes to the sun. Then the sun makes room for him, like the hole of a Lambara,[1333] and through it he mounts higher. He comes to the moon. Then the moon makes room for him, like the hole of a drum, and through it he mounts higher, and arrives at the world where there is no sorrow, no snow.[1334] There he dwells eternal years.

ELEVENTH BRÂHMA*N*A.

This is indeed the highest penance, if a man, laid up with sickness, suffers pain.[1335] He who knows this, conquers the highest world.

This is indeed the highest penance, if they carry a dead person into the forest.[1336] He who knows this, conquers the highest world.

This is indeed the highest penance, if they place a dead person on the fire.[1337] He who knows this, conquers the highest world.

[1332] There are two udders, the Svâhâ and Vasha*t*, on which the gods feed, i.e. words with which oblations are given to the gods. With Hanta they are given to men, with Svadhâ to the fathers.

[1333] A musical instrument.

[1334] The commentator explains hima by bodily pain, but snow is much more characteristic.

[1335] The meaning is that, while he is suffering pain from illness, he should think that he was performing penance. If he does that, he obtains the same reward for his sickness which he would have obtained for similar pain inflicted on himself for the sake of performing penance.

[1336] This is like the penance of leaving the village and living in the forest.

[1337] This is like the penance of entering into the fire.

TWELFTH BRÂHMA*N*A.

1. Some say that food is Brahman, but this is not so, for food decays without life (prâ*n*a). Others say that life (prâ*n*a) is Brahman, but this is not so, for life dries up without food. Then these two deities (food and life), when they have become one, reach that highest state (i.e. are Brahman). Thereupon Prât*ri*da said to his father: 'Shall I be able to do any good to one who knows this, or shall I be able to do him any harm?'[1338] The father said to him, beckoning with his hand: 'Not so, O Prât*ri*da; for who could reach the highest state, if he has only got to the oneness of these two?' He then said to him: 'Vi; verily, food is Vi, for all these beings rest (vish*t*âni) on food.' He then said: 'Ram; verily, life is Ram, for all these beings delight (ramante) in life. All beings rest on him, all beings delight in him who knows this.'

THIRTEENTH BRÂHMA*N*A.

1. Next follows the Uktha.[1339]. Verily, breath (prâ*n*a) is Uktha, for breath raises up (utthâpayati) all this. From him who knows this, there is raised a wise son, knowing the Uktha; he obtains union and oneness with the Uktha.

2. Next follows the Yagus. Verily, breath is Yagus, for all these beings are joined in breath.[1340] For him who knows this, all beings are joined to procure his excellence; he obtains union and oneness with the Yagus.

3. Next follows the Sâman. Verily, breath is the Sâman, for all these beings meet in breath. For him who knows this, all beings meet to procure his excellence; he obtains union and oneness with the Sâman.

4. Next follows the Kshatra. Verily, breath is the Kshatra, for breath is Kshatra, i.e. breath protects (trâyate) him from being hurt (ksha*n*ito*h*). He who knows this, obtains Kshatra (power), which requires no protection; he obtains union and oneness with Kshatra.[1341]

1338 That is, is he not so perfect in knowledge that nothing can harm him?

1339 Meditation on the hymn called uktha. On the uktha, as the principal part in the Mahâvrata, see Kaush. Up. III, 3; Ait. Âr. II, 1, 2. The uktha, yagus, sâman, &c. are here represented as forms under which prâ*n*a or life, and indirectly Brahman, is to be meditated on.

1340 Without life or breath nothing can join anything else; therefore life is called yagus, as it were yugus.

1341 Instead of Kshatram atram, another *S*âkhâ, i.e. the Mâdhyandina, reads Kshatramâtram, which Dvivedagaṅga explains as, he obtains the nature of the Kshatra, or he obtains the Kshatra which protects (Kshatram âtram).

FOURTEENTH BRÂHMA*N*A.

1. The words Bhûmi (earth), Antariksha (sky), and Dyu[1342] (heaven) form eight syllables. One foot of the Gâyatrî consists of eight syllables. This (one foot) of it is that (i.e. the three worlds). And he who thus knows that foot of it, conquers as far as the three worlds extend.

2. The *Ri*kas, the Yagû*m*shi, and the Sâmâni form eight syllables. One foot (the second) of the Gâyatrî consists of eight syllables. This (one foot) of it is that (i.e. the three Vedas, the *Ri*g-veda, Yagur-veda, and Sama-veda). And he who thus knows that foot of it, conquers as far as that threefold knowledge extends.

3. The Prâ*n*a (the up-breathing), the Apâna (the down-breathing), and the Vyâna (the back-breathing) form eight syllables. One foot (the third) of the Gâyatrî consists of eight syllables. This (one foot) of it is that (i.e. the three vital breaths). And he who thus knows that foot of it, conquers as far as there is anything that breathes. And of that (Gâyatrî, or speech) this indeed is the fourth (turîya), the bright (dar*s*ata) foot, shining high above the skies.[1343] What is here called turîya (the fourth) is meant for *k*aturtha (the fourth); what is called dar*s*atam padam (the bright foot) is meant for him who is as it were seen (the person in the sun); and what is called paroragas (he who shines high above the skies) is meant for him who shines higher and higher above every sky. And he who thus knows that foot of the Gâyatrî, shines thus himself also with happiness and glory.

4. That Gâyatrî (as described before with its three feet) rests on that fourth foot, the bright one, high above the sky. And that again rests on the True (satyam), and the True is the eye, for the eye is (known to be) true. And therefore even now, if two persons come disputing, the one saying, I saw, the other, I heard, then we should trust the one who says, I saw. And the True again rests on force (balam), and force is life (prâ*n*a), and that (the True) rests on life.[1344] Therefore they say, force is stronger than the True. Thus does that Gâyatrî rest with respect to the self (as life). That Gâyatrî protects (tatre) the vital breaths (gayas); the gayas are the prâ*n*as (vital breaths), and it protects them. And because it protects (tatre) the vital breaths (gayas), therefore it is called Gâyatrî. And that Savit*ri* verse which the teacher teaches,[1345] that is it (the life,

---

[1342] Dyu, nom. Dyaus, must be pronounced Diyaus.

[1343] Paronagas, masc., should be taken as one word, like paroksha, viz. he who is beyond all ragas, all visible skies.

[1344] *S*aṅkara understood the True (satyam) by tad, not the balam, the force.

[1345] The teacher teaches his pupil, who is brought to him when eight years old, the Sâvitrî verse, making him repeat each word, and each half verse, till he knows the whole, and by teaching him that Sâvitrî, he is supposed to teach him really the prâ*n*a, the life, as the self of the world.

the prâ*n*a, and indirectly the Gâyatrî); and whomsoever he teaches, he protects his vital breaths.

5. Some teach that Sâvitrî as an Anush*t*ubh[1346] verse, saying that speech is Anush*t*ubh, and that we teach that speech. Let no one do this, but let him teach the Gâyatrî as Sâvitrî.[1347] And even if one who knows this receives what seems to be much as his reward (as a teacher), yet this is not equal to one foot of the Gâyatrî.

6. If a man (a teacher) were to receive as his fee these three worlds full of all things, he would obtain that first foot of the Gâyatrî. And if a man were to receive as his fee everything as far as this threefold knowledge extends, he would obtain that second foot of the Gâyatrî. And if a man were to receive as his fee everything whatsoever breathes, he would obtain that third foot of the Gâyatrî. But 'that fourth bright foot, shining high above the skies'[1348] cannot be obtained by anybody—whence then could one receive such a fee?

7. The adoration[1349] of that (Gâyatrî):

'O Gâyatrî, thou hast one foot, two feet, three feet, four feet.[1350] Thou art footless, for thou art not known. Worship to thy fourth bright foot above the skies.' If[1351] one (who knows this) hates some one and says, 'May he not obtain this,' or 'May this wish not be accomplished to him,' then that wish is not accomplished to him against whom he thus prays, or if he says, 'May I obtain this.'

8. And thus *G*anaka Vaideha spoke on this point to Bu*d*ila Â*s*vatarâ*s*vi:[1352] 'How is it that thou who spokest thus as knowing the Gâyatrî, hast become an elephant and carriest me?' He answered: 'Your Majesty, I did not know its mouth. Agni, fire, is indeed its mouth; and if people pile even what seems much (wood) on the fire, it consumes it all. And thus a man who knows this, even if he commits what seems

---

1346 The verse would be, *Ri*g-veda V, 82, 1:

> Tat savitur v*rin*îmahe vaya*m* devasya bhoganam
> *S*resh*th*am sarvadhâtama*m* turam bhagasya dhîmahi.

1347 Because Gâyatrî represents life, and the pupil receives life when be learns the Gâyatrî.

1348 See before, § 2.

1349 Upasthâna is the act of approaching the gods, προσκύνησις Angehen, with a view of obtaining a request. Here the application is of two kinds, abhi*k*ârika, imprecatory against another, and abhyudayika, auspicious for oneself. The former has two formulas, the latter one. An upasthâna is here represented as effective, if connected with the Gâyatrî.

1350 Consisting of the three worlds, the threefold knowledge, the threefold vital breaths, and the fourth foot, as described before.

1351 I have translated this paragraph very freely, and differently from *S*aṅkara. The question is, whether dvishyât with iti can be used in the sense of abhi*k*âra, or imprecation. if not, I do not see how the words should be construed. The expression yasmâ upatish*th*ate is rightly explained by Dvivedagaṅga, yadartham evam upatish*th*ate.

1352 A*s*vatarasyâ*s*vasyâpatyam, *S*aṅkara.

much evil, consumes it all and becomes pure, clean, and free from decay and death.'

FIFTEENTH BRÂHMA*N*A.

1.[1353] The face of the True (the Brahman) is covered with a golden disk.[1354] Open that, O Pûshan,[1355] that we may see the nature of the True.[1356]

2. O Pûshan, only seer, Yama (judge), Sûrya (sun), son of Pragâpati,[1357] spread thy rays and gather them!

The light which is thy fairest form, I see it. I am what he is (viz. the person in the sun).

3. Breath to air and to the immortal! Then this my body ends in ashes. Om! Mind, remember! Remember thy deeds! Mind, remember! Remember thy deeds![1358]

4. Agni, lead us on to wealth (beatitude) by a good path,[1359] thou, O God, who knowest all things! Keep far from us crooked evil, and we shall offer thee the fullest praise! (Rv. I, 189, 1.)

SIXTH ADHYÂYA.

FIRST BRÂHMANA[1360].

1. Hari*h*, Om. He who knows the first and the best, becomes himself the first and the best among his people. Breath is indeed the first and the best. He who knows this, becomes the first and the best among his people, and among whomsoever he wishes to be so.

2. He who knows the richest,[1361] becomes himself the richest

---

[1353] These verses, which are omitted here in the Mâdhyandina text, are found at the end of the Vâgasaneyi-upanishad 15-18. They are supposed to be a prayer addressed to Âditya by a dying person.

[1354] Mahîdhara on verse 17: The face of the true (purusha in the sun), is covered by a golden disk.' *S*añkara explains here mukha, face, by mukhya*m* svarûpam, the principal form or nature.

[1355] Pûshan is here explained as a name of Savit*ri*, the sun; likewise all the names in the next verse.

[1356] Cf. Maitr. Up. VI, 35.

[1357] Of Î*s*vara or Hira*n*yagarbha.

[1358] The Vâgasaneyi-sa*m*hitâ reads: Om, krato smara, *kl*ibe smara, k*ri*ta*m* smara. Uva*t*a holds that Agni, fire, who has been worshipped in youth and manhood, is here invoked in the form of mind, or that kratu is meant for sacrifice. 'Agni, remember me 'Think of the world! Remember my deeds!' K*l*ibe is explained by Mahîdhara as a dative of k*l*ip, k*l*ip meaning loka, world, what is made to be enjoyed (kalpyate bhogâya).

[1359] Not by the Southern path, the dark, from which there is a fresh return to life.

[1360] This Brâhma*n*a, also called a Khila (p. 1010, l. 8; p. 1029, l. 8), occurs in the Mâdhyandina-*s*âkhâ XIV, 9, 2. It should be compared with the *Kh*ândogya-upanishad V, 1 (Sacred Books of the East, vol. i, p. 72); also with the Ait. Âr. II, 4; Kaush. Up. III, 3; and the Pra*s*ña Up. II, 3.

among his people. Speech is the richest. He who knows this, becomes the richest among his people, and among whomsoever he wishes to be so.

3. He who knows the firm rest, becomes himself firm on even and uneven ground. The eye indeed is the firm rest, for by means of the eye a man stands firm on even and uneven ground. He who knows this, stands firm on even and uneven ground.

4. He who knows success, whatever desire he desires, it succeeds to him. The ear indeed is success. For in the ear are all these Vedas successful. He who knows this, whatever desire he desires, it succeeds to him.

5. He who knows the home, becomes a home of his own people, a home of all men. The mind indeed is the home. He who knows this, becomes a home of his own people and a home of all men.

6. He who knows generation,[1362] becomes rich in offspring and cattle. Seed indeed is generation. He who knows this, becomes rich in offspring and cattle.

7. These Prâ*n*as (senses), when quarrelling together as to who was the best, went to Brahman[1363] and said: 'Who is the richest of us?' He replied: 'He by whose departure this body seems worst, he is the richest.'

8. The tongue (speech) departed, and having been absent for a year, it came back and said: 'How have you been able to live without me?' They replied: 'Like unto people, not speaking with the tongue, but breathing with breath, seeing with the eye, hearing with the ear, knowing with the mind, generating with seed. Thus we have lived.' Then speech entered in.

9. The eye (sight) departed, and having been absent for a year, it came back and said: 'How have you been able to live without me?' They replied: 'Like blind people, not seeing with the eye, but breathing with the breath, speaking with the tongue, hearing with the ear, knowing with the mind, generating with seed. Thus we have lived.' Then the eye entered in.

10. The ear (hearing) departed, and having been absent for a year, it came back and said: 'How have you been able to live without me?' They replied: 'Like deaf people, not hearing with the ear, but breathing with the breath, speaking with the tongue, seeing with the eye, knowing with the mind, generating with seed. Thus we have lived.' Then the ear entered in.

11. The mind departed, and having been absent for a year, it came

---

[1361] Here used as a feminine, while in the *Kh*ând. Up. V, 1, it is vasish*th*a.

[1362] This is wanting in the *Kh*ând. Up. Roer and Poley read Pragâpati for pragâti. MS, I. O. 3 75 has pragâti, MS. I. O. 1973 pragâpati.

[1363] Here we have Pragâpati, instead of Brahman, in the *Kh*ând. Up.; also sresh*th*a instead of vasish*th*a.

back and said: 'How have you been able to live without me?' They replied: 'Like fools, not knowing with their mind, but breathing with the breath, seeing with the eye, hearing with the ear, generating with seed. Thus we have lived.' Then the mind entered in.

12. The seed departed, and having been absent for a year, it came back and said: 'How have you been able to live without me?' They replied: 'Like impotent people, not generating with seed, but breathing with the breath, seeing with the eye, hearing with the ear, knowing with the mind. Thus we have lived.' Then the seed entered in.

13. The (vital) breath, when on the point of departing, tore up these senses, as a great, excellent horse of the Sindhu country might tare up the pegs to which he is tethered. They said to him: 'Sir, do not depart. We shall not be able to live without thee.' He said: 'Then make me an offering.' They said: 'Let it be so.'

14. Then the tongue said: 'If I am the richest, then thou art the richest by it.' The eye said: 'If I am the firm rest, then thou art possessed of firm rest by it.' The ear said: 'If I am success, then thou art possessed of success by it.' The mind said: 'If I am the home, thou art the home by it.' The seed said: 'If I am generation, thou art possessed of generation by it.' He said: 'What shall be food, what shall be dress for me?'

They replied: 'Whatever there is, even unto dogs, worms, insects, and birds,[1364] that is thy food, and water thy dress. He who thus knows the food of Ana (the breath),[1365] by him nothing is eaten that is not (proper) food, nothing is received that is not (proper) food. *S*rotriyas (Vedic theologians) who know this, rinse the mouth with water when they are going to eat, and rinse the mouth with water after they have eaten, thinking that thereby they make the breath dressed (with water).'

SECOND BRÂHMA*N*A[1366].

1. *S*vetaketu Âru*n*eya went to the settlement of the Pa*ñk*âlas. He came near to Pravâha*n*a *G*aivali,[1367] who was walking about (surrounded by his men). As soon as he (the king) saw him, he said: 'My boy!' *S*vetaketu replied: 'Sir!'

Then the king said: 'Have you been taught by your father!' 'Yes,'

[1364] It may mean, every kind of food, such as is eaten by dogs, worms, insects, and birds.

[1365] We must read, with MS. I. O. 375, anasyânnam, not annasyânnam, as MS. I. O. 1973, Roer, and Poley read. Weber has the right reading, which is clearly suggested by *Kh*ând. Up. V, 2, 1.

[1366] See *Kh*ând. Up. V, 3; Muir, Original Sanskrit Texts, I, 433; Deussen, Vedânta, p. 390. The commentator treats this chapter as a supplement, to explain the ways that lead to the pit*ri*loka and the devaloka.

[1367] The MSS. I. O. 375 and 1973 give *G*aivali, others *G*aibali. He is a Kshatriya sage, who appears also in *Kh*ând. Up. I, 8, 1, as silencing Brâhma*n*as.

he replied.

2. The king said: 'Do you know how men, when they depart from here, separate from each other?' 'No,' he replied.

'Do you know how they come back to this world?' 'No,' he replied.[1368]

'Do you know how that world does never become full with the many who again and again depart thither?' 'No,' he replied.

'Do you know at the offering of which libation the waters become endowed with a human voice and rise and speak?' 'No,' he replied.

'Do you know the access to the path leading to the Devas and to the path leading to the Fathers, i.e. by what deeds men gain access to the path leading to the Devas or to that leading to the Fathers? For we have heard even the saying of a *Ri*shi: "I heard of two paths for men, one leading to the Fathers, the other leading to the Devas. On those paths all that lives moves on, whatever there is between father (sky) and mother (earth)."'

*S*vetaketu said: 'I do not know even one of all these questions.'

3. Then the king invited him to stay and accept his hospitality. But the boy, not caring for hospitality, ran away, went back to his father, and said: 'Thus then you called me formerly well-instructed!' The father said: 'What then, you sage?' The son replied: 'That fellow of a Râganya asked me five questions, and I did not know one of them.'

'What were they?' said the father.

'These were they,' the son replied, mentioning the different heads.

4. The father said: 'You know me, child, that whatever I know, I told you. But come, we shall go thither, and dwell there as students.'

'You may go, Sir,' the son replied.

Then Gautama went where (the place of) Pravâha*n*a Gaivali was, and the king offered him a seat, ordered water for him, and gave him the proper offerings. Then he said to him: 'Sir, we offer a boon to Gautama.'

5. Gautama said: 'That boon is promised to me; tell me the same speech which you made in the presence of my boy.'

6. He said: 'That belongs to divine boons, name one of the human boons.'

7. He said: 'You know well that I have plenty of gold, plenty of cows, horses, slaves, attendants, and apparel; do not heap on me[1369]

[1368] The same question is repeated in Roer's edition, only substituting sampadyante for âpadyante. The MSS. I. O. 375 and 1973 do not support this.

[1369] Abhyavadânya is explained as niggardly, or unwilling to give, and derived from vadânya, liberal, a-vadânya, illiberal, and abhi, towards. This, however, is an impossible form in Sanskrit. Vadânya means liberal, and stands for avadânya, this being derived from avadâna, lit. what is cut off, then a morsel, a gift. In abhyavadânya the original a reappears, so that abhyavadânya means, not niggardly, but on the contrary, liberal, i.e. giving more than is required. Avadânya has never been met with in the sense of niggardly, and though a rule of Pâ*n*ini sanctions the formation of a-vadânya, it does not

what I have already in plenty, in abundance, and superabundance.'

The king said: 'Gautama, do you wish (for instruction from me) in the proper way?'

Gautama replied: 'I come to you as a pupil.'

In word only have former sages (though Brahmans) come as pupils (to people of lower rank), but Gautama actually dwelt as a pupil (of Pravâha*n*a, who was a Râganya) in order to obtain the fame of having respectfully served his master.[1370]

8. The king said: 'Do not be offended with us, neither you nor your forefathers, because this knowledge has before now never dwelt with any Brâhma*n*a.[1371] But I shall tell it to you, for who could refuse you when you speak thus?

9. 'The altar (fire), O Gautama, is that world (heaven);[1372] the fuel is the sun itself, the smoke his rays, the light the day, the coals the quarters, the sparks the intermediate quarters. On that altar the Devas offer the *s*raddhâ libation (consisting of water[1373]). From that oblation rises Soma, the king (the moon).

10. 'The altar, O Gautama, is Parganya (the god of rain); the fuel is the year itself, the smoke the clouds, the light the lightning, the coals the thunderbolt, the sparks the thunderings. On that altar the Devas offer Soma, the king (the moon). From that oblation rises rain.

11. 'The altar, O Gautama, is this world;[1374] the fuel is the earth itself, the smoke the fire, the light the night, the coals the moon, the sparks the stars. On that altar the Devas offer rain. From that oblation rises food.

12. 'The altar, O Gautama, is man; the fuel the opened mouth, the smoke the breath, the light the tongue, the coals the eye, the sparks the ear. On that altar the Devas offer food. From that oblation rises seed.

13. 'The altar, O Gautama, is woman.[1375] On that altar the Devas offer seed. From that oblation rises man. He lives so long as he lives, and then when he dies,

14. 'They take him to the fire (the funeral pile), and then the altar-fire is indeed fire, the fuel fuel, the smoke smoke, the light light, the

---

say in what sense. Abhyavadâ in the sense of cutting off in addition occurs in *S*atap. Br. II, 5, 2, 40; avadâna*m* karoti, in the sense of making a present, occurs Maitr. Up. VI, 33.

[1370] The commentator takes the opposite view. In times of distress, he says, former sages, belonging to a higher caste, have submitted to become pupils to teachers of a lower caste, not, however, in order to learn, but simply in order to live. Therefore Gautama also becomes a pupil in name only, for it would be against all law to act otherwise. See Gautama, Dharma-sûtras VII, i, ed, Stenzler; translated by Bühler, p. 209.

[1371] Here, too, my translation is hypothetical, and differs widely from *S*aṅkara.

[1372] Cf. *Kh*ând. Up. V, 4.

[1373] Deussen translates In diesem Feuer opfern die Götter den Glauben.'

[1374] Here a distinction is made between aya*m* loka, this world, and p*ri*thivî, earth, while in the *Kh*ând. Up. aya*m* loka is the earth, asau loka the heaven.

[1375] Tasyâ upastha eva samil, lomâni dhûmo, yonir ar*k*ir, yad anta*h*karoti te 'ṅgârâ, abhinandâ visphuliṅgâ*h*.

coals coals, the sparks sparks. In that very altar-fire the Devas offer man, and from that oblation man rises, brilliant in colour.

15. 'Those who thus know this (even G*ri*hasthas), and those who in the forest worship faith and the True[1376] (Brahman Hira*n*yagarbha), go to light (ar*k*is), from light to day, from day to the increasing half, from the increasing half to the six months when the sun goes to the north, from those six months to the world of the Devas (Devaloka), from the world of the Devas to the sun, from the sun to the place of lightning. When they have thus reached the place of lightning a spirit[1377] comes near them, and leads them to the worlds of the (conditioned) Brahman. In these worlds of Brahman they dwell exalted for ages. There is no returning for them.

16. 'But they who conquer the worlds (future states) by means of sacrifice, charity, and austerity, go to smoke, from smoke to night, from night to the decreasing half of the moon, from the decreasing half of the moon to the six months when the sun goes to the south, from these months to the world of the fathers, from the world of the fathers to the moon. Having reached the moon, they become food, and then the Devas feed on them there, as sacrificers feed on Soma, as it increases and decreases.[1378] But when this (the result of their good works on earth) ceases, they return again to that ether, from ether to the air, from the air to rain, from rain to the earth. And when they have reached the earth, they become food, they are offered again in the altar-fire, which is man (see § 11), and thence are born in the fire of woman. Thus they rise up towards the worlds, and go the same round as before.

'Those, however, who know neither of these two paths, become worms, birds, and creeping things.'

THIRD BRÂHMA*N*A[1379].

1. If a man wishes to reach greatness (wealth for performing sacrifices), he performs the upasad rule during twelve days[1380] (i.e. he lives on small quantities of milk), beginning on an auspicious day of the light half of the moon during the northern progress of the sun, collecting at the same time in a cup or a dish made of Udumbara wood all sorts of herbs, including fruits. He sweeps the floor (near the house-

---

[1376] *S*a*n*kara translates, 'those who with faith worship the True,' and this seems better.

[1377] 'A person living in the Brahma-world, sent forth, i.e. created, by Brahman, by the mind,' *S*a*n*kara. 'Der ist nicht wie ein Mensch,' Deussen, p. 392.

[1378] See note 4 on *Kh*ând. Up. V, 10, and Deussen, Vedânta, p. 393. *S*a*n*kara guards against taking âpyâyasvâpakshîyasva as a mantra. A similar construction is *g*âyasva m*ri*yasva, see *Kh*ând. Up. V, 10, 8.

[1379] Mâdhyandina text, p. 1103; cf. *Kh*ând. Up. V, 2, 4-8; Kaush. Up. II, 3.

[1380] Yasmin pu*n*ye 'nukûle 'hni karma *k*ikîrshati tata*h* prâk pu*n*yâham evârabhya dvâda*s*âham upasadvratî.

altar, âvasathya), sprinkles it, lays the fire, spreads grass round it according to rule,[1381] prepares the clarified butter (âgya), and on a day, presided over by a male star (nakshatra), after having properly mixed the Mantha[1382] (the herbs, fruits, milk, honey, &c.), he sacrifices (he pours âgya into the fire), saying:[1383] 'O *G*âtavedas, whatever adverse gods there are in thee, who defeat the desires of men, to them I offer this portion; may they, being pleased, please me with all desires.' Svâhâ!

'That cross deity who lies down,[1384] thinking that all things are kept asunder by her, I worship thee as propitious with this stream of ghee.' Svâhâ!

2. He then says, Svâhâ to the First, Svâhâ to the Best, pours ghee into the fire, and throws what remains into the Mantha (mortar).

He then says, Svâhâ to Breath, Svâhâ to her who is the richest, pours ghee into the fire, and throws what remains into the Mantha (mortar).

He then says, Svâhâ to Speech, Svâhâ to the Support, pours ghee into the fire, and throws what remains into the Mantha (mortar).

He then says, Svâhâ to the Eye, Svâhâ to Success, pours ghee into the fire, and throws what remains into the Mantha (mortar).

He then says, Svâhâ to the Ear, Svâhâ to the Home, pours ghee into the fire, and throws what remains into the Mantha (mortar).

He then says, Svâhâ to the Mind, Svâhâ to Offspring, pours ghee into the fire, and throws what remains into the Mantha (mortar).

He then says, Svâhâ to Seed, pours ghee into the fire, and throws what remains into the Mantha (mortar).

3. He then says, Svâhâ to Agni (fire), pours ghee into the fire, and throws what remains into the Mantha (mortar).

He then says, Svâhâ to Soma, pours ghee into the fire, and throws what remains into the Mantha (mortar).

He then says, Bhû*h* (earth), Svâhâ, pours ghee into the fire, and throws what remains into the Mantha (mortar).

He then says, Bhuva*h* (sky), Svâhâ, pours ghee into the fire, and throws what remains into the Mantha (mortar).

He then says, Sva*h* (heaven), Svâhâ, pours ghee into the fire, and throws what remains into the Mantha (mortar).

He then says, Bhûr, Bhuva*h*, Sva*h*, Svâhâ, pours ghee into the fire, and throws what remains into the Mantha (mortar).

[1381] As the whole act is considered smârta, not *s*rauta, the order to be observed (âv*r*it) is that of the sthâlîpâka.

[1382] Dravadravye prakshiptâ mathitâ*h* saktava*h* is the explanation of Mantha, given in *G*aimin. N. M. V. p. 406.

[1383] These verses are not explained by *S*aṅkara, and they are absent in the *Kh*ând. Up. V, 2, 6, 4.

[1384] The Mâdhyandinas read nipadyase.

He then says, Svâhâ to Brahman (the priesthood), pours ghee into the fire, and throws what remains into the Mantha (mortar).

He then says, Svâhâ to Kshatra (the knighthood), pours ghee into the fire, and throws what remains into the Mantha (mortar).

He then says, Svâhâ to the Past, pours ghee into the fire, and throws what remains into the Mantha (mortar).

He then says, Svâhâ to the Future, pours ghee into the fire, and throws what remains into the Mantha (mortar).

He then says, Svâhâ to the Universe, pours ghee into the fire, and throws what remains into the Mantha (mortar).

He then says, Svâhâ to all things, pours ghee into the fire, and throws what remains into the Mantha (mortar).

He then says, Svâhâ to Pragâpati, pours ghee into the fire, and throws what remains into the Mantha (mortar).

4. Then he touches it (the Mantha, which is dedicated to Prâ*n*a, breath), saying: 'Thou art fleet (as breath). Thou art burning (as fire). Thou art full (as Brahman). Thou art firm (as the sky). Thou art the abode of all (as the earth). Thou hast been saluted with Hiṅ (at the beginning of the sacrifice by the prastot*ri*). Thou art saluted with Hiṅ (in the middle of the sacrifice by the prastot*ri*). Thou hast been sung (by the udgât*ri* at the beginning of the sacrifice). Thou art sung (by the udgât*ri* in the middle of the sacrifice). Thou hast been celebrated (by the adhvaryu at the beginning of the sacrifice). Thou art celebrated again (by the âgnîdhra in the middle of the sacrifice). Thou art bright in the wet (cloud). Thou art great. Thou art powerful. Thou art food (as Soma). Thou art light (as Agni, fire, the eater). Thou art the end. Thou art the absorption (of all things).'

5. Then he holds it (the Mantha) forth, saying: 'Thou[1385] knowest all, we know thy greatness. He is indeed a king, a ruler, the highest lord. May that king, that ruler make me the highest lord.'

6. Then he eats it, saying: 'Tat savitur vare*n*yam[1386] (We meditate on that adorable light)—The winds drop honey for the righteous, the rivers drop honey, may our plants be sweet as honey! Bhû*h* (earth) Svâhâ!

'Bhargo devasya dhîmahi (of the divine Savit*ri*)—May the night be honey in the morning, may the air above the earth, may heaven, our father, be honey! Bhuva*h* (sky) Svâhâ!

'Dhiyo yo nah pro*k*odayât (who should rouse our thoughts)—May the tree be full of honey, may the sun be full of honey, may our cows

[1385] These curious words â ma*m*si â ma*m*hi te mahi are not explained by *S*aṅkara. Ânandagiri explains them as I have translated them. They correspond to 'amo, nâmâsy ama hi te sarvam idam' in the *Kh*ând. Up. V, 2, 6, 6. The Mâdhyandinas read: 'âmo 'sy âma*m* hi te mayi, sa hi râgâ, &c. Dvivedagaṅga translates: thou art the knower, thy knowledge extends to me.'

[1386] Rv. III, 62, 10.

be sweet like honey! Sva*h* (heaven) Svâhâ!'

He repeats the whole Sâvitrî verse, and all the verses about the honey, thinking, May I be all this! Bhûr, Bhuva*h*, Sva*h*, Svâhâ! Having thus swallowed all, he washes his hands, and sits down behind the altar, turning his head to the East. In the morning he worships Âditya (the sun), with the hymn, 'Thou art the best lotus of the four quarters, may I become the best lotus among men.' Then returning as he came, he sits down behind the altar and recites the genealogical list.[1387]

7. Uddâlaka Âruni told this (Mantha-doctrine) to his pupil Vâgasaneya Yâg*ñ*avalkya, and said: 'If a man were to pour it on a dry stick, branches would grow, and leaves spring forth.'

8. Vâgasaneya Yâg*ñ*avalkya told the same to his pupil Madhuka Paiṅgya, and said: 'If a man were to pour it on a dry stick, branches would grow, and leaves spring forth.'

9. Madhuka Paiṅgya told the same to his pupil *K*ûla Bhâgavitti, and said: 'If a man were to pour it on a dry stick, branches would grow, and leaves spring forth.'

10. *K*ûla Bhâgavitti told the same to his pupil *G*ânaki Âyasthû*n*a, and said: 'If a man were to pour it on a dry stick, branches would grow, and leaves spring forth.'

11. *G*ânaki Âyasthû*n*a told the same to his pupil Satyakâma *G*âbâla, and said: 'If a man were to pour it on a dry stick, branches would grow, and leaves spring forth.'

12. Satyakâma *G*âbâla told the same to his pupils, and said: 'If a man were to pour it on a dry stick, branches would grow, and leaves spring forth.'

Let no one tell this[1388] to any one, except to a son or to a pupil.[1389]

13. Four things are made of the wood of the Udumbara tree, the sacrificial ladle (sruva), the cup (*k*amasa), the fuel, and the two churning sticks.

There are ten kinds of village (cultivated) seeds, viz. rice and barley (brîhiyavâs), sesamum and kidney-beans (tilamâshâs), millet and panic seed (a*n*upriyaṅgavas), wheat (godhûmâs), lentils (masûrâs), pulse (khalvâs), and vetches (khalakulâs[1390]). After having ground these he sprinkles them with curds (dadhi), honey, and ghee, and then offers

---

[1387] This probably refers to the list immediately following.

[1388] The Mantha-doctrine with the prâ*n*adar*s*ana. Comm.

[1389] It probably means to no one except to one's own son and to one's own disciple. Cf. *S*vet. Up. VI, 22.

[1390] I have given the English names after Roer, who, living in India, had the best opportunity of identifying the various kinds of plants here mentioned. The commentators do not help us much. *S*aṅkara says that in some places Priyaṅgu (panic seed or millet) is called Kaṅgu; that Khalva, pulse, is also called Nishpâva and Valla, and Khalakula, vetches, commonly Kulattha. Dvivedagaṅga adds that A*n*u is called in Guzerat Moriya, Priyaṅgu Kaṅgu, Khalva, as nishpâva, Valla, and Khalakula Kulattha.

(the proper portions) of clarified butter[1391] (âgya).

FOURTH BRÂHMA*N*A[1392].

1. The earth is the essence of all these things, water is the essence of the earth, plants of water, flowers of plants, fruits of flowers, man of fruits, seed of man.

2. And Pragâpati thought, let me make an abode for him, and he created a woman (*S*atarûpâ).

Tâ*m*[1393] s*r*ish*t*vâdha upâsta, tasmât striyam adha upâsîta. Sa etam prâ*ñk*a*m* grâvâ*n*am âtmana eva samudapârayat, tenainâm abhyas*r*igat.

3. Tasyâ vedir upastho, lomâni barhi*s*, *k*armâdhishava*n*e, samiddho[1394] madhyatas, tau mushkau. Sa yâvân ha vai vâgapeyena yagamânasya loko bhavati tâvân asya loko bhavati ya eva*m* vidvân adhopahâsa*m* *k*araty a sa[1395] strî*n*a*m* suk*r*ita*m* v*r*iṅkte 'tha ya idam avidvân adhopahâsa*m* *k*araty âsya striya*h* suk*r*ita*m* v*r*iñgate.

4. Etad dha sma vai tadvidvân Uddâlaka Âru*n*ir âhaitad dha sma vai tadvidvân Nâko Maudgalya âhaitad dha sma vai tadvidvân Kumârahârita âha, bahavo maryâ brâhma*n*âyanâ[1396] nirindriyâ visuk*r*ito'smâl lokât prayanti[1397] ya ida*m* avidvâ*m*so 'dhopahâsa*m* *k*arantîti. Bahu vâ[1398] ida*m* suptasya va gâgrato vâ reta*h* skandati,

5. Tad abhim*r*i*s*ed anu vâ mantrayeta yan me 'dya reta*h* p*r*ithivîm askântsîd yad oshadhîr apy asarad yad apa*h*, idam aha*m* tad reta âdade

---

[1391] According to the rules laid down in the proper Grihya-sûtras.

[1392] This Brâhma*n*a is inserted here because there is supposed to be some similarity between the preparation of the *S*rîmantha and the Putramantha, or because a person who has performed the *S*rîmantha is fit to perform the Putramantha. Thus *S*aṅkara says: Prâ*n*adar*s*ina*h* *s*rîmantha*m* karma k*r*itavata*h* putramanthe 'dhikâra*h*. Yadâ putramantha*m* *k*ikîrshati tadâ srîmantha*m* k*r*itvâ *r*itukâla*m* patnyâ*h* (brahma*k*arye*n*a) pratîkshata iti.

[1393] I have given those portions of the text which did not admit of translation into English, in Sanskrit. It was not easy, however, to determine always the text of the Kânva-*s*âkhâ. Poley's text is not always correct, and Roer seems simply to repeat it. *S*aṅkara's commentary, which is meant for the Kânva text, becomes very short towards the end of the Upanishad. It is quite sufficient for the purpose of a translation, but by no means always for restoring a correct text. MS. Wilson 369, which has been assigned to the Kâ*n*va-*s*âkhâ, and which our Catalogue attributes to the same school, gives the Mâdhyandina text, and so does MS. Mill 108. I have therefore collated two MSS. of the India Office, which Dr. Rost had the kindness to select for me, MS. 375 and MS. 1973, which I call A. and B.

[1394] Roer reads samidho, but *S*aṅkara and Dvivedagaṅga clearly presuppose samiddho, which is in A. and B.

[1395] Roer has âsâ*m* sa strî*n*âm, Poley, A. and B. have âsâ*m* strî*n*âm. *S*aṅkara. (MS. Mill 64) read â sa strî*n*âm, and later on âsya striya*h*, though both Roer and Poley leave out the â here too (â asyeti *kh*eda*h*).

[1396] Brâhma*n*âyanâ*h*, the same as brahmabandhava*h*, i.e. Brâhmans by descent only, not by knowledge.

[1397] Naraka*m* ga*kkh*antîtyartha*h*. Dvivedagaṅga.

[1398] Bahu vâ svalpa*m* vâ.

punar mâm aitv indriyam punas tega*h* punar bhaga*h*, punar agnayo[1399] dhish*n*yâ yathâsthâna*m* kalpantâm, ity anâmikâṅgush*th*âbhyâm âdâyântare*n*a stanau vâ bhruvau vâ nim*riñg*yât[1400].

6. If a man see himself in the water,[1401], he should recite the following verse: 'May there be in me splendour, strength, glory, wealth, virtue.'

She is the best of women whose garments are pure.[1402] Therefore let him approach a woman whose garments are pure, and whose fame is pure, and address her.

7. If she do not give in,[1403] let him, as he likes, bribe her (with presents). And if she then do not give in, let him, as he likes, beat her with a stick or with his hand, and overcome her,[1404] saying: 'With manly strength and glory I take away thy glory,'—and thus she becomes unglorious.[1405]

8. If she give in, he says: 'With manly strength and glory I give thee glory,'—and thus they both become glorious.

9. Sa yâm i*kkh*et kâmayeta meti tasyâm artha*m* nish*t*âya[1406] mukhena mukha*m* sandhâyopastham asyâ abhim*ris*ya *g*aped aṅgâdaṅgât sambhavasi h*ri*dayâd adhi *g*âyase, sa tvam aṅgakashâyo[1407] 'si digdhaviddhâm[1408] iva mâdayemâm amûm mayîti.[1409]

10. Atha yâm i*kkh*en na garbha*m* dadhîteti[1410] tasyâm artha*m* nish*t*âya mukhena mukha*m* sandhâyâbhiprâ*n*yâpânyâd indriye*n*a te retasâ reta âdada ity aretâ[1411] eva bhavati.

11. Atha yâm i*kkh*ed garbha*m* dadhîteti tasyâm artha*m* nish*t*âya mukhena mukha*m* sandhâyâpânyâbhiprâ*n*yâd indriye*n*a te retâsa reta âdadhâmîti garbhi*n*y eva bhavati.

12. Now again, if a man's wife has a lover and the husband hates him, let him (according to rule)[1412] place fire by an unbaked jar, spread

---

[1399] The Mâdhyandina text has agnayo, and Dvivedagaṅga explains it by dhîsh*n*yâ agnaya*h s*arîrasthitâ*h*. Poley and Roer have punar agnir dhish*n*yâ, and so have A. and B.

[1400] Nirm*rig*yât, A.; nim*riñg*yât, B.

[1401] Dvivedagaṅga adds, retoyonâv udake reta*h*si*k*as tatra sva*kkh*âyâdar*s*ane prâya*sk*ittam âha.

[1402] Trirâtravrata*m* k*ri*tvâ *k*aturtha 'hni snâtâm.

[1403] Instead of connecting kâmam with dadyât, Dvivedagaṅga explains it by yathâ*s*akti.

[1404] Atikram, scil. maithunâya.

[1405] Bandhyâ durbhagâ.

[1406] Nish*t*âya, A. B.; nish*th*âya, Roer, Poley; the same in § 10.

[1407] Sa tvam aṅgânâ*m* kashâyo raso 'si.

[1408] Vishalipta*s*araviddhâm m*ri*gîm iva.

[1409] Mâdayeti is the reading of the Mâdhyandina text. Poley, Roer, A. and B. read mâdayemâm amûm mayîti. Ânandagiri has m*ri*gîm ivâmûm madiyâ*m* striyam me mâdaya madva*s*â*m* kurv ityartha*h*. Dvivedagaṅga explains mâdayeti.

[1410] Rûpabhra*ms*ayauvanahânibhayât.

[1411] Agarbhi*n*î.

[1412] Âvasathyâgnim eva pragvâlya.

a layer of arrows in inverse order,[1413] anoint these three arrow-heads[1414] with butter in inverse order, and sacrifice, saying: 'Thou hast sacrificed in my fire, I take away thy up and down breathing, I here.'[1415]

'Thou hast sacrificed in my fire, I take away thy sons and cattle, I here.'

'Thou hast sacrificed in my fire, I take away thy sacred and thy good works, I here.'

'Thou hast sacrificed in my fire, I take away thy hope and expectation, I here.'

He whom a Brâhma*n*a who knows this curses, departs from this world without strength and without good works. Therefore let no one wish even for sport with the wife of a *S*rotriya[1416] who knows this, for he who knows this, is a dangerous enemy.

13. When the monthly illness seizes his wife, she should for three days not drink from a metal vessel, and wear a fresh dress. Let no V*ri*shala or V*ri*shalî (a *S*ûdra man or woman) touch her. At the end of the three days, when she has bathed, the husband should make her pound rice.[1417]

14. And if a man wishes that a white son should be born to him, and that he should know one Veda, and live to his full age, then, after having prepared boiled rice with milk and butter, they should both eat, being fit to have offspring.

15. And if a man wishes that a reddish[1418] son with tawny eyes should be born to him, and that he should know two Vedas, and live to his full age, then, after having prepared boiled rice with coagulated milk and butter, they should both eat, being fit to have offspring.

16. And if a man wishes that a dark son should be born to him with red eyes, and that he should know three Vedas, and live to his full age, then, after having prepared boiled rice with water and butter, they should both eat, being fit to have offspring.

17. And if a man wishes that a learned daughter should be born to him, and that she should live to her full age, then, after having prepared boiled rice with sesamum and butter, they should both eat, being fit to

---

[1413] Pa*sk*imâgra*m* dakshi*n*âgra*m* vâ yathâ syât tathâ.

[1414] Tisra*h* is left out by Roer and Poley, by A. and B.

[1415] I have translated according to the Kâ*n*va text, as far as it could be made out. As there are four imprecations, it is but natural that tisra*h* should be left out in the Kâ*n*va text. It is found in the Mâdhyandina text, because there the imprecations are only three in number, viz. the taking away of hope and expectation, of sons and cattle, and of up and down breathing. Instead of asâv iti, which is sufficient, the Mâdhyandina text has asâv iti nâma g*ri*h*n*âti, and both Ânandagiri and Dvivedagaṅga allow the alternative, âtmana*h* *s*atror vâ nâma grih*n*âti, though asau can really refer to the speaker only.

[1416] Roer reads dvâre*n*a; Poley, A. and B. dâre*n*a; the Mâdhyandinas gâyâyâ. *S*aṅkara, according to Roer, interprets dvâre*n*a, but it seems that dvâre*n*a is used here in the singular, instead of the plural. See Pâraskara G*ri*hya-sûtras I, 11.

[1417] To be used for the ceremony described in § 14 seq.

[1418] Kapilo var*n*ata*h* piṅgala*h* piṅgâksha*h*.

have offspring.

18. And if a man wishes that a learned son should be born to him, famous, a public man, a popular speaker, that he should know all the Vedas, and that he should live to his full age, then, after having prepared boiled rice with meat and butter, they should both eat, being fit to have offspring. The meat should be of a young or of an old bull.

19. And then toward morning, after having, according to the rule of the Sthâlîpâka (pot-boiling), performed the preparation of the Âgya (clarified butter[1419]), he sacrifices from the Sthâlîpâka bit by bit, saying: 'This is for Agni, Svâhâ! This is for Anumati, Svâhâ! This is for the divine Savit*ri*, the true creator, Svâhâ!' Having sacrificed, he takes out the rest of the rice and eats it, and after having eaten, he gives it to his wife. Then he washes his hands, fills a water-jar, and sprinkles her thrice with it, saying: 'Rise hence, O Vi*s*vâvasu,[1420] seek another blooming girl, a wife with her husband.'

20. Then he embraces her, and says: 'I am Ama (breath), thou art Sâ (speech).[1421] Thou art Sâ (speech), I am Ama (breath). I am the Sâman, thou art the *Rik*.[1422] I am the sky, thou art the earth. Come, let us strive together, that a male child may be begotten.'[1423]

21. Athâsyâ ûrû vihâpayati, vigihîthâ*m* dyâvâp*ri*thivî iti tasyâm artha*m* nish*t*âya mukhena mukha*m* sandhâya trir enâm anulomâm[1424] anumârsh*t*i, Vish*n*ur yoni*m* kalpayatu, Tvash*t*â rûpâ*n*i pi*m*satu, âsi*ñk*atu Pragâpatir Dhâtâ garbha*m* dadhatu te. Garbha*m* dhehi Sinîvâli, garbha*m* dhehi p*ri*thush*t*uke, garbha*m* te A*s*vinau devâv âdhattâm pushkarasragau.

22. Hira*n*mayî ara*n*î yâbhyâ*m* nirmanthatâm[1425] a*s*vinau,[1426] ta*m* te

---

[1419] Karu*m* *s*rapayitvâ.

[1420] Name of a Gandharva, as god of love. See *Ri*g-veda X, 85, 22. Dvivedagaṅga explains the verse differently, so that the last words imply, I come together with my own wife.

[1421] Because speech is dependent on breath, as the wife is on the husband. See *Kh*ând. Up. I, 6, 1.

[1422] Because the Sâma-veda rests on the *Ri*g-veda.

[1423] This is a verse which is often quoted and explained. It occurs in the Atharva-veda XIV, 71, as 'amo 'ham asmi si tva*m*, sâmâham asmy *ri*k tvam, dyaur aham p*ri*thivî tvam; tâv iha sam bhavâva pragâm â ganayâvahai.'

Here we have the opposition between ama*h* and sâ, while in the Ait. Brâhma*n*a VIII, 27, we have amo 'ham asmi sa tvam, giving ama*h* in opposition to sa. It seems not unlikely that this was an old proverbial formula, and that it meant originally no more than 'I am he, and thou art she.' But this meaning was soon forgotten. In the *Kh*ând. Up. I, 6, 1, we find sâ explained as earth, ama as fire (Sacred Books of the East, vol. i, p. 13). In the Ait. Brâhma*n*a sâ is explained as *Rik*, ama as Sâman. I have therefore in our passage also followed the interpretation of the commentary, instead of rendering it, 'I am he, and thou art she; thou art she, and I am he.'

[1424] Anulomam, mûrdhânam ârabhya pâdântam.

[1425] Nirmathitavantau.

[1426] A*s*vinau devau, Mâdhyandina text.

garbha*m* havâmahe[1427] da*s*ame mâsi sûtave. Yathâgnigarbhâ p*ri*thivî, yathâ dyaur indre*n*a garbhi*n*î, vâyur di*s*â*m* yathâ garbha eva*m* garbha*m* dadhâ*m*î te 'sav iti.[1428]

23. Soshyantîm[1429] adbhir abhyukshati. Yathâ vâyu*h*[1430] pushkari*n*î*m* sami*ñg*ayati sarvata*h*, evâ te garbha egatu sahâvaitu garâyu*n*â. Indrasyâya*m* vraga*h* k*ri*ta*h* sârga*l*a*h*[1431] saparі*s*raya*h*,[1432] tam indra nirgahi garbhe*n*a sâvarâ*m*[1433] saheti.

24.[1434] When the child is born, he prepares the fire, places the child on his lap, and having poured p*ri*shadâgya, i.e. dadhi (thick milk) mixed with gh*ri*ta (clarified butter) into a metal jug, he sacrifices bit by bit of that p*ri*shadâgya, saying: 'May I, as I increase in this my house, nourish a thousand! May fortune never fail in his race, with offspring and cattle, Svâhâ!'

'I offer to thee. in my mind the vital breaths which are in me, Svâhâ!'

'Whatever[1435] in my work I have done too much, or whatever I have here done too little, may the wise Agni Svish*t*ak*ri*t make this right and proper for us, Svâhâ!'

25. Then putting his mouth near the child's right ear, he says thrice, Speech, speech![1436] After that he pours together thick milk, honey, and clarified butter, and feeds the child with (a ladle of) pure

---

[1427] Dadhâmahe, Mâdhyandina text. Instead of sûtave, A. has sûyate, B. sûtaye.

[1428] Iti nâma g*ri*h*n*âti, Mâdhyandina text. *S*aṅkara says, asâv iti tasyâ*h*. Ânandagiri says, asâv iti patyur vâ nirde*s*a*h*; tasyâ nâma g*ri*h*n*âtîti pûrve*n*a sambandha*h*. Dvivedagaṅga says, ante bhartâsâv aham iti svâtmano nâma g*ri*h*n*âti, bhâryâyâ vâ.

[1429] See Pâraskara G*ri*hya-sûtra I. 16 seq.

[1430] Vatâ*h*, M.

[1431] Argadayâ nirodhena saha vartamâna*h* sârga*d*a*h*, Dvivedagaṅga.

[1432] Sapari*s*raya*h*, pari*s*raye*n*a parivesh*t*anena garâyu*n*â sahita*h*, Dvivedagaṅga.

[1433] Sâvarâm is the reading given by Poley, Roer, A. and B. Ânandagiri explains: garbhani*h*sara*n*ânantara*m* yâ mâ*m*sape*s*î nirga*kkh*ati sâvarâ, tâ*m* *k*a nirgamayety artha*h*. Dvivedagaṅga (ed. Weber) writes: nirgamyamânamâ*m*sape*s*î sâ-avara*s*abdavâ*k*yâ, ta*m* sâvara*m* *k*a nirgamaya.

[1434] These as well as the preceding rules refer to matters generally treated in the G*ri*hya-sûtras; see Â*s*valâyana, G*ri*hya-sûtras I, 13 seq.; Pâraskara, G*ri*hya-sûtras I, 11 seq.; *S*âṅkâkyana, G*ri*hya-sûtras I, 19 seq. It is curious, however, that Â*s*valâyana I, 13, 1, refers distinctly to the Upanishad as the place where the pu*m*savana and similar matters were treated. This shows that the Upanishads were known before the composition of the G*ri*hya-sûtras, and explains perhaps, at least partially, why the Upanishads were considered as rahasya. Â*s*valâyana says, 'Conception, begetting of a boy, and guarding the embryo are to be found in the Upanishad. But if a man does not read the Upanishad, let him know that he should feed his wife,' &c. Nârâya*n*a explains that Â*s*valâyana here refers to an Upanishad which does not exist in his own *S*âkhâ, but he objects to the conclusion that therefore the garbhâdhâna and other ceremonies need not be performed, and adds that some hold it should be performed, as prescribed by *S*aunaka and others.

[1435] Â*s*valâyana, G*ri*hya-sûtra I, 10, 23.

[1436] Trayîlaksha*n*â vâk tvayi pravi*s*atv iti *g*apato 'bhiprâya*h*.

gold,[1437] saying: 'I give thee Bhû*h*, I give thee Bhuva*h*, I give thee Sva*h*.[1438] Bhûr, Bhuva*h*, Sva*h*, I give thee all.'[1439]

26.[1440] Then he gives him his name, saying: 'Thou art Veda;' but this is his secret name.[1441]

27. Then he hands the boy to his mother and gives him her breast, saying: 'O Sarasvatî, that breast of thine which is inexhaustible, delightful, abundant, wealthy, generous, by which thou cherishest all blessings, make that to flow here.'[1442]

28.[1443] Then he addresses the mother of the boy:

'Thou art I*l*â Maitrâvaru*n*î: thou strong woman hast born a strong boy. Be thou blessed with strong children thou who hast blessed me with a strong child.'

And they say of such a boy: 'Ah, thou art better than thy father; ah, thou art better than thy grandfather. Truly he has reached the highest point in happiness, praise, and Vedic glory who is born as the son of a Brâhma*n*a that knows this.'

[1437] Cf. Pâraskara G*r*ihya-sûtras I, 16, 4, anâmikayâ suvar*n*ântarhitayâ; *S*âṅkhâyana, G*r*ihya-sûtras I, 24, prâ*s*ayeg gâtarupe*n*a.

[1438] Bhûr bhuva*h* sva*h* are explained by Dvivedagaṅga as the *R*ig-veda, Yagur-veda, and Sâma-veda. They might also be earth, air, and heaven. See *S*âṅkhâyana, G*r*ihya-sûtras 1, 24; Bhur *r*igveda*m* tvayi dadhâmi, &c.

[1439] The Mâdhyandinas add here another verse, which the father recites while he strokes his boy: 'Be a stone, be an axe, be pure gold. Thou art my Self, called my son; live a hundred harvests.' The same verse occurs in the Â*s*valâyana G*r*ihya-sûtras I, 15, 3.

[1440] The two ceremonies, here described, are the âyushya-karman and the medhâganana. They are here treated rather confusedly. Pâraskara (G*r*ihya-sûtras I, 16, 3) distinguishes the medhâganana and the âyushya. He treats the medhâganana first, which consists in feeding the boy with honey and clarified butter, and saying to him bhûs tvayi dadhâmi, &c. The âyushya consists in repeating certain verses in the boy's ear, wishing him a long life, &c. In Â*s*valâyana's G*r*ihya-sûtras, I, 15, 1 contains the âyushya, I, 15, 2 the medhâganana. *S*âṅkhâyana also (I, 24) treats the âyushya first, and the medhâganana afterwards, and the same order prevails in the Mâdhyandina text of the B*r*ihadâranyaka-upanishad.

[1441] In the Mâdhyandina text these acts are differently arranged.

[1442] *R*ig-veda I, 164, 49.

[1443] These verses are differently explained by various commentators. Ânandagiri explains i*l*â as stutyâ, bhogyâ. He derives Maitrâvaru*n*î from Maitrâvaru*n*a, i.e. Vasish*th*a, the son of Mitrâvaru*n*au, and identifies her with Arundhatî. Dvivedagaṅga takes i*d*â as bhogyâ, or i*d*âpâtrî, or p*r*ithivîrûpâ, and admits that she may be called Maitrâvaru*n*î, because born of Mitrâvaru*n*au. Vîre is rightly taken as a vocative by Dvivedagaṅga, while Ânandagiri explains it as a locative, mayi nimittabhûte. One expects agîgana*h* instead of agîganat, which is the reading of A. and B. The reading of the Mâdhyandinas, âgîganathâ*h*, is right grammatically, but it offends against the metre, and is a theoretical rather than a real form. If we read agîgana*h*, we must also read akara*h*, unless we are prepared to follow the commentator, who supplies bhavatî.

FIFTH BRÂHMANA.

1. Now follows the stem:[1444]

1. Pautimâshîputra from Kâtyâyanîputra,
2. Kâtyâyanîputra from Gotamîputra,
3. Gotamîputra from Bhâradvâ*g*îputra,
4. Bhâradvâ*g*îputra from Pârâ*s*arîputra,
5. Pârâ*s*arîputra from Aupasvatîputra,
6. Aupasvatîputra from Pârâ*s*arîputra,
7. Pârâ*s*arîputra from Kâtyâyanîputra,
8. Kâtyâyanîputra from Kau*s*ikîputra,
9. Kau*s*ikîputra from Âlambîputra and Vaiyâghrapadîputra,
10. Âlambîputra and Vaiyâghrapadîputra from Kâ*n*vîputra,
11. Kâ*n*vîputra from Kâpîputra,
12. Kâpîputra

2. from Âtreyîputra,

13. Âtreyîputra from Gautamîputra,
14. Gautamîputra from Bhâradvâ*g*îputra,
15. Bhâradvâ*g*îputra from Pâra*s*arîputra,
16. Pâra*s*arîputra from Vâtsîputra,
17. Vâtsîputra from Pâra*s*arîputra,
18.[1445] Pâra*s*arîputra from Vârkâru*n*îputra,
19. Vârkâru*n*îputra from Vârkâru*n*îputra,
20. Vârkâru*n*îputra from Ârtabhagîputra,
21. Ârtabhagîputra from *S*auṅgîputra,
22. *S*auṅgîputra from Sâṅk*ri*tîputra,
23.[1446] Sâṅk*ri*tîputra from Âlambâyanîputra,
24. Âlambâyanîputra from Âlambîputra,
25. Âlambîputra from *G*ayantîputra,
26. *G*ayantîputra from Mâ*nd*ûkâyanîputra,
27. Mâ*nd*ûkâyanîputra from Mâ*nd*ûkîputra,
28. Mâ*nd*ûkîputra from *S*â*nd*ilîputra,

[1444] The Mâdhyandinas begin with vayam, we, then 1. Bhâradvâ*g*îputra, 2. Vâtsîma*nd*avîputra, 3. Pâra*s*arîputra, 4. Gârgîputra, 5. Pârâ*s*arî-kau*nd*inîputra, 6. Gârgîputra, 7. Gârgîputra, 8. Bâ*d*eyîputra, 9. Maushikîputra, 10. Hârikar*n*îputra, 11. Bhâradvâ*g*îputra, 12. Paiṅgîputra, 13. *S*aunakîputra, 14. Kâ*s*yapî-bâlâkyâ-mâ*th*arîputra, 15. Kautsîputra, 16. Baudhîputra, 17. *S*âlaṅkâyanîputra, 18. Vârshaga*n*îputra, 19. Gautamîputra, 20. Âtreyîputra, 21. Gautamîputra, 22. Vâtsîputra, 23. Bhâradvâgîputra, 24. Pârâ*s*arîputra, 25. Vârkâru*n*îputra; then from No. 20 as in the Kâ*n*va text.

This stem is called by *S*aṅkara, Samastaprava*k*anava*ms*a*h*, and Ânandagiri adds, pûrvau va*ms*au purushavi*s*eshitau, t*ri*tîyas tu strîviseshita*h*, strîprâdhâ*n*yât. Dvivedagaṅga writes, putramanthakarma*n*a*h* strîsa*m*skârârthatvenoktatvât tatsannidhânâd aya*m* va*m*sa*h* strîprâdhânyeno*k*yate.

[1445] M. has only one.

[1446] M. inverts 23 and 24.

29. *S*â*nd*ilîputra from Râthîtarîputra,
30.[1447] Râthîtarîputra from Bhâlukîputra,
31. Bhâlukîputra from Krau*ñk*ikîputrau,
32. Krau*ñk*ikîputrau from Vai*tt*abhatîputra,[1448]
33. Vai*tt*abhatîputra from Kâr*s*akeyîputra,[1449]
34. Kâr*s*akeyîputra from Prâ*k*înayogîputra,
35. Prâ*k*înayogîputra from Sâ*ñ*gîvîputra,[1450]
36. Sâ*ñ*gîvîputra from Prâ*s*ñîputra Âsurivâsin,
37. Prâ*s*ñîputra Âsurivâsin from Âsurâya*n*a,
38. Âsurâya*n*a from Âsuri,
39. Âsuri

3. from Yâ*g*ñavalkya,
40. Yâ*g*ñavalkya from Uddâlaka,
41. Uddâlaka from Aru*n*a,
42. Aru*n*a from Upave*s*i,
43. Upave*s*i from Ku*s*ri,
44. Ku*s*ri from Vâga*s*ravas,
45. Vâga*s*ravas from *G*ihvâvat Vâdhyoga,
46. *G*ihvâvat Vâdhyoga from Asita Vârshaga*n*a,
47. Asita Vârshaga*n*a from Harita Ka*s*yapa,
48. Harita Ka*s*yapa from *S*ilpa Kasyapa,
49. *S*ilpa Kasyapa from Ka*s*yapa Naidhruvi,
50. Ka*s*yapa Naidhruvi from Vâ*k*,
51. Vâ*k* from Ambhi*n*î,
52. Ambhi*n*î from Âditya, the Sun.

As coming from Âditya, the Sun, these pure[1451] Yagus verses have been proclaimed by Yâgñavalkya Vâgasaneya.

4.[1452] The same as far as Sâñgîvîputra (No. 36), then
36. Sâñgîvîputra from Mâ*nd*ûkâyani,
37. Mâ*nd*ûkâyani from Mâ*nd*avya,
38. Mâ*nd*avya from Kautsa,

[1447] Deest in M.

[1448] Vaidabh*r*itîputra, M.

[1449] Bhâlukîputra, M.

[1450] Kâr*s*akeyîputra after 35 in M.

[1451] They are called *s*uklâni, white or pure, because they are not mixed with Brâhma*n*as, avyâmi*s*râ*n*i brâhmaṅena (doshair asaṅkîr*n*âni, paurusheyatvadoshad-vârâbhâvâd ityartha*h*). Or they are ayâtayâmâni, unimpaired. Ânandagiri adds, Pragâpatim ârabhya Sâ*ñ*gîvîputraparyanta*m* (No. 36) Vâgasaneyi*s*âkhâsu sarvâsv eko va*m*sa ityâha samânam iti. Dvivedagaṅga says: Vâgisâkhâva*kkh*innânâ*m* yagushâ*m* Sûrye*n*opadish*t*atva*m* Yâ*g*ñavalkyena prâptatvam *k*a purâ*n*eshu prasiddham.

[1452] This last paragraph is wanting in the Mâdhyandina text, but a very similar paragraph occurs in *S*atapatha-brâhma*n*a X, 6, 5, 9, where, however, Vâtsya comes before Sândilya.

39. Kautsa from Mâhitthi,
40. Mâhitthi from Vâmakakshâya*n*a,
41. Vâmakakshâya*n*a from *S*â*nd*ilya,
42. *S*â*nd*ilya from Vâtsya,
43. Vâtsya from Ku*s*ri,
44. Ku*s*ri from Yag*ñ*ava*k*as Râgastambâyana,
45. Yag*ñ*ava*k*as Râgastambâyana from Tura Kâvasheya,
46. Tura Kâvasheya from Pragâpati,
47. Pragâpati from Brahman,
48. Brahman is Svayambhu, self-existent.

Adoration to Brahman!

*S*VETÂ*S*VATARA-UPANISHAD.

FIRST ADHYÂYA.

1. The Brahma-students say: Is Brahman the cause?[1453] Whence are we born? Whereby do we live, and whither do we go? O ye who know Brahman, (tell us) at whose command we abide, whether in pain or in pleasure?

2. Should time, or nature,[1454] or necessity, or chance, or the elements be considered as the cause, or he who is called the person (purusha, vig*ñ*ânâtmâ)? It cannot be their union either, because that is not self-dependent,[1455] and the self also is powerless, because there is (independent of him) a cause of good and evil.[1456]

[1453] This translation seems the one which *S*aṅkara himself prefers, for on p. 277, when recapitulating, he says, kim brahma kâra*n*am âhosvit kâlâdi. In comparing former translations, whether by Weber, Roer, Gough, and others, it will be seen that my own differs considerably from every one of them, and differs equally from *S*aṅkara's interpretation. It would occupy too much space to criticise former translations, nor would it seem fair, considering how long ago they were made, and how imperfect were the materials which were then accessible. All I wish my readers to understand is that, if I differ from my predecessors, I do so after having carefully examined their renderings. Unfortunately, Roer's edition of both the text and the commentary is often far from correct. Thus in the very first verse of the *S*vetâ*s*vatara-upanishad, I think we ought to read sampratish*th*â*h*, instead of sampratish*th*itâ*h*. In the commentary the reading is right. Vyavasyâm is a misprint for vyavasthâm. In the second verse we must separate kâla*h* and svabhâva*h*. Yad*rikhh*â no very unusual word, meaning chance, was formerly taken for a name of the moon! Instead of na tvâtmabhâvât, both sense and metre require that we should read anâtmabhâvât, though the commentators take a different view. They say, because there is a self, and then go on to say that even that would not suffice. Such matters, however, belong to a critical commentary on the Upanishads rather than to a translation, and I can refer to them in cases of absolute necessity only, and where the readings of the two MSS., A. and B, seem to offer some help.

[1454] Svabhâva, their own nature or independent character.

[1455] Union presupposes a uniter.

[1456] Âtmâ is explained by *S*aṅkara as the *g*îva*h*, the living self, and as that living self is in his present state determined by karman, work belonging to a former existence, it cannot be thought of as an independent cause.

3. The sages, devoted to meditation and concentration, have seen the power belonging to God himself,[1457] hidden in its own qualities (gu*n*a). He, being one, superintends all those causes, time, self, and the rest.[1458]

4.[1459] We meditate on him who (like a wheel) has one felly with three tires, sixteen ends, fifty spokes, with twenty counter-spokes, and six sets of eight; whose one rope is manifold, who proceeds on three different roads, and whose illusion arises from two causes.

[1457] Devâtma*s*akti is a very important term, differently explained by the commentators, but meaning a power belonging to the Deva, the Î*s*vara, the Lord, not independent of him, as the *S*âṅkhyas represent Prak*ri*ti or nature. Herein lies the important distinction between Vedanta and *S*â*n*khya.

[1458] Kâlâtmabhyâ*m* yuktâni, kâlapurushasa*m*yuktâni svabhâvâdini. Âtman is here taken as synonymous with purusha in verse 2.

[1459] It is difficult to say whether this verse was written as a summing up of certain technicalities recognised in systems of philosophy existing at the time, or whether it is a mere play of fancy. I prefer the former view, and subjoin the explanation given by *S*aṅkara, though it is quite possible that on certain points he may be mistaken. The Î*s*vara or deva is represented as a wheel with one felly, which would seem to be the phenomenal world. It is called triv*ri*t, threefold, or rather having three tires, three bands or hoops to bind the felly, these tires being intended for the three gu*n*as of the prak*ri*ti, the Sattva, Ragas, and Tamas. In the Brahmopanishad (Bibl. Ind. p. 251) the triv*ri*t sûtram is mentioned. Next follows sho*d*a*s*ântam, ending in the sixteen. These sixteen are differently explained. They may be meant for the five elements and the eleven indriyas or organs (the five receptive and the five active senses, together with manas, the common sensory); or for the sixteen kalâs, mentioned in the Pra*s*ñopanishad, VI, 1, p. 283. Then follows a new interpretation. The one felly may be meant for the chaos, the undeveloped state of things, and the sixteen would then be the two products in a general form, the Virâ*g* and the Sûtrâtman, while the remaining fourteen would be the individual products, the bhuvanas or worlds beginning with Bhû*h*.

Next follows *s*atârdhâram, having fifty spokes. These fifty spokes are supposed to produce the motion of the mundane wheel, and are explained by *S*aṅkara as follows:

1. The five Viparyayas, misconceptions, different kinds of ignorance or doubt, viz. Tamas, Moha, Mahâmoha, Tâmisra, Andhatâmisra, or, according to Patañgali, ignorance, self-love, love, hatred, and fear (Yoga-sûtras I, 8; II, 2; Sâṅkhya-sûtras III, 37).

2. The twenty-eight A*s*aktis, disabilities, causes of misconception. (See Sâṅkhya-sûtras III, 38.)

3. The nine inversions of the Tush*t*is, satisfactions. (Sâṅkhya-sûtras III, 39.)

4. The eight inversions of the Siddhis, perfections. (Sâṅkhya-sûtras III, 40.)

These are afterwards explained singly. There are 8 kinds of Tamas, 8 kinds of Moha, 10 kinds of Mahâmoha, 18 kinds of Tâmisra, and 18 kinds of Andhatâmisra, making 62 in all. More information on the A*s*aktis, the Tush*t*is, and Siddhis may be found in the Sâṅkhya-sûtras III, 37-45; Sâṅkhya-kârikâ 47 seq.; Yoga-sûtras II, 2 seq.

Then follow the 20 pratyaras, the counter-spokes, or wedges to strengthen the spokes, viz. the 10 senses and their 10 objects.

The six ash*t*akas or ogdoads are explained as the ogdoads of Prak*ri*ti, of substances (dhâtu), of powers (ai*s*varya), of states (bhâva), of gods (deva), of virtues (âtmagu*n*a).

The one, though manifold cord, is love or desire, Kâma, whether of food, children, heaven or anything else.

The three paths are explained as righteousness, unrighteousness, and knowledge, and the one deception arising from two causes is ignorance of self, produced by good or bad works.

5.[1460] We meditate on the river whose water consists of the five streams, which is wild and winding with its five springs, whose waves are the five vital breaths, whose fountain head is the mind, the course of the five kinds of perceptions. It has five whirlpools, its rapids are the five pains; it has fifty kinds of suffering, and five branches.

6. In that vast Brahma-wheel, in which all things live and rest, the bird flutters about, so long as he thinks that the self (in him) is different from the mover (the god, the lord). When he has been blessed by him, then he gains immortality.[1461]

7. But what is praised (in the Upanishads) is the Highest Brahman, and in it there is the triad.[1462] The Highest Brahman is the safe support, it is imperishable. The Brahma-students,[1463] when they have known what is within this (world), are devoted and merged in the Brahman, free from birth.[1464]

8. The Lord (îsa) supports all this together, the perishable and the imperishable, the developed and the undeveloped. The (living) self, not being a lord, is bound,[1465] because he has to enjoy (the fruits of works); but when he has known the god (deva), he is freed from all fetters.

9. There are two, one knowing (îsvara), the other not-knowing (gîva), both unborn, one strong, the other weak;[1466] there is she, the unborn, through whom each man receives the recompense of his works;[1467] and there is the infinite Self (appearing) under all forms, but himself inactive. When a man finds out these three, that is Brahma.[1468]

[1460] Here again, where the Îsvara is likened to a stream, the minute coincidences are explained by *S*aṅkara in accordance with certain systems of philosophy. The five streams are the five receptive organs, the five springs are the five elements, the five waves are the five active organs. The head is the manas, the mind, or common sensory, from which the perceptions of the five senses spring. The five whirlpools are the objects of the five senses, the five rapids are the five pains of being in the womb, being born, growing old, growing ill, and dying. The next adjective pa*ñk*â*s*adbhedâm is not fully explained by *S*aṅkara. He only mentions the five divisions of the kle*s*a (see Yoga-sûtras II, 2), but does not show how their number is raised to fifty. Dr. Roer proposes to read pa*ñk*akle*s*a-bhedâm, but that would not agree with the metre. The five parvans or branches are not explained, and may refer to the fifty kinds of suffering (kle*s*a). The whole river, like the wheel in the preceding verse, is meant for the Brahman as kâryakâra*n*âtmaka, in the form of cause and effect, as the phenomenal, not the absolutely real world.

[1461] If he has been blessed by the Î*s*vara, i.e. when he has been accepted by the Lord, when he has discovered his own true self in the Lord. It must be remembered, however, that both the Î*s*vara, the Lord, and the purusha, the individual soul, are phenomenal only, and that the Brahma-wheel is meant for the prapa*ñk*a, the manifest, but unreal world.

[1462] The subject (bhokt*ri*), the object (bhogya), and the mover (prerit*ri*), see verse 12.

[1463] B. has Vedavido, those who know the Vedas.

[1464] Tasmin pralîyate tv âtmâ samâdhi*h* sa udâh*ri*ta*h*.

[1465] Read badhyate for budhyate.

[1466] The form î*s*anî*s*au is explained as *kh*ândasa; likewise brahmam for brahma.

[1467] Cf. *S*vet. Up. IV, 5, bhuktabhogyâm.

[1468] The three are (1) the lord, the personal god, the creator and ruler; (2) the individual soul or souls; and (3) the power of creation, the devâtma*s*akti of verse 3. All

10. That which is perishable[1469] is the Pradhâna[1470] (the first), the immortal and imperishable is Hara.[1471] The one god rules the perishable (the pradhâna) and the (living) self.[1472] From meditating on him, from joining him, from becoming one with him there is further cessation of all illusion in the end.

11. When that god is known, all fetters fall off, sufferings are destroyed, and birth and death cease. From meditating on him there arises, on the dissolution of the body, the third state, that of universal lordship;[1473] but he only who is alone, is satisfied.[1474]

12. This, which rests eternally within the self, should be known; and beyond this not anything has to be known. By knowing the enjoyer,[1475] the enjoyed, and the ruler, everything has been declared to be threefold, and this is Brahman.

13. As the form of fire, while it exists in the under-wood,[1476] is not seen, nor is its seed destroyed, but it has to be seized again and again by means of the stick and the under-wood, so it is in both cases, and the Self has to be seized in the body by means of the pra*n*ava (the syllable

---

three are contained in Brahman; see verses 7, 12. So 'pi mâyî parame*s*varo mâyopâdhisannidhes tadvân iva.

[1469] See verse 8.

[1470] The recognised name for Prak*ri*ti, or here Devâtma*s*akti, in the later Sâṅkhya philosophy.

[1471] Hara, one of the names of *S*iva or Rudra, is here explained as avidyâder hara*n*ât, taking away ignorance. He would seem to be meant for the Î*s*vara or deva, the one god, though immediately afterwards he is taken for the true Brahman, and not for its phenomenal divine personification only.

[1472] The self, Âtman, used here, as before, for purusha, the individual soul, or rather the individual souls.

[1473] A blissful state in the Brahma-world, which, however, is not yet perfect freedom, but may lead on to it. Thus it is said in the *S*ivadharmottara:

Dhyânâd ai*s*varyam, atulam ai*s*varyât sukham uttamam,
*Gñ*ânena tat parityagya videho muktim âpnuyât.

[1474] This alone-ness, kevalatvam, is produced by the knowledge that the individual self is one with the divine self, and that both the individual and the divine self are only phenomenal forms of the true Self, the Brahman.

[1475] Bhoktâ, possibly for bhoktrâ, unless it is a *Kh*ândasa form. It was quoted before, Bibl. Ind. p. 292, l. 5. The enjoyer is the purusha, the individual soul, the subject; the enjoyed is prak*ri*ti, nature, the object; and the ruler is the Î*s*vara, that is, Brahman, as god. I take brahmam etat in the same sense here as in verse 9.

[1476] This metaphor, like most philosophical metaphors in Sanskrit, is rather obscure at first sight, but very exact when once understood. Fire, as produced by a fire drill, is compared to the Self. It is not seen at first, yet it must be there all the time; its liṅga or subtle body cannot have been destroyed, because as soon as the stick, the indhana, is drilled in the under-wood, the yoni, the fire becomes visible. In the same way the Self, though invisible during a state of ignorance, is there all the time, and is perceived when the body has been drilled by the Pra*n*ava, that is, after, by a constant repetition of the sacred syllable Om, the body has been subdued, and the ecstatic vision of the Self has been achieved.

Indhana, the stick used for drilling, and yoni, the under-wood, in which the stick is drilled, are the two ara*n*is, the fire-sticks used for kindling fire. See Tylor, Anthropology, p. 260.

Om).

14. By making his body the under-wood, and the syllable Om the upper-wood, man, after repeating the drill of meditation, will perceive the bright god, like the spark hidden in the wood.[1477]

15. As oil in seeds, as butter in cream, as water in (dry) river-beds,[1478] as fire in wood, so is the Self seized within the self, if man looks for him by truthfulness and penance;[1479]

16. (If he looks) for the Self that pervades everything, as butter is contained in milk, and the roots whereof are self-knowledge and penance. That is the Brahman taught by the Upanishad.

SECOND ADHYÂYA.

1.[1480] Savit*ri* (the sun), having first collected his mind and expanded his thoughts, brought Agni (fire), when he had discovered his light, above the earth.

2.[1481] With collected minds we are at the command of the divine

---

[1477] Cf. Dhyânavindûpan. verse 20; Brahmopanishad, p. 256.

[1478] Srotas, a stream, seems to mean here the dry bed of a stream, which, if dug into, will yield water.

[1479] The construction is correct, if we remember that he who is seized is the same as he who looks for the hidden Self. But the metre would be much improved if we accepted the reading of the Brahmopanishad, evam âtmâ âtmani g*ri*hyate 'sau, which is confirmed by B. The last line would be improved by reading, satyenaina*m* ye 'nupa*s*yanti dhîrâ*h*.

[1480] The seven introductory verses are taken from hymns addressed to Savit*ri* as the rising sun. They have been so twisted by *S*aṅkara, in order to make them applicable to the teachings of the Yoga philosophy, as to become almost nonsensical. I have given a few specimens of *S*aṅkara's renderings in the notes, but have translated the verses, as much as possible, in their original character. As they are merely introductory, I do not understand why the collector of the Upanishad should have seen in them anything but an invocation of Savit*ri*.

These verses are taken from various Sa*m*hitâs. The first yu*ñ*gâna*h* prathamam is from Taitt. Sa*m*h. IV, 1, 1, 1, 1; Vâg. Sa*m*h. XI, 1; see also *S*at. Br. VI, 3, 1, 12. The Taittirîya-text agrees with the Upanishad, the Vâgasaneyi-text has dhiyam for dhiya*h*, and agne*h* for agnim. Both texts take tatvâya as a participle of tan, while the Upanishad reads tattvâya, as a dative of tattva, truth. I have translated the verse in its natural sense. *S*aṅkara, in explaining the Upanishad, translates: 'At the beginning of our meditation, joining the mind with the Highest Self, also the other prâ*n*as, or the knowledge of outward things, for the sake of truth, Savit*ri*, out of the knowledge of outward things, brought Agni, after having discovered his brightness, above the earth, in this body.' He explains it: 'May Savit*ri*, taking our thoughts away from outward things, in order to concentrate them on the Highest Self, produce in our speech and in our other senses that power which can lighten all objects, which proceeds from Agni and from the other favourable deities.' He adds that 'by the favour of Savit*ri*, Yoga may be obtained.'

[1481] The second verse is from Taitt. Sa*m*h. IV, 1, 1, 1, 3; Vâg. Sa*m*h. XI, 2. The Vâgasaneyi-text has svargyâya for svargeyâya, and *s*aktyâ for *s*aktyai. *S*aṅkara explains: 'With a mind that has been joined by Savit*ri* to the Highest Self, we, with the sanction of that Savit*ri*, devote ourselves to the work of meditation, which leads to the obtainment of Svarga, according to our power.' He explains Svarga by Paramâtman. Sâya*n*a in his commentary on the Taittirîya-sa*m*hitâ explains svargeyâya by svargaloke gîyamânasyâgne*h* sampâdanâya; *S*aṅkara, by svargaprâptihetubhûtâya dhyânakarma*n*e.

Savit*ri*, that we may obtain blessedness.

3.[1482] May Savit*ri*, after he has reached with his mind the gods as they rise up to the sky, and with his thoughts (has reached) heaven, grant these gods to make a great light to shine.

4.[1483] The wise sages of the great sage collect their mind and collect their thoughts. He who alone knows the law (Savit*ri*) has ordered the invocations; great is the praise of the divine Savit*ri*.

5.[1484] Your old prayer has to be joined[1485] with praises. Let my song go forth like the path of the sun! May all the sons of the Immortal listen, they who have reached their heavenly homes.

---

*S*aktyai is explained by *S*añkara by yathâsâmarthyam; by Sâya*n*a, by *s*aktâ bhûyâsma. Mahîdhara explains *s*aktyâ by svasâmarthyena. I believe that the original reading was svargyâya *s*aktyai, and that we must take *s*aktyai as an infinitive, like ityai, construed with a dative, like d*ri*saye sûryâya, for the seeing of the sun. The two attracted datives would be governed by save, 'we are under the command of Savit*ri*,' svargyâya *s*aktyai, 'that we may obtain svargya, life in Svarga or blessedness.'

[1482] The third verse is from Taitt. Sa*m*h. IV, 1, 1, 1, 2; Vâg. Sa*m*h. XI, 3. The Taittirîyas read yuktvâya manasâ; the Vâgasaneyins, yuktvâya savitâ. *S*añkara translates: 'Again he prays that Savit*ri*, having directed the devas, i.e. the senses, which are moving towards Brahman, and which by knowledge are going to brighten up the heavenly light of Brahman, may order them to do so; that is, he prays that, by the favour of Savit*ri*, our senses should be turned away from outward things to Brahman or the Self.' Taking the hymn as addressed to Savit*ri*, I have translated deva by gods, not by senses, suvaryata*h* by rising to the sky, namely, in the morning. The opposition between manasâ and dhiyâ is the same here as in verse 1, and again in verse 4.

[1483] This verse is from Taitt. Sa*m*h. IV, 1, 1, 1, 4; I, 2, 13, 1, 1; Vâg. Sa*m*h. V, 14; XI, 4; XXXVII, 2; *R*ig-veda V, 81, 1; *S*at. Br. III, 5, 3, 11; VI, 3, 1, 16. *S*añkara explains this verse again in the same manner as he did the former verses, while the *S*atapatha-brâhma*n*a supplies two different ritual explanations.

[1484] For this verse, see Taitt. Sa*m*h. IV, 1, 1, 2, 1; Vâg. Sa*m*h. XI, 5; Atharva-veda XVIII, 3, 39; *R*ig-veda X, 13, 1. The Vâgasaneyins read vi *s*loka etu for vi *s*lokâ yanti; sûre*h* for sûrâ*h*; *s*ri*n*vantu for *s*ri*n*vanti; and the *R*ig-veda agrees with them. The dual vâm is accounted for by the verse belonging to a hymn celebrating the two *s*akatas, carts, bearing the offerings (havirdhâne); most likely, however, the dual referred originally to the dual deities of heaven and earth. I prefer the text of the *R*ig-veda and the Vâgasaneyins to that of the Taittirîyas, and have translated the verse accordingly. In the Atharva-veda XVIII, 39, if we may trust the edition, the verse begins with svâsasthe bhavatam indave na*h*, which is really the end of the next verse (Rv. X, 13, 2), while the second line is, vi *s*loka eti pathyeva sûri*h* *s*ri*n*vantu vi*s*ve am*ri*tâsa etat. I see no sense in pathyeva sûrâ*h*. *S*añkara explains pathyeva by pathi sanmârge, athavâ pathyâ kîrti*h*, while his later commentary, giving *s*ri*n*vantu and putrâ*h* sûrâtmano hira*n*yagarbhasya, leads one to suppose that he read sûre*h* *s*ri*n*vantu. *S*âyana (Taitt. Sa*m*h. IV, 1, 1, 2) explains pathyâ sûrâ iva by gîrvâ*n*amârga antarikshe sûryara*s*mayo yathâ prasaranti tadvat. The same, when commenting on the *R*ig-veda (X, 13, 1), Says: pathyâ-iva sûre*h*, yathâ stotu*h* svabhûtâ pathyâ pari*n*âmasukhâvahâhutir vi*s*vân devân prati vividha*m* ga*kkh*ati tadvat. Mahîdhara (Vâg. Sa*m*h. XI, 5) refers sûre*h* (pa*n*ditasya) to *s*loka*h*, and explains pathyeva by patho 'napetâ pathyâ ya*gñ*amârgaprav*ri*ttâhuti*h*.

[1485] Yugé cannot stand for yu*ñ*ge, as all commentators and translators suppose, but is a datival infinitive. Neither can yu*ñ*gate in the following verse stand for yuñkte (see Boehtlingk, s. v.), or be explained as a subjunctive form. A. reads adhirudhyate, B. abhirudhyate, with a marginal note abhinudyate. It is difficult to say whether in lighting the fire the wind should be directed towards it, or kept from it.

6. Where the fire is rubbed[1486], where the wind is checked, where the Soma flows over, there the mind is born.

7. Let us love the old Brahman by the grace of Savit*ri*; if thou make thy dwelling there, the path will not hurt thee.[1487]

8. If a wise man hold his body with its three erect parts (chest, neck, and head) even,[1488] and turn his senses with the mind towards the heart, he will then in the boat of Brahman[1489] cross all the torrents which cause fear.

9. Compressing his breathings let him, who has subdued all motions, breathe forth through the nose with gentle breath.[1490] Let the wise man without fail restrain his mind, that chariot yoked with vicious horses.[1491]

10. Let him perform his exercises in a place[1492] level, pure, free from pebbles, fire, and dust, delightful by its sounds, its water, and bowers, not painful to the eye, and full of shelters and caves.

11. When Yoga is being performed, the forms which come first, producing apparitions in Brahman, are those of misty smoke, sun, fire, wind, fire-flies, lightnings, and a crystal moon.[1493]

12. When, as earth, water, light, heat, and ether arise, the fivefold quality of Yoga takes place,[1494] then there is no longer illness, old age,

---

1486 That is, at the Soma sacrifice, after the fire has been kindled and stirred by the wind, the poets, on partaking of the juice, are inspirited for new songs. *S*aṅkara, however, suggests another explanation as more appropriate for the Upanishad, namely, 'Where the fire, i.e. the Highest Self, which burns all ignorance, has been kindled (in the body, where it has been rubbed with the syllable Om), and where the breath has acted, i.e. has made the sound peculiar to the initial stages of Yoga, there Brahman is produced.' In fact, what was intended to be taught was this, that we must begin with sacrificial acts, then practise yoga, then reach samâdhi, perfect knowledge, and lastly bliss.

1487 We must read k*rin*avase, in the sense of 'do this and nothing will hurt thee,' or, if thou do this, thy former deeds will no longer hurt thee.

1488 Cf. Bhagavadgîtâ VI, 13. Sama*m* kâya*s*irogrîva*m* dhârayan. *S*aṅkara says: trî*n*y unnatâny urogrîva*s*irâ*m*sy unnatâni yasmin *s*arire.

1489 Explained by *S*aṅkara as the syllable Om.

1490 Cf. Bhagavadgîtâ V, 27. Prâ*n*âpânau samau k*ri*tvâ nâsâbhyantara *k*âri*n*au. See Telang's notes, Sacred Books of the East, vol. viii, p. 68 seq.

1491 A similar metaphor in Ka*th*. Up. III, 4-6; Sacred Books of the East, vol. xv, p. 13.

1492 The question is whether *s*abdagalâsrayâdibhi*h* should be referred to mano 'nukûle, as I have translated it, or to vivargite, as *S*aṅkara seems to take it, because he renders *s*abda, sound, by noise, and â*s*raya by ma*nd*apa, a booth. See Bhagavadgîtâ VI, 11. In the Maitr. Up. VI, 30, Râmatîrtha explains su*k*au de*s*e by girinadîpulinaguhâdi*s*uddhastâne. See also Â*s*v. G*ri*hya-sûtras III, 2, 2.

1493 Or, it may be, a crystal and the moon.

1494 The Yogagu*n*a is described as the quality of each element, i.e. smell of the earth, taste of water, &c. It seems that the perception of these gunas is called yogaprav*ri*tti. Thus by fixing the thought on the tip of the nose, a perception of heavenly scent is produced; by fixing it on the tip of the tongue, a perception of heavenly taste; by fixing it on the point of the palate, a heavenly colour; by fixing it on the middle of the tongue, a heavenly touch; by fixing it on the roof of the tongue, a heavenly sound. By

or pain[1495] for him who has obtained a body, produced by the fire of Yoga.

13. The first results of Yoga they call lightness, healthiness, steadiness, a good complexion, an easy pronunciation, a sweet odour, and slight excretions.

14. As a metal disk (mirror), tarnished by dust, shines bright again after it has been cleaned, so is the one incarnate person satisfied and free from grief, after he has seen the real nature of the Self.[1496]

15. And when by means of the real nature of his self he sees, as by a lamp, the real nature of Brahman, then having known the unborn, eternal god, who is beyond all natures,[1497] he is freed from all fetters.

16. He indeed is the god who pervades all regions: he is the first-born (as Hira*n*yagarbha), and he is in the womb. He has been born, and he will be born.[1498] He stands behind all persons, looking everywhere.

17. The god[1499] who is in the fire, the god who is in the water, the god who has entered into the whole world, the god who is in plants, the god who is in trees, adoration be to that god, adoration!

THIRD ADHYÂYA.[1500]

1. The snarer[1501] who rules alone by his powers, who rules all the worlds by his powers, who is one and the same, while things arise and exist,[1502]—they who know this are immortal.

2. For there is one Rudra only, they do not allow a second, who rules all the worlds by his powers. He stands behind all persons,[1503] and

---

means of these perceptions the mind is supposed to be steadied, because it is no longer attracted by the outward objects themselves. See Yoga-sûtras I, 35.

[1495] Or no death, na m*ri*tyu*h*, B.

[1496] Pareshâm pâ*th*e tadvat sa tattvam prasamîkshya dehîti.

[1497] Sarvatattvair avidyâtatkâryair vi*s*uddham asa*m*sp*ri*sh*t*am.

[1498] This verse is found in the Vâg. Sa*m*h. XXXII, 4; Taitt. Âr. X, 1, 3, with slight modifications. The Vâgasaneyins read esho ha (so do A. B.) for esha hi; sa eva gâta*h* (A. B.) for sa vigâta*h*; ganâs (A. B.) for ganâ*m*s. The Âra*n*yaka has sa vigâyamâna*h* for sa vigâta*h*, pratyanmukhâs for pratya*ñ*ganâ*m*s, and vi*s*vatomukha*h* for sarvatomukha*h*. Colebrooke (Essays, I, 57) gives a translation of it. If we read ganâ*h*, we must take it as a vocative.

[1499] B. (not A.) reads yo rudro yo 'gnau.

[1500] This Adhyâya represents the Highest Self as the personified deity, as the lord, î*s*a, or Rudra, under the sway of his own creative power, prak*ri*ti or mâyâ.

[1501] *S*ankara explains gâla, snare, by mâyâ. The verse must be corrected, according to *S*ankara's commentary:

> ya eko gâlavân î*s*ata î*s*anîbhi*h*
> sarvâñ llokân î*s*ata î*s*anîbhi*h*.

[1502] Sambhava, in the sense of Vergehen, perishing, rests on no authority.

[1503] Here again the MSS. A. B. read ganâs, as a vocative.

after having created all worlds he, the protector, rolls it up[1504] at the end of time.

3.[1505] That one god, having his eyes, his face, his arms, and his feet in every place, when producing heaven and earth, forges them together with his arms and his wings.[1506]

4. He,[1507] the creator and supporter of the gods, Rudra, the great seer, the lord of all, he who formerly gave birth to Hira*n*yagarbha, may he endow us with good thoughts.

5.[1508] O Rudra, thou dweller in the mountains, look upon us with that most blessed form of thine which is auspicious, not terrible, and reveals no evil!

6.[1509] O lord of the mountains, make lucky that arrow which thou, a dweller in the mountains, holdest in thy hand to shoot. Do not hurt man or beast!

7. Those who know beyond this the High Brahman, the vast, hidden in the bodies of all creatures, and alone enveloping everything, as the Lord, they become immortal.[1510]

8.[1511] I know that great person (purusha) of sunlike lustre beyond the darkness.[1512] A man who knows him truly, passes over death; there is no other path to go.[1513]

9. This whole universe is filled by this person (purusha), to whom there is nothing superior, from whom there is nothing different, than whom there is nothing smaller or larger, who stands alone, fixed like a tree in the sky.[1514]

10. That which is beyond this world is without form and without

---

[1504] I prefer sa*m*ku*k*o*k*a to sa*m*kukopa, which gives us th e meaning that Rudra, after having created all things, draws together, i.e. takes them all back into himself, at the end of time. I have translated sa*msrig*ya by having created, because Boehtlingk and Roth give other instances of sa*msrig* with that sense. Otherwise, 'having mixed them together again,' would seem more appropriate. A. and B. read sa*mk*uko*k*a.

[1505] This is a very popular verse, and occurs *Ri*g-veda X, 81, 3; Vâg. Sa*m*h. XVII, 19; Ath.-veda XIII, 2, 26; Taitt. Sa*m*h. IV, 6, 2, 4; Taitt. Âr. X, 1, 3.

[1506] *S*aṅkara takes dhamati in the sense of sa*m*yogayati, i.e. he joins men with arms, birds with wings.

[1507] See IV, 12.

[1508] See Vâg. Sa*m*h. XVI, 2; Taitt. Sa*m*h. IV, 5, 1, 1.

[1509] See Vâg. Sa*m*h. XVI, 3; Taitt. Sa*m*h. IV, 5, 1, 1; Nîlarudropan. p. 274.

[1510] The knowledge consists in knowing either that Brahman is Î*s*a or that Î*s*a is Brahman. But in either case the gender of the adjectives is difficult. The *S*vetâ*s*vatara-upanishad seems to use b*ri*hanta as an adjective, instead of b*ri*hat. I should prefer to translate: Beyond this is the High Brahman, the vast. Those who know Î*s*a, the Lord, hidden in all things and embracing all things to be this (Brahman), become immortal. See also Muir, Metrical Translations, p. 196, whose translation of these verses I have adopted with few exceptions.

[1511] Cf. Vâg. Sa*m*h. XXX, 18; Taitt. Âr. III, 12, 3.

[1512] Cf. Bhagavadgîtâ VIII, 9.

[1513] Cf. *S*vet. Up. VI, 15.

[1514] Divi, the sky, is explained by *S*aṅkara as dyotanâtmani svamahimni.

suffering. They who know it, become immortal, but others suffer pain indeed.[1515]

11. That Bhagavat[1516] exists in the faces, the heads, the necks of all, he dwells in the cave (of the heart) of all beings, he is all-pervading, therefore he is the omnipresent *S*iva.

12. That person (purusha) is the great lord; he is the mover of existence,[1517] he possesses that purest power of reaching everything,[1518] he is light, he is undecaying.

13.[1519] The person (purusha), not larger than a thumb, dwelling within, always dwelling in the heart of man, is perceived by the heart, the thought,[1520] the mind; they who know it become immortal.

14.[1521] The person (purusha) with a thousand heads. a thousand eyes, a thousand feet, having compassed the earth on every side, extends beyond it by ten fingers' breadth.

15. That person alone (purusha) is all this, what has been and what will be; he is also the lord of immortality; he is whatever grows by food.[1522]

[1515] The pain of sa*m*sâra, or transmigration. See B*ri*had. Up. IV, 3, 20.

[1516] I feel doubtful whether the two names Bhagavat and *S*iva should here be preserved, or whether the former should be rendered by holy, the latter by happy. The commentator explains Bhagavat by

> ai*s*varyasya samagrasya vîryasya ya*s*asa*h s*riya*h*
> *G*ñânavairâgyayo*s k*aiva sha*nn*âm bhaga itira*n*â.

Wilson, in his Essay on the Religious Sects of the Hindus, published in 1828, in the Asiatic Researches, XVI, p. 11, pointed out that this verse and another (*S*vet. Up. II, 2) were cited by the *S*aivas as Vedic authorities for their teaching. He remarked that these citations would scarcely have been made, if not authentic, and that they probably did occur in the Vedas. In the new edition of this Essay by Dr. Rost, 1862, the references should have been added.

[1517] *S*ankara explains sattvasya by anta*h*kara*n*asya.

[1518] I take prâpti, like other terms occurring in this Upanishad, in its technical sense. Prâpti is one of the vibhûtis or ai*s*varyas, viz. the power of touching anything at will, as touching the moon with the tip of one's finger. See Yoga-sûtras, ed. Rajendralal Mitra, p. 121.

[1519] Cf. Taitt. Âr. X, 71 (Anuv. 38, p. 858). Ka*th*. Up. IV, 12-13; above.

[1520] The text has manvî*s*a, which *S*ankara explains by *g*ñâne*s*a. But Weber has conjectured rightly, I believe, that the original text must have been manîshâ. The difficulty is to understand how so common a word as manîshâ could have been changed into so unusual a word as manvî*s*a. See IV, 20.

[1521] This is a famous verse of the *R*ig-veda, X, 90, 1; repeated in the Atharva-veda, XIX, 6, 1; Vâg. Sa*m*h. XXXI, 1; Taitt. Âr. III, 12, 1. *S*ankara explains ten fingers' breadth by endless; or, he says, it may be meant for the heart, which is ten fingers above the navel.

[1522] Sâya*n*a, in his commentary on the Rig-veda and the Taitt. Âr., gives another explanation, viz. he is also the lord of all the immortals, i.e. the gods, because they grow to their exceeding state by means of food, or for the sake of food.

16. Its[1523] hands and feet are everywhere, its eyes and head are everywhere, its ears are everywhere, it stands encompassing all in the world.[1524]

17. Separate from all the senses, yet reflecting the qualities of all the senses, it is the lord and ruler of all, it is the great refuge of all.

18. The embodied spirit within the town with nine gates,[1525] the bird, flutters outwards, the ruler of the whole world, of all that rests and of all that moves.

19. Grasping without hands, hasting without feet, he sees without eyes, he hears without ears. He knows what can be known, but no one knows him; they call him the first, the great person (purusha).

20.[1526] The Self, smaller than small, greater than great, is hidden in the heart of the creature. A man who has left all grief behind, sees the majesty, the Lord, the passionless, by the grace of the creator (the Lord).

21.[1527] I know[1528] this undecaying, ancient one, the self of all things, being infinite and omnipresent. They declare that in him all birth is stopped, for the Brahma-students proclaim him to be eternal.[1529]

FOURTH ADHYÂYA.

1. He, the sun, without any colour, who with set purpose[1530] by means of his power (*s*akti) produces endless colours,[1531] in whom all this comes together in the beginning, and comes asunder in the end—may he, the god, endow us with good thoughts.[1532]

2. That (Self) indeed is Agni (fire), it is Âditya (sun), it is Vâyu (wind), it is *K*andramas (moon); the same also is the starry

[1523] The gender changes frequently, according as the author thinks either of the Brahman, or of its impersonation as Î*s*a, Lord.

[1524] *S*añkara explains loka by nikâya, body.

[1525] Cf. Ka*th*. Up. V, 1.

[1526] Cf. Taitt. Âr. X, 12 (10), p. 800; Ka*th*. Up. II, 20; above. The translation had to be slightly altered, because the *S*vetâ*s*vataras, as Taittirîyas, read akratum for akratu*h*, and î*s*am for âtmana*h*.

[1527] Cf. Taitt. Âr. III, 13, 1; III, 12, 7.

[1528] A. reads vedârû*dh*am, not B.

[1529] A. and B. read brahmavâdino hi pravadanti.

[1530] Nihitârtha, explained by *S*añkara as g*ri*hîtaprayogana*h* svârthanirapeksha*h*. This may mean with set purpose, but if we read ag*ri*hîtaprayogana*h* it would mean the contrary, namely, without any definite object, irrespective of his own objects. This is possible, and perhaps more in accordance with the idea of creation as propounded by those to whom the devâtma*s*akti is mâyâ. Nihita would then mean hidden.

[1531] Colour is intended for qualities, differences, &c.

[1532] This verse has been translated very freely. As it stands, vi *k*aiti *k*ânte vi*s*vam âdau sa deva*h*, it does not construe, in spite of all attempts to the contrary, made by *S*añkara. What is intended is yasminn ida*m* sa*m* *k*a vi *k*aiti sarvam (IV, 11); but how so simple a line should have been changed into what we read now, is difficult to say.

firmament,[1533] it is Brahman (Hira*n*yagarbha), it is water, it is Pragâpati (Virâg).

3. Thou art woman, thou art man; thou art youth, thou art maiden; thou, as an old man, totterest[1534] along on thy staff; thou art born with thy face turned everywhere.

4. Thou art the dark-blue bee, thou art the green parrot with red eyes, thou art the thunder-cloud, the seasons, the seas. Thou art without beginning,[1535] because thou art infinite, thou from whom all worlds are born.

5.[1536] There is one unborn being (female), red, white, and black, uniform, but producing manifold offspring. There is one unborn being (male) who loves her and lies by her; there is another who leaves her, while she is eating what has to be eaten.

6.[1537] Two birds, inseparable friends, cling to the same tree. One of them eats the sweet fruit, the other looks on without eating.

7. On the same tree man sits grieving, immersed, bewildered, by his own impotence (an-îsâ). But when he sees the other lord (îsa) contented, and knows his glory, then his grief passes away.

8.[1538] He who does not know that indestructible being of the *Ri*g-

---

[1533] This is the explanation of *S*aṅkara, and probably that of the Yoga schools in India at his time. But to take *s*ukram for dîptiman nakshatrâdi, brahma for Hira*n*yagarbha, and Pragâpati for Virâg seems suggested by this verse only.

[1534] Va*ñk*ayasi, an exceptional form, instead of va*ñk*asi (A. B.)

[1535] We see throughout the constant change from the masculine to the neuter gender, in addressing either the lord or his true essence.

[1536] This is again one of the famous verses of our Upanishad, because it formed for a long time a bone of contention between Vedânta and Sâṅkhya philosophers. The Sâṅkhyas admit two principles, the Purusha, the absolute subject, and the Prak*ri*ti, generally translated by nature. The Vedanta philosophers admit nothing but the one absolute subject, and look upon nature as due to a power inherent in that subject. The later Sâṅkhyas therefore, who are as anxious as the Vedântins to find authoritative passages in the Veda, confirming their opinions, appeal to this and other passages, to show that their view of Prak*ri*ti, as an independent power, is supported by the Veda. The whole question is fully discussed in the Vedânta-sûtras I, 4, 8. Here we read rohita-k*ri*sh*n*a-*s*uklâm, which seems preferable to lohita-k*ri*sh*n*a-var*n*âm, at least from a Vedânta point of view, for the three colours, red, black, and white, are explained as signifying either the three gunas, ragas, sattva, and tamas, or better (*Kh*ând. Up. VI, 3, 1), the three elements, tegas (fire), ap (water), and anna (earth). A. reads rohita*s*uklak*ri*sh*n*âm; B. lohita*s*uklakrish*n*â (sic). We also find in A. and B. bhuktabhogâm for bhuktabhogyâm, but the latter seems technically the more correct reading. It would be quite wrong to imagine that aga and agâ are meant here for he-goat and she-goat. These words, in the sense of unborn, are recognised as early as the hymns of the *Ri*g-veda, and they occurred in our Upanishad I, 9, where the two agas are mentioned in the same sense as here. But there is, no doubt, a play on the words, and the poet wished to convey the second meaning of he-goat and she-goat, only not as the primary, but as the secondary intention.

[1537] The same verses occur in the Mundaka Up. III, 1.

[1538] It is difficult to see how this verse comes in here. In the Taitt. Âr. II, 11, 6, it is quoted in connection with the syllable Om, the Akshara, in which all the Vedas are comprehended. It is similarly used in the N*ri*si*m*ha-pûrva-tâpanî, IV, 2; V, 2. In our

Veda, that highest ether-like (Self) wherein all the gods reside, of what use is the *Ri*g-Veda to him? Those only who know it, rest contented.

9. That from which the maker (mâyin[1539]) sends forth all this—the sacred verses, the offerings, the sacrifices, the panaceas, the past, the future, and all that the Vedas declare—in that the other is bound up through that mâyâ.

10. Know then Prak*ri*ti (nature) is Mâyâ (art), and the great Lord the Mâyin (maker); the whole world is filled with what are his members.

11. If a man has discerned him, who being one only, rules over every germ (cause), in whom all this comes together and comes asunder again, who is the lord, the bestower of blessing, the adorable god, then he passes for ever into that peace.

12.[1540] He, the creator and supporter of the gods, Rudra, the great seer, the lord of all, who saw,[1541] Hira*n*yagarbha being born, may he endow us with good thoughts.

13. He who is the sovereign of the gods, he in whom all the worlds[1542] rest, he who rules over all two-footed and four-footed beings, to that god[1543] let us sacrifice an oblation.

14. He who has known him who is more subtile than subtile, in the midst of chaos, creating all things, having many forms, alone enveloping everything,[1544] the happy one (*S*iva), passes into peace for ever.

15. He also was in time[1545] the guardian of this world, the lord of

---

passage, however, akshara is referred by *S*aṅkara to the paramâtman, and I have translated it accordingly. *Rikah* is explained as a genitive singular, but it may also be taken as a nom. plur., and in that case both the verses of the Veda and the gods are said to reside in the Akshara, whether we take it for the Paramâtman or for the Om. In the latter case, parame vyoman is explained by utk*ri*sh*t*e and rakshake.

[1539] It is impossible to find terms corresponding to mâyâ and mâyin. Mâyâ means making, or art, but as all making or creating, so far as the Supreme Self is concerned, is phenomenal only or mere illusion, mâyâ conveys at the same time the sense of illusion. In the same manner mâyin is the maker, the artist, but also the magician or juggler. What seems intended by our verse is that from the akshara which corresponds to brahman, all proceeds, whatever exists or seems to exist, but that the actual creator or the author of all emanations is Î*s*a, the Lord, who, as creator, is acting through mâyâ or devâtma*s*akti. Possibly, however, anya, the other, may be meant for the individual purusha.

[1540] See before, III, 4.

[1541] *S*aṅkara does not explain this verse again, though it differs from III, 4. Vig*ñ*ânâtman explains pa*s*yata by apa*s*yata, and qualifies the Âtmanepada as irregular.

[1542] B. reads yasmin devâ*h*, not A.

[1543] I read tasmai instead of kasmai, a various reading mentioned by Vig*ñ*ânâtman. It was easy to change tasmai into kasmai, because of the well-known line in the *Ri*g-veda, kasmai devâya havishâ vidhema. Those who read kasmai, explain it as a dative of Ka, a name of Pragâpati, which in the dative should be kâya, and not kasmai. It would be better to take kasmai as the dative of the interrogative pronoun. See M. M., History of Ancient Sanskrit Literature, p. 433; and Vitâna-sutras IV, 22.

[1544] Cf. III, 7.

[1545] In former ages, *S*aṅkara.

all, hidden in all beings. In him the Brahmarshis and the deities are united,[1546] and he who knows him cuts the fetters of death asunder.

16. He who knows *S*iva (the blessed) hidden in all beings, like the subtile film that rises from out the clarified butter,[1547] alone enveloping everything,—he who knows the god, is freed from all fetters.

17. That god, the maker of all things, the great Self,[1548] always dwelling in the heart of man, is perceived by the heart, the soul, the mind;[1549]—they who know it become immortal.

18. When the light has risen,[1550] there is no day, no night, neither existence nor non-existence;[1551] *S*iva (the blessed) alone is there. That is the eternal, the adorable light of Savit*ri*,[1552]—and the ancient wisdom proceeded thence.

19. No one has grasped him above, or across, or in the middle.[1553] There is no image of him whose name is Great Glory.

20. His form cannot be seen, no one perceives him with the eye. Those[1554] who through heart and mind know him thus abiding in the heart, become immortal.

21. 'Thou art unborn,' with these words some one comes near to thee, trembling. O Rudra, let thy gracious[1555] face protect me for ever!

22.[1556] O Rudra! hurt us not in our offspring and descendants, hurt us not in our own lives, nor in our cows, nor in our horses! Do not slay our men in thy wrath, for, holding oblations, we call on thee always.

[1546] Because both the Brahmarshis, the holy seers, and the deities find their true essence in Brahman.

[1547] We should say, like cream from milk.

[1548] Or the high-minded.

[1549] See III, 13.

[1550] Atamas, no darkness, i.e. light of knowledge.

[1551] See on the difficulty of translating sat and asat, τὸ ὄν and τὸ μή ὄν, the remarks in the Preface.

[1552] Referring to the Gâyatrî, *Ri*g-veda III, 62, 10; see also *S*vet. Up. V, 4.

[1553] See Muir, Metrical Translations, p. 198; Maitr. Up. VI, 17.

[1554] B. reads h*ri*dâ manîshâ manasâbhik*l*ipto, yat tad vidur; A. h*ri*di h*ri*distham manasâya enam eva*m* vidur.

[1555] Dakshina is explained either as invigorating, exhilarating, or turned towards the south.

[1556] See Colebrooke, Miscellaneous Essays, I, p. 141; *Ri*g-veda I, 114, 8; Taitt. Sa*m*h. IV, 5, 10, 3; Vâg. Sa*m*h. XVI, 16. The various readings are curious. Âyushi in the *S*vet. Up., instead of âyau in the *Ri*g-veda, is supported by the Taitt. Sa*m*h. and the Vâg. Sa*m*h.; but Vig*ñ*ânâtman reads âyau. As to bhâmito, it seems the right reading, being supported by the *Ri*g-veda, the Taitt. Sa*m*h., and the *S*vet. Up., while bhâvito in Roer's edition is a misprint. The Vâg. Sa*m*h. alone reads bhâmino, which Mahîdhara refers to virân. The last verse in the *Ri*g-veda and Vâg. Sa*m*h. is havishmanta*h* sadam it tvâ havâmahe; in the Taitt. Sa*m*h. havishmanto namasâ vidhema te. In the *S*vet. Up. havishmantah sadasi tvâ havâmahe, as printed by Roer, seems to rest on *S*aṅkara's authority only. The other commentators, *S*aṅkarânanda and Vig*ñ*ânâtman, read and interpret sadam it.

FIFTH ADHYÂYA.

1. In the imperishable and infinite Highest Brahman,[1557] wherein the two, knowledge and ignorance, are hidden,[1558] the one, ignorance, perishes,[1559] the other, knowledge, is immortal; but he who controls both, knowledge and ignorance, is another.[1560]

2. It is he who, being one only, rules over every germ (cause), over all forms, and over all germs; it is he who, in the beginning, bears[1561] in his thoughts the wise son, the fiery, whom he wishes to look on[1562] while he is born.[1563]

3.[1564] In that field[1565] in which the god, after spreading out one net after another[1566] in various ways, draws it together again, the Lord, the great Self,[1567] having further created the lords,[1568] thus carries on his lordship over all.

4. As the car (of the sun) shines, lighting up all quarters, above, below, and across, thus does that god, the holy, the adorable, being one, rule over all that has the nature of a germ.[1569]

5. He, being one, rules over all and everything, so that the universal germ ripens its nature, diversifies all natures that can be ripened,[1570] and determines all qualities.[1571]

[1557] *S*aṅkara explains Brahmapare by brahma*n*o hira*n*yagarbhât pare, or by parasmin brahma*n*i, which comes to the same. Vig*ñ*ânâtman adds *kh*ândasa*h* paranipâta*h*. As the termination e may belong to the locative singular or to the nom. dual, commentators vary in referring some of the adjectives either to brahman or to vidyâvidye.

[1558] Gû*dh*e, lokair *g*ñâtum a*s*akye, *S*aṅkarânanda.

[1559] *S*aṅkara explains ksharam, by sa*msr*itikâra*n*am, am*r*itam by mokshahetu*h*.

[1560] *S*aṅkara explains that he is different from them, being only the sâkshin, or witness. *S*aṅkarânanda seems to have read Somya, i.e. Somavatpriyadar*s*ana, as if *S*vetâ*s*vatvara addressed his pupil.

[1561] Like a mother, see I, 9.

[1562] Like a father.

[1563] See on this verse the remarks made in the Introduction.

[1564] The MSS. read yasmin for asmin, and patayas for yatayas, which the commentator explains by patîn.

[1565] The world, or the mûlaprak*r*iti, the net being the sa*m*sâra.

[1566] *S*aṅkara explains ekaikam by pratyekam, i.e. for every creature, such as gods, men, beasts, &c.

[1567] I doubt whether mahâtmâ should be translated by the great Self, or whether great would not be sufficient. The whole verse is extremely difficult.

[1568] From Hira*n*yagarbha to insects; or beginning with Marî*k*i.

[1569] Cf. IV, 11; V, 2.

[1570] MS. B. has prâ*k*yân, and explains it by pûrvotpannân.

[1571] This is again a very difficult verse. I have taken vi*s*vayoni*h* as a name for Brahman, possessed of that devâtma*s*akti which was mentioned before, but I feel by no means satisfied. The commentators do not help, because they do not see the difficulty of the construction. If one might conjecture, I should prefer pa*k*et for pa*k*ati, and should write parinâmayed yat, and viniyogayed yat, unless we changed ya*kk*a into ya*s* *k*a.

6.[1572] Brahma (Hira*n*yagarbha) knows this, which is hidden in the Upanishads, which are hidden in the Vedas, as the Brahma-germ. The ancient gods and poets who knew it, they became it and were immortal.

7.[1573] But he who is endowed with qualities, and performs works that are to bear fruit, and enjoys the reward of whatever he has done, migrates through his own works, the lord of life, assuming all forms, led by the three Gu*n*as, and following the three paths.[1574]

8.[1575] That lower one also, not larger than a thumb, but brilliant like the sun, who is endowed with personality and thoughts, with the quality of mind and the quality of body, is seen small even like the point of a goad.

9. That living soul is to be known as part of the hundredth part of the point of a hair,[1576] divided a hundred times, and yet it is to be infinite.

10. It is not woman, it is not man, nor is it neuter; whatever body it takes, with that it is joined[1577] (only).

11.[1578] By means of thoughts, touching, seeing, and passions the incarnate Self assumes successively in various places various forms,[1579]

[1572] This verse admits of various translations, and requires also some metrical emendations. Thus Vig*ñ*ânâtman explains vedaguhyopanishatsu very ingeniously by the Veda, i.e. that part of it which teaches sacrifices and their rewards; the Guhya, i.e. the Âra*n*yaka, which teaches the worship of Brahman under various legendary aspects; and the Upanishads, which teach the knowledge of Brahman without qualities. These three divisions would correspond to the karmakâ*nd*a, yogakâ*nd*a, and *g*ñânakâ*nd*a (*G*aimini, Pata*ñ*gali, Bâdarâyana). See Deussen, Vedânta, p. 20. Mr. Gough and Dr. Roer take Brahmayoni as 'the source of the Veda,' or as the source of Hira*n*yagarbha. The irregular form vedate may be due to a corruption of vedânte.

[1573] Here begins the description of what is called the tvam (thou), as opposed to the tat (that), i.e. the living soul, as opposed to the Highest Brahman.

[1574] The paths of vice, virtue, and knowledge.

[1575] Both MSS. (A. and B.) read ârâgramâtro by avaro 'pi d*r*ish*th*a*h*.

[1576] An expression of frequent occurrence in Buddhist literature.

[1577] A. and B. read yugyate. A. explains yugyate by sambadhyate. B. explains adyate bhakshyate tirobhûta*h* kriyate. *S*aṅkara explains rakshyate, sa*m*rakshyate, tattaddharmân âtmany adhyasyâbhimanyate.

[1578] The MSS. vary considerably. Instead of mohair, A. and B. read homair. They read grâsâmbuv*r*ish*t*ya *k*âtma. A. reads âtmaviv*r*iddhiganma, B. âtmaniv*r*iddhaganmâ. A. has abhisamprapadye, B. abhisamprapadyate. My translation follows *S*aṅkara, who seems to have read âtmaviv*r*iddhiganma, taking the whole line as a simile and in an adverbial form. Vig*ñ*ânâtman, however, differs considerably. He reads homai*h*, and explains homa as the act of throwing oblations into the fire, as in the Agnihotra. This action of the hands, he thinks, stands for all actions of the various members of the body. Grâsâmbuv*r*ish*t*i he takes to mean free distribution of food and drink, and then explains the whole sentence by 'he whose self is born unto some states or declines from them again, namely, according as he has showered food and drink, and has used his hands, eyes, feelings, and thoughts.' *S*aṅkarânanda takes a similar view, only he construes saṅkalpanam and spar*s*anam as two d*r*ish*t*is, te eva d*r*ish*t*î, tayor âtmâgnau prakshepâ homâ*h*; and then goes on, na kevalam etai*h*, ki*m* tv asmin sthâne *s*arire grâsâmbuv*r*ish*t*yâ ka. He seems to read âtmaviv*r*iddhaganmâ, but afterwards explains viv*r*iddhi by vividhâ v*r*iddhi*h*.

[1579] Forms as high as Hira*n*yagarbha or as low as beasts.

in accordance with his deeds, just as the body grows when food and drink are poured into it.

12. That incarnate Self, according to his own qualities, chooses (assumes) many shapes, coarse or subtile, and having himself caused his union with them, he is seen as another and another,[1580] through the qualities of his acts, and through the qualities of his body.

13.[1581] He who knows him who has no beginning and no end, in the midst of chaos, creating all things, having many forms, alone enveloping everything, is freed from all fetters.

14. Those who know him who is to be grasped by the mind, who is not to be called the nest (the body[1582]), who makes existence and non-existence, the happy one (*S*iva), who also creates the elements,[1583] they have left the body.

SIXTH ADHYÂYA.

1.[1584] Some wise men, deluded, speak of Nature, and others of Time (as the cause of everything[1585]); but it is the greatness of God by which this Brahma-wheel is made to turn.

2. It is at the command of him who always covers this world, the knower, the time of time,[1586] who assumes qualities and all knowledge,[1587] it is at his command that this work (creation) unfolds itself, which is called earth, water, fire, air, and ether;

3.[1588] He who, after he has done that work and rested again, and after he has brought together one essence (the self) with the other (matter), with one, two, three, or eight, with time also and with the subtile qualities of the mind,

4. Who, after starting[1589] the works endowed with (the three)

1580 Instead of aparo, B. reads avaro, but explains aparo.

1581 Cf. III, 7; IV, 14, 16.

1582 Nî*d*a is explained as the body, but *S*aṅkarânanda reads anilâkhyam, who is called the wind, as being prâ*n*asya prâ*n*am, the breath of the breath.

1583 *S*aṅkara explains kalâsargakaram by he who creates the sixteen kalâs, mentioned by the Âtharva*n*ikas, beginning with prâ*n*a, and ending with nâman; see Pra*sñ*a Up. VI, 4. Vi*gñ*ânâtman suggests two other explanations, 'he who creates by means of the kalâ, i.e. his inherent power;' or 'he who creates the Vedas and other sciences.' The sixteen kalâs are, according to *S*aṅkarânanda, prâ*n*a, *s*raddhâ, kha, vâyu, gyoti*h*, ap, p*ri*thivî, indriya, mana*h*, anna, vîrya, tapa*h*, mantra, karman, kâla (?), nâman. See also before, I, 4.

1584 See Muir, Metrical Translations, p. 198.

1585 See before, 1, 2.

1586 The destroyer of time. Vi*gñ*ânâtman reads kâlâkâlo, and explains it by kâlasya niyantâ, upahartâ. *S*aṅkarânanda explains kâla*h* sarvavinâ*s*akârî, tasyâpi vinâsakara*h*. See also verse 16.

1587 Or sarvavid ya*h*.

1588 Instead of vinivartya, Vi*gñ*ânâtman and *S*aṅkarânanda read viniv*ri*tya.

1589 Âruhya for ârabhya, *S*aṅkarânanda.

qualities, can order all things, yet when, in the absence of all these, he has caused the destruction of the work, goes on, being in truth[1590]

[1590] These two verses are again extremely obscure, and the explanations of the commentators throw little light on their real, original meaning. To begin with *S*aṅkara, he assumes the subject to be the same as he at whose command this work unfolds itself, and explains tattvasya tattvena sametya yogam by âtmano bhûmyâdinâ yoga*m* sa*m*gamayya. As the eight Tattvas he gives earth, water, fire, air, ether, mind, thought, personality, while the Âtmagu*n*as are, according to him, the affections of the mind, love, anger, &c. In the second verse, however, *S*aṅkara seems to assume a different subject. 'If a man,' he says, 'having done works, infected by qualities, should transfer them on Î*s*vara, the Lord, there would be destruction of the works formerly done by him, because there would be no more connection with the self.' Something is left out, but that this is *S*aṅkara's idea, appears from the verses which he quotes in support, and which are intended to show that Yogins, transferring all their acts, good, bad, or indifferent, on Brahman, are no longer affected by them. 'That person,' *S*aṅkara, continues, 'his works being destroyed and his nature purified, moves on, different from all things (tattva), from all the results of ignorance, knowing himself to be Brahman.' 'Or,' he adds, 'if we read anyad, it means, he goes to that Brahman which is different from all things.'

*S*aṅkarânanda takes a different view. He says: 'If a man has performed sacrifices, and has finished them, or, has turned away from them again as vain, and if he has obtained union with that which is the real of the (apparently) real, &c.' The commentator then asks what is that with which he obtains union, and replies, 'the one, i.e. ignorance; the two, i.e. right and wrong; the three, i.e. the three colours, red, white, and black; and the eight, i.e. the five elements, with mind, thought, and personality; also with time, and with the subtile affections of the mind.' He then goes on, 'If that man, after having begun qualified works, should take on himself all states (resulting from ignorance), yet, when these states cease, there would be an end of the work, good or bad, done by him, and when his work has come to an end, he abides in truth (according to the Veda); while the other, who differs from the Veda, is wrong.' *S*aṅkarânanda, however, evidently feels that this is a doubtful interpretation, and he suggests another, viz. 'If the Lord himself,' he says, 'determined these states (bhâva), it would seem that there would be no end of sa*m*sâra. He therefore says, that when these states, ignorance &c., cease, the work done by man ceases; and when the work done ceases, the living soul gets free of sa*m*sâra, being in truth another, i.e. different from ignorance and its products.'

Vig*ñ*ânâtman says: 'If a man, having done work, turns away from it, and obtains union of one tattva (the tvam, or self) with the real tattva (the tat, or the Lord);—and how? By means of the one, i.e. the teaching of the Guru; the two, i.e. love of the Guru and of the Lord; the three, i.e. hearing, remembering, and meditating; the eight, i.e. restraint, penance, postures, regulation of the breath, abstraction, devotion, contemplation, and meditation (Yoga-sûtras II, 2 9); by time, i.e. the right time for work; by the qualities of the self, i.e. pity, &c.; by the subtile ones, i.e. the good dispositions for knowledge, then (we must supply) he becomes free.' And this he explains more fully in the next verse. 'If, after having done qualified works, i.e. works to please the Lord, a Yati discards all things, and recognises the phenomenal character of all states, and traces them back to their real source in Mûlaprak*ri*ti and, in the end, in the Sa*kk*idânanda, he becomes free. If they (the states) cease, i.e. are known in their real source, the work done ceases also in its effects, and when the work has been annihilated, he goes to freedom, being another in truth; or, if we read anyat, he goes to what is different from all these things, namely, to the Lord; or, he goes to a state of perfect lordship in truth, having discovered the highest truth, the oneness of the self with the Highest Self.'

I think that, judging from the context, the subject is really the same in both verses, viz. the Lord, as passing through different states, and at last knowing himself to be above them all. Yet, the other explanations may be defended, and if the subject were taken to be different in each verse, some difficulties would disappear.

different (from all he has produced);

5. He is the beginning, producing the causes which unite (the soul with the body), and, being above the three kinds of time (past, present, future), he is seen as without parts,[1591] after we have first worshipped that adorable god, who has many forms, and who is the true source (of all things), as dwelling in our own mind.

6. He is beyond all the forms of the tree[1592] (of the world) and of time, he is the other, from whom this world moves round, when[1593] one has known him who brings good and removes evil, the lord of bliss, as dwelling within the self, the immortal, the support of all.

7. Let us know that highest great lord of lords,[1594] the highest deity of deities, the master of masters, the highest above, as god, the lord of the world, the adorable.

8. There is no effect and no cause known of him, no one is seen like unto him or better; his high power is revealed as manifold, as inherent, acting as force and knowledge.

9. There is no master of his in the world, no ruler of his, not even a sign of him.[1595] He is the cause, the lord of the lords of the organs,[1596] and there is of him neither parent nor lord.

10. That only god who spontaneously covered himself, like a spider, with threads drawn from the first cause (pradhâna), grant us entrance into Brahman.[1597]

11. He is the one God, hidden in all beings, all-pervading, the self within all beings, watching over all works, dwelling in all beings, the witness, the perceiver,[1598] the only one, free from qualities.

12.[1599] He is the one ruler of many who (seem to act, but really do)

[1591] Vig*ñ*ânâtman and *S*aṅkarânanda read akalo 'pi, without parts, and *S*aṅkara, too, presupposes that reading, though the text is corrupt in Roer's edition.

[1592] Explained as samsâravr*i*ksha, the world-tree, as described in the Ka*th*a Up. VI, 1.

[1593] It seems possible to translate this verse in analogy with the former, and without supplying the verb either from yâti, in verse 4, or from vidâma, in verse 7. The poet seems to have said, he is that, he is seen as that, when one has worshipped him, or when one has known him within oneself.

[1594] *S*aṅkara thinks that the lords are Vaivasvata &c.; the deities, Indra &c.; the masters, the Pragâpatis. Vig*ñ*ânâtman explains the lords as Brahman, Vish*n*u, Rudra, &c.; the deities as Indra, &c.; the masters as Hira*n*yagarbha, &c. *S*aṅkarânanda sees in the lords Hira*n*yagarbha &c., in the deities Agni &c., in the masters the Pragâpatis, such as Ka*s*yapa.

[1595] If he could be inferred from a sign, there would be no necessity for the Veda to reveal him.

[1596] Kara*n*a, instrument, is explained as organ of sense. The lords of such organs would be all living beings, and their lord the true Lord.

[1597] Besides brahmâpyayam, i.e. brahma*n*y apyayam, ekîbhâvam, another reading is brahmâvyayam, i.e. brahma *k*âvyaya*m* *k*a.

[1598] All the MSS. seem to read *k*etâ, not *k*ettâ.

[1599] See Ka*th*a-upanishad V, 12-15.

not act;[1600] he makes the one seed manifold. The wise who perceive him within their self, to them belongs eternal happiness, not to others.

13.[1601] He is the eternal among eternals, the thinker among thinkers, who, though one, fulfils the desires of many. He who has known that cause which is to be apprehended by *S*âṅkhya (philosophy) and Yoga (religious discipline), he is freed from all fetters.

14. The[1602] sun does not shine there, nor the moon and the stars, nor these lightnings, and much less this fire. When he shines, everything shines after him; by his light all this is lightened.

15. He is the one bird[1603] in the midst of the world; he is also (like) the fire (of the sun) that has set in the ocean. A man who knows him truly, passes over death;[1604] there is no other path to go.

16. He makes all, he knows all, the self-caused, the knower,[1605] the time of time (destroyer of time), who assumes qualities and knows everything, the master of nature and of man,[1606] the lord of the three qualities (gu*n*a), the cause of the bondage, the existence, and the liberation of the world.[1607]

17. He who has become that,[1608] he is the immortal, remaining the lord, the knower, the ever-present guardian of this world, who rules this world for ever, for no one else is able to rule it.

18. Seeking for freedom I go for refuge to that God who is the light

---

[1600] *S*aṅkara explains that the acts of living beings are due to their organs, but do not affect the Highest Self, which always remains passive (nishkriya).

[1601] I have formerly translated this verse, according to the reading nityo 'nityânâ*m* *k*etana*s* *k*etanânâm, the eternal thinker of non-eternal thoughts. This would be a true description of the Highest Self who, though himself eternal and passive, has to think (gîvâtman) non-eternal thoughts. I took the first *k*etana*h* in the sense of *k*ettâ, the second in the sense of *k*etana*m*. The. commentators, however, take a different, and it may be, from their point, a more correct view. *S*aṅkara says: 'He is the eternal of the eternals, i.e. as he possesses eternity among living souls (gîvas), these living souls also may claim eternity. Or the eternals may be meant for earth, water, &c. And in the same way he is the thinker among thinkers.'

*S*aṅkarânanda says: 'He is eternal, imperishable, among eternal, imperishable things, such as the ether, &c. He is thinking among thinkers.'

Vig*ñ*ânâtman says: 'The Highest Lord is the cause of eternity in eternal things on earth, and the cause of thought in the thinkers on earth.' But he allows another construction, namely, that he is the eternal thinker of those who on earth are endowed with eternity and thought. In the end all these interpretations come to the same, viz. that there is only one eternal, and only one thinker, from whom all that is (or seems to be) eternal and all that is thought on earth is derived.

[1602] See Ka*th*. Up. V, 15; Mu*nd*. Up. II, 2, 10; Bhagavadgîtâ XV, 6.

[1603] Ha*m*sa, frequently used for the Highest Self, is explained here as hanty avidyâdibandhakâra*n*am iti ha*m*sa*h*.

[1604] Cf. III, 8.

[1605] Again the MSS. read kâlakâlo, as in verse 2. They also agree in putting *gñ*ah before kâlakâlo, as in verse 2.

[1606] Pradhânam avyaktam, kshetra*gñ*o vi*gñ*ânâtmâ.

[1607] He binds, sustains, and dissolves worldly existence.

[1608] He who seems to exist for a time in the form of kshetra*gñ*a and pradhâna.

of his own thoughts,[1609] he who first creates Brahman (m.)[1610] and delivers the Vedas to him;

19. Who is without parts, without actions, tranquil, without fault, without taint,[1611] the highest bridge to immortality—like a fire that has consumed its fuel.

20. Only when men shall roll up the sky like a hide, will there be an end of misery, unless God has first been known.[1612]

21. Through the power of his penance and through the grace of God[1613] has the wise *S*vetâ*s*vatara truly[1614] proclaimed Brahman, the highest and holiest, to the best of ascetics,[1615] as approved by the company of *Ri*shis.

22. This highest mystery in the Vedânta, delivered in a former age, should not be given to one whose passions have not been subdued, nor to one who is not a son, or who is not a pupil.[1616]

23. If these truths have been told to a high-minded man, who feels the highest devotion for God, and for his Guru as for God, then they will shine forth,—then they will shine forth indeed.

[1609] The MSS. vary between âtmabuddhiprakâ*s*am and âtmabuddhiprasâdam. The former reading is here explained by *S*ankarânanda as svabuddhisâkshi*n*am.

[1610] Explained as Hira*n*yagarbha.

[1611] Nira*ñ*gana*m* nirlepam.

[1612] *S*ankarânanda reads tadâ *s*ivam avig*ñ*âya du*h*khasyânto bhavishyati; Vig*ñ*ânâtman retains devam but mentions *s*ivam as a various reading. Both have anto, not antam, like Roer. *S*ankara seems to have found na before bhavishyati, or to have read du*h*khânto na bhavishyati, for he explains that there will be no end of misery, unless God has first been known. It is possible, however, that the same idea may be expressed in the text as we read it, so that it should mean, Only when the impossible shall happen, such as the sky being rolled up by men, will misery cease, unless God has been discovered in the heart.

[1613] The MSS, read devaprasâdât, which is more in keeping with the character of this Upanishad.

[1614] Samyak may be both adverb and adjective in this sentence, kâkâkshinyâyena.

[1615] Atyâ*s*ramin is explained by *S*ankara as atyantam pûgyatamâ*s*ramibhya*h*; and he adds, *k*aturvidhâ bhikshava*s* *k*a bahûdakaku*t*î*k*akau, Ha*m*sa*h* paramaha*m*sa*s* *k*a yo ya*h* pa*s*kât sa uttama*h*. Weber (Indische Studien, II, 109) has himself corrected his mistake of reading antyâ*s*ramibhya*h*, and translating it by neighbouring hermits.

These four stages in the life of a Sannyâsin are the same to-day as they were in the time of the Upanishads, and Dayânanda Sarasvatî describes them in his autobiography, though in a different order: 1. Ku*t*î*k*aka, living in a hut, or in a desolate place, and wearing a red-ochre coloured garment, carrying a three-knotted bamboo rod, and wearing the hair in the centre of the crown of the head, having the sacred thread, and devoting oneself to the contemplation of Parabrahma. 2. Bahûdaka, one who lives quite apart from his family and the world, maintains himself on alms collected at seven houses, and wears the same kind of reddish garment. 3. Ha*m*sa, the same as in the preceding case, except the carrying of only a one-knotted bamboo. 4. Paramaha*m*sa, the same as the others; but the ascetic wears the sacred thread, and his hair and beard are quite long. This is the highest of all orders. A Paramaha*m*sa who shows himself worthy is on the very threshold of becoming a Dîkshita.

[1616] Cf. B*ri*h. Up. VI, 3, 12; Maitr. Up. VI, 2 9.

PRAS*Ñ*A-UPANISHAD.

FIRST QUESTION.

Adoration to the Highest Self! Hari*h*, Om!

1. Suke*s*as[1617] Bhâradvâga,[1618] and *S*aivya Satyakâma, and Sauryâya*n*in[1619] Gârgya, and Kausalya[1620] Â*s*valâyana, and Bhârgava Vaidarbhi,[1621] and Kabandhin Kâtyâyana, these were devoted to Brahman, firm in Brahman, seeking for the Highest Brahman. They thought that the venerable Pippalâda could tell them all that, and they therefore took fuel in their hands (like pupils), and approached him.

2. That *R*ishi said to them: 'Stay here a year longer, with penance, abstinence, and faith; then you may ask questions according to your pleasure, and if we know them, we shall tell you all.'

3. Then[1622] Kabandhin Kâtyâyana approached him and asked: 'Sir, from whence may these creatures be born?'

4. He replied: 'Pragâpati (the lord of creatures) was desirous of creatures (pragâ*h*). He performed penance',[1623] and having performed penance, he produces a pair, matter (rayi) and spirit (prâ*n*a), thinking that they together should produce creatures for him in many ways.

5.[1624] The sun is spirit, matter is the moon. All this, what has body and what has no body, is matter, and therefore body indeed is matter.

6. Now Âditya, the sun, when he rises, goes toward the East, and thus receives the Eastern spirits into his rays. And when he illuminates the South, the West, the North, the Zenith, the Nadir, the intermediate quarters, and everything, he thus receives all spirits into his rays.

7. Thus he rises, as Vai*s*vânara, (belonging to all men,) assuming all forms, as spirit, as fire. This has been said in the following verse:

8.[1625] (They knew) him who assumes all forms, the golden,[1626] who

---

[1617] Suke*s*as seems better than Suke*s*an, and he is so called in the sixth Pra*sñ*a, in MS. Mill 74.

[1618] Bhâradvâ*g*a, *S*aivya, Gârgya, Âsvalâyana, Bhârgava, and Kâtyâyana are, according to *S*a*n*kara, names of gotras or families.

[1619] Sûryasyâpatya*m* Saurya*h*, tadapatya*m* *S*auryâya*nih*. Dîrgha*h* sulopa*s* *k*a *kh*ândasa iti sa eva Sauryâya*n*î.

[1620] Kausalyo nâmata*h*, kosalâyâm bhavo vâ.

[1621] Vaidarbhi is explained as vidarbhe*h* prabhava*h*, or Vidarbheshu prabhava*h*. Vidarbha, a country, south of the Vindhya mountains, with Ku*nd*ina as its capital. Vaidarbha, a king of the Vidarbhas, is mentioned in the Ait. Brâhm. VII, 34. Vaidarbhi is a patronymic of Vidarbha. See B. R. s. v.

[1622] After the year was over.

[1623] Or he meditated; see Upanishads, vol. i, n. 587.

[1624] *S*a*n*kara explains, or rather obscures, this by saying that the sun is breath, or the eater, or Agni, while matter is the food, namely, Soma.

[1625] Cf. Maitr. Up. VI, 8.

knows all things, who ascends highest, alone in his splendour, and warms us; the thousand-rayed, who abides in a hundred places, the spirit of all creatures, the Sun, rises.

9. The year indeed is Pragâpati, and there are two paths thereof, the Southern and the Northern. Now those who here believe in sacrifices and pious gifts as work done, gain the moon only as their (future) world, and return again. Therefore the *Ri*shis who desire offspring, go to the South, and that path of the Fathers is matter (rayi).

10. But those who have sought the Self by penance, abstinence, faith, and knowledge, gain by the Northern path Âditya, the sun. This is the home of the spirits, the immortal, free from danger, the highest. From thence they do not return, for it is the end. Thus says the *S*loka:[1627]

11. Some call him the father with five feet (the five seasons), and with twelve shapes (the twelve months), the giver of rain in the highest half of heaven; others again say that the sage is placed in the lower half, in the chariot[1628] with seven wheels and six spokes.

12. The month is Pragâpati; its dark half is matter, its bright half spirit. Therefore some *Ri*shis perform sacrifice in the bright half, others in the other half.

13. Day and Night[1629] are Pragâpati; its day is spirit, its night matter. Those who unite in love by day waste their spirit, but to unite in love by night is right.

14. Food is Pragâpati. Hence proceeds seed, and from it these creatures are born.

15. Those therefore who observe this rule of Pragâpati (as laid down in § 13), produce a pair, and to them belongs this Brahma-world here.[1630] But those in whom dwell penance, abstinence, and truth,

16. To them belongs that pure Brahma-world, to them, namely, in whom there is nothing crooked, nothing false, and no guile.'

SECOND QUESTION.

1. Then Bhârgava Vaidarbhi asked him: 'Sir, How many gods[1631] keep what has thus been created, how many manifest this,[1632] and who is the best of them?'

2. He replied: 'The ether is that god, the wind, fire, water, earth,

---

[1626] Hari*n*am is explained as ra*s*mimantam, or as harati sarveshâm prâ*n*inâm âyû*m*shi bhaumân vâ rasân iti hari*nah*. I prefer to take it in the sense of yellow, or golden.

[1627] *Ri*g-veda I, 164, 12. We ought to read upare vi*k*aksha*n*am.

[1628] Sapta*k*akre, i.e. rathe. The seven wheels are explained as the rays or horses of the sun; or as half-years, seasons, months, half-months, days, nights, and muhûrtas.

[1629] Taken as one, as a Nychthemeron.

[1630] In the moon, reached by the path of the Fathers.

[1631] Devâ*h*, powers, organs, senses.

[1632] Their respective power.

speech, mind, eye, and ear. These, when they have manifested (their power), contend and say: We (each of us) support this body and keep it.[1633]'

3.[1634] Then Prâ*n*a (breath, spirit, life), as the best, said to them: 'Be not deceived, I alone, dividing myself fivefold, support this body and keep it.'

4. They were incredulous; so he, from pride, did as if he were going out from above. Thereupon, as he went out, all the others went out, and as he returned, all the others returned. As bees go out when their queen[1635] goes out, and return when she returns, thus (did) speech, mind, eye, and ear; and, being satisfied, they praise Prâ*n*a, saying:

5. 'He is Agni (fire), he shines as Sûrya (sun), he is Parganya (rain), the powerful (Indra), he is Vâyu, (wind), he is the earth, he is matter, he is God—he is what is and what is not, and what is immortal.

6. 'As spokes in the nave of a wheel, everything is fixed in Prâ*n*a, the verses of the *R*ig-veda, Yagur-veda, Sâma-veda, the sacrifice, the Kshatriyas, and the Brâhmans.

7. 'As Pragâpati (lord of creatures) thou movest about in the womb, thou indeed art born again. To thee, the Prâ*n*a, these creatures bring offerings, to thee who dwellest with the other prâ*n*as (the organs of sense).

8. 'Thou art the best carrier for the Gods, thou art the first offering[1636] to the Fathers. Thou art the true work of the Rishis,[1637] of the Atharvâṅgiras.

9. 'O Prâ*n*a, thou art Indra by thy light, thou art Rudra, as a protector; thou movest in the sky, thou art the sun, the lord of lights.

10. 'When thou showerest down rain, then, O Prâ*n*a, these creatures of thine are delighted,[1638] hoping that there will be food, as much as they desire.

11. 'Thou art a Vrâtya,[1639] O Prâ*n*a, the only *R*ishi,[1640] the

---

[1633] This is *S*aṅkara's explanation, in which bâ*n*a is taken to mean the same as *s*arîra, body. But there seems to be no authority for such a meaning, and Ânandagiri tries in vain to find an etymological excuse for it. Bâ*n*a or Vâ*n*a generally means an arrow, or, particularly in Brâhma*n*a writings, a harp with many strings. I do not see how an arrow could be used as an appropriate simile here, but a harp might, if we take avash*t*abhya in the sense of holding the frame of the instrument, and vidhârayâma*h* in the sense of stretching and thereby modulating it.

[1634] On this dispute of the organs of sense, see B*r*ih. Up. VI, 1, p. 201; *Kh*ând. Up. V, 1 (S. B. E., vol. i, p. 72).

[1635] In Sanskrit it is madhukararâga, king of the bees.

[1636] When a *s*râddha is offered to the Pit*r*is.

[1637] Explained as the eye and the other organs of sense which the chief Prâ*n*a supports; but it is probably an old verse, here applied to a special purpose.

[1638] Another reading is prâ*n*ate, they breathe.

[1639] A person for whom the sa*m*skâras, the sacramental and initiatory rites, have not been performed. *S*aṅkara says that, as he was the first born, there was no one to perform

consumer of everything, the good lord. We are the givers of what thou hast to consume, thou, O Mâtarisva,[1641] art our father.

12. 'Make propitious that body of thine which dwells in speech, in the ear, in the eye, and which pervades the mind; do not go away!

13. 'All this is in the power of Prâna, whatever exists in the three heavens. Protect us like a mother her sons, and give us happiness and wisdom.'

THIRD QUESTION.

1. Then Kausalya Âsvalâyana asked: 'Sir, whence is that Prâna (spirit) born? How does it come into this body? And how does it abide, after it has divided itself? How does it go out? How does it support what is without,[1642] and how what is within?'

2. He replied: 'You ask questions more difficult, but you are very fond of Brahman, therefore I shall tell it you.

3. 'This Prâna (spirit) is born of the Self. Like the shadow thrown on a man, this (the prâna) is spread out over it (the Brahman).[1643] By the work of the mind[1644] does it come into this body.

4. 'As a king commands officials, saying to them: Rule these villages or those, so does that Prâna (spirit) dispose the other prânas, each for their separate work.

5. 'The Apâna (the down-breathing) in the organs of excretion and generation; the Prâna himself dwells in eye and ear, passing through mouth and nose. In the middle is the Samâna[1645] (the on-breathing); it carries what has been sacrificed as food equally (over the body), and the seven lights proceed from it.

6. 'The Self[1646] is in the heart. There are the 101 arteries, and in each of them there are a hundred (smaller veins), and for each of these

---

them for him, and that he is called Vrâtya, because he was pure by nature. This is all very doubtful.

[1640] Agni is said to be the *Ri*shi of the Âtharva*n*as.

[1641] Instead of the irregular vocative Mâtari*s*va, there is another reading, Mâtari*s*vana*h*, i.e. thou art the father of Mâtari*s*van, the wind, and therefore of the whole world.

[1642] All creatures and the gods.

[1643] Over Brahman, i.e. the Self, the parama purusha, the akshara, the satya. The prâ*n*a being called a shadow, is thereby implied to be unreal (an*ri*ta). *S*aṅkara.

[1644] Manok*ri*ta is explained as an ârsha sandhi. It means the good or evil deeds, which are the work of the mind.

[1645] I keep to the usual translation of Samâna by on-breathing, though it is here explained in a different sense. Samâna is here supposed to be between prâ*n*a and apâna, and to distribute the food equally, samam, over the body. The seven lights are explained as the two eyes, the two ears, the two nostrils, and the mouth.

[1646] Here the Liṅgâtmâ or *G*îvâtmâ.

branches there are 72,000.[1647] In these the Vyâna (the back-breathing) moves.

7. 'Through one of them, the Udâna (the out-breathing) leads (us) upwards to the good world by good work, to the bad world by bad work, to the world of men by both.

8. 'The sun rises as the external Prâ*n*a, for it assists the Prâ*n*a in the eye.[1648] The deity that exists in the earth, is there in support of man's Apâna (down-breathing). The ether between (sun and earth) is the Samâna (on-breathing), the air is Vyâna (back-breathing).

9. 'Light is the Udâna (out-breathing), and therefore he whose light has gone out comes to a new birth with his senses absorbed in the mind.

10. 'Whatever his thought (at the time of death) with that he goes back to Prâ*n*a, and the Prâ*n*a, united with light,[1649] together with the self (the *g*îvâtmâ) leads on to the world, as deserved.

11. 'He who, thus knowing, knows Prâ*n*a, his offspring does not perish, and he becomes immortal. Thus says the *S*loka:

12. 'He who has known the origin,[1650] the entry, the place, the fivefold distribution, and the internal state[1651] of the Prâ*n*a, obtains immortality, yes, obtains immortality.'

FOURTH QUESTION.

1. Then Sauryâya*n*in Gârgya asked: 'Sir, What are they that sleep in this man, and what are they that are awake in him? What power (deva) is it that sees dreams? Whose is the happiness? On what do all these depend?'

2. He replied: 'O Gârgya, As all the rays of the sun, when it sets, are gathered up in that disc of light, and as they, when the sun rises again and again, come forth, so is all this (all the senses) gathered up in the highest faculty (deva),[1652] the mind. Therefore at that time that man does not hear, see, smell, taste, touch, he does not speak, he does not take, does not enjoy, does not evacuate, does not move about. He

---

[1647] A hundred times 101 would give us 10,100, and each multiplied by 72,000 would give us a sum total of 727,200,000 veins, or, if we add the principal veins, 727,210,201. Ânandagiri makes the sum total, 72 ko*t*is, 72 lakshas, six thousands, two hundred and one, where the six of the thousands seems to be a mistake for da*s*asahasram. In the B*ri*hadâr. Upanishad II, 1, 19, we read of 72,000 arteries, likewise in Yâ*gñ*avalkya III, 108. See also B*ri*h. Up. IV, 3, 20; *Kh*ând. Up. VI, 5, 3, comm.; Kaush. Up. IV, 20; Ka*th*a Up. VI, 16.

[1648] Without the sun the eye could not see.

[1649] With Udâna, the out-breathing.

[1650] This refers to the questions asked in verse 1, and answered in the verses which follow.

[1651] The adhyâtma, as opposed to the vâhya, mentioned in verse 1. Ayati instead of âyâti is explained by *kh*ândasa*m* hrasvatvam.

[1652] See note to verse 5.

sleeps, that is what people say.

3. 'The fires of the prâ*n*as are, as it were,[1653] awake in that town (the body). The Apâna is the Gârhapatya fire, the Vyâna the Anvâhâryapa*k*ana fire; and because it is taken out of the Gârhapatya fire, which is fire for taking out,[1654] therefore the Prâ*n*a is the Âhavanîya fire.[1655]

'Now the Apâna is identified with the Gârhapatya fire, no reason being given except afterwards, when it is said that the Prâ*n*a is the Âhavanîya fire, being taken out of the Gârhapatya, here called pra*n*ayana, in the same manner as the prâ*n*a proceeds in sleep from the apâna. The Vyâna is identified with the Dakshi*n*âgni, the Southern fire, because it issues from the heart through an aperture on the right.

4. Because it carries equally these two oblations, the out-breathing and the in-breathing, the Samâna is he (the Hot*ri* priest).[1656] The mind is the sacrificer, the Udâna is the reward of the sacrifice, and it leads the sacrificer every day (in deep sleep) to Brahman.

5. 'There that god[1657] (the mind) enjoys in sleep greatness. What has been seen, he[1657] sees again; what has been heard, he hears again; what has been enjoyed in different countries and quarters, he enjoys again; what has been seen and not seen, heard and not heard, enjoyed and not enjoyed, he sees it all; he, being all, sees.

6. 'And when he is overpowered by light,[1658] then that god sees no dreams, and at that time that happiness arises in his body.

7. 'And, O friend, as birds go to a tree to roost, thus all this rests in the Highest Âtman,—

8. 'The earth and its subtile elements, the water and its subtile elements, the light and its subtile elements, the air and its subtile elements, the ether and its subtile elements; the eye and what can be seen, the ear and what can be heard, the nose and what can be smelled, the taste and what can be tasted, the skin and what can be touched, the voice and what can be spoken, the hands and what can be grasped, the

---

[1653] We ought to read agnaya iva.

[1654] Pra*n*ayana, pra*n*îyate 'smâd iti pra*n*ayano gârhapatyo 'gni*h*.

[1655] The comparison between the prâ*n*as and the fires or altars is not very clear. As to the fires or altars, there is the Gârhapatya, placed in the South-west, the household fire, which is always kept burning, from which the fire is taken to the other altars. The Anvâhâryapa*k*ana, commonly called the Dakshi*n*a fire, placed in the South, used chiefly for oblations to the forefathers. The Âhavanîya fire, placed in the East, and used for sacrifices to the gods.

[1656] The name of the Hot*ri* priest must be supplied. He is supposed to carry two oblations equally to the Âhavanîya, and in the same way the Vyâna, combines the two breathings, the in and out breathings.

[1657] The gîvâtman under the guise of manas. The Sanskrit word is deva, god, used in the sense of an invisible power, but as a masculine. The commentator uses manodeva*h*, p. 212, l. 5. I generally translate deva, if used in this sense, by faculty, but the context required a masculine. See verse 2.

[1658] In the state of profound sleep or sushupti.

feet and what can be walked, the mind and what can be perceived, intellect (buddhi) and what can be conceived, personality and what can be personified, thought and what can be thought, light and what can be lighted up, the Prâ*n*a and what is to be supported by it.

9. 'For he it is who sees, hears, smells, tastes, perceives, conceives, acts, he whose essence is knowledge,[1659] the person, and he dwells in the highest, indestructible Self,—

10. 'He who knows that indestructible being, obtains (what is) the highest and indestructible, he without a shadow, without a body, without colour, bright,—yes, O friend, he who knows it, becomes all-knowing, becomes all. On this there is this *S*loka:

11. 'He, O friend, who knows that indestructible being wherein the true knower, the vital spirits (prâ*n*as), together with all the powers (deva), and the elements rest, he, being all-knowing, has penetrated all.'

FIFTH QUESTION.

1. Then *S*aivya Satyakâma asked him:—'Sir, if some one among men should meditate here until death on the syllable Om, what would he obtain by it?'

2. He replied: 'O Satyakâma, the syllable Om (AUM) is the highest and also the other Brahman; therefore he who knows it arrives by the same means[1660] at one of the two.

3. 'If he meditate on one Mâtrâ (the A),[1661] then, being enlightened by that only, he arrives quickly at the earth.[1662] The *Rik*-verses lead him to the world of men, and being endowed there with penance, abstinence, and faith, he enjoys greatness.

4. 'If he meditate with[1663] two Mâtrâs (A + U) he arrives at the Manas,[1664] and is led up by the Yagus-verses to the sky, to the Soma-world. Having enjoyed greatness in the Soma-world, he returns again.

5. 'Again, he who meditates with this syllable AUM of three Mâtrâs, on the Highest Person, he comes to light and to the sun. And as a snake is freed from its skin, so is he freed from evil. He is led up by the Sâman-verses to the Brahma-world;[1665] and from him, full of life

---

[1659] Buddhi and the rest are the instruments of knowledge, but there is the knower, the person, in the Highest Self.

[1660] Âyatanena, âlambanena.

[1661] Dîpikâyâ*m* Vâ*k*aspatinaivâkâramâtram ityeva vyâkhyâtam.

[1662] Sampadyate prâpnoti *g*anmeti *s*esha*h*.

[1663] *S*rutau t*ri*tîyâ dvitîyârthe.

[1664] Literally the mind, but here meant for the moon, as before. It is clear that manasi belongs to sampadyate, not, as the Dîpikâ and Roer think, to dhyâyîta. Some take it for svapnâbhimânî Hira*n*yagarbha*h*.

[1665] The world of Hira*n*yagarbha*h*, called the Satyaloka.

(Hira*n*yagarbha, the lord of the Satya-loka[1666]), he learns[1667] to see the all-pervading, the Highest Person. And there are these two *S*lokas:

6. 'The three Mâtrâs (A + U + M), if employed separate, and only joined one to another, are mortal;[1668] but in acts, external, internal, or intermediate, if well performed, the sage trembles not.[1669]

7. 'Through the *Rik*-verses he arrives at this world, through the Yagus-verses at the sky, through the Sâman-verses at that which the poets teach,—he arrives at this by means of the Oṅkâra; the wise arrives at that which is at rest, free from decay, from death, from fear,—the Highest.'

SIXTH QUESTION.

1. Then Suke*s*as Bhâradvâga asked him, saying: 'Sir, Hira*n*yanâbha, the prince of Kosalâ,[1670] came to me and asked this question: Do you know the person of sixteen parts, O Bhâradvâga? I said to the prince: I do not know him; if I knew him, how should I not tell you? Surely, he who speaks what is untrue withers away to the very root; therefore I will not say what is untrue. Then he mounted his chariot and went away silently. Now I ask you, where is that person?'

2. He replied: 'Friend, that person is here within the body, he in whom these sixteen parts arise.'

3. He reflected: 'What is it by whose departure I shall depart, and by whose staying I shall stay?'

4. He sent forth (created) Prâ*n*a (spirit);[1671] from Prâ*n*a *S*raddhâ (faith),[1672] ether, air, light, water, earth, sense, mind, food; from food came vigour, penance, hymns, sacrifice, the worlds, and in the worlds the name[1673] also.

5. As these flowing rivers[1674] that go towards the ocean, when they have reached the ocean, sink into it, their name and form are broken,

---

[1666] On a later addition, bringing in the Om as consisting of three Mâtrâs and a half, see Weber, Ind. Stud. I, p. 453; Roer, p. 238.

[1667] Tadupade*s*eneti yâvat.

[1668] Because in their separate form, A, U, M, they do not mean the Highest Brahman.

[1669] The three acts are explained as waking, slumbering, and deep sleep; or as three kinds of pronunciation, târa-mandra-madhyama. They are probably meant for Yoga exercises in which the three Mâtrâs of Om are used as one word, and as an emblem of the Highest Brahman.

[1670] *S*aṅkara explains Kausalya by Kosalâyâm bhava*h*. Ânandatîrtha gives the same explanation. Kosalâ is the capital, generally called Ayodhyâ. There is no authority for the palatal s.

[1671] *S*aṅkara explains prâ*n*a by sarvaprâ*n*o Hira*n*yagarbha (sarvaprâ*n*ikara*n*âdhâram antarâtmânam).

[1672] Faith is supposed to make all beings act rightly.

[1673] Nâma stands here for nâmarûpe, name (concept) and form. See before.

[1674] Cf. Mu*nd*. Up. IV, 2, 8; *Kh*ând. Up. VIII, 10.

and people speak of the ocean only, exactly thus these sixteen parts of the spectator that go towards the person (purusha), when they have reached the person, sink into him, their name and form are broken, and people speak of the person only, and he becomes without parts and immortal. On this there is this verse:

6. 'That person who is to be known, he in whom these parts rest, like spokes in the nave of a wheel, you know him, lest death should hurt you.'

7. Then he (Pippalâda) said to them: 'So far do I know this Highest Brahman, there is nothing higher than it.'

8. And they praising him, said: 'You, indeed, are our father, you who carry us from our ignorance to the other shore.'

Adoration to the highest *Ri*shis!

Adoration to the highest *Ri*shis!

Tat sat. Hari*h*, Om!

MAITRÂYA*N*A-BRÂHMA*N*A-UPANISHAD

FIRST PRAPÂTHAKA.

1. The laying of the formerly-described sacrificial fires[1675] is indeed the sacrifice of Brahman. Therefore let the sacrificer, after he has laid those fires, meditate on the Self. Thus only does the sacrificer become complete and faultless.

But who is to be meditated on? He who is called Prâ*n*a (breath). Of him there is this story:

2. A King, named B*ri*hadratha, having established his son in his sovereignty,[1676] went into the forest, because he considered this body as transient, and had obtained freedom from all desires. Having performed the highest penance, he stands there, with uplifted arms, looking up to the sun. At the end of a thousand (days),[1677] the Saint Sâkâyanya,[1678] who knew the Self, came near,[1679] burning with splendour, like a fire without smoke. He said to the King: 'Rise, rise! Choose a boon!'

The King, bowing before him, said: 'O Saint, I know not the Self,

---

1675 The performance of all the sacrifices, described in the Maitrâya*n*a-brâhma*n*a, is to lead up in the end to a knowledge of Brahman, by rendering a man fit for receiving the highest knowledge. See Manu VI, 82: 'All that has been declared (above) depends on meditation; for he who is not proficient in the knowledge of the Self reaps not the full reward of the performance of rites.'

1676 Instead of virâgye, a doubtful word, and occurring nowhere else, m. reads vairâgye.

1677 Or years, if we read sahasrasya instead of sahasrâhasya.

1678 The descendant of *S*âkâyana. Saint is perhaps too strong; it means a holy, venerable man, and is frequently applied to a Buddha.

1679 Both M. and m. add mune*h* before antikam, whereas the commentary has râg*ñ*a*h*.

thou knowest the essence (of the Self). We have heard so. Teach it us.'

*S*âkâyanya replied: 'This was achieved of yore; but what thou askest is difficult to obtain.[1680] O Aikshvâka, choose other pleasures.'

The King, touching the Saint's feet with his head, recited this Gâthâ:

3. 'O Saint, What is the use of the enjoyment of pleasures in this offensive, pithless body—a mere mass of bones, skin, sinews, marrow,[1681] flesh, seed, blood, mucus, tears, phlegm, ordure, water,[1682] bile, and slime! What is the use of the enjoyment of pleasures in this body which is assailed by lust, hatred, greed, delusion, fear, anguish, jealousy, separation from what is loved, union with what is not loved,[1683] hunger, thirst, old age, death, illness, grief, and other evils!

4. 'And we see that all this is perishable, as these flies, gnats, and other insects, as herbs and trees,[1684] growing and decaying. And what of these? There are other great ones, mighty wielders of bows, rulers of empires, Sudyumna, Bhûridyumna, Indradyumna, Kuvalayâ*s*va, Yauvanâ*s*va, Vadhrya*s*va, A*s*vapati,[1685] *S*a*s*abindu, Hari*sk*andra, Ambarîsha,[1686] Nahusha, Anânata, *S*aryâti, Yayâti, Anara*n*ya,[1687] Ukshasena,[1688] &c., and kings such as Marutta, Bharata (Daushyanti), and others, who before the eyes of their whole family surrendered the greatest happiness, and passed on from this world to that. And what of these? There are other great ones. We see the destruction[1689] of Gandharvas, Asuras,[1690] Yakshas, Râkshasas, Bhûtas, Ga*n*as, Pi*s*â*k*as, snakes, and vampires. And what of these? There is the drying up of other great oceans, the falling of mountains, the moving of the pole-star, the cutting of the wind-ropes (that hold the stars), the submergence

[1680] Though the commentator must have read etad v*ri*ttam purastâd du*hs*akyam etat pra*s*ñam, yet pra*s*ñam as a neuter is very strange. M. reads etad v*ri*ttam purastât, du*ss*akama pri*kkh*a pra*s*ñam; m. reads etad vratam purastâd a*s*akyam mâ pri*kh*a prasñam aikshvâka, &c. This suggests the reading, etad v*ri*ttam purastâd du*hs*akam mi prikkha pra*s*ñam, i.e. this was settled formerly, do not ask a difficult or an impossible question.

[1681] Read maggâ.

[1682] M. adds vâta before pitta; not m.

[1683] An expression that often occurs in Buddhist literature. See also Manu VI, 62: 'On their separation from those whom they love, and their union with those whom they hate; on their strength overpowered by old age, and their bodies racked with disease.'

[1684] The Sandhi vanaspatayodbhûta for vanaspataya udbhûta is anomalous. M. reads vanaspatayo bhûtapradhva*m*sina*h*.

[1685] M. carries on a*s*vapati*s*a*s*abinduhari*sk*andrâmbarîsha.

[1686] After Ambarîsha, M. reads Nabhushânanutu*s*ayyâtiyayâtyanara*n*yâkshasenâdayo. Nahusha (Naghusha?) is the father of *S*aryâti; Nâbhâga, the father of Ambarîsha. These names are so carelessly written that even the commentator says that the text is either *kh*ândasa or prâmâdika. Anânata is a mere conjecture. It occurs as the name of a *R*ishi in *R*ig-veda IX, 111.

[1687] Anaranya, mentioned in the Mahâbhârata, I, 230.

[1688] M. reads anara*n*yâkshasena.

[1689] M. and m. read nirodhanam.

[1690] M. adds Apsarasas.

of the earth, and the departure of the gods (suras) from their place. In such a world as this, what is the use of the enjoyment of pleasures, if he who has fed[1691] on them is seen[1692] to return (to this world) again and again! Deign therefore to take me out! In this world I am like a frog in a dry well. O Saint, thou art my way, thou art my way.'

SECOND PRAPÂTHAKA.

1. Then the Saint *S*âkâyanya, well pleased, said to the King: 'Great King B*ri*hadratha, thou banner of the race of Ikshvâku, quickly obtaining a knowledge of Self, thou art happy, and art renowned by the name of Marut, the wind.[1693] This indeed is thy Self.'[1694]

'Which,[1695] O Saint,' said the King.

Then the Saint said to him:

2. 'He[1696] who, without stopping the out-breathing,[1697] proceeds upwards (from the sthûla to the sûkshma *s*arîra), and who, modified (by impressions), and yet not modified,[1698] drives away the darkness (of error), he is the Self. Thus said the Saint Maitri.'[1699] And *S*âkâyanya said to the King B*ri*hadratha: 'He who in perfect rest, rising from this body (both from the sthûla and sûkshma), and reaching the highest light,[1700] comes forth in his own form, he is the Self[1701] (thus said *S*âkâyanya); this is the immortal, the fearless, this is Brahman.'

3. 'Now then this is the science of Brahman, and the science of all Upanishads, O King, which was told us by the Saint Maitri.[1702] I shall tell it to thee:

'We hear (in the sacred records) that there were once the Vâlakhilyas,[1703] who had left off all evil, who were vigorous and passionless. They said to the Pragâpati Kratu: "O Saint, this body is without intelligence, like a cart. To what supernatural being belongs

---

[1691] AL and m. read â*s*ritasya, but the commentator explains a*s*itasya.

[1692] Here we have the Maitrâya*n*a Sandhi, d*ris*yatâ iti, instead of d*ris*yata iti; see von Schroeder, Maitrâya*n*î Sa*m*hitâ, p. xxviii. M. and m. read drisyata.

[1693] P*ri*shadasva in the Veda is another name of the Maruts, the storm gods. Afterwards the king is called Marut, VI, 30.

[1694] This sentence is called a Sûtra by the commentator to VI, 32.

[1695] M. reads Kathaya me katamo bhavân iti.

[1696] M. leaves out atha.

[1697] One might read âvish*t*ambhanena, in the sense of while preventing the departure of the vital breath, as in the B*ri*h. Âr. VI, 3, prâ*n*ena rakshann avaram kulâyam.

[1698] M. reads vyathamâno 'vyathamânas.

[1699] M. leaves out Maitri*h*-ity eva*m* hyâha. The commentator explains Maitrir by mitrâyâ apatyam *ri*shir maitrir maitreya. In a later passage (II, 3) M. reads Bhagavatâ Maitre*n*a, likewise the Anubhûtiprakâ*s*a.

[1700] M. adds svaya*m* gyotir upasampadya.

[1701] M. reads esha for ity esha, which seems better.

[1702] M. reads Maitre*n*a vyâkhyâtâ.

[1703] M. M., Translation of Rig-veda, Preface, p. xxxiv.

this great power by which such a body has been made intelligent? Or who is the driver? What thou knowest, O Saint, tell us that."'[1704] Pragâpati answered and said:

4. 'He who in the Sruti is called "Standing above," like passionless ascetics[1705] amidst the objects of the world, he, indeed, the pure, clean, undeveloped, tranquil, breathless, bodiless,[1706] endless, imperishable, firm, everlasting, unborn, independent one, stands in his own greatness, and by him has this body been made intelligent, and he is also the driver of it.'

They said: 'O Saint, How has this been made intelligent by such a being as this which has no desires,[1707] and how is he its driver?' He answered them and said:

5. 'That Self which is very small, invisible, incomprehensible, called Purusha, dwells of his own will here in part;[1708] just as a man who is fast asleep awakes of his own will.[1709] And this part (of the Self) which is entirely intelligent, reflected in man (as the sun in different vessels of water), knowing the body (kshetragña), attested by his conceiving, willing, and believing,[1710] is Pragâpati (lord of creatures), called Visva. By him, the intelligent, is this body made intelligent, and he is the driver thereof.'

They said to him: 'O Saint,[1711] if this has been made intelligent by such a being as this, which has no desires, and if he is the driver thereof, how was it?' He answered them and said:

6. 'In the beginning Pragâpati (the lord of creatures) stood alone. He had no happiness, when alone. Meditating[1712] on himself, he created many creatures. He looked on them and saw they were, like a stone, without understanding, and standing like a lifeless post. He had no

---

[1704] M. adds: brûhîti te ho*k*ur Bhagavan katham anena vâsya*m* yat Bhagavan vetsy etad asmâka*m* brûhîti tân hovâ*k*eti.

[1705] The commentator allows ûtrdhvaretasasa*h* to be taken as a vocative also.

[1706] Nirâtmâ is explained by the commentator as thoughtless, without volition, &c. But âtmâ is frequently used for body also, and this seems more appropriate here. M., however, reads anî*s*âtmâ, and this is the reading explained in the Anubhûtiprakâsa, p. 228, ver. 60. This might mean the Âtman which has not yet assumed the quality of a personal god. See VI, 28; VI, 31.

[1707] The reading anish*th*ena is explained by the commentator as free from any local habitation or attachment. He also mentions the various readings anish*t*ena, free from wishes, and anish*th*ena, the smallest. M. reads ani*kkh*ena, and this seems better than anish*t*ena. The Anubhûtiprakâ*s*a reads likewise ani*kkh*asya.

[1708] I read buddhipûrvam, and again with M. suptasyeva buddhipûrvam. I also read a*m*sena without iti, as in M. The simile seems to be that a man, if he likes, can wake himself at any time of night, and this 'if he likes' is expressed by buddhipûrvam. See Anubhûtiprakâ*s*a, vv. 67, 68.

[1709] M. reads vibodhayati, atha.

[1710] See Maitr. Up. V, 2; Cowell's Translation, pp. 246, 256; Vedântaparibhâshâ, ed. A. Venis, in the Pandit, IV, p. 100.

[1711] M. adds: bhagavann îd*ris*asya katham a*ms*ena vartanam iti tân hovâ*k*a.

[1712] AT. reads abhidhyâyan.

happiness. He thought, I shall enter[1713] within, that they may awake. Making himself like air (vâyu)[1714] he entered within. Being one, he could not do it. Then dividing himself fivefold, he is called Prâ*n*a, Apâna, Samâna, Udâna, Vyâna. Now that[1715] air which rises upwards, is Prâ*n*a. That which moves downwards, is Apâna. That by which these two are supposed to be held, is Vyâna. That[1716] which carries the grosser material of food to the Apâna, and brings the subtler material to each limb, has the name Samâna. [After these (Prâ*n*a, Apâna, Samâna) comes the work of the Vyâna, and between them (the Prâ*n*a, Apâna, and Samâna on one side and the Vyâna on the other) comes the rising of the Udâna.] That which brings up or carries down[1717] what has been drunk and eaten, is the Udâna.[1718]

'Now the Upâ*m*su-vessel (or prâ*n*a) depends on the Antaryâma-vessel (apâna) and the Antaryâma-vessel (apâna) on the Upâ*m*su-vessel[1719] (prâ*n*a), and between these two the self-resplendent (Self) produced heat.[1720] This heat is the purusha (person), and this purusha is Agni Vai*s*vânara. And thus it is said elsewhere:[1721] "Agni Vai*s*vânara is the fire within man by which the food that is eaten is cooked, i.e. digested. Its noise is that which one hears, if one covers one's ears. When a man is on the point of departing this life, he does not hear that noise."

'Now he,[1722] having divided himself fivefold, is hidden in a secret place (buddhi), assuming the nature of mind, having the prâ*n*as as his body, resplendent, having true concepts, and free like ether.[1723] Feeling even thus that he has not attained his object, he thinks from within the

---

1713 It is better to read with M. vi*s*ânîti.

1714 M. vâyum iva.

1715 M. Atha yo 'yam.

1716 M. reads: yo 'ya*m* sthavish*th*am anna*m* dhâtum annasyâpâne sthâpayaty a*n*ish*tham* *k*âṅge 'ṅge sa*m*nayati esha vâva sa samâno 'tha yo 'yam. Leaving, out annam, this seems the right reading. The whole sentence from uttaram to udânasya is left out in M.

1717 M. nigirati *k*aisho vâva sa udâno 'tha yenaitâs sirâ anuvyâptâ esha vâva sa vyâna*h*.

1718 The views of these five kinds of wind differ considerably. Here the commentator explains that the prâ*n*a and apâna, the up-breathing and down-breathing, keep the bodily warmth alive, as bellows keep up a fire. The food cooked in it is distributed by the Samâna, so that the coarse material becomes ordure, the middle flesh, the subtle material mind (manas). The udâna brings up phlegm, &c., while the Vyâna gives strength to the whole body.

1719 Two sacrificial vessels (graha) placed on either side of the stone on which the Soma is squeezed, and here compared to the Prâ*n*a and Apâna, between which the Self (*k*aitanyâtmâ) assumes heat.

1720 M. reads tayor antarâ*l*e *k*aush*n*yam prâsuvat.

1721 See B*r*ihadâra*n*yaka Up. V, 9; *Kh*ând. Up. III, 13, 8.

1722 The Vai*s*vânara or purusha, according to the commentator, but originally the Pragâpati, who had made himself like air, and divided himself into five vital airs.

1723 Thus the âtmâ, with his own qualities and those which he assumes, becomes a living being.

interior of the heart,[1724] "Let me enjoy objects." Therefore, having first broken open these five apertures (of the senses), he enjoys the objects by means of the five reins. This means that these perceptive organs (ear, skin, eye, tongue, nose) are his reins; the active organs (tongue (for speaking), hands, feet, anus, generative organ) his horses; the body his chariot, the mind the charioteer, the whip being the temperament. Driven by that whip, this body goes round like the wheel driven by the potter. This body is made intelligent, and he is the driver thereof.

'This[1725] is indeed the Self, who seeming to be filled with desires, and seeming to be overcome[1726] by bright or dark fruits of action, wanders about in every body (himself remaining free). Because he is not manifest, because he is infinitely small, because he is invisible, because he cannot be grasped, because he is attached to nothing, therefore he, seeming to be changing, an agent in that which is not (prak*ri*ti), is in reality not an agent and unchanging. He is pure, firm, stable, undefiled,[1727] unmoved, free from desire, remaining a spectator, resting in himself Having concealed himself in the cloak of the three qualities he appears as the enjoyer of *ri*ta, as the enjoyer of *ri*ta (of his good works).'

THIRD PRAPÂ*TH*AKA.

1. The Vâlakhilyas said to Pragâpati Kratu: 'O Saint, if thou thus showest the greatness of that Self, then who is that other different one, also called Self,[1728] who really overcome by bright and dark fruits of action, enters on a good or bad birth? Downward or upward is his course,[1729] and overcome by the pairs (distinction between hot and cold, pleasure and pain, &c.) he roams about.'[1730]

2. Pragâpati Kratu replied: 'There is indeed that other[1731] different one, called the elemental Self (Bhûtâtmâ), who, overcome by bright and dark fruits of action, enters on a good or bad birth: downward or upward is his course, and overcome by the pairs he roams about. And

---

[1724] M. reads esho 'sya h*ri*dantare tish*th*ann.

[1725] M. reads: Sa vâ esha âtmeti ho*s*ann iva sitâsitai*h*. This seems better than u*s*anti kavaya*h*, which hardly construes.

[1726] M. reads abhibhûyamânay iva, which again is better than anabhibhûta iva, for he seems to be overcome, but is not, just as he seems to be an agent, but is not. See also III, 1.

[1727] M. has alepo.

[1728] The pure Self, called âtmâ, brahma, *k*inmâtram, prag*ñ*ânaghanam, &c., after entering what he had himself created, and no longer distinguishing himself from the created things (bhûta), is called Bhûtâtmâ.

[1729] M. reads here and afterwards avâkam ûrdhva*m* vâ gatidvandvai*h*.

[1730] M. adds at the end, paribhramatîti katama esha iti, tân hovâ*k*eti, and leaves it out at the end of § 2.

[1731] M. here reads avara.

this is his explanation: The five Tanmâtrâs[1732] (sound, touch, form, taste, smell) are called Bhûta; also the five Mahâbhûtas (gross elements) are called Bhûta. Then the aggregate[1733] of all these is called *s*arîra, body.[1734] And lastly he of whom it was said that he dwelt in the body,[1735] he is called Bhûtâtmâ, the elemental Self. Thus his immortal Self[1736] is like a drop of water on a lotus leaf,[1737] and he himself is overcome by the qualities of nature. Then,[1738] because he is thus overcome, he becomes bewildered, and because he is bewildered, he saw not the creator, the holy Lord, abiding within himself. Carried along by the waves of the qualities,[1739] darkened in his imaginations, unstable, fickle, crippled, full of desires, vacillating, he enters into belief, believing "I am he," "this is mine;"[1740] he binds his Self by his Self, as a bird with a net, and overcome afterwards by the fruits of what he has done, he enters on a good and bad birth; downward or upward is his course, and overcome by the pairs he roams about.'

They asked: 'Which is it?' And he answered them:

3. 'This also has elsewhere been said: He who acts, is the elemental Self; he who causes to act by means of the organs,[1741] is the inner man (anta*h*purusha). Now as even a ball of iron, pervaded (overcome) by fire, and hammered by smiths, becomes manifold (assumes different forms, such as crooked, round, large, small[1742]), thus the elemental Self, pervaded (overcome) by the inner man, and hammered by the qualities, becomes manifold.[1743] And the four tribes (mammals, birds, &c.), the fourteen worlds (Bhûr, &c.), with all the number of beings, multiplied eighty-four times,[1744] all this appears as manifoldness. And those multiplied things are impelled by man (purusha) as the wheel by the potter.[1745] And as when the ball of iron is hammered, the fire is not overcome, so the (inner) man is not overcome, but the elemental Self is overcome, because it has united

[1732] M. reads tanmâtrâ*n*i.

[1733] M. reads teshâ*m* samudayas ta*kkh*arîram.

[1734] The commentator distinguishes between liṅga-*s*arîra, consisting of prâ*n*as, indriyas, the anta*h*karana, and the sûkshmabhûtas; and the sthûla-*s*arîra, consisting of the five Mahâbhûtas.

[1735] M. reads *s*arîram ity uktam.

[1736] M. reads athâsti tasyâ*h* bindur iva.

[1737] It sticks to it, yet it can easily run off again.

[1738] M. reads Ato, and the commentator explains atho by ata*h* kâra*n*ât, adding sandhi*h kh*ândasa*h*.

[1739] See VI, 30.

[1740] M. reads aha*m* so mamedam.

[1741] M. anta*h*kara*n*ai*h*.

[1742] See commentary, p. 48, l. 7.

[1743] AI. reads upety atha trigu*n*a*m k*aturgâlam.

[1744] M. reads *k*aturas*i*tilakshayonipari*n*atam. See also Anubhûtiprakâ*s*a, ver. 118.

[1745] M*ri*tyava seems an impossible word, though the commentator twice explains it as kulâla, potter. M. reads *k*akri*n*eti, which seems preferable. Weber conjectures m*ri*tpa*k*a.

itself (with the elements).

4. 'And it has been said elsewhere:[1746] This body produced from marriage, and endowed with growth[1747] in darkness, came forth by the urinary passage, was built up with bones, bedaubed with flesh, thatched with skin, filled with ordure, urine, bile, slime, marrow, fat, oil,[1748] and many impurities besides, like a treasury full of treasures.[1749]

5. 'And it has been said elsewhere: Bewilderment, fear, grief, sleep, sloth, carelessness, decay, sorrow, hunger, thirst, niggardliness, wrath, infidelity, ignorance, envy, cruelty,[1750] folly, shamelessness, meanness,[1751] pride, changeability,[1752] these are the results of the quality of darkness (tama*h*).[1753]

'Inward thirst, fondness, passion, covetousness, unkindness, love, hatred, deceit,[1754] jealousy, vain restlessness, fickleness,[1755] unstableness, emulation, greed, patronising of friends, family pride, aversion to disagreeable objects, devotion to agreeable objects, whispering,[1756] prodigality, these are the results of the quality of passion (ragas).

'By these he is filled, by these he is overcome, and therefore this elemental Self assumes manifold forms, yes, manifold forms.'

FOURTH PRAPÂ*TH*AKA.

1. The Vâlakhilyas, whose passions were subdued, approached him full of amazement and said: 'O Saint, we bow before thee; teach thou, for thou art the way, and there is no other for us. What process is there

---

[1746] Part of this passage has been before the mind of the author of the Mânava-dharma*s*âstra, when writing, VI, 76, 77: asthisthû*n*a*m* snâyuyutam mâ*m*sa*s*o*n*italepanam, *k*armâvanaddha*m* durgandhi pûr*n*am mûtrapurîshayo*h*, garâ*s*okasamâvish*ta*m rogâyatanam âturam ragasvalam anitya*m* *k*a bhûtâvâsam ima*m* tyaget. The same verses occur in the Mahâbhârata XII, 12463-4, only with tyaga at the end, instead of tyaget. The rendering of asthibhi*s* *k*itam by asthisthû*n*am shows that *k*ita was understood to mean piled or built up, i.e. supported by bones.

[1747] Instead of sa*m*v*ri*ddhyupetam M. reads sa*m*viddhyapetam.

[1748] M. adds snâyu after vasâ, and instead of âmayai*h* reads malai*h*. This reading, malai*h*, would seem preferable, though Manu's rogâyatanam might be quoted in support of âmayai*h*. The exact meaning of vasâ is given in the Âryavidyâsudhâkara, p. 82, l. 9.

[1749] Therefore should wise people not identify their true Self with the body. M. reads vasuneti.

[1750] M. reads vaikâru*n*yam.

[1751] Instead of nirâk*ri*tityam M. reads nik*ri*tatvam, which is decidedly preferable. We may take it to mean either meanness, as opposed to uddhatatvam, overbearing, or knavery, the usual meaning of nik*ri*ti.

[1752] M. reads asatvam, possibly for asattvam.

[1753] M. reads tâmasânvitai*h*, and afterwards râgasânvitai*h*; also t*ri*shnâ instead of antast*ri*shnâ.

[1754] M. reads vyavartatvam.

[1755] It should be ka*ñk*alatvam.

[1756] M. reads mattasvaro.

for the elemental Self, by which, after leaving this (identity with the elemental body), he obtains union[1757] with the (true) Self?' Pragâpati Kratu said to them:

2. 'It has been said elsewhere: Like the waves in large rivers, that which has been done before, cannot be turned back, and, like the tide of the sea, the approach of death is hard to stem. Bound[1758] by the fetters of the fruits of good and evil, like a cripple; without freedom, like a man in prison; beset by many fears, like one standing before Yama (the judge of the dead); intoxicated by the wine of illusion, like one intoxicated by wine; rushing about, like one possessed by an evil spirit; bitten by the world, like one bitten by a great serpent; darkened by passion, like the night; illusory, like magic; false, like a dream; pithless, like the inside of the Kadalî; changing its dress in a moment, like an actor;[1759] fair in appearance, like a painted wall, thus they call him; and therefore it is said:

'Sound,[1760] touch, and other things are like nothings; if the elemental Self is attached to them, it will not remember the Highest Place.[1761]

3. 'This is indeed the remedy for the elemental Self: Acquirement of the knowledge of the Veda, performance of one's own duty, therefore conformity on the part of each man to the order to which he happens to belong. This[1762] is indeed the rule for one's own duty, other performances are like the mere branches of a stem.[1763] Through it one obtains the Highest above, otherwise one falls downward.[1764] Thus is one's own duty declared, which is to be found in the Vedas. No one belongs truly to an order (â*s*rama) who transgresses his own law.[1765] And if people say, that a man does not belong to any of the orders, and that he is an ascetic,[1766] this is wrong, though, on the other hand, no one who is not an ascetic brings his sacrificial works to perfection or obtains knowledge of the Highest Self.[1767] For thus it is said:

1757 Instead of the irregular sâyogyam, M. always reads sâyugyam.

1758 It is not quite clear what is the subject to which all these adjectives refer. M. reads baddho for baddham, but afterwards agrees with the text as published by Cowell.

1759 M. reads na*t*avat.

1760 M. reads ye 'rthâ anarthâ iva te sthitâ*h*, esham.

1761 M. reads na smaret paramam padam.

1762 M. reads svadharma eva sarva*m* dhatte, stambha*s*âkhevetarâni.

1763 The commentator considers the other sacrificial performances as hurtful, and to be avoided.

1764 M. reads anyathâdha*h* pataty, esha.

1765 The rules of the order to which he belongs.

1766 A Tapasvin is free from the restrictions of the preceding âsramas, but he must have obeyed them first, before he can become a real Tapasvin.

1767 M. reads â*s*rameshv evâvasthitas tapasvî *k*ety u*k*yata ity, etad apy uktam, &c. This would mean, 'For it is said that he only who has dwelt in the â*s*ramas is also called a Tapasvin, a real ascetic; and this also has been said, that no one obtains self-knowledge

'By ascetic penance goodness is obtained, from goodness understanding is reached, from understanding the Self is obtained, and he who has obtained that, does not return.[1768]

4. '"Brahman is," thus said one who knew the science of Brahman; and this penance is the door to Brahman, thus said one who by penance had cast off all sin. The syllable Om is the manifest greatness of Brahman, thus said one who well grounded (in Brahman) always meditates on it. Therefore by knowledge, by penance, and by meditation is Brahman gained. Thus one goes beyond[1769] Brahman (Hira*n*yagarbha), and to a divinity higher than the gods; nay, he who knows this, and worships Brahman by these three (by knowledge, penance, and meditation), obtains bliss imperishable, infinite, and unchangeable. Then freed from those things (the senses of the body, &c.) by which he was filled and overcome, a mere charioteer,[1770] he obtains union with the Self.'

5. The Vâlakhilyas said: 'O Saint, thou art the teacher, thou art the teacher.[1771] What thou hast said, has been properly laid up in our mind. Now answer us a further question: Agni, Vâyu, Âditya, Time (kâla) which is Breath (prâ*n*a[1772]), Food (anna), Brahmâ,[1773] Rudra, Vish*n*u, thus do some meditate on one, some on another. Say which of these is the best for us.' He said to them:

6. 'These are but the chief manifestations of the highest, the immortal, the incorporeal Brahman. He who is devoted to one, rejoices here in his world (presence), thus he said. Brahman indeed is all this, and a man may meditate on, worship, or discard also those which[1774] are its chief manifestations. With these (deities) he proceeds to higher and higher worlds, and when all things perish, he becomes one with the Purusha, yes, with the Purusha.'

---

except an ascetic.' This is not impossible, but the commentator follows the text as printed by Cowell. AI. reads âtmag*ñ*ânenâdhigama*h*, karma*s*uddhi.

[1768] M. reads manasâ prâpyate tv âtmâ hy âtmâptyâ na nivartata iti.

[1769] M. reads pura eta, which may be right.

[1770] Rathita*h* is a very strange word, but, like everything else, it is explained by the commentator, viz. as ratham prâpito rathitva*m* *k*a prâpita iti yâvat. Nevertheless the reading of M. seems to me preferable, viz. atha yai*h* paripûr*n*o 'bhibhûto 'ya*m* tathaitai*s* *k*a, tai*h* sarvair vimukta svâtmany eva sâyugyam upaiti. I should prefer vimuktas tv âtmany eva, and translate, 'But then, freed from all those things by which he was filled and likewise was overcome by them, he obtains union with the Self.'

[1771] M. reads the second time abhivâdy asmîti, which is no improvement. It might have been ativâdyasîti.

[1772] M. reads Yama*h* prâ*n*o.

[1773] This is, of course, the personal Brahmâ of the Hindu triad. To distinguish this personal Brahmâ from the impersonal, I sometimes give his name in the nom. masc., Brahmâ, and not the grammatical base, Brahman.

[1774] M. reads yâ vâ asyâ. The commentator explains yâ vâsyâ*h* by vâsayogyâ*h*; or yâ vâ yâ*h* by kâ*s*kit, admitting a Vedic irregularity which is not quite clear.

FIFTH PRAPÂ*TH*AKA[1775].

1. Next follows Kutsâyana's hymn of praise:

'Thou art Brahmâ, and thou art Vish*n*u, thou art Rudra, thou Pragâpati,[1776] thou art Agni, Varu*n*a, Vâyu, thou art Indra, thou the Moon.

'Thou art Anna[1777] (the food or the eater), thou art Yama, thou art the Earth, thou art All, thou art the Imperishable. In thee all things exist in many forms, whether for their natural or for their own (higher) ends.

'Lord of the Universe, glory to thee! Thou art the Self of All, thou art the maker of All, the enjoyer of All; thou art all life, and the lord of all pleasure and joy.[1778] Glory to thee, the tranquil, the deeply hidden, the incomprehensible, the immeasurable, without beginning and without end.'

2. 'In the beginning[1779] darkness (tamas) alone was this. It was in the Highest, and, moved by the Highest, it becomes uneven. Thus it becomes obscurity (ragas).[1780] Then this obscurity, being moved, becomes uneven. Thus it becomes goodness (sattva). Then this goodness, being moved, the essence flowed forth.[1781] This is that part (or state of Self) which is entirely intelligent, reflected in man (as the sun is in different vessels of water) knowing the body (kshetrag*ñ*a), attested by his conceiving, willing, and believing, it is Pragâpati, called Vi*s*va. His manifestations have been declared before.[1782] Now that part of him which belongs to darkness, that, O students,[1783] is he who is called Rudra. That part of him which belongs to obscurity, that, O

[1775] At the beginning of the fifth Prapâ*th*aka my MS. gives the *S*lokas which in the printed edition are found in VI, 34, Atreme *s*lokâ bhavanti, yathâ nirindhano vahnir, &c., to nirvishaya*m* sm*ri*tam. Then follows as § 2, Atha yatheda*m* Kautsyâyanistutis, tvam, &c.

[1776] The commentator explains Brahmâ by Hira*ny*agarbha and Pragâpati by Virâg.

[1777] M. reads tvam Manus, tva*m* Yama*s* *k*a tvam, p*ri*thivî tvam athâ*k*yuta*h*, which is so clearly the right reading that it is difficult to understand how the mistakes arose which are presupposed by the commentary. See Taitt. Up. II, 2.

[1778] M. reads vi*s*vakrî*d*ârati*h* prabhu*h*, which seems better.

[1779] M. reads tamo vâ idam ekam âsta tat paro syât tat pare*n*eritam. It may have been tat pare 'sthât.

[1780] M. reads etad vai ragaso rûpam, which is better, or, at least, more in accordance with what follows.

[1781] M. reads sattvam everitarasas sa*m* prâs*ri*vat.

[1782] A reference to Maitr. Up. II, 5, would have saved the commentator much trouble. M. has a better text. It leaves out vi*s*veti or vi*s*vâkhyas after pragâpati, which may be wrong, but then goes on: tasya proktâ agryâs tanavo brahmâ rudro vish*n*ur iti. In enumerating the three agryâs tanava*h*, however, M. is less consistent, for it begins with ragas or Brahmâ, then goes on to tamas or Rudra, and ends with sattva or Vish*n*u. The Anubhûtiprakâsa, verse 142, has the right succession.

[1783] This vocative, brahma*k*ârino, is always left out in M.

students, is he who is called Brahmâ. That part of him which belongs to goodness, that, O students, is he who is called Vish*n*u. He being one, becomes three, becomes eight,[1784] becomes eleven,[1785] becomes twelve, becomes infinite. Because[1786] he thus came to be, he is the Being (neut.), he moves about, having entered all beings, he has become the Lord of all beings. He is the Self within and without, yes, within and without.'

SIXTH PRAPÂ*TH*AKA[1787].

1. He (the Self) bears the Self in two ways,[1788] as he who is Prâ*n*a (breath), and as he who is Âditya (the sun). Therefore there are two paths for him,[1789] within and without, and they both turn back in a day and night. The Sun is the outer Self, the inner Self is Breath. Hence the motion of the inner Self is inferred from the motion of the outer Self[1790] For thus it is said:

'He who knows, and has thrown off all evil, the overseer of the senses,[1791] the pure-minded, firmly grounded (in the Self) and looking away (from all earthly objects), he is the same.' Likewise the motion of the outer Self is inferred from the motion of the inner Self. For thus it is said:

'He who within the sun is the golden person, who looks upon this earth from his golden place, he is the same who, after entering the inner lotus of the heart,[1792] devours food (perceives sensuous objects, &c.)'

[1784] The five prâ*n*as, the sun, moon, and asterisms.

[1785] The eleven organs of sense and action, which, by dividing manas and buddhi, become twelve.

[1786] M. reads aparimitadhâ *k*odbhûtatvâd bhûteshu *k*arati pravish*t*a*h* sarvabhûtânâm.

[1787] The commentator describes the sixth and seventh chapters as Khila, supplementary, and does not think that they are closely connected with the chief object of the Upanishad. This chief object was to show that there is only one thinking Self (*k*idâtmâ) to be known, and that the same is to be meditated on as manifested in the different forms of Rudra, Brahmâ, Vish*n*u, &c. Thus the highest object of those who wish for final liberation has been explained before, as well as the proper means of obtaining that liberation. What follows are statements of the greatness of the various manifestations of the Âtman, and advice how to worship them. My MS. gives the beginning of the sixth Prapâ*th*aka, but ends with the end of the eighth paragraph. The verses in paragraph 34, as mentioned before, are given in my MS. at the end of the fourth Prapâ*th*aka. My translation deviates considerably from the commentary. The text is obscure and not always correct. My rule has been throughout to begin a new sentence with eva*m* hy âha, 'for thus it is said,' which introduces proofs of what has been said before. The passages thus quoted as proofs from the Veda are often difficult to understand, nor do they always consist of a complete sentence. My translation therefore is often purely tentative.

[1788] M. reads dvitîyâ for dvidhâ.

[1789] M. reads dvau vâ etâv asya pa*ñk*adhâ nâmântar bahi*s* *k*âhorâtre tau vyâvartete.

[1790] While the sun goes round Meru in a day and a night, the breath performs 21,000 breathings, or, more exactly, 21,600. M. reads bahirâtmagatyâ.

[1791] M. reads adhyaksha, not akshâdhyaksha.

[1792] M. reads sa esho 'nta*h* pushkare h*ri*tpushkare vâ*s*rito.

2. And he who having entered the inner lotus of the heart, devours food, the same, having gone te, the sky as the fire of the sun, called Time, and being invisible, devours all beings as his food.

What is that lotus and of what is it made? (the Vâlakhilyas ask.[1793])

That lotus is the same as the ether; the four quarters, and the four intermediate points are its leaves.[1794]

These two, Breath and the Sun, move on near to each other (in the heart and in the ether). Let him worship these two, with the syllable Om, with the Vyâh*ri*ti words (bhû*h*, bhuva*h*, svar), and with the Sâvitrî hymn.

3. There are two forms of Brahman,[1795] the material (effect) and the immaterial (cause). The material is false, the immaterial is true. That which is true is Brahman, that which is Brahman is light, and that which is light is the Sun.[1796] And this Sun became the Self of that Om.

He divided himself threefold, for Om consists of three letters, a + u + m. Through them all this[1797] is contained in him as warp and woof. For thus it is said:

'Meditate on that Sun as Om, join your Self (the breath) with the (Self of the) Sun.'

4. And thus it has been said elsewhere: The Udgîtha (of the Sâma-veda) is the Pra*n*ava[1798] (of the *Ri*g-veda), and the Pra*n*ava is the Udgîtha, and thus the Sun is Udgîtha, and he is Pra*n*ava or Om. For thus it is said:[1799]

'The Udgîtha, called Pra*n*ava, the leader (in the performance of sacrifices), the bright,[1800] the sleepless, free from old age and death, three-footed,[1801] consisting of three letters (a + u + m), and likewise to be known as fivefold (five prâ*n*as) placed in the cave.' And it is also said:

'The three-footed Brahman has its root upward,[1802] the branches are ether, wind, fire, water, earth, &c. This one Asvattha[1803] by name, the world, is Brahman, and of it that is the light which is called the Sun,

---

[1793] The commentator ascribes the dialogue still to the Vâlakhilyas and Pragâpati Kratu.

[1794] M. reads dalasa*m*sthâ âsur vâgni*h* parata etai*h* prâ*n*âdityâv etâ.

[1795] See B*ri*h. Up. II, 3, 1.

[1796] Professor Cowell, after giving the various readings of his MSS., says, 'the true reading would seem to be yat satya*m* tad brahma, yad brahma ta*g* *g*yotir, yad *g*yotis sa âditya*h*.' This is exactly the reading of my own MS.

[1797] M. reads *k*aivâsminn ity evam hyâha.

[1798] The mystic syllable Om.

[1799] See *Kh*ândogyopanishad I, 5; Maitr. Up. VI, 25.

[1800] M. reads nâmarûpam.

[1801] The three feet of the prâ*n*a are waking, slumber, and deep sleep; the three feet of the sun, the three worlds, bhû*h*, bhuva*h*, svar, as in VII, 11. See also *Kh*ând. Up. III, 12.

[1802] Cf. Ka*th*. Up. VI, 1.

[1803] A*s*vattha, lit. fig-tree, then frequently used metaphorically as a name of the world. Here explained as, it will not stand till to-morrow.'

and it is also the light of that syllable Om. Therefore let him for ever worship that (breath and sun, as manifestations of Brahman) with the syllable Om.'

He alone enlightens us. For thus it is said:

'This alone is the pure syllable, this alone is the highest syllable; he who knows that syllable only, whatever he desires, is his.'[1804]

5. And thus it has been said elsewhere: This Om[1805] is the sound-endowed body of him (Prâ*n*âdityâtman). This is his gender-endowed body, viz. feminine, masculine, neuter. This is his light-endowed body, viz. Agni, Vâyu, Âditya. This is his lord-endowed body, viz. Brahmâ, Rudra, Vish*n*u. This is his mouth-endowed body, viz. Gârhapatya, Dakshi*n*âgni, Âhavanîya.[1806] This is his knowledge-endowed body, viz. *Rik*, Yagus, Sâman. This is his world-endowed body, viz. Bhû*h*, Bhuva*h*, Svar. This is his time-endowed body, viz. Past, Present, Future. This is his heat-endowed body, viz. Breath, Fire, Sun. This is his growth-endowed body, viz. Food, Water, Moon. This is his thought-endowed body, viz. intellect, mind, personality. This is his breath-endowed body, viz. Prâ*n*a, Apâna, Vyâna. Therefore by the aforesaid syllable Om are all these here enumerated bodies praised and identified (with the Prâ*n*âdityâtman). For thus it is said:[1807]

'O Satyakâma, the syllable Om is the high and the low Brahman.'

6. This[1808] (world) was unuttered.[1809] Then forsooth Pragâpati, having brooded, uttered it in the words Bhû*h*, Bhuva*h*, Svar. This is the grossest body of that Pragâpati, consisting of the three worlds.[1810] Of that body Svar is the head, Bhuva*h* the navel, Bhû*h* the feet, the sun the eye. For in the eye is fixed man's great measure, because with the eye he makes all measurements. The eye is truth (satyam), for the person (purusha) dwelling in the eye proceeds to all things (knows all objects with certainty). Therefore let a man worship with the Vyâh*ri*tis, Bhû*h*, Bhuva*h*, Svar, for thus Pragâpati, the Self of All, is worshipped as the (sun, the) Eye of All.[1811] For thus it is said:

'This (the sun) is Pragâpati's all-supporting body, for in it this all[1812] is hid (by the light of the sun); and in this all it (the light) is hid.

[1804] Ka*th*. Up. II, 16.

[1805] M. reads tanûr yom iti.

[1806] The fires on the three altars.

[1807] Pras*ñ*a Up. V, 2.

[1808] M. reads atha vyâttam.

[1809] So far the pra*n*ava or Om has been explained; now follows the explanation of the Vyâh*ri*tis; cf. VI, 2. Vyâh*ri*ti is derived from vyâhar, and means an utterance.

[1810] Cf. VI, 5.

[1811] M. reads vi*s*vata*s*kakshur.

[1812] Pragâpati, according to the commentator, is identified with Satya, the true, because sat means the three worlds, and these (bhû*h*, bhuva*h*, svar) are said to be his body. Hence probably the insertion of Satyam before Pragâpati at the beginning of the paragraph. Then he argues, as the eye has been called satya, and as the eye is Âditya, therefore Pragâpati also, being Satya, is Âditya, the sun. And again, if the sun is

Therefore this is worshipped.'[1813]

7. (The Sâvitrî begins:[1814]) Tat Savitur vare*n*yam, i.e. 'this of Savit*ri*, to be chosen.' Here the Âditya (sun) is Savit*ri*, and the same is to be chosen by the love(r) of Self, thus say the Brahma-teachers.

(Then follows the next foot in the Savit*ri*): Bhargo devasya dhîmahi, i.e. 'the splendour of the god we meditate on.' Here the god is Savit*ri*, and therefore he who is called his splendour, him I meditate on, thus say the Brahma-teachers.

(Then follows the last foot): Dhiyo yo na*h* pra*k*odayât, i.e. 'who should stir up our thoughts.' Here the dhiya*h* are thoughts, and he should stir these up for us, thus say the Brahma-teachers.

(He now explains the word bhargas). Now he who is called bhargas is he who is placed in yonder Âditya (sun), or he who is the pupil in the eye.[1815] And he is so called, because his going (gati) is by rays (bhâbhi*h*); or because he parches (bhargayati) and makes the world to shrivel up. Rudra is called Bhargas, thus say the Brahma-teachers. Or bha means that he lights up these worlds; ra, that he delights these beings, ga that these creatures go to him and come from him; therefore being a bha-ra-ga, he is called Bhargas.

Sûrya[1816] (sun) is so called, because Soma is continually squeezed out (su). Savit*ri* (sun) is so called, because he brings forth (su). Âditya (sun) is so called, because he takes up (âdâ, scil. vapour, or the life of man). Pâvana[1817] is so called, because he purifies (pu). Apas, water, is so called, because it nourishes (pyâ).

And it is said:

'Surely the Self (absorbed in Prâ*n*a, breath), which is called Immortal,[1818] is the thinker, the perceiver, the goer, the evacuator,[1819] the delighter, the doer, the speaker, the taster, the smeller, the seer, the hearer, and he touches. He is Vibhu (the pervader), who has entered into the body.' And it is said:

'When the knowledge is twofold (subjective and objective), then he hears, sees, smells, tastes, and touches (something), for it is the Self

---

worshipped (by the vyâh*ri*tis) then, like the sun, the eye of all, Pragâpati also, the self of all, is worshipped.

[1813] Eshopasîta is impossible. We must either read, with the commentator, etam upâsîta, or with M. eshopasiteti.

[1814] He now proceeds to explain the worship of the Sâvitrî verse, which had been mentioned in VI, 2, after the Om and the Vyâh*ri*tis, as the third mode of worshipping Prâ*n*a (breath) and Âditya (sun), these being two correlative embodiments of the Self. The Sâvitrî is found in *Ri*g-veda III, 6 2, 10, but it is here explained in a purely philosophical sense. See also B*ri*h. Up. VI, 3, 6.

[1815] M. reads târake 'ksh*n*i.

[1816] Sûrya is considered as the daily performer of the Prâta*h*savana, &c., the sacrifice at which Soma is squeezed out as an offering.

[1817] M. reads pavamânât pavamâna*h*.

[1818] M. reads am*ri*tâkhya*s* *k*etâkhya*s* *k*etâ.

[1819] M. reads gantâ s*ri*sh*t*â.

that knows everything.'

But when the knowledge is not twofold (subjective only), without effect, cause, and action,[1820] without a name, without a comparison, without a predicate[1821]—what is that? It cannot be told.[1822]

8. And the same Self is also called I*s*âna (lord), *S*ambhu, Bhava, Rudra (tâmasa); Pragâpati (lord of creatures), Vi*s*vas*rig* (creator of all), Hira*n*yagarbha, Satyam (truth), Prâ*n*a, (breath), Ha*m*sa (râgasa); *S*âst*ri* (ruler), Vish*n*u, Nârâya*n*a (sâttvika); Arka, Savit*ri*, Dhât*ri* (supporter), Vidhât*ri*[1823] (creator), Samrâg (king), Indra, Indu (moon). He is also he who warms, the Sun, hidden by the thousand-eyed golden egg, as one fire by another. He is to be thought after, he is to be sought after. Having said farewell to all living beings, having gone to the forest, and having renounced all sensuous objects, let man perceive the Self[1824] from his own body.

'(See him)[1825] who assumes all forms, the golden, who knows all things, who ascends highest, alone in his splendour, and warms us; the thousand-rayed, who abides in a hundred places, the spirit of all creatures, the Sun, rises.'[1826]

9. Therefore he who by knowing this has become the Self of both Breath and Sun, meditates (while meditating on them) on his Self, sacrifices (while sacrificing to them) to his Self-this meditation, the mind thus absorbed in these acts, is praised by the wise.

Then let him purify the contamination of the mind by the verse U*kkh*ish*t*opahatam, &c.:[1827] 'Be it food left, or food defiled by left food, be it food given by a sinner, food coming from a dead person, or from one impure from childbirth, may the purifying power of Vasu, may Agni, and the rays of Savit*ri*, purify it, and all my sin.'[1828]

First (before eating) he surrounds (the offered food) with water (in rincing his mouth[1829]). Then saying, Svâhâ to Prâ*n*a, Svâhâ to Apâna, Svâhâ to Vyâna, Svâhâ to Samâna, Svâhâ to Udâna, he offers (the food)

[1820] M. reads kâryakăra*n*akarmavinirmuktam.

[1821] Nirupâkhyam, rightly translated by Cowell by 'without a predicate,' and rendered by the commentator by apramaya, i.e. not to be measured, not to be classed, i.e. without a predicate.

[1822] I have translated this in accordance with a well-known passage, quoted by the commentator from the B*ri*hadâranyaka, rather than in accordance with his own interpretation.

[1823] M. leaves out vidhâtâ.

[1824] Instead of the peculiar Maitrâya*n*i reading, svâ*ñ* *s*ârîrâd, AI. reads svâ*s* *kh*arîrâd.

[1825] The oneness of the Sun and the Breath is proclaimed in the following verse of the Pra*sñ*a Upanishad I, 8.

[1826] Here ends the M. manuscript, with the following title: iti *s*rîyagu*ss*âkhâyâm Maitrâya*n*îyabrâhma*n*opanishadi shash*th*a*h* prapâ*th*aka*h*. Samâptâ.

[1827] In the following paragraphs the taking of food is represented as a sacrifice offered by the Self to the Self (âtmayaganarûpam bhoganam, p. 106, l. 13).

[1828] Several words have been inserted in this verse, spoiling the metre.

[1829] See *Kh*ând. Up. V, 2.

with five invocations (in the fire of the mouth). What is over, he eats in silence, and then he surrounds (the food) once more afterwards with water (rincing the mouth after his meal). Having washed let him, after sacrificing to himself, meditate on his Self with these two verses, Prâ*n*o 'gni*h* and Vi*s*vo 'si, viz. 'May the Highest Self as breath, as fire (digestive heat), as consisting of the five vital airs, having entered (the body), himself satisfied, satisfy all, he who protects all.' 'Thou art Vi*s*va (all), thou art Vai*s*vânara (fire), all that is born is upheld by thee; may all offerings enter into thee; creatures live where thou grantest immortality to all.' He who eats according to this rule, does not in turn become food for others.

10. There is something else to be known. There is a further modification of this Self-sacrifice (the eating), namely, the food and the eater thereof. This is the explanation. The thinking Purusha (person), when he abides within the Pradhâna (nature), is the feeder who feeds on the food supplied by Prak*ri*ti (nature). The elemental Self[1830] is truly his food, his maker being Pradhâna (nature[1831]). Therefore what is composed of the three qualities (gu*n*as) is the food, but the person within is the feeder. And for this the evidence is supplied by the senses. For animals spring from seed, and as the seed is the food, therefore it is clear that what is food is Pradhâna (the seed or cause of everything). Therefore, as has been said, the Purusha (person) is the eater, Prak*ri*ti, the food; and abiding within it he feeds. All that begins with the Mahat[1832] (power of intellect) and ends with the Vi*s*eshas (elements[1833]), being developed from the distinction of nature with its three qualities, is the sign (that there must be a Purusha, an intelligent subject). And in this manner the way with its fourteen steps has been explained.[1834] (This is comprehended in the following verse): 'This world is indeed the food, called pleasure, pain, and error (the result of the three qualities); there is no laying hold of the taste of the seed (cause), so long as there is no development (in the shape of effect).' And in its three stages also it has the character of food, as childhood, youth, and old age; for, because these are developed, therefore there is in them the character of food.[1835]

And in the following manner does the perception of Pradhâna (nature) take place, after it has become manifest:—Intellect and the rest, such as determination, conception, consciousness, are for the

---

[1830] See before, III, 3.

[1831] This is very doubtful, in fact, unintelligible. The commentator says, asya bhûtâtmana*h* kartâ pradhâna*h* pûrvokta*h*, so 'pi bhogya ity artha*h*.

[1832] Technical terms, afterwards adopted by the Sâṅkhya philosophers.

[1833] Professor Cowell observes that the term vi*s*esha, as here applied to the five gross elements, occurs in the Sâṅkhya-kârika, ver. 38.

[1834] Five receptive, five active organs, and four kinds of consciousness.

[1835] Its very development proves it to be food. Cowell.

tasting (of the effects of Pradhâna). Then there are the five (perceptive organs) intended for the (five) objects of senses, for to taste them. And thus are all acts of the five active organs, and the acts of the five Prâ*n*as or vital airs (for the tasting of their corresponding objects). Thus what is manifest (of nature) is food, and what is not manifest is food. The enjoyer of it is without qualities, but because he has the quality of being an enjoyer, it follows that he possesses intelligence.

As Agni (fire) is the food-eater among the gods, and Soma the food, so he who knows this eats food by Agni (is not defiled by food, as little as Agni, the sacrificial fire). This elemental Self, called Soma (food), is also called Agni, as having undeveloped nature for its mouth (as enjoying through nature, and being independent of it), because it is said, 'The Purusha (person) enjoys nature with its three qualities, by the mouth of undeveloped nature.' He who knows this, is an ascetic, a yogin, he is a performer of the Self-sacrifice (see before). And he who does not touch the objects of the senses when they intrude on him, as no one would touch women intruding into an empty house, he is an ascetic, a yogin, a performer of the Self-sacrifice.

11. This is the highest form of Self, viz. food, for this Prâ*n*a (this body) subsists on food. If it eats not, it cannot perceive, hear, touch, see, smell, taste, and it loses the vital airs.[1836] For thus it is said:

'If it eats, then in full possession of the vital airs, it can perceive, hear, touch, speak, taste, smell, see.' And thus it is said:

'From food are born all creatures that live on earth; afterwards they live on food, and in the end (when they die) they return to it.'[1837]

12. And thus it is said elsewhere: Surely all these creatures run about day and night, wishing to catch food. The sun takes food with his rays, and by it he shines. These vital airs digest, when sprinkled with food. Fire flares up by food, and by Brahmâ (Pragâpati), desirous of food, has all this been made. Therefore let a man worship food as his Self. For thus it is said:

'From food creatures are born, by food they grow when born; because it is eaten and because it cats creatures, therefore it is called food (annam).'

13. And thus it is said elsewhere: This food is the body of the blessed Vish*n*u, called Vi*s*vabh*ri*t (all-sustaining). Breath is the essence of food, mind of breath, knowledge of mind, joy of knowledge. He who knows this is possessed of food, breath, mind, knowledge, and joy. Whatever creatures here on earth eat food, abiding in them he, who knows this, eats food. Food has been called undecaying, food has been called worshipful; food is the breath of animals, food is the oldest, food has been called the physician.

[1836] *Kh*ând. Up. VII, 9, 1.

[1837] Taitt. Up. II, 2.

14. And thus it has been said elsewhere: Food is the cause of all this, time of food, and the sun is the cause of time.[1838] The (visible) form of time is the year, consisting of twelve months, made up of Nimeshas (twinklings) and other measures. Of the year one half (when the sun moves northward) belongs to Agni, the other to Varu*n*a (when the sun moves southward). That which belongs to Agni begins with the asterism of Maghâ, and ends with half of the asterism of Sravish*th*â, the sun stepping down northward. That which belongs to Soma (instead of Varu*n*a) begins with the asterism (of A*s*leshâ), sacred to the Serpents, and ends with half of the asterism of Sravish*th*â, the sun stepping up southward. And then there (are the months) one by one, belonging to the year, each consisting of nine-fourths of asterisms (two asterisms and a quarter being the twelfth part of the passage of the sun through the twenty-seven Nakshatras), each determined by the sun moving together with the asterisms. Because time is imperceptible by sense, therefore this (the progress of the sun, &c.) is its evidence, and by it alone is time proved to exist. Without proof there is no apprehension of what is to be proved; but even what is to be proved can become proof, for the sake of making itself known, if the parts (the twinklings, &c.) can be distinguished from the whole (time[1839]). For thus it is said:

'As many portions of time as there are, through them the sun proceeds: he who worships time as Brahman, from him time moves away very far.' And thus it is said:

'From time all beings flow, from time they grow; in time they obtain rest; time is visible (sun) and invisible (moments).'

15. There are two forms of Brahman, time and non-time. That which was before the (existence of the) sun is non-time and has no parts. That which had its beginning from the sun is time and has parts. Of that which has parts, the year is the form, and from the year are born all creatures; when produced by the year they grow, and go again to rest in the year. Therefore the year is Pragâpati, is time, is food, is the nest of Brahman, is Self. Thus it is said:

'Time ripens and dissolves all beings in the great Self, but he who knows into what time itself is dissolved, he is the knower of the Veda.'

16. This manifest time is the great ocean of creatures. He who is called Savit*ri* (the sun, as begetter) dwells in it, from whence the moon, stars, planets, the year, and the rest are begotten. From them again comes all this, and thus, whatever of good or evil is seen in this world, comes from them. Therefore Brahman is the Self of the sun, and a man should worship the sun under the name of time. Some say the sun is

---

[1838] As food depends on time, therefore time is praised, which again depends on the sun, which is a form of the Self.

[1839] Thus, the commentator says, the existence of the lamp can be proved by the light of the lamp, as the existence of time is proved by what we see, the rising of the sun. All this is very obscure.

Brahman, and thus it is said:

'The sacrificer, the deity that enjoys the sacrifice, the oblation, the hymn, the sacrifice, Vish*n*u, Pragâpati, all this is the Lord, the witness, that shines in yonder orb.'

17. In the beginning Brahman was all this.[1840] He was one, and infinite; infinite in the East, infinite in the South, infinite in the West, infinite in the North, above and below and everywhere infinite. East and the other regions do not exist for him, nor across, nor below, nor above. The Highest Self is not to be fixed, he is unlimited, unborn, not to be reasoned about, not to be conceived. He is like the ether (everywhere), and at the destruction of the universe, he alone is awake. Thus from that ether he wakes all this world, which consists of thought only, and by him alone is all this meditated on, and in him it is dissolved. His is that luminous form which shines in the sun, and the manifold light in the smokeless fire, and the heat which in the stomach digests the food. Thus it is said:

'He who is in the fire, and he who is in the heart, and he who is in the sun, they are one and the same.'

He who knows this becomes one with the one.

18. This is the rule for achieving it (viz. concentration of the mind on the object of meditation): restraint of the breath, restraint of the senses, meditation, fixed attention, investigation, absorption, these are called the sixfold Yoga.[1841] When beholding by this Yoga, he beholds the gold-coloured maker, the lord, the person, Brahman, the cause, then the sage, leaving behind good and evil, makes everything (breath, organs of sense, body, &c.) to be one in the Highest Indestructible (in the pratyagâtman or Brahman). And thus it is said:

'As birds and deer do not approach a burning mountain, so sins never approach those who know Brahman.'

19. And thus it is said elsewhere: When he who knows has, while he is still Prâ*n*a (breath), restrained his mind, and placed all objects of the senses far away from himself, then let him remain without any conceptions. And because the living person, called Prâ*n*a (breath), has been produced here on earth from that which is not Prâ*n*a (the thinking Self), therefore let this Prâ*n*a merge the Prâ*n*a (himself) in what is called the fourth.[1842] And thus it is said:

'What is without thought, though placed in the centre of thought, what cannot be thought, the hidden, the highest—let a man merge his thought there: then will this living being (liṅga) be without

[1840] Brahman used as neuter, but immediately followed by eko 'nanta*h*, &c.

[1841] After having explained the form of what is to be meditated on and the mode of meditation, the Upanishad now teaches the Yoga which serves to keep our thoughts in subjection, and to fix our thoughts on the object of meditation. See Yoga-Sûtras II, 29.

[1842] The fourth stage is meant for the thinking Self, the earlier stages being waking, slumbering, and sleep.

attachment.'[1843]

20. And thus it has been said elsewhere: There is the superior fixed attention (dhâra*n*â) for him, viz. if he presses the tip of the tongue down the palate and restrains voice, mind, and breath, he sees Brahman by discrimination (tarka). And when, after the cessation of mind,[1844] he sees his own Self, smaller than small, and shining, as the Highest Self,[1845] then having seen his Self as the Self, he becomes Self-less, and because he is Self-less, he is without limit, without cause, absorbed in thought. This is the highest mystery, viz. final liberation. And thus it is said:

'Through the serenity of the thought he kills all actions, good or bad; his Self serene, abiding in the Self, obtains imperishable bliss.'

21. And thus it has been said elsewhere: The artery, called Sushumnâ, going upwards (from the heart to the Brahmarandhra), serving as the passage of the Prâ*n*a, is divided within the palate. Through that artery, when it has been joined by the breath (held in subjection), by the sacred syllable Om, and by the mind (absorbed in the contemplation of Brahman), let him proceed upwards,[1846] and after turning the tip of the tongue to the palate, without[1847] using any of the organs of sense, let greatness perceive greatness.[1848] From thence he goes to selflessness, and through selflessness he ceases to be an enjoyer of pleasure and pain, he obtains aloneness (kevalatva, final deliverance). And thus it is said:

'Having successively fixed the breath, after it had been restrained, in the palate, thence having crossed the limit (the life), let him join himself afterwards to the limitless (Brahman) in the crown of the head.'

22. And thus it has been said elsewhere: Two Brahmans have to be meditated on, the word and the non-word. By the word alone is the non-word revealed. Now there is the word Om. Moving upward by it (where all words and all what is meant by them ceases), he arrives at absorption in the non-word (Brahman). This is the way, this is the immortal, this is union, and this is bliss. And as the spider, moving upward by the thread, gains free space, thus also he who meditates,

---

[1843] Professor Cowell offers two renderings of this difficult passage: 'This which is called prâ*n*a, i.e. the individual soul as characterised by the subtil body, will thus no longer appear in its separate individuality from the absence of any conscious subject; or, this subtil body bearing the name of intellect will thus become void of all objects.'

[1844] The commentator remarks that this process is called Lambikâyoga, and the state produced by it Unmanî or Unmanîbhâva; see amanîbhâva, in VI, 34, ver. 7.

[1845] I should have preferred to translate âtmânam âtmanâ pa*s*yati by 'he sees his Self by his Self,' but the commentator takes a slightly different view, and says itthambhâve t*r*itîyâ; paramâtmarûpe*n*a pa*s*yati.

[1846] Cf. Ka*th*a Up. V I, 16 Pra*sñ*a Up. III, 6.

[1847] If we read sa*m*yogya we must follow the commentator in translating by 'uniting the senses with the prâ*n*a and the manas.'

[1848] Let the Self perceive the Self.

moving upward by the syllable Om, gains independence.

Other teachers of the word (as Brahman) think otherwise. They listen to the sound of the ether within the heart while they stop the ears with the thumbs. They compare it to seven noises, like rivers, like a bell, like a brazen vessel, like the wheels of a carriage, like the croaking of frogs, like rain, and as if a man speaks in a cavern. Having passed beyond this variously apprehended sound, and having settled in the supreme, soundless (non-word), unmanifested Brahman, they become undistinguished and undistinguishable, as various flavours of the flowers are lost in the taste of honey. And thus it is said:

'Two Brahmans are to be known, the word-Brahman and the highest Brahman; he who is perfect in the word-Brahman attains the highest Brahman.'[1849]

23. And thus it has been said elsewhere: The syllable Om is what is called the word. And its end is the silent, the soundless, fearless, sorrowless, joyful, satisfied, firm, unwavering, immortal, immovable, certain (Brahman), called Vish*n*u. Let him worship these two, that he may obtain what is higher than everything (final deliverance). For thus it is said:

'He who is the high and the highest god,[1850] by name Om-kâra, he is soundless and free from all distinctions: therefore let a man dwell on him in the crown of his head.'

24. And thus it has been said elsewhere: The body is the bow, the syllable Om is the arrow, its point is the mind. Having cut through the darkness, which consists of ignorance,[1851] it approaches that which is not covered by darkness.[1852] Then having cut through that which was covered (the personal soul), he saw Brahman, flashing like a wheel on fire, bright like the sun, vigorous, beyond all darkness, that which shines forth in yonder sun, in the moon, in the fire, in the lightning.[1853] And having seen him, he obtains immortality. And thus it has been said:

'Meditation is directed to the highest Being (Brahman) within, and (before) to the objects (body, Om, mind); thence the indistinct understanding becomes distinct.

'And when the works of the mind are dissolved, then that bliss which requires no other witness, that is Brahman (Âtman), the immortal, the brilliant, that is the way, that is the (true) world.'

[1849] Cf. Mahâbhârata XII, 8540; Sarvadar*s*ana-saṅgraha, p. 147; Cowell's Translation, p. 271.

[1850] The commentator takes devâ as deva*h*, though the accent is against it; see Schroeder, Über die Maitrâya*n*î Sa*m*hitâ, p. 9, l. 11.

[1851] Should it not be, 'darkness is the mark?'

[1852] Atamâvish*t*a, explained as an irregular compound, atama-âvish*t*am, tama-âve*s*anarahitam.

[1853] Cf. Bhagavadgîtâ XV, 12.

25. And thus it has been said elsewhere: He who has his senses hidden as in sleep, and who, while in the cavern of his senses (his body), but no longer ruled by them, sees, as in a dream, with the purest intellect, Him who is called Pra*n*ava (Om), the leader,[1854] the bright, the sleepless, free from old age, from death, and sorrow, he is himself also called Pra*n*ava, and becomes a leader, bright, sleepless, free from old age, from death, and sorrow. And thus it is said:

'Because in this manner he joins the Prâ*n*a (breath), the Om, and this Universe in its manifold forms, or because they join themselves (to him), therefore this (process of meditation) is called Yoga (joining).

'The oneness of breath, mind, and senses, and then the surrendering of all conceptions, that is called Yoga.'

26. And thus it has also been said elsewhere: As a sportsman, after drawing out the denizens of the waters with a net, offers them (as a sacrifice) in the fire of his stomach, thus are these Prâ*n*as (vital airs), after they have been drawn out with the syllable Om, offered in the faultless fire (Brahman).[1855]

Hence he is like a heated vessel (full of clarified butter); for as the clarified butter in the heated vessel lights up, when touched with grass and sticks, thus does this being which is called Not-breath (Âtman) light up, when touched by the Prâ*n*as (the vital airs).[1856] And that which flares up, that is the manifest form of Brahman, that is the highest place of Vish*n*u,[1857] that is the essence of Rudra. And this, dividing his Self in endless ways, fills all these worlds. And thus it is said:

'As the sparks from the fire, and as the rays from the sun, thus do his Prâ*n*as and the rest in proper order again and again proceed from him here on earth.'[1858]

27. And thus it has also been said elsewhere: This is the heat of the highest, the immortal, the incorporeal Brahman, viz. the warmth of the body. And this body is the clarified butter (poured on it, by which the heat of Brahman, otherwise invisible, is lighted up). Then, being manifest, it is placed in the ether (of the heart). Then by concentration they thus remove that ether which is within the heart, so that its light appears, as it were.[1859] Therefore the worshipper becomes identified with that light without much delay. As a ball of iron, if placed in the

---

[1854] Cf. VI, 4.

[1855] Cf. *S*vetâ*s*vatara-upanishad III, 10.

[1856] As the fire which exists invisibly in a heated vessel becomes visible when the heated vessel is touched with sticks dipped in butter, thus the Âtman in the body appears only when the Prâ*n*as are diffused in it. Or, as the clarified butter, heated together with the vessel, lights up grass that comes in contact with it, so does this Âtman (called Not-breath), by heating its two bodies which are pervaded by the reflections of the thinker, light up everything brought in contact with it, viz. the world.

[1857] See Ka*th*a Up. III, 9.

[1858] See VI, 31; B*ri*h. Up. II, 1, 10.

[1859] The light was always there, but it seems then only to appear.

earth, becomes earth without much delay, and as, when it has once become a clod of earth, fire and smiths have nothing more to do with that ball of iron, thus does thought (without delay) disappear, together with its support.[1860] And thus it is said:

'The shrine which consists of the ether in the heart, the blissful, the highest retreat, that is our own, that is our goal, and that is the heat and brightness of the fire and the sun.'

28. And thus it has been said elsewhere: After having left behind the body, the organs of sense, and the objects of sense (as no longer belonging to us), and having seized the bow whose stick is fortitude and whose string is asceticism, having struck down also with the arrow, which consists in freedom from egotism, the first guardian of the door of Brahman (for if man looks at the world egotistically, then, taking the diadem of passion, the earrings of greed and envy, and the staff of sloth, sleep, and sin, and having seized the bow whose string is anger, and whose stick is lust, he destroys with the arrow which consists of wishes, all beings)—having therefore killed that guardian, he crosses by means of the boat Om to the other side of the ether within the heart, and when the ether becomes revealed (as Brahman), he enters slowly, as a miner seeking minerals in a mine, into the Hall of Brahman. After that let him, by means of the doctrine of his teacher, break through the shrine of Brahman, which consists of the four nets (of food, breath, mind, knowledge, till he reaches the last shrine, that of blessedness and identity with Brahman). Thenceforth pure, clean, undeveloped, tranquil, breathless, bodiless, endless, imperishable, firm, everlasting, unborn and independent, he stands on his own greatness,[1861] and having seen (the Self), standing in his own greatness, he looks on the wheel of the world as one (who has alighted from a chariot) looks on its revolving wheel. And thus it is said:

'If a man practises Yoga for six months and is thoroughly free (from the outer world), then the perfect Yoga (union), which is endless, high, and hidden, is accomplished.

'But if a man, though well enlightened (by instruction), is still pierced by (the gu*n*as of) passion and darkness, and attached to his children, wife, and house, then perfect Yoga is never accomplished.'[1862]

29. After he had thus spoken (to B*ri*hadratha), *S*âkâyanya,

---

[1860] The commentator explains this differently. He says that the similes are intended to show how, as soon as the impediment is removed, the worshipper obtains his true form, i.e. becomes Brahman. Afterwards he explains *k*ittam, thought, by the individual thinker, and declares that he vanishes together with the thought, which forms the â*s*raya, the place, or the upâdhi, the outward form. Or again, he says that the *k*itta, the mind, vanishes with its outward sign, viz. the thoughts and imaginations.

[1861] See Maitr. Up. II, 4; VI, 31.

[1862] This would seem to have been the end of the dialogue between Pragâpati and the Vâlakhilyas, which, as related by *S*âkâyanya to King B*ri*hadratha, began in II, 3. See, however, VII, 8.

absorbed in thought, bowed before him, and said: 'O King, by means of this Brahma-knowledge have the sons of Pragâpati (the Vâlakhilyas) gone to the road of Brahman. Through the practice of Yoga a man obtains contentment, power to endure good and evil, and tranquillity. Let no man preach this most secret doctrine to any one who is not his son or his pupil,[1863] and who is not of a serene mind. To him alone who is devoted to his teacher only, and endowed with all necessary qualities, may he communicate it.[1864]

30. 'Om! Having settled down in a pure place let him, being pure himself, and firm in goodness, study the truth, speak the truth, think the truth, and offer sacrifice to the truth.[1865] Henceforth he has become another; by obtaining the reward of Brahman his fetters are cut asunder, he knows no hope, no fear from others as little as from himself, he knows no desires; and having attained imperishable, infinite happiness, he stands blessed in the true Brahman, who longs for a true man.[1866] Freedom from desires is, as it were, the highest prize to be taken from the best treasure (Brahman). For a man full of all desires, being possessed of will, imagination, and belief, is a slave; but he who is the opposite, is free.

'Here some say, it is the Gu*n*a[1867] (i.e. the so-called Mahat, the principle of intellect which, according to the Sâṅkhyas, is the result of the Gu*n*as or qualities), which, through the differences of nature (acquired in the former states of existence), goes into bondage to the will, and that deliverance takes place (for the Gu*n*a) when the fault of the will has been removed. (But this is not our view), because (call it gu*n*a, intellect, buddhi, manas, mind, ahaṅkâra, egotism, it is not the mind that acts, but) he sees by the mind (as his instrument), he hears by the mind; and all that we call desire, imagination, doubt, belief, unbelief, certainty, uncertainty, shame, thought, fear, all that is but mind (manas). Carried along by the waves of the qualities, darkened in his imaginations, unstable, fickle, crippled, full of desires, vacillating, he enters into belief, believing I am he, this is mine, and he binds his Self by his Self, as a bird with a net.[1868] Therefore a man, being possessed of will, imagination, and belief, is a slave, but he who is the opposite is free. For this reason let a man stand free from will,

---

[1863] *S*vet. Up. VI, 22; B*r*ih. Up. VI. 3, 12.

[1864] Here may have been the end of a chapter, but the story of *S*âkâyanya and B*r*ihadratha is continued to VI, 30.

[1865] The truth or the true are explained by, (1) the book which teaches the Highest Self; (2) by Brahman, who is to be spoken about; (3) by Brahman, who is to be meditated on; (4) by Brahman, who is to be worshipped in thought.

[1866] I have translated this according to the commentary, but I should prefer to read satyâbhilâshi*n*i.

[1867] The passages within brackets had to be added from the commentary in order to make the text intelligible, at least according to Râmatîrtha's views.

[1868] See III, 2.

imagination, and belief—this is the sign of liberty, this is the path that leads to Brahman, this is the opening of the door, and through it he will go to the other shore of darkness. All desires are there fulfilled. And for this they quote a verse:

'"When the five instruments of knowledge stand still together with the mind, and when the intellect does not move, that is called the highest state."'[1869]

Having thus said, Sâkâyanya became absorbed in thought. Then Marut (i.e. the King B*ri*hadratha),[1870] having bowed before him and duly worshipped him, went full of contentment to the Northern Path,[1871] for there is no way thither by any side-road. This is the path to Brahman. Having burst open the solar door, he rose on high and went away. And here they quote:

'There are endless rays (arteries) for the Self who, like a lamp, dwells in the heart: white and black, brown and blue, tawny and reddish.[1872]

'One of them (the Sushumnâ) leads upwards, piercing the solar orb: by it, having stepped beyond the world of Brahman, they go to the highest path.

'The other hundred rays[1873] rise upwards also, and on them the worshipper reaches the mansions belonging to the different bodies of gods.

'But the manifest rays of dim colour which lead downwards, by them a man travels on and on helplessly, to enjoy the fruits of his actions here.'

Therefore it is said that the holy Âditya (sun) is the cause of new births (to those who do not worship him), of heaven (to those who worship him as a god), of liberty (to those who worship him as Brahman).[1874]

31. Some one asks: 'Of what nature are those organs of sense that go forth (towards their objects)? Who sends them out here, or who holds them back?'

Another answers: 'Their nature is the Self; the Self sends them out, or holds them back; also the Apsaras (enticing objects of sense), and the solar rays (and other deities presiding over the senses).'

Now the Self devours the objects by the five rays (the organs of

---

[1869] See the same verse in Ka*th*a Up. VI, 10.

[1870] See before, II, 1.

[1871] See Pras*ñ*a Up. I, 10,' But those who have sought the Self by penance, abstinence, faith, and knowledge, gain by the Northern Path Âditya, the sun.'

[1872] See *Kh*ând. Up. VIII, 6.

[1873] A similar verse, but with characteristic variations, occurs in the *Kh*ând. Up. VIII, 6, 6, and in the Ka*th*a Up. VI, 16.

[1874] Here ends the story of *S*âkâyanya, which began I, 2, and was carried on through chap. VI, though that chapter and the seventh are called Khilas, or supplements, and though the MS. M. also ends, as we saw, with the eighth paragraph of the sixth chapter.

sense); then who is the Self?

He who has been defined by the terms pure, clean, undeveloped, tranquil,[1875] &c., who is to be apprehended independently by his own peculiar signs. That sign of him who has no signs, is like what the pervading heat is of fire, the purest taste of water; thus say some.[1876] It is speech, hearing, sight, mind, breath; thus say others.[1877] It is intellect, retention, remembering, knowledge; thus say others.[1878] Now all these are signs of the Self in the same sense in which here on earth shoots are the signs of seed, or smoke, light, and sparks of fire. And for this they quote:[1879]

'As the sparks from the fire, and as the rays from the sun, thus do his Prâ*n*as and the rest in proper order again and again proceed from him here on earth.'

32. From this very Self, abiding within his Self, come forth all Prâ*n*as (speech, &c.), all worlds, all Vedas, all gods, and all beings; its Upanishad (revelation)[1880] is that it is 'the true of the true.' Now as from a fire of green wood, when kindled, clouds of smoke come forth by themselves (though belonging to the fire), thus from that great Being has been breathed forth all this which is the *Ri*g-veda, the Yagur-veda, the Sama-veda, the Atharvâṅgirasas (Atharva-veda), the Itihâsa (legendary stories), the Purâ*n*a (accounts of the creation, &c.), Vidyâ (ceremonial doctrines), the Upanishads, the *S*lokas (verses interspersed in the Upanishads, &c.), the Sûtras (compendious statements), the Anuvyâkhyânas (explanatory notes), the Vyâkhyânas (elucidations)[1881]—all these things are his.

33. This fire (the Gârhapatya-fire) with five bricks is the year. And its five bricks are spring, summer, rainy season, autumn, winter; and by them the fire has a head, two sides, a centre, and a tail. This earth (the Gârhapatya-fire) here is the first sacrificial pile for Pragâpati, who

---

[1875] See before, II, 4; VI, 13.

[1876] See *S*vet. Up. VI, 13.

[1877] See Ken. Up. 2.

[1878] See Ait. Up. III, 2. Here we find dh*ri*ti (holding), sm*ri*ti (remembering), prag*ñ*ânam (knowledge), but not buddhi. Prag*ñ*ânam seems the right reading, and is supported by M.

[1879] See before, VI, 26.

[1880] Revelation is here the rendering of Upanishad, upanigamayit*ri*tvât sâkshâdrahasyam, and the true (sattya) is explained first by the five elements, and then by that which is their real essence.

[1881] See *Kh*ând. Up. VI, 1. The explanations given of these literary titles are on the whole the same as those we had before in similar passages. What is peculiar to Râmatîrtha is that he explains Upanishad by such passages as we had just now, viz. its Upanishad is that it is the true of the true. The *S*lokas are, explained as verses like those in VI, 19, a*k*itta*m* *k*ittamadhyastham. The Sûtras are explained as comprehensive sentences, such as II, 2, aya*m* vâva khalv âtmâ te. Anuvyâkhyânas are taken as explanations following on the Sûtra in II, 2, beginning with atha ya esho*kkh*vâsâvish*t*ambhanena. The Vyâkhyânas are taken as fuller statements of the meaning contained in the Sûtra, such as the dialogue between the Vâlakhilyas and Kratu.

knows the Purusha (the Virâ*g*). It presented the sacrificer to Vâyu, (the wind) by lifting him with the hands to the sky. That Vâyu is Prâ*n*a (Hira*n*yagarbha).

Prâ*n*a is Agni (the Dakshi*n*âgni-fire), and its bricks are the five vital breaths, Prâ*n*a, Vyâna, Apâna, Samâna, Udâna; and by them the fire has a head, two sides, a centre, and a tail. This sky (the Dakshi*n*âgni-fire) here is the second sacrificial pile for Pragâpati, who knows the Purusha. It presented the sacrificer to Indra, by lifting him with the hands to heaven. That Indra is Âditya, the sun.

That (Indra) is the Agni (the Âhavanîya-fire), and its bricks are the *Rik*, the Yagush, the Sâman, the Atharvâṅgirasas, the Itihâsa, and the Purâ*n*a; and by them the fire has a head, two sides, a tail, and a centre. This heaven (Âhavanîya-fire) is the third sacrificial pile for Pragâpati, who knows the Purusha. With the hands it makes a present of the sacrificer to the Knower of the Self (Pragâpati); then the Knower of the Self, lifting him up, presented him to Brahman. In him he becomes full of happiness and joy.

34. The earth is the Gârhapatya-fire, the sky the Dakshina-fire, the heaven the Âhavanîya-fire; and therefore they are also the Pavamâna (pure), the Pâvaka (purifying), and the *S*u*k*i (bright).[1882]. By this (by the three deities, Pavamâna, Pâvaka, and *S*u*k*i) the sacrifice (of the three fires, the Gârhapatya, Dakshi*n*a, and Âhavanîya) is manifested. And because the digestive fire also is a compound of the Pavamâna, Pâvaka, and *S*u*k*i, therefore that fire is to receive oblations, is to be laid with bricks, is to be praised, and to be meditated on. The sacrificer, when he has seized the oblation, wishes[1883] to perform his meditation of the deity:

'The gold-coloured bird abides in the heart, and in the sun—a diver bird, a swan, strong in splendour; him we worship in the fire.'

Having recited the verse, he discovers its meaning, viz. the adorable splendour of Savit*ri* (sun) is to be meditated on by him who, abiding within his mind, meditates thereon. Here he attains the place of rest for the mind, he holds it within his own Self. On this there are the following verses:

(1) As a fire without fuel becomes quiet in its place,[1884] thus do the thoughts, when all activity ceases, become quiet[1885] in their place.

(2) Even in a mind which loves the truth[1886] and has gone to rest in itself there arise, when it is deluded by the objects of sense, wrongs

[1882] Epithets of Agni, the sacrificial-fire, pavamâna applying to the Gârhapatya-fire, pâvaka to the Dakshi*n*a-fire, and *suk*i to the Âhavanîya-fire. The construction of the sentence, however, is imperfect.

[1883] This means, he ought to perform it.

[1884] Dies in the fireplace.

[1885] M. reads upa*s*âmyati twice.

[1886] M. reads satyakâmina*h*.

resulting from former acts.[1887]

(3) For thoughts alone cause the round of births;[1888] let a man strive to purify his thoughts. What a man thinks, that he is: this is the old secret.[1889]

(4) By the serenity of his thoughts a man blots out all actions, whether good or bad. Dwelling within his Self with serene thoughts, he obtains imperishable happiness.

(5) If the thoughts of a man were so fixed on Brahman as they are on the things of this world, who would not then be freed from bondage?

(6) The mind, it is said, is of two kinds, pure or impure; impure from the contact with lust, pure when free from lust.[1890]

(7) When a man, having freed his mind from sloth, distraction, and vacillation, becomes as it were delivered from his mind,[1891] that is the highest point.

(8) The mind must be restrained in the heart till it comes to an end;—that is knowledge, that is liberty: all the rest are extensions of the ties[1892] (which bind us to this life).

(9) That happiness which belongs to a mind which by deep meditation has been washed[1893] clean from all impurity and has entered within the Self, cannot be described here by words; it can be felt by the inward power only.[1894]

(10) Water in water, fire in fire, ether in ether, no one can distinguish them; likewise a man whose mind has entered (till it cannot be distinguished from the Self), attains liberty.

(11) Mind alone is the cause of bondage and liberty for men; if attached to the world, it becomes bound; if free from the world, that is liberty.[1895]

Therefore those who do not offer the Agnihotra (as described above), who do not lay the fires (with the bricks, as described above), who are ignorant (of the mind being the cause of the round of births), who do not meditate (on the Self in the solar orb) are debarred from remembering the ethereal place of Brahman. Therefore that fire is to receive oblations, is to be laid with bricks, is to be praised, to be

---

[1887] The commentator inserts a negative.

[1888] M. reads sa*m*sâra*h*.

[1889] This is very like the teaching of the Dhammapada, I, 1.

[1890] Cf. Ind. Stud. II, 60. Brahmavindu Up. v. 1, where we read kâmasaṅkalpam, as in MS. M.

[1891] See note to VI, 20.

[1892] M. reads moksha*sk*a and *s*eshâs tu. The commentator says that this line is easy, but it is so by no means. Professor Cowell translates granthavistarâ*h* by book-prolixity, but this sounds very strange in an Upanishad. I am not satisfied with my own translation, but it may stand till a better one is found. M. reads g*ri*ndhavistarâ*h*. The granthis are mentioned in *Kh*ând. Up. VII, 26; Ka*th*. Up. VI, 15.

[1893] M. reads nirdhûta.

[1894] M. reads kara*n*eti.

[1895] M. reads vishayâsaktam muktyai.

meditated on.

35.[1896] Adoration to Agni, the dweller on earth, who remembers his world. Grant that world to this thy worshipper!

Adoration to Vâyu, the dweller in the sky, who remembers his world. Grant that world to this thy worshipper!

Adoration to Âditya, the dweller in heaven, who remembers his world. Grant that world to this thy worshipper!

Adoration to Brahman, who dwells everywhere, who remembers all. Grant all to this thy worshipper!

The mouth of the true (Brahman) is covered with a golden lid; open that, O Pûshan (sun), that we may go to the true one, who pervades all (Vish*n*u).[1897]

He who is the person in the sun, I am he.[1898]

And what is meant by the true one is the essence of the sun, that which is bright, personal, sexless;[1899] a portion (only) of the light which pervades the ether; which is, as it were, in the midst of the sun, and in the eye, and in the fire. That is Brahman, that is immortal, that is splendour.

That is the true one, a portion (only) of the light which pervades the ether, which is in the midst of the sun, the immortal, of which Soma (the moon) and the vital breaths also are offshoots: that is Brahman, that is immortal, that is splendour.

That is the true one, a portion (only) of the light which pervades the ether, which in the midst of the sun shines as Yagus, viz. as Om, as water, light, essence, immortal, Brahman, Bhû*h*, Bhuva*h*, Svar, Om.

'The eight-footed,[1900] the bright, the swan, bound with three threads, the infinitely small, the imperishable, blind for good and evil, kindled with light—he who sees him, sees everything.'

A portion (only) of the light which pervades the ether, are the two rays rising in the midst of the sun. That is the knower[1901] (the Sun), the true one. That is the Yagus, that is the heat, that is Agni (fire), that is Vâyu (wind), that is breath, that is water, that is the moon, that is bright, that is immortal, that is the place of Brahman, that is the ocean of light. In that ocean the sacrificers are dissolved[1902] like salt, and that is oneness with Brahman, for all desires are there fulfilled. And here

---

1896 Next follow invocations to be addressed to the deities.

1897 The verse occurs in a more original form in Tal. Up. 15.

1898 The commentator adds iti after aham.

1899 *Kh*ând. Up. I, 6, 6; *S*vet. Up. V, 10.

1900 The eight feet are explained as the eight regions, or âroga and the rest. The swan is the sun. The three threads are the three Vedas; see *K*ûl. Up. I, 1; Ind. Stud. IX, 11—ash*t*apâda*m* *s*u*k*ir ha*m*sa*m* trisûtram ma*n*im avyayam, dvivartamâna*m* taigasaiddha*m* sarva*h* pa*s*yan na pa*s*yati. Here the eight feet are explained as the five elements, manas, buddhi, and aha*n*kâra.

1901 Savit for savit*ri*.

1902 Vlîyante for vilîyante.

they quote:

'Like a lamp, moved by a gentle wind, he who dwells within the gods shines forth. He who knows this, he is the knower, he knows the difference (between the high and the highest Brahman); having obtained unity, he becomes identified with it.

'They who rise up in endless number, like spray drops (from the sea), like lightnings from the light within the clouds in the highest heaven, they, when they have entered into the light of glory (Brahman), appear like so many flame-crests in the track of fire.'

36. There are two manifestations of the Brahma-light: one is tranquil, the other lively. Of that which is tranquil, the ether is the support; of that which is lively, food. Therefore (to the former) sacrifice must be offered on the house-altar with hymns, herbs, ghee, meat, cakes, sthâlîpâka, and other things; to the latter, with meat and drinks (belonging to the great sacrifices) thrown into the mouth, for the mouth is the Âhavanîya-fire; and this is done to increase our bodily vigour, to gain the world of purity, and for the sake of immortality. And here they quote:

'Let him who longs for heaven, offer an Agnihotra. By an Agnish*t*oma he wins the kingdom of Yama; by Uktha, the kingdom of Soma; by a Sho*d*asin-sacrifice, the kingdom of Sûrya; by an Atirâtra-sacrifice, the kingdom of Indra; by the sacrifices beginning with the twelve-night sacrifice and ending with the thousand years' sacrifice, the world of Pragâpati.

'As a lamp burns so long as the vessel that holds the wick is filled with oil, these two, the Self and the bright Sun, remain so long as the egg (of the world) and he who dwells within it hold together.'

37. Therefore let a man perform all these ceremonies with the syllable Om (at the beginning). Its splendour is endless, and it is declared to be threefold, in the fire (of the altar), in the sun (the deity), in the breath (the sacrificer). Now this is the channel to increase the food, which makes what is offered in the fire ascend to the sun. The sap which flows from thence, rains down as with the sound of a hymn. 'By it there are vital breaths, from them there is offspring. And here they quote:

'"The offering which is offered in the fire, goes to the sun; the sun rains it down by his rays; thus food comes, and from food the birth of living beings."'[1903]

And thus he said:

'The oblation which is properly thrown on the fire, goes toward the sun; from the sun comes rain, from rain food, from food living beings.'

38. He who offers the Agnihotra breaks through the net of desire. Then, cutting through bewilderment, never approving of anger,

[1903] See Manu III, 76.

meditating on one desire (that of liberty), he breaks through the shrine of Brahman with its four nets, and proceeds thence to the ether. For having there broken through the (four) spheres of the Sun, the Moon, the Fire, and Goodness, he then, being purified himself, beholds dwelling in goodness, immovable, immortal, indestructible, firm, bearing the name of Vish*n*u, the highest abode, endowed with love of truth and omniscience, the self-dependent Intelligence (Brahman), standing in its own greatness. And here they quote:

'In the midst of the sun stands the moon, in the midst of the moon the fire, in the midst of fire goodness, in the midst of goodness the Eternal.'

Having meditated on him who has the breadth of a thumb within the span (of the heart) in the body, who is smaller than small, he obtains the nature of the Highest; there all desires are fulfilled. And on this they quote:

'Having the breadth of a thumb within the span (of the heart) in the body, like the flame of a lamp, burning twofold or threefold, that glorified Brahman, the great God, has entered into all the worlds. Om! Adoration to Brahman! Adoration!'

SEVENTH PRAPÂTHAKA.

1. Agni, the Gâyatra (metre), the Triv*ri*t (hymn), the Rathantara (song), the spring, the upward breath (prâ*n*a), the Nakshatras, the Vasus (deities)—these rise in the East; they warm, they rain, they praise[1904] (the sun), they enter again into him (the sun), they look out from him (the sun). He (the sun) is inconceivable, without form, deep, covered, blameless, solid, unfathomable, without qualities, pure, brilliant, enjoying the play of the three qualities, awful, not caused, a master-magician,[1905] the omniscient, the mighty, immeasurable, without beginning or end, blissful, unborn, wise, indescribable, the creator of all things, the self of all things, the enjoyer of all things, the ruler of all things, the centre of the centre of all things.

2. Indra, the Trish*t*ubh (metre), the Pa*ñk*adasa (hymn), the B*ri*hat (song), the summer, the through-going breath (Vyâna), Soma, the Rudras—these rise in the South; they warm, they rain, they praise, they enter again into him, they look out from him. He (the sun) is without end or beginning, unmeasured, unlimited, not to be moved by another, self-dependent, without sign, without form, of endless power, the creator, the maker of light.

3. The Maruts, the *G*agatî (metre), the Saptada*s*a (hymn), the Vairupa (song), the rainy season, the downward breath (apâna), *S*ukra,

[1904] Other MSS. read sruvanti, which seems better.

[1905] See VII, 11, abhidhyâtur vist*ri*tir iva.

the Âdityas—these rise in the West; they warm, they rain, they praise, they enter again into him, they look out from him. That is the tranquil, the soundless, fearless, sorrowless, joyful, satisfied, firm, immovable, immortal, eternal, true, the highest abode, bearing the name of Vish*n*u.

4. The Vi*s*ve Devas, the Anush*t*ubh (metre), the Ekavi*m*sa (hymn), the Vairâga (song), the autumn, the equal breath (samâna), Varu*n*a, the Sâdhyas—these rise in the North; they warm, they rain, they praise, they enter again into him, they look out from him. He is pure within, purifying, undeveloped, tranquil, breathless, selfless, endless.

5. Mitrâ-Varu*n*au, the Pańkti (metre), the Tri*n*avatrayastri*m*sa (hymns), the *S*âkvara-raivata (songs), the snowy and dewy seasons, the out-going breath (udâna), the Ańgiras, the Moon—these rise above; they warm, they rain, they praise, they enter again into him, they look out from him—who is called Pra*n*ava (Om), the leader, consisting of light, without sleep, old age, death, and sorrow.

6. *S*ani (Saturn), Rahu and Ketu (the ascending and descending nodes), the serpents, Rakshas, Yakshas, men, birds, *s*arabhas, elephants, &c.—these rise below; they warm, they rain, they praise, they enter again into him, they look out from him—he who is wise, who keeps things in their right place, the centre of all, the imperishable, the pure, the purifier, the bright, the patient, the tranquil.

7. And he is indeed the Self, smaller (than small) within the heart, kindled like fire, endowed with all forms. Of him is all this food, within him all creatures are woven. That Self is free from sin,[1906] free from old age, from death and grief, from hunger and thirst, imagining nothing but what it ought to imagine, and desiring nothing but what it ought to desire. He is the highest lord, he is the supreme master of all beings, the guardian of all beings, a boundary keeping all things apart in their right places.[1907] He the Self, the lord, is indeed Sambhu, Bhava, Rudra, Pragâpati, the creator of all, Hira*n*yagarbha, the true, breath, the swan, the ruler, the eternal, Vish*n*u, Nârâya*n*a. And he who abides in the fire, and he who abides in the heart, and he who abides in the sun, they are one and the same. To thee who art this, endowed with all forms, settled in the true ether, be adoration!

8. Now follow the impediments in the way of knowledge, O King![1908] This is indeed the origin of the net of bewilderment, that one who is worthy of heaven lives with those who are not worthy of heaven. That is it. Though they have been told that there is a grove before them, they cling to a small shrub. And others also who are always merry, always abroad, always begging, always making a living by handiwork; and others who are begging in towns, performing

---

[1906] See *Kh*ând. Up. VIII, 7, 1.

[1907] See *Kh*ând. Up. VIII, 4, 1, where we find setur vidh*r*itir eshâ*m* lokânâm.

[1908] This king is not meant for B*ri*hadratha.

sacrifices for those who are not allowed to offer sacrifices, who make themselves the pupils of *S*ûdras, and *S*ûdras who know the sacred books; and others who are malignant, who use bad language, dancers, prize-fighters, travelling mendicants, actors, those who have been degraded in the king's service; and others who for money pretend that they can lay (the evil influences) of Yakshas, Râkshasas, ghosts, goblins, devils, serpents, imps, &c.; and others who falsely wear red dresses,[1909] earrings, and skulls; and others who wish to entice by the jugglery of false arguments, mere comparisons and paralogisms, the believers in the Veda—with all these he should not live together. They are clearly thieves, and unworthy of heaven. And thus it is said:

'The world unsettled by the paralogisms of the denial of Self, by false comparisons and arguments, does not know what is the difference between Veda and philosophy.'[1910]

9. B*ri*haspati, having become *S*ukra, brought forth that false knowledge for the safety of Indra and for the destruction of the Asuras. By it they show that good is evil, and that evil is good. They say that we ought to ponder on the (new) law, which upsets the Veda and the other sacred books.[1911] Therefore let no one ponder on that false knowledge: it is wrong, it is, as it were, barren. Its reward lasts only as long as the pleasure lasts, as with one who has fallen from his caste. Let that false science not be attempted, for thus it is said:

(i) Widely opposed and divergent are these two, the one known as false knowledge, the other as knowledge. I (Yama) believe Na*k*iketas to be possessed by a desire of knowledge; even many pleasures do not move thee.[1912]

(2) He who knows at the same time both the imperfect (sacrifice, &c.) and the perfect knowledge (of the Self), he crosses death by means of the imperfect, and obtains immortality by means of the perfect knowledge.[1913]

(3) Those who are wrapped up[1914] in the midst of imperfect knowledge, fancying themselves alone wise and learned, they wander about floundering and deceived, like the blind led by the blind.[1915]

[1909] This refers to people who claim the privileges and licence of Sannyâsins without having passed through the discipline of the preceding â*s*ramas, As this was one of the chief complaints made against the followers of *S*âkyamuni, it might refer to Buddhists, but it ought to be borne in mind that there were Buddhists before Buddha.

[1910] If we translate thus, the use of vidyâ for v*ri*thâ vidyâ is unusual; if we follow the commentary, we should have to translate, he does not know the Veda and the other knowledge.

[1911] All this may refer to Buddhists, but not by necessity, for there were heretics, such as B*ri*haspati, long before *S*âkyamuni.

[1912] See Ka*th*. Up. II, 4.

[1913] See Vâ*g*. Up. 11.

[1914] Vesh*t*yamânâ*h*, instead of vartamânâ*h*.

[1915] See Ka*th*. Up. II, 5.

10. The gods and the demons, wishing to know the Self, went into the presence of Brahman (their father, Pragâpati).[1916] Having bowed before him, they said: 'O blessed one, we wish to know the Self, do thou tell us.' Then, after having pondered a long while, he thought, these demons are not yet self-subdued;[1917] therefore a very different Self was told to them (from what was told to the gods). On that Self these deluded demons take their stand, clinging to it, destroying the true means of salvation (the Veda), preaching untruth. What is untrue they see as true, as in jugglery. Therefore, what is taught in the Vedas, that is true. What is said in the Vedas, on that the wise keep their stand. Therefore let a Brâhman not read what is not of the Veda, or this will be the result.

11. This is indeed the nature of it (the Veda), the supreme light of the ether which is within the heart. This is taught as threefold, in the fire, in the sun, in the breath. This is indeed the nature of it, the syllable Om, of the ether which is within the heart. By it (by the Om) that (light) starts, rises, breathes forth, becomes for ever the means of the worship and knowledge of Brahman. That (light, in the shape of Om), when there is breathing, takes the place of the internal heat, free from all brightness.[1918] This is like the action of smoke; for when there is a breath of air, the smoke, first rising to the sky in one column, follows afterwards every bough, envelopes it and takes its shape.[1919] It is like throwing salt (into water), like heating ghee.[1920] The Veda comes and goes like the dissolving view of a master-magician.[1921] And here they quote:

'Why then is it called "like lightning?" Because as soon as it comes forth (as Om) it lights up the whole body. Therefore let a man worship that boundless light by the syllable Om.'

(1) The man in the eye who abides in the right eye, he is Indra, and

---

[1916] Cf. *Kh*ând. Up. VIII, 8.

[1917] I prefer ayatâtmâna*h*, though it is the easier (sugama) reading, as compared with anyatâtmâna*h*, those who seek for the Self elsewhere, namely, in the body. It seems to me to refer to those who, without having subdued the passions of their body, wish to obtain the knowledge of the Highest Self. Possibly, however, the author may have intended a climax from anyatâtmâna*h* to anyatamam.

[1918] This seems to be the meaning adopted by the commentator; but may it not be, sending forth brightness?

[1919] The simile is not very clear. The light of Brahman is below the sphere of fire in the body. That sphere of fire becoming heated, the light of Brahman becomes manifest. When the fire has been fanned by the wind of sonant breath, then the light of Brahman, embodying itself in the wind and the fire, manifests itself first in the mere sound of Om, but afterwards, checked by throat, palate, &c., it assumes the form of articulate letters, and ends by becoming the Veda in its many branches.

[1920] As these are outwardly changed, without losing their nature, thus the light of Brahman, though assuming the different forms of the Veda, remains itself.

[1921] See before, VII, 1.

his wife abides in the left eye.[1922]

(2) The union of these two takes place in the cavity within the heart, and the ball of blood which is there, that is indeed the vigour and life of these two.

(3) There is a channel going from the heart so far, and fixed in that eye; that is the artery for both of them, being one, divided into two.

(4) The mind excites the fire of the body, that fire stirs the breath, and the breath, moving in the chest, produces the low sound.

(5) Brought forth by the touch of the fire, as with a churning-stick, it is at first a minim, from the minim it becomes in the throat a double minim; on the tip of the tongue know that it is a treble minim, and, when uttered, they call it the alphabet (στοιχεῖα).[1923]

(6) He who sees this, does not see death, nor disease, nor misery, for seeing he sees all (objectively, not as affecting him subjectively); he becomes all everywhere (he becomes Brahman).

(7) There is the person in the eye, there is he who walks as in sleep, he who is sound asleep, and he who is above the sleeper: these are the four conditions (of the Self), and the fourth is greater than all.[1924]

(8) Brahman with one foot moves in the three, and Brahman with three feet is in the last.

It is that both the true (in the fourth condition) and the untrue (in the three conditions) may have their desert, that the Great Self (seems to) become two, yes, that he (seems to) become two.[1925]

THE END

[1922] See B*ri*h. Up. IV, 2, 2, 3, where Indra is explained as Indha.

[1923] A comparison of this verse with *Kh*ând. Up. VII, 26, shows the great freedom with which the wording of these ancient verses was treated. Instead of—

> Na pasyan m*ri*tyum pa*s*yati na roga*m* nota du*h*khatâm,
> Sarva*m* hi pa*s*yan pa*s*yati sarvam âpnoti sarva*s*a*h*,

the *Kh*ândogya Up. reads:

> Na pa*s*yo m*ri*tyum pa*s*yati na roga*m* nota du*h*khatâm,
> Sarva*m* ha pa*s*ya*h* pa*s*yati sarvam âpnoti sarva*s*a*h*.

[1924] The conditions here described are sometimes called the Vi*s*va (Vai*s*vânara), Taigasa, Prâg*ñ*a, and Turîya. In the first state the Self is awake, and enjoys the world; in the second he sees everything as in a dream; in the third the two former states cease, and he is absorbed in sleep; in the fourth he becomes again the pure Self. In the first state the Self has the disguise of a coarse material body; in the second of a subtle material body; in the third its disguise is potential only; in the fourth it has no disguise, either potential or realised.

[1925] 'By reason of the experience of the false and the true, the great Soul appears possessed of duality.' Cowell.

www.ingramcontent.com/pod-product-compliance
Lightning Source LLC
Chambersburg PA
CBHW021207090426
42740CB00006B/161
* 9 7 8 1 4 2 0 9 7 4 7 0 6 *